# Provide & Protect

## Important Life Decisions

**A. CHARLES SCHULTZ**
*Attorney-at-Law*

ISBN: 978-0-9845321-0-0

Library of Congress Cataloging

Published by Crescendo Interactive, Inc., Camarillo, CA

Printed in Oxnard, CA

# WELCOME TO
## *Provide & Protect*

You are about to start a journey that will have great importance to you and your family. In fact, the first chapter has the title "Important Life Decisions." I know you will enjoy the discussion about the estate planning process. This book covers four sections: "You & Your Family," "Your Contacts & Healthcare," "Your Finances" and "Your Estate Plan."

"You & Your Family" is a great place to start. You will learn how to provide for children, grandchildren, nephews, nieces and other family members in ways that are truly helpful. The final section on the family letter shows how you can share essential information with your loved ones and also close with a family blessing.

"Your Contacts & Healthcare" is a critical area—both during life and for your estate. You need to be sure your advisors are prepared to make crucial decisions for your care if you become incapacitated. If you have minor children, you will want to learn how to select reliable guardians and trustees to provide for them.

One of the most popular sections is "Your Finances." Understanding property ownership methods and listing all of your assets are essential for good planning. Only after gathering your property information will you be ready to make key estate planning decisions.

Finally, with careful efforts you may accumulate a substantial estate. "Your Estate Plan" explains many planning options. I know you will enjoy a new understanding of the different estate strategies that can help you provide for your family. You may be interested in a plan to help family and also support the charitable causes that matter to you. Several plans allow you to take care of both your immediate family and the larger family of friends and those in need served by your favorite charities.

As you read, you might begin thinking about your own family and estate planning goals. To help you further, the organization whose name appears on the cover of this book offers additional resources. Please visit their website to download a complimentary "Wills Planning Guide." If their website includes an "Online Wills Planner," you can create an online account to begin developing your own estate plan and find answers to each of the quizzes contained in this book.

Many of the chapters include examples that will be helpful in explaining different concepts to you. The examples are based on real people, but the names of the families involved have been changed. Some of the examples include tax rates and brackets that are updated by the government each year. To view updated chapters with the latest government tax information, please visit the web address on the cover of this book, select "Plan Your Will" and read the latest version located in the "Provide & Protect" section of the "Wills Planner."

I want to dedicate this book to my sweetheart and wife, Ardis Schultz. She is the heart and life for all that we do at Crescendo Interactive, Inc. I also express my appreciation to my daughter Kristen Schultz Jaarda and the other attorneys at Crescendo—Christopher Jaarda and Charles Van Patten for their review, suggestions and support. Finally, my thanks to Heidi Lundgren for her role as designer and manager of this project.

Enjoy your journey! I know you will have a great experience.

Cordially yours,

A. Charles Schultz
*Attorney-at-Law*

# TABLE OF CONTENTS

Introduction                                                    1

Table of Contents                                               3

About the Author                                                6

**SECTION I** *You & Your Family*                               7

**Chapter 1**  Important Life Decisions                         9

**Chapter 2**  Who Will Receive Your Property?                 13

**Chapter 3**  Caring for Minor Children                       19

**Chapter 4**  Seven Questions on Gifts to Children            23

**Chapter 5**  How to Give Property to Children                31

**Chapter 6**  Do You Have a Difficult Family?                 37

**Chapter 7**  Helping Children Today                          43

**Chapter 8**  Helping Children Tomorrow                       47

**Chapter 9**  Integrity and Initiative                        51

**Chapter 10** Your Family Letter — Memorial Services          57

Application and Action                                          63

**SECTION II** *Your Contacts & Healthcare*                    65

**Chapter 11** Living Wills and Advance Directives             67

**Chapter 12** Planning with a Serious Illness                 73

**Chapter 13** Your Plan for Senior Care                       79

**CHRONIC ILLNESS**

    **Chapter 14**  Part I — Care of Your Person     85

    **Chapter 15**  Part II — Care of Your Property     91

    Application and Action     97

**SECTION III**  *Your Finances*     **99**

    **Chapter 16**  What Do You Own?     101

    **Chapter 17**  Separate and Joint Property     107

    **Chapter 18**  Married Couples and Property     111

    **Chapter 19**  Social Security     115

    **Chapter 20**  401(k) Retirement Plans     121

  **IRAs**

    **Chapter 21**  Regular and Roth     127

    **Chapter 22**  IRA and 401(k) Designated Beneficiary Options     131

    Application and Action     137

**SECTION IV**  *Your Estate Plan*     **139**

  **WILLS**

    **Chapter 23**  Perils of Probate     141

    **Chapter 24**  Good and Bad     147

    **Chapter 25**  Passing Unequal Shares In Your Will     153

    **Chapter 26**  Ten Reasons to Update Your Estate Plan     159

    **Chapter 27**  Living Trusts vs. Wills     165

    **Chapter 28**  Online Accounts     171

    **Chapter 29**  Bequests to Your Favorite Charity     177

  **TRUSTS**

    **Chapter 30**  Your Living Trust Choices     183

    **Chapter 31**  Living Trust — Life and Death Decisions     187

    **Chapter 32**  How to Fund Your Living Trust     191

    **Chapter 33**  Income for Surviving Spouse     197

**Chapter 34** For Surviving Spouse      201

**Chapter 35** To Protect Children      207

**Chapter 36** For Creative Spenders      213

**Chapter 37** "Give It Twice" Trust      219

**Chapter 38** "Wait A While" Trust      223

**LIFE INSURANCE**

**Chapter 39** Costs and Benefits      229

**Chapter 40** Irrevocable Life Insurance Trust (ILIT)      237

**LIFETIME PLANS**

**Chapter 41** Gifts of Cash      243

**Chapter 42** Gifts of Stock      249

**Chapter 43** Gifts of Land      253

**Chapter 44** Gifts of Homes      259

**Chapter 45** Gifts with Life Income      265

The Shortest Day      271

Index      275

# ABOUT THE AUTHOR

A. Charles Schultz is a California attorney who specializes in charitable giving and estate planning. He is President of Crescendo Interactive, Inc. and is the principal author of the Crescendo Planned Giving Software and the GiftLegacy Pro eMarketing System. In addition, he is editor for the GiftLaw.com charitable tax planning website, the GiftLaw Pro charitable tax service, and also edits the weekly GiftLaw and GiftLegacy eNewsletters.

Charles writes, speaks and publishes extensively. He teaches more than 30 planned giving seminars per year and is the creator of GiftCollege.com, an internet education program for gift planners and professional advisors. Charles assists a select group of business owners/ trustees of major charities in charitable estate planning. He received his law degree from the University of Michigan. Charles is on the Board of the Christian Foundation of the West.

# You & Your Family

# IMPORTANT LIFE DECISIONS

"How can I plan?" asked Mary. "We just sold our home and bought a retirement condo. Our older child just moved across the country and our younger child will be getting married later this year. With so much change, how can we make plans?"

## Life Changes Quickly

In each of our lives, change comes very quickly. You are going to face new circumstances every year.

Yet planning exists to prepare for life—and to give your family members better lives. It is essential to create goals that help your family live better in the midst of new circumstances.

Planning for the future is a key part of a successful life. Even if you or your family are going through major changes, there are several basic steps that will help you succeed in your plans.

## Set Goals

Step one for a successful life is to have goals. It has been said, "If you don't know where you're going, you're not likely to get there." This is very true about goals for your family and for your estate.

Often, single persons or couples meet with a professional advisor and have not considered setting specific goals. Your advisor in this circumstance will try to be helpful and suggest "typical" goals.

However, think about goal-setting as though you are purchasing a birthday gift for a family member in a clothing store. You might look at many different shirts or pants for that person. A clothing store might have 20, 30, or even 50 different sizes. One size does not fit all in the area of clothing, and it also doesn't work for your family and estate plan.

How do you find the "right size?" That shirt or slacks for a family member must fit properly. In your planning for family, it's important to decide the right time and amounts for an inheritance to be most beneficial for your children, nephews and nieces. Your other goals may include the age for heirs to receive property and reducing costs and death taxes.

### What Do You Own?

Can you write down a list of all the property you own? A single person will often own items outright, although there may be a mortgage or other debt obligation against real property. However, married couples have at least three different types of potential ownership. Property could be owned individually by spouses or owned jointly. In some states, the property could be held in a type of joint ownership called community property.

Understanding your property starts with listing all of your assets including your savings account, certificates of deposit, home, IRA, 401(k) and personal assets.

### Children, Nephews and Nieces

Your plan to benefit family through your estate will vary greatly, depending upon the ages and circumstances of your children and their needs. For parents with minor children, a key decision is to select a guardian. Minor children also need to have property held in trust, so there is appropriate investment and expenditure of those funds. For adult children, it's important to think through the right time, right amount and right type of inheritance. Many families find that a trust that pays income for a number of years to adult children is also a very helpful method to provide added security for them.

## Wills and Trusts

Do you have a will? Is it current? You should review your will periodically and discuss your plan with your attorney. If you have a substantial estate, a will with a trust may be appropriate. Because a will does not provide for your care in a medical emergency, you will want to make sure that your estate planning includes a will, a durable power of attorney for healthcare and a living will to handle end-of-life issues.

## Planning for Probate

How can you avoid probate? Generally, most individuals can avoid probate for a large portion of their assets.

The probate process is important because when a person passes away, his or her property must first be used to pay bills, expenses and debts. An executor or personal representative is appointed to gather an inventory of all assets, conserve assets for all beneficiaries and make certain to carry out the decedent's intentions as written in his or her will.

The probate process specifically applies to assets transferred under your will. However, many types of assets are transferred through other means. Trusts, IRAs and insurance are subject to the terms of the agreement or beneficiary designation. Property held in joint tenancy with right of survivorship is transferred to the survivor whose name is on title.

Pay-on-death and other types of accounts can also avoid probate. However, all parts of your entire plan need to work together. When a plan has not been carefully developed to meet your goals, there may be an expensive and heart-rending fight over property by your heirs. A good plan will give one of the best possible gifts to your family— the gift of peace.

**CHAPTER 1**

IMPORTANT LIFE DECISIONS

# QUIZ

**1.** Because of the uncertainty of life, it is best not to set goals.

☐ True        ☐ False

**2.** Setting goals will help to determine the right inheritance at the right time for children, nephews or nieces.

☐ True        ☐ False

**3.** Most married couples understand their property and the type of ownership.

☐ True        ☐ False

**4.** Estate planning is much more than a will.

☐ True        ☐ False

**5.** It is usually a good idea to avoid probate.

☐ True        ☐ False

**Answers:** To view the quiz answers online, please use the website on the front cover. On that site select "Plan Your Will" and logon to your free Wills Planner account. Select the "Provide & Protect Resources" button on the right and "I. You & Your Family." Select "#1" and view the Quiz Answers at the bottom. You may also enjoy the three-minute video explanation.

# WHO WILL RECEIVE YOUR PROPERTY?

"Who should receive my property?" asked Helen to her attorney, Clara. "There are so many decisions to make. Since Morgan passed away, I need to make these decisions myself. Should I give property to the children outright or in trust? Is there a best age for them to receive the property? And what if one of them were to pass away before I do? The grandchildren are still too young to manage property. I also have made a loan to one of the children. Should I forgive that loan? And what about my dog Rover? Who will take care of Rover?"

## Beneficiaries of Your Will

Helen has questions that are very common. She is trying to decide who should be the beneficiary of her will. Plus, there are questions about how old children or other heirs should be when they receive her property or how she can best plan for someone to take care of the family dog.

You might have several different types of beneficiaries. There could be primary beneficiaries, contingent beneficiaries, life estate and remainder recipients, minors who receive income from a trust, debtor beneficiaries who receive forgiveness and restricted beneficiaries.

A famous American who included all of these types of gifts in his will was Benjamin Franklin.

### Primary Beneficiaries

Ben Franklin gave his son William all of his property in Nova Scotia "to hold to him, his heirs and designs forever." Because William received the property outright, he was a primary beneficiary.

You might own specific property such as land, a home, or a family heirloom that you want transferred to a primary beneficiary. This is often the starting point for planning your estate distributions.

### Life Estate

Franklin owned three homes on Market Street in Philadelphia, other property within Philadelphia and pasture land on Hickory Lane next to the city. He transferred the right to use that property together with his "silver plate, pictures and household goods" to his daughter Sarah Bache and her husband Richard Bache for use "during their natural lives."

This bequest created a life estate. You may have a home or other real property and desire for a person to use that property for his or her lifetime. A life estate is an excellent way to give a person life use of property.

### Final Beneficiary

After the lives of Sarah and Richard Bache, the property in Philadelphia that they used was transferred to their children. This property was then solely owned by the children.

Following a life estate, the property is usually transferred outright to the remainder or final beneficiaries. If you create a life estate for a person, then you may also designate a person or perhaps a charitable organization to own the property after your life tenant passes away.

### Contingent Beneficiary

Ben Franklin wanted to transfer property to his daughter and son-in-law for life, with the final distribution to their children. But what if one of the children were to pass away prior to the demise of both parents? Franklin indicated that if one of the children were "to die under age, and without issue," that share would be "equally divided among the survivors."

A contingent beneficiary is the person who will receive the property if the first person is not living at the time of the transfer. For example, you may wish to give a gift through your will to a brother or sister. But if he or she passes away before you do, then it is important to select another person to receive the property.

**Trust for Minors**

Ben Franklin understood that some of the children of his daughter Sarah might be quite young at the time when both parents pass away. He stated that some of them are "under age" and "may not have capacity" to manage the property. Therefore, he ordered the Supreme Court of Pennsylvania to select "three honest, intelligent, impartial men" to manage the property.

If you plan to assist young children, you will want to create a trust to manage property for the benefit of the children. Primarily, the trust will distribute income and, if needed, principal to the child until each recipient reaches your designated age for distribution of the assets.

**Debtor Beneficiaries**

Ben Franklin was like many parents in that he made loans to his children. As is quite often the case, he decided to forgive the loans and indicated he would discharge his son-in-law "from all claim and rent of moneys due to me."

If you have made loans to friends or family members, it is very possible that you may choose to forgive those loans. In effect, you are forgiving the debt and giving back the note or other obligation.

**Pet Beneficiaries**

Ben Franklin gave away his printing materials and books and left several other bequests. However, it appears that he decided not to make any provision for a pet.

During the past few years, more than half of the state legislatures in the United States have permitted a plan to benefit a pet. The simple solution is for you to transfer a family pet to a friend and make a gift of sufficient funds to provide for care of the animal. Of course, you are trusting your friend to provide that care and to use the funds appropriately.

Some states also allow you to create a pet trust. A trust can be managed by a bank or a commercial trustee, or you can select a private trustee. The property that is transferred to the trust will be used for the care of your pet.

There have been cases in which a trust was created and the trustee was directed to continue payments to the pet caregiver as long as the pet should live. Perhaps not surprisingly, Rover seemed to survive for an unusual period of time. When each Rover passed away, the family replaced Rover with a dog of similar appearance and breed. So long as the new "Rovers" kept appearing, the trust income payments were made to the family.

**CHAPTER 2**

WHO WILL RECEIVE YOUR PROPERTY?

# QUIZ

**1.** Your beneficiaries who receive bequests of specific property are called primary beneficiaries.

☐ True    ☐ False

**2.** You must always select a contingent beneficiary.

☐ True    ☐ False

**3.** A person who receives a life estate in property pays the maintenance, insurance and taxes.

☐ True    ☐ False

**4.** It is good planning to create a trust for minor beneficiaries.

☐ True    ☐ False

**5.** It is quite common to forgive debts.

☐ True    ☐ False

**Answers:** To view the quiz answers online, please use the website on the front cover. On that site select "Plan Your Will" and logon to your free Wills Planner account. Select the "Provide & Protect Resources" button on the right and "I. You & Your Family." Select "#2" and view the Quiz Answers at the bottom. You may also enjoy the three-minute video explanation.

## CHAPTER 3

# CARING FOR MINOR CHILDREN

"Who would take our children? I am not sure anyone would be willing to take them," remarked Shelly to her attorney, Jim. "It's not that they aren't good children. They are all fine, but there are 11 of them! If something happens to Pat and me, who will take them?"

### Personal Guardian for Minor Children

One very important decision for you to make when creating a plan is to decide who would be the guardian of your minor children. When you write your first will, it is very possible that you still have minor children at home. While you may not have 11 children and face the challenge that confronted Shelly and Pat, this is still a very crucial and important decision.

Your guardian will raise the children, teach them values, select the schools they attend and perform the functions of a parent. If you do not have a guardian selected in a will, a court may select a person. That person may not share your cultural background, your religion, your general world view, or any other aspects of the character that you think important for the person who raises your children. By selecting a guardian and an alternate in your will, you have a much better prospect of finding someone that you think is the right person to raise your children.

**Two Parents**

If there are two parents, normally the survivor will be selected as the guardian of the children. But if both were to pass away, then it would be necessary to select a guardian.

Even if you select a guardian, there could still be an objection or contest by other family members. The probate judge usually will approve your selection unless there is strong evidence that indicates the person is not qualified. For example, evidence of alcoholism, criminal background or a history of child abuse could lead the judge to select another person. However, in nearly all cases the person that you select is chosen because he or she is the best possible individual to raise your children.

**Single Parent**

There are several reasons why a person may be a single parent in our society. A single parent may never have been married, there could have been a divorce, or the spouse could have passed away. In all three cases, it is especially important for single parents to have carefully selected a guardian.

**Blended Family**

If you have divorced and remarried, it may be your desire to have your new spouse as the guardian for children from your first marriage.

Normally, children are placed with their biological parent. However, if you can show good reasons why it is in "the best interest of the child" for your new spouse to be guardian, the court may permit him or her to raise your children. It is desirable for you to write a letter that is retained with your will to explain your reasons why the biological parent is not a good choice and how your current spouse would be the best person to raise your children.

**Property for Your Children**

If you have a high level of trust in the person selected to be guardian, it is possible to transfer property outright to him or her. However, if you choose to entrust a guardian with your property, you need to recognize that the guardian will have complete control and may choose to use the property for other purposes. This may be an acceptable solution if you have moderate resources, but if your property is substantial, a trust may be a better choice.

**Trust for Children**

With a moderate to substantial amount of property, it is quite common to create a trust. One person is selected as trustee to manage the property. He or she then transfers the income and, if required, principal to the guardian. The combination of one person managing the property and the guardian raising the children provides checks and balances that achieve the best result for the child.

**CHAPTER 3**

CARING FOR MINOR CHILDREN

# QUIZ

**1.** Selecting a guardian is one of the most important estate planning decisions for parents of minor children.

☐ True     ☐ False

**2.** If my spouse practices a different religion, I can select another person as guardian.

☐ True     ☐ False

**3.** A single parent may select a guardian who is not the biological parent if he or she can show that the biological parent is not the appropriate guardian.

☐ True     ☐ False

**4.** It is helpful to provide a letter or other means to show the reason for selecting a guardian if there is a blended family situation.

☐ True     ☐ False

**5.** Even with a substantial inheritance for the child, it is perfectly appropriate to transfer both guardianship and the inheritance to the same person.

☐ True     ☐ False

**Answers:** To view the quiz answers online, please use the website on the front cover. On that site select "Plan Your Will" and logon to your free Wills Planner account. Select the "Provide & Protect Resources" button on the right and "I. You & Your Family." Select "#3" and view the Quiz Answers at the bottom. You may also enjoy the three-minute video explanation.

# SEVEN QUESTIONS ON GIFTS TO CHILDREN

Many questions arise when we consider the options for giving to children. Why should we give? When, what and how should we give? Will gifts impact the self-esteem and initiative of the child? Can a gift plan transfer values to children?

These are all very important questions. Clearly there are better ways to give and a prudent parent will consider carefully the manner, nature and amount of gifts. If the gifts are given in a proper way, they can be very beneficial for the child. Alternatively, gifts given at the wrong time or in the wrong amounts can lessen the initiative and even weaken the character of the child. Thus, it is important to make gifts in the optimum manner at the right time.

### Why Give to Children?

There are several reasons why you may choose to make gifts to children during life. Some parents wish to start the inheritance process. If they have substantial resources, it is desirable to begin the inheritance while the children are in their 30s, 40s and 50s. Many children can use the help at that time to start careers, purchase a home and assist in the cost of raising their own children.

Another reason for making gifts is to teach conservation. Most parents who have significant resources have been careful to conserve their assets and build them up during life. By making transfers of assets during life, the parents can see how the children handle those assets and, in turn, offer advice and encouragement. In addition, when the parents have the opportunity to see the effect of inheritance on children, it helps to clarify the parents' goals. Goals for inheritance should include the amount transferred during life, the time of transfer, the principal and income amounts and times for transfer of those items to family in the estate.

Starting the property transfer process during life enables parents to understand how to plan for the optimum inheritance for children.

### When Should a Parent Start Giving?

There is both an easy answer and a difficult answer to this question. First, parents should start giving to children when they reach the "age of financial responsibility." But what is that age? Some children reach the "age of financial responsibility" at 25, while others might not attain that status at age 75.

Another factor that affects the "when to give" question is the resources of the parent. Many people in our society live to be age 80, 90 or even older. The parents should make certain that they have sufficient assets to provide for long-term care, if that is needed. Some parents may wish to purchase long-term care insurance prior to making gifts to children. Alternatively, other parents of retirement age may determine that they have adequate resources to provide for their long-term care and can make gifts to family members. In making this determination, you will want to consider pensions, Social Security, IRAs and other assets.

If a parent determines that there are sufficient assets and that the children have reached an appropriate age (which in most cases is when children are in their 30s, 40s and 50s), then the parent may choose to start making gifts.

### What Should I Give?

In the book *The Millionaire Next Door*, the authors studied the impact of gifts of cash to children in their 30s and 40s. The essence of their research was that, for most children, gifts of cash are typically spent.

Furthermore, with the exception of elementary school teachers and college professors, children in other professions who received cash gifts actually had less in savings by retirement age than those who received no gifts. Those who received cash gifts not only spent the gifts, but also continued to spend other personal cash and ended up with smaller estates than those who had received no gifts.

If parents are not concerned about whether or not the gift is spent, then the gift of cash is appropriate. However, many parents make gifts to children with the hope that the child will invest and build up some reserve assets. If the hope is that children will invest and begin to build their estates, then gifts of property show much more promise.

For example, many parents hold stock and can transfer shares by gift to the children. Alternatively, some parents hold real property or have created family limited partnerships and can transfer either the real property or the partnership units to children.

If the gifts are less than the annual exclusion amount per parent, per child each year ($14,000 in 2017 and potentially higher in future years), then the gift is not subject to gift tax. It should be noted that the child takes the cost basis of the parent when property is gifted. Thus, if the child were to sell the appreciated stock or land, he or she would have to pay a capital gains tax. Many parents actually look at this as a favorable circumstance, since their intention is for the child to hold the asset. If there is significant appreciation, these parents deem it beneficial since that potential gain could dissuade children from selling the asset, paying the capital gains tax, and spending the money.

How much can be transferred using annual gift exclusions? There are cases in which appreciated stock gifts were held by family members and there was significant value transferred. After a ten-year period, the stock transferred with annual exclusions may be worth several hundred thousand dollars. In one case, the parents used gift exclusions over a period of 30 years and the children held the gifted stock. At the conclusion of that gifting program, the children were all multimillionaires—and all with zero gift or estate tax!

**Should I Give Different Amounts?**

Most parents will attempt to treat all children equally. From the perspective of the child, the gift is viewed as a representation of the love of the parent. Thus, it seems appropriate in most circumstances for there to be equal transfers to the children.

However, most rules have reasonable and logical exceptions. The two most common exceptions in this area are the special needs trust and a family business. If one child has a disability, the rest of the family understands the need for additional provision for that child through what is commonly called a special needs trust. This is a trust with an independent trustee who has discretion to make distributions to the child, but is not normally required to do so. The special needs trust makes provision for the maximum benefit of the child and could potentially allow some beneficiaries to also receive government benefits.

The other exception to equal treatment for children may occur with a family business. If some children are involved in the business and other children are not, it is desirable to provide a substantial inheritance for all children. However, maintaining business viability may require the transfer of a majority of the business interest to the child that is involved in the business.

In addition, many parents believe that transfer is fair because the efforts of the children in the business have contributed to the overall growth of the business and the overall growth of the parents' estate. These are delicate questions to which parents should give careful thought, but in the case of the special needs trust and the family business, it is common for one child to receive a greater benefit than the other children.

**Will My Gift Decrease Motivation and Self-esteem?**

This is a concern of all parents. If an estate is substantial, it is a very important issue to consider. Nearly everyone knows of cases where a large inheritance was transferred to an individual and it was spent in very unhealthy ways. Indeed, sometimes the size of the inheritance contributes to tearing down rather than building up the child's character.

Perhaps the best gift most parents and grandparents should consider is education, which can be used during an entire lifetime. Because one competes with other students in the class, education is also a very good character-building exercise.

A second very fine gift that may not involve significant financial resources is help with a career or business. Many businesspeople are able to assist their children in starting careers or businesses through advice and financing. These opportunities are excellent because the child then has the self-esteem derived from building a career or a business of his or her own.

Another strategy is to wait for a reasonable level of maturity. Some parents wait until the children are in their 40s or 50s to start gifting programs. At that time, values are more likely to be established for the children and they are more likely to make productive use of the property.

**Why Don't My Children Think Like Me?**

This question surely has crossed the mind of nearly all parents. A parent may consider a particular property or asset and say, "If I had that property, this is what I would do with it."

As all parents know, children quite often hold different opinions. They have generally not been tested in as many different circumstances as their parents. The children need "time to learn." When transferring an inheritance to children, parents need to remember that they have quite often acquired that property over 30 or 40 years. The parents had many opportunities to learn the value of thrift, conservation, investment and careful planning.

Children will not learn these principles from a ten-minute discussion with their parents. They will need to learn some of these lessons out in the real world, operating with real money and real property. It is inevitable that some children will make mistakes. However, their parents also made mistakes along the way. This is the educational part of the gift process.

Parents should be willing to provide "opportunity to make mistakes" property to their children. This does not necessarily mean that the property must have enormous value. However, there must be some value to the property. This "opportunity to make mistakes" property can best be gifted during life. After one or two such episodes, the children may suddenly have a greater understanding of some of the values held by the parents.

### How Do I Support Charity and Transfer Values to Children?

One goal of parents is to teach values to children. We all hope that our children will be honest, loving, loyal, faithful, true and upright. How do you teach those values? First, values are caught and not taught. Fortunately, many parents have shared the lesson of the importance of family and extended family with the children. The family includes children and, in some cases, nephew, nieces and other relatives. The extended family includes the wider group of individuals who are helped by charities that the parents support.

One especially effective way to teach the principle of helping others is to model that behavior through support of charities that benefit the extended family. Children realize that they are here on Earth not just to acquire the best homes, fastest cars and most exotic vacations, but also to find a sense of purpose and value through assisting others. The extended family example of the parents is one of the best lessons that encourage children to acquire values similar to the parents. This lesson is taught during life both through contribution of time and gifts of cash and property to charity.

In addition, a very effective teaching method is to use planned giving concepts. These planned giving opportunities can provide benefits for children and a remainder to charity. In using these gift plans, the parent teaches the child to consider both the family and the extended family in planning. If major benefit for the extended family can be realized through tax savings, this becomes a particularly powerful lesson.

Gifts to children during life can accomplish many goals and objectives. Parents need to give careful thought to the children's needs and opportunities. If your assets permit, you may have the ability to give children "time to learn," provide them the "opportunity-to-make-mistakes" property and to facilitate the transfer of values. Truly, these objectives make giving during life an important part of your efforts to "help the child become a better person."

**CHAPTER 4**

SEVEN QUESTIONS ON GIFTS TO CHILDREN

# QUIZ

**1.** A primary reason for making gifts to children is to teach them to invest and use funds responsibly.

☐ True     ☐ False

**2.** For most children, gifts of cash are saved for retirement.

☐ True     ☐ False

**3.** The best gifts to children are typically property rather than cash.

☐ True     ☐ False

**4.** The age of financial responsibility is always reached by age 40.

☐ True     ☐ False

**5.** Gifts that are too large may harm self-esteem.

☐ True     ☐ False

**Answers:** To view the quiz answers online, please use the website on the front cover. On that site select "Plan Your Will" and logon to your free Wills Planner account. Select the "Provide & Protect Resources" button on the right and "I. You & Your Family." Select "#4" and view the Quiz Answers at the bottom. You may also enjoy the three-minute video explanation.

# HOW TO GIVE PROPERTY TO CHILDREN

Parents have a number of reasons for making gifts to children. First, a parent should have sufficient resources for retirement and for long-term care needs before making substantial gifts. Once you have acquired a reasonable level of security, you might consider making gifts to children.

Your gifts to children will enable two types of education. First, your children will have the ability to learn to manage and hopefully invest the gifts to start building their estate. In addition, you will be able to understand better how a child will manage or use the gift property.

Finally, if you have a larger estate, the use of annual gift exclusions can be a very good strategy to save potential future estate taxes.

**There are Seven Different Ways that Gifts Can be Made to Children.**

1. **Cash Gifts:** You can simply write a check to children. Some parents give an amount up to the annual gift exclusion ($14,000 per child, per parent in 2017 and larger amounts in future years). This is a very easy and convenient way to make a gift.

However, there are some concerns about cash gifts that you should understand. When gifts to children are in cash, they are quite frequently spent rather than being invested. If the regular gifts are made over a period of years, it may encourage your children to live at a higher than normal lifestyle. In many cases the child will benefit more from a gift of a property investment, rather than a gift of cash.

2. **Stock Gifts:** While it is possible for you to hold stock certificates, the overwhelming majority of stock is now held in a street account by a brokerage firm. The easiest method for transfer of stock is for the child to create an account with the same firm. The brokerage firm has the documentation necessary to make a transfer from your account to your child's account.

With a property gift, you will need to know the gift value. Because public stock is valued at the mean between the high and low prices on the date of the transfer, the value is quite easy to determine. Most parents will make stock gifts to children with value below the annual exclusion amount. Each parent will have one annual exclusion for each child, so the total given each year for a couple is double the exclusion. In addition, larger gifts can be made by filing an IRS Form 709 Gift Tax Return and using part of your lifetime gift exemption.

If stock or other appreciated property is transferred to children by gift, they take the same cost basis as the parents. Although the stock may be appreciated, there is no capital gains tax payable when the stock is transferred. However, the child has the same basis as the parent. If the stock is sold, the child will pay capital gains tax on the increase in value.

The dividends or income from the stock will be distributed to the child. If he or she is under age 19 or is a student under age 24, then in most cases the income will be taxed to the child at the parent's tax rate. You may have heard this concept called the "kiddie" tax.

3. **Mutual Funds:** Many parents own mutual funds that are managed by a financial services firm. These may be a very good candidate for a gift to children. You can create a new mutual fund account and use the appropriate form from the financial services company to make a gift to the child. If the mutual fund is appreciated, then the potential capital gain and income tax rules are similar to those described for the gifts of stock.

4. **Gifts of Land or Home:** A gift of real property is accomplished through a deed. Depending upon your state's rules, a warranty

or grant deed is normally used, but in some cases a quitclaim deed may be appropriate. You will identify the property being transferred on the deed. After you sign the gift deed, it will be notarized and recorded with the county registrar of deeds. This will produce clear evidence that the property has been given to your children.

In order to qualify for the gift exclusion limit, you may choose to transfer partial interests in property. This is called an "undivided interest" in the property. For example, if a property is worth $100,000 a parent might deed 10% of that property each year for ten years to a child. The gifts will be less than the gift exclusion and after ten years the child owns the property. If the real property is substantial in value and gifts exceed the annual exclusion, then you will need an appraisal so that the property transferred can be correctly valued on IRS Form 709, Federal Gift Tax Return.

5. **Uniform Transfers to Minors Act (UTMA):** Under the UTMA, you may transfer property or assets to a custodian for the benefit of a child who is a minor. The custodian serves as the manager of the asset and can invest and spend funds as he or she considers advisable for the use and benefit of the minor. The custodian must maintain tax records and the income is taxed to the child.

When the child reaches legal age (18 in some states, although age 21 is required or permissible in most states), the child then has ownership of the assets.

The UTMA is convenient and relatively easy to manage. If assets are likely to be used for the child's education by age 21, the UTMA can be a good planning strategy. However, if there are fairly substantial assets you may be reluctant to permit a 21-year-old child to have access to large principal amounts.

6. **Trust for Children:** A child's trust can be quite flexible. Many parents have created trusts for the benefit of one child or even a "family pot" trust for multiple children. The trustee is frequently given permission to use the trust income for the education, living expenses and health needs of the child.

Trustees frequently have broad discretion over trust investments and the use of the funds. The goal of the parents is to provide for the needs of the child yet protect the funds until the child has reached the age of financial responsibility. As a parent, you have the ability to decide what the general guidelines on distributions will be for your trustee and at what age your children will receive their principal from the trust.

7. **Tax-free Sale Trust for Children:** An attractive option if you have appreciated property is to create a charitable remainder unitrust for a term of 20 years with income payable to children. For example, John and Mary Jones had three children and owned property with a value of $250,000. Because they had paid $50,000 for the property, they were reluctant to sell and pay a capital gains tax of over $45,000.

A much better plan for John and Mary was to transfer the property to a charitable remainder trust paying 6% to their three children for 20 years. They received an income tax deduction of approximately $75,000 and bypassed the capital gains tax. The children each received one-third of the 6% income for 20 years and their total income was approximately $330,000. After the 20 years, the trust had grown to $305,000 and it benefited the favorite charities of John and Mary.

John and Mary were able to enjoy very large tax savings now, transfer an income stream to children for 20 years and eventually benefit their favorite charities. Mary particularly appreciated the ability to give an income stream because one of the three children tended to "spend money like water" and had the opportunity over 20 years to acquire better financial management skills.

**CHAPTER 5**

HOW TO GIVE PROPERTY TO CHILDREN

# QUIZ

**1.** If you give appreciated stock to your child and he or she sells the stock, there will be no tax payable.

☐ True ☐ False

**2.** In making gifts of land, it is possible to use undivided interests in order to give amounts that are within the annual exclusion.

☐ True ☐ False

**3.** Under the Uniform Transfers to Minors Act (UTMA), you can transfer stock to a custodian for a minor and protect the stock until he or she is age 30.

☐ True ☐ False

**4.** If you create and fund a family trust, the trustee can have great discretion over the distribution of income or principal to your child.

☐ True ☐ False

**5.** A term-of-years unitrust is an excellent way to combine tax savings with income for children.

☐ True ☐ False

**Answers:** To view the quiz answers online, please use the website on the front cover. On that site select "Plan Your Will" and logon to your free Wills Planner account. Select the "Provide & Protect Resources" button on the right and "I. You & Your Family." Select "#5" and view the Quiz Answers at the bottom. You may also enjoy the three-minute video explanation.

# DO YOU HAVE A DIFFICULT FAMILY?

A businessman with a $2.5 billion estate passed away in 1976. He was single and many individuals, mostly unrelated to him, filed more than 40 wills with the probate court. Not surprisingly, the individuals who filed the 40 wills hoped to become beneficiaries of a large portion of the estate.

Twenty-two cousins fought with all of the other individuals claiming a share of the estate. In the end, the wills were all ruled invalid and the 22 cousins plus the federal government divided up the estate.

Your estate may not be $2.5 billion, but if you have a reasonable level of resources and a difficult family member, there could be a will contest. This may occur because one of your family members or potential heirs might believe that he or she can receive a larger portion of the estate. Some beneficiaries will receive a larger share if your will is valid and some will gain if the will is determined invalid. The difficult person is likely to sue if he or she can gain a larger part of your estate.

### How Will a Difficult Person Attack Your Plan?

There are several ways to challenge your will. He or she will claim that you have a lack of capacity, that there were unqualified or improper witnesses, or that there has been undue influence that invalidates the will.

## What is Capacity?

Capacity is a legal term that means you are qualified to sign a will. Fortunately, you don't lose capacity simply because you have a "senior moment" or a brief period of forgetfulness. Rather, your capacity is defined as (i) your ability to understand that your will transfers your estate, (ii) that you know the general type and nature of your property, and (iii) you can identify the family members who are your potential heirs.

## What Questions May the Attorney Ask?

Your attorney will be very interested in making certain that the will is properly signed and qualified to transfer your property. He or she may ask general questions to enable you to show that you're qualified to sign the will. The questions may include, "Why are you here?" and "What do you own?" and "Who are the members of your family?"

You should briefly respond to each of the questions. The attorney and the witnesses will then be able to testify about your capacity if a difficult person claims that you were not capable of signing a proper will.

You should be able to affirm that you understand a will transfers your property and in a general way identify the major assets in your estate. You do not need to explain specifically all the property or the exact value, but a general explanation is necessary.

The people you describe as potential heirs will typically be your spouse, children, brothers, sisters, grandchildren, other relatives and special friends. If you are specifically including or excluding someone, you may wish to mention that fact.

In some cases, a doctor is asked to provide additional explanation. He or she may describe your general mental and physical condition and any medications you are currently taking.

The key day is the date you actually sign the will. Even if you just have a "lucid interval" on that day, you generally will be qualified to sign the will. The attorney and witnesses may later be called to testify and can describe your general conduct and statements to assist the court in determining whether you are qualified on that date to sign the will.

### What is Undue Influence?

As we become more senior, we tend to have less physical and mental strength. In very senior years, we may have a level of weakness that permits another person to impose their will upon us. The action of a child or caregiver in causing us to sign a will that reflects his or her intent rather than our intent is called "undue influence."

Your child or caregiver may encourage you to sign a new will that would disinherit other children or other beneficiaries and give the estate to him or her. In some cases, the child or caregiver has paid the attorney for a new will that makes him or her the sole beneficiary.

### What are the Flags to Watch For?

There are three specific flags or conditions that you should understand. First, if you have physical and mental weakness, you may be more vulnerable. Second, be cautious if the influencer approaches you and offers to obtain the document or pay the attorney. Third, it is a red flag if the influencer is going to receive a larger than normal benefit under the new will.

### Is it Acceptable to Sign Your Will if You are in the Hospital?

Because many individuals discover a need to update their will after they become ill, it is very common to sign a will or trust in the hospital. However, there are some cautions or steps that you should take.

First, when you sign the will or trust, the attorney, witnesses and medical staff may be in the room, but the beneficiaries should not be in your presence. The advisors and medical staff in the room are there for your protection and welfare and are objective because they are not receiving a bequest or inheritance.

Second, it is important for you to explain to the attorney, the witnesses and any medical staff present that you understand the will, you have thought through the reasons for rewriting the will and you disclose the name of any person who suggests that you rewrite the will.

While these steps cannot guarantee that a difficult person will not file a claim, you have now taken significant steps to decrease the risk of a will contest.

### Does a No-contest Clause Work?

In many states, it is permitted for you to write a no-contest clause into your will. For example, if you have four children who each receive one-fourth of the estate, you might write a provision into the will that says if one of them contests the will, he or she will lose that one-fourth share.

No-contest clauses have often been upheld. One strategy that some individuals use is to provide a reasonable bequest in the will for a difficult heir. If the child or other heir contests the will and loses, he or she will be giving up some meaningful benefit. This may discourage a child or other heir from contesting the will.

### Summary

Your will is designed to carry out your intent. If you sign a new will in your very senior years when you are not in the strongest mental and physical health, it can still be valid and upheld. However, taking a few common sense steps to increase the likelihood that there will not be a contest by a difficult family member is quite easy and good judgment on your part.

## CHAPTER 6

DO YOU HAVE A DIFFICULT FAMILY?

# QUIZ

1. Many larger estates will experience a claim by a difficult person.

   ☐ True ☐ False

2. To sign a valid will you need to know the general nature of your property.

   ☐ True ☐ False

3. For your will to be valid, you must know the value of your assets.

   ☐ True ☐ False

4. Your attorney should ask general questions at the will signing to enable you to show your capacity.

   ☐ True ☐ False

5. Undue influence can occur if someone else imposes their will on you and causes you to sign a new will or trust.

   ☐ True ☐ False

**Answers:** To view the quiz answers online, please use the website on the front cover. On that site select "Plan Your Will" and logon to your free Wills Planner account. Select the "Provide & Protect Resources" button on the right and "I. You & Your Family." Select "#6" and view the Quiz Answers at the bottom. You may also enjoy the three-minute video explanation.

# HELPING CHILDREN TODAY

When children are in their 30s and 40s, they frequently are starting a new career or beginning a family. Many are still paying off school debts. For these reasons they could benefit from some additional help.

If parents have appreciated property, a special trust that helps children could be very beneficial. The parents will receive substantial tax savings, while the children can benefit from 20 years of income from the trust.

Kris and Jill have raised three children. When the children were young, Kris and Jill did what many parents do in their mid-40s—they bought a new home. However, rather than selling their old home, they turned it into a rental unit.

After renting that home for 20 years, Kris and Jill are now 65. Their three children have all moved out and are starting families. Kris and Jill own their current home, have recently sold their business and enjoy good retirement income.

Their oldest child is a daughter with two children. The middle son is married with three children and their younger son has two children. Kris and Jill especially enjoy visiting their seven grandchildren.

As they considered their situation, Kris and Jill decided they would like to help their children. However, they are seeking a solution that will also save taxes. The rental home was initially purchased for $200,000. Their CPA has taken depreciation during the time they have owned it. In today's real estate market, it is worth about $400,000.

Kris and Jill are now ready to sell and move on with life. Therefore, they sat down to discuss options with their CPA, Sam.

**Kris:** "Sam, you know that we bought the new house when we were both 45 and we kept this as a rental. Now after 20 years, we are tired of tenants and ready to move on. Jill wants to spend our time visiting the grandchildren and doing some traveling. But I know that this home is now worth much more today, so there would be a big tax if we were to sell. Is there a way we can help the children without paying tax?"

**Sam:** "I understand that it's now time to consider moving on. Your retirement income is good, you own your home and have no debt. You are well positioned to do something to help your children. It would also be great if we could reduce your income taxes for the next five years. That would provide additional ability for you to save and invest more for the future."

**Jill:** "Yes, we are in good shape but our children are now trying to start families. They need some extra help. With the cost of education, clothes and other items for our grandchildren, we would like to give them some assistance."

**Sam:** "You could set up a special trust that allows you to sell this property tax free. That would leave the full value available to earn income for your children. I could run an illustration that shows how we could set that trust up for 20 years and sell without tax. In addition, you receive a charitable deduction of approximately $150,000. We probably would spread that over about five years. Each year you could reduce your personal income taxes by over a third with that deduction."

**Kris:** "That's the ticket—helping children and saving taxes at the same time. How much income would we transfer to the children?"

**Sam:** "It looks like that trust would pay over $500,000 to the children over the 20 years. That's quite a bit of education and clothes!"

**Jill:** "And after the 20 years of payments to children, can we then pick the charities that will receive the trust property?"

Sam: "Yes. You can select one or more charities that will receive a very nice gift."

Kris: "But who will manage the property? We're going to start traveling and we don't want to have management responsibilities."

Sam: "We can talk to a charity or a trust company to serve as trustee. A trustee will invest the proceeds after the property is sold and pay the income to your three children. If you would like, I will make contact with a trustee and we can get the process started."

Jill: "I think it is time to move forward, so let's go ahead and set up this plan."

**CHAPTER 7**

HELPING CHILDREN TODAY

# QUIZ

**1.** If the rental home is sold through a charitable remainder trust, there is a bypass of capital gain.

☐ True    ☐ False

**2.** If Kris and Jill sold the rental home, they could qualify for the $500,000 exclusion for sale of a principal residence.

☐ True    ☐ False

**3.** A charitable deduction may be spread over five years.

☐ True    ☐ False

**4.** As the children receive the income, it is tax free to them.

☐ True    ☐ False

**5.** The rental home will be transferred to the unitrust and then a sale contract will be signed by the trustee.

☐ True    ☐ False

**Answers:** To view the quiz answers online, please use the website on the front cover. On that site select "Plan Your Will" and logon to your free Wills Planner account. Select the "Provide & Protect Resources" button on the right and "I. You & Your Family." Select "#7" and view the Quiz Answers at the bottom. You may also enjoy the three-minute video explanation.

# HELPING CHILDREN TOMORROW

Parents and children often have a different perspective on saving and spending. Parents of retirement age today were born during the Great Depression or during the 1940s and have a strong desire to save and invest in order to increase economic security.

Some of their children may have a different perspective. Because their children did not grow up during adverse economic times, they tend to consume more and save less. Understandably, many of these parents hope that their children could have greater economic security during retirement.

Mike and Kristi are recently retired. They have two children, John and Mary. Mike and Kristi bought a lot on an inland waterway when they were in their 40s. But the next year, Mike accepted a position in a state that was quite a distance from the waterfront lot. They've owned the lot for more than 20 years, but never built on the property because of the distance.

Mike and Kristi recently retired at age 65. They have good retirement income, a home that is paid for and good savings. Recently, Mike received a very good offer from a person who would like to purchase the waterfront lot. After receiving the offer, Mike and Kristi contacted their attorney, Steve, to discuss the best way to maximize benefits for them and their children.

**Mike:** "We have been very fortunate. Kristi and I have just retired and we have good income. We both get Social Security and also have two pensions. With that retirement income and our house paid for, we're doing fine."

**Kristi:** "You might remember that we mentioned buying this lot on the intracoastal waterway years ago. But after we moved south for Mike's new job, it was just too far to travel. We never ended up building our vacation home on that property. Now we've had an offer to buy that property at a great price. We told the person that we weren't quite ready to sell yet, but he still seems to be very interested."

**Steve:** "That sounds like a good offer and a good opportunity. It may be the right time to sell that lot. But you know that there is a lot of appreciation and you will pay a large capital gains tax."

**Mike:** "Yes, I know. We were doing some research and a friend of ours who is a gift planner for a charity said that we could save a bundle with a special trust. He called it a charitable remainder trust. We did some reading online and it seems like a good idea. But we don't actually need the income ourselves."

**Kristi:** "Mike and I like the tax savings. But we thought that maybe what we should do is give the income to John and Mary. They just don't save the way we have. I am very concerned about them. If they don't save more, they are going to need added income during their retirement. With all the financial uncertainty in America today, we would like to see if there is a way to help them."

**Steve:** "Many parents share your desire to provide some added retirement income for their children. You mentioned that charitable trust. Let me show you how a special version of that trust could help John and Mary.

"That trust is usually called a unitrust. I am going to explain how a retirement version of that unitrust could work for them. With your offer of $400,000, we could transfer the lot into the trust and after it is transferred, accept the offer. I suggest the $400,000 in the trust be invested for 20 years. With growth over those 20 years, it could increase to perhaps $1.2 million in value. That's of course depending on how the investments would be during that time, but that's quite possible. If we are able to grow to that level, the trust then would pay approximately $2.5 million to John and Mary during their retirement years. In addition, you would receive a tax deduction today of about $42,000 that could save another $14,000 in tax."

**Mike:** "So if we use that special retirement version of the unitrust, we sell tax free, get a deduction, and the trust grows until John and Mary retire. Then it pays a very good amount to John and Mary. That will very nicely supplement their other retirement income."

**Kristi:** "This sounds like a great use of that lot. It will answer my question on how to provide added retirement income for the children. Let's move forward with this trust."

**Mike:** "Plus, while it's a very long time into the future, there eventually will be a good gift to our favorite charity."

**CHAPTER 8**

HELPING CHILDREN TOMORROW

# QUIZ

**1.** With an offer on the lot, it's still possible to fund a charitable remainder trust.

☐ True ☐ False

**2.** A charitable trust can transfer income to children.

☐ True ☐ False

**3.** A unitrust must always make the required 5% or more payout.

☐ True ☐ False

**4.** All the income from the trust will be ordinary income for John and Mary.

☐ True ☐ False

**5.** A long-term charitable remainder trust is normally set at 5%.

☐ True ☐ False

**Answers:** To view the quiz answers online, please use the website on the front cover. On that site select "Plan Your Will" and logon to your free Wills Planner account. Select the "Provide & Protect Resources" button on the right and "I. You & Your Family." Select "#8" and view the Quiz Answers at the bottom. You may also enjoy the three-minute video explanation.

# INTEGRITY AND INITIATIVE

Pat and Allen were talking about their three children. They are empty nesters and the three children are off making their way in the world.

**Pat:** "I've been thinking about our three children. They are all doing fine, but we want to make sure that the inheritance we give them helps them to be better people. The inheritance some of our friends gave to their children was substantial, but the children just didn't use it very well. In fact, when an uncle of mine passed away, the inheritance was used very poorly by his children."

**Allen:** "But how do we make sure that the inheritance for our children leads to a good result? We need to do some research to make sure that our plan works effectively."

Pat and Allen did their homework. They read articles and spoke with several advisors, seeking wisdom. The result of their study is an inheritance plan that helps the child to be a better person. It is summarized as the "Integrity And Initiative" or "Twin I's" plan.

## Goals of Parents

Your primary goal as a parent is to help each child be a successful person—not just financially, but also in his or her career, family life and social status. While attorneys and CPAs are trained to help you transfer property to children, a good inheritance plan is much more than just transferring property. As Pat noted, there are many plans that are successful in transferring property but lead to a very bad result.

Yes, a successful plan transfers property. But good planning transfers it at the right time, the right way and in the right amount so that it achieves a good result. While a good result cannot be guaranteed, the "Integrity And Initiative" plan will increase the probability of that favorable result.

### Time to Learn

Principle one of the twin I's plan is to spread the resources out over time. This gives children some time to learn.

Parents have usually acquired an estate over 20, 30 or even 40 years. If you ask a person of retirement age to recall their early years, they will frequently share stories about the challenges they faced. For most people of retirement age, those challenges were financial "bumps in the road" that were very educational. Without that education, they would not have been as successful in life or in their finances.

Children who will receive a substantial inheritance also need time to learn. An inheritance can be stretched over a period of time. This may enhance the overall probability that the inheritance will facilitate development of integrity and initiative.

A good "Integrity And Initiative" plan could transfer property in four ways:

1. Gifts during life
2. Principal after the parents pass away
3. Income for a period of years
4. Delayed principal

### Gifts During Life

When should a parent start making gifts to children? The easy answer is as soon as the children reach the age of financial responsibility.

But what is that age? That will vary, but most children in their 30s, 40s or 50s do reach that point of maturity.

At that time, parents frequently start by making gifts using the annual gift exclusion. This exclusion amount may be gifted with no tax or reporting to the IRS. The annual exclusion in 2017 is $14,000 per child and is adjusted every two to four years.

Generally, it is better to give property rather than cash. Cash tends to be spent fairly quickly. Regular gifts of cash may result in a child acquiring a taste for expensive items that are above his or her normal lifestyle. This can lead to problems later on in life.

By making gifts of stock, land or other types of property, parents encourage children to invest and build their assets. Therefore, a good gift is a gift of property.

### Principal When the Parents Pass Away

The second gift strategy is to transfer principal after both parents pass away. This can be a bequest from the estate of the surviving spouse. The principal could also be a distribution from an insurance trust that pays to the children after both spouses have passed away. The transfer of principal could be a specific property such as a home, land or securities or it could be simply a portion of the estate.

### Income For a Term of Years

A very popular third option is to create a trust that pays income for a period of 15 or 20 years to the children. For larger estates this is usually a charitable remainder unitrust. The trust is funded after both parents have passed away. It pays a 5% or 6% annual income to the children. In many cases, it is very advantageous to fund the trust with an IRA or other qualified plan. The trust earns income for the family for the selected number of years. At the end of the 15 or 20 years, the trust is then transferred to favorite charities.

The combination of some principal and income for a term of years is very helpful. Parents can treat their children equally; however, there are some children who may require a longer period of time to mature in their financial management. The combination of principal and income for a period of years allows these children the time to learn better money-management skills.

**Delayed Principal**

The fourth concept is an additional payment of principal when the children have become more mature. Following the expiration of the payouts for the unitrust term of years, an additional amount can be distributed. This frequently is done through the "Wait A While" trust. Your attorney may have another name for that trust—the charitable annuity lead trust.

For the term of years that the children were receiving unitrust income under the third part of the plan, the charities receive the payouts from the lead trust. After the unitrust income payments have been made to children and that trust terminates, the children receive their delayed principal distribution from the lead trust.

**Keys to Successful Planning**

A successful "Twin I's" plan is created by understanding the four transfer options and then setting goals. These goals will frequently include a target amount for the inheritance for the children at each level. In addition, it is useful to create a total inheritance target amount per child.

For example, one parent wanted the children to receive $25,000 each year in income. Because a unitrust funded with $500,000 paying a 5% payout produces $25,000, the family decided to set up a unitrust of that amount for each child.

Over the 20 years, the trust paid more than $500,000 as income to each child with the remainder then distributed to charity.

## Conclusion

Allen and Pat carefully thought through the four different options. They established the overall target inheritance number for each child. After learning about the different options, they decided to use the first three options. With a combination of gifts during life, some principal from an insurance trust when both parents pass away, plus income from a unitrust for a term of 20 years, they were able to achieve all of their objectives.

Pat concluded, "We now feel that we have a much better plan. We are not just transferring property to our children, but we have carefully thought through the ways in which the inheritance will help the children. With the combination of gifts during life, some principal, and then income for a term of 20 years, we are giving our children the best possible opportunity to develop integrity and initiative."

## CHAPTER 9
### INTEGRITY AND INITIATIVE

# QUIZ

**1.** The "Integrity And Initiative" plan usually involves an inheritance distributed over a longer period of time.

☐ True ☐ False

**2.** CPAs and attorneys are trained to help parents transfer good character to children through the inheritance.

☐ True ☐ False

**3.** Gifts of property are generally preferred over gifts of cash.

☐ True ☐ False

**4.** The transfer of principal when parents pass away may be through a bequest from the second estate or an insurance trust.

☐ True ☐ False

**5.** The charitable remainder trust that produces income is often funded with an IRA.

☐ True ☐ False

**Answers:** To view the quiz answers online, please use the website on the front cover. On that site select "Plan Your Will" and logon to your free Wills Planner account. Select the "Provide & Protect Resources" button on the right and "I. You & Your Family." Select "#9" and view the Quiz Answers at the bottom. You may also enjoy the three-minute video explanation.

# YOUR FAMILY LETTER
## Memorial Services

A family letter is a key part of a good estate plan. It is much more personal than many of your estate documents. A family letter allows you to share your heart and show appreciation and gratitude to family members. During a time when family members are grieving, it also helps them to complete many practical steps to protect your property.

The family letter may have up to ten different sections. Each section will cover an important but separate topic.

### Estate Data

Your estate organizer usually has four parts. It will explain the family names and key information, identify your attorney, CPA and other financial and health advisors, cover all of your assets and financial information and outline your estate planning choices.

The estate organizer may be printed or you may use an online version. Your family letter should explain where the information is located. If you are using an online estate planner, it's important to know your account name and password so the information will be available.

### Important Documents

Your important documents will generally be safeguarded in three different ways. First, many individuals have a safe deposit box. The safe deposit box typically holds birth certificates, death certificates, degrees and other legal agreements, marriage or divorce documents, military discharge records, property deeds, a personal property inventory, stock and bond certificates and vehicle titles.

Second, you may have a fireproof box at home. This box will frequently include your insurance policies, your living will, medical power of attorney or advance directive, trust documents and your will.

Third, there are some items that should be left with your attorney, friend, agent or another trusted person. These are items that may be needed while you are still living or will be necessary very soon after you pass away. These documents (or copies of documents) could include your financial power of attorney, a durable power of attorney for healthcare or advance directive, your living will, trusts and your will.

### Accounts and Passwords

Because an increasing number of records and information are retained online in personal accounts, you will want to be certain that your personal letter lists all accounts. You may decide to include passwords with the personal letter. Alternatively, if you are entrusting all of this information to a specific person or other location, that should be identified.

With the rapid movement to online banking, online mutual funds and securities accounts, donor advised fund accounts, health savings accounts and your email accounts, you may have six to 10 accounts with various passwords. It will be important to have all of this information recorded.

### Your Family History

While your estate organizer will include basic information about you and your family members, there is an excellent opportunity in your family letter to discuss your family history. This can include a few short paragraphs that give the names and background of your parents. List all of their children or other key relatives in your family. Your history may discuss marriages, divorces and any blended family relationships. Finally, the family history will show the date of death for persons who have passed away.

Family history can include discussions of your activities, interests and career. It enables all of your extended family to have a good picture of your entire life.

## Care for Children, Grandchildren or Pets

If you are responsible for any children, grandchildren or pets, this is an opportunity for you to explain your plan for their care. While your estate planning documents will normally appoint guardians for your children or grandchildren who are under your care, it still may be beneficial for the guardian to receive recommendations from you on their education and other areas of development that you understand very well. If someone is to care for pets, you may have recommendations on the way in which that is done.

## Memberships

You may have memberships in a number of organizations. Some memberships, such as those in a golf course or in a club that purchases various types of sporting event tickets, are transferable to heirs. It would be helpful to your family for you to list any memberships that you have so they can handle them properly.

## Care of Your Body

When you pass away, your body may be in the custody of a medical center or nursing home. If you have previously decided to make any organ donations, it is helpful to explain that decision in your family letter. The requirements for making organ donations are typically covered under state law. In many cases, decisions on organ donations are made when you sign your living will or advance medical directive.

## Funeral or Memorial Services

The cost of many funerals now exceeds $10,000. If you would like to assist family members in the decisions surrounding your funeral or memorial service, the family letter is an excellent way to do so.

First, your family will need to decide whether to have a burial in a cemetery with a casket or to use cremation services and an urn. You may have personal or religious reasons for preferring one or the other.

With a casket and burial in a cemetery, your family will generally make use of a funeral home. Because there now is significant competition in the industry, funeral homes are starting to offer advance prices and package services. If you desire a specific range of services, type of casket or prefer not to be embalmed, those directions are helpful to your family.

There are funeral consumers' alliances in many locations. Your family may find assistance and guidance on www.funerals.org. This guidance may help them make good decisions during a very difficult time in the midst of grief over your loss.

If you are a veteran, your family may want to contact the Department of Veterans Affairs. You may qualify for a gravesite at no cost in one of the 130 national cemeteries for veterans and their spouses.

## Obituary

In your funeral or memorial service, there will be eulogies. It is also customary to have a printed description of your lifetime. This will frequently include your basic history, awards, achievements, military service and lifetime employment. If you have specific requests for information to be included in the obituary, it is helpful to your family to give them guidance. You may have certain principles or values that are important to you that you would like to share through the obituary. This is an opportunity for you to communicate your values to the public.

## Final Words and Blessings for Family

Your family letter may conclude with a word of blessing. It is a tradition in many cultures for the elders to provide a blessing for the next generation. This is frequently done when the elder is still living, but certainly your family letter provides a similar way to bless your children, grandchildren, nephews, nieces and other family members.

Your final words of wisdom and blessing for family members will be of great comfort as they grieve for your loss. It is an appropriate and fitting way to conclude your family letter.

**CHAPTER 10**

YOUR FAMILY LETTER — Memorial Services

# QUIZ

**1.** You should keep your signed will in a safety deposit box.

☐ True     ☐ False

**2.** It is important for you to record account names, locations and passwords.

☐ True     ☐ False

**3.** Medical papers and a living will should be kept in your safety deposit box.

☐ True     ☐ False

**4.** There are several options for funeral services and caskets.

☐ True     ☐ False

**5.** You may want to conclude your family letter with words of blessing.

☐ True     ☐ False

**Answers:** To view the quiz answers online, please use the website on the front cover. On that site select "Plan Your Will" and logon to your free Wills Planner account. Select the "Provide & Protect Resources" button on the right and "I. You & Your Family." Select "#10" and view the Quiz Answers at the bottom. You may also enjoy the three-minute video explanation.

# APPLICATION AND ACTION

As you finish reading the family section of *Provide & Protect*, we encourage you to take the first steps in establishing or updating your estate plans. As a service to you and your personal attorney, we have an online Wills Planner. You may go online to the web address on the front cover and select the "Plan Your Will" link. The free online Wills Planner permits you to have your own personal secure account. Please feel free to call us if you need help in setting up your online account.

There are several easy steps to setting up your account and entering the information online. After you have finished entering the information, you will be able to return at any time and update it as needed.

1. Go to the website on the front cover.

2. You will see the home page for gift planning. Look for the link with the title "Plan Your Will."

3. After you click "Plan Your Will," you will view the Wills Planner access page. If you do not yet have a Wills Planner account, select "Create Your Account" and enter your data. After you create your account, you may enter your username and password to view your personal, secure account on the Wills Planner website.

4. Once you have entered the website, you will see four different sections. The first is the "You and Your Family" section. Click on that section and enter your family information. There are also sections on "Your Contacts & Healthcare", "Your Finances" and "Your Estate Plan." You may save and view your information at any time.

5. You may want to view some of the *Provide & Protect* chapters and videos. Click the "*Provide & Protect*" button. You may view the entire updated version of the *Provide & Protect* multi-media book online. Each chapter includes a short video and quiz with answers. Some of our friends like to read a chapter each week, watch the video and take the quiz. In just one year, you may cover the entire book.

6. Finally, please feel free to call or email us at any time if we can help you with a short online phone tutorial.

# Your Contacts & Healthcare

# LIVING WILLS AND ADVANCE DIRECTIVES

As you approach end-of-life decisions, there are several steps that should be taken to make sure you receive the right type and level of care. To assist you in these decisions, most states now permit either an advance directive or a living will. These documents are designed to assist your family and doctors in making the decisions that you prefer at that time.

## Senior Medical Planning

There are three important background areas that you should learn about before entering into senior medical care. These are the medical oath and principles of your care providers, the rules created by Congress to ensure your medical information is protected and the decisions by your state on the specific document that you use to convey your wishes.

Doctors will frequently follow a set of principles that were originally called the Hippocratic Oath. The first oath was written by Hippocrates, a Greek doctor who is considered the father of modern medicine.

A modern version of the Hippocratic Oath typically states, "To practice and prescribe to the best of my ability for the good of my patients." Following this principle, your doctor will attempt to restore you to good health.

Because of modern improvements in medicine, it is possible to prolong your life through the use of ventilators, intravenous feeding and other devices. While you certainly want your doctors and nurses to provide very good care, you also will need to offer some guidance on how extensively your family and doctors should use modern technology to prolong your life.

A second major area to understand is called HIPAA. The Health Insurance Portability and Accountability Act (HIPAA) was passed by Congress in 1996. It is designed to provide protection for you and to keep your health information private.

Under the HIPAA rules, you have the right to see your health records, but you must give your permission before the records are released to other individuals. The information provided by doctors or nurses about your care, medications or other personal information is protected. However, you will want to be certain that your designated healthcare proxy or person who will assist in making decisions has the right to review these records. There is a HIPAA release form that you will need to sign in order to enable your advisors to give proper recommendations to your doctors and nurses.

Finally, you must understand the specific documents of your state. Some states use an advance directive in which you would choose a combination of a durable power of attorney for healthcare and a living will. Other states have separate documents. It is very important that you use the appropriate document that is best for your state.

## The Advance Directive

Your first key advisor is the person who will make your medical decisions if you are incapacitated. This individual is frequently called the healthcare proxy. He or she is your agent and holds your power of attorney for healthcare.

You will want to list the person, their address and phone number so he or she can be easily contacted. It is also quite common to select a second or third person to serve if the first person is unable or unwilling to serve.

Part of this section will also explain the level of authority that you have given. Your healthcare proxy usually does not have the authority to make decisions unless, in the view of your doctor, you are no longer able to make decisions yourself. However, many forms allow you to sign and empower that person immediately. The authority of your healthcare proxy may also extend after you pass away so that he or she can make appropriate decisions at that time.

Your healthcare proxy may be called upon to make significant decisions for your care. For example, it may be necessary to decide whether or not to use morphine or other types of pain medication. If the decision is to make use of morphine, then a second decision will be made on the use of a low dose or a high dose. With a lower dose of morphine or other types of pain medication, you may have greater clarity of mind but may be less comfortable. If you receive higher doses of medication, you may not be as clear-headed, even though you are at a higher comfort level. These decisions can only be made based on your condition at a given time, but they do directly impact the quality of your life in that circumstance.

A healthcare proxy may also be called upon to make very significant decisions about the hospital, nursing home or other care facility and the level of treatment. For example, some seniors have suffered broken hips or limbs at a time when their demise was near. A healthcare proxy will need to make decisions about the appropriate level of care or treatment under those circumstances.

A second section of an advance directive allows you to give counsel on the level of measures and technology that will be used to prolong your life. If you have an incurable or irreversible condition that will result in your death within a relatively short time, there are medical devices that can significantly prolong your life.

These are sometimes referred to as "heroic measures." If you desire all reasonable measures to be taken, you can generally request that care. If you do so, your life may be extended to the greatest extent possible under "generally accepted healthcare standards."

Your healthcare guidelines expressed in your advance directive will discuss the level of nutrition and hydration. If you prefer to receive nutrition and hydration through intravenous methods, you may specifically request those.

It is helpful for medical providers to have some level of direction for your pain management. If you prefer a higher level of pain management even though that gives you less clarity of thought, you may so indicate.

A third, fairly typical section of the advance directive covers donation of organs and designation of your primary doctor. If you would like to provide specific organs or designate specific purposes for the use of your body, you may identify the particular organs or discuss purposes. Common purposes include transplantation, therapy, research and education.

Advance directives and living wills may, under state law, be witnessed in a manner similar to the witnessing of your will. Some states require two witnesses and a notary to witness your advance directive. Check with your state law to make certain that you have complied with those requirements. A helpful website with state law requirements is www.caringinfo.org. It is maintained by the National Hospice and Palliative Care Organization and seeks to improve care at the end of life.

## Action Steps

After completing your living will or advance directive, you will sign and typically have witnesses for your original document. Prepare several copies of your advance directive. You will want to give a copy to your healthcare agent, your family, clergy, your doctors and other advisors who may be involved in assisting with your medical decisions.

At any time you may revoke the living will or advance directive. It generally is best to revoke the entire document and complete a new document. If you attempt to amend different parts of the advance directive, there is a risk that you may sign provisions that conflict or are inconsistent. If you are in need of urgent care or treatment, you do not want any conflicting provisions in your living will or advance directive.

Your living will or advance directive is a very important part of your personal planning. It is designed to help you receive the best possible care at the end of your life and still comply to the greatest extent with your personal healthcare preferences.

**CHAPTER 11**

LIVING WILLS AND ADVANCE DIRECTIVES

# QUIZ

1. Under the HIPAA rules, you need to verbally tell your healthcare proxy that he or she has the right to make your medical decisions and has access to your medical records.

   ☐ True      ☐ False

2. All states allow you to express preferences on end-of-life care through an advance directive.

   ☐ True      ☐ False

3. With an advance directive, you normally will select a close family member or advisor who lives in your area as your healthcare agent.

   ☐ True      ☐ False

4. With modern technology, you can be kept alive for an extended period if you so request.

   ☐ True      ☐ False

5. Your personal preferences on pain management can have substantial impact on your end-of-life care.

   ☐ True      ☐ False

**Answers:** To view the quiz answers online, please use the website on the front cover. On that site select "Plan Your Will" and log on to your free Wills Planner account. Select the "Provide & Protect Resources" button on the right and "II. Your Contacts & Healthcare." Select "#11" and view the Quiz Answers at the bottom. You may also enjoy the three-minute video explanation.

# PLANNING WITH A SERIOUS ILLNESS

If at some point in life you have a serious illness, there are a number of planning options that should be considered.

With a serious illness, there are emotional, physical and mental challenges. The illness may be primarily physical, but the person will eventually start to suffer discouragement and even depression. His or her mental capabilities may also start to fail due to deterioration of the body.

Given these serious issues, it is important to consider the care of the person, care of his or her property, financial decisions, potential actions and securing assistance from advisors and family.

## Care of the Person

There are several areas that are important in thinking through care of the person. You should check to make sure you have a current durable power of attorney for healthcare or advance directive. This document needs to be shared with the person who is designated as your healthcare proxy. A serious illness could lead to your hospitalization and a need for the healthcare proxy to make important medical decisions.

There also are potential physical changes for a home or a vehicle. If you have an illness but can operate a motorized wheelchair, it may be appropriate to modify or remodel your home to make it handicap accessible. Similarly, you may suffer from a major illness but are still capable of driving. However, it may be necessary to obtain or modify a vehicle so that you can still drive.

A primary concern for the ill person is, "Who will be the caregiver?" Initially, the seriously ill person may stay at home and a family member may be caregiver. However, you should have a plan to move to assisted living, a nursing home or even a hospital if needed.

### Care of Your Property

If you have a serious illness, it will be important to have either a person who has a power of attorney to manage your property or a revocable living trust. With a revocable living trust, your property is transferred by deed or other document to the trustee. While you may be the initial trustee, your trust also lists a successor trustee to take over if you are no longer able to manage property. With a serious illness, you may wish to resign and have the successor trustee take over while you still have the ability to offer advice and counsel.

If you have a home with valuable art or other valuable collections, it will be important to prepare for management of your property. At any time in the future, you may need to move to nursing care or the hospital. Valuable property will need to be protected and preserved for your estate beneficiaries.

With a serious illness, it is a good time to review your will and all trusts. If you have a trust, you should make certain that the title and ownership of property is correct. The trust is effective only if property is legally transferred to the trustee. Similarly, some individuals hold property as joint tenants with right of survivorship with other family members. If this is the case and you pass away, the surviving family member will own the property outright. If that is your intention, this method is fine. However, you should check all titles to make sure that they are correct for the plan that you have created.

### Financial Accounts

You may have bank accounts, securities accounts and other business accounts. Check to be certain that all of the accounts are listed on your financial records. If you have online access to the accounts, a trusted advisor should know all of the passwords. If you are in the hospital or nursing home, your advisor will need access to your accounts.

## Potential Actions

You may have a current pattern of gifts to family or gifts to charity. If you wish to have your successor trustee or the person holding your power of attorney continue that gifting pattern, there will need to be a specific direction in your living trust or power of attorney to achieve that result.

In some states, there could be very significant income and estate taxes. Even though you have a serious illness, it may be worth considering changing your domicile to a state with a lower tax structure. This will require that you establish a new residence, change your driver's license and auto registration, file your income taxes and show that you are a permanent resident of the new state.

## Advisors and Family

Particularly if you have a substantial estate and are quite ill, it is important to make sure that you have reliable and trustworthy advisors. Far too many elders who have substantial assets become weak and are victims of elder abuse. A group of trusted advisors and family members will protect you and your property.

Your advisors will discuss your vehicle use. There are several cases where seniors felt able to drive vehicles, but were progressively less capable. One individual in her 80s drove regularly to visit her daughter just one mile away. However, one day she made a wrong turn and became disoriented. A day and a half later, the highway patrol discovered the car idling at the side of the road several hundred miles away. Fortunately, she did not become lost during the winter or she very easily could have frozen to death before being discovered.

Advisors and family members will need to discuss with the seriously ill person the arrangements for transportation and the possibility of higher levels of care. This could mean moving from your home into an assisted living facility or nursing home. These discussions are best undertaken while the seriously ill person is still able to think clearly and make good decisions.

Planning with a serious illness is a challenging process. Yet it is much better for the person and for the protection of the estate that the process is entered into openly and willingly by the individual and his or her advisors and family.

**CHAPTER 12**

PLANNING WITH A SERIOUS ILLNESS

# QUIZ

1. With a serious illness, the first concern is care of the person.

   ☐ True  ☐ False

2. With a serious illness, you should have a plan with guidance for the time when you will move to higher care levels.

   ☐ True  ☐ False

3. The person who holds the durable power of attorney for healthcare will decide your care levels.

   ☐ True  ☐ False

4. If you have a home with a valuable art collection, it is fine to select one heir to manage it if you are moved to a nursing home.

   ☐ True  ☐ False

5. A successor trustee will need specific authorization to continue your pattern of gifts to family and charity.

   ☐ True  ☐ False

**Answers:** To view the quiz answers online, please use the website on the front cover. On that site select "Plan Your Will" and log on to your free Wills Planner account. Select the "Provide & Protect Resources" button on the right and "II. Your Contacts & Healthcare." Select "#12" and view the Quiz Answers at the bottom. You may also enjoy the three-minute video explanation.

# PLANNING FOR SENIOR CARE

Planning for retirement and senior care is very important. The activities of daily living for a senior person include eating, dressing, bathing and walking or moving. At some point, every senior will likely need assistance in one or more of these areas.

An important consideration will be the cost of providing that care. By retirement, it is helpful for you to own your home, be debt free, and have retirement income and savings. Retirement income will frequently include Social Security, your IRA or 401(k), a pension plan and investment earnings.

Typically, there are four different levels of care utilized by seniors. The first level includes "in-home care" which includes moderate assistance with certain living functions, such as meal delivery. In home care often progresses to "home healthcare," defined as assistance with the activities of daily living by a home healthcare aid or nurse. The next level is a more formal assisted living or independent living facility. In an assisted living facility, there are more staff and a higher level of assistance. Finally, the fourth level is skilled nursing care. This is 24-hour nursing care in a facility that is designed to provide a higher level of medical assistance.

## Independent Home Care

Independent home care is popular for several reasons. First, it is the least expensive of the four levels of care. Independent home care, or "home care" typically provides a senior with assistance for one or more life functions that does not include healthcare.

With home care, seniors are able to live independently in their home. Seniors with home care might, for example, benefit from a program that delivers a daily meal to their home. If they are not able to maintain their driver's license, they might also participate in a ride-sharing program once or twice per week so they can go to the store to buy certain essentials.

There are a number of local charities that provide services to assist with home care and outreach services. In addition, friends and family can create a schedule to provide assistance to their senior loved one.

Finally, home care very often includes a home monitoring system that allows seniors to contact the monitoring service if they are injured. This service might also require seniors to check in at the same time every morning when an alert sounds so that the monitoring service can contact a relative who lives nearby if the senior does not respond.

### Home Healthcare

The next level of care, home healthcare, involves a greater degree of assistance to seniors and includes healthcare services that are provided in the senior's home. Home healthcare will vary significantly depending on the level of services provided. However, it frequently will cost from $10,000 to $30,000 per year.

Home healthcare is preferred to assisted living or nursing home care because the person receiving care will be able to maintain his or her independence. While the cost is generally reasonable, there are many organizations and providers who can give you good quality care. A key decision for home healthcare is the person who will be the caregiver. Family is often the first option. If you have a child or other relative who is willing to provide assistance, you may be able to live quite comfortably in a family home or perhaps in an attached apartment.

The next level will frequently be a service provider such as a home healthcare aide. The aides visit on a regular basis and provide assistance. Many individuals are able to manage well by themselves as long as they have a home healthcare aide who makes regular visits.

A third level of home healthcare may involve visits by a practical nurse or registered nurse. The nurse may assist you with various types of care and check to see that you are using your medications or other types of therapy in a beneficial manner.

There are safeguards that should be carefully considered for home healthcare. The organizations that provide home healthcare are generally licensed by each state. You can check into their certification and also their reputation. It's also helpful to have a family member who is in regular contact with the senior person who is receiving home healthcare.

As you age and become more senior, it may be appropriate for you to stop driving and to depend on others for transportation. In addition, the family protector can watch to see that you do not make inappropriate expenditures or become vulnerable to any type of abuse.

### Independent or Assisted Living

The next level of care is independent or assisted living which typically has a cost of $40,000 to $65,000 per year. Many facilities provide both independent and assisted living. Independent living permits the individual to live in a residential facility, but to have a reasonably high level of control of his or her life. With independent living, the person will live in his or her own apartment or small residence and frequently retains a vehicle and the ability to drive. Independent living often offers a meals plan so that the resident can choose to eat in a common dining area.

Assisted living occurs in a more structured residence with a higher level of staff services. The assisted living facility will involve staff who regularly assist residents with the activities of daily living.

### Long-term Care

Long-term care includes several levels of care. The two most common levels are skilled nursing and intermediate care. Skilled nursing will provide around-the-clock care from a licensed practical nurse or registered nurse. The cost of skilled nursing care may be $90,000 to $110,000 per year.

Intermediate care facilities also are intended to care for residents that have chronic illnesses or impairments of health. These facilities offer 24-hour staff care. However, they will not always have a registered nurse and may use vocational or practical nurse staff.

It is extremely important with long-term care to examine the facility. Is the facility owned and managed by a for-profit or a nonprofit? What is the affiliation of the organization?

A person may be in a skilled nursing home for several years. Because the costs are very significant, the financial strength of the organization is quite important. If the organization at some point in the future has a financial shortfall, it may find it necessary to reduce services. This could have great impact on the care of a senior person.

Other areas to consider are the facility and the services. What is the location of the facility? You should review the cleanliness of the rooms and the public areas and try to determine the general feelings of current residents toward the facility. Many care facilities offer a number of different types of services. Some of these are social or recreational while others are therapeutic and health related.

Finally, how are the levels of staffing and the food service for the facility? A good facility will have a caring and adequate staff and food service team for the number of residents.

## Alzheimer's Care

Alzheimer's is a challenging disease because it leads progressively to very high care requirements. Because of the staff and facility requirements, Alzheimer's care can cost $100,000 or more per year.

There are three general levels of Alzheimer's. Early-stage Alzheimer's involves some short-term memory loss, difficulties with routine tasks and mood swings. Middle-stage Alzheimer's patients may start to show confusion about time and place, loss of memory and wandering. With late-stage Alzheimer's, there is a loss of cognitive function and eventual physical deterioration.

Home care is possible for early-stage Alzheimer's. A family member can provide the level of care needed. It is important that the caregiver understands the risks and takes protective actions to minimize the potential for the senior person to wander off and become lost.

The next level of care is an organized senior residence with a measure of independence. This will provide available 24-hour care, but still enables an early or middle-stage Alzheimer's patient to have some level of control of his or her activities.

Finally, for advanced stages of Alzheimer's, the senior person will need 24-hour residential care. Family members should examine the rooms, consider the staffing levels and review the policies regarding medication for those Alzheimer's patients.

**CHAPTER 13**

YOUR PLAN FOR SENIOR CARE

# QUIZ

1. Home healthcare is popular both for reasons of acceptable costs and good quality care through trained home healthcare aides.

   ☐ True       ☐ False

2. Assisted living care will provide 24-hour nursing assistance.

   ☐ True       ☐ False

3. In a facility that has both assisted living and skilled nursing, the decision to move from one area to the other is completely up to the senior person.

   ☐ True       ☐ False

4. A person in a facility with independent living, assisted living and skilled nursing may generally remain in the independent living area if he or she can complete two of four activities of daily living, does not present a danger to himself or other residents and does not require physical control.

   ☐ True       ☐ False

5. Home healthcare for early-stage Alzheimer's seniors is demanding but possible.

   ☐ True       ☐ False

**Answers:** To view the quiz answers online, please use the website on the front cover. On that site select "Plan Your Will" and log on to your free Wills Planner account. Select the "Provide & Protect Resources" button on the right and "II. Your Contacts & Healthcare." Select "#13" and view the Quiz Answers at the bottom. You may also enjoy the three-minute video explanation.

# CHRONIC ILLNESS
## Care of Your Person

If you have a chronic illness, your personal planning will need to involve careful consideration of your condition. Many Americans experience ALS disease, Alzheimer's, Huntington's disease, Parkinson's disease, multiple sclerosis (MS) or other types of chronic diseases.

If you or a loved one has one of these conditions, it is important to communicate with your attorney and other advisors about your condition. There are specific planning options both during life and for your testamentary plan that should be considered.

ALS (Lou Gehrig's disease) is a disease that progressively affects a person's ability to control muscle movement. Symptoms include muscle twitching and cramping. Most ALS victims will eventually need a ventilator for breathing, but often will be quite clear-headed during their lifetime.

Alzheimer's is a disease with a progressive reduction in mental capacity. Mild Alzheimer's may be identified by memory lapse and forgetfulness. As Alzheimer's progresses, the individual begins to lose speech facility, forgets to follow normal personal cleanliness habits and loses control. Often, the Alzheimer's sufferer eventually loses the ability to recognize family members and other loved ones.

Huntington's disease is an inherited disorder. The person with Huntington's disease may have great difficulty with coordination and eventually will suffer from dementia and require full-time care.

Parkinson's disease is a disorder of the nervous system. It can lead to progressive deterioration of both the physical body and mental capabilities. Because there is great variation with the disease, some individuals with treatment are able to live reasonably long lives.

Multiple sclerosis (MS) is also a disorder of the nervous system. There is progressive damage to nerve fibers that leads to physical and mental disability. MS may be fairly moderate at first but tends to lead to attacks that can cause progressive deterioration. MS may range from fairly mild to quite severe and very debilitating.

These five and other chronic diseases are all unique and different. Some afflict the body and others reduce the capabilities of the mind. For example, Alzheimer's has greater impact on mental ability, while ALS victims are often suffering in body but may be quite clear in mind.

Your attorney and other advisors need to understand the conditions sufficiently well so that your documents and plans reflect your particular circumstance.

The principal documents for any chronic illness are a durable power of attorney for healthcare, a living will and a HIPAA release. In many states, the durable power of attorney for healthcare and living will are combined into one document described as an advance directive.

### Durable Power of Attorney for Healthcare

If you have a chronic illness, particularly one that leads to loss of mental capacity, it is very important to have a designated person who can make medical decisions for you. In the event that you are unable to reason or communicate, your designated advisor must discuss your medical care with doctors and hospital staff.

A durable power of attorney for healthcare allows you to designate a trusted person to speak to the doctors on your behalf. This power in some states is a separate document. In others, it is the first portion of an advance directive. Many states refer to the person holding the durable power of attorney as your "healthcare proxy."

Regardless of the form of the document or the name of your agent, this person is qualified to make your medical decisions if required.

## Whom Should You Appoint?

For a person with a chronic illness, this can be a challenging decision. You would like to select someone who understands your medical condition and your preferences about care. This could be a family member or friend.

Adult children are often selected, but may experience great emotional trauma in making an end-of-life decision. A friend may be a good choice if you do not have a child who feels willing or emotionally capable of making those decisions.

Generally, you will select a healthcare proxy agent and a successor. It is usually best not to select two persons as your proxy agent—they might disagree at a critical time while you are in need of an immediate decision.

### Living Will

A person with chronic illness needs both a healthcare proxy agent and a living will. Your healthcare proxy agent can make decisions regarding your care, even if you are not near death. The function of the living will is to describe your preferences for care if you are potentially in your last weeks or days of life.

The advance of medical science has enabled doctors to keep people alive for extended periods of time, even if there is virtually no possibility of recovery. If you are in this circumstance, your living will provides guidance to your doctors.

For example, the living will can discuss whether or not heroic measures will be taken to sustain your life. If you have an irreversible condition with no chance of recovery, the living will also specifies whether nutrition and hydration will be maintained.

If you suffer from one of the chronic illnesses that affects mental capacity, it may be important for you to sign your living will before you have mental deterioration. Many Alzheimer's patients and other individuals with great mental deterioration are no longer capable of signing a living will.

## Health Insurance Portability and Accountability Act (HIPAA)

In 1996, Congress passed the Health Insurance Portability and Accountability Act. HIPAA was designed to protect your rights to medical information. Your doctor and other medical providers will frequently acquire extensive background information and treatment information for your chronic illness. Under the HIPAA rules, there are safeguards to protect your personal medical information. A doctor, medical center, or other provider may not disclose this information, particularly to someone who will use it for marketing or similar purposes.

However, you may wish to have your medical information released to your professional advisors so they can make appropriate decisions for you. In order to receive this information, your healthcare proxy must have a formal release from you.

The HIPAA release, which will be in writing, should describe the health information that may be released to the person. It may provide a general list of medical centers or providers or could have an open-ended release for any hospital or medical provider and may include a termination date. After you sign your HIPAA release, you can always revoke that release and sign a new one.

Many states have specific forms for advance directives, living wills, or durable powers of attorney for healthcare. You will want to be certain that you have signed the correct form for your state.

**CHAPTER 14**

CHRONIC ILLNESS — Care of Your Person

# QUIZ

1. A durable power of attorney for healthcare in some states is called an advance directive.

   ☐ True      ☐ False

2. It is perfectly acceptable to appoint two individuals as co-agents to serve as your healthcare proxies.

   ☐ True      ☐ False

3. A durable power of attorney for healthcare is used to advise your doctors about end-of-life decisions.

   ☐ True      ☐ False

4. The living will is applicable if you are in a near death circumstance.

   ☐ True      ☐ False

5. If your advisor does not have a HIPAA release, the medical center may refuse to release your records to him or her.

   ☐ True      ☐ False

**Answers:** To view the quiz answers online, please use the website on the front cover. On that site select "Plan Your Will" and log on to your free Wills Planner account. Select the "Provide & Protect Resources" button on the right and "II. Your Contacts & Healthcare." Select "#14" and view the Quiz Answers at the bottom. You may also enjoy the three-minute video explanation.

# CHRONIC ILLNESS
## Care of Your Property

If you have a chronic illness, you will need to care both for your person and for your property. This article will explain some of the specific preparations that are important to care for your property. With a chronic illness, you may have a higher probability that you will not be able to manage your property and will need assistance during your lifetime. In addition, there will be a need to make sure that your testamentary transfers are upheld if a relative questions your ability or your capacity to make those decisions.

### Power of Attorney

There are several types of powers of attorney for managing your property. With a chronic illness, you may not have the physical or mental capability to manage your property. A designated person can be of great assistance to you in making sure that your property is managed and used for your best care.

A general power of attorney will permit your selected representatives to have complete control over all of your financial affairs. It is quite powerful, but must also be granted carefully so that the person uses that broad power appropriately. You must have a high level of trust in the person to give him or her general power of attorney.

A special power of attorney is a grant of limited rights. For example, a person may have the right to lease or sell your principal residence. If you are transferred to a care facility and will no longer be able to return home, it may be good to give a person the legal right to sell your residence.

A "springing" power of attorney can be particularly useful if you have a chronic illness. In the event that you are incapacitated or unable to function effectively, then your selected agent may assume the rights under your power of attorney. With a springing power, there can be difficulty in determining whether the lower level of incapacity is sufficient to trigger the power. For this reason, some states have specific requirements and restrictions on springing powers.

If your designated agent for the power of attorney has fairly broad power, you may wish to include the ability for that person to make gifts to family or gifts to charity. Typically, the right to make gifts enables your agent to continue your current pattern of gifts to family or to charity. Your agent will decide if the resources in your estate allow both the making of gifts and providing for your care.

### Capacity to Make a Will

With a chronic illness, your basic estate planning document is still a will. While you may also have a revocable living trust, a will is needed to distribute any property not owned by the trust when you pass away.

Many of your assets will pass to beneficiaries outside the probate process and will not be owned inside your trust. These include your qualified IRA and other retirement plans, life insurance policies that are transferred by beneficiary designation and any real property owned as joint tenants with right of survivorship. That real property will be transferred under property law to the surviving person.

However, if your designated beneficiary under a qualified retirement plan or a life insurance policy passes away before you, or the other joint tenant with a real property asset passes away prior to your demise, the assets could be distributed to your estate and be subject to your will. Therefore, it is essential to have a proper will.

With some types of chronic illness, you may have a loss of either physical or mental abilities. In this case, an heir could claim that you did not have proper capacity to sign the will and could contest it. Therefore, it may be helpful to emphasize to your witnesses that you clearly understand the process and have a good understanding both of your property and of the general provisions of the will. In addition, some individuals obtain records from their physicians that explain the various types of treatment. Your doctor may also discuss your ability to have control of your mental facilities during the estate planning process.

## Revocable Living Trust

A revocable living trust is strongly recommended if you have a chronic illness. It is much more flexible than a durable power of attorney.

If you suffer from a disability or become incapacitated, upon the recommendation of one or two physicians your successor trustee will be empowered to manage your assets.

With no revocable living trust, a family member may instead be required to obtain permission from the probate court to create a conservatorship. This will require expensive and repeated visits to the court for approval of expenditures, sale of most real property and other actions. It will greatly increase the expense and the difficulties for the person who is acting as your conservator.

A successor trustee under a revocable living trust is far more flexible and less expensive. Compared with a conservatorship, the cost of creating the revocable living trust may be recovered in the first few months of the time when you need someone else to manage your property.

Revocable living trusts are a legal agreement. You specify the management powers of the trustee, the general provisions for distribution of income and principal and select your successor trustee. Ordinarily, you will serve as the initial trustee. If you are incapacitated, the successor trustee will take over and manage the property. Your property will be legally transferred with a deed for real property and by creating trust accounts for mutual funds, securities and cash. It is essential to make sure that title to the selected property is properly transferred under state law rules to you as trustee of the living trust.

## Assemble Your Records

Even if you have a power of attorney to help manage your property, have signed a valid will and have created a revocable living trust, it will help your advisors if you have an organized system for your records.

The first set of records should include all of the above planning documents. In addition, the documents for the care of your person, such as a durable power of attorney for healthcare, a HIPAA release, a living will or an advance directive should be included.

The second set of documents will be all of your financial records. Many people with a chronic disease have placed their records on computer. Through a combination of online banking and records from your brokerage and securities accounts, all of your financial data can be accessible in one location.

The third category of record is your family information and personal history. This could include marriage certificates, insurance records and other various types of medical reports.

**CHAPTER 15**

CHRONIC ILLNESS — Care of Your Property

# QUIZ

1. A general power of attorney should be given only to a person with whom you have a high level of trust.

   ☐ True     ☐ False

2. If your power of attorney does not include the power to make gifts to family or charity, most agents will refuse to make any gifts.

   ☐ True     ☐ False

3. If you have all of your assets in a revocable living trust, or have designated beneficiaries for your IRA or other qualified retirement plan and hold property as joint tenants with right of survivorship, you do not need a will.

   ☐ True     ☐ False

4. A revocable living trust could save a person with a chronic illness thousands of dollars.

   ☐ True     ☐ False

5. A revocable living trust eliminates all estate tax.

   ☐ True     ☐ False

**Answers:** To view the quiz answers online, please use the website on the front cover. On that site select "Plan Your Will" and log on to your free Wills Planner account. Select the "Provide & Protect Resources" button on the right and "II. Your Contacts & Healthcare." Select "#15" and view the Quiz Answers at the bottom. You may also enjoy the three-minute video explanation.

# APPLICATION AND ACTION

Congratulations on reading this far! By now you know about many of your healthcare options. You may want to complete the "Your Contacts & Healthcare" section of your online Wills Planner. After you have finished entering your healthcare choices, you will be able to return at any time and update it as needed.

1. Go to the website on the front cover.

2. You will see the home page for gift planning. Look for the link with the title "Plan Your Will."

3. After you click "Plan Your Will," you will view the Wills Planner access page. If you do not yet have a Wills Planner account, select "Create Your Account" and enter your data. After you create your account, you may enter your username and password to view your personal, secure account on the Wills Planner website.

4. Once you have entered the website, you will see four different sections. The first is the "You and Your Family" section. Click on that section and enter your family information. There are also sections on "Your Contacts & Healthcare", "Your Finances" and "Your Estate Plan." You may save and view your information at any time.

5. You may want to view some of the *Provide & Protect* chapters and videos. Click the "*Provide & Protect*" button. You may view the entire updated version of the *Provide & Protect* multi-media book online. Each chapter includes a short video and quiz with answers. Some of our friends like to read a chapter each week, watch the video and take the quiz. In just one year, you may cover the entire book.

6. Finally, please feel free to call or email us at any time if we can help you with a short online phone tutorial.

# Your Finances

# WHAT DO YOU OWN?

John and Helen have been thinking about updating their estate plan. They called and made an appointment with their attorney, Clara.

John and Helen updated Clara on their current family situation. They have three children who are now on their own and successfully pursuing careers. After listening to the short update on the three children, Clara turned to a review of John's and Helen's property.

**Clara:** "Before we update your plan, we need to make sure we have a complete list of your property. Let's start with a few questions. Do you have a home? Are there bank or security accounts?"

**John:** "Well, we do have our home. It's in both of our names. There is our joint checking account and a savings account. Both of us also have some other accounts. I have one savings account with myself and our son Bill. Helen has a savings account with our daughter Susan and another one for Helen and our daughter Linda. We have some mutual funds with a large financial company. I think that's in both our names."

**Clara:** "That's a very good start. Now most people also have a pension or retirement plan and some life insurance. Do you have both of those?"

**John:** "Yes, I have a 401(k) at my work and Helen has an IRA. She had a 401(k) at one time and we rolled it over into an IRA when she changed jobs. I have a life insurance policy and I think it pays Helen $300,000 if something happens to me."

**Clara:** "So you have a life insurance policy. Do you know if it is a whole life, universal life or a term insurance plan? If it is a whole life or a universal life, it probably has a certain amount of cash value now."

**John:** "I am not real sure but it probably is a whole life plan. We bought the policy about ten years ago and I make payments every month."

**Clara:** "Is there any other real estate or other securities accounts?"

**Helen:** "When my dad passed away, he owned 640 acres of timberland. It was divided three ways between my brother, my sister and me. My share is still in my name. We don't get income from the timberland because we only cut enough timber to pay the property taxes."

**Clara:** "Thanks, Helen. That's helpful to know. What about personal possessions? You probably have automobiles, furniture, perhaps a collection of items or a recreational vehicle?"

**John:** "Yes, we have two cars. I think my car is in my name and Helen's car is in her name. Of course, we have furniture in all of the rooms of our four-bedroom home. We also have an RV that we use to take trips in the summer. I think it is in both our names."

**Clara:** "And are there any other types of ownership interests or business interests? Are either of you likely to receive an inheritance in the near future?"

**Helen:** "Yes, my mother is still living. John's parents have passed away and we received a moderate inheritance when his mom passed away. When my mother passes away, I will probably receive some additional property. When dad passed away, half of the timberland was given to the three of us and mother has the other half. When she passes away, I would guess that the three children would each receive a third of the timberland that she owns."

**Clara:** "This is a very good list of the assets. Let's now try to estimate the values of your property. The value will not be the initial amount you paid for each property, but a general estimate of what they are worth today."

(John, Helen, and Clara spent 20 minutes estimating the value of all of their property before moving on to discuss their debts.)

**Clara:** "John and Helen, there is just one more part to this inventory process. While I know you both are very careful and conservative in your financial affairs, some people have debt. Do you have a home mortgage? Is there a loan on a car or on your recreational vehicle? And do you have an ongoing credit card balance?"

**John:** "Yes, we do have a mortgage on the home. It still has a balance of $100,000. There is a loan on my car of about $3,000. Helen's car is paid off and we pay off our credit cards each month."

**Clara:** "Thanks very much for patiently working through the inventory with me. This is going to be very important as we make decisions about your estate plan."

### Why the Inventory Process is Important

It takes time and effort to make a list of your property. However, there are several important reasons why that property list is a crucial part of a successful plan. The list enables you to identify your assets, estimate the value, understand the best potential benefits for your children or other heirs, plan to reduce your taxes and set up goals for your children.

Identification of your property is very important. If both John and Helen pass away, the first responsibility of their executor or personal representative is to identify and list all of their assets. The inventory will be an excellent guide for the executor. Without an inventory, some assets might be forgotten, lost or eventually abandoned and transferred to state government.

Valuation is important. The values are estimates, but frequently the total value is significantly larger than you may realize. Values also need to reflect the potential reductions for liabilities. Most families are similar to John and Helen in that they have fairly modest liabilities and quite substantial total values at the time of retirement.

## Benefits For Children and Other Heirs

Benefits for children and other heirs are best determined after you list all of your property values. It's also extremely important to understand how the property is owned. Some of the property in joint ownership will be transferred under state property law to the survivor. Only the property subject to the probate process is transferred by your will.

Because many people have substantial assets in their 401(k), IRA, other retirement plan or life insurance, and these assets are all transferred by the beneficiary designation, it is essential to help your attorney know how the property is titled and who the beneficiary is of the various retirement and insurance plans. The correct beneficiary designation enables your children or other heirs to receive benefits.

Estate taxes may be applicable for those with larger estates. Because some individuals have property that may have increased in value (the timberland owned by Helen had increased greatly in value over the past 30 years), and because there may be an inheritance that increases the estate yet further, it is important to consider the potential impact of estate taxes. A good plan can save thousands and even millions in future estate tax.

A final benefit of the inventory process is that the parents now have a much clearer picture of their assets. This enables them to make decisions that will be important for deciding the amount and type of inheritance for their children. There may be specific assets, such as family heirlooms or land, that should be transferred to one child rather than the others. Because parents frequently are interested in treating children equally, knowing the approximate values of the property enables them to make plans for transfer of some assets to specific children and to maintain overall fairness in the plan.

**CHAPTER 16**

WHAT DO YOU OWN?

# QUIZ

**1.** Most people value their property quite accurately.

☐ True   ☐ False

**2.** The assets of an estate are fairly easy to value.

☐ True   ☐ False

**3.** With life insurance it is important to consider both the current cash value and the death benefit.

☐ True   ☐ False

**4.** The type of ownership can have great impact on the estate plan.

☐ True   ☐ False

**5.** Liabilities can have major impact on estate planning.

☐ True   ☐ False

**Answers:** To view the quiz answers online, please use the website on the front cover. On that site select "Plan Your Will" and logon to your free Wills Planner account. Select the "Provide & Protect Resources" button on the right and "III. Your Finances." Select "#16" and view the Quiz Answers at the bottom. You may also enjoy the three-minute video explanation.

# SEPARATE AND JOINT PROPERTY

"My brother, Pete and I own a ranch together," said Joe to his advisor. "We inherited the four sections of our ranch from my mother. As a single person, I think that I will plan to leave 50% of my share to Pete and the other half to my favorite charity. Of course, if Pete dies, he is married and probably wants to leave his share to his spouse and children."

Do Pete and Joe need to review their estate plans? Yes! These two rancher brothers held title as joint tenants with right of survivorship. If the single brother (Joe) were to pass away, Pete would inherit his brother's half of the ranch. Even though Joe stated that half of his share should go to his favorite charity, nothing will be given to charity.

On the other hand, if the married brother (Pete) were to pass away, under the joint tenancy with right of survivorship rules the ranch now belongs in its entirety to Joe. Pete's spouse and children would have no benefit, with the exception of some states in which a forced spousal share might provide some relief.

Do you know how your property is owned? This can make a huge difference in your plan, just as it did for Pete and Joe. Property can be owned outright, as tenants in common, as joint tenants with right of survivorship or in a trust.

## Outright Ownership

Joe is a single person and also owns a home in a small community close to the ranch. He has complete title to the property in his name.

The legal term for owning property outright is "fee simple" title. Because Joe owns the property outright in his name, he is obligated to personally pay the taxes, mortgage interest and any other costs of maintaining the property. However, he has complete use of the property and may transfer it during life or through his estate to any person or charity.

## Tenants in Common

With property held as tenants in common, each person has an undivided interest in his or her portion. For example, Pete and Joe could change the title to the ranch to tenants in common. Each would still own 50% of the entire ranch. The taxes, the mortgage payments or any other costs would be divided between the brothers. However, because the ranch is held as tenants in common, each person may make transfers of the property during life or through his estate. Joe could decide to leave 50% of his half to Pete and 50% to favorite charity. Pete could leave his 50% of the ranch to his spouse and children.

## Joint Tenancy with Right of Survivorship

The property could be held jointly, but under state law the surviving tenant receives title to the property when the first passes away. For example, if Pete were to pass away while the property is held as joint tenants with right of survivorship, Joe then would own the entire ranch. Both Pete and Joe would pay their share of taxes and the mortgage during life, but the property is transferred by state law to the surviving joint tenant, not according to the will of the first to pass away. For anyone other than a surviving spouse, joint tenancy with right of survivorship may result in an accidental disinheritance.

## Trusts

It is possible to transfer real estate and other assets into a trust. Each person deeds his or her portion into the trust. The trustee owns the entire property for the benefit of the income and remainder recipients. The trustee will manage the property, collect income and distribute it according to the terms of the trust document. A trust is especially useful if you own property in different states.

Therefore, it is very important to understand how your property is owned. When you are creating your estate plan or are considering a transfer or gift during life, you need to be certain that you first understand the ownership. Then you will be able to make a legal transfer to the intended beneficiary.

Many estate lawsuits have occurred because individuals thought they had the right to transfer property by will, but there was a joint tenancy with right of survivorship that transferred the property to a surviving owner. If one person receives under the will and another by right of survivorship, litigation is quite likely. By understanding the way in which your property is titled, you can be certain that your intentions are carried out according to your plan.

## CHAPTER 17
SEPARATE AND JOINT PROPERTY

# QUIZ

1. Property that is owned outright or in fee simple may be given during life or at death to any person or a charity.

   ☐ True      ☐ False

2. If you own property as a joint tenant with right of survivorship, you may transfer it by your will.

   ☐ True      ☐ False

3. When property is held by two persons as tenants in common, each individual pays 50% of the taxes, 50% of the mortgage and receives 50% of the net income.

   ☐ True      ☐ False

4. If property is held by two persons as tenants in common, either one can transfer his or her 50% of the property by will.

   ☐ True      ☐ False

5. Property held in a trust must be deeded to the trustee.

   ☐ True      ☐ False

**Answers:** To view the quiz answers online, please use the website on the front cover. On that site select "Plan Your Will" and logon to your free Wills Planner account. Select the "Provide & Protect Resources" button on the right and "III. Your Finances." Select "#17" and view the Quiz Answers at the bottom. You may also enjoy the three-minute video explanation.

# MARRIED COUPLES AND PROPERTY

Mary was a surviving spouse. She and her first spouse, Ryan owned a lovely home and placed it into joint tenancy with right of survivorship. After Ryan passed away, Mary met Logan and they were married. Because she had the house in joint tenancy before, Mary changed the title to joint tenancy with right of survivorship, with Logan as the other joint tenant.

Unfortunately, Mary passed away two years later. Her will gave all of her property to the children of her first marriage. However, their children, Sam and Susan, did not receive the largest asset in her estate—Mary's home. Logan was the surviving tenant and under state law he owned the home outright. He later passed on the valuable home to children from his first marriage.

Joint tenancy for married couples is very simple and quite common. However, it is not always the best plan, especially if there is a second marriage or blended family.

For first marriages, joint tenancy with right of survivorship is a very convenient way to own a home, bank account, stocks or mutual funds. However, couples should understand that there are some potential risks in holding property as joint tenants with right of survivorship. If the couple is planning to fund trusts or the estate increases to a level that it is important to create a special tax-saving trust called the bypass trust, then joint tenancy can conflict with the will or living trust provisions. Joint tenancy may also disinherit a beneficiary under the will. While joint tenancy is very simple and common, it should be used with caution.

### Joint or Separate Property

Joint property is typical for any assets acquired during marriage. However, property that is inherited or brought into a marriage is usually separate property. Separate property in most states may be transferred to persons other than the surviving spouse. If a spouse inherits separate property and plans to keep it separate for inheritance purposes, it's also important to avoid commingling the separate property with other assets. If the separate property is commingled with joint property or treated as joint property by paying the taxes and other costs out of a joint checking account, then the separate property may be converted to jointly held property. This could significantly change the estate plan result.

### Community Property

Several states allow a married couple to own property as community property. Property acquired during a marriage in Alaska (with a written agreement), California, Idaho, Washington, Nevada, New Mexico, Texas or Wisconsin will be owned equally by husband and wife.

In Alaska, Arizona, California, Nevada, Texas and Wisconsin, the community property may be held with right of survivorship. In other states, the property is owned in joint tenancy with right of survivorship, but there is a separate agreement that states the property is community property. In both cases, when the first spouse passes away, the second spouse is now the owner without a probate process.

### Saving Capital Gains Tax

There is a very important capital gains tax benefit for the surviving spouse if it is possible to hold the property as community property. When property that has been acquired appreciates in value, there is a capital gains tax due upon sale. For example, if stock were purchased for $25 and increased in value over several years to $100, upon sale the $75 of appreciation would be taxed as long-term capital gain.

If stock or land passes through an estate, then the person receiving the property may benefit from a step-up in basis. For example, if a share of stock bought for $25 and worth $100 now is transferred through an estate, then the cost basis to the beneficiary is also $100. He or she may sell the stock for that amount with no capital gains tax.

### Tax-free Sale

With community property, a married couple could jointly purchase 100 shares of stock for $50. The 100 shares then appreciate to $200. If one spouse passes away and the 50 shares are given to the surviving spouse, he or she receives a step-up in basis on both portions and now may sell the stock for $200 with no tax.

However, in a state that does not follow the community property rules, with joint tenancy only the 50% of the stock owned by the deceased spouse gets a stepped-up basis. In effect, the stock is divided in half and the cost basis is $25 on that share with a fair market value of $100. When that stock passes through the estate, the basis is stepped up to $100 and it may be sold with no tax. But when the surviving spouse also sells the stock for $100, he or she still has $25 of cost basis and $75 of taxable gain on the stock.

Therefore, if community property status is available and a surviving spouse might desire to sell assets without paying any capital gains tax, it's important to be sure that the community property title is created.

**CHAPTER 18**

MARRIED COUPLES AND PROPERTY

# QUIZ

**1.** Married couples use joint tenancy because it is simple.

☐ True    ☐ False

**2.** Community property is a method of building assets during the marriage that are owned 50% by one spouse and 50% by the other spouse.

☐ True    ☐ False

**3.** If the one spouse inherits property during their lifetime, it automatically becomes joint or community property.

☐ True    ☐ False

**4.** Joint tenancy is better than community property for reducing the potential capital gains taxes of a surviving spouse who receives land or stock.

☐ True    ☐ False

**5.** A married couple may use joint tenancy to own stocks or bank accounts.

☐ True    ☐ False

**Answers:** To view the quiz answers online, please use the website on the front cover. On that site select "Plan Your Will" and logon to your free Wills Planner account. Select the "Provide & Protect Resources" button on the right and "III. Your Finances." Select "#18" and view the Quiz Answers at the bottom. You may also enjoy the three-minute video explanation.

# SOCIAL SECURITY

Linda asked, "When should I take my Social Security? I will turn 57 this year and have a strong earnings history, having paid into Social Security for nearly 35 years. Given the year I was born, my 'regular' retirement age for purposes of Social Security will be age 67 but I can take 'early' benefits starting at age 62 or even wait until age 70. Which is better for me?"

## Social Security Benefits

The average American retires and receives Social Security to cover part of his or her retirement expenses. A typical Social Security payment replaces approximately 40% of your pre-retirement income. To qualify for Social Security, you need to have contributed to the fund for 40 quarters or 10 years. Your Social Security payout will be dependent on your highest earning years.

## Full Payments at Age 67

In the 1980s, Congress decided to slowly increase the age for full Social Security benefits from 65 to 67. For anyone born after 1960, the full Social Security retirement benefit is available at age 67.

Based on the tables, Linda would qualify for $2,825 per month (in current dollars). If she waits until that age to start payouts, she receives a larger amount than if she selects an early payout at age 62 and it will be adjusted for inflation.

The favorable news for Linda is that she would receive this larger amount plus cost-of-living increases for her lifetime. In addition, if she works after age 67, there's no reduction in her Social Security payment. She can continue to receive the full income of her work and the Social Security benefit. Of course, because both she and her employer are contributing to the Social Security system while she is working, her actual Social Security benefit is significantly reduced. Her Social Security payout will be taxed and her net after-tax benefit will be reduced.

Because Linda is still working, she is contributing about $600 per month of after-tax income to Social Security. Her employer is also contributing a similar sum. The net Social Security benefit to her, after payment of income taxes on her contribution and the contribution by her employer from her salary, is now approximately $300 to $600 of added after-tax monthly income.

### Early Payout at Age 62

Linda could join most Americans and start taking payments when she is age 62. Based on the current Social Security tables, her maximum payment would be 30% lower than the full benefits she would receive at age 67.

This amount will be adjusted every year based on the Social Security cost-of-living increase. While her benefit is adjusted for inflation, the actual value or purchasing power of this amount will not change. Linda's mother is still living and her grandmother lived to be 96, so she may be wise to plan for a fairly long retirement.

There is one other challenge for Linda. If she continues to work, and many individuals do work until their late 60s, she will lose part of her Social Security payment. For every $3 in income (over an indexed limit) she earns between age 62 and her full retirement age, she loses $1 in Social Security benefits. By taking her payment at age 62, she receives both a lower payout for her lifetime and reduced payments for the years until her full retirement age.

### Delaying Payments to Age 70

If Linda continues with her present employment and does not need her Social Security income, she can receive an increased benefit by delaying the start of payments to age 70. The benefit starting at age 70 for Linda is currently 24% higher than what she would receive at age 67. With inflation adjustments, Linda's benefit could be even higher by the time she reaches age 70.

This represents a significant increase over her normal retirement amount. The amount increases by about 8% per year because the government has held her funds longer and she has a shorter period of time before beginning to receive her payments.

If Linda lives to her mid 80s, then she will have received a greater total Social Security benefit. If she joins her long-lived relatives who have survived to their mid 90s, her net economic benefit from Social Security by delaying the first payouts to age 70 is dramatically greater than her total payouts starting at age 62 or 67.

**Tax-free Social Security Payouts**

Individuals with lower incomes do not pay any federal tax on Social Security. Generally, single people with incomes under $25,000 per year do not pay tax.

**50% of Social Security Taxable**

For many Social Security recipients, their income is in the middle range and 50% is taxable. For example, a single person with taxable income of approximately $25,000 to $34,000 would pay tax on half of his or her Social Security. The taxable income is called the modified adjusted gross income and includes adjustments for some types of tax-free income.

Because Linda has a substantial IRA, she expects to have a higher level of income.

**85% of Social Security Taxable**

With other pension income and IRA income, Linda anticipates a modified adjusted gross income of over $36,000 per year. As a result, 85% of her Social Security is taxable.

Linda is not very pleased with this plan. Because she already paid tax on her half of the Social Security, she feels that this is a very substantial tax. However, with the increasing need to fund Social Security in the future, the high probability is that Linda will pay tax on 85% of her Social Security during her lifetime.

## Social Security for Spouses

A spouse may have different options for receiving Social Security. First, if he or she qualifies based on employment, then the best choice may be to take his or her normal benefit at the selected retirement age.

However, a surviving spouse can receive a reduced spousal benefit starting at age 60. At a later date they may transition to a full benefit under their own qualification. Former spouses may also receive benefits after age 62.

**CHAPTER 19**

SOCIAL SECURITY

# QUIZ

**1.** Even with an IRA and a pension from your company, you may also qualify for Social Security benefits.

☐ True ☐ False

**2.** Most Americans take Social Security at the earliest age of 62.

☐ True ☐ False

**3.** If you take Social Security benefits at age 62, the retirement benefit is reduced by 10%.

☐ True ☐ False

**4.** If you take retirement benefits at age 62, you may continue to work and receive the full amount.

☐ True ☐ False

**5.** If you have good income and your parents lived a long and full life, it may be better for you to wait until age 70 to start Social Security payments.

☐ True ☐ False

**Answers:** To view the quiz answers online, please use the website on the front cover. On that site select "Plan Your Will" and logon to your free Wills Planner account. Select the "Provide & Protect Resources" button on the right and "III. Your Finances." Select "#19" and view the Quiz Answers at the bottom. You may also enjoy the three-minute video explanation..

# 401(k) RETIREMENT PLANS

The 401(k) is rapidly becoming the most popular qualified retirement plan. More than 90% of large companies now offer a 401(k). With a 401(k), each employee has an individual account and is permitted to transfer a portion of his or her salary directly into the account each year.

Most 401(k) plans qualify for excluding the contribution from your taxable income each year. However, some employers have created a "Roth 401(k)" plan in which your contributions are after tax.

To encourage employees to fund a 401(k), some employers also create a matching fund. The employer determines the amount of match and the maximum. While many different plans are selected by employers, a fairly typical employer match is $1 for $2 of contribution to 6% of the employee's salary. With this plan, an employee who contributes the full 6% would receive a 3% employer match. Therefore, the total 401(k) contribution that year would be equal to 9% of the employee's income.

## Contribution Limits

There are several potential contribution limits for employees. This year, the voluntary contribution by the employee is limited to $18,000. However, employees over age 50 during the year are permitted to add a "catch up" contribution of $6,000. The total annual employee contribution for those over age 50 is $24,000 this year. Both limits are indexed for inflation and increase in $500 increments. Some companies also will add a match or other company contribution to that amount.

Most companies have highly compensated employees (HCE) who are subject to specific rules. To make certain that the contributions are fair, the employees with income above a certain threshold and owners of more than 5% of a business are limited in their contributions. There are various "safe harbor" provisions that allow the HCEs to contribute without worrying about the annual contribution tests. For example, if there is a non-elective contribution by the company of 3% or more for all employees, then the plan does not have to meet specific standards for highly compensated employees.

## 401(k) Investments

The employer will select a custodian of the 401(k) and typically there will be a group of mutual funds for the 401(k) investments. The employee will have opportunity to select from the various mutual funds. These mutual funds are usually in four general categories.

The first category is stock mutual funds. Stocks have a long-term return of approximately 10%. For investments of 20 years or more, a percentage of the 401(k) in stocks will usually be a good decision. Stock funds generally include large cap, medium cap and small capitalization companies. Some funds may favor domestic companies and some foreign.

Stock funds should be fairly diversified to minimize the risk of loss if a company were to fail. A portfolio of large, midsized and small company mutual funds may own shares in 1,000 or more companies.

Bonds are the second type of investment fund. Mid-term and long-term bonds have returned approximately 5.5% during the past 75 years. Because bond values change much more slowly than stock values, the bonds are a more stable investment than stocks and are appropriate for shorter timeframes before retirement. As 401(k) owners move into their 50s, 60s and 70s, the percentage of bonds normally increases and that of stocks decreases. Some advisors suggest that the percentage of bonds should match your age. For example, a person age 60 may choose to hold 60% in bonds and 40% in stocks.

Cash is the third investment option. Most 401(k) plans permit a money market fund or similar option. Returns on cash funds are frequently 1% to 3%, but these cash options preserve principal in a downturn.

Real estate is the fourth investment type. Some 401(k) plans permit real estate investment trust (REIT) investments. Real estate may be a good long-term investment, but also involves substantial potential risk.

### 401(k) Distributions

There are three general periods of time of importance to 401(k) owners. Prior to age 59½, there is a 10% excise tax on distributions. For a regular 401(k), the owner who takes early distributions would pay both income tax plus the additional 10% excise tax. There are exceptions for disability, substantially equal payments over a lifetime or economic hardship, but most individuals attempt to avoid early withdrawals if possible.

Between age 59½ and age 70½, there is a voluntary distribution option. As a 401(k) owner, you may choose to take distributions to cover living expenses. The distributions may be any amount from the regular 401(k), but will be reported by you as taxable income.

After age 70½ (by April 1 of the following year), you must take at least the required minimum distribution (RMD). Your required minimum distribution starts at approximately 3.8% at age 71 and increases to nearly 8.8% by age 90. With one exception, the distributions by a 401(k) owner are governed by this schedule under the IRS Uniform Table. The exception is a husband and wife in which one spouse is more than 10 years younger. A special table applies in that case.

### 401(k) Loans

A 401(k) plan document may permit you to take a loan from your account. Loans are limited to the lesser of 50% of your plan or $50,000, and must be repaid within five years (except for purchase of a primary residence). A reasonable rate of interest is charged. While your loan is repaid with after-tax dollars, your 401(k) account will grow by the amount of the loan interest.

## 401(k) Balances

Because the required initial withdrawal amount at age 71 is approximately 3.8%, many individuals with 401(k)s will find that their total fund balance increases until their early to mid 80s. Even with some reduction in balance during ages 85 to 95 because the withdrawal percentages continue to increase, many 401(k) owners will pass away with substantial balances.

Because there is likely to be a significant balance in your 401(k) when you pass away, careful selection of your designated beneficiaries is important. If you pass away with a substantial 401(k) balance, then a significant amount will be distributed to your designated primary or contingent beneficiary. In most cases, your designated beneficiary will have the option of taking distribution of your 401(k) over a term of years.

**CHAPTER 20**

401(k) RETIREMENT PLANS

# QUIZ

1. A 401(k) plan is an example of a self-directed retirement plan.

   ☐ True        ☐ False

2. An employee may contribute $10,000 or more from salary to a regular 401(k) plan and reduce taxable income by that amount.

   ☐ True        ☐ False

3. If the 401(k) owner is over 50, he or she may contribute an additional $6,000.

   ☐ True        ☐ False

4. The 401(k) owner is permitted to select investments.

   ☐ True        ☐ False

5. As the 401(k) employee grows older and is closer to retirement, he or she should select more stocks rather than bonds because stocks produce a higher rate of return.

   ☐ True        ☐ False

**Answers:** To view the quiz answers online, please use the website on the front cover. On that site select "Plan Your Will" and logon to your free Wills Planner account. Select the "Provide & Protect Resources" button on the right and "III. Your Finances." Select "#20" and view the Quiz Answers at the bottom. You may also enjoy the three-minute video explanation.

# IRAs
# Regular and Roth

While Social Security will provide approximately 40% of the average person's retirement income, an Individual Retirement Account (IRA) is an essential addition for a successful retirement. Your IRA has two main benefits—contributions to a regular IRA are from pre-tax income and there is tax-free growth. There is another version of an IRA called a Roth IRA that is funded with after-tax income.

Linda is in her middle working years and anticipates receiving Social Security when she retires. But she has several questions about whether she should also start funding an IRA.

- How should I fund my IRA?
- Is it a good idea to do an IRA rollover?
- At what age should I start taking IRA distributions?
- Should I take the minimum required distribution or a larger amount?

### Funding the IRA

If you are not actively participating in another type of qualified retirement plan and are within an adjusted gross income limit, you may qualify to transfer a substantial sum each year into an IRA. The IRA contribution amount is $5,500 this year. If you are over age 50, you may also make an additional $1,000 "catch-up" contribution. The maximum IRA contribution amounts are indexed for inflation in increments of $500. In future years, the contribution amount will increase.

Because Linda is over age 50, she is able to contribute $5,500 and her catch-up amount of $1,000, for a total of $6,500 to her IRA this year.

Linda considers the options to create a regular IRA or a Roth IRA. Because she wants to receive the income tax deduction, she transfers the funds into a regular IRA and deducts the $6,500 on her federal tax returns.

## IRA Rollovers

The majority of larger IRAs are funded through rollovers from retirement plans through your employer. If you have a qualified plan through your employment, upon separation from service or reaching a specific age, such as 70, you will usually have an option to rollover to a self-directed IRA.

Normally, your qualified plan through a business has been funded with pretax income. The IRA account also benefits from tax-free growth. Therefore, the rollover will be from the other qualified plan into a regular IRA. Your IRA will continue to grow tax free, but future distributions to you will be taxable.

IRAs may be rolled over to a new custodian. The preferred method is to have a custodian-to-custodian transfer. If the funds are transferred directly from one IRA custodian to the new custodian, there is no tax.

While it is permissible for your custodian to transfer funds to you and then for you to make the rollover, your IRA custodian will withhold 20%. Because of the 20% withholding requirement, virtually all IRA rollovers are completed with the custodian-to-custodian method.

An IRA to Roth IRA rollover may also be permissible for you. Generally speaking, people with any adjusted gross income are permitted to transfer a regular IRA to a Roth IRA. The value of the IRA will be included in your taxable income, so you may owe a substantial income tax for the conversion.

The primary benefit of the conversion to the Roth is that a Roth IRA does not have a mandatory distribution requirement at age 70½. The funds may be permitted to grow tax free and, at the discretion of the owner, may be withdrawn tax free during retirement years. If the owner of a Roth IRA does not make withdrawals, then the Roth may be transferred to children, who may make tax free withdrawals over their life expectancy.

## IRA Distributions

For a regular IRA, there are specific rules on both contributions and withdrawals. Withdrawals for distributions are generally not taken before age 59½. With limited exceptions—such as uniform distributions over a lifetime, disability, separation from employment after age 55, or other exceptions—there is a 10% excise tax in addition to the regular ordinary income tax on withdrawals before age 59½. Therefore, very few individuals take early withdrawals before age 59½.

Between ages 59½ and 70½, there is an optional period for withdrawals. The withdrawals are not required, but you may take withdrawal of any amount. Of course, for a regular IRA the amount withdrawn is taxable to you and no longer grows tax free in the fund. Therefore, you may not want to take withdrawals unless you actually need the funds for living expenses.

After you reach age 70½, there are required minimum distributions (RMDs). The distributions start at approximately 3.8% at age 71 but increase with age each year. The distribution is calculated using your balance on December 31 multiplied by the appropriate percentage, and must be taken by the end of the next year. If you fail to take your distribution, there is a 50% penalty, so an error or an intentional disregard of the RMD rules is quite rare.

**CHAPTER 21**

IRAs — Regular and Roth

# QUIZ

**1.** I can fund a regular IRA and deduct $5,500 in 2017.

☐ True ☐ False

**2.** The two primary benefits of a regular IRA are tax-free contribution and tax-free growth.

☐ True ☐ False

**3.** A Roth IRA may also be funded with pre-tax income.

☐ True ☐ False

**4.** If I need the funds, I may take a distribution before age 59½ without penalty.

☐ True ☐ False

**5.** After age 70½, I will have to take a required minimum distribution.

☐ True ☐ False

**Answers:** To view the quiz answers online, please use the website on the front cover. On that site select "Plan Your Will" and logon to your free Wills Planner account. Select the "Provide & Protect Resources" button on the right and "III. Your Finances." Select "#21" and view the Quiz Answers at the bottom. You may also enjoy the three-minute video explanation.

# IRA and 401(k) Designated Beneficiary Options

Each year, IRA and 401(k)s are subject to required minimum distributions (RMDs). Because the distributions start at just under 4% at age 71 and then slowly increase, many IRA and 401(k) plans will continue to grow. While the distributions will eventually become larger, most individuals will eventually pass away with an IRA or 401(k) balance reasonably close to the value of their plan at age 70.

For this reason, the eventual distribution options for an IRA or 401(k) are quite important. For you and many other readers, the IRA or 401(k) may be the largest asset in your estate.

IRA and 401(k)s are transferred through a designated beneficiary that you select on your IRA or 401(k) custodian's form. The five common choices for designated beneficiary are the surviving spouse, children, charity, a trust for children or a trust for spouse and children.

## 1. Spouse as Beneficiary

The most common choice for a married couple is to select the surviving spouse as the designated beneficiary of an IRA or 401(k). When the IRA or 401(k) owner passes away, the surviving spouse has two choices with an IRA. He or she can receive payments under a one-life expectancy schedule or the IRA can be rolled over into his or her IRA.

Because the payments under the IRA schedule are frequently double the required payments with the rollover, nearly everyone rolls over the IRA into his or her own plan.

Assume that Harry Smith is the IRA owner and he passes away with Helen Smith as his designated beneficiary. Helen is age 68 when Harry passes away and rolls over the IRA into her plan.

When Helen reaches age 70½, she must start taking required minimum distributions. The minimum distribution must be taken by April 1 of the next year and is just under 4%. Her distribution will steadily increase as she becomes more senior.

Because Helen rolled over Harry's IRA into her IRA, she qualifies for the lower required minimum distributions under the uniform table. Helen often selects children or charities as designated beneficiaries.

If you are in a community property state and plan to leave your IRA to a trust or other beneficiary that is not your spouse, then it is essential to obtain a written consent from your spouse. In many states, attorneys who prepare estate plans will frequently use a waiver if the spouse is not the designated beneficiary of an IRA.

## 2. Children

For the surviving spouse, or in cases where there is a blended family, an IRA or 401(k), or any portion thereof, may be transferred to children.

There are two typical methods for designating children as beneficiaries. First, if each child receives a fraction of the plan, then each child may take distributions based on his or her own life expectancy.

Second, if there is a class designation with the IRA designated to a group of children or other heirs, then the age of the oldest beneficiary is used to determine the payouts.

It is best with several children to allocate a fractional share to each child. The opportunity to use the separate share method is quite important because of the payout calculation method. If a 60-year-old child is the beneficiary of an IRA, then he or she may take distributions over approximately 25 years. The distributions would start at age 61 at approximately 1/25th or 4%. Using a method of subtracting one from the denominator each year, the payments would steadily increase until the entire IRA is distributed at approximately age 86.

Does your child have to take the stretch payout? No, and frequently children do not. Many CPAs have indicated to the author that their clients have passed away and given the children an opportunity to stretch out the payouts.

However, this plan is often not successful. Approximately one-half of the children take the distribution early, even though that means paying the income tax earlier and losing the benefit of the tax-free growth for the life expectancy of the child. Parents who wish to encourage lifetime IRA distribution for the child may choose to use a testamentary trust to hold the IRA and payout over the child's life expectancy.

### 3. Charity

For the IRA or 401(k) owner, the qualified plan is a wonderful benefit and a very good asset. However, for children, the IRA or 401(k) is transferred with a large "you owe the IRS" tax bill attached (with the exception of a Roth IRA that is income tax free). For the vast majority of qualified plans, the child will pay income tax. Worse yet, the IRA or 401(k) distributions may even push the child into a higher tax bracket.

With the income tax on the IRA or 401(k) and no income tax paid on the home, land or stocks, for children the IRA or 401(k) is a less desirable asset. In fact, many will consider this a "bad asset" because of the income tax on most IRA payouts to children.

For this reason, children would far prefer to receive a home, land or stock because there is no income tax bill attached. The wise planning decision is to transfer the home, stocks or land (the good assets) to children and the IRA or 401(k) to charity (the bad assets due to the income tax bill to children).

Because charities are tax exempt, there is no payment of income tax or estate tax. The charity receives the full value tax free. By transferring the IRA or 401(k) to charity, it is possible to turn a bad asset into a good asset.

## 4. "Give It Twice" Trust

A very good plan for parents who have made lifetime gifts to charity is to combine a benefit to children with a future benefit to charity. This plan is called a "Give It Twice" trust.

A charitable remainder trust may receive the IRA or 401(k) with no payment of income tax. The full value of the IRA or 401(k) may be invested for a term of up to 20 years. Income earned is taxable and that new income is paid to children for the selected term of years. At the end of the selected term, the charity receives the trust principal.

For example, Mary Smith had an $800,000 estate. She lived in a home worth $200,000, had a CD for $200,000 and $400,000 in her IRA. Her IRA was substantial because when her husband Bill passed away, she rolled over his IRA into hers so the combined IRA is now half of her estate.

Mary has two children and decides to transfer the home and CDs to the children in equal shares when she passes away. They each receive $200,000 in value from the home and CDs with no income or estate tax.

After Mary passes away, the $400,000 IRA is transferred into a charitable remainder trust. It receives the IRA proceeds and invests the full $400,000. The trust pays 5%, which is divided between the two children for a term of 20 years. At the end of 20 years, the trust principal plus growth is given to charity.

Mary felt very pleased because she had achieved several goals. First, she had provided both principal and income to her children. This is a very good plan because some children will need a period of time to improve their money management skills. Second, she saved all of the income tax on the IRA. Because the unitrust is tax exempt, it receives the entire IRA tax free. The trust earns income for the children for a term of 20 years and is then transferred tax free to charity.

Because the trust benefits the children with more than $400,000 in income and then is given to charity, it truly may be called a "Give It Twice" trust.

## 5. Trust for Spouse and Children

For individuals with larger estates, it may make good sense to create a trust for surviving spouse and then a term of years for children. The IRA is transferred after the first person passes away into the trust for the surviving spouse. The trust will distribute income for his or her lifetime and then to the children for a term of 20 years. Following the life of spouse plus 20 years for the children, the trust remainder is distributed to charity.

This trust has several benefits. First, it may save very large income taxes because the trust is tax exempt. Second, the trust can be a "net plus makeup" plan that allows the spouse to choose to save taxes by taking reduced income during life. This will allow the IRA to continue to grow and build up the trust so there is greater income to the children.

This plan is an excellent way to benefit the surviving spouse, children and charity.

**CHAPTER 22**

IRA and 401(k) — Designated Beneficiary Options

# QUIZ

1. The typical plan for an IRA or 401(k) is to select the surviving spouse as designated beneficiary, and then for the spouse to eventually pass the plan on to children.

   ☐ True ☐ False

2. Sam is a single person with two nephews, Bill and Tom. In his IRA, Sam selects Bill as his designated beneficiary. However, three years later, he selects Tom in his will as the recipient of his IRA. Because the will is signed later, it will control the distribution.

   ☐ True ☐ False

3. Transferring an IRA or 401(k) to charity saves both income and estate tax.

   ☐ True ☐ False

4. A trust for children and charity is often called a "Give It Twice" trust.

   ☐ True ☐ False

5. If an IRA is transferred to a family trust, it is income-tax free.

   ☐ True ☐ False

**Answers:** To view the quiz answers online, please use the website on the front cover. On that site select "Plan Your Will" and logon to your free Wills Planner account. Select the "Provide & Protect Resources" button on the right and "III. Your Finances." Select "#22" and view the Quiz Answers at the bottom. You may also enjoy the three-minute video explanation.

# APPLICATION AND ACTION

Congratulations on finishing this section. By now you know about different financial options. You may want to complete the "Your Finances" section of your online Wills Planner. After you have finished entering your financial information, you will be able to return at any time and update it as needed.

1. Go to the website on the front cover.

2. You will see the home page for gift planning. Look for the link with the title "Plan Your Will."

3. After you click "Plan Your Will," you will view the Wills Planner access page. If you do not yet have a Wills Planner account, select "Create Your Account" and enter your data. After you create your account, you may enter your username and password to view your personal, secure account on the Wills Planner website.

4. Once you have entered the website, you will see four different sections. The first is the "You and Your Family" section. Click on that section and enter your family information. There are also sections on "Your Contacts & Healthcare", "Your Finances" and "Your Estate Plan." You may save and view your information at any time.

5. You may want to view some of the *Provide & Protect* chapters and videos. Click the *"Provide & Protect"* button. You may view the entire updated version of the *Provide & Protect* multi-media book online. Each chapter includes a short video and quiz with answers. Some of our friends like to read a chapter each week, watch the video and take the quiz. In just one year, you may cover the entire book.

6. Finally, please feel free to call or email us at any time if we can help you with a short online phone tutorial.

# Your Estate Plan

# WILLS
## Perils of Probate

"I am an heir of the decedent and here is his will."

Potential Heir

Business Owner passed away on April 5, 1976, with an estate of $2.5 billion. Many people appeared claiming, "I am Business Owner's heir" and submitted wills with themselves as beneficiaries. The court finally determined seven years later that none of the wills were valid and split the estate among 22 of the decedent's cousins. The costs and fees paid to lawyers during administration of Business Owner's estate were in the millions of dollars.

### Probate Process

When a person passes away, it is important to have an organized process to transfer his or her property. The probate process is an organized method to gather all of the property of the individual, pay all of his or her bills, determine the appropriate beneficiaries to receive the property and make the actual transfer.

The probate process can be quite easy and rapid for small estates or can last for many years with larger or more complicated estates. Most people do not spend much time thinking about probate. However, if they are potential beneficiaries, probate is a topic of great interest. To the 22 cousins who received multimillion-dollar inheritances, Business Owner's probate process was very interesting.

**Probate Players**

There are at least four general categories of probate players. First, an executor or personal representative is the manager of the estate. Second, an estate attorney is involved to advise the executor or personal representative on all probate and legal matters.

Third, a probate judge will rule on the validity of any will, review many of the actions of the executor, and approve the final distributions. Finally, heirs will be the beneficiaries of the estate.

**Probate Process**

The probate process involves eight separate steps to ensure an orderly transfer of all of the property to the right individuals. Let's assume that Ed Executor and Ellen Attorney are probating the estate of Business Owner.

1. **Accept the Will:** Ed or Ellen will normally submit the will to the court for probate. Usually, there is one final will that is accepted. However, there are many cases in which individuals wrote their own wills or there was a question about the validity of a given will, resulting in a wills contest. Eventually, the court will determine the validity and meaning of the will. However, for Business Owner's estate, none of the wills were valid and state law determined who received the $2.5 billion.

2. **Locate Heirs:** Because Business Owner did not have a valid will, Ed Executor needed to locate all of the heirs. But, the 22 cousins still needed to be approved by the court. Under state law, Business Owner's estate was transferred to his relatives. With $2.5 billion at stake, all of them had attorneys to ensure that each cousin received the proper share. Even if Business Owner had signed a valid will, it would have been essential to locate all the heirs. In some cases, the selected recipients had passed away and property was distributed to their children or other relatives.

3. **Determine the Estate Assets and Values:** Ed Executor is responsible for finding all of Business Owner's estate assets. The assets included real estate, bank accounts, securities accounts and

other property. Because Business Owner's estate was taxable, all property was valued so that federal taxes could be paid. Finally, the balance of the estate was distributed to the 22 cousins.

4. **Pay Executor and Attorney:** Not surprisingly, Ed Executor and Ellen Attorney were paid a large fee from Business Owner's estate. The costs for the probate process may be quite substantial and the executor and attorney are always paid. Costs may be as low as 2% of the estate value or may range up to 7% or 8% of estate value. However, if there is an estate contest, costs can consume a large portion of the entire estate.

5. **Make Debt Payments:** After determining the nature of the property and the approximate value of Business Owner's estate, Ed Executor will also advertise for any claims by creditors. The state probate law determines the period of time and the type of public notice to be given. If creditors do not file claims against the estate, they risk losing their ability to collect their debts. All debts and taxes are paid before the final distribution.

6. **Resolve Controversies:** Seven years of controversies in Business Owner's estate required continuous attention from Ed Executor and Ellen Attorney. Most of the controversies centered around the submitted wills. If there are any controversies, such as a claim that the final will is invalid due to undue influence of a party who obtained the will, then the court must determine the rights of all parties under the will and applicable state law. After seven years, the court decided that none of the wills in Business Owner's estate were valid.

7. **File Income and Estate tax Returns:** Because Business Owner's estate was $2.5 billion and produced income each year, Ed Executor had to file the final income tax return for Business Owner and annual returns for the estate. Based on the appraised valuation, Ed and Ellen also filed the estate tax return and paid the estate tax to the IRS.

8. **Distribute Assets to Heirs:** After seven years of court proceedings, payment of estate taxes, court costs, executor fees, and attorney fees, the probate judge approved the final distribution order and the 22 cousins of Business Owner received their inheritance.

## Probate Problems

There are several negative results for which probate has a deservedly bad reputation. First, the process is public. Anyone can obtain the will of Jacqueline Kennedy Onassis and read her provisions for children John Jr. and Caroline.

As was true for Business Owner's estate, the probate process may be both lengthy and expensive. Both time and money can be easily wasted in the bureaucracy of the process.

Probate is also as good and as bad as the judge who is involved. Judges are people, with the good and bad characteristics of humanity. Some are very dedicated and capable and some are primarily interested in an early exit to the golf course in the afternoon. Depending upon the quality of the judge, the probate process can be easy or quite challenging for the executor and estate attorney.

Finally, the existence of a substantial estate (such as that of Business Owner) invites relatives to submit claims and is fertile ground for developing probate controversies. If there is any question about the validity of the will, or there are conflicting methods of transfer of the same property (joint tenancy with one person and attempting to transfer the same property through a will to a second person), a will contest and probate battle may occur.

## Avoiding Probate

There are multiple methods that are used to avoid probate. These can be quite successful, but all methods must be coordinated carefully to be certain that the overall plan works correctly.

1. **Joint Tenancy with Right of Survivorship:** Under property law, the surviving joint tenant owns the real estate.

2. **Designated Beneficiary:** An insurance policy, an IRA, a 401(k) or other qualified plan is transferred to the designated beneficiary. There is a contract with the insurance company or the retirement plan custodian and that person agrees to make the transfer to the individual or organization selected by the owner. Typical forms permit the selection of a primary beneficiary and also a contingent beneficiary.

3. **Pay-on-Death (POD) Accounts:** Most states that follow the Uniform Probate Code may allow a "POD" account. Most savings accounts, checking accounts and certificates of deposit are under state law permitted to be transferred to the "payable-on-death" recipient.

4. **Revocable Living Trust:** Perhaps the most popular method for avoiding probate is a revocable living trust. The grantor is taxable on the assets of the trust, but frequently will transfer a personal residence, securities accounts and other major assets into the trust. The assets in the trust avoid the probate process.

**CHAPTER 23**

WILLS — Perils of Probate

# QUIZ

1. Probate is a simple and quick process to transfer property.

   ☐ True      ☐ False

2. The key parties in a probate process are the executor or personal representative, the estate attorney and a probate judge.

   ☐ True      ☐ False

3. A principal function of the executor is to complete the inventory and advertise the willingness of the estate to make payments to creditors of the deceased.

   ☐ True      ☐ False

4. The biggest negative for the probate process is the cost involved.

   ☐ True      ☐ False

5. There are both efficient and effective ways of avoiding probate.

   ☐ True      ☐ False

**Answers:** To view the quiz answers online, please use the website on the front cover. On that site select "Plan Your Will" and logon to your free Wills Planner account. Select the "Provide & Protect Resources" button on the right and "IV. Your Estate Plan." Under "Wills" Select "#23" and view the Quiz Answers at the bottom. You may also enjoy the three-minute video explanation.

# WILLS
## Good and Bad

### Where is the Missing Will?

More than 40 wills were submitted to the probate court, with a multitude of potential heirs each claiming to be the true recipient of a wealthy business owner who passed away in 1976. With a $2.5 billion estate at stake, there was intense interest in the decision of the court.

After extensive review of the 40 documents, the court finally determined that none of the 40 wills were valid. Because there was no valid will, the court divided the $2.5 billion estate among 22 relatives. Court costs, attorney costs and estate taxes were enormous, but the 22 heirs still each received millions of dollars.

### Why is a Will Important?

There are at least seven reasons for creating a will. A "peace of mind" estate plan starts with your will. The will passes your property to family, friends and favored organizations, could direct distribution of a recent inheritance, may fix errors in living trust funding, allows you to select a guardian, enables you to disinherit a child or other relative, permits you to select your executor and may help with a simplified probate.

1. **Transfer of Property:** There are some types of property that are best transferred by will. Many types of personal assets are difficult to transfer through a living trust or are not appropriate for a "pay on death" transfer. Because vehicles and other personal assets are likely to be bought and sold, it is much easier to keep vehicles,

furniture, collections and other items in the probate estate and transfer them by will.

2. **Potential Inheritance:** You might be planning to receive an inheritance from a parent or other relative, but the inheritance could be delayed by the probate process, potential estate issues or other reasons. Therefore, when you finally receive title to the property, there may not be a convenient time or opportunity to transfer the assets into a revocable living trust. As a result, the inheritance will form part of your estate.

   There also have been cases in which a person passes away in a tragic accident. The estate may receive an insurance settlement or a claim under a wrongful death action. These assets would become part of the probate estate and are transferred under the residuary clause of your will.

3. **Living Trust Errors:** A living trust is a very appropriate way of avoiding the probate process. However, in too many cases a person has a valid living trust but has not properly transferred the real estate, securities accounts or other assets to the trust. As a result, the property that has not been legally transferred to the trust will be part of the probate estate covered by your will.

4. **Guardian for Minors:** The selection of a guardian for minor children is done through your will. Most states do not permit you to use a living trust (there are a few exceptions) for this purpose, so it is very important to designate the guardian in your will. When you create the will and designate the guardian of the person, it is also quite common to establish a family trust for the minor children and appoint the trustee.

5. **Disinherit Someone:** It is possible to disinherit a child or other heir. The appropriate place to explain that disinheritance or explain why the inheritance is a nominal amount (such as $1.00) is in your will.

6. **Select the Executor:** Your executor is a key person for a successful estate property transition. The executor will inventory your estate,

advertise for creditors, pay bills and taxes, submit your will to the probate court and obtain the court's approval for the final distribution. Your will is the document in which you will name your executor. Even if you have a revocable living trust with a trustee and a successor, it is essential to select an executor who will manage your probate property.

7. **Simplify Probate:** In many states it is possible for people who pass away with modest to moderate resources to have a simplified or summary probate. This permits your executor to manage your property and make distribution of it with very minimal contact with the probate courts. For example, California allows many estates with assets valued under $150,000 to use a simplified probate process. The executor will follow the directions in your will and distribute your property accordingly. In most cases, this will simplify administration and reduce your estate costs.

## Good and Bad Wills

As was the case in the estate of Business Owner, there are many submitted wills that are not deemed valid or legal. In order to have a valid or legal will, you need to comply with the state law requirements for wills. While there is some variation between the states, most states will follow several guidelines.

1. **Legal Age:** In most states you must be 18 years old to sign a will.

2. **Sound Mind:** As we become more senior, we do not have as clear a mind as we had back in our youth. Most states permit you to create a will if you have "lucid intervals" and understand the nature of your property and the fact that the will is going to direct the transfer of that property to your selected recipients.

3. **Typed or Printed:** A will normally is either typed or printed. While some states permit handwritten or other types of wills, the vast majority of wills will be typed or printed and will contain at least one substantive transfer of property.

4. **Date and Sign:** Your will must be dated and signed. The date is essential in order to make certain that this is your final will.

Many individuals might write and sign two or more wills during a lifetime. Only your final will is going to be used by the probate court to distribute your property.

5. **Witnesses:** Under your state law, you will need to sign your will in the presence and hearing of two witnesses. Your witnesses must be adults who are of sound mind and should not be beneficiaries under the will. They need to be told that this is a will, but you do not need to disclose the contents of your will to the witnesses.

6. **Self-Proving Will:** In some states, it is permissible to have a notary or an affidavit witness form in which the will is either notarized or the person pledges under perjury that this is a valid will. If the will is "self-proved," it will simplify the probate process. Ordinarily, the witness is not required to testify in the probate court with a self-proved will.

**CHAPTER 24**

WILLS — Good and Bad

# QUIZ

**1.** Even with a small estate, it is important to have a will.

☐ True    ☐ False

**2.** All states allow you to select a guardian in your will.

☐ True    ☐ False

**3.** With a living trust, you don't need a will.

☐ True    ☐ False

**4.** If you wish to disinherit a child or other relative, it is very desirable to make that clear in your will.

☐ True    ☐ False

**5.** You may sign a valid will if you have a lucid interval.

☐ True    ☐ False

**Answers:** To view the quiz answers online, please use the website on the front cover. On that site select "Plan Your Will" and logon to your free Wills Planner account. Select the "Provide & Protect Resources" button on the right and "IV. Your Estate Plan." Under "Wills" Select "#24" and view the Quiz Answers at the bottom. You may also enjoy the three-minute video explanation.

# WILLS
## Passing Unequal Shares in Your Will

Because children look at the inheritance as a representation of their parents' love, most parents leave children equal shares of their estate. However, there are a number of good reasons why a parent might leave unequal shares. These reasons consider the needs of children, the potential large financial success of one child, a benefit previously given to a child that will be balanced in the estate, estrangement from a child or a blended family.

You will want to discuss carefully these circumstances with your attorney and other advisors. After thinking through your situation, you may decide that there are good reasons for making an unequal distribution of property to children.

### Special Needs Child

Mary is a single mother with three children. Her oldest daughter, Jane is age 30 and is a nurse. She is married with two children.

Son Joe is age 27, single and pursuing a career in sales. The third child, Kara, is age 17 and is disabled. She lives at home with Mary.

Mary has been financially careful and is building her estate. She owns her home, has an insurance policy that will be sufficient to pay off the mortgage on the home and provide an additional benefit for her children, and has a good retirement plan.

Because Mary does not have a huge estate, she wants to be certain that Kara has sufficient resources. Both Jane and Joe are successful in their careers and do not need assistance for their present lifestyle. While Mary would like to provide some inheritance for them, her primary concern is to make certain that Kara receives needed care.

Therefore, Mary makes provision for a modest bequest of cash to Jane and Joe in her will. She also leaves a small bequest to a favorite charity. However, the majority of Mary's estate is transferred to a "special needs trust" for the benefit of Kara.

The benefit of the special needs trust is that the trustee may receive the property and use it at his or her discretion for Kara's benefit. If the special needs trust is correctly written, it will not reduce Kara's potential qualification for state or federal benefits.

The special needs trust also permits the trustee to pay for Kara's care as he or she determines appropriate. After Kara passes away, the special needs trust will be divided between the grandchildren of Mary and her favorite charity.

### Favored Child

Sue and Tom have raised three children and are now empty nesters. Their oldest child Sam attended a very fine university, followed by an excellent medical school, and is now a surgeon. Their younger children Julie and Linda both graduated from a state university.

Because Sue and Tom provided much greater financial support for Sam that enabled him to complete medical school and become a surgeon, they decided to transfer a larger proportion of their estate to Julie and Linda. While Julie and Linda both are successful and graduated from the state university, Sue and Tom believe that giving them a larger portion of the estate will create balance when compared with the benefits previously received by Sam.

Sue and Tom recognize that it's not possible to be perfectly equal in these circumstances, but hope the larger inheritance for Julie and Linda will make the total distribution as fair as possible.

### Great Success Child

Tara and Jim have two children. Their oldest son Harvey has always had strong technical skills. After Harvey completed his engineering degree in college, he began working as a software programmer for a small company. In just a few years, he received shares of stock and the company went public. Harvey now has substantial wealth.

Harvey's sister, Lynn, also completed school and teaches third grade. She lives by herself in an apartment and has many friends at her school. However, Lynn has a very modest lifestyle and earnings in comparison to Harvey.

Tara and Jim thought carefully through the situation and talked to their attorney Harold. He explained that Harvey now has a large estate that could be subject to a significant future estate tax. If Tara and Jim were to transfer more property to Harvey, it simply makes his estate tax problem more difficult.

Because Lynn has comparatively modest resources, Tara and Jim decided that the vast majority of the estate would be transferred to her. However, they do have a family heirloom—a grandfather clock that has been handed down through four generations. While the grandfather clock does not have huge value, it is an important family memento. Tara and Jim decided to transfer the grandfather clock to Harvey and the balance of the estate to Lynn.

### Estranged Child

Peter and Janet have raised two children. The oldest is a son named Bill and their daughter is Nancy. While Bill was in his early 20s, he dropped out of college and left without making contact with his parents or his sister Nancy. Bill was gone for 12 years and no one knew his location. After 12 years of wandering and traveling, Bill returned to his hometown community. However, he has not reached out to his parents or his sister. When they have attempted to contact him, Bill has avoided contact with his family.

While this is a difficult situation and brings sadness to Peter and Janet, they feel that Bill has quite deliberately separated himself from the rest of the family. Given Bill's decision to go his separate way, Peter and Janet believe that their inheritance can be used most productively by Nancy.

They are also concerned that if Bill receives an inheritance, he will not use it for good purposes. Therefore, Peter and Janet have decided to leave their estate to daughter Nancy.

### Blended Family

Joe was a very successful bachelor entrepreneur and businessman. He invested very well and built a number of commercial buildings.

When Joe met Helen, she was divorced and had two children from her first marriage. Her children William and Lorraine were in their early 20s when Joe and Helen were married. They have had very minimal contact with Joe since the marriage.

Joe and Helen had a son named Steve. Helen's third child is quite diligent and has always been a good student. He completed college and recently passed his CPA exam.

When Joe and Helen were married, Joe was already in possession of a very large estate. His attorney recommended that they create a prenuptial agreement. Under this agreement, Helen would receive a substantial amount in trust for her lifetime. When she passes away, the trust assets will be distributed by the terms of the qualified terminable interest property trust created in Joe's estate plan.

Joe and Helen discussed their situation. Joe would like a larger portion of the estate to be transferred to their son Steve. Because the estate is quite large, there are more than sufficient resources to take care of Helen.

After discussion with their attorney Clara, Joe and Helen decided that if he were to pass away first, one-half of his estate would be transferred to Steve. The other half will be placed in a marital deduction trust to benefit Helen. She will have the income and, if needed for her care, the principal from that trust.

When Helen passes away, that marital trust will be divided with one-third to each of the three children.

While this plan provides a much larger inheritance for Steve, the other two children from Helen's first marriage will still also receive substantial assets.

### Discussions with Children

These five plans all show specific reasons why a parent may choose to leave unequal amounts. While the reasons are apparent to the parent, they may not always be as easily understood by the children.

Many parents choose to explain and disclose an "unequal shares" plan during life. A meeting is frequently set up at the office of the family attorney. The entire family is invited. The parents explain the reasons why they have decided to create the estate plan with different amounts. Children have the ability to discuss the plan with the parents and ask questions of the financial advisors.

Later, many parents also will meet individually with children to explain the situation and circumstances. With the exception of the estranged child in the "Peter and Janet" example, most children will understand their parents' reasoning. The children may not always agree with their parents, but it usually is helpful for future family harmony for children to discuss their parents' decisions about inheritance.

Therefore, if you as a parent are thinking about passing an unequal amount to children, it may be wise to discuss a possible family meeting with your attorney, CPA or other financial advisor.

**CHAPTER 25**

WILLS — Passing Unequal Shares in Your Will

# QUIZ

1. Because children look at the inheritance as a representation of the love of the parent, most parents will leave equal amounts to children even though they know that there are economic differences among the children.

   ☐ True      ☐ False

2. With a special needs trust, the child is ordinarily able to benefit from the trust and still receive federal or state benefits.

   ☐ True      ☐ False

3. If a child is very successful, it is best if the successful child learns that he or she will not receive inheritance until the will is read.

   ☐ True      ☐ False

4. With an estranged child, it is good to make contact and tell them they are disinherited.

   ☐ True      ☐ False

5. A blended family will almost always treat all children the same.

   ☐ True      ☐ False

**Answers:** To view the quiz answers online, please use the website on the front cover. On that site select "Plan Your Will" and logon to your free Wills Planner account. Select the "Provide & Protect Resources" button on the right and "IV. Your Estate Plan." Under "Wills" Select "#25" and view the Quiz Answers at the bottom. You may also enjoy the three-minute video explanation.

# WILLS
## Ten Reasons to Update Your Estate Plan

You have completed a will and perhaps a revocable living trust. Your durable power of attorney for healthcare and a living will are accompanied by a HIPAA release. All of your records are safely in place and carefully organized.

So you now are finished with your estate planning. Or are you? Will there be changes in your circumstances or your family that should lead to a review of your plan? Could some events cause you to need to revise or update the plan?

Yes, there are a number of reasons to consider revising or updating your plan. These include any of the following reasons:

### 1. New Children, Grandchildren or Other Heirs

Your estate plan almost certainly makes provision for children and other heirs who are living when you pass away. If you have a specific transfer to one child, a new child may receive a smaller than intended inheritance.

For example, John Smith had a $1 million estate and left a $400,000 residence to child A. He then divided the balance of the estate with 1/6 of the balance to child A and 5/6 to child B. If a third child is born, depending upon state law, the child might receive nothing or perhaps would benefit from a portion of the residue. In either case, the uncertainty could lead to estate litigation or to family strife.

If you have a sizeable estate and there are large specific bequests, the arrival of a new heir is a good time to review your plan. One option is to transfer assets to the heirs "then living" when you pass away.

If the estate is $1 million, in some states a child C who is born later would receive 1/3 of the estate. This could dramatically change the benefit for child B and leave her with a reduced inheritance. In addition, child C could be a minor or a very young adult and not be capable of managing his or her property. For several reasons, the arrival of a new heir makes a review of your plan very important.

## 2. Move to a Different State

If you are married and move to a different state, there may be a change in the laws that affect ownership. Some states are called "common law" property states and some are "community property." If you move from one state to another and change in either direction, it may be important to clarify the ownership of your property as separate property or joint property.

For individuals with moderate to larger estates, there could be significant estate or inheritance taxes. Several states have inheritance taxes that will apply at lower levels than the federal exemption per person. Depending on who among your relatives receives your property, a new state may have a substantial tax.

Finally, many states have specific rules on durable powers of attorney for healthcare, living wills or advance directives or even the HIPAA release. If you acquire permanent legal residence in the state, your doctors will expect that your medical planning documents reflect their state law.

## 3. Sale or Purchase of a Major Asset

You may have a major real estate asset or a business that is to be transferred to one of your heirs. If that property is sold or substantially increases in value, your entire plan could change. For example, if a property greatly increases in value and there is a large estate tax that is paid out of the residue of your estate, the beneficiary of that specific property could receive a much larger inheritance than you intend. Those children or other heirs who are receiving the residue could find their inheritance greatly reduced by estate tax paid on the asset transferred to the first child.

Alternatively, if the first asset is sold, then a child may receive a smaller than intended inheritance. Therefore, a significant sale or purchase is a good time for an estate planning review.

### 4. Reaching Age 70½

The four types of estate property are generally cash and cash equivalents, stocks, real estate and qualified plans. Over the years, your qualified retirement plan may become a large portion of your estate. Your IRA, 401(k) or other qualified plan will require distributions to start on April 1 of the year after you reach age 70½.

If you pass away before the entire plan is paid out to you during your retirement years, the balance is transferred to your designated beneficiary. Because retirement plans have grown substantially over the past decade (even with a reduction in plan value during the 2008 downturn), it's very important to review your beneficiary designations. Many individuals pass away and the plan value is transferred to beneficiaries who have been selected 10, 15, and even 25 years earlier. There could be many reasons why you would want to update that beneficiary designation, and age 70½ is a logical time to do so.

### 5. Your Selected Beneficiary is Deceased

In many families there are unmarried brothers or sisters. It is quite common for these individuals to receive an inheritance and to remember the surviving brothers and sisters in their plans. However, even if there are two or three unmarried brothers or sisters, one will inevitably be the survivor and hold most of the assets. If you are remembering a sibling in your plan, there is a substantial possibility that he or she will pass away before you do. In that case, it is useful to revise the plan and select a new recipient of that share of your estate.

## 6. Divorce or Remarriage

Estate plans for single persons are quite different from those of married couples. A single person who transfers assets to a former spouse will not qualify for the unlimited marital deduction. While property settlements are typically handled during the dissolution of marriage proceedings, there are many cases where individuals forget to change beneficiary designations on retirement plans and insurance policies. Particularly if you later remarry and then pass away with a new spouse, there is a high likelihood of litigation between the ex-spouse and the new spouse if you have forgotten to update your beneficiary designations. Therefore, your plan and your beneficiary designations should always be reviewed in the event of a divorce or remarriage.

## 7. Substantial Change in Value

If your estate increases or decreases significantly in value, there can be major impact on beneficiaries. For example, mother has children A, B and C. She leaves a home valued at $300,000 to child A, a farm valued at $800,000 to child B and the liquid assets to child C. While she is in a nursing home and no longer able to change the will, oil is discovered on the farm. When mother passes away, child B receives not $800,000 but $8 million. To add insult to injury, the estate is now larger than the estate exemption and each child must pay estate tax on his or her inheritance. While child B with the largest inheritance will under most state tax apportionment laws pay the largest tax, it will be a matter of considerable sibling unhappiness for the two children who receive the smaller shares and still have to pay a large estate tax on their portion.

## 8. Adding a Major Property to a Living Trust

If you have a substantial estate, you may hold your real estate in a living trust. If you invest in real estate or acquire a major new property and transfer that to the living trust, it will be useful to review the plan. In some circumstances, there may be different beneficiaries for the living trust than for your qualified plans and life insurance. The addition of a high value asset to the living trust could increase the benefits for the persons receiving shares from the trust in comparison to the rest of your heirs.

## 9. Selected Executor or Trustee Not Available

With a will or a revocable living trust, you may also select a successor executor or trustee. While this usually will handle the situation in which the primary executor or trustee predeceases you, it still is useful to review your plan if one of these persons passes away. You can easily select a new primary executor or trustee with an appropriate backup person.

## 10. Passage of Time

Estate plans are affected by changes in your asset value, by changes in your family, and potentially by changes in federal or state law. Therefore, it is useful every three to five years for you to sit down with your attorney and review your plan. Given all the potential areas that can change, it's quite likely that you may wish to modify some portion of the plan.

**CHAPTER 26**

WILLS — Ten Reasons to Update Your Estate Plan

# QUIZ

1. If I divide a property or income from a trust among my grandchildren, my document should say "distribute assets to the then-living" grandchildren.

   ☐ True ☐ False

2. If you acquire a major real property asset and your will indicates that the residue will be divided equally among three children, you do not need to review your plan.

   ☐ True ☐ False

3. Most IRA owners periodically review their beneficiary designations.

   ☐ True ☐ False

4. If you have a plan to distribute principal or income to a brother or sister and he or she passes away, it is very good to review your plan.

   ☐ True ☐ False

5. So long as the residue is divided equally among "then-living" heirs, the plan will work fine even if there is a large change in value.

   ☐ True ☐ False

**Answers:** To view the quiz answers online, please use the website on the front cover. On that site select "Plan Your Will" and logon to your free Wills Planner account. Select the "Provide & Protect Resources" button on the right and "IV. Your Estate Plan." Under "Wills" Select "#26" and view the Quiz Answers at the bottom. You may also enjoy the three-minute video explanation.

# WILLS
## Living Trusts Versus Wills

Jacqueline Kennedy Onassis was diagnosed with cancer in January 1994. She signed a will in the New York offices of a large law firm on March 22, 1994. She passed away just two months later on May 19 at the age of 64.

Because a will is a public document, her will is available on the internet. In the will she remembered family members, several friends and planned to make a substantial transfer to a charitable lead trust. However, because the children received the family personal property and promptly sold the items for the unexpectedly large sum of $35,000,000, the residue of the estate was used to pay the estate taxes on this large transfer of value to children and the charitable trust was not funded.

Bing Crosby passed away on October 14, 1977, with a trust. When his first wife Dixie Lee passed away from cancer in 1952, she had a will that transferred her separate and community property. Bing Crosby was very upset that his financial circumstances were disclosed to the public through the probate process. After marrying his second wife Kathryn, Crosby created a number of trusts for the children from his first marriage, for Kathryn and for children from his second marriage. He greatly appreciated the privacy benefit of creating a living trust.

You may not have the fame of Jacqueline Onassis or the assets of Bing Crosby (along with Lawrence Welk and Bob Hope, he was one of the wealthiest actors at the time of his death), but you can learn from both of them in deciding whether or not to create a will or a living trust.

### When Wills are a Good Choice

There are a number of reasons why a person frequently starts the estate planning process with a will. These include youth, cost, the estate size, the ability to transfer assets outside of probate and a hesitation to select a trustee.

### Young and Healthy

If you are in your 30s or 40s and have good health, a will is the common starting point for estate planning. Your will is much more simple than a living trust. The property subject to a will goes through probate, but that could be many decades in the future.

As you acquire other property, it can be covered by your will. You can modify your will at any time, and you save the effort necessary to retitle and track property inside a living trust.

For a young person, the cost savings are significant. Wills frequently cost from $250 to $800, while a living trust may involve costs of $1,000 to $2,500. A young person may be reluctant to spend the funds necessary to create a living trust, but can start his or her estate plan quite reasonably with a will.

### Modest or Moderate Estate

A second characteristic of people who choose a will is that they have a fairly modest or moderate estate. As the estate becomes larger and more complicated, a trust is more important. For individuals who have more moderate assets, the will is a good starting point. As the estate grows, they can use some of the increase in resources to add a living trust to their plan.

### Using Transfer Methods that Avoid Probate

Another option is to create a will then transfer most assets without probate. Your IRA, qualified pension plan, life insurance and property held in joint tenancy with right of survivorship all avoid the probate process. For individuals who have a modest or moderate estate and are willing to transfer most assets through contract or property law methods that avoid probate, a will is a good solution.

### Do Not Want to Select a Trustee

With a living trust, it is necessary to select a trustee to manage your property. This trustee frequently will end up managing your assets during the senior years of your life and after you pass away.

Some people do not like the concept of a trustee managing their property. They would rather own the property themselves outright during life and transfer the property outright to family members. For this person, a will is often a preferred planning method.

### When a Living Trust is a Good Choice

For those individuals who can afford a living trust, it is a very good choice. The living trust facilitates management of property during life, protection of the grantor, transfer of assets and income to family members and management of real estate.

### Senior Age Care

What if I become too ill to manage property? One of the concerns you may have is that you may eventually become a senior person with a major illness. For medical reasons, you may be unable to manage your property. A major benefit of a living trust is that you select a successor trustee. If you are no longer able to serve as trustee and manage the property, your successor trustee can manage your property. He or she can make certain that the expenses of your medical care or long-term care needs are covered through trust payments.

### Larger Estate or Real Estate

If you have a more substantial estate, a living trust can have multiple benefits. The living trust may include various provisions for handling the management of real estate or personal business interests. Particularly if you have real estate in multiple states, it is advantageous to transfer that property to a living trust. This property can then be managed for the benefit of both you and your heirs.

If you have property in multiple states and pass away with a will, it is necessary to conduct a probate administration in each state where you own property. This entails hiring professionals to manage the probate in each estate and considerably increases the total cost. With a living trust holding real estate in different states, there is no need for multiple and expensive probate proceedings.

### Bypassing Probate

One of the major benefits of a living trust is that the trust assets bypass the probate process. In most states, there are savings in probate costs that may be many thousands of dollars.

Not only are there savings in probate costs, but your estate may also avoid the delays that frequently occur in the probate process. If there are claims against the estate, the probate process can take from two to ten years. While some large estates have been tied up in probate for many years, other similarly sized estates with a living trust can continue to manage the property and pay income and principal to beneficiaries.

### Privacy

As Bing Crosby discovered, a living trust is generally a private document. While wills are public documents (the will of Jacqueline Kennedy Onassis and many other famous individuals are readily available through internet search sites), a living trust is a private document. Even if a financial institution requests the trust in order to invest property owned by the trust, generally only a small portion of the trust is required to be disclosed to the institution. For most purposes the living trust is private.

### Reduced Risk of Estate Contest

Larger estates are understandably more vulnerable to a probate contest. When the document and a large estate are public, as is the case with the will, the target is very tempting. Distant relatives come out of the woodwork to determine whether they have a potential claim against the estate.

One of the most disheartening aspects of a will contest is that there frequently are lifelong hard feelings among family members. In many cases, the bitterness from a will contest is carried by children, grandchildren, cousins, nephews and nieces to their grave.

A living trust is a private document. Because it is a private document and does not have to meet the specific standards for signature and witnesses that are applicable to a will, it is less likely to be attacked.

With a large estate, the living trust is generally safer. In addition, if a senior person needs someone to manage the estate, the successor trustee has been previously designated. The successor trustee frequently protects the senior person from potential undue influence of heirs or caregivers. Therefore, the living trust reduces the probability of an estate contest.

**CHAPTER 27**

WILLS — Living Trusts Versus Wills

# QUIZ

1. For a young person with a modest estate, a will is usually more reasonable than a trust.

   ☐ True     ☐ False

2. Because you can use IRA beneficiary designations, joint tenancy with right of survivorship and other types of nonprobate transfers, a will is not needed.

   ☐ True     ☐ False

3. An excellent living trust benefit is the ability to protect you in your very senior years.

   ☐ True     ☐ False

4. With substantial holdings of real estate, a living trust is not needed.

   ☐ True     ☐ False

5. Privacy is a major benefit of a living trust.

   ☐ True     ☐ False

**Answers:** To view the quiz answers online, please use the website on the front cover. On that site select "Plan Your Will" and logon to your free Wills Planner account. Select the "Provide & Protect Resources" button on the right and "IV. Your Estate Plan." Under "Wills" Select "#27" and view the Quiz Answers at the bottom. You may also enjoy the three-minute video explanation.

# ONLINE ACCOUNTS

At any given time, the average American maintains between 30 and 50 online accounts. These may be with banks, financial institutions, utility companies, email providers, social media outlets, commercial shopping or travel sites and accounts unique to technology such as an account to purchase apps for a smartphone.

Modern estate plans should include an "ePlan" to manage online accounts and online data. There are four specific steps to creating an effective ePlan. These include compiling a list of each account along with an explanation of how each is used, developing a plan for storing electronic information, naming an executor to manage the accounts and providing appropriate direction to your executor.

### 1. Compile a List of Accounts and How to Access Them

The first part of an effective ePlan is to gather information and to compile a list of your accounts together with information about the accounts. Your list should specify the username, password account number and a description of what is included in each account. Because passwords frequently change, you should be sure to keep this list up to date.

There are four major types of online accounts: personal, financial, business and social media. Examples of personal accounts include email accounts and those used in conjunction with photos, videos, music and apps for smartphones or tablets. The information associated with these accounts is typically backed up on a computer hard drive, a backup drive or cloud account.

Financial accounts might include savings and checking accounts, retirement accounts, utility accounts, and accounts related to travel and shopping. Increasingly, people are using electronic devices to bank online, including linking accounts for automatic payments, to manage retirement and investment accounts, and to shop online at sites such as Amazon, eBay, airlines and other companies. Online financial accounts also allow for the management of digital currency such as Bitcoin. In many cases, the estate executor will need the account holder's username, password and account number to identify and access any online financial accounts and to ensure that they can be left to family.

Business related accounts could include intellectual property that is part of a website or blog, including written work, photos, videos and musical compositions and software. If you own business assets like these, be sure to discuss these specific assets with your attorney.

Examples of social media accounts are Facebook, Twitter, and LinkedIn. These accounts may be valuable or sufficiently sentimental because they contain photos and comments that should be passed on to family. A good ePlan will instruct the executor how to dispose of these assets, such as whether the executor should copy the data from these accounts to share with family and whether to wind down and close these accounts.

### 2. Store and Protect Your Information

The second part of an effective ePlan is the development of a plan for storing information. This will involve saving the list that you compiled as well as backing up important data files and account information.

Because an ePlan account list contains sensitive information such as usernames and passwords, it is essential to maintain the security and confidentiality of this list. There are three basic options for securing an ePlan account list. First, this list could be handwritten and stored in a safe place. Second, it could be in electronic format such as a spreadsheet saved to a thumb drive. Extra security measures can be taken to password protect or encrypt the file or drive. Third, there are programs that manage, save and encrypt passwords. These programs allow people to connect multiple devices to a password management program and the program will keep the passwords up to date on each device. If you password protect a file, encrypt a drive or use a password management program, be sure to provide your executor or a loved one with the file password or encryption key or with access to one of your devices so your executor can access the password program.

For purposes of security, and in order to keep the list up to date, maintain a single list. Avoid saving the list on a computer in case of data loss or a data breach. Do not include this list in a will or living trust; these documents may become public. Save the list in a secure location such as in a locked, fireproof home safe or safety deposit box. Some states require that a safety deposit box cannot be opened after the owner passes away without the approval of the probate court. Ask your attorney if you live in one of these states. If you do, consider storing your list in a home safe.

There are several options for maintaining a backup of important electronic information such as pictures, videos, music and archived email. You can back up this information on your personal computer, in a cloud account or on an external backup drive, thumb drive or DVD, which can then be stored in a home safe or safety deposit box.

### 3. Select Your Digital Executor

After compiling a list and selecting a storage method, the third part of an ePlan will be the selection of a digital executor. Many states have passed laws that give access to online accounts to the executor of an estate. In some cases, however, state law may limit access if the executor does not have the password or an estate plan does not clearly grant powers to the executor to access these accounts. Accordingly, your estate plan should be explicit in the granting of authority with respect to online accounts, and the ePlan should provide the necessary passwords to the executor. Institutions that provide online account access may give the executor access upon a showing of appropriate authorization in the estate plan or, in some cases, may require an order from the probate court. For some accounts such as Bitcoin, the executor will need the password to access the account.

### 4. Provide Your Executor with "Digital Directions"

The fourth and final part of an ePlan includes a letter of instruction to the digital executor. This letter will tell the executor how to manage your online accounts and digital assets. It may also provide recommendations for the distribution of various accounts, assets, files and information to family. Information in personal accounts, such as photos and videos, can easily be duplicated. Accordingly, the letter may instruct the executor to produce copies of those files to share broadly with family. Assets in any financial accounts will be transferred to your chosen heirs according to your will, trust or beneficiary designation form, after which the financial institutions will close your accounts. A letter can also tell the executor how to manage social media accounts. Options for dealing with social media accounts include transferring account management to a loved one so that the account can remain active and serve as a memorial to the original account holder, or the account can simply be closed down.

### Account Specific Information

Google, Facebook, Twitter, Apple and other companies have adopted policies to address the situation when an account holder has passed away. These policies may allow an account holder to designate a "Legacy Contact" to manage the account, require specific documentation before a deceased person's account can be closed, such as a copy of a death certificate, court order, notarized letter or obituary, or automatically close an account after an extended period of inactivity, such as three to twelve months. These policies are subject to change, so a digital executor should familiarize themselves with the policies of each account provider and may need to act quickly to preserve important and sentimental information for family and loved ones.

### Protecting Your Digital Assets

Digital estate planning is a new and rapidly changing field. By incorporating an ePlan into your estate plan, you can ensure that your executor will take the right steps to preserve and protect these accounts and that valuable and sentimental data can be passed on to family and loved ones.

## CHAPTER 28
## ONLINE ACCOUNTS

# QUIZ

1. The four general types of online accounts are personal accounts, financial accounts, business electronic assets and online dating records.

   ☐ True      ☐ False

2. You should not place your list of online accounts and passwords in a will or living trust.

   ☐ True      ☐ False

3. Storing your account and password list in a safety deposit box may limit access by your executor.

   ☐ True      ☐ False

4. A password management program is a good option for managing your online accounts and password list.

   ☐ True      ☐ False

5. A digital executor should view the terms of service for social media when someone passes away.

   ☐ True      ☐ False

**Answers:** To view the quiz answers online, please use the website on the front cover. On that site select "Plan Your Will" and logon to your free Wills Planner account. Select the "Provide & Protect Resources" button on the right and "IV. Your Estate Plan." Under "Wills" Select "#28" and view the Quiz Answers at the bottom. You may also enjoy the three-minute video explanation.

# WILLS
## Bequests to Your Favorite Charity

Bequests to charity are the most popular type of planned gift. A donor may retain assets during life and then leave a bequest to a charity.

A bequest to a charity should include the full legal name, city and state of the charity—particularly if there are chapters of a national organization or religious organizations with similar names. An attorney who drafts the will should be certain that he or she has correctly identified the intended charity by legal name, city and state.

### Specific Bequests

As a donor, you may choose to leave a specific item or amount to a charity. For example, some friends of charities have left a bequest of land or property adjacent to the campus of the charity. The usual purpose is for the charity to be able to use that property for future additions or expansion.

If you own art or a specific item that may be used by a charity for its exempt purpose, that asset may be a good choice for a specific bequest. Once again, it is important to identify the exact item and the charity by legal name, city and state. Some donors may also choose to list an alternative gift if they leave a specific bequest. If for any reason your estate no longer owns the specific bequest property at your death, you may wish to designate another item or an amount of cash to the charity.

Another option is a specific bequest of an amount of cash. This allows you to know the exact amount that will be transferred from your estate to charity. There is one planning issue to consider with a bequest of a specific amount of cash. If you transfer a specific amount of cash to a charity and your estate is much larger or much smaller than the present value, this bequest to charity may be a larger or smaller part of the estate than you intend. If this is a reasonable prospect, you may wish to leave a percentage of the estate to your favorite charity.

### Gift of Part of the Residue of the Estate

After all of the specific bequests have been made and your estate costs and taxes have been paid, the balance of the estate is called the residue. You probably will choose to distribute the residue on a percentage basis. Many donors decide to leave a percentage of the residue to charity.

Some donors give charity a specific percentage, such as 5%, 10% or more. Another option is to give to all of your charities a share that is equal to the share of your children, nephews, nieces or other beneficiaries.

For example, one donor had two children and divided her estate into three shares. Each child received one share and the charities collectively divided the third share. Another parent with three children divided the estate into four shares and did the same. Treating your charities as one child and simply dividing the estate with one share for each child and one share for favorite charities is a very convenient way to benefit your favorite charities.

### IRA or 401(k)

If your estate includes an IRA or 401(k) in addition to your home, CDs and other securities, you might consider a beneficiary designation to charity.

From your perspective, your IRA is a very good asset. For most IRAs, other than a Roth IRA, the plan is funded with pretax dollars. It also grows tax free. However, you or your beneficiary will pay income tax when you withdraw the funds.

For you, the IRA is an excellent plan. Everyone should have a qualified plan such as an IRA, 401(k), or other retirement plan. Your IRA is funded with pre-tax dollars and grows tax free. This is an excellent plan for your future security.

If you pass away with a fairly substantial balance in your regular IRA or 401(k), that could be an excellent opportunity to make a charitable bequest. For the vast majority of Americans who have an estate that is not subject to estate tax, the only tax paid by the family will be income tax. Your home, CDs, stocks and bonds can be transferred to children without tax.

However, if you give family members your IRA, it comes with a large "you-owe-the-IRS" tax bill attached. When children or other heirs receive your IRA, they pay tax at their highest rate on their IRA distributions. This can be a sum of many tens of thousands of dollars.

Therefore, if you are planning to leave assets to charity, the transfer of an IRA may be a good plan.

Joe is an IRA owner and was speaking with his tax advisor Harry about the options for leaving a bequest to his favorite charity.

**Joe:** "Harry, I've been thinking about leaving a bequest to charity. You know, I've always thought that I would leave most of my estate to my two nephews and three nieces. But as I've thought about it, I have supported my favorite charity for many years and would like to do something for them."

**Harry:** "Well, you have a home, some CDs, some stocks and bonds and your IRA. Right now, the other assets are worth about $600,000 in total and your IRA is $200,000. How much were you thinking of leaving to the charity?"

**Joe:** "I thought I would give them about one-fourth of the estate and transfer the rest to my five nieces and nephews."

**Harry:** "You know, Joe, if you give them the home, stocks and bonds and CDs they will pay zero estate and income tax. But if you give them the IRA, they would have to pay income tax. A better plan might be to give the IRA to charity. Because a charity is tax exempt, it doesn't pay the income tax. In your case, that's a savings of over $60,000."

**Joe:** "That sounds like a great idea. How do I make that gift?"

**Harry:** "Your IRA is transferred by a beneficiary designation. We will obtain the form from your IRA custodian and designate your favorite charity. The nice part about a beneficiary designation is that it avoids probate."

## Bequest for a Purpose

A bequest of assets through a will, a revocable living trust, or a beneficiary designation of a retirement plan also enables you to select a purpose. In most cases, donors simply leave a bequest for the general purposes of the charity. Because your bequest may occur many years after you sign your will, it is good to give the board of directors of the charity opportunity to select the best and most effective use of the bequest.

However, if you wish to benefit a specific area within your favorite charity, that is perfectly fine. You may designate the purpose for the use of your funds. In selecting a purpose, it is still best to give a general category for the use of the funds, so that the organization can continue to make the best possible use of your bequest.

**CHAPTER 29**

WILLS — Bequests to Your Favorite Charity

# QUIZ

**1.** With a gift to a religious charity or a local chapter of a national charity, there is seldom a name problem.

☐ True    ☐ False

**2.** A gift of the residue to charity is frequently better than a specific bequest.

☐ True    ☐ False

**3.** A possible plan for the charitably minded is to give the charities the same share as children, nephews or nieces.

☐ True    ☐ False

**4.** An IRA is usually transferred by will.

☐ True    ☐ False

**5.** A major benefit of a bequest of IRA to charity is that you save potential income tax.

☐ True    ☐ False

**Answers:** To view the quiz answers online, please use the website on the front cover. On that site select "Plan Your Will" and logon to your free Wills Planner account. Select the "Provide & Protect Resources" button on the right and "IV. Your Estate Plan." Under "Wills" Select "#29" and view the Quiz Answers at the bottom. You may also enjoy the three-minute video explanation.

# TRUSTS
## Your Living Trust Choices

The living trust is becoming quite a popular estate planning strategy. It costs more than a will, but includes many features that are helpful during life and in your estate. Let's review some of the basic principles of the living trust.

### Living Trust Basics

A trust is created by transferring property to a trustee. The trustee is required to follow the provisions of a written trust document. That document identifies the individuals who will receive the income. In most cases, there are reasons or grounds for invading the principal for the benefit of named income recipients. After a period of time, such as the life of the income recipients, the trust remainder is then distributed or held in trust for the benefit of other persons.

### Living Trust Example—Bill and Clara

Assume that Bill and Clara are married with three children. They create a living trust with themselves as the initial trustees. Bill and Clara transfer their home, mutual fund accounts and other assets into the trust. They will receive the income from the assets for their lifetime and have the ability to invade the trust or distribute assets back to themselves at any time. When they pass away, their selected successor trustee will manage the property and use it for the benefit of their three children.

## Trust Creation

There are several steps in the process for Bill and Clara to create their trust. They will need to visit with their attorney and discuss the basic provisions for payment of income, invasion of principal, and distribution of their remainder. The remainder is the term to describe the value of the trust after both Bill and Clara pass away.

After they have discussed the living trust provisions and their attorney has drafted the trust agreement, they will then sign the trust both as the grantors and as the initial trustees. In order to have property to manage, the next step is to actually fund the trust or transfer assets to it.

The trust document will explain that Bill and Clara have the right to receive income for life from the trust. They can revoke the trust in whole or in part and transfer assets back to themselves as individuals. The trust will name one or more successor trustees. The successor will manage the trust if they are ill and are unable to manage or if they simply are no longer willing to undertake that responsibility. Finally, the trust document will explain who receives trust property after they pass away.

## Living Trust Income Taxes

Because Bill and Clara have the right to receive the income from the trust and also can revoke the trust, they will report all of the income on their personal IRS Form 1040. The IRS does not regard the living trust as a separate taxpayer. For tax purposes, living trust income, capital gains and deductions flow through to their personal tax return.

For example, they may transfer their residence into the trust. If the residence has a mortgage, they will still be permitted to pay the mortgage and deduct the home mortgage interest on their tax return. In addition, if the trust transfers the property to a qualified exempt charity, Bill and Clara will be permitted to report the charitable deduction on their personal tax return.

## Funding the Trust

Each type of asset will need to be transferred into the trust. Legal title to real estate is transferred through a deed (typically a warranty or grant deed depending upon your state). Bill and Clara signed deeds that transferred their personal residence from themselves to the trust with them as trustees. The deeds were filed with the local county registrar of deeds.

Stocks, bonds and mutual funds can be transferred into new accounts created by the trustee. In some cases, the financial services firm will require proof that you have the ability to transfer these items into the trust. Your attorney can create an "affidavit of trust" that you will sign. It will authorize the financial services company to create a new account for the trust and transfer the securities or mutual funds into that account.

Your cars, furniture and other tangible personal property are frequently retained in your personal name rather than being transferred to the trust account. If you do transfer vehicles through your appropriate state title into the trust, then it will be necessary to be certain that any purchases or sales of vehicles in the future are correctly titled in the name of the trust.

## Estate Taxes

Because Bill and Clara have the right to receive trust income and the ability to invade the trust, it will be included in their estate. You may have heard that a living trust avoids probate. This is true. But, it is most important to realize that the federal government includes both your probate estate and other assets of which you have ownership in your taxable estate.

The taxable estate includes your assets probated under your will, your IRA, most insurance policies and your living trust assets. Therefore, if you have a large estate your attorney will ensure that your planning avoids probate to save probate costs, but is also designed to reduce estate taxes on the total assets in your probate estate and living trust.

**CHAPTER 30**

TRUSTS — Your Living Trust Choices

# QUIZ

1. With a living trust, the trust grantors also frequently serve as the initial trustees.

   ☐ True ☐ False

2. Once you sign the living trust you have completed your estate planning process.

   ☐ True ☐ False

3. With a living trust, you can revoke part or all of the trust.

   ☐ True ☐ False

4. If you have stock or land in your living trust and sell that property for a gain, the trust will pay the capital gains tax.

   ☐ True ☐ False

5. The living trust avoids all estate tax.

   ☐ True ☐ False

**Answers:** To view the quiz answers online, please use the website on the front cover. On that site select "Plan Your Will" and logon to your free Wills Planner account. Select the "Provide & Protect Resources" button on the right and "IV. Your Estate Plan." Under "Trusts" Select "#30" and view the Quiz Answers at the bottom. You may also enjoy the three-minute video explanation.

# LIVING TRUSTS
## Life and Death Decisions

In discussing your living trust with your attorney, there are several very important decisions for you to consider. Some of your decisions affect the management of property during life, and others will determine how your successor trustee manages your property for the benefit of family, friends and charity after you pass away.

### Medical Care Planning

The living trust works together with other important estate planning documents in the event that you have a medical crisis or emergency. When you sign a living trust, your attorney will also prepare an advance directive or, in some states, a durable power of attorney for healthcare and a living will.

These documents will be different in the various states, but have the same general purpose. The durable power of attorney for healthcare enables you to select a person who will make medical decisions if you are not able to advise the doctors yourself. A living will explains the circumstances that will be surrounding your final weeks or days and makes requests to the attending doctors and nurses concerning your preferences for care at that time.

While these medical documents are important to ensure that you receive the best care, the living trust also contains provisions that make certain your property is managed for your benefit. If you are ill, your designated successor trustee may manage your property, pay bills and ensure good medical care for you.

## Trust for Minor Children

If you are a single parent or a couple with minor children, then the living trust will usually include a family trust for the benefit of those children. If both parents have passed away, the successor trustee will manage the family trust for the children.

The trust provisions frequently permit the trustee to allocate the income to the children based on his or her understanding of their individual needs. Unless the trust is quite substantial, it is common for the entire family trust for minors to be used to provide for the room, board, tuition and medical expenses of the minors until the youngest child reaches the age for distribution. For many parents, this is when the youngest child is age 25 or older.

During the existence of the trust, a trustee of a family trust for minors generally has quite broad discretion. For example, the trustee may distribute income to any of the children and may invade principal for medical expenses, educational expenses or other needed items. The parent will frequently provide a general statement of guidance for distributions, especially of principal, but the trustee will often have broad discretion. Therefore, it is common to select a trusted friend, advisor or family member as trustee of the trust for minor children.

If your estate is substantial, you may want to select one person as guardian of your children and another as successor trustee of your property. In this way, you build a "check and balance" into the plan that encourages both your guardian and trustee to use the assets to best benefit your children.

## Single Person—"Give It Twice" Trust

The living trust directs the distribution of assets after the demise of a single person. Frequently, the assets are distributed to family and favorite charities. The family could be children, but many times includes nephews and nieces.

A single person may choose to create a trust for nephews and nieces. One trust that is gaining popularity is a "Give It Twice" trust. The trust pays income to the nephews or nieces until the initial value of the trust has been paid out as income. Trust principal is then distributed to charity.

For example, a single person with four nephews and nieces passed away and transferred $500,000 into the "Give It Twice" trust. The trust paid approximately $500,000 of income over a term of 18 years to the four nephews and nieces. After that time, the trust principal of $500,000 was distributed to a favorite charity.

### Planning by Married Couples

If married couples have minor children, then a family trust for minors is appropriate. However, particularly if the married couples have a larger estate, then your advisor may suggest a plan with two trusts. With a larger estate, your advisor may recommend a combination of a qualified terminable interest property trust (QTIP) for the surviving spouse and a bypass trust.

The QTIP distributes all income to the surviving spouse. It can be invaded, but only for the benefit of the surviving spouse. After the surviving spouse passes away, the assets are distributed under the will of the first person to pass away. This distribution is frequently made to children, but may also include favorite charities. The QTIP protects both the surviving spouse and the children from the first marriage.

The second trust is the bypass trust. It is normally funded with the amount of the exemption equivalent. This trust usually distributes income to the surviving spouse. There is also a limited power to invade principal for the benefit of the surviving spouse if needed for health, education, maintenance or support.

Because this trust uses the exemption of the first to pass away and follows the appropriate guidelines, it is not subject to tax in the estate of surviving spouse. Only the QTIP and the other personally owned assets will be subject to estate tax from the assets of the surviving spouse.

**CHAPTER 31**

LIVING TRUSTS — Life and Death Decisions

# QUIZ

1. The living trust is designed to provide for your personal care in the event of a medical emergency.

   ☐ True ☐ False

2. It is important to select a successor trustee and determine the circumstances in which he or she takes over the trust if there is a medical emergency.

   ☐ True ☐ False

3. If you create a trust for minor children in your living trust, you need to be very thoughtful in your selection of the successor trustee.

   ☐ True ☐ False

4. In funding a trust for nieces or nephews, a single person will often set up a "Give It Twice" trust funded with an IRA or pension plan.

   ☐ True ☐ False

5. A married couple with a substantial estate may create a QTIP and bypass trust plan, and both trusts will qualify for the marital deduction.

   ☐ True ☐ False

**Answers:** To view the quiz answers online, please use the website on the front cover. On that site select "Plan Your Will" and logon to your free Wills Planner account. Select the "Provide & Protect Resources" button on the right and "IV. Your Estate Plan." Under "Trusts" Select "#31" and view the Quiz Answers at the bottom. You may also enjoy the three-minute video explanation.

# TRUSTS
## How to Fund Your Living Trust

A revocable living trust is one of the principal estate planning methods. While everyone should have a will, there are many benefits of a revocable living trust. For individuals who have moderate or larger estates, the revocable living trust can receive and own your property. For that reason, a revocable living trust is a good centralized method for managing your property.

If you as a senior person are unable or unwilling to manage your assets, the individual you've selected as successor trustee will take over and manage property for you. Not only does this protect you, the property will eventually pass to your heirs and bypass probate. The probate savings could be many tens of thousands of dollars.

A primary benefit of the living trust is that it avoids a conservatorship. If you have only a will, own substantial assets, and become unable to manage your property, it may be necessary to conduct an expensive and lengthy court process to appoint a conservator of your assets.

For example, comedian Groucho Marx had a will. But in his mid-eighties, he no longer was competent to manage his property. There was a major court battle between his family members and a long-time companion over who should be appointed conservator of both him and his property. The court battles consumed large sums of money and led to a very awkward and humiliating spectacle that was bewildering to Groucho Marx.

If Groucho Marx had created a living trust and transferred his property to that trust, then his selected successor trustee could have managed his property during his senior years.

### Funded or Unfunded Living Trust?

It is possible to create a living trust that is unfunded during life. Together with the living trust, you would then sign a pour-over will. The assets that you possess at death would go through the probate process. However, the pour-over will may transfer those properties to the living trust. This property is then used according to your trust provisions to benefit your selected heirs.

The disadvantage of the unfunded trust is that you do not avoid probate. Your estate will pay the full probate costs. In addition, you give up the potential protection of a successor trustee during life. It is only if your assets are transferred to the trust that a successor trustee can then manage them for your benefit. The unfunded living trust, therefore, could lead to a conservatorship, as was the case with Groucho Marx.

### Funded Living Trust

There are several different types of assets that will be transferred to a living trust. You will need to work with your attorney and other advisors to make certain that your property is correctly placed into the trust.

Title to your property is determined by state law. You will need to comply with the appropriate agreements or documents to make sure that title is held by the trustee. In most cases, you will serve as the initial trustee of the revocable living trust. Therefore, real property and other assets will be transferred from you as an individual to you as trustee of the trust.

Real estate is often the principal asset that is transferred to the trust. This is normally accomplished through a warranty deed or grant deed, depending upon your state. The property is transferred directly from you as an individual to you as trustee. Deeds are notarized and then recorded at the county registrar of deeds.

There are considerations that you should discuss with your attorney before transferring your home or other real property into your trust through a deed. There may be a reassessment or increase in the property tax, or there may be transfer taxes when deeds are recorded. In most states, the popular living trust has been protected from an increase in property taxes. However, you should check with your attorney.

### Guidelines for Living Trust Property Transfers

1. **Your Home:** Even though your home is transferred to a living trust, you still qualify to deduct the mortgage interest paid on the home. If you later sell the home and have made it your principal residence for two of the past five years, you will be able to exclude $250,000 for a single person or $500,000 of capital gain for a married couple. In addition, most states permit you to live in the home and qualify for a homestead exemption reduction in your property tax, even though the home is now titled under the living trust.

2. **Securities:** Public stocks and bonds can be transferred directly to the trust. You may hold title to the bonds in trust or you may create a trust securities account that holds stocks and bonds.

3. **Safe Deposit Box:** If you have a safe deposit box, that can be taken out in the name of the trust. However, some institutions that maintain safe deposit boxes require a certified copy of the trust to be kept on file. Another option may be to give your successor trustee signing authority on your safe deposit box.

4. **Real Estate:** If you own real estate in your home state or other states, it should be transferred to the trust. If you pass away with real estate owned in your individual name in another state, it will require a rather expensive probate proceeding in that state to transfer the real estate. However, if it is transferred to your revocable trust, then you avoid that foreign state probate proceeding and cost.

When your home or other real estate is transferred to the trust, there may be a requirement to send a copy of the trust to your lender. Most title companies and lenders will accept a short "affidavit of trust" that can be prepared by your attorney. This indicates that the trust is a qualified living trust and the trustees have the power to transfer real estate.

5. **Tangible Personal Property:** A common question is whether tangible personal property should be included in the trust. It is possible to transfer your cars, boats, recreational vehicles or art and other collections to the trust. However, many individuals choose to retain personal ownership of tangible personal property. This is frequently the case because you may periodically buy or sell vehicles or other tangible personal items. By not transferring tangible personal property to the trust, it simplifies lifetime transfer of those items. However, if there is extremely valuable tangible personal property that would be subject to substantial probate cost through your will, then it may be appropriate to transfer that property to the trust.

What if you would like to sell trust property? It is entirely possible to transfer property from the trust to a new person. The trustee may simply deed the property directly to an individual.

In some circumstances, your attorney may think that it is better for title insurance purposes for you to sign two deeds. One deed is from you as trustee to you as an individual. The second deed would be from you as an individual to the new buyer. There may be a modest transfer tax cost for both deeds, but this is an acceptable strategy for simplifying the transfer of real property.

**CHAPTER 32**

TRUSTS — How to Fund Your Living Trust

# QUIZ

1. A living trust provides protection both for your property and for your person, and this protection justifies the cost for most people.

   ☐ True      ☐ False

2. An unfunded living trust may be used together with a pour-over will to protect your property and avoid a conservatorship.

   ☐ True      ☐ False

3. With a living trust, you will normally fund the trust by transferring a deed to your family residence to yourself as trustee.

   ☐ True      ☐ False

4. If you own real estate in other states, a living trust is a good plan.

   ☐ True      ☐ False

5. Tangible personal property is often not transferred to the living trust.

   ☐ True      ☐ False

**Answers:** To view the quiz answers online, please use the website on the front cover. On that site select "Plan Your Will" and logon to your free Wills Planner account. Select the "Provide & Protect Resources" button on the right and "IV. Your Estate Plan." Under "Trusts" Select "#32" and view the Quiz Answers at the bottom. You may also enjoy the three-minute video explanation.

# TRUSTS
## Income for Surviving Spouse

Elliot and Alexis were concerned about planning for the future. They had built a substantial estate of $1,200,000. When Elliot was 70, he rolled over his $400,000 qualified retirement plan into an IRA. Because he is now over age 70½, Elliot is taking distributions.

Alexis also has an IRA. They jointly own their home, which is debt free, and have savings accounts, stocks and bonds.

If Elliot were to pass away first, Alexis would like to avoid paying additional tax. In addition to the IRA, Alexis already receives income from their investments.

Alexis said, "We seem to be paying a lot of income tax. When Elliot takes distributions from his IRA, that just pushes our income up higher and we pay more and more tax. Is there a way that I could reduce my income tax if Elliot passed away?"

### A Solution for Alexis

Elliot could name Alexis as the designated beneficiary of his IRA. After Elliot passes away, Alexis may roll the IRA over. Alexis is age 70, and will soon be required to start distributions from the IRA. The added income would significantly increase Alexis's taxes.

A solution that gives Alexis protection and good flexibility is for Elliot to transfer his IRA to a special trust when he passes away. Under the design of this trust, Alexis could receive a 5% income payout or could encourage the trustee to invest for growth.

If Alexis decides to let the income grow inside the trust, it will grow tax free until more income is desired. At a future date, Alexis may decide that the balance of the estate is not producing as much income as desired, and could encourage the trustee to start making the payments. By that time, it is quite possible that the $400,000 would have grown and the trust payouts could be significantly greater.

### How to Create the Trust

The trust has a special name. It is called a net income plus makeup charitable remainder unitrust. Elliot and Alexis talked to their attorney, George. He prepared a trust document that Elliot and Alexis signed.

Under their state law, this trust document is valid even though it is not yet funded. Elliot then selected the trust as the designated beneficiary for his IRA and Alexis consented in writing to that designation.

### When Elliot Passes Away

If Elliot passes away first, Alexis will own the family home outright and will inherit their other assets, except the IRA. Elliot's IRA will be transferred directly to the unitrust. Because it is a net plus makeup unitrust, the trustee may discuss her goals with Alexis and then invest the $400,000.

### Alexis's Options

Alexis may choose to allow the trust to grow for a period of time, if there is sufficient income from the IRA, Social Security and pension. However, if Alexis prefers to receive income from the $400,000 unitrust, then the trustee can invest to produce at least the 5% income and pay that amount to Alexis.

Alexis may decide to allow the trust to grow because there are modest expenses, no debt and sufficient income to enjoy annual traveling. At a future date Alexis could request the trustee change the investments from growth to income. For now, Alexis is comfortable with the trust investments in growth securities.

## Saving Income Taxes

Because the growth of the trust is tax free and Alexis is not receiving substantial income from the trust, the income will be lower and there will be substantial tax savings. Alexis shared with their attorney, George, "I have more than enough and I could always spend a portion of my CDs if needed. It is a relief not to have the extra income and have to pay those high income taxes. Plus, I know that the trust is growing and I could receive a larger income in the future if needed."

## Benefits for Family and Charity

If necessary in the future, Alexis will receive the income from the unitrust. However, Alexis may choose to allow the trust to grow and live on other income. When Alexis passes away, the trust principal plus growth will go to three favorite charities of Elliot and Alexis.

In addition, the children of Elliot and Alexis will also receive a substantial inheritance. The balance of the estate, including their home, CDs, stocks and bonds, will be divided between their two children.

Alexis is very pleased that income taxes will be reduced, and the estate total will be larger. Over time, the trust could grow quite substantially. The combination of security for Alexis, trust growth for charity and the benefits to family from the inheritance of the balance of the estate create a very good plan for Elliot and Alexis.

**CHAPTER 33**

TRUSTS — Income for Surviving Spouse

# QUIZ

1. If an IRA is transferred to a surviving spouse, he or she may roll over the IRA into his or her own plan.

   ☐ True      ☐ False

2. If a surviving spouse rolls over the IRA, he or she will be required to take distributions at age 70½.

   ☐ True      ☐ False

3. With a charitable remainder unitrust, the trustee must make an annual payment of 5% or more.

   ☐ True      ☐ False

4. With a net income unitrust, the trustee has the option of investing for growth or for income.

   ☐ True      ☐ False

5. If a unitrust grows, it may benefit both the surviving spouse and charity.

   ☐ True      ☐ False

**Answers:** To view the quiz answers online, please use the website on the front cover. On that site select "Plan Your Will" and logon to your free Wills Planner account. Select the "Provide & Protect Resources" button on the right and "IV. Your Estate Plan." Under "Trusts" Select "#33" and view the Quiz Answers at the bottom. You may also enjoy the three-minute video explanation.

# TRUSTS
## For Surviving Spouse

There are three different basic types of trusts for a surviving spouse: a qualified terminable interest property trust (QTIP), a qualified domestic trust (QDOT) or a charitable remainder trust (CRT). All three of these trusts may qualify for the marital deduction. However, there are many specific reasons for choosing one of these three trust types.

### QTIP Trust

The QTIP trust is the most common marital deduction trust. There are four basic rules for the QTIP trust:

1. All income must be paid to the surviving spouse.

2. The surviving spouse may require the trustee to invest in assets that produce income.

3. The principal may be invaded only for the benefit of the surviving spouse.

4. The trust remainder will be distributed to the beneficiaries designated under the will of the first to pass away.

A QTIP trust is excellent for protecting the children of a first marriage. The trust can benefit the surviving spouse and then will be transferred to those children.

### Example—Jane Lost Everything but Betty Was Protected

Joe and Jane were married and had two children. On Saturday evenings, they often went to dinner with their friends Bill and Betty.

Joe passed away first and had a simple will. He left his estate outright to Jane. It qualified for the estate marital deduction so there was no estate tax.

Subsequently, Jane married John Speculator. John was involved in a Brazilian gold mining adventure. The entire estate of Jane was soon invested far south of the border, never to return. Jane and her children lost everything.

Bill and Betty decided to protect their estate. Bill created a QTIP trust for his half of the estate. When Bill passed away, Betty was the beneficiary of the QTIP trust. After a few years, she married Sam Speculator. While Sam was involved in the Brazilian gold mining adventure, the QTIP created by Bill provided income and protection for Betty for her lifetime. In addition, the QTIP principal was protected.

### QTIP Powers and Election

There are several powers that are permitted for a QTIP. First, the required provisions are that the income be paid to the surviving spouse and principal can be invaded only for the surviving spouse. However, the trustee may choose to transfer the greater of 5% of trust assets or $5,000 each year to the surviving spouse. In addition, it is permitted to allow the surviving spouse to appoint the remainder. If the surviving spouse holds the power to appoint, he or she can direct the trust to children from the first marriage, but also could give trust assets to other persons.

A QTIP must be elected on the Form 706 Federal Estate Tax Return. It is also possible to make a partial QTIP election and to create a transfer of the balance that is taxable in the first estate. The benefit of this plan is that this amount will be tax free to family in the second estate.

### QDOT Trusts

If a spouse is not a U.S. citizen, then a transfer will not qualify for the federal marital deduction. In this case it is possible to create a qualified domestic trust (QDOT).

With a QDOT, the surviving spouse will receive all income. There must be at least one trustee that is a U.S. citizen or corporation. If the surviving spouse receives distributions of principal, those will be subject to estate tax, with one exception. There is a "hardship" exception that may allow tax-free principal distributions for emergency medical care or other extraordinary circumstances.

If the surviving spouse desires to qualify for the regular marital deduction, he or she may become a U.S. citizen prior to the date for filing the federal Form 706 Estate Tax Return.

### Charitable Remainder Trust (CRT)

The third option for a qualified marital deduction trust is a charitable remainder trust. The trust may be created as a two-life agreement during the joint lifetimes of the spouses or it could be created in a will or living trust to benefit the surviving spouse.

There are two different payout options for this CRT. A standard CRT pays 5% or more each year to the surviving spouse. This payout is made from income and, if necessary, from trust principal. An attractive benefit of a CRT is that it may grow tax free during the life of the surviving spouse.

Part of the CRT payments may be distributed at the lower capital gain rates. Finally, because the assets are stepped up to fair market value in the estate, the potential exists to invest in municipal bonds and pay out tax-free income to the spouse.

A second payout method is a net-income-plus-makeup unitrust. This trust method can enable the principal to be invested for growth rather than income. Because the growth inside the trust is tax free, the surviving spouse may dramatically lower income taxes if he or she does not need the income. Rather than taking the full CRT payout and paying income tax, the spouse permits the trustee to invest for growth for his or her lifetime. If income is needed at a higher level later in life, the trustee may reinvest for income and pay the regular income plus make up the prior shortfall.

With a CRT, after the surviving spouse passes away the remainder is distributed to qualified exempt charities. The charities may be designated by the first spouse to pass away, or a power can be given to the surviving spouse to designate the charities.

**CHAPTER 34**

TRUSTS — For Surviving Spouse

# QUIZ

**1.** The three most popular types of marital deduction trusts are the QTIP, the QDOT and the CRT.

☐ True    ☐ False

**2.** With a QTIP trust, if there is a medical emergency for the children, it is permitted to make distributions to children or pay for their medical care.

☐ True    ☐ False

**3.** With a QTIP, it is usually the objective to protect the inheritance for the benefit of the children of the first marriage.

☐ True    ☐ False

**4.** With a charitable remainder trust for the surviving spouse, you may select either a standard or a net-plus-makeup payout method.

☐ True    ☐ False

**5.** With a charitable remainder trust, it will qualify for a marital deduction if the surviving spouse is the only permitted recipient.

☐ True    ☐ False

**Answers:** To view the quiz answers online, please use the website on the front cover. On that site select "Plan Your Will" and logon to your free Wills Planner account. Select the "Provide & Protect Resources" button on the right and "IV. Your Estate Plan." Under "Trusts" Select "#34" and view the Quiz Answers at the bottom. You may also enjoy the three-minute video explanation.

# TRUSTS
## To Protect Children

Trusts are an excellent way to provide for the support and care of children while protecting them. Two important reasons to create a trust are to care for minor children or for a special needs child. In both circumstances, trusts can be an essential part of making plans to provide the best possible care.

### How Trusts Work

There are several people and terms that you should know about to understand how trusts work. Let's examine the different people or terms that will be useful in setting up and operating a trust for children.

**Trustee:** A trustee will be charged with managing the property under the terms of a trust document. The three choices for trustee are a bank or trust company, a private trustee or a charitable trustee for a trust that benefits charity.

A trustee has a particular name—a fiduciary. This means that the trustee is required under state law to provide appropriate management of the trust. Based on the trust document that you sign as the trust grantor, the trustee will do his or her best to follow your intent.

**Property:** The trust exists to hold and manage property. While in many states a trust is legally in existence after you sign the trust document, it doesn't actually have any purpose until it receives property. Your trustee refers to this as the "funding" of the trust.

The trustee will manage the property according to the terms of your trust document.

**Investments:** Under state law, your trustee is required to follow the standards of a prudent investor. In most cases, the trustee will invest in a portfolio of stocks and bonds. Approximately 50% to 60% of the typical trust portfolio is invested in a diversified group of stocks, with the balance invested in bonds.

Under the prudent investor rules, the trustee is obligated to diversify. Through diversification the risk of loss will be reduced and the probability that the trust will function as you intend is greater.

**Income:** Income is defined under the law as either ordinary income or capital gain. The interest from bonds and mortgage notes is ordinary income. Historically, trusts have paid out their ordinary income. However, because many trustees now have more than half of the trust property invested in stocks, trusts now may pay out a portion of recognized capital gain as income.

**Capital Gain:** Capital gain is the other type of earnings of a trust. While a portion of the capital gain represents principal and will be retained in the trust to benefit the remainder recipient, part of the gain under modern investment strategies is typically allocated to income. The trustee will look at the trust document to determine who will receive the income. Normally, the trustee will pay out on a quarterly basis the ordinary income and part of the recognized capital gains.

**Remainder:** Under the trust document, the trust will pay income for a period of time, such as a life of a person or a term of years. After all of the income payments have been completed, the trust principal or remainder is usually transferred to the beneficiaries.

For example, a trust was funded with $300,000 and paid income to children Billy, Susie and Linda until they were age 30. At that time, the trust remainder value of $300,000 was divided between the three children. Because each received one-third of the remainder, the inheritance amount for each child was $100,000.

## Trusts for Minor Children

Parents correctly understand that a minor child is not ready to receive a substantial inheritance. Therefore, it is very common for parents to create in their will or living trust a plan to set up a trust for minor children.

The trust for minor children frequently permits the trustee broad latitude to pay income and principal to the children or spend it for their healthcare or other needs. Because of this flexibility, the trustee of the trust for minor children is frequently a family member or professional advisor for the family. After all of the children reach a particular age, the trust is then usually distributed in equal shares to the then-living children.

## Trust for Children Billy and Mary

Bill and Clara Jones are 36 and 34. They have two children—Billy (age four) and Mary (age one).

After visiting with their attorney, Bill and Clara signed their first will. If one of them should pass away, estate property and guardianship of the children will pass to the survivor. However, if they both pass away, then they have selected Clara's brother, Harold, and his wife as the guardians for the children. They also have selected Bill's sister, Susan, who is a CPA, as the trustee of their family trust for Billy and Mary.

CPA Susan has discretion under the trust instrument to make distributions of income or principal to Billy and Mary or to pay providers for their support or medical care. In order to provide maximum protection for Mary, the entire trust principal is retained until Mary is age 30. By that time, Bill and Clara believe that Mary will have completed her education and be well established in life. Even though Billy will be 33 and Mary will be 30, the trust principal will be divided equally between the two of them at that time.

With a family trust for minor children, the assets of the family are typically not large. Most trusts for minor children are funded primarily by term life insurance on the lives of Bill and Clara. Therefore, it is very common for the trust to continue in existence until the youngest child reaches the desired age. While this means that older children may have to wait longer for their inheritance, that is a secondary goal to making sure that the youngest children are all taken care of until they reach the selected age.

### Special Needs Trust

A child with a disability or special need will require both a caregiver and financial resources.

During the lives of the parents, they are often able to provide the required care for a special needs child. However, after they pass away, there may need to be a more structured option that involves a special facility for that child.

To plan for the case when both parents pass away, arrangements for the care facility and financial requirements of a special needs child should be made in advance. A special needs child often has no major assets and therefore is qualified for the Social Security SSI Program or for Medicaid.

However, if the parents were to give the child an inheritance outright or a vested income stream, then those funds will all be expended before the child could receive federal benefits. As a result, the special needs trust was designed to allow parents to provide help for children, even though the child may be receiving federal or state benefits.

The key to the special needs trust is that the trustee has complete discretion over principal and income. He or she may add the income back to the trust corpus, or may make distributions to the child or for the benefit of the child.

Because the special needs trust depends on federal and state laws that regularly change, an attorney who specializes in these trusts is often used to draft the specific provisions. However, there generally are several items the trustee can provide the special needs child and still maintain his or her qualification for federal and state benefits. These include a vehicle, a home, furnishings, property for self-support, medical care and educational expenses.

The special needs trust also should have an intention to preserve the trust for a remainder beneficiary. Even though the special needs child may receive income and principal that actually does exhaust the trust, the hope that another entity or person would benefit from the remainder is quite helpful.

**CHAPTER 35**

TRUSTS — To Protect Children

# QUIZ

1. A trustee under state law is required to follow the prudent investor standard.

   ☐ True ☐ False

2. Minor children can receive principal or income from the trust that allows the trustee discretion to make distributions.

   ☐ True ☐ False

3. Children who are beneficiaries of a trust for minor children will each receive their prorated shares at age 30.

   ☐ True ☐ False

4. With a special needs trust a child may qualify for government benefits and still receive payments from the trust.

   ☐ True ☐ False

5. The trustee of a special needs trust must make payments of all income to the child.

   ☐ True ☐ False

**Answers:** To view the quiz answers online, please use the website on the front cover. On that site select "Plan Your Will" and logon to your free Wills Planner account. Select the "Provide & Protect Resources" button on the right and "IV. Your Estate Plan." Under "Trusts" Select "#35" and view the Quiz Answers at the bottom. You may also enjoy the three-minute video explanation.

# TRUSTS
## For Creative Spenders

Trusts can be quite useful for protecting children. However, for some children, the trust serves an additional function: It protects the principal from being rapidly spent by a child. These trusts have a specific name—they are called "spendthrift" trusts.

Marla was visiting with her attorney Elizabeth shortly after her husband Harry passed away. She shared her concern for her youngest child, Joe.

**Marla:** "Harry and I were very fortunate to have four great children. I love each one of them very much. However, when it comes time to making decisions about inheritance, I have a big problem. Our older children Sam and Linda are quite good with financial matters. The third child Lynn is average, but our youngest son Joe is very carefree. If Joe has money, it is gone in a flash. What can I do?"

**Elizabeth:** "This is a fairly common situation. Many parents would like to treat their children equally, but some children are very good managers and one or two are not. In your case, we hope that Joe eventually learns to become more responsible. But for the present plan, it makes good sense to provide Joe with spendthrift trust provisions."

### The Spendthrift Trust Concept

A spendthrift trust allows a parent to protect a certain amount of inheritance. If you have a circumstance like Marla, it may be appropriate to transfer inheritance outright to some of your children and the same amount of property into a spendthrift trust for the "creative spender" child.

A spendthrift trust will need to be managed by a trustee who can make good decisions. For a larger trust, this could be a bank or trust company. In many circumstances a private trustee is selected, such as one of the family financial advisors or even one of the other children.

The trustee will have the usual power to invest and manage the trust assets. The first important provision for the trustee is his or her power over income. The spendthrift trust normally includes seven different provisions that apply to the income:

1. Income may be paid to the child.

2. Income may be paid to persons or organizations providing benefits to the child. For a spendthrift child, it frequently is necessary to make the payment directly to the provider or the child would simply spend the money.

3. The child may not demand the payment of the income. A spendthrift child may desire to purchase some item and would simply demand income if that right existed.

4. The child may not pledge or borrow against the trust income or principal. Once again, if the child could pledge or borrow against the trust, they could quickly deplete the trust through those loans.

5. The trustee usually has complete discretion over distributions. A parent may indicate the general purposes of the trust, but a trustee is better able to protect the principal and the beneficiary if he or she has complete discretion.

6. Trust principal may be used by the trustee for the education, healthcare needs or support of the child.

7. Some trusts create incentive plans. In these trusts, the trustee is authorized to distribute income that will match the income of the child.

## Spendthrift Trusts and Distributions of Principal

With a spendthrift trust, distribution of principal is also subject to specific requirements. While the parents are given a reasonable level of flexibility in setting forth the distribution rules, there are several general guidelines that are usually followed.

1. The trustee will have discretion to distribute principal over the duration of the trust. The trustee normally has quite broad powers to make distribution of principal. In order to protect the child, this is quite important. However, the child may have a very good investment or business opportunity for which he or she needs principal. If the trustee is convinced that the child can use principal responsibly, then the distribution may be made.

2. The trust principal is normally held in trust for life or until a fairly senior age, such as 50 or older. If the child eventually acquires the capability of managing assets properly, the trustee can use the discretionary power to move the assets to the child. However, because the parent is concerned that the child may never acquire a high level of management expertise, the trust often lasts for life.

3. The child has no right to demand principal. The principal is controlled by the trustee for the protection of the child.

4. The child may not pledge the trust principal or borrow against the principal. Because the trustee is not obligated to make payment on any loans by the child, the banks or other lenders will not make loans using the trust income or principal as collateral.

## A Solution for "Creative Bill"

Sam and Sandy have an estate of $1 million. Their children—Alice, Jim and Bill—are all in their mid-thirties. Alice is age 38 and Jim is age 37. They are both solid and responsible. However, Bill is 33 and is quite a creative person. Sandy says that "If Bill had a million dollars, he would use it creatively in three weeks."

Because of their desire to treat everyone equally and to protect Bill from his creative spending habits, Sam and Sandy created a fairly typical plan for their circumstances. If one spouse passes away, the $1 million estate will be transferred to the survivor. When the survivor passes away, their favorite charity will receive a bequest of 10% of the estate. The other 90% will be divided. Alice and Jim will receive their shares outright. However, the third share will be transferred into a spendthrift trust with family advisor Steven as trustee. There will also be a successor trustee—First Bank from their local community.

As trustee of the spendthrift trust, Steven will receive approximately $300,000. He will invest this amount in a diversified portfolio of stocks and bonds. Steven will have discretion to distribute income and/or principal to Bill. When Bill reaches age 55, he will then receive the full inheritance. Sam and Sandy believe that by that time he will be responsible in managing the property.

**CHAPTER 36**

TRUSTS — For Creative Spenders

# QUIZ

**1.** If you have three or four children, there is a high probability that you have at least one creative spender.

☐ True ☐ False

**2.** With a spendthrift trust, a family advisor may frequently serve as trustee.

☐ True ☐ False

**3.** With a spendthrift trust, a child may demand payment.

☐ True ☐ False

**4.** With a spendthrift trust, the child may pledge trust assets for a personal loan.

☐ True ☐ False

**5.** A spendthrift trust often lasts for the lifetime of the child.

☐ True ☐ False

**Answers:** To view the quiz answers online, please use the website on the front cover. On that site select "Plan Your Will" and logon to your free Wills Planner account. Select the "Provide & Protect Resources" button on the right and "IV. Your Estate Plan." Under "Trusts" Select "#36" and view the Quiz Answers at the bottom. You may also enjoy the three-minute video explanation.

# TRUSTS
## "Give It Twice" Trust

A very popular option for a parent with children is called the "Give It Twice" trust. This is a trust funded when the surviving parent passes away. Part of the estate is transferred outright to children. The balance is placed in a special "Give It Twice" trust.

The trust pays income to children for a term of years—usually 20 years. The income can be divided equally among the children for that period of time. Following the selected term of years, the trust principal is then transferred to charity.

In effect, the property has been used twice—once to benefit children with income and the second time to help charity at the end of the trust.

Cindy is a surviving spouse. Her spouse, Michael, passed away four years ago. She is doing fine and combined both IRAs into one. Cindy's estate is now approximately $800,000. Her home, CDs and other property are valued at $400,000, and the combination of IRAs is also about $400,000.

She was reading online about the "Give It Twice" trust. Because Cindy is debt free and has Social Security plus pension income, she thinks that her estate, when she passes away, is likely to be fairly close to its current value. Cindy sat down with her attorney, David, to discuss the possibility of creating a trust.

**Cindy:** "David, I was reading an article online about this special "Give It Twice" trust. It sounds like you can give an asset once to children through the income stream and then transfer the trust property to charity."

**Attorney:** "Yes, Cindy, that can be done."

**Cindy:** "Before Michael passed away, we talked about this. We agreed to treat each of our four children equally and also provide a benefit to our favorite charity."

**Attorney:** "With your estate of $800,000, you have the ability to do something pretty significant for both your family and favorite charity."

**Cindy:** "Yes, but there is one big problem. Our three older children—Bill, Sue and Pete—do fine. They are quite financially responsible. But our youngest son Ted is very creative. He spends money like water. If we gave him one-fourth of the estate or $200,000, I am afraid he would spend that very quickly. We need to figure out a way to protect at least part of his inheritance."

**Attorney:** "That 'Give It Twice' plan could be very helpful. You can benefit all four children equally with an initial amount. For example, you could transfer the $400,000 to them when you pass away. That would be $100,000 per child. The other $400,000 could go to the trust. They would each receive one-fourth of that income for 20 years. That would give Ted a chance to learn to save and invest. In addition, if you transfer the IRA into that trust, you can save all that income tax because the special trust is tax exempt."

**Cindy:** "This sounds like a great plan. When I pass away, I could transfer my IRA into the "Give It Twice" trust and benefit my four children and my favorite charity. But how do I do that?"

**Attorney:** "I can write a trust that you sign. It's called an unfunded trust because there are no assets at present. Then we will contact your IRA custodian and select this charitable remainder trust as the designated beneficiary for your IRA. When you pass away, the IRA balance will be transferred to the trustee of your 'Give It Twice' trust."

**Cindy:** "This is very exciting. It is going to be great for my family and we will also be able to help our favorite charity after the term of years. I especially like the way that this will help Ted to learn to save and invest. Let's move forward as quickly as possible."

**CHAPTER 37**

TRUSTS — "Give It Twice" Trust

# QUIZ

1. A "Give It Twice" trust is designed to benefit both children and charity.

   ☐ True      ☐ False

2. The "Give It Twice" trust is good for families where there is "a creative" child.

   ☐ True      ☐ False

3. A "Give It Twice" trust is primarily designed for larger estates.

   ☐ True      ☐ False

4. A "Give It Twice" trust must be funded with an IRA or a 401(k).

   ☐ True      ☐ False

5. A benefit of a "Give It Twice" trust is that the IRA may be transferred and the trust is still tax exempt.

   ☐ True      ☐ False

**Answers:** To view the quiz answers online, please use the website on the front cover. On that site select "Plan Your Will" and logon to your free Wills Planner account. Select the "Provide & Protect Resources" button on the right and "IV. Your Estate Plan." Under "Trusts" Select "#37" and view the Quiz Answers at the bottom. You may also enjoy the three-minute video explanation.

# TRUSTS
## "Wait A While" Trust

Bill and Clara were talking to their attorney Susan about their family.

**Clara:** "It may be time to start the inheritance process. Our children are now ages 35, 37 and 38. We might want to give them something during the next few years."

**Bill:** "Susan, when we spoke by phone, you thought that we might consider a 'Wait A While' trust."

**Clara:** "How does that work?"

**Bill:** "Well, the trust is funded with property and pays a fixed amount to charity for a period of years."

**Susan:** "We might think about a trust that pays for 12 years. You already make gifts to charity so we just would make those same gifts out of the trust. After 12 years, the trust will be distributed to the children. They will then be ages 47, 49 and 50."

**Clara:** "That's probably a very good time to pass property to them. They may still have children in college and they also will be thinking seriously about investing for their future retirement."

**Bill:** "Is this the right time to consider a 'Wait A While' trust?"

**Susan:** "You have come at a good time. Your estate is continuing to grow, both of you have prepared very well for your retirement and this is a good time to think about this trust."

**Clara:** "Is 12 years a typical length of time for this trust? As I understand the trust, our children will receive our inheritance after that period of time."

**Susan:** "You may choose the time. Twelve years is a very good option. We can fund the trust with a fairly substantial amount so that there will be a good start to their inheritance at that time. When we fund the trust, there will be a requirement to file a gift tax return and use part of the gift exemption that each of you have. However, you won't actually have to pay any gift tax at that time. In addition, this may save future estate tax. While it's very difficult to know exactly what the estate tax picture will be like in the future, there is a good probability that there will be an estate tax and this trust will produce large tax savings."

**Bill:** "Is this the primary reason to set up this lead trust? Our desire is to start planning for our children's inheritance."

**Susan:** "It is a very good reason. Another reason is to help your favorite charities with the payouts for the 12 years."

**Clara:** "I like the idea of starting the inheritance for children. With our growing estate, there will eventually be a larger distribution. By the time the children receive this first inheritance, they will be more mature. In addition, we'll still be here to offer advice and counsel."

**Bill:** "We thought that we might start this with about $500,000. We have a portfolio of stocks and bonds that has grown over the years. With this amount and some potential growth in the trust, each of our three children would receive about $200,000 after the trust has made the 12 years of payments to charity."

**Susan:** "A good idea is to transfer a securities portfolio that is comprised of around 60% stocks and 40% bonds. The bond income will be used first to pay the charities. With the bond income and stock dividends, we can take care of most of the payout. I suggest that the trust pay an annuity amount equal to 5% of the value. If you fund the trust with $500,000, then there would be $25,000 paid to charity each year. If we can earn more than 5% each year, the growth will be transferred to children at the end of 12 years."

Clara: "This sounds like a very good idea. Bill, let's move forward and ask Susan to prepare the documents. I know that this will be great for our children and for our favorite charities."

### Charitable Lead Trust Solution

The "Wait a While" trust is called a charitable lead annuity trust. Bill and Clara plan to transfer $500,000 in stocks and bonds to the trust. Because it is an annuity trust, it pays an initial 5% of $500,000 or $25,000 fixed amount to the charity. Over a period of 12 years, the trust will pay $300,000 to charity.

Bill and Clara may select the charities when the trust is created or they may permit children to select charities each year. While most donors select the charities, it's also permissible to allow children to select part or all of the charities to receive the distribution.

The trust's stocks and bonds will continue to be invested. If the total return is 6.5%, it would grow to $630,000 over the 12 year period. Each of the three children would then receive approximately $210,000.

The trust may be funded with appreciated property. When the children receive their initial inheritance, there may be appreciation. However, the children will have two easy solutions to avoid paying any capital gains tax. If they are making gifts to charity, they may retain their cash income and use the appreciated stocks to make their charitable gifts. This will bypass the capital gain. Alternatively, if they do wish to sell, they could sell part for cash and transfer the balance into a two-life charitable remainder unitrust. The charitable savings from the trust would offset the gain on the part sold and again there would be no capital gains tax paid by the children.

### Gift and Estate Taxes

Attorney Susan will file a Form 709 Gift Tax Return. She will report a gift of $500,000 with a charitable gift deduction of $245,000. There will be a taxable transfer of $255,000. However, this is significantly less than the $5.49 million gift exemption available to each spouse. Therefore, there will be no payment of gift tax now. Because the amount of the gift is fixed, if there is a substantial estate tax when Bill and Clara pass away, there will be added estate tax savings.

## Summary

The "Wait A While" trust is an excellent plan to start an inheritance. It allows Bill and Clara to continue to benefit favorite charities for a period of years and then transfer the principal to children or other family members.

Their attorney Susan will file a gift tax return, but in virtually all cases there will be no gift tax payable because of the gift exemption. In all probability, the "Wait A While" trust will save a major future estate tax. Finally, it allows Bill and Clara to start an inheritance for the children and to give them advice and counsel on the best use of the funds.

**CHAPTER 38**

TRUSTS —"Wait A While" Trust

# QUIZ

**1.** The primary reason for a "Wait A While" trust is to start the inheritance process.

☐ True    ☐ False

**2.** With a lead trust, there is a fixed amount or percentage paid to charity.

☐ True    ☐ False

**3.** With a lead trust, the donor must select charities when the trust is created.

☐ True    ☐ False

**4.** With a lead trust, most donors will pay gift taxes.

☐ True    ☐ False

**5.** A lead trust is likely to save future estate tax.

☐ True    ☐ False

**Answers:** To view the quiz answers online, please use the website on the front cover. On that site select "Plan Your Will" and logon to your free Wills Planner account. Select the "Provide & Protect Resources" button on the right and "IV. Your Estate Plan." Under "Trusts" Select "#38" and view the Quiz Answers at the bottom. You may also enjoy the three-minute video explanation.

# LIFE INSURANCE
## Costs and Benefits

Let's look at the "top five" reasons people give for not owning life insurance.

1. Too Expensive. "I just cannot afford life insurance right now."

2. Confusing. "We looked at proposals from three companies—page after page of numbers. What does it all mean? I haven't the slightest idea!"

3. Too Many Types. "I checked into term insurance, whole life insurance, universal life, variable life, single premium, and survivorship insurance. But which one is right for me?"

4. No Trust. "Those big insurance companies claim to have billions of reserve funds. But one of the biggest insurance companies has been on the ropes for months. Who can you trust?"

5. Don't Plan to Die. "Someday when I plan to die, I will consider life insurance. But for now—don't worry, be happy!"

**Five Reasons to Own Life Insurance**

There are several reasons for you to purchase life insurance. If you were to pass away, the life insurance death benefits could provide resources that are quite important to your family. The various benefits include payment of your funeral and final expenses, paying off mortgages or other debts, living expenses or income for a surviving spouse, inheritance for children and payment of estate taxes.

1. **Final Expenses and Funeral Costs.** Usually there are medical expenses during the last weeks of life. These frequently will range from $5,000 to $10,000. Your memorial service preparation and costs can also easily exceed $10,000. Total final expenses can often be more than $20,000.

2. **Pay Debts and Mortgages.** The payment of debts or a mortgage is a one-time expense. Depending upon the amount of your mortgage, this could cost anywhere from a few thousand dollars to many hundreds of thousands of dollars.

3. **Living Expenses for Spouse.** The largest amount of insurance is typically purchased to provide both economic security and an investment that will add to the spouse's other annual income. A reasonable method is to estimate a 5% return on the investment. For example, if a spouse needed another $25,000 of income over and above the amount paid by retirement funds, Social Security and other earnings, then insurance equal to $500,000 invested at 5% would produce this amount.

4. **Inheritance for Children.** Permanent insurance is frequently used as a method of providing an inheritance for children. Many parents who make substantial gifts to charity plan to use life insurance as a means of providing additional inheritance for children or other family members.

5. **Estate Taxes.** If your estate is large, there may be a substantial payment of federal or state estate tax. If you own a family business or other assets that are intended to be transferred to family, then your estate could be subject to estate tax. Life insurance can be an excellent method to provide funds for payment of estate tax. Normally, for larger estates the life insurance is owned by an irrevocable life insurance trust so the insurance itself is not subject to estate tax.

#### Determining the Life Insurance Amount

A fairly simple way for you to determine the total amount of needed insurance is to add up your one-time expenses, then calculate the amount of insurance invested at 5% necessary to benefit a surviving spouse, children or other family members. For example, if your one-time expenses are $200,000 and your spouse desires additional income of $25,000, then the total insurance would be $700,000. This amount includes $200,000 for expenses and $500,000 invested at 5% to produce the annual income.

More sophisticated calculations are available online. Use your favorite search site to look for "life insurance needs calculator," and select from the available free public calculators.

### How Life Insurance Works

Life insurance started because individuals were concerned that they might pass away and not provide sufficient resources for family. Because young families typically need a substantial fund and lack the ability to save enough in a short period of time, the concept of life insurance was created.

If many thousands of individuals pay premiums and those funds are invested, then a pool of funds will be available to compensate individuals. The life insurance company hires actuaries who determine the probable number of individuals who will pass away in a given year. Especially for younger persons, out of a pool of 100,000 only a few will pass away in a given year. As a result, the insurance company is able to receive all the premiums and invest them in the insurance reserve fund. The earnings and a portion of the funds are distributed each year to pay claims for those who pass away.

The insurance funds are primarily invested in bonds. The insurance company generally receives 1% to 1.2% to cover all of their overhead and costs. The balance is returned through insurance proceeds to beneficiaries.

### Life Insurance Policy Categories

Insurance is generally divided into two categories—term insurance and permanent insurance.

## Term Insurance

Term insurance is the least expensive type of insurance and is favored by younger people and many financial planners. The term insurance is available with an annual renewable term (ART) or with a fixed payment for five years, 10 years, 15 years or longer.

Because term insurance does not include any investment or cash value, it enables the largest potential policy to be purchased for the least cost. Due to intense competition within the insurance industry, prices on term policies and level-pay term policies have moved lower in recent years.

Some types of term policies also include the ability to convert to whole life or universal life at a future time. If the conversion is elected, then there will be a substantial increase in the premium.

## Permanent Insurance

Permanent insurance includes several types. The traditional favorite is whole life insurance, but there are also universal life, variable life and survivorship life insurance.

**Whole Life.** The traditional whole life policy involves both insurance and a cash value. The premiums are substantially higher than term insurance because the policy will build a savings element or cash value. During the first year, much of the cash value may be used by the insurance company to cover the commission payment to the sales representative, but over time the cash value may increase. The owner of the policy has the right to borrow against the cash value at favorable rates.

Whole life is frequently fixed in terms of premiums paid and death benefit. The insurance company is determining the probable return of its reserve fund and, based on the age and health of the insured person, calculates and commits to a fixed benefit in exchange for a certain premium.

**Universal Life.** Universal life was created to provide an option for people who would consider purchasing term insurance and invest an additional amount in mutual funds. With universal life, the policy is invested and a cash reserve is built up. The insurance reserve growth covers the cost of the insurance policy. Universal life policies may include flexible options for increasing or decreasing premium payments. Of course, the cash value of the policy will change with a modification of the premium schedule.

**Variable Universal Life.** If the insured desires to own life insurance but also potentially gain from investments in stocks and bonds, a variable policy may be appropriate. With a variable policy the insured typically is permitted to invest in different mutual funds managed by the financial services company. If the mutual funds increase in value, the policy cash value will increase.

**Survivorship Life.** For a couple, an attractive option is to purchase a survivorship policy. This policy pays a death benefit after both husband and wife pass away. Because two persons are insured, it frequently is possible to obtain insurance even if one spouse is in poor health. Quite often, this insurance can be purchased at a more reasonable premium because two persons must pass away before the death benefit is paid. It is particularly useful for providing funds to pay for taxes if a business is to be transferred from parents to children after they both pass away.

### Life Insurance Beneficiaries

In most estates, life insurance does not pass through the probate process. The insurance policy is a contract between the insured and the insurance company. The person who purchases the insurance has the right to name the beneficiaries. Normally, a primary and a secondary beneficiary are named. It's also possible to divide the insurance policy among several children or other beneficiaries.

A common beneficiary designation is for the spouse to be a primary beneficiary and the children to be the contingent beneficiaries with equal shares. If the spouse were to predecease the insured or they were to pass away in a common accident, then the children would receive the insurance proceeds.

Minor children should usually not be the beneficiaries of a policy. In many states, if a minor child receives a substantial inheritance, a conservator must be appointed to manage the assets. This is quite expensive and also has the disadvantage of transferring the assets to the minor child when he or she becomes an adult.

A much better arrangement is to transfer the policy to a living trust for the benefit of the minor children, or to create a trust and a will for the benefit of the minor children and transfer the policy to the estate to fund that trust.

### Prudent Purchase of Insurance

Life insurance is an important decision, and it is helpful to learn about the different types of insurance. Most individuals will also visit with a chartered life underwriter (CLU) or other representative of a financial services company.

The representative can conduct an insurance needs analysis and suggest the appropriate type of insurance. It is helpful for you to do sufficient research to understand the reasons why many individuals choose term insurance or permanent insurance. In addition, the use of online calculators to determine insurance funding will also provide you with a better understanding of the appropriate amount of insurance. The amount of insurance recommended by online calculators can vary greatly, so understanding your probable needs is quite important.

### Insurance Company Ratings

Insurance companies are rated by several sources. A.M. Best, Weiss, Moody's and other ratings services are available. You should be certain to ask for the ratings of any company if a representative suggests purchasing a policy from them. It is also easy to go online and do a search for "insurance company ratings" and obtain the actual ratings for most financial services companies.

**CHAPTER 39**

LIFE INSURANCE — Costs and Benefits

# QUIZ

**1.** The typical motivating cause for the purchase of insurance is the need for income for survivors.

☐ True ☐ False

**2.** Insurance needs are generally equal to three times current income.

☐ True ☐ False

**3.** Young families frequently purchase term insurance.

☐ True ☐ False

**4.** During times of financial uncertainty, whole life is frequently preferred to variable life insurance.

☐ True ☐ False

**5.** There are several companies that rate life insurance companies.

☐ True ☐ False

**Answers:** To view the quiz answers online, please use the website on the front cover. On that site select "Plan Your Will" and logon to your free Wills Planner account. Select the "Provide & Protect Resources" button on the right and "IV. Your Estate Plan." Under "Life Insurance" Select "#39" and view the Quiz Answers at the bottom. You may also enjoy the three-minute video explanation.

## CHAPTER 40

# LIFE INSURANCE
# Irrevocable Life Insurance Trust (ILIT)

Susan and Steve had been talking to their tax attorney, Elizabeth, about plans for their family. Susan is very concerned about their family:

**Susan:** "I wish that we had a perfect family, but we must admit we don't. We have three children. Our first child is out on his own, has a good job and is doing fine. But our second child has had substance abuse problems and recently was released from rehabilitation. He now seems fine but he has had relapses before. Our third child is a very sweet young woman who unfortunately has been married, divorced and is now remarried. But she is now going through some real rough spots in her new marriage. How can we protect our three children with so many risks?"

**Steve:** "We've been very fortunate and our business has grown quite large. We have an offer for the business and have been told that we could sell it tax free through a special charitable trust. That sounds like a great idea, but we need to set up an inheritance for the children and it must be done in a way that protects them. How can we do this? What's the best way to sell our business tax free and replace the inheritance for the children?"

**Elizabeth:** "We have a great plan that achieves all of those goals. You will be able to sell your business tax free and set up a special trust that holds an insurance policy for the benefit of your children. After both of you pass away, the trust will receive the insurance proceeds income and estate tax free. The full amount can be invested to provide new taxable income for the lives of your children."

## When to Use a Life Insurance Trust

A very beneficial estate planning strategy to protect your "less-than-perfect" family is to create a trust that owns life insurance. To gain the maximum benefit from this trust, it is irrevocable after it is created. Your advisor will usually call this an irrevocable life insurance trust (ILIT).

## Benefits of an ILIT

**Management.** If you have a substantial estate and plan to pass a significant inheritance to children, a trust enables you to select the child or the financial institution that will be best qualified to manage significant assets.

**Income Rather Than Principal.** Many parents are faced with Steve and Susan's problem. They have one or more children who will act in harmful ways with a substantial amount of principal. So the best solution is to provide income to everyone for a term of years or for life. A trust is an excellent method for this purpose. The trustee can also have discretion to distribute principal, or at an age you select the trust property can be given to your children.

**Tax Savings.** If your estate is more than the federal exemption, it may in future years be subject to taxes at a very high rate. For individuals who support charity, a great plan is to create a trust or make charitable gifts with the majority of the estate and replace the gifted property with an insurance trust. Steve and Susan can create a two-life charitable remainder trust and benefit from a tax-free sale and life income for themselves. After they pass away, their children will benefit from the insurance proceeds in the ILIT.

## How Does the ILIT Work?

ILIT Goals. If you have a large estate, a very important goal is to make sure the ILIT is not subject to estate tax. In order to protect the ILIT from taxes, Steve and Susan cannot retain specific powers over the trust or the life insurance. Specifically, they cannot have the right to cash in the policy, to borrow against it, or even to designate the beneficiaries. The policy is purchased with the trust as the beneficiary and will not be changed after it is first acquired by the trust.

**Gift of Premiums.** Steve and Susan will need to make annual gifts to the ILIT to pay the insurance premiums. Because they can use their annual exclusion, they are able to fund a very substantial policy ($14,000 for each parent times three children equals as much as $84,000 per year in 2017—with indexing of the annual exclusion, it may be more in future years). When they transfer the premium amount to the trustee, their children each receive a special right known as a "Crummey" power, named after the first person to use this concept. Under their Crummey power, the children have 30 days to spend the money. With appropriate parental guidance, the children do not spend the money and it may then be used for payment of insurance premiums. Because the annual exclusion gift of $14,000 requires the child to be able to spend the money for a short period of time, the Crummey power is an essential part of the ILIT.

**ILIT Insurance Policies.** There are two ways for the insurance policy to be transferred to the ILIT. The first and preferred method is for the ILIT to actually purchase a new policy. However, if you or your spouse are not insurable, in some cases an existing policy is given to the ILIT. If you give an existing policy to the ILIT, in order for the ILIT to be estate tax free you must survive for at least three years.

### Trustee

**Child as Trustee.** Many parents will select one of the children as trustee, preferably one with good financial skills. The child frequently serves for a reduced fee or no fee. The disadvantage for the child serving as trustee is that he or she may have conflicts with other siblings.

**Financial Institution as Trustee.** The second option is for a bank or trust company to serve as trustee. If the insurance trust is quite large, the objective nature of the bank or trust institution may make this a good option. In considering a bank or financial institution as trustee, Steve and Susan should understand the costs for the investment and administration services of the bank after the insurance proceeds have been received and the trust is funded.

## ILIT Options

**Income.** After the demise of Steve and Susan, the trustee will invest the insurance proceeds and pay income to the beneficiaries. Some trusts last until the beneficiary has reached a specific age, or the trust may last for their lifetimes. With the concern about protecting a child with a substance abuse problem and the marital relationship problems of their daughter, Steve and Susan decided to continue the income stream for the lives of their children. The primary goal of many parents is to provide an additional level of economic security for the children. This income stream will provide payouts for the rest of their lifetimes.

**Ability to Distribute Principal.** The trustee may be given permission to distribute principal. This could be based upon such standards as health, education, maintenance and support, or may be discretionary with the trustee. Steve and Susan permitted their trustee to make distributions for medical care but not for enhanced lifestyle. Steve asked, "What is likely to be the result if two of our children receive principal?" Based on the belief that principal distributions will be used for unneeded and perhaps unhealthy purposes, their trust will pay income and, if required, medical expenses.

**Income Taxes on New Trust Income.** While the insurance proceeds are tax free to the trust as long as there has been no violation of the insurance guidelines, the new income that is earned and distributed to the children will be taxable. If the income were retained in the trust, the trust would pay the tax. However, because most income would be distributed to the children, they will pay the ordinary income or capital gains tax on their trust distributions.

**CHAPTER 40**

LIFE INSURANCE — Irrevocable Life Insurance Trust

# QUIZ

**1.** A major reason for creating an ILIT is management of the insurance proceeds.

☐ True      ☐ False

**2.** The ILIT is frequently set up for people with modest estates.

☐ True      ☐ False

**3.** The ILIT can qualify for a transfer to children that is estate-tax free.

☐ True      ☐ False

**4.** When the ILIT is created, there is usually provision for a special power known as a "Crummey" power.

☐ True      ☐ False

**5.** The ILIT may last for the life of the children.

☐ True      ☐ False

**Answers:** To view the quiz answers online, please use the website on the front cover. On that site select "Plan Your Will" and logon to your free Wills Planner account. Select the "Provide & Protect Resources" button on the right and "IV. Your Estate Plan." Under "Life Insurance" Select "#40" and view the Quiz Answers at the bottom. You may also enjoy the three-minute video explanation.

# LIFETIME PLANS
## Gifts of Cash

Many people use the annual exclusion amount as part of their overall estate planning strategy.

**Sara:** "We had a pretty good year this year. After all the financial changes last year, we decided it was a good time to be more careful. So we watched our budget, took a less expensive vacation, and we actually have substantial savings at the end of this year."

**Jane:** "Yes. Joe and I were also careful. We have been talking. After setting aside part of our cash savings, we could maybe make some gifts this year. Next Tuesday, we're planning to meet with our tax advisor to discuss some gifts."

**Sara:** "Harry and I met with our advisor last week to talk about some end-of-year gifts. We plan to make some gifts to the children and also some gifts to charity."

### Gifts to Children and Other Heirs

Sara is wise to consider gifts to children or other heirs. This year, she and Harry can make gifts of $14,000 each to their children or other beneficiaries using their annual gift exclusions. Sara and Harry decide to make gifts to their two children. Based upon the $14,000 annual exclusion for two donors and two children, they could give $56,000 with no gift tax and no requirement to file a gift tax return.

One good strategy that many parents use is to make a gift of property and to save the cash themselves. For example, if Sara and Harry have some shares of public stock it makes good sense for them to make gifts of their appreciated stock to their children or other heirs. They can then invest the cash themselves and replace the gifted property.

There are two benefits for Sara and Harry if they make the gift of stock. First, the basis in the stock flows through to the children. If the children later sell the stock, they will pay the capital gains tax. However, Harry and Sara have avoided paying the tax themselves and recognition of the gain may be deferred for many years. Sara and Harry can place the cash in their investment fund and replace the stock given to children or other heirs.

Second, it frequently is desirable for children and other heirs to receive property rather than cash. Children tend to spend cash quickly for consumer items. Harry and Sara would like their children to learn to save and invest. A gift of stock is much more likely to lead the children to follow the example of Harry and Sara.

### Gifts to Charity

Both Sara and Jane are considering gifts to charity. It is a very good time for them to consider a cash gift. Because they were careful in budgeting this year, both Sara and Jane have a greater opportunity to make a substantial cash gift this year.

Making a cash gift is quite easy. You can simply write a check to your favorite charity. But it is important to make sure that you follow the requirements of the IRS in order to receive your appropriate tax savings for your gift.

### Cash Gifts and the IRS

A cash gift saves tax at your top tax rate. For example, if you are in the 33% tax bracket, then a gift of $100 produces a charitable deduction of that amount. Multiplying the $100 times your 33% tax bracket produces an actual tax savings of $33. Of course, in some states you will also save state income taxes.

Your gift by check may be mailed to the charity. If you place the check in the U.S. mail by December 31 of this year and the check clears, it will be deducted in 2017 even though the charity receives the check next year.

If you make a gift of more than $250 to a charity, you must receive what the IRS calls "contemporaneous written acknowledgment" and what you probably refer to as a receipt. The charity will send you a receipt when the gift is made or at the end of the year when you are preparing to file your tax returns. You should keep the receipt or a copy for your records so that you can prove that the gift qualifies for a charitable deduction.

If you make charitable gifts using payroll deductions, you will be permitted to claim the charitable deduction. In that case, you must retain a pay stub or a Form W-2 from your employer that shows the amount given to charity.

You may also spend cash amounts that are deductible as volunteer expenses. In this case, you should make records of each expenditure that shows the services that were rendered to the charity. It also is important to note whether any goods or services have been transferred by the charity back to you.

Charities sometimes make transfers back to donors. A common type of transfer back is a charity dinner. For example, if the charity charges $100 for a dinner event and the value of the dinner is $18, then the charity will send you a receipt that shows a charitable gift of $82. The IRS has a special name for this gift. They call it a "quid pro quo" gift. If the charity is giving something substantial back to you, such as a dinner, the amount of your deduction is just the charitable part of the payment.

Another possible option is for a charity to give you a token gift. If the charity gives a donor a "low value" item that has the logo, colors or identification of the charity on it, it will be disregarded.

For 2017, donors who make gifts of $53.50 or more may receive items with the name or logo of the charity that are valued at less than $10.70.

For donors who make fairly large gifts, the token item may generally have a value up to 2% of the amount of the gift with a limit on the token item value at $107. In the future, those numbers will increase slightly.

## Summary

If you have been careful in budgeting this year like Sara and Jane, it may also be a very good time to make an end-of-year cash gift. By following the guidelines that are set forth, you can make sure that you have provided a very nice benefit for a favorite charity and also receive your full charitable deduction on your income taxes.

## CHAPTER 41

LIFETIME PLANS — Gifts of Cash

# QUIZ

1. The annual gift exclusion applies only to gifts of cash to children or other heirs.

   ☐ True     ☐ False

2. If you give cash to children in an amount less than the annual exclusion, they must be able to spend the cash.

   ☐ True     ☐ False

3. If you make a charitable gift of $500 to a charity, you must receive a receipt prior to filing your IRS Form 1040 Income Tax Return.

   ☐ True     ☐ False

4. If I mail a check in the post office prior to December 31, I may deduct that gift this tax year even though the charity receives the gift in January.

   ☐ True     ☐ False

5. If I make a gift this year of $70 and receive a mug with the logo of my favorite charity valued at $12, I still can deduct the full $70.

   ☐ True     ☐ False

**Answers:** To view the quiz answers online, please use the website on the front cover. On that site select "Plan Your Will" and logon to your free Wills Planner account. Select the "Provide & Protect Resources" button on the right and "IV. Your Estate Plan." Under "Lifetime Plans" Select "#41" and view the Quiz Answers at the bottom. You may also enjoy the three-minute video explanation.

# LIFETIME PLANS
## Gifts of Stock

What will the market do this year? Perhaps the best answer is, "It will go up and down." Stock returns vary to a significant degree each year. However, long-term stock returns have been reasonably substantial.

Between 1990 and 2010, the average stock return was about 6%. While there was a very substantial increase during 1990 – 2000 and decreases during 2002 and 2008, the total return over two decades was approximately 6%.

Longer holding periods have generally resulted in higher total returns. The total stock return for seven decades between 1945 and 2015 was about 10%. Returns for long periods of time have paralleled this amount.

Because many stocks have increased in value over time, you may hold stocks with substantial appreciation. If you're considering a major gift or end-of-year gift, a gift of public company stock to charity provides two major benefits. First, there is a charitable deduction for the value of the stock. Second, the charity does not pay tax on the sale of the stock so you bypass the capital gain.

Two fairly common reasons for making a substantial gift of stock are that you may have sold an appreciated asset with a large capital gain or you have good income. If you have a large gain or substantial income, you may want to offset that gain or income with a charitable deduction through a gift of stock. Because you receive both the charitable deduction and a bypass of capital gains tax, there is a double benefit for your gift of stock.

### Lisa Considers a Stock Gift

Lisa was considering a gift of stock. She had purchased stock 10 years ago in a well-known company with many retail stores. With the worldwide expansion of this company, the stock had increased from her original purchase price of $50,000 to a total of $100,000 in value.

Lisa decided to visit with CPA Susan about the potential gift.

**Lisa:** "Susan, I bought the stock years ago and earlier this year my broker suggested that I sell half of the stock. I sold $50,000 of the $100,000 of the stock. I still have $50,000 left."

**Susan:** "Under the IRS rules, Lisa, you are required to divide your $50,000 cost basis between the half you sold and the half that remains. That means that half of the gain or $25,000 is going to be reported as income this year. However, if you decide to give the other half to your favorite charity, you will receive a deduction for $50,000. The deduction is based on the value of the stock on the gift date. The IRS calls that value the mean between the high and low sale price on that day. In addition, you will save capital gains tax because you bypass the gain on the half that you've given to your favorite charity."

**Lisa:** "That sounds like a great plan. If I make that gift, I'll be able to benefit from a large tax deduction that will more than offset the tax on my gain. Plus, the charity won't have to pay the tax on my stock when it sells. Finally, my charity will enjoy a very nice major gift."

### Bill has Good Income This Year

Another reason for making a stock gift is that you may have a very substantial income that could cause you to pay a large income tax. Bill had purchased stock in a company recommended by his son eight years ago. His son used a computer made by this company and said to his dad that this would be a good stock to own. During that eight-year time, Bill's $15,000 initial investment had grown to a value of

$165,000. Bill also had a very good year with a large income and was talking to his CPA Tom about a charitable deduction.

**Bill:** "Tom, I had a great year this year and I have been thinking about making a charitable gift with my stock in the computer company. It has gone way up in value and now is worth $165,000. I could sure use that deduction."

**Tom:** "Yes, that would be the right property to give. You will be able to claim a large deduction. Because you have a high income this year, you can take the full write-off. Plus, by giving the stock you bypass the gain. If you later would like to take your tax savings and make another stock investment, that is perfectly fine."

Bill decided to make the gift. While there is a limit of a deduction in one year to 30% of Bill's adjusted gross income, he has a high income this year and is able to take the full charitable deduction.

### How to Make a Stock Gift

Most stock is held in an account at a brokerage firm. Relatively few people now wish to hold the actual certificates in their safety deposit box. If you hold actual certificates, you may mail the certificate and a signed stock power in separate envelopes to the charity.

Because most stock is held by the brokerage firm, the stock is transferred directly from the account at the brokerage firm to an account for the charity. For any gift more than $250, the charity will issue a receipt. With that receipt and the information on the stock, CPA Susan and CPA Tom will include IRS Form 8283 with the tax returns for Lisa and Bill. The gift of stock will produce a large deduction that will save huge income taxes this year.

**CHAPTER 42**

LIFETIME PLANS — Gifts of Stock

# QUIZ

1. A gift of stock is deductible at fair market value.

   ☐ True        ☐ False

2. A gift of public stock will require a qualified appraisal.

   ☐ True        ☐ False

3. A charitable deduction from a gift of stock is always taken in the year of the gift.

   ☐ True        ☐ False

4. A stock gift has a second benefit because the charity bypasses the gain.

   ☐ True        ☐ False

5. Most stock is held in electronic brokerage accounts.

   ☐ True        ☐ False

**Answers:** To view the quiz answers online, please use the website on the front cover. On that site select "Plan Your Will" and logon to your free Wills Planner account. Select the "Provide & Protect Resources" button on the right and "IV. Your Estate Plan." Under "Lifetime Plans" Select "#42" and view the Quiz Answers at the bottom. You may also enjoy the three-minute video explanation.

# LIFETIME PLANS
## Gifts of Land

Many friends of charities have benefited from a gift of land or a gift of land with a building or other structure. There are two main benefits for this gift. First, there is a charitable deduction, normally for the fair market value at the time of the gift. Second, if the real estate has appreciated the gift to a qualified public charity bypasses or avoids the capital gains tax.

The combination of a substantial charitable deduction and a bypass of capital gain is an excellent double benefit. Many donors who sell other property or have substantial income will be able to use this charitable deduction to reduce their income taxes.

There are several reasons why you might consider a gift of property. You may have recently sold another property and could use the charitable deduction. If you have commercial or rental real estate, eventually your rental income increases while your depreciation is gradually reduced. With increased rents and reduced depreciation, you may have a very substantial income tax problem.

### Lisa's Land and the Developers

Lisa purchased property 10 years ago for $100,000. It was vacant land in a commercial area and now has a value of $200,000. She has paid off the debt and it is now free and clear. Lisa contacted her CPA Susan because she had started to receive some inquiries about the property from a developer. The developer was interested in building a commercial building on the property.

**Lisa:** "I have owned this property for 10 years and it has now appreciated. With that appreciation, will I pay a large tax if I sell the property?"

**Susan:** "Yes, Lisa. You purchased it for $100,000 and it is now worth $200,000. You will pay the federal capital gains tax plus a state capital gains tax because you live in a state that levies that tax. You should also consider that you have already sold another property and have a very large capital gain this year."

**Lisa:** "Yes, I have been thinking about that other sale. With that large capital gain, I sure could use a large charitable deduction. What would happen if I give this property to charity?"

**Susan:** "You can transfer a property to charity the same way that you would sell the property, by signing a deed to transfer the property to the charity. The deed will be recorded and you can qualify for a charitable deduction. The $200,000 deduction would offset a substantial part of your gain. We might be able to offset the entire capital gains tax payable on the other sale that you completed earlier this year. In addition to your income tax deduction that will offset tax on that other sale, you bypass the gain on the gift of this property. With both tax benefits, you will save about $100,000."

**Lisa:** "Great! That's almost as much as I paid for it in the first place. Plus, I could help my favorite charity with a very nice gift this year. That sounds like just the ticket for me."

Lisa contacted her favorite charity and deeded the land to that nonprofit. She was careful to be certain that she had not signed a contract or agreed to a sale of the property before the gift. After the deed was recorded, the charity then made contact with several developers and sold the property for $200,000.

## Bill's Declining Depreciation Solution

Another gift option could be a gift of a commercial property. Bill bought a small commercial building 14 years ago for $200,000. During that period of time, he paid off the debt. His CPA Tom took straight-line depreciation and his cost basis in the building is now $120,000. Fortunately, over that period of time the property appreciated to a value of $320,000.

Bill owns many rental homes and commercial buildings and receives rental income on those properties. Because he has owned them for quite a few years, the depreciation deductions are now lower and his rental income continues to go up. As a result, Bill now has a large income and pays a very large income tax.

**Bill Meets with His CPA Tom to Discuss his Plans for This Year.**

**Bill:** "You know, Tom, I keep getting better rents every year, but I now have less and less depreciation. The income taxes are going to wallop me this year."

**Tom:** "Yes, Bill. Because you've owned properties for quite a long period of time, your income is now much more than the depreciation and your taxes are going to be much higher."

**Bill:** "Well, maybe I should just give this rental home to my favorite charity. They are in the middle of a fairly large fund drive and could sure use the gift. Would that help?"

**Tom:** "Yes, you would receive a very substantial deduction. The current value of that building is about $320,000. That deduction could save taxes this year, and perhaps for the next two or three years. You can take that kind of charitable deduction over as many as six years. Based on your tax situation, I think you could take the deduction over about three years. This would save over $100,000 in income taxes. In addition, by giving it to charity you would not pay tax on the $200,000 of gain in that rental home, which represents a savings of another $40,000 or more."

**Bill:** "This sounds like a very good plan. I have been looking for ways to reduce my taxes and help my favorite charity with that fund drive. Let's go ahead and do this."

## Appraisal Requirements

Lisa and Bill both decided to make gifts of property to a favorite charity. These gifts will offset the large capital gain for Lisa and the higher income for Bill. However, for a gift of property valued at more than $5,000 they will need a qualified appraisal.

Their CPAs secured the services of Arnold Appraiser. He is certified as a Member of the Appraisal Institute (MAI) and specializes in real estate appraisals. Arnold appraised both properties and gave the two CPAs the appraisals, complete with comparables and other important appraisal information.

CPA Susan and CPA Tom also had the charities and Appraiser Arnold sign an IRS Form 8283. This form is necessary to qualify them to report the charitable deductions on their tax returns.

After making these two gifts of property, Lisa and Bill enjoyed both major benefits. They saved very substantial income taxes and also bypassed the capital gain on the property that was gifted. A gift of land can be a very fine gift with great benefits both for the donors and for the charitable organization.

## CHAPTER 43

LIFETIME PLANS — Gifts of Land

# QUIZ

**1.** A gift of land produces a charitable deduction at fair market value.

☐ True    ☐ False

**2.** You can always use your charitable deduction in one year.

☐ True    ☐ False

**3.** A gift of real estate to charity will bypass the potential capital gain on the property.

☐ True    ☐ False

**4.** If property is gifted and it is more than $5,000 in value, there must be a qualified appraisal.

☐ True    ☐ False

**5.** It is best if the property that is gifted to charity does not have debt.

☐ True    ☐ False

**Answers:** To view the quiz answers online, please use the website on the front cover. On that site select "Plan Your Will" and logon to your free Wills Planner account. Select the "Provide & Protect Resources" button on the right and "IV. Your Estate Plan." Under "Lifetime Plans" Select "#43" and view the Quiz Answers at the bottom. You may also enjoy the three-minute video explanation.

# LIFETIME PLANS
## Gifts of Homes

Most families purchase their largest personal residence in their mid-forties. Families with children often need the additional space. Other families think they want to purchase a home that they can enjoy for many years.

By the time you reach retirement age, you probably have an empty nest. The children or other family members have now moved on and are creating their own homes. Some individuals at that point decide they like their home in their neighborhood and would like to stay there for their lifetime. Others might want to sell the larger property and move to a condo or retirement community.

### Stay-at-Home Sam

Sam is a single person and enjoys his home. He bought the residence when he was 48 because he loved the neighborhood.

Sam has cheerfully planted shrubs and flowers on his lot. He loves to spend time outside taking care of the property. Sam enjoys the neighborhood and plans to live there for the rest of his life. He just turned 75 this year and is in very good health.

He has a pension from his company, his Social Security and an IRA that was created by rolling over a qualified retirement plan. With income from all three sources, Sam now has no deductions other than his charitable gifts and is paying very substantial income taxes. As a result, he is very interested in finding a way to reduce his tax burden.

Sam bought the home for $200,000. It now has increased in value to $450,000. Sam also has been a regular supporter of two community charities that assist young people. He would like to eventually leave his home to charity to benefit youth in his community.

### Sam Decides to Visit With His CPA Jim.

**Sam:** "You know, Jim, I've lived in my home for many years and I like it here. I live in a great neighborhood and I know these neighbors. So I would like to stay here, but as you know, I keep paying more and more income tax each year. It would be great to have a way to save some taxes and eventually pass the home to charity."

**Jim:** "Yes, we've talked several times about different ideas to save taxes. Since you like your home and would like eventually to transfer it to a charity, there is a way that you could save a large amount of taxes today. The gift plan is called a transfer with a life estate. You deed the right to own the home after you pass away to your favorite two charities and retain the right to live there for your lifetime. Based on your age and home value, you would receive a charitable deduction of around $250,000. This would save taxes for you over as many as the next five years. In fact, with some cash gifts plus this deduction, you could cut your tax bill in half."

**Sam:** "Cutting my taxes in half is a great idea. And I do want to help these young people through these charities eventually. But what if 10 years from now I want to move to a retirement community? What happens then?"

**Jim:** "There are some rollover options at that time. Each year, as you get older, the value of the life interest goes down slightly. Still, you will have a substantial value. You could later have a joint sale with the charity and receive your portion for the life interest in cash. Another option is to transfer your life interest portion to the charity in exchange for a gift annuity."

**Sam:** "This sounds like a great plan. Let's contact the gift planner at my favorite charity to get the ball rolling."

### Clara Buys a Condo

Clara and Frank were married for 58 years. Frank passed away two years ago, leaving Clara and their three children who are now all adults.

When Clara and Frank were both 43, they bought a four-bedroom home. With two parents and three children at home, the atmosphere was very lively and eventful. When Clara and Frank reached their 50s, the children moved out and now are raising their own families.

Clara and Frank bought the home for $200,000. It is in a very nice neighborhood and has appreciated over the years to $800,000 in value. Clara decided to sit down with her CPA, Alice, to discuss the possibility of selling her home and moving to a condo.

**Clara:** "You know, Alice, Frank and I really needed the large house when the three children were at home. With five of us, we filled that four-bedroom house and there were always friends of our children visiting overnight. But now, with Frank gone and the children on their own, I don't need that big four-bedroom house. In fact, it's becoming a burden to maintain it. I would be much happier in a nice two-bedroom condo. I have been looking around and I think I have found one for $300,000 that would be just right for me."

**Alice:** "Yes, we all get to a point where it may make good sense to downsize. With the initial purchase price of your home and then an increase in basis when Frank passed away, you have a basis of about $400,000 in your home. If you were to sell it for $800,000, the gain would be $400,000. You would use your $250,000 exclusion for sale of your principal residence and $150,000 would be taxable."

**Clara:** "Well, I am not sure I want to pay tax on that much gain. I was thinking about making a gift to the charity that Frank and I have always supported. They are building a new wing on one of their facilities, and Frank and I had always talked about making a gift large enough that it could be named in our honor."

**Alice:** "How much is the naming opportunity?"

**Clara:** "It is a fairly large gift proposal and yet there is the value in the home. Plus, I have an IRA and other investments. The gift opportunity is $100,000. I was thinking that I could give 1/8 of the value of the home to the charity. The remaining $700,000 would more than cover the condo, plus I could add $400,000 to my current CDs."

**Alice:** "That actually works quite well. With your $250,000 exclusion, it reduces the taxable gain on your $700,000 home sale of your part to $100,000. If we transfer the 1/8 by deed to the charity just before the sale, you will bypass tax on the $100,000 and have a charitable deduction. The tax savings on your charitable deduction will more than offset the tax payable on your gain. You will end up with no tax on this transfer and $700,000 cash. After you buy the condo for $300,000, you are exactly right that you will have $400,000 to add to your CDs or other investments."

**Clara:** "That looks like exactly the right solution. Let's contact my attorney Bill and we will set up the gift. We can also list the home and find a buyer. I'm very excited about moving to the new condo in this retirement community. There are several friends from my social group in that community and I know I will enjoy living there."

**CHAPTER 44**

LIFETIME PLANS — Gifts of Homes

# QUIZ

1. If Sam sets up a life estate, he will be able to receive a charitable deduction for the value of the remainder.

   ☐ True     ☐ False

2. With a life estate, the charity will take care of the maintenance, insurance and taxes.

   ☐ True     ☐ False

3. In the future, Sam could sell his life interest.

   ☐ True     ☐ False

4. Clara Condo can use her $250,000 exclusion for sale of a personal residence even though she is not selling the entire property.

   ☐ True     ☐ False

5. Clara Condo will get the same tax benefits if she waits and makes a cash gift after the sale.

   ☐ True     ☐ False

**Answers:** To view the quiz answers online, please use the website on the front cover. On that site select "Plan Your Will" and logon to your free Wills Planner account. Select the "Provide & Protect Resources" button on the right and "IV. Your Estate Plan." Under "Lifetime Plans" Select "#44" and view the Quiz Answers at the bottom. You may also enjoy the three-minute video explanation.

# LIFETIME PLANS
## Gifts with Life Income

Many friends of charity have acquired appreciated property over time. A great way to use this appreciated property is for a charitable gift. A donor of appreciated property receives a charitable tax deduction and also benefits from bypassing capital gains tax on that gift property.

But some friends also want to increase their income. Two agreements that are popular for this purpose are a gift of appreciated stock for a charitable gift annuity or a gift of real estate into a special trust called a charitable remainder unitrust.

If you make a transfer into a gift plan that pays you income for life, you may receive both a charitable tax deduction and favorable capital gains benefits. Because you receive income, your charitable deduction is for a portion of the value in your property.

With most life-income gifts, your selected charity will need to wait until you pass away until it receives the actual gift. The IRS has periodically approved these plans in letters and rulings.

Therefore, a gift annuity or charitable remainder trust is a very good way to combine a charitable deduction now, income for one or two lives and an eventual significant benefit to a favorite charity.

### Susan Seeks Secure, Fixed Payments

After taking her car in to have it repaired, Susan looked at the cost of the parts for that repair and thought that the auto parts business would be a good investment. She did some research and purchased stock about 10 years ago in a mid-sized company that had auto parts stores throughout the nation.

Susan thought that people will always need replacement parts for their autos and other vehicles. She proved to be a good investor, and the stock increased from the $20,000 she paid to its present value of $50,000.

Because Susan is now in her 70s and not getting as much income from her CDs and other investments that she desires, she is exploring ways to increase her income. The stock has increased in value to $50,000, but pays a dividend between 1% and 2%.

Susan read about a charitable gift annuity. It appeared to her that based on her age she could receive fixed payments of 6.3%. She was quite excited and called her CPA Margie to discuss setting up a gift annuity.

**Susan:** "Margie, I bought this stock 10 years ago after I had a car repair done. It was a bit of a shock to me when I saw the cost of the auto parts. But I thought about that and decided that an auto parts store might be a good investment. I invested $20,000 in a mid-sized company and that stock is now worth $50,000. I was reading the website of my favorite charity and it seems that I can set up a charitable gift annuity with this stock."

**Margie:** "Yes, a charitable gift annuity is a contract between you and the charity. I ran your $50,000 number on the website calculator and you will receive a 6.3% payout for life. That's $3,150 each year."

**Susan:** "That's great! Do I also get any tax savings? I sure could use a deduction this year."

**Margie:** "There is good news about tax savings. You get a charitable tax deduction of about $20,000. In addition, around 30% of your annual payment will be tax free."

**Susan:** "This is going to increase my income and at the same time reduce my taxes. It sounds like just the right plan. I will call the charity today."

### Steve and Linda are Tired of Tenants

Steve and Linda bought a rental home 10 years ago. They're both 65 now and would like to retire.

Because they want to travel, they hope to sell the rental property and be freed of the management responsibility. Last month they finished paying off the mortgage and the property is now debt free.

Steve and Linda called their attorney Bill to discuss the best way to sell so they can start traveling.

**Steve:** "We bought this years ago and actually have not taken income. All of the rental payments have gone to pay off the debt. Our CPA says that the original $200,000 cost has now been depreciated down to around $125,000. But the home has gradually increased in value and we think it is worth about $300,000."

**Bill:** "I understand why both of you are ready to sell. It certainly is an effort to manage tenant issues. You could sell the property, invest the proceeds and have greater freedom to travel."

**Steve:** "We heard that you can sell tax free and we don't want to pay any tax. How does that plan work?"

**Bill:** "Several of my clients have set up a special charitable trust to sell property tax free. You and Linda could transfer your rental home to the trust. The trustee then will sell tax free. Plus, you get a charitable deduction of around $100,000 if you take a 5% payout. That's the minimum payout, but it is a very good idea. Most of my financial planner friends recommend a 5% payout for the best long-term investment security. So I usually suggest a 5% trust. We have a special name for that trust. It is called a unitrust."

**Linda:** "So we can sell tax free and get 5% payments for both our lives. If Steve passes away, will I receive the full 5%?"

**Bill:** "Yes. The income will be paid jointly to you during life and then to the survivor for his or her lifetime. Hopefully, the trust will earn more than 5% and will grow. If the trust principal grows, your 5% income can grow and give you some inflation protection. Because you might live for 25 years, 30 years or even longer, that is quite important."

**Linda:** "After we both pass away, then my understanding is that the trust will be given to one or more favorite charities."

**Bill:** "Yes, you can select the charity or charities to benefit from your unitrust."

**Steve:** "This sounds like quite a good idea. Bill, go ahead and draft the charitable trust. We already have a stack of travel brochures on our coffee table. We're ready to start moving now."

**CHAPTER 45**

LIFETIME PLANS — Gifts with Life Income

# QUIZ

1. A charitable gift annuity pays a fixed amount for life.

   ☐ True   ☐ False

2. If you fund a charitable gift annuity with $20,000, you will receive that much in charitable deduction.

   ☐ True   ☐ False

3. A charitable remainder unitrust must pay a minimum of 5%.

   ☐ True   ☐ False

4. You may transfer assets to a unitrust and sell tax free if there is no sale contract before the trust is funded.

   ☐ True   ☐ False

5. The growth of the assets inside a charitable remainder unitrust is tax free.

   ☐ True   ☐ False

**Answers:** To view the quiz answers online, please use the website on the front cover. On that site select "Plan Your Will" and logon to your free Wills Planner account. Select the "Provide & Protect Resources" button on the right and "IV. Your Estate Plan." Under "Lifetime Plans" Select "#45" and view the Quiz Answers at the bottom. You may also enjoy the three-minute video explanation.

# THE SHORTEST DAY

Every day has 24 hours—1,440 minutes—86,400 seconds. Or does it? A short day is coming for all of us—a day when we will not reach the 86,400[th] second of that day and will pass on to our final reward.

We may have lived a long and useful life, filled with great memories. First, the "learning" years—youthful and vibrant time spent in school with classmates. Second, the "earning" years—that first job, building a career and meeting many friends and business associates. Third, the "retirement" years—finally having time to enjoy visits with all of your family and friends.

In many ways you have made a difference for family, friends and countless others during your lifetime. Yet, there is one more part of life—the chance through your estate to make a meaningful difference in the lives of those in need. And so I invite you to consider this story.

John D. Rockefeller founded Standard Oil in 1870 and became the richest man on the planet. When he passed away, his accountant was asked,

"How much of an estate did he leave?"

His accountant's answer was, "All of it."

During his lifetime John D. Rockefeller accumulated many assets. He also gave generously both during his lifetime and through his estate.

You also have accumulated and given. Yet, in your estate the accumulation period is over. As was true with John D. Rockefeller, everything will be given to someone or for some purpose.

Thank you for your gifts during life. I know you have carefully thought about how much to give, to whom to give and how to give. Now I invite you to think about a "living legacy."

It is called a "living legacy" from your estate because through this gift you live on—your lifelong efforts for accumulation continue to bear fruit in helping others.

Many of our friends find great joy and satisfaction during life, knowing that their estate will someday make a great difference in the lives of others. By completing this guide and a will with benefits for family and charity, you too can join in that happiness.

"The Shortest Day" may be coming soon or may be many years into the future. But your chance for the satisfaction of a legacy that touches many others can be here today.

Thank you again for your generous support of those in need!

# INDEX

**A**

annual gift tax exclusion, 25, 31 – 33, 53, 239, 243

appreciated property. See property

asset inventory, 11, 57, 58, 103, 104, 148

**B**

bequests, 14, 15, 39, 40, 53, 153, 154, 159, 160, 177 – 180

**C**

capital gains tax. See tax

**Care**

    level of, 67, 69, 79, 80, 81, 83

charitable gift annuity, 265, 266

charitable lead trust. See trusts

charitable remainder unitrust (CRT). See trusts

**Children**

    estranged child, 155 – 157

    gifts to, 23 – 29, 31 – 34

    guardian of. See minor children

    helping, 43 – 45, 47 – 49

    loans to, 15

    minor. See minor children

    special needs, 26, 153, 154, 207, 210, 211

**D**

debt, 10, 11, 15, 43, 44, 79, 103, 143, 197, 198, 219, 230, 253, 255, 267

disinheritance, 39, 112, 147, 148
    accidental, 108, 111

## E

email, 58, 171, 174

## F

family business, 26, 230
family limited partnership (FLP), 25

## G

**Gifts**
    of cash, 24, 25, 28, 31, 53, 243 – 246
    of home, 259 – 262
    of land, 32, 253 – 256
    of stock, 25, 32, 53, 249 – 251
    to charity, 177 – 180
    to children, 23 – 29, 31 – 34

## H

**Healthcare,** 65
    advance directive, 58, 67 – 71
    durable power of attorney, 11, 58, 68, 73, 86, 93, 94, 159, 187
    healthcare proxy agent, 86, 87
    HIPAA, 68, 86, 88, 94, 159, 160
    living will, 11, 58, 59, 67 – 71, 86 – 88, 94, 159, 160, 187
    revocable living trust, 74, 91– 94, 145

## I

inheritance, 9 –11, 23 –29, 51–54, 102, 104, 148, 153 –157,
    159 –163, 208 –210, 213 –216, 223 –226, 228, 234, 237, 238

## L

life estate, 13, 14, 260
**Life insurance,** 229– 234
    irrevocable life insurance trust (ILIT), 237 – 240
**Living trust,** 74, 75, 93, 145, 147–149, 159, 162, 163, 173,
    183 – 185, 187 – 189
    funding, 185, 191 – 194
living trust and will, differences between, 165 – 169

# M

**Minor children**

    guardian, 9 –11, 19 – 21, 59, 147, 148

    trust, 13, 15, 31 – 34, 188, 207– 211

# P

**Pets**

    providing for, 15, 16, 59

**Probate**, 141 – 145

    planning for, 11

**Property**

    appreciated, 32, 34, 43 – 45, 249 – 251, 253 – 256,
        263 – 266, 265 – 268

    types of, 107 – 109, 111 – 113

# Q

qualified marital deduction trust (QDOT). See *trusts*

qualified terminable interest property (QTIP), 156, 189, 201 – 204

# R

real estate retirement unitrust. See *trusts*

residue, 159 – 161, 165, 178

**Retirement**

    401(k), 10, 79, 101, 104, 121 – 124, 161, 178, 179

    designated beneficiary, 131 – 135, 145

    IRA, 10, 11, 24, 53, 79, 92, 101, 104, 117, 127 – 129, 131 – 133

    planning for, 79 – 83

    social security, 115 – 118

# S

social media, 171 – 174

special needs trust. See *trusts*

spendthrift trust. See *trusts*

stock. See *gifts*

# T

**Tax**

    capital gains tax, 112, 113

    domicile, 75

estate tax, 25, 31, 75, 104, 133, 134, 143, 144, 147, 155, 160 – 162, 165, 179, 185

**Trusts**

bypass trust, 112, 189

charitable lead trust, 53, 54, 165, 223 – 226

charitable remainder unitrust (CRT), 34, 47 – 49, 53 – 55, 134, 197 – 199, 201 – 204, 219 – 221, 265 – 267

for minor children. See minor children

irrevocable life insurance trust (ILIT). See life insurance

living trust. See living trust

qualified marital deduction trust (QDOT), 201 – 204

special needs trust, 26, 153, 154, 210, 211

spendthrift trust, 213 – 216

real estate retirement unitrust, 47 – 49

## U

uniform transfers to minors act (UTMA), 33

## W

**Wills**

beneficiaries, 153 – 157, 177 – 180

blended family, 20, 156, 157

capacity, 37, 38, 85 – 87, 91, 92, 149, 150

sound mind, 149, 150

contest, 37 – 40, 168, 169

estranged child, 155, 156

guidelines, 149, 150

living wills. See healthcare

reasons to update, 159 – 163

undue influence, 37

unequal shares, 153 – 157

Creation, Life and Beauty,

undone by death and wrongdoing,

regained by God's surprising victory,

AS TOLD IN THE BOOKS OF **THE**
# NEW TESTAMENT,
# PSALMS AND PROVERBS
NEW INTERNATIONAL VERSION®

# ZONDERVAN®

Biblica provides God's Word to people through translation, publishing and Bible
engagement in Africa, Asia Pacific, Europe, Latin America, Middle East, and North
America. Through its worldwide reach, Biblica engages people with God's Word so
that their lives are transformed through a relationship with Jesus Christ.

THE STORY OF GOD AND THE WORLD,
INVITING YOU TO

TAKE UP YOUR ROLE IN THE
DRAMA
OF THE BIBLE

"... this is how God fulfilled what he had foretold through all the prophets, saying that his Messiah would suffer. Repent, then, and turn to God, so that your sins may be wiped out, that times of refreshing may come from the Lord, and that he may send the Messiah, who has been appointed for you—even Jesus. Heaven must receive him until the time comes for God to restore everything, as he promised long ago through his holy prophets."

The book of Acts

# THE DRAMA
## OF THE BIBLE
## IN SIX ACTS

The Bible is a collection of letters, poems, stories, visions, prophetic oracles, wisdom and other kinds of writing. The first step to good Bible reading and understanding is to engage these collected works as the different kinds of writing that they are, and to read them as whole books. We encourage you to read big, to not merely take in little fragments of the Bible. The introductions at the start of each book will help you to do this.

But it is also important not to view the Bible as a gathering of unrelated writings. Overall, the Bible is a narrative. These books come together to tell God's true story and his plan to set the world right again. This story of the Bible falls naturally into six key major acts, which are briefly summarized below.

> "I had always felt life first as a story: and if there is a story, there is a story-teller."
>
> G.K. Chesterton

But even more precisely, we can say the story of the Bible is a drama. The key to a drama is that it has to be acted out, performed, lived. It can't remain as only words on a page. A drama is an activated story. The Bible was written so we could enter into its story. It is meant to be lived.

All of us, without exception, live our lives as a drama. We are on stage every single day. What will we say? What will we do? According to which story will we live? If we are not answering these questions with the biblical script, we will follow another. We can't avoid living by someone's stage instructions, even if merely our own.

This is why another key to engaging the Bible well is to recognize that its story has not ended. God's saving action continues. We are all invited to take up our own roles in this ongoing story of redemption and new creation. So, welcome to the drama of the Bible. Welcome to the story of how God intends to renew your life, and the life of the world. God himself is calling you to engage with his word.

# Act 1: GOD'S INTENTION

 The drama begins (in the first pages of the book of Genesis) with God already on the stage creating a world. He makes a man and a woman, Adam and Eve, and places them in the Garden of Eden to work it and take care of it. The earth is created to be their home. God's intention is for humanity to be in close, trusting relationship with him and in harmony with the rest of creation that surrounds them.

In a startling passage, the Bible tells us that human beings are God's image-bearers, created to share in the task of bringing God's wise and beneficial rule to the rest of the world. Male and female together, we are significant, decision-making, world-shaping beings. This is our vocation, our purpose as defined in the biblical story.

An equally remarkable part of Act 1 is the description of God as coming into the garden to be with the first human beings. Not only is the earth the God-intended place for humanity, God himself comes to make the beautiful new creation his home as well.

God then gives his own assessment of the whole creation: *God saw all that he had made, and it was very good.* Act 1 reveals God's original desire for the world. It shows us that life itself is a gift from the Creator. It tells us what we were made for and provides the setting for all the action that follows.

# Act 2: EXILE

Tension and conflict are introduced to the story when Adam and Eve decide to go their own way and seek their own wisdom. They listen to the deceptive voice of God's enemy, Satan, and doubt God's trustworthiness. They decide to live apart from the word that God himself has given them. They decide to be a law to themselves.

The disobedience of Adam and Eve—the introduction of sin into our world—is presented in the Bible as having devastating consequences. Humans were created for healthy, life-giving relationship: with God, with each other, and with the rest of creation. But now humanity must live with the fracturing of all these relations and with the resulting shame, brokenness, pain, loneliness—and death.

Heaven and earth—God's realm and our realm— were intended to be united. God's desire from the beginning was clearly to live with us in the world he made. But now God is hidden. Now it is possible to be in our world and not know him, not experience his presence, not follow his ways, not live in gratitude.

As a result of this rebellion, the first exile in the story takes place. The humans are driven away from God's presence. Their offspring throughout history will seek to find their way back to the source of life. They will devise any number of philosophies and religions, trying to make sense of a fallen, yet haunting world. But death now stalks them, and they will find that they cannot escape it. Having attempted to live apart from God and his good word, humans will find they have neither God nor life.

New questions arise in the drama: Can the curse on creation be overcome and the relationship between God and humanity restored? Can heaven and earth be reunited? Or did God's enemy effectively end the plan and subvert the story?

# Act 3: CALLING ISRAEL TO A MISSION

 We see the direction of God's redemptive plan when he calls Abraham, promising to make him into a great nation. God narrows his focus and concentrates on one group of people. But the ultimate goal remains the same: to bless all the peoples on earth and remove the curse from creation.

When Abraham's descendants are enslaved in Egypt, a central pattern in the story is set: God hears their cries for help and comes to set them free. God makes a covenant with this new nation of Israel at Mt. Sinai. Israel is called by God to be a light to the nations, showing the world what it means to follow God's ways for living. If they will do this, he will bless them in their new land and will come to live with them.

However, God also warns them that if they are

not faithful to the covenant, he will send them away, just as he did with Adam and Eve. In spite of God's repeated warnings through his prophets, Israel seems determined to break the covenant. So God abandons the holy temple—the sign of his presence with his people—and it is smashed by pagan invaders. Israel's capital city Jerusalem is sacked and burned.

Abraham's descendants, chosen to reverse the failure of Adam, have now apparently also failed. The problem this poses in the biblical story is profound. Israel, sent as the divine answer to Adam's fall, cannot escape Adam's sin. God, however, remains committed to his people and his plan, so he sows the seed of a different outcome. He promises to send a new king, a descendant of Israel's great King David, who will lead the nation back to its destiny. The very prophets who warned Israel of the dire consequences of its wrongdoing also pledge that the good news of God's victory will be heard in Israel once again.

Act 3 ends tragically, with God apparently absent and the pagan nations ruling over Israel. But the hope of a promise remains. There is one true God. He has chosen Israel. He will return to his people to live with them again. He will bring justice, peace and healing to Israel, and then to the world. He will do this in a final and climactic way. God will send his anointed one—the Messiah. He has given his word on this.

# Act 4: THE SURPRISING VICTORY OF JESUS

 "He is the god made manifest . . . the universal savior of human life." These words referring to Caesar Augustus (found in a Roman inscription from 4 BC in Ephesus) proclaim the gospel of the Roman Empire. This version of the good news announces that Caesar is the lord who brings peace and prosperity to the world.

Into this empire a son of David is born, and he announces the gospel of God's kingdom. Jesus of Nazareth brings the good news of the coming of God's reign. He begins to show what God's new creation looks like. He announces the end of Israel's exile and the forgiveness of sins. He heals the sick and raises the dead. He overcomes the dark spiritual powers. He welcomes sinners and those considered unclean. Jesus renews the nation, rebuilding the twelve tribes of Israel around himself in a symbolic way.

But the established religious leaders are threatened by Jesus and his kingdom, so they have him brought before the Roman governor. During the very week that the Jews were remembering and celebrating Passover—God's ancient rescue of his people from slavery in Egypt—the Romans nail Jesus to a cross and kill him as a false king.

But the Bible claims that this defeat is actually

God's greatest victory. How? Jesus willingly gives up his life as a sacrifice on behalf of the nation, on behalf of the world. Jesus takes onto himself the full force of evil and empties it of its power. In this surprising way, Jesus fights and wins Israel's ultimate battle. The real enemy was never Rome, but the spiritual powers that lie behind Rome and every other kingdom whose weapon is death. Through his blood Jesus pays the price and reconciles everything in heaven and on earth to God.

God then publicly declares this victory by reversing Jesus' death sentence and raising him back to life. The resurrection of Israel's king shows that the great enemies of God's creation—sin and death—really have been defeated. The resurrection is the great sign that the new creation has begun.

Jesus is the fulfillment of Israel's story and a new start for the entire human race. Death came through the first man, Adam. The resurrection of the dead comes through the new man, Jesus. God's original intention is being reclaimed.

# Act 5: THE RENEWED PEOPLE OF GOD

If the key victory has already been secured, why is there an Act 5? The answer is that God wants the victory of Jesus to spread to all the nations of the world. The risen Jesus says to his disciples, *"Peace be with you! As the Father has sent me, I am sending you."* So this new act in the drama tells the story of how the earliest followers of Jesus began to spread the good news of God's reign.

According to the New Testament, all those who belong to Israel's Messiah are children of Abraham, heirs of both the ancient promises and the ancient mission. The task of bringing blessing to the peoples of the world has been given again to Abraham's family. Their mission is to live out the liberating message of the good news of God's kingdom.

God is gathering people from all around the world and forming them into assemblies of Jesus-followers— his church. Together they are God's new temple, the place where his Spirit lives. They are the community of those who have pledged their allegiance to Jesus as the true Lord of the world. They have crossed from death into new life, through the power of God's Spirit. They demonstrate God's love across the usual boundaries of race, class, tribe and nation.

Forgiveness of sins and reconciliation with God can now be announced to all. Following in the steps of Jesus, his followers proclaim this gospel in both word and deed. The power of this new, God-given life breaking into the world is meant to be shown by the real-world actions of the Christian community. But the message also has a warning. When the Messiah returns, he will come as the rightful judge of the world.

The Bible is the story of the central struggle weaving its way through the history of the world. And now the story arrives at our own time, enveloping us in its drama.

So the challenge of a decision confronts us. What will we do? How will we fit into this story? What role will we play? God is inviting us to be a part of his mission of re-creation—of bringing restoration, justice and forgiveness. We are to join in the task of making things new, to be a living sign of what is to come when the drama is complete.

# Act 6: GOD COMES HOME

God's future has come into our world through the work of Jesus the Messiah. But for now, the present evil age also continues. Brokenness, wrongdoing, sickness and even death remain. We live in the time of the overlap of the ages, the time of in-between. The final Act is coming, but it has not yet arrived.

We live in the time of invitation, when the call of the gospel goes out to every creature. Of course, many still live as though God doesn't exist. They do not acknowledge the rule of the Messiah. But the day is coming when Jesus will return to earth and the reign of God will become an uncontested reality throughout the world.

God's presence will be fully and openly with us once again, as it was at the beginning of the drama. God's plan of redemption will reach its goal. The creation will experience its own Exodus, finding freedom from its bondage to decay. Pain and tears, regret and shame, suffering and death will be no more.

When the day of resurrection arrives God's people will find that their hope has been realized. The dynamic force of an indestructible life will course through their bodies. Empowered by the Spirit, and unhindered by sin and death, we will pursue our original vocation as a renewed humanity. We will be culture makers, under God but over the world. Having been remade in the image of Christ, we will share in bringing his wise, caring rule to the earth.

At the center of it all will be God himself. He will return and make his home with us, this time in a new heavens and a new earth. We, along with the rest of creation, will worship him perfectly and fulfill our true calling. God will be all in all, and the whole world will be full of his glory.

## WHAT NOW?

The preceding overview of the drama of the Bible is meant to give you a framework so you can begin to read the books that make up the story. The summary we've provided is merely an invitation for you to engage the sacred books themselves.

Many people today follow the practice of reading only small, fragmentary snippets of the Bible—verses—and often in isolation from the books of which they are a part. This does not lead to good Bible understanding. We encourage you instead to take in whole books, the way their authors wrote them. This is really the only way to gain deep insight to the Scriptures.

Go deep and read big.

The more you immerse yourself in the script of this drama, the better you will be able to find your own place in the story. The following page, called *Living the Script*, will help you with practical next steps for taking up your role in the Bible's drama of renewal.

# LIVING
## THE SCRIPT

From the beginning God made it clear that he intends for us to be significant players in his drama. No doubt, it is first and foremost God's story. But we can't passively sit back and just watch what happens. At every stage he invites humans to participate with him.

Here are three key steps to finding your place in the drama:

## 1. IMMERSE YOURSELF IN THE BIBLE

If we are unfamiliar with the text of the drama itself, there's no chance of living our parts well. Only when we read both deeply and widely in the Bible, marinating in it and letting it soak into our lives, will we be prepared to effectively take up our roles. The more we read the Bible, the better readers we will become. Rather than skimming the surface, we will become skilled at interpreting and practicing what we read.

## 2. COMMIT TO FOLLOW JESUS

We've all taken part in the brokenness and wrongdoing that came into the story in Act 2. The victory of Jesus in Act 4 now offers us the opportunity to have our lives turned around. Our sins can be forgiven. We can become part of God's story of new creation.

Turn away from your wrongdoing. God has acted through the death and resurrection of the Messiah to deal decisively with evil—in your life and in the life of the world. His death was a sacrifice, and his resurrection a new beginning. Acknowledge that Jesus is the rightful ruler of the world, and commit to follow him and join with God's people.

## 3. LIVE YOUR PART

Followers of Jesus are gospel players in local communities living out the biblical drama together. But we do not have an exact script for our lines and actions in the drama today. Our history has not yet been written. And we can't just repeat lines from earlier acts in the drama. So what do we do?

We read the Bible to understand what God has already done, especially through Jesus the Messiah, and to know how we carry this story forward. *The Bible helps us answer the key question about everything we say and do: Is this an appropriate and fitting way to live out the story of Jesus today?* This is how we put the Scriptures into action. Life's choices can be messy, but God has given us his word and promised us his Spirit to guide us on the way. You are God's artwork, created to do good works. May your life be a gift of beauty back to him.

ACT 1

ACT 3

God's Intention: Creation

Calling Israel to a Mission: Abraham ca. 2100 BC

Exile: The Fall into Sin

ACT 4

ACT 2

Jesus Dies ca. AD 30; 3 Days Later He Rises from the Dead

The Surprising Victory of Jesus

WORLD EVENTS

Pyramids built, 2500's BC
Hinduism gains influence in India, 1100's BC
Buddhism founded in India, 500's BC
Alexander the Great begins rule, 336 BC
China begins construction on The Great Wall, 214 BC
Rise of the Roman Empire, 27 BC

# THE DRAMA OF THE BIBLE:
## A Visual Chronology

Beginning of Kings' Rule
ca. 1000 BC

Kingdoms Exiled
Israel 722 BC
Judah 586 BC

Moses Leads Israel
out of Slavery

Temple Rebuilt
516 BC

The Church
Today

ACT 5

God Comes Home

The Renewed People of God

ACT 6

## IN THE FRONT...

The Drama of the Bible in Six Acts . . . iii
Living the Script . . . xvi
A Visual Chronology of the Drama . . . xviii
Mapping the Story—the Setting of the Drama . . . xxiv

# A GUIDE TO
# THE BOOKS OF THE
# NEW TESTAMENT, PSALMS AND PROVERBS

(pause and pray before you read the Scriptures)

## STORIES ABOUT JESUS

MATTHEW  1

MARK  43

LUKE  69

JOHN  114

ACTS  148
(and the story of the early Jesus-followers)

## LETTERS FROM PAUL

| | | | |
|---|---|---|---|
| ROMANS | 191 | 1 THESSALONIANS | 265 |
| 1 CORINTHIANS | 211 | 2 THESSALONIANS | 269 |
| 2 CORINTHIANS | 229 | 1 TIMOTHY | 272 |
| GALATIANS | 241 | 2 TIMOTHY | 278 |
| EPHESIANS | 248 | TITUS | 282 |
| PHILIPPIANS | 255 | PHILEMON | 285 |
| COLOSSIANS | 260 | | |

Messages on
## STAYING FAITHFUL

HEBREWS  287

## WISDOM TEACHINGS

JAMES  302

## LETTERS from other leaders

| | | | |
|---|---|---|---|
| 1 PETER | 307 | 2 JOHN | 322 |
| 2 PETER | 313 | 3 JOHN | 323 |
| 1 JOHN | 317 | JUDE | 324 |

## AN APOCALYPSE

REVELATION  326

## ISRAEL'S SONG BOOK

PSALMS  351

## ISRAEL'S WISDOM SAYINGS

PROVERBS  468

AT THE BACK...

Table of Weights & Measures . . . 509

About the NIV . . . . . . . . . . . . . . . . 511

Israel's continuing story and its climax in

# THE LIFE, DEATH AND RESURRECTION OF JESUS THE MESSIAH,

the announcement of

# GOD'S VICTORY OVER HUMANITY'S ENEMIES SIN AND DEATH,

and the invitation for

# ALL PEOPLES TO BE RECONCILED TO GOD

and to share in his

# RESTORATION OF ALL THINGS,

PRESENTED IN THE BOOKS OF **THE NEW TESTAMENT**

THE WORLD OF JESUS
Israel in the First Century

THE GOSPEL GOES OUT
TO THE FIRST CENTURY WORLD

ITALY

Rome

MACEDONIA

Philippi

Thessalonica

GALATIA

ASIA

Ephesus • Colossae

Corinth

ACHAIA

PATMOS

CRETE

MALTA

MEDITERRANEAN SEA

Antioch

Damascus

CYPRUS

Caesarea

ISRAEL

Jerusalem

JUDEA

EGYPT

# MATTHEW

Matthew's purpose is to show that God has kept his ancient promises to Israel through the life, death and resurrection of Jesus the Messiah. The long-expected reign of heaven is now coming to earth, bringing the Jewish story to its climax. Matthew begins by highlighting that Jesus was the son of David, Israel's most famous king, and the son of Abraham, Israel's founding patriarch. Jesus is the true Israelite and God's promised Messiah.

The Messiah is shown as reliving the story of Israel—going down into the Jordan River, facing temptation in the wilderness, gathering twelve disciples as twelve new tribes, ascending a mountain to deliver a new Torah, etc. The author highlights the idea of Jesus as a new Moses by collecting his teachings into five long speeches. These are marked off by some variation of the phrase *When Jesus had finished saying these things*. Just as the Torah had five books, Matthew presents five major sections.

The book concludes by telling how Jesus brought about the great new act of redemption for his people. As in the story of Israel's Exodus, a Passover meal is celebrated and then deliverance comes. Jesus gives his life for the sake of the world and is then raised from the dead. At the beginning of the book, Jesus is given the name *Immanuel*, meaning "God with us." At the end, Jesus sends his followers into the world with the promise that *surely I am with you always*.

---

1 This is the genealogy[a] of Jesus the Messiah[b] the son of David, the son of Abraham:

2 Abraham was the father of Isaac,
Isaac the father of Jacob,
Jacob the father of Judah and his brothers,
3 Judah the father of Perez and Zerah, whose mother was Tamar,
Perez the father of Hezron,
Hezron the father of Ram,
4 Ram the father of Amminadab,
Amminadab the father of Nahshon,
Nahshon the father of Salmon,

5 Salmon the father of Boaz, whose mother was Rahab,
Boaz the father of Obed, whose mother was Ruth,
Obed the father of Jesse,
6 and Jesse the father of King David.

David was the father of Solomon, whose mother had been Uriah's wife,
7 Solomon the father of Rehoboam,
Rehoboam the father of Abijah,
Abijah the father of Asa,
8 Asa the father of Jehoshaphat,
Jehoshaphat the father of Jehoram,

---

*a 1* Or *is an account of the origin*   *b 1* Or *Jesus Christ. Messiah* (Hebrew) and *Christ* (Greek) both mean *Anointed One*; also in verse 18.

Jehoram the father of Uzziah,

[9] Uzziah the father of Jotham,
Jotham the father of Ahaz,
Ahaz the father of Hezekiah,

[10] Hezekiah the father of Ma-
nasseh,
Manasseh the father of
Amon,
Amon the father of Josiah,

[11] and Josiah the father of Jeconiah[a] and his brothers at
the time of the exile to Babylon.

[12] After the exile to Babylon:
Jeconiah was the father of
Shealtiel,
Shealtiel the father of Zerub-
babel,

[13] Zerubbabel the father of Abi-
hud,
Abihud the father of Eliakim,
Eliakim the father of Azor,

[14] Azor the father of Zadok,
Zadok the father of Akim,
Akim the father of Elihud,

[15] Elihud the father of Eleazar,
Eleazar the father of Mat-
than,
Matthan the father of Jacob,

[16] and Jacob the father of Joseph, the husband of Mary,
and Mary was the mother
of Jesus who was called the
Messiah.

[17] Thus there were fourteen generations in all from Abraham to
David, fourteen from David to the
exile to Babylon, and fourteen from
the exile to Babylon to the Messiah.

[18] This is how the birth of Jesus
the Messiah came about[b]: His
mother Mary was pledged to be
married to Joseph, but before they
came together, she was found to be
pregnant through the Holy Spirit.
[19] Because Joseph her husband was
faithful to the law, and yet[c] did not
want to expose her to public disgrace, he had in mind to divorce
her quietly.

[20] But after he had considered
this, an angel of the Lord appeared
to him in a dream and said, "Joseph
son of David, do not be afraid to take
Mary home as your wife, because
what is conceived in her is from the
Holy Spirit. [21] She will give birth to
a son, and you are to give him the
name Jesus,[d] because he will save
his people from their sins."

[22] All this took place to fulfill
what the Lord had said through the
prophet: [23] "The virgin will conceive
and give birth to a son, and they will
call him Immanuel"[e] (which means
"God with us").

[24] When Joseph woke up, he did
what the angel of the Lord had
commanded him and took Mary
home as his wife. [25] But he did not
consummate their marriage until
she gave birth to a son. And he gave
him the name Jesus.

2 After Jesus was born in Bethlehem in Judea, during the time
of King Herod, Magi[f] from the east
came to Jerusalem [2] and asked,
"Where is the one who has been
born king of the Jews? We saw his
star when it rose and have come to
worship him."

[3] When King Herod heard this he
was disturbed, and all Jerusalem
with him. [4] When he had called together all the people's chief priests
and teachers of the law, he asked
them where the Messiah was to be

---

[a] 11 That is, Jehoiachin; also in verse 12      [b] 18 Or The origin of Jesus the Messiah was like this
[c] 19 Or was a righteous man and      [d] 21 Jesus is the Greek form of Joshua, which means the LORD
saves.      [e] 23 Isaiah 7:14      [f] 1 Traditionally wise men

born. [5]"In Bethlehem in Judea," they replied, "for this is what the prophet has written:

[6] " 'But you, Bethlehem, in the
        land of Judah,
    are by no means least among
        the rulers of Judah;
    for out of you will come a ruler
        who will shepherd my people
        Israel.'[a]

[7]Then Herod called the Magi secretly and found out from them the exact time the star had appeared. [8]He sent them to Bethlehem and said, "Go and search carefully for the child. As soon as you find him, report to me, so that I too may go and worship him."

[9]After they had heard the king, they went on their way, and the star they had seen when it rose went ahead of them until it stopped over the place where the child was. [10]When they saw the star, they were overjoyed. [11]On coming to the house, they saw the child with his mother Mary, and they bowed down and worshiped him. Then they opened their treasures and presented him with gifts of gold, frankincense and myrrh. [12]And having been warned in a dream not to go back to Herod, they returned to their country by another route.

[13]When they had gone, an angel of the Lord appeared to Joseph in a dream. "Get up," he said, "take the child and his mother and escape to Egypt. Stay there until I tell you, for Herod is going to search for the child to kill him."

[14]So he got up, took the child and his mother during the night and left for Egypt, [15]where he stayed until the death of Herod. And so was fulfilled what the Lord had said

through the prophet: "Out of Egypt I called my son."[b]

[16]When Herod realized that he had been outwitted by the Magi, he was furious, and he gave orders to kill all the boys in Bethlehem and its vicinity who were two years old and under, in accordance with the time he had learned from the Magi. [17]Then what was said through the prophet Jeremiah was fulfilled:

[18]"A voice is heard in Ramah,
        weeping and great mourning,
    Rachel weeping for her children
        and refusing to be comforted,
        because they are no more."[c]

[19]After Herod died, an angel of the Lord appeared in a dream to Joseph in Egypt [20]and said, "Get up, take the child and his mother and go to the land of Israel, for those who were trying to take the child's life are dead."

[21]So he got up, took the child and his mother and went to the land of Israel. [22]But when he heard that Archelaus was reigning in Judea in place of his father Herod, he was afraid to go there. Having been warned in a dream, he withdrew to the district of Galilee, [23]and he went and lived in a town called Nazareth. So was fulfilled what was said through the prophets, that he would be called a Nazarene.

3 In those days John the Baptist came, preaching in the wilderness of Judea [2]and saying, "Repent, for the kingdom of heaven has come near." [3]This is he who was spoken of through the prophet Isaiah:

"A voice of one calling in the
        wilderness,
    'Prepare the way for the Lord,
        make straight paths for him.' "[d]

---

[a] 6 Micah 5:2,4    [b] 15 Hosea 11:1    [c] 18 Jer. 31:15    [d] 3 Isaiah 40:3

[4] John's clothes were made of camel's hair, and he had a leather belt around his waist. His food was locusts and wild honey. [5] People went out to him from Jerusalem and all Judea and the whole region of the Jordan. [6] Confessing their sins, they were baptized by him in the Jordan River.

[7] But when he saw many of the Pharisees and Sadducees coming to where he was baptizing, he said to them: "You brood of vipers! Who warned you to flee from the coming wrath? [8] Produce fruit in keeping with repentance. [9] And do not think you can say to yourselves, 'We have Abraham as our father.' I tell you that out of these stones God can raise up children for Abraham. [10] The ax is already at the root of the trees, and every tree that does not produce good fruit will be cut down and thrown into the fire.

[11] "I baptize you with[a] water for repentance. But after me comes one who is more powerful than I, whose sandals I am not worthy to carry. He will baptize you with[a] the Holy Spirit and fire. [12] His winnowing fork is in his hand, and he will clear his threshing floor, gathering his wheat into the barn and burning up the chaff with unquenchable fire."

[13] Then Jesus came from Galilee to the Jordan to be baptized by John. [14] But John tried to deter him, saying, "I need to be baptized by you, and do you come to me?"

[15] Jesus replied, "Let it be so now; it is proper for us to do this to fulfill all righteousness." Then John consented.

[16] As soon as Jesus was baptized, he went up out of the water. At that moment heaven was opened, and he saw the Spirit of God descending like a dove and alighting on him. [17] And a voice from heaven said, "This is my Son, whom I love; with him I am well pleased."

4 Then Jesus was led by the Spirit into the wilderness to be tempted[b] by the devil. [2] After fasting forty days and forty nights, he was hungry. [3] The tempter came to him and said, "If you are the Son of God, tell these stones to become bread."

[4] Jesus answered, "It is written: 'Man shall not live on bread alone, but on every word that comes from the mouth of God.'[c]"

[5] Then the devil took him to the holy city and had him stand on the highest point of the temple. [6] "If you are the Son of God," he said, "throw yourself down. For it is written:

" 'He will command his angels concerning you,
and they will lift you up in their hands,
so that you will not strike your foot against a stone.'[d]"

[7] Jesus answered him, "It is also written: 'Do not put the Lord your God to the test.'[e]"

[8] Again, the devil took him to a very high mountain and showed him all the kingdoms of the world and their splendor. [9] "All this I will give you," he said, "if you will bow down and worship me."

[10] Jesus said to him, "Away from me, Satan! For it is written: 'Worship the Lord your God, and serve him only.'[f]"

[11] Then the devil left him, and angels came and attended him.

[12] When Jesus heard that John had been put in prison, he withdrew to Galilee. [13] Leaving Nazareth, he

[a] 11 Or in    [b] 1 The Greek for *tempted* can also mean *tested*.    [c] 4 Deut. 8:3
[d] 6 Psalm 91:11,12    [e] 7 Deut. 6:16    [f] 10 Deut. 6:13

went and lived in Capernaum, which was by the lake in the area of Zebulun and Naphtali— ¹⁴to fulfill what was said through the prophet Isaiah:

¹⁵ "Land of Zebulun and land of
            Naphtali,
        the Way of the Sea, beyond the
            Jordan,
        Galilee of the Gentiles—
¹⁶ the people living in darkness
        have seen a great light;
    on those living in the land of the
            shadow of death
        a light has dawned."ᵃ

¹⁷From that time on Jesus began to preach, "Repent, for the kingdom of heaven has come near."

¹⁸As Jesus was walking beside the Sea of Galilee, he saw two brothers, Simon called Peter and his brother Andrew. They were casting a net into the lake, for they were fishermen. ¹⁹"Come, follow me," Jesus said, "and I will send you out to fish for people." ²⁰At once they left their nets and followed him.

²¹Going on from there, he saw two other brothers, James son of Zebedee and his brother John. They were in a boat with their father Zebedee, preparing their nets. Jesus called them, ²²and immediately they left the boat and their father and followed him.

²³Jesus went throughout Galilee, teaching in their synagogues, proclaiming the good news of the kingdom, and healing every disease and sickness among the people. ²⁴News about him spread all over Syria, and people brought to him all who were ill with various diseases, those suffering severe pain, the demon-possessed, those having seizures, and the paralyzed; and he healed them.

²⁵Large crowds from Galilee, the Decapolis,ᵇ Jerusalem, Judea and the region across the Jordan followed him.

5 Now when Jesus saw the crowds, he went up on a mountainside and sat down. His disciples came to him, ²and he began to teach them. He said:

³ "Blessed are the poor in spirit,
        for theirs is the kingdom of
            heaven.
⁴ Blessed are those who mourn,
        for they will be comforted.
⁵ Blessed are the meek,
        for they will inherit the earth.
⁶ Blessed are those who
            hunger and thirst for
            righteousness,
        for they will be filled.
⁷ Blessed are the merciful,
        for they will be shown mercy.
⁸ Blessed are the pure in heart,
        for they will see God.
⁹ Blessed are the peacemakers,
        for they will be called children
            of God.
¹⁰ Blessed are those who are
            persecuted because of
            righteousness,
        for theirs is the kingdom of
            heaven.

¹¹ "Blessed are you when people insult you, persecute you and falsely say all kinds of evil against you because of me. ¹²Rejoice and be glad, because great is your reward in heaven, for in the same way they persecuted the prophets who were before you.

¹³"You are the salt of the earth. But if the salt loses its saltiness, how can it be made salty again? It is no longer good for anything, except to be thrown out and trampled underfoot.

---

ᵃ 16 Isaiah 9:1,2      ᵇ 25 That is, the Ten Cities

14 "You are the light of the world. A town built on a hill cannot be hidden. 15 Neither do people light a lamp and put it under a bowl. Instead they put it on its stand, and it gives light to everyone in the house. 16 In the same way, let your light shine before others, that they may see your good deeds and glorify your Father in heaven.

17 "Do not think that I have come to abolish the Law or the Prophets; I have not come to abolish them but to fulfill them. 18 For truly I tell you, until heaven and earth disappear, not the smallest letter, not the least stroke of a pen, will by any means disappear from the Law until everything is accomplished. 19 Therefore anyone who sets aside one of the least of these commands and teaches others accordingly will be called least in the kingdom of heaven, but whoever practices and teaches these commands will be called great in the kingdom of heaven. 20 For I tell you that unless your righteousness surpasses that of the Pharisees and the teachers of the law, you will certainly not enter the kingdom of heaven.

21 "You have heard that it was said to the people long ago, 'You shall not murder,[a] and anyone who murders will be subject to judgment.' 22 But I tell you that anyone who is angry with a brother or sister[b][c] will be subject to judgment. Again, anyone who says to a brother or sister, 'Raca,'[d] is answerable to the court. And anyone who says, 'You fool!' will be in danger of the fire of hell.

23 "Therefore, if you are offering your gift at the altar and there remember that your brother or sister has something against you, 24 leave your gift there in front of the altar. First go and be reconciled to them; then come and offer your gift.

25 "Settle matters quickly with your adversary who is taking you to court. Do it while you are still together on the way, or your adversary may hand you over to the judge, and the judge may hand you over to the officer, and you may be thrown into prison. 26 Truly I tell you, you will not get out until you have paid the last penny.

27 "You have heard that it was said, 'You shall not commit adultery.'[e] 28 But I tell you that anyone who looks at a woman lustfully has already committed adultery with her in his heart. 29 If your right eye causes you to stumble, gouge it out and throw it away. It is better for you to lose one part of your body than for your whole body to be thrown into hell. 30 And if your right hand causes you to stumble, cut it off and throw it away. It is better for you to lose one part of your body than for your whole body to go into hell.

31 "It has been said, 'Anyone who divorces his wife must give her a certificate of divorce.'[f] 32 But I tell you that anyone who divorces his wife, except for sexual immorality, makes her the victim of adultery, and anyone who marries a divorced woman commits adultery.

33 "Again, you have heard that it was said to the people long ago, 'Do not break your oath, but fulfill to the Lord the vows you have made.' 34 But I tell you, do not swear an oath at all: either by heaven, for it is God's throne; 35 or by the earth, for it is his footstool; or by Jerusalem, for it is the city of the Great King. 36 And

---

a 21 Exodus 20:13    b 22 The Greek word for brother or sister (adelphos) refers here to a fellow disciple, whether man or woman; also in verse 23.    c 22 Some manuscripts brother or sister without cause    d 22 An Aramaic term of contempt    e 27 Exodus 20:14    f 31 Deut. 24:1

do not swear by your head, for you cannot make even one hair white or black. 37 "All you need to say is simply 'Yes' or 'No'; anything beyond this comes from the evil one.[a]

38 "You have heard that it was said, 'Eye for eye, and tooth for tooth.'[b] 39 But I tell you, do not resist an evil person. If anyone slaps you on the right cheek, turn to them the other cheek also. 40 And if anyone wants to sue you and take your shirt, hand over your coat as well. 41 If anyone forces you to go one mile, go with them two miles. 42 Give to the one who asks you, and do not turn away from the one who wants to borrow from you.

43 "You have heard that it was said, 'Love your neighbor[c] and hate your enemy.' 44 But I tell you, love your enemies and pray for those who persecute you, 45 that you may be children of your Father in heaven. He causes his sun to rise on the evil and the good, and sends rain on the righteous and the unrighteous. 46 If you love those who love you, what reward will you get? Are not even the tax collectors doing that? 47 And if you greet only your own people, what are you doing more than others? Do not even pagans do that? 48 Be perfect, therefore, as your heavenly Father is perfect.

6 "Be careful not to practice your righteousness in front of others to be seen by them. If you do, you will have no reward from your Father in heaven.

2 "So when you give to the needy, do not announce it with trumpets, as the hypocrites do in the synagogues and on the streets, to be honored by others. Truly I tell you, they

have received their reward in full. 3 But when you give to the needy, do not let your left hand know what your right hand is doing, 4 so that your giving may be in secret. Then your Father, who sees what is done in secret, will reward you.

5 "And when you pray, do not be like the hypocrites, for they love to pray standing in the synagogues and on the street corners to be seen by others. Truly I tell you, they have received their reward in full. 6 But when you pray, go into your room, close the door and pray to your Father, who is unseen. Then your Father, who sees what is done in secret, will reward you. 7 And when you pray, do not keep on babbling like pagans, for they think they will be heard because of their many words. 8 Do not be like them, for your Father knows what you need before you ask him.

9 "This, then, is how you should pray:

"'Our Father in heaven,
    hallowed be your name,
10 your kingdom come,
    your will be done,
        on earth as it is in heaven.
11 Give us today our daily bread.
12 And forgive us our debts,
    as we also have forgiven our
        debtors.
13 And lead us not into temptation,[d]
    but deliver us from the evil
        one.[e]'

14 For if you forgive other people when they sin against you, your heavenly Father will also forgive you. 15 But if you do not forgive others their sins, your Father will not forgive your sins.

---

[a] 37 Or from evil     [b] 38 Exodus 21:24; Lev. 24:20; Deut. 19:21     [c] 43 Lev. 19:18
[d] 13 The Greek for temptation can also mean testing.     [e] 13 Or from evil; some late manuscripts one, / for yours is the kingdom and the power and the glory forever. Amen.

¹⁶"When you fast, do not look somber as the hypocrites do, for they disfigure their faces to show others they are fasting. Truly I tell you, they have received their reward in full. ¹⁷But when you fast, put oil on your head and wash your face, ¹⁸so that it will not be obvious to others that you are fasting, but only to your Father, who is unseen; and your Father, who sees what is done in secret, will reward you.

¹⁹"Do not store up for yourselves treasures on earth, where moths and vermin destroy, and where thieves break in and steal. ²⁰But store up for yourselves treasures in heaven, where moths and vermin do not destroy, and where thieves do not break in and steal. ²¹For where your treasure is, there your heart will be also.

²²"The eye is the lamp of the body. If your eyes are healthy,ᵃ your whole body will be full of light. ²³But if your eyes are unhealthy,ᵇ your whole body will be full of darkness. If then the light within you is darkness, how great is that darkness!

²⁴"No one can serve two masters. Either you will hate the one and love the other, or you will be devoted to the one and despise the other. You cannot serve both God and money.

²⁵"Therefore I tell you, do not worry about your life, what you will eat or drink; or about your body, what you will wear. Is not life more than food, and the body more than clothes? ²⁶Look at the birds of the air; they do not sow or reap or store away in barns, and yet your heavenly Father feeds them. Are you not much more valuable than they? ²⁷Can any one of you by worrying add a single hour to your life?ᶜ

²⁸"And why do you worry about clothes? See how the flowers of the field grow. They do not labor or spin. ²⁹Yet I tell you that not even Solomon in all his splendor was dressed like one of these. ³⁰If that is how God clothes the grass of the field, which is here today and tomorrow is thrown into the fire, will he not much more clothe you—you of little faith? ³¹So do not worry, saying, 'What shall we eat?' or 'What shall we drink?' or 'What shall we wear?' ³²For the pagans run after all these things, and your heavenly Father knows that you need them. ³³But seek first his kingdom and his righteousness, and all these things will be given to you as well. ³⁴Therefore do not worry about tomorrow, for tomorrow will worry about itself. Each day has enough trouble of its own.

7 "Do not judge, or you too will be judged. ²For in the same way you judge others, you will be judged, and with the measure you use, it will be measured to you.

³"Why do you look at the speck of sawdust in your brother's eye and pay no attention to the plank in your own eye? ⁴How can you say to your brother, 'Let me take the speck out of your eye,' when all the time there is a plank in your own eye? ⁵You hypocrite, first take the plank out of your own eye, and then you will see clearly to remove the speck from your brother's eye.

⁶"Do not give dogs what is sacred; do not throw your pearls to pigs. If you do, they may trample them under their feet, and turn and tear you to pieces.

⁷"Ask and it will be given to you; seek and you will find; knock and

---

ᵃ 22 The Greek for *healthy* here implies *generous*.    ᵇ 23 The Greek for *unhealthy* here implies
*stingy.*    ᶜ 27 Or *single cubit to your height*

the door will be opened to you. 8For everyone who asks receives; the one who seeks finds; and to the one who knocks, the door will be opened.

9"Which of you, if your son asks for bread, will give him a stone? 10Or if he asks for a fish, will give him a snake? 11If you, then, though you are evil, know how to give good gifts to your children, how much more will your Father in heaven give good gifts to those who ask him! 12So in everything, do to others what you would have them do to you, for this sums up the Law and the Prophets.

13"Enter through the narrow gate. For wide is the gate and broad is the road that leads to destruction, and many enter through it. 14But small is the gate and narrow the road that leads to life, and only a few find it.

15"Watch out for false prophets. They come to you in sheep's clothing, but inwardly they are ferocious wolves. 16By their fruit you will recognize them. Do people pick grapes from thornbushes, or figs from thistles? 17Likewise, every good tree bears good fruit, but a bad tree bears bad fruit. 18A good tree cannot bear bad fruit, and a bad tree cannot bear good fruit. 19Every tree that does not bear good fruit is cut down and thrown into the fire. 20Thus, by their fruit you will recognize them.

21"Not everyone who says to me, 'Lord, Lord,' will enter the kingdom of heaven, but only the one who does the will of my Father who is in heaven. 22Many will say to me on that day, 'Lord, Lord, did we not prophesy in your name and in your name drive out demons and in your name perform many miracles?'

23Then I will tell them plainly, 'I never knew you. Away from me, you evildoers!'

24"Therefore everyone who hears these words of mine and puts them into practice is like a wise man who built his house on the rock. 25The rain came down, the streams rose, and the winds blew and beat against that house; yet it did not fall, because it had its foundation on the rock. 26But everyone who hears these words of mine and does not put them into practice is like a foolish man who built his house on sand. 27The rain came down, the streams rose, and the winds blew and beat against that house, and it fell with a great crash."

28When Jesus had finished saying these things, the crowds were amazed at his teaching, 29because he taught as one who had authority, and not as their teachers of the law.

8 When Jesus came down from the mountainside, large crowds followed him. 2A man with leprosy[a] came and knelt before him and said, "Lord, if you are willing, you can make me clean."

3Jesus reached out his hand and touched the man. "I am willing," he said. "Be clean!" Immediately he was cleansed of his leprosy. 4Then Jesus said to him, "See that you don't tell anyone. But go, show yourself to the priest and offer the gift Moses commanded, as a testimony to them."

5When Jesus had entered Capernaum, a centurion came to him, asking for help. 6"Lord," he said, "my servant lies at home paralyzed, suffering terribly."

---

[a] 2 The Greek word traditionally translated *leprosy* was used for various diseases affecting the skin.

⁷Jesus said to him, "Shall I come and heal him?"

⁸The centurion replied, "Lord, I do not deserve to have you come under my roof. But just say the word, and my servant will be healed. ⁹For I myself am a man under authority, with soldiers under me. I tell this one, 'Go,' and he goes; and that one, 'Come,' and he comes. I say to my servant, 'Do this,' and he does it."

¹⁰When Jesus heard this, he was amazed and said to those following him, "Truly I tell you, I have not found anyone in Israel with such great faith. ¹¹I say to you that many will come from the east and the west, and will take their places at the feast with Abraham, Isaac and Jacob in the kingdom of heaven. ¹²But the subjects of the kingdom will be thrown outside, into the darkness, where there will be weeping and gnashing of teeth."

¹³Then Jesus said to the centurion, "Go! Let it be done just as you believed it would." And his servant was healed at that moment.

¹⁴When Jesus came into Peter's house, he saw Peter's mother-in-law lying in bed with a fever. ¹⁵He touched her hand and the fever left her, and she got up and began to wait on him.

¹⁶When evening came, many who were demon-possessed were brought to him, and he drove out the spirits with a word and healed all the sick. ¹⁷This was to fulfill what was spoken through the prophet Isaiah:

"He took up our infirmities
　and bore our diseases."ᵃ

¹⁸When Jesus saw the crowd around him, he gave orders to cross

to the other side of the lake. ¹⁹Then a teacher of the law came to him and said, "Teacher, I will follow you wherever you go."

²⁰Jesus replied, "Foxes have dens and birds have nests, but the Son of Man has no place to lay his head."

²¹Another disciple said to him, "Lord, first let me go and bury my father."

²²But Jesus told him, "Follow me, and let the dead bury their own dead."

²³Then he got into the boat and his disciples followed him. ²⁴Suddenly a furious storm came up on the lake, so that the waves swept over the boat. But Jesus was sleeping. ²⁵The disciples went and woke him, saying, "Lord, save us! We're going to drown!"

²⁶He replied, "You of little faith, why are you so afraid?" Then he got up and rebuked the winds and the waves, and it was completely calm.

²⁷The men were amazed and asked, "What kind of man is this? Even the winds and the waves obey him!"

²⁸When he arrived at the other side in the region of the Gadarenes,ᵇ two demon-possessed men coming from the tombs met him. They were so violent that no one could pass that way. ²⁹"What do you want with us, Son of God?" they shouted. "Have you come here to torture us before the appointed time?"

³⁰Some distance from them a large herd of pigs was feeding. ³¹The demons begged Jesus, "If you drive us out, send us into the herd of pigs."

³²He said to them, "Go!" So they came out and went into the pigs, and the whole herd rushed down

ᵃ 17 Isaiah 53:4 (see Septuagint)　　ᵇ 28 Some manuscripts Gergesenes; other manuscripts Gerasenes the steep bank into the lake and died in the water. 33Those tending the pigs ran off, went into the town and reported all this, including what had happened to the demon-possessed men. 34Then the whole town went out to meet Jesus. And when they saw him, they pleaded with him to leave their region.

9 Jesus stepped into a boat, crossed over and came to his own town. 2Some men brought to him a paralyzed man, lying on a mat. When Jesus saw their faith, he said to the man, "Take heart, son; your sins are forgiven."

3At this, some of the teachers of the law said to themselves, "This fellow is blaspheming!"

4Knowing their thoughts, Jesus said, "Why do you entertain evil thoughts in your hearts? 5Which is easier: to say, 'Your sins are forgiven,' or to say, 'Get up and walk'? 6But I want you to know that the Son of Man has authority on earth to forgive sins." So he said to the paralyzed man, "Get up, take your mat and go home." 7Then the man got up and went home. 8When the crowd saw this, they were filled with awe; and they praised God, who had given such authority to man.

9As Jesus went on from there, he saw a man named Matthew sitting at the tax collector's booth. "Follow me," he told him, and Matthew got up and followed him.

10While Jesus was having dinner at Matthew's house, many tax collectors and sinners came and ate with him and his disciples. 11When the Pharisees saw this, they asked his disciples, "Why does your teacher eat with tax collectors and sinners?"

12On hearing this, Jesus said, "It is not the healthy who need a doctor, but the sick. 13But go and learn what this means: 'I desire mercy, not sacrifice.'ᵃ For I have not come to call the righteous, but sinners."

14Then John's disciples came and asked him, "How is it that we and the Pharisees fast often, but your disciples do not fast?"

15Jesus answered, "How can the guests of the bridegroom mourn while he is with them? The time will come when the bridegroom will be taken from them; then they will fast.

16"No one sews a patch of unshrunk cloth on an old garment, for the patch will pull away from the garment, making the tear worse. 17Neither do people pour new wine into old wineskins. If they do, the skins will burst; the wine will run out and the wineskins will be ruined. No, they pour new wine into new wineskins, and both are preserved."

18While he was saying this, a synagogue leader came and knelt before him and said, "My daughter has just died. But come and put your hand on her, and she will live." 19Jesus got up and went with him, and so did his disciples.

20Just then a woman who had been subject to bleeding for twelve years came up behind him and touched the edge of his cloak. 21She said to herself, "If I only touch his cloak, I will be healed."

22Jesus turned and saw her. "Take heart, daughter," he said, "your faith has healed you." And the woman was healed at that moment.

23When Jesus entered the synagogue leader's house and saw the noisy crowd and people playing pipes, 24he said, "Go away. The girl

ᵃ 13 Hosea 6:6

is not dead but asleep." But they laughed at him. 25After the crowd had been put outside, he went in and took the girl by the hand, and she got up. 26News of this spread through all that region.

27As Jesus went on from there, two blind men followed him, calling out, "Have mercy on us, Son of David!"

28When he had gone indoors, the blind men came to him, and he asked them, "Do you believe that I am able to do this?"

"Yes, Lord," they replied.

29Then he touched their eyes and said, "According to your faith let it be done to you"; 30and their sight was restored. Jesus warned them sternly, "See that no one knows about this." 31But they went out and spread the news about him all over that region.

32While they were going out, a man who was demon-possessed and could not talk was brought to Jesus. 33And when the demon was driven out, the man who had been mute spoke. The crowd was amazed and said, "Nothing like this has ever been seen in Israel."

34But the Pharisees said, "It is by the prince of demons that he drives out demons."

35Jesus went through all the towns and villages, teaching in their synagogues, proclaiming the good news of the kingdom and healing every disease and sickness. 36When he saw the crowds, he had compassion on them, because they were harassed and helpless, like sheep without a shepherd. 37Then he said to his disciples, "The harvest is plentiful but the workers are few. 38Ask the Lord of the harvest, therefore, to send out workers into his harvest field."

10 Jesus called his twelve disciples to him and gave them authority to drive out impure spirits and to heal every disease and sickness.

2These are the names of the twelve apostles: first, Simon (who is called Peter) and his brother Andrew; James son of Zebedee, and his brother John; 3Philip and Bartholomew; Thomas and Matthew the tax collector; James son of Alphaeus, and Thaddaeus; 4Simon the Zealot and Judas Iscariot, who betrayed him.

5These twelve Jesus sent out with the following instructions: "Do not go among the Gentiles or enter any town of the Samaritans. 6Go rather to the lost sheep of Israel. 7As you go, proclaim this message: 'The kingdom of heaven has come near.' 8Heal the sick, raise the dead, cleanse those who have leprosy,a drive out demons. Freely you have received; freely give.

9"Do not get any gold or silver or copper to take with you in your belts— 10no bag for the journey or extra shirt or sandals or a staff, for the worker is worth his keep. 11Whatever town or village you enter, search there for some worthy person and stay at their house until you leave. 12As you enter the home, give it your greeting. 13If the home is deserving, let your peace rest on it; if it is not, let your peace return to you. 14If anyone will not welcome you or listen to your words, leave that home or town and shake the dust off your feet. 15Truly I tell you, it will be more bearable for Sodom and Gomorrah on the day of judgment than for that town.

a 8  The Greek word traditionally translated *leprosy* was used for various diseases affecting the skin.

¹⁶"I am sending you out like sheep among wolves. Therefore be as shrewd as snakes and as innocent as doves. ¹⁷Be on your guard; you will be handed over to the local councils and be flogged in the synagogues. ¹⁸On my account you will be brought before governors and kings as witnesses to them and to the Gentiles. ¹⁹But when they arrest you, do not worry about what to say or how to say it. At that time you will be given what to say, ²⁰for it will not be you speaking, but the Spirit of your Father speaking through you.

²¹"Brother will betray brother to death, and a father his child; children will rebel against their parents and have them put to death. ²²You will be hated by everyone because of me, but the one who stands firm to the end will be saved. ²³When you are persecuted in one place, flee to another. Truly I tell you, you will not finish going through the towns of Israel before the Son of Man comes.

²⁴"The student is not above the teacher, nor a servant above his master. ²⁵It is enough for students to be like their teachers, and servants like their masters. If the head of the house has been called Beelzebul, how much more the members of his household!

²⁶"So do not be afraid of them, for there is nothing concealed that will not be disclosed, or hidden that will not be made known. ²⁷What I tell you in the dark, speak in the daylight; what is whispered in your ear, proclaim from the roofs. ²⁸Do not be afraid of those who kill the body but cannot kill the soul. Rather, be afraid of the One who can destroy both soul and body in hell. ²⁹Are not two sparrows sold for a penny? Yet not one of them will fall to the

ground outside your Father's care.ᵃ ³⁰And even the very hairs of your head are all numbered. ³¹So don't be afraid; you are worth more than many sparrows.

³²"Whoever acknowledges me before others, I will also acknowledge before my Father in heaven. ³³But whoever disowns me before others, I will disown before my Father in heaven.

³⁴"Do not suppose that I have come to bring peace to the earth. I did not come to bring peace, but a sword. ³⁵For I have come to turn

" 'a man against his father,
    a daughter against her mother,
a daughter-in-law against her
      mother-in-law—
³⁶  a man's enemies will be the
      members of his own
      household.'ᵇ

³⁷"Anyone who loves their father or mother more than me is not worthy of me; anyone who loves their son or daughter more than me is not worthy of me. ³⁸Whoever does not take up their cross and follow me is not worthy of me. ³⁹Whoever finds their life will lose it, and whoever loses their life for my sake will find it.

⁴⁰"Anyone who welcomes you welcomes me, and anyone who welcomes me welcomes the one who sent me. ⁴¹Whoever welcomes a prophet as a prophet will receive a prophet's reward, and whoever welcomes a righteous person as a righteous person will receive a righteous person's reward. ⁴²And if anyone gives even a cup of cold water to one of these little ones who is my disciple, truly I tell you, that person will certainly not lose their reward."

ᵃ 29 Or will; or knowledge      ᵇ 36 Micah 7:6

11 After Jesus had finished instructing his twelve disciples, he went on from there to teach and preach in the towns of Galilee.[a]

2 When John, who was in prison, heard about the deeds of the Messiah, he sent his disciples 3 to ask him, "Are you the one who is to come, or should we expect someone else?"

4 Jesus replied, "Go back and report to John what you hear and see: 5 The blind receive sight, the lame walk, those who have leprosy[b] are cleansed, the deaf hear, the dead are raised, and the good news is proclaimed to the poor. 6 Blessed is anyone who does not stumble on account of me."

7 As John's disciples were leaving, Jesus began to speak to the crowd about John: "What did you go out into the wilderness to see? A reed swayed by the wind? 8 If not, what did you go out to see? A man dressed in fine clothes? No, those who wear fine clothes are in kings' palaces. 9 Then what did you go out to see? A prophet? Yes, I tell you, and more than a prophet. 10 This is the one about whom it is written:

" 'I will send my messenger
    ahead of you,
who will prepare your way
    before you.'[c]

11 Truly I tell you, among those born of women there has not risen anyone greater than John the Baptist; yet whoever is least in the kingdom of heaven is greater than he. 12 From the days of John the Baptist until now, the kingdom of heaven has been subjected to violence,[d] and violent people have been raiding it. 13 For all the Prophets and the

Law prophesied until John. 14 And if you are willing to accept it, he is the Elijah who was to come. 15 Whoever has ears, let them hear.

16 "To what can I compare this generation? They are like children sitting in the marketplaces and calling out to others:

17 " 'We played the pipe for you,
    and you did not dance;
we sang a dirge,
    and you did not mourn.'

18 For John came neither eating nor drinking, and they say, 'He has a demon.' 19 The Son of Man came eating and drinking, and they say, 'Here is a glutton and a drunkard, a friend of tax collectors and sinners.' But wisdom is proved right by her deeds."

20 Then Jesus began to denounce the towns in which most of his miracles had been performed, because they did not repent. 21 "Woe to you, Chorazin! Woe to you, Bethsaida! For if the miracles that were performed in you had been performed in Tyre and Sidon, they would have repented long ago in sackcloth and ashes. 22 But I tell you, it will be more bearable for Tyre and Sidon on the day of judgment than for you. 23 And you, Capernaum, will you be lifted to the heavens? No, you will go down to Hades.[e] For if the miracles that were performed in you had been performed in Sodom, it would have remained to this day. 24 But I tell you that it will be more bearable for Sodom on the day of judgment than for you."

25 At that time Jesus said, "I praise you, Father, Lord of heaven and earth, because you have hidden

a 1 Greek in their towns    b 5 The Greek word traditionally translated leprosy was used for various diseases affecting the skin.    c 10 Mal. 3:1    d 12 Or been forcefully advancing    e 23 That is, the realm of the dead these things from the wise and learned, and revealed them to little children. ²⁶Yes, Father, for this is what you were pleased to do.

²⁷"All things have been committed to me by my Father. No one knows the Son except the Father, and no one knows the Father except the Son and those to whom the Son chooses to reveal him.

²⁸"Come to me, all you who are weary and burdened, and I will give you rest. ²⁹Take my yoke upon you and learn from me, for I am gentle and humble in heart, and you will find rest for your souls. ³⁰For my yoke is easy and my burden is light."

12 At that time Jesus went through the grainfields on the Sabbath. His disciples were hungry and began to pick some heads of grain and eat them. ²When the Pharisees saw this, they said to him, "Look! Your disciples are doing what is unlawful on the Sabbath."

³He answered, "Haven't you read what David did when he and his companions were hungry? ⁴He entered the house of God, and he and his companions ate the consecrated bread — which was not lawful for them to do, but only for the priests. ⁵Or haven't you read in the Law that the priests on Sabbath duty in the temple desecrate the Sabbath and yet are innocent? ⁶I tell you that something greater than the temple is here. ⁷If you had known what these words mean, 'I desire mercy, not sacrifice,'ᵃ you would not have condemned the innocent. ⁸For the Son of Man is Lord of the Sabbath."

⁹Going on from that place, he went into their synagogue, ¹⁰and a man with a shriveled hand was there. Looking for a reason to bring charges against Jesus, they asked him, "Is it lawful to heal on the Sabbath?"

¹¹He said to them, "If any of you has a sheep and it falls into a pit on the Sabbath, will you not take hold of it and lift it out? ¹²How much more valuable is a person than a sheep! Therefore it is lawful to do good on the Sabbath."

¹³Then he said to the man, "Stretch out your hand." So he stretched it out and it was completely restored, just as sound as the other. ¹⁴But the Pharisees went out and plotted how they might kill Jesus.

¹⁵Aware of this, Jesus withdrew from that place. A large crowd followed him, and he healed all who were ill. ¹⁶He warned them not to tell others about him. ¹⁷This was to fulfill what was spoken through the prophet Isaiah:

¹⁸ "Here is my servant whom I have
        chosen,
    the one I love, in whom I
        delight;
  I will put my Spirit on him,
    and he will proclaim justice to
        the nations.
¹⁹He will not quarrel or cry out;
    no one will hear his voice in
        the streets.
²⁰A bruised reed he will not break,
    and a smoldering wick he will
        not snuff out,
  till he has brought justice
        through to victory.
²¹   In his name the nations will
        put their hope."ᵇ

²²Then they brought him a demon-possessed man who was blind and mute, and Jesus healed him, so that he could both talk and see. ²³All the people were astonished and said, "Could this be the Son of David?"

---

ᵃ 7 Hosea 6:6    ᵇ 21 Isaiah 42:1-4

24But when the Pharisees heard this, they said, "It is only by Beelzebul, the prince of demons, that this fellow drives out demons."

25Jesus knew their thoughts and said to them, "Every kingdom divided against itself will be ruined, and every city or household divided against itself will not stand. 26If Satan drives out Satan, he is divided against himself. How then can his kingdom stand? 27And if I drive out demons by Beelzebul, by whom do your people drive them out? So then, they will be your judges. 28But if it is by the Spirit of God that I drive out demons, then the kingdom of God has come upon you.

29"Or again, how can anyone enter a strong man's house and carry off his possessions unless he first ties up the strong man? Then he can plunder his house.

30"Whoever is not with me is against me, and whoever does not gather with me scatters. 31And so I tell you, every kind of sin and slander can be forgiven, but blasphemy against the Spirit will not be forgiven. 32Anyone who speaks a word against the Son of Man will be forgiven, but anyone who speaks against the Holy Spirit will not be forgiven, either in this age or in the age to come.

33"Make a tree good and its fruit will be good, or make a tree bad and its fruit will be bad, for a tree is recognized by its fruit. 34You brood of vipers, how can you who are evil say anything good? For the mouth speaks what the heart is full of. 35A good man brings good things out of the good stored up in him, and an evil man brings evil things out of the evil stored up in him. 36But I tell you that everyone will have to give account on the day of judgment for every empty word they have spoken. 37For by your words you will be acquitted, and by your words you will be condemned."

38Then some of the Pharisees and teachers of the law said to him, "Teacher, we want to see a sign from you."

39He answered, "A wicked and adulterous generation asks for a sign! But none will be given it except the sign of the prophet Jonah. 40For as Jonah was three days and three nights in the belly of a huge fish, so the Son of Man will be three days and three nights in the heart of the earth. 41The men of Nineveh will stand up at the judgment with this generation and condemn it; for they repented at the preaching of Jonah, and now something greater than Jonah is here. 42The Queen of the South will rise at the judgment with this generation and condemn it; for she came from the ends of the earth to listen to Solomon's wisdom, and now something greater than Solomon is here.

43"When an impure spirit comes out of a person, it goes through arid places seeking rest and does not find it. 44Then it says, 'I will return to the house I left.' When it arrives, it finds the house unoccupied, swept clean and put in order. 45Then it goes and takes with it seven other spirits more wicked than itself, and they go in and live there. And the final condition of that person is worse than the first. That is how it will be with this wicked generation."

46While Jesus was still talking to the crowd, his mother and brothers stood outside, wanting to speak to him. 47Someone told him, "Your mother and brothers are standing outside, wanting to speak to you."

⁴⁸He replied to him, "Who is my mother, and who are my brothers?" ⁴⁹Pointing to his disciples, he said, "Here are my mother and my brothers. ⁵⁰For whoever does the will of my Father in heaven is my brother and sister and mother."

13 That same day Jesus went out of the house and sat by the lake. ²Such large crowds gathered around him that he got into a boat and sat in it, while all the people stood on the shore. ³Then he told them many things in parables, saying: "A farmer went out to sow his seed. ⁴As he was scattering the seed, some fell along the path, and the birds came and ate it up. ⁵Some fell on rocky places, where it did not have much soil. It sprang up quickly, because the soil was shallow. ⁶But when the sun came up, the plants were scorched, and they withered because they had no root. ⁷Other seed fell among thorns, which grew up and choked the plants. ⁸Still other seed fell on good soil, where it produced a crop—a hundred, sixty or thirty times what was sown. ⁹Whoever has ears, let them hear."

¹⁰The disciples came to him and asked, "Why do you speak to the people in parables?"

¹¹He replied, "Because the knowledge of the secrets of the kingdom of heaven has been given to you, but not to them. ¹²Whoever has will be given more, and they will have an abundance. Whoever does not have, even what they have will be taken from them. ¹³This is why I speak to them in parables:

"Though seeing, they do not see;
    though hearing, they do not
        hear or understand.

¹⁴In them is fulfilled the prophecy of Isaiah:

" 'You will be ever hearing but
        never understanding;
    you will be ever seeing but
        never perceiving.
¹⁵For this people's heart has
        become calloused;
    they hardly hear with their
        ears,
    and they have closed their
        eyes.
Otherwise they might see with
        their eyes,
    hear with their ears,
    understand with their hearts
and turn, and I would heal
        them.'ᵃ

¹⁶But blessed are your eyes because they see, and your ears because they hear. ¹⁷For truly I tell you, many prophets and righteous people longed to see what you see but did not see it, and to hear what you hear but did not hear it.

¹⁸"Listen then to what the parable of the sower means: ¹⁹When anyone hears the message about the kingdom and does not understand it, the evil one comes and snatches away what was sown in their heart. This is the seed sown along the path. ²⁰The seed falling on rocky ground refers to someone who hears the word and at once receives it with joy. ²¹But since they have no root, they last only a short time. When trouble or persecution comes because of the word, they quickly fall away. ²²The seed falling among the thorns refers to someone who hears the word, but the worries of this life and the deceitfulness of wealth choke the word, making it unfruitful. ²³But the seed falling on good soil refers to someone who hears

ᵃ 15 Isaiah 6:9,10 (see Septuagint)

the word and understands it. This is the one who produces a crop, yielding a hundred, sixty or thirty times what was sown."

24Jesus told them another parable: "The kingdom of heaven is like a man who sowed good seed in his field. 25But while everyone was sleeping, his enemy came and sowed weeds among the wheat, and went away. 26When the wheat sprouted and formed heads, then the weeds also appeared.

27"The owner's servants came to him and said, 'Sir, didn't you sow good seed in your field? Where then did the weeds come from?'

28"'An enemy did this,' he replied.

"The servants asked him, 'Do you want us to go and pull them up?'

29"'No,' he answered, 'because while you are pulling the weeds, you may uproot the wheat with them. 30Let both grow together until the harvest. At that time I will tell the harvesters: First collect the weeds and tie them in bundles to be burned; then gather the wheat and bring it into my barn.'"

31He told them another parable: "The kingdom of heaven is like a mustard seed, which a man took and planted in his field. 32Though it is the smallest of all seeds, yet when it grows, it is the largest of garden plants and becomes a tree, so that the birds come and perch in its branches."

33He told them still another parable: "The kingdom of heaven is like yeast that a woman took and mixed into about sixty pounds[a] of flour until it worked all through the dough."

34Jesus spoke all these things to the crowd in parables; he did not say anything to them without using a parable. 35So was fulfilled what was spoken through the prophet:

"I will open my mouth in
        parables,
    I will utter things hidden since
        the creation of the world."[b]

36Then he left the crowd and went into the house. His disciples came to him and said, "Explain to us the parable of the weeds in the field."

37He answered, "The one who sowed the good seed is the Son of Man. 38The field is the world, and the good seed stands for the people of the kingdom. The weeds are the people of the evil one, 39and the enemy who sows them is the devil. The harvest is the end of the age, and the harvesters are angels.

40"As the weeds are pulled up and burned in the fire, so it will be at the end of the age. 41The Son of Man will send out his angels, and they will weed out of his kingdom everything that causes sin and all who do evil. 42They will throw them into the blazing furnace, where there will be weeping and gnashing of teeth. 43Then the righteous will shine like the sun in the kingdom of their Father. Whoever has ears, let them hear.

44"The kingdom of heaven is like treasure hidden in a field. When a man found it, he hid it again, and then in his joy went and sold all he had and bought that field.

45"Again, the kingdom of heaven is like a merchant looking for fine pearls. 46When he found one of great value, he went away and sold everything he had and bought it.

47"Once again, the kingdom of heaven is like a net that was let down into the lake and caught all

---

[a] 33 Or about 27 kilograms    [b] 35 Psalm 78:2

kinds of fish. 48When it was full, the fishermen pulled it up on the shore. Then they sat down and collected the good fish in baskets, but threw the bad away. 49This is how it will be at the end of the age. The angels will come and separate the wicked from the righteous 50and throw them into the blazing furnace, where there will be weeping and gnashing of teeth.

51"Have you understood all these things?" Jesus asked.

"Yes," they replied.

52He said to them, "Therefore every teacher of the law who has become a disciple in the kingdom of heaven is like the owner of a house who brings out of his storeroom new treasures as well as old."

53When Jesus had finished these parables, he moved on from there. 54Coming to his hometown, he began teaching the people in their synagogue, and they were amazed. "Where did this man get this wisdom and these miraculous powers?" they asked. 55"Isn't this the carpenter's son? Isn't his mother's name Mary, and aren't his brothers James, Joseph, Simon and Judas? 56Aren't all his sisters with us? Where then did this man get all these things?" 57And they took offense at him.

But Jesus said to them, "A prophet is not without honor except in his own town and in his own home."

58And he did not do many miracles there because of their lack of faith.

14 At that time Herod the tetrarch heard the reports about Jesus, 2and he said to his attendants, "This is John the Baptist; he has risen from the dead! That is why miraculous powers are at work in him."

3Now Herod had arrested John and bound him and put him in prison because of Herodias, his brother Philip's wife, 4for John had been saying to him: "It is not lawful for you to have her." 5Herod wanted to kill John, but he was afraid of the people, because they considered John a prophet.

6On Herod's birthday the daughter of Herodias danced for the guests and pleased Herod so much 7that he promised with an oath to give her whatever she asked. 8Prompted by her mother, she said, "Give me here on a platter the head of John the Baptist." 9The king was distressed, but because of his oaths and his dinner guests, he ordered that her request be granted 10and had John beheaded in the prison. 11His head was brought in on a platter and given to the girl, who carried it to her mother. 12John's disciples came and took his body and buried it. Then they went and told Jesus.

13When Jesus heard what had happened, he withdrew by boat privately to a solitary place. Hearing of this, the crowds followed him on foot from the towns. 14When Jesus landed and saw a large crowd, he had compassion on them and healed their sick.

15As evening approached, the disciples came to him and said, "This is a remote place, and it's already getting late. Send the crowds away, so they can go to the villages and buy themselves some food."

16Jesus replied, "They do not need to go away. You give them something to eat."

17"We have here only five loaves of bread and two fish," they answered.

18"Bring them here to me," he

said. ¹⁹And he directed the people to sit down on the grass. Taking the five loaves and the two fish and looking up to heaven, he gave thanks and broke the loaves. Then he gave them to the disciples, and the disciples gave them to the people. ²⁰They all ate and were satisfied, and the disciples picked up twelve basketfuls of broken pieces that were left over. ²¹The number of those who ate was about five thousand men, besides women and children.

²²Immediately Jesus made the disciples get into the boat and go on ahead of him to the other side, while he dismissed the crowd. ²³After he had dismissed them, he went up on a mountainside by himself to pray. Later that night, he was there alone, ²⁴and the boat was already a considerable distance from land, buffeted by the waves because the wind was against it.

²⁵Shortly before dawn Jesus went out to them, walking on the lake. ²⁶When the disciples saw him walking on the lake, they were terrified. "It's a ghost," they said, and cried out in fear.

²⁷But Jesus immediately said to them: "Take courage! It is I. Don't be afraid."

²⁸"Lord, if it's you," Peter replied, "tell me to come to you on the water."

²⁹"Come," he said.

Then Peter got down out of the boat, walked on the water and came toward Jesus. ³⁰But when he saw the wind, he was afraid and, beginning to sink, cried out, "Lord, save me!"

³¹Immediately Jesus reached out his hand and caught him. "You of little faith," he said, "why did you doubt?"

³²And when they climbed into the boat, the wind died down. ³³Then those who were in the boat worshiped him, saying, "Truly you are the Son of God."

³⁴When they had crossed over, they landed at Gennesaret. ³⁵And when the men of that place recognized Jesus, they sent word to all the surrounding country. People brought all their sick to him ³⁶and begged him to let the sick just touch the edge of his cloak, and all who touched it were healed.

15 Then some Pharisees and teachers of the law came to Jesus from Jerusalem and asked, ²"Why do your disciples break the tradition of the elders? They don't wash their hands before they eat!"

³Jesus replied, "And why do you break the command of God for the sake of your tradition? ⁴For God said, 'Honor your father and mother'ᵃ and 'Anyone who curses their father or mother is to be put to death.'ᵇ ⁵But you say that if anyone declares that what might have been used to help their father or mother is 'devoted to God,' ⁶they are not to 'honor their father or mother' with it. Thus you nullify the word of God for the sake of your tradition. ⁷You hypocrites! Isaiah was right when he prophesied about you:

⁸ "'These people honor me with
　　　their lips,
　but their hearts are far from
　　　me.
⁹They worship me in vain;
　their teachings are merely
　　　human rules.'ᶜ"

¹⁰Jesus called the crowd to him and said, "Listen and understand. ¹¹What goes into someone's mouth does not defile them, but what

ᵃ 4 Exodus 20:12; Deut. 5:16　ᵇ 4 Exodus 21:17; Lev. 20:9　ᶜ 9 Isaiah 29:13

comes out of their mouth, that is what defiles them."

¹²Then the disciples came to him and asked, "Do you know that the Pharisees were offended when they heard this?"

¹³He replied, "Every plant that my heavenly Father has not planted will be pulled up by the roots. ¹⁴Leave them; they are blind guides.ᵃ If the blind lead the blind, both will fall into a pit."

¹⁵Peter said, "Explain the parable to us."

¹⁶"Are you still so dull?" Jesus asked them. ¹⁷"Don't you see that whatever enters the mouth goes into the stomach and then out of the body? ¹⁸But the things that come out of a person's mouth come from the heart, and these defile them. ¹⁹For out of the heart come evil thoughts—murder, adultery, sexual immorality, theft, false testimony, slander. ²⁰These are what defile a person; but eating with unwashed hands does not defile them."

²¹Leaving that place, Jesus withdrew to the region of Tyre and Sidon. ²²A Canaanite woman from that vicinity came to him, crying out, "Lord, Son of David, have mercy on me! My daughter is demon-possessed and suffering terribly."

²³Jesus did not answer a word. So his disciples came to him and urged him, "Send her away, for she keeps crying out after us."

²⁴He answered, "I was sent only to the lost sheep of Israel."

²⁵The woman came and knelt before him. "Lord, help me!" she said.

²⁶He replied, "It is not right to take the children's bread and toss it to the dogs."

²⁷"Yes it is, Lord," she said. "Even the dogs eat the crumbs that fall from their master's table."

²⁸Then Jesus said to her, "Woman, you have great faith! Your request is granted." And her daughter was healed at that moment.

²⁹Jesus left there and went along the Sea of Galilee. Then he went up on a mountainside and sat down. ³⁰Great crowds came to him, bringing the lame, the blind, the crippled, the mute and many others, and laid them at his feet; and he healed them. ³¹The people were amazed when they saw the mute speaking, the crippled made well, the lame walking and the blind seeing. And they praised the God of Israel.

³²Jesus called his disciples to him and said, "I have compassion for these people; they have already been with me three days and have nothing to eat. I do not want to send them away hungry, or they may collapse on the way."

³³His disciples answered, "Where could we get enough bread in this remote place to feed such a crowd?"

³⁴"How many loaves do you have?" Jesus asked.

"Seven," they replied, "and a few small fish."

³⁵He told the crowd to sit down on the ground. ³⁶Then he took the seven loaves and the fish, and when he had given thanks, he broke them and gave them to the disciples, and they in turn to the people. ³⁷They all ate and were satisfied. Afterward the disciples picked up seven basketfuls of broken pieces that were left over. ³⁸The number of those who ate was four thousand men, besides women and children. ³⁹After Jesus had sent the crowd away,

---

ᵃ 14 Some manuscripts *blind guides of the blind*

he got into the boat and went to the vicinity of Magadan.

16 The Pharisees and Sadducees came to Jesus and tested him by asking him to show them a sign from heaven.

2 He replied, "When evening comes, you say, 'It will be fair weather, for the sky is red,' 3 and in the morning, 'Today it will be stormy, for the sky is red and overcast.' You know how to interpret the appearance of the sky, but you cannot interpret the signs of the times.[a] 4 A wicked and adulterous generation looks for a sign, but none will be given it except the sign of Jonah." Jesus then left them and went away.

5 When they went across the lake, the disciples forgot to take bread. 6 "Be careful," Jesus said to them. "Be on your guard against the yeast of the Pharisees and Sadducees."

7 They discussed this among themselves and said, "It is because we didn't bring any bread."

8 Aware of their discussion, Jesus asked, "You of little faith, why are you talking among yourselves about having no bread? 9 Do you still not understand? Don't you remember the five loaves for the five thousand, and how many basketfuls you gathered? 10 Or the seven loaves for the four thousand, and how many basketfuls you gathered? 11 How is it you don't understand that I was not talking to you about bread? But be on your guard against the yeast of the Pharisees and Sadducees."

12 Then they understood that he was not telling them to guard against the yeast used in bread, but against the teaching of the Pharisees and Sadducees.

13 When Jesus came to the region of Caesarea Philippi, he asked his disciples, "Who do people say the Son of Man is?"

14 They replied, "Some say John the Baptist; others say Elijah; and still others, Jeremiah or one of the prophets."

15 "But what about you?" he asked. "Who do you say I am?"

16 Simon Peter answered, "You are the Messiah, the Son of the living God."

17 Jesus replied, "Blessed are you, Simon son of Jonah, for this was not revealed to you by flesh and blood, but by my Father in heaven. 18 And I tell you that you are Peter,[b] and on this rock I will build my church, and the gates of Hades[c] will not overcome it. 19 I will give you the keys of the kingdom of heaven; whatever you bind on earth will be[d] bound in heaven, and whatever you loose on earth will be[d] loosed in heaven." 20 Then he ordered his disciples not to tell anyone that he was the Messiah.

21 From that time on Jesus began to explain to his disciples that he must go to Jerusalem and suffer many things at the hands of the elders, the chief priests and the teachers of the law, and that he must be killed and on the third day be raised to life.

22 Peter took him aside and began to rebuke him. "Never, Lord!" he said. "This shall never happen to you!"

23 Jesus turned and said to Peter, "Get behind me, Satan! You are a stumbling block to me; you do not have in mind the concerns of God, but merely human concerns."

24 Then Jesus said to his disciples, "Whoever wants to be my

---

*a 2,3* Some early manuscripts do not have *When evening comes . . . of the times.*   *b 18* The Greek word for *Peter* means *rock.*   *c 18* That is, the realm of the dead   *d 19* Or *will have been* disciple must deny themselves and take up their cross and follow me. ²⁵For whoever wants to save their life*a* will lose it, but whoever loses their life for me will find it. ²⁶What good will it be for someone to gain the whole world, yet forfeit their soul? Or what can anyone give in exchange for their soul? ²⁷For the Son of Man is going to come in his Father's glory with his angels, and then he will reward each person according to what they have done.

²⁸"Truly I tell you, some who are standing here will not taste death before they see the Son of Man coming in his kingdom."

17 After six days Jesus took with him Peter, James and John the brother of James, and led them up a high mountain by themselves. ²There he was transfigured before them. His face shone like the sun, and his clothes became as white as the light. ³Just then there appeared before them Moses and Elijah, talking with Jesus.

⁴Peter said to Jesus, "Lord, it is good for us to be here. If you wish, I will put up three shelters—one for you, one for Moses and one for Elijah."

⁵While he was still speaking, a bright cloud covered them, and a voice from the cloud said, "This is my Son, whom I love; with him I am well pleased. Listen to him!"

⁶When the disciples heard this, they fell facedown to the ground, terrified. ⁷But Jesus came and touched them. "Get up," he said. "Don't be afraid." ⁸When they looked up, they saw no one except Jesus.

⁹As they were coming down the mountain, Jesus instructed them,

"Don't tell anyone what you have seen, until the Son of Man has been raised from the dead."

¹⁰The disciples asked him, "Why then do the teachers of the law say that Elijah must come first?"

¹¹Jesus replied, "To be sure, Elijah comes and will restore all things. ¹²But I tell you, Elijah has already come, and they did not recognize him, but have done to him everything they wished. In the same way the Son of Man is going to suffer at their hands." ¹³Then the disciples understood that he was talking to them about John the Baptist.

¹⁴When they came to the crowd, a man approached Jesus and knelt before him. ¹⁵"Lord, have mercy on my son," he said. "He has seizures and is suffering greatly. He often falls into the fire or into the water. ¹⁶I brought him to your disciples, but they could not heal him."

¹⁷"You unbelieving and perverse generation," Jesus replied, "how long shall I stay with you? How long shall I put up with you? Bring the boy here to me." ¹⁸Jesus rebuked the demon, and it came out of the boy, and he was healed at that moment.

¹⁹Then the disciples came to Jesus in private and asked, "Why couldn't we drive it out?"

²⁰He replied, "Because you have so little faith. Truly I tell you, if you have faith as small as a mustard seed, you can say to this mountain, 'Move from here to there,' and it will move. Nothing will be impossible for you." [21]*b*

²²When they came together in Galilee, he said to them, "The Son of Man is going to be delivered into the hands of men. ²³They will kill

*a 25* The Greek word means either *life* or *soul*; also in verse 26.   *b 21* Some manuscripts include here words similar to Mark 9:29.

him, and on the third day he will be raised to life." And the disciples were filled with grief.

24After Jesus and his disciples arrived in Capernaum, the collectors of the two-drachma temple tax came to Peter and asked, "Doesn't your teacher pay the temple tax?"

25"Yes, he does," he replied.

When Peter came into the house, Jesus was the first to speak. "What do you think, Simon?" he asked. "From whom do the kings of the earth collect duty and taxes — from their own children or from others?"

26"From others," Peter answered.

"Then the children are exempt," Jesus said to him. 27"But so that we may not cause offense, go to the lake and throw out your line. Take the first fish you catch; open its mouth and you will find a four-drachma coin. Take it and give it to them for my tax and yours."

18 At that time the disciples came to Jesus and asked, "Who, then, is the greatest in the kingdom of heaven?"

2He called a little child to him, and placed the child among them. 3And he said: "Truly I tell you, unless you change and become like little children, you will never enter the kingdom of heaven. 4Therefore, whoever takes the lowly position of this child is the greatest in the kingdom of heaven. 5And whoever welcomes one such child in my name welcomes me.

6"If anyone causes one of these little ones — those who believe in me — to stumble, it would be better for them to have a large millstone hung around their neck and to be drowned in the depths of the sea.

7Woe to the world because of the things that cause people to stumble! Such things must come, but woe to the person through whom they come! 8If your hand or your foot causes you to stumble, cut it off and throw it away. It is better for you to enter life maimed or crippled than to have two hands or two feet and be thrown into eternal fire. 9And if your eye causes you to stumble, gouge it out and throw it away. It is better for you to enter life with one eye than to have two eyes and be thrown into the fire of hell.

10"See that you do not despise one of these little ones. For I tell you that their angels in heaven always see the face of my Father in heaven. [11]a

12"What do you think? If a man owns a hundred sheep, and one of them wanders away, will he not leave the ninety-nine on the hills and go to look for the one that wandered off? 13And if he finds it, truly I tell you, he is happier about that one sheep than about the ninety-nine that did not wander off. 14In the same way your Father in heaven is not willing that any of these little ones should perish.

15"If your brother or sisterb sins,c go and point out their fault, just between the two of you. If they listen to you, you have won them over. 16But if they will not listen, take one or two others along, so that 'every matter may be established by the testimony of two or three witnesses.'d 17If they still refuse to listen, tell it to the church; and if they refuse to listen even to the church, treat them as you would a pagan or a tax collector.

a 11 Some manuscripts include here the words of Luke 19:10.    b 15 The Greek word for brother or sister (adelphos) refers here to a fellow disciple, whether man or woman; also in verses 21 and 35.    c 15 Some manuscripts sins against you    d 16 Deut. 19:15

18 "Truly I tell you, whatever you bind on earth will be[a] bound in heaven, and whatever you loose on earth will be[a] loosed in heaven.

19 "Again, truly I tell you that if two of you on earth agree about anything they ask for, it will be done for them by my Father in heaven. 20 For where two or three gather in my name, there am I with them."

21 Then Peter came to Jesus and asked, "Lord, how many times shall I forgive my brother or sister who sins against me? Up to seven times?"

22 Jesus answered, "I tell you, not seven times, but seventy-seven times.[b]

23 "Therefore, the kingdom of heaven is like a king who wanted to settle accounts with his servants. 24 As he began the settlement, a man who owed him ten thousand bags of gold[c] was brought to him. 25 Since he was not able to pay, the master ordered that he and his wife and his children and all that he had be sold to repay the debt.

26 "At this the servant fell on his knees before him. 'Be patient with me,' he begged, 'and I will pay back everything.' 27 The servant's master took pity on him, canceled the debt and let him go.

28 "But when that servant went out, he found one of his fellow servants who owed him a hundred silver coins.[d] He grabbed him and began to choke him. 'Pay back what you owe me!' he demanded.

29 "His fellow servant fell to his knees and begged him, 'Be patient with me, and I will pay it back.'

30 "But he refused. Instead, he went off and had the man thrown into prison until he could pay the debt. 31 When the other servants saw what had happened, they were outraged and went and told their master everything that had happened.

32 "Then the master called the servant in. 'You wicked servant,' he said, 'I canceled all that debt of yours because you begged me to. 33 Shouldn't you have had mercy on your fellow servant just as I had on you?' 34 In anger his master handed him over to the jailers to be tortured, until he should pay back all he owed.

35 "This is how my heavenly Father will treat each of you unless you forgive your brother or sister from your heart."

19 When Jesus had finished saying these things, he left Galilee and went into the region of Judea to the other side of the Jordan. 2 Large crowds followed him, and he healed them there.

3 Some Pharisees came to him to test him. They asked, "Is it lawful for a man to divorce his wife for any and every reason?"

4 "Haven't you read," he replied, "that at the beginning the Creator 'made them male and female,'[e] 5 and said, 'For this reason a man will leave his father and mother and be united to his wife, and the two will become one flesh'[f]? 6 So they are no longer two, but one flesh. Therefore what God has joined together, let no one separate."

7 "Why then," they asked, "did Moses command that a man give his wife a certificate of divorce and send her away?"

---

a 18 Or *will have been*   b 22 Or *seventy times seven* was worth about 20 years of a day laborer's wages. was the usual daily wage of a day laborer (see 20:2).   c 24 Greek *ten thousand talents*; a talent   d 28 Greek *a hundred denarii*; a denarius   e 4 Gen. 1:27   f 5 Gen. 2:24

8 Jesus replied, "Moses permitted you to divorce your wives because your hearts were hard. But it was not this way from the beginning. 9 I tell you that anyone who divorces his wife, except for sexual immorality, and marries another woman commits adultery."

10 The disciples said to him, "If this is the situation between a husband and wife, it is better not to marry."

11 Jesus replied, "Not everyone can accept this word, but only those to whom it has been given. 12 For there are eunuchs who were born that way, and there are eunuchs who have been made eunuchs by others — and there are those who choose to live like eunuchs for the sake of the kingdom of heaven. The one who can accept this should accept it."

13 Then people brought little children to Jesus for him to place his hands on them and pray for them. But the disciples rebuked them.

14 Jesus said, "Let the little children come to me, and do not hinder them, for the kingdom of heaven belongs to such as these." 15 When he had placed his hands on them, he went on from there.

16 Just then a man came up to Jesus and asked, "Teacher, what good thing must I do to get eternal life?"

17 "Why do you ask me about what is good?" Jesus replied. "There is only One who is good. If you want to enter life, keep the commandments."

18 "Which ones?" he inquired.

Jesus replied, " 'You shall not murder, you shall not commit adultery, you shall not steal, you shall not give false testimony, 19 honor your father and mother,'ᵃ and 'love your neighbor as yourself.'ᵇ"

20 "All these I have kept," the young man said. "What do I still lack?"

21 Jesus answered, "If you want to be perfect, go, sell your possessions and give to the poor, and you will have treasure in heaven. Then come, follow me."

22 When the young man heard this, he went away sad, because he had great wealth.

23 Then Jesus said to his disciples, "Truly I tell you, it is hard for someone who is rich to enter the kingdom of heaven. 24 Again I tell you, it is easier for a camel to go through the eye of a needle than for someone who is rich to enter the kingdom of God."

25 When the disciples heard this, they were greatly astonished and asked, "Who then can be saved?"

26 Jesus looked at them and said, "With man this is impossible, but with God all things are possible."

27 Peter answered him, "We have left everything to follow you! What then will there be for us?"

28 Jesus said to them, "Truly I tell you, at the renewal of all things, when the Son of Man sits on his glorious throne, you who have followed me will also sit on twelve thrones, judging the twelve tribes of Israel. 29 And everyone who has left houses or brothers or sisters or father or mother or wifeᶜ or children or fields for my sake will receive a hundred times as much and will inherit eternal life. 30 But many who are first will be last, and many who are last will be first.

20 "For the kingdom of heaven is like a landowner who went out

---

ᵃ 19 Exodus 20:12-16; Deut. 5:16-20    ᵇ 19 Lev. 19:18    ᶜ 29 Some manuscripts do not have or wife.

early in the morning to hire workers for his vineyard. [2]He agreed to pay them a denarius[a] for the day and sent them into his vineyard.

[3]"About nine in the morning he went out and saw others standing in the marketplace doing nothing. [4]He told them, 'You also go and work in my vineyard, and I will pay you whatever is right.' [5]So they went.

"He went out again about noon and about three in the afternoon and did the same thing. [6]About five in the afternoon he went out and found still others standing around. He asked them, 'Why have you been standing here all day long doing nothing?'

[7]"'Because no one has hired us,' they answered.

"He said to them, 'You also go and work in my vineyard.'

[8]"When evening came, the owner of the vineyard said to his foreman, 'Call the workers and pay them their wages, beginning with the last ones hired and going on to the first.'

[9]"The workers who were hired about five in the afternoon came and each received a denarius. [10]So when those came who were hired first, they expected to receive more. But each one of them also received a denarius. [11]When they received it, they began to grumble against the landowner. [12]'These who were hired last worked only one hour,' they said, 'and you have made them equal to us who have borne the burden of the work and the heat of the day.'

[13]"But he answered one of them, 'I am not being unfair to you, friend. Didn't you agree to work for a denarius? [14]Take your pay and go. I want to give the one who was hired last the same as I gave you. [15]Don't I

have the right to do what I want with my own money? Or are you envious because I am generous?'

[16]"So the last will be first, and the first will be last."

[17]Now Jesus was going up to Jerusalem. On the way, he took the Twelve aside and said to them, [18]"We are going up to Jerusalem, and the Son of Man will be delivered over to the chief priests and the teachers of the law. They will condemn him to death [19]and will hand him over to the Gentiles to be mocked and flogged and crucified. On the third day he will be raised to life!"

[20]Then the mother of Zebedee's sons came to Jesus with her sons and, kneeling down, asked a favor of him.

[21]"What is it you want?" he asked.

She said, "Grant that one of these two sons of mine may sit at your right and the other at your left in your kingdom."

[22]"You don't know what you are asking," Jesus said to them. "Can you drink the cup I am going to drink?"

"We can," they answered.

[23]Jesus said to them, "You will indeed drink from my cup, but to sit at my right or left is not for me to grant. These places belong to those for whom they have been prepared by my Father."

[24]When the ten heard about this, they were indignant with the two brothers. [25]Jesus called them together and said, "You know that the rulers of the Gentiles lord it over them, and their high officials exercise authority over them. [26]Not so with you. Instead, whoever wants to become great among you must be your

---

[a] 2 A denarius was the usual daily wage of a day laborer.

servant, 27and whoever wants to be first must be your slave— 28just as the Son of Man did not come to be served, but to serve, and to give his life as a ransom for many."

29As Jesus and his disciples were leaving Jericho, a large crowd followed him. 30Two blind men were sitting by the roadside, and when they heard that Jesus was going by, they shouted, "Lord, Son of David, have mercy on us!"

31The crowd rebuked them and told them to be quiet, but they shouted all the louder, "Lord, Son of David, have mercy on us!"

32Jesus stopped and called them. "What do you want me to do for you?" he asked.

33"Lord," they answered, "we want our sight."

34Jesus had compassion on them and touched their eyes. Immediately they received their sight and followed him.

21 As they approached Jerusalem and came to Bethphage on the Mount of Olives, Jesus sent two disciples, 2saying to them, "Go to the village ahead of you, and at once you will find a donkey tied there, with her colt by her. Untie them and bring them to me. 3If anyone says anything to you, say that the Lord needs them, and he will send them right away."

4This took place to fulfill what was spoken through the prophet:

5 "Say to Daughter Zion,
  'See, your king comes to you,
gentle and riding on a donkey,
  and on a colt, the foal of a
    donkey.'"[a]

6The disciples went and did as Jesus had instructed them. 7They brought the donkey and the colt and placed their cloaks on them for Jesus to sit on. 8A very large crowd spread their cloaks on the road, while others cut branches from the trees and spread them on the road. 9The crowds that went ahead of him and those that followed shouted,

  "Hosanna[b] to the Son of David!"

  "Blessed is he who comes in the
    name of the Lord!"[c]

  "Hosanna[b] in the highest
    heaven!"

10When Jesus entered Jerusalem, the whole city was stirred and asked, "Who is this?"

11The crowds answered, "This is Jesus, the prophet from Nazareth in Galilee."

12Jesus entered the temple courts and drove out all who were buying and selling there. He overturned the tables of the money changers and the benches of those selling doves. 13"It is written," he said to them, "'My house will be called a house of prayer,'[d] but you are making it 'a den of robbers.'[e]"

14The blind and the lame came to him at the temple, and he healed them. 15But when the chief priests and the teachers of the law saw the wonderful things he did and the children shouting in the temple courts, "Hosanna to the Son of David," they were indignant.

16"Do you hear what these children are saying?" they asked him.

"Yes," replied Jesus, "have you never read,

  "'From the lips of children and
    infants

---

[a] 5 Zech. 9:9   [b] 9 A Hebrew expression meaning "Save!" which became an exclamation of praise; also in verse 15   [c] 9 Psalm 118:25,26   [d] 13 Isaiah 56:7   [e] 13 Jer. 7:11

you, Lord, have called forth
     your praise'*a*?"

17 And he left them and went out
of the city to Bethany, where he
spent the night.

18 Early in the morning, as Jesus
was on his way back to the city, he
was hungry. 19 Seeing a fig tree by
the road, he went up to it but found
nothing on it except leaves. Then
he said to it, "May you never bear
fruit again!" Immediately the tree
withered.

20 When the disciples saw this,
they were amazed. "How did the
fig tree wither so quickly?" they
asked.

21 Jesus replied, "Truly I tell you, if
you have faith and do not doubt, not
only can you do what was done to
the fig tree, but also you can say to
this mountain, 'Go, throw yourself
into the sea,' and it will be done. 22 If
you believe, you will receive whatever you ask for in prayer."

23 Jesus entered the temple courts,
and, while he was teaching, the
chief priests and the elders of the
people came to him. "By what authority are you doing these things?"
they asked. "And who gave you this
authority?"

24 Jesus replied, "I will also ask
you one question. If you answer
me, I will tell you by what authority I am doing these things. 25 John's
baptism—where did it come from?
Was it from heaven, or of human
origin?"

They discussed it among themselves and said, "If we say, 'From
heaven,' he will ask, 'Then why
didn't you believe him?' 26 But if
we say, 'Of human origin'—we are
afraid of the people, for they all hold
that John was a prophet."

27 So they answered Jesus, "We
don't know."

Then he said, "Neither will I tell
you by what authority I am doing
these things.

28 "What do you think? There was
a man who had two sons. He went to
the first and said, 'Son, go and work
today in the vineyard.'

29 "'I will not,' he answered, but
later he changed his mind and
went.

30 "Then the father went to the
other son and said the same thing.
He answered, 'I will, sir,' but he did
not go.

31 "Which of the two did what his
father wanted?"

"The first," they answered.

Jesus said to them, "Truly I tell
you, the tax collectors and the prostitutes are entering the kingdom of
God ahead of you. 32 For John came
to you to show you the way of righteousness, and you did not believe
him, but the tax collectors and the
prostitutes did. And even after you
saw this, you did not repent and believe him.

33 "Listen to another parable:
There was a landowner who planted a vineyard. He put a wall around
it, dug a winepress in it and built
a watchtower. Then he rented the
vineyard to some farmers and
moved to another place. 34 When
the harvest time approached, he
sent his servants to the tenants to
collect his fruit.

35 "The tenants seized his servants; they beat one, killed another,
and stoned a third. 36 Then he sent
other servants to them, more than
the first time, and the tenants treated them the same way. 37 Last of all,
he sent his son to them. 'They will
respect my son,' he said.

*a 16* Psalm 8:2 (see Septuagint)

38 "But when the tenants saw the son, they said to each other, 'This is the heir. Come, let's kill him and take his inheritance.' 39 So they took him and threw him out of the vineyard and killed him.

40 "Therefore, when the owner of the vineyard comes, what will he do to those tenants?"

41 "He will bring those wretches to a wretched end," they replied, "and he will rent the vineyard to other tenants, who will give him his share of the crop at harvest time."

42 Jesus said to them, "Have you never read in the Scriptures:

" 'The stone the builders rejected
    has become the cornerstone;
the Lord has done this,
    and it is marvelous in our
        eyes'*a*?

43 "Therefore I tell you that the kingdom of God will be taken away from you and given to a people who will produce its fruit. 44 Anyone who falls on this stone will be broken to pieces; anyone on whom it falls will be crushed."*b*

45 When the chief priests and the Pharisees heard Jesus' parables, they knew he was talking about them. 46 They looked for a way to arrest him, but they were afraid of the crowd because the people held that he was a prophet.

22 Jesus spoke to them again in parables, saying: 2 "The kingdom of heaven is like a king who prepared a wedding banquet for his son. 3 He sent his servants to those who had been invited to the banquet to tell them to come, but they refused to come.

4 "Then he sent some more servants and said, 'Tell those who have been invited that I have prepared

my dinner: My oxen and fattened cattle have been butchered, and everything is ready. Come to the wedding banquet.'

5 "But they paid no attention and went off—one to his field, another to his business. 6 The rest seized his servants, mistreated them and killed them. 7 The king was enraged. He sent his army and destroyed those murderers and burned their city.

8 "Then he said to his servants, 'The wedding banquet is ready, but those I invited did not deserve to come. 9 So go to the street corners and invite to the banquet anyone you find.' 10 So the servants went out into the streets and gathered all the people they could find, the bad as well as the good, and the wedding hall was filled with guests.

11 "But when the king came in to see the guests, he noticed a man there who was not wearing wedding clothes. 12 He asked, 'How did you get in here without wedding clothes, friend?' The man was speechless.

13 "Then the king told the attendants, 'Tie him hand and foot, and throw him outside, into the darkness, where there will be weeping and gnashing of teeth.'

14 "For many are invited, but few are chosen."

15 Then the Pharisees went out and laid plans to trap him in his words. 16 They sent their disciples to him along with the Herodians. "Teacher," they said, "we know that you are a man of integrity and that you teach the way of God in accordance with the truth. You aren't swayed by others, because you pay no attention to who they are. 17 Tell us then, what is your opinion? Is

---

*a* 42 Psalm 118:22,23    *b* 44 Some manuscripts do not have verse 44.

it right to pay the imperial tax[a] to Caesar or not?"

18 But Jesus, knowing their evil intent, said, "You hypocrites, why are you trying to trap me? 19 Show me the coin used for paying the tax." They brought him a denarius, 20 and he asked them, "Whose image is this? And whose inscription?"

21 "Caesar's," they replied.

Then he said to them, "So give back to Caesar what is Caesar's, and to God what is God's."

22 When they heard this, they were amazed. So they left him and went away.

23 That same day the Sadducees, who say there is no resurrection, came to him with a question. 24 "Teacher," they said, "Moses told us that if a man dies without having children, his brother must marry the widow and raise up offspring for him. 25 Now there were seven brothers among us. The first one married and died, and since he had no children, he left his wife to his brother. 26 The same thing happened to the second and third brother, right on down to the seventh. 27 Finally, the woman died. 28 Now then, at the resurrection, whose wife will she be of the seven, since all of them were married to her?"

29 Jesus replied, "You are in error because you do not know the Scriptures or the power of God. 30 At the resurrection people will neither marry nor be given in marriage; they will be like the angels in heaven. 31 But about the resurrection of the dead—have you not read what God said to you, 32 'I am the God of Abraham, the God of Isaac, and the God of Jacob'[b]? He is not the God of the dead but of the living."

33 When the crowds heard this, they were astonished at his teaching.

34 Hearing that Jesus had silenced the Sadducees, the Pharisees got together. 35 One of them, an expert in the law, tested him with this question: 36 "Teacher, which is the greatest commandment in the Law?"

37 Jesus replied: "'Love the Lord your God with all your heart and with all your soul and with all your mind.'[c] 38 This is the first and greatest commandment. 39 And the second is like it: 'Love your neighbor as yourself.'[d] 40 All the Law and the Prophets hang on these two commandments."

41 While the Pharisees were gathered together, Jesus asked them, 42 "What do you think about the Messiah? Whose son is he?"

"The son of David," they replied.

43 He said to them, "How is it then that David, speaking by the Spirit, calls him 'Lord'? For he says,

44 "'The Lord said to my Lord:
    "Sit at my right hand
until I put your enemies
    under your feet."'[e]

45 If then David calls him 'Lord,' how can he be his son?" 46 No one could say a word in reply, and from that day on no one dared to ask him any more questions.

23 Then Jesus said to the crowds and to his disciples: 2 "The teachers of the law and the Pharisees sit in Moses' seat. 3 So you must be careful to do everything they tell you. But do not do what they do, for they do not practice what they preach. 4 They tie up heavy, cumbersome loads and put them on other people's shoulders, but they

---

a 17 A special tax levied on subject peoples, not on Roman citizens    b 32 Exodus 3:6
c 37 Deut. 6:5    d 39 Lev. 19:18    e 44 Psalm 110:1

themselves are not willing to lift a finger to move them.

5 "Everything they do is done for people to see: They make their phylacteries[a] wide and the tassels on their garments long; 6 they love the place of honor at banquets and the most important seats in the synagogues; 7 they love to be greeted with respect in the marketplaces and to be called 'Rabbi' by others.

8 "But you are not to be called 'Rabbi,' for you have one Teacher, and you are all brothers. 9 And do not call anyone on earth 'father,' for you have one Father, and he is in heaven. 10 Nor are you to be called instructors, for you have one Instructor, the Messiah. 11 The greatest among you will be your servant. 12 For those who exalt themselves will be humbled, and those who humble themselves will be exalted.

13 "Woe to you, teachers of the law and Pharisees, you hypocrites! You shut the door of the kingdom of heaven in people's faces. You yourselves do not enter, nor will you let those enter who are trying to. [14][b]

15 "Woe to you, teachers of the law and Pharisees, you hypocrites! You travel over land and sea to win a single convert, and when you have succeeded, you make them twice as much a child of hell as you are.

16 "Woe to you, blind guides! You say, 'If anyone swears by the temple, it means nothing; but anyone who swears by the gold of the temple is bound by that oath.' 17 You blind fools! Which is greater: the gold, or the temple that makes the gold sacred? 18 You also say, 'If anyone swears by the altar, it means nothing; but anyone who swears by the gift on the altar is bound by that oath.' 19 You blind men! Which is greater: the gift, or the altar that makes the gift sacred? 20 Therefore, anyone who swears by the altar swears by it and by everything on it. 21 And anyone who swears by the temple swears by it and by the one who dwells in it. 22 And anyone who swears by heaven swears by God's throne and by the one who sits on it.

23 "Woe to you, teachers of the law and Pharisees, you hypocrites! You give a tenth of your spices — mint, dill and cumin. But you have neglected the more important matters of the law — justice, mercy and faithfulness. You should have practiced the latter, without neglecting the former. 24 You blind guides! You strain out a gnat but swallow a camel.

25 "Woe to you, teachers of the law and Pharisees, you hypocrites! You clean the outside of the cup and dish, but inside they are full of greed and self-indulgence. 26 Blind Pharisee! First clean the inside of the cup and dish, and then the outside also will be clean.

27 "Woe to you, teachers of the law and Pharisees, you hypocrites! You are like whitewashed tombs, which look beautiful on the outside but on the inside are full of the bones of the dead and everything unclean. 28 In the same way, on the outside you appear to people as righteous but on the inside you are full of hypocrisy and wickedness.

29 "Woe to you, teachers of the law and Pharisees, you hypocrites! You build tombs for the prophets and decorate the graves of the righteous. 30 And you say, 'If we had lived in the days of our ancestors,

---

[a] 5 That is, boxes containing Scripture verses, worn on forehead and arm    [b] 14 Some manuscripts include here words similar to Mark 12:40 and Luke 20:47.

we would not have taken part with them in shedding the blood of the prophets.' ³¹So you testify against yourselves that you are the descendants of those who murdered the prophets. ³²Go ahead, then, and complete what your ancestors started!

³³"You snakes! You brood of vipers! How will you escape being condemned to hell? ³⁴Therefore I am sending you prophets and sages and teachers. Some of them you will kill and crucify; others you will flog in your synagogues and pursue from town to town. ³⁵And so upon you will come all the righteous blood that has been shed on earth, from the blood of righteous Abel to the blood of Zechariah son of Berekiah, whom you murdered between the temple and the altar. ³⁶Truly I tell you, all this will come on this generation.

³⁷"Jerusalem, Jerusalem, you who kill the prophets and stone those sent to you, how often I have longed to gather your children together, as a hen gathers her chicks under her wings, and you were not willing. ³⁸Look, your house is left to you desolate. ³⁹For I tell you, you will not see me again until you say, 'Blessed is he who comes in the name of the Lord.'ᵃ"

24 Jesus left *the temple* and was *walking* away when his disciples came up to him to call his attention to its buildings. ²"Do you see all these things?" he asked. "Truly I tell you, not one stone here will be left on another; every one will be thrown down."

³As Jesus was sitting on the Mount of Olives, the disciples came to him privately. "Tell us," they said, "when will this happen, and what will be the sign of your coming and of the end of the age?"

⁴Jesus answered: "Watch out that no one deceives you. ⁵For many will come in my name, claiming, 'I am the Messiah,' and will deceive many. ⁶You will hear of wars and rumors of wars, but see to it that you are not alarmed. Such things must happen, but the end is still to come. ⁷Nation will rise against nation, and kingdom against kingdom. There will be famines and earthquakes in various places. ⁸All these are the beginning of birth pains.

⁹"Then you will be handed over to be persecuted and put to death, and you will be hated by all nations because of me. ¹⁰At that time many will turn away from the faith and will betray and hate each other, ¹¹and many false prophets will appear and deceive many people. ¹²Because of the increase of wickedness, the love of most will grow cold, ¹³but the one who stands firm to the end will be saved. ¹⁴And this gospel of the kingdom will be preached in the whole world as a testimony to all nations, and then the end will come.

¹⁵"So when you see standing in the holy place 'the abomination that causes desolation,'ᵇ spoken of through the prophet Daniel—let the reader understand—¹⁶then let those who are in Judea flee to the mountains. ¹⁷Let no one on the housetop go down to take anything out of the house. ¹⁸Let no one in the field go back to get their cloak. ¹⁹How dreadful it will be in those days for pregnant women and nursing mothers! ²⁰Pray that your flight will not take place in winter or on the Sabbath. ²¹For then there will be great distress, unequaled from

ᵃ 39 Psalm 118:26    ᵇ 15 Daniel 9:27; 11:31; 12:11

the beginning of the world until now—and never to be equaled again.

22 "If those days had not been cut short, no one would survive, but for the sake of the elect those days will be shortened. 23 At that time if anyone says to you, 'Look, here is the Messiah!' or, 'There he is!' do not believe it. 24 For false messiahs and false prophets will appear and perform great signs and wonders to deceive, if possible, even the elect. 25 See, I have told you ahead of time.

26 "So if anyone tells you, 'There he is, out in the wilderness,' do not go out; or, 'Here he is, in the inner rooms,' do not believe it. 27 For as lightning that comes from the east is visible even in the west, so will be the coming of the Son of Man. 28 Wherever there is a carcass, there the vultures will gather.

29 "Immediately after the distress of those days

" 'the sun will be darkened,
    and the moon will not give its
        light;
the stars will fall from the sky,
    and the heavenly bodies will
        be shaken.'*a*

30 "Then will appear the sign of the Son of Man in heaven. And then all the peoples of the earth*b* will mourn when they see the Son of Man coming on the clouds of heaven, with power and great glory.*c* 31 And he will send his angels with a loud trumpet call, and they will gather his elect from the four winds, from one end of the heavens to the other.

32 "Now learn this lesson *from* the fig tree: As soon as its twigs get tender and its leaves come out, you know that summer is near. 33 Even so, when you see all these things, you know that it*d* is near, right at the door. 34 Truly I tell you, this generation will certainly not pass away until all these things have happened. 35 Heaven and earth will pass away, but my words will never pass away.

36 "But about that day or hour no one knows, not even the angels in heaven, nor the Son,*e* but only the Father. 37 As it was in the days of Noah, so it will be at the coming of the Son of Man. 38 For in the days before the flood, people were eating and drinking, marrying and giving in marriage, up to the day Noah entered the ark; 39 and they knew nothing about what would happen until the flood came and took them all away. That is how it will be at the coming of the Son of Man. 40 Two men will be in the field; one will be taken and the other left. 41 Two women will be grinding with a hand mill; one will be taken and the other left.

42 "Therefore keep watch, because you do not know on what day your Lord will come. 43 But understand this: If the owner of the house had known at what time of night the thief was coming, he would have kept watch and would not have let his house be broken into. 44 So you also must be ready, because the Son of Man will come at an hour when you do not expect him.

45 "Who then is the faithful and wise servant, whom the master has put in charge of the servants in his household to give them their food at the proper time? 46 It will be good for that servant whose master finds him doing so when he returns.

---

*a* 29 Isaiah 13:10; 34:4    *b* 30 Or *the tribes of the land*    *c* 30 See Daniel 7:13-14.    *d* 33 Or *he*
*e* 36 Some manuscripts do not have *nor the Son.*

⁴⁷Truly I tell you, he will put him in charge of all his possessions. ⁴⁸But suppose that servant is wicked and says to himself, 'My master is staying away a long time,' ⁴⁹and he then begins to beat his fellow servants and to eat and drink with drunkards. ⁵⁰The master of that servant will come on a day when he does not expect him and at an hour he is not aware of. ⁵¹He will cut him to pieces and assign him a place with the hypocrites, where there will be weeping and gnashing of teeth.

25 "At that time the kingdom of heaven will be like ten virgins who took their lamps and went out to meet the bridegroom. ²Five of them were foolish and five were wise. ³The foolish ones took their lamps but did not take any oil with them. ⁴The wise ones, however, took oil in jars along with their lamps. ⁵The bridegroom was a long time in coming, and they all became drowsy and fell asleep.

⁶"At midnight the cry rang out: 'Here's the bridegroom! Come out to meet him!'

⁷"Then all the virgins woke up and trimmed their lamps. ⁸The foolish ones said to the wise, 'Give us some of your oil; our lamps are going out.'

⁹"'No,' they replied, 'there may not be enough for both us and you. Instead, go to those who sell oil and buy some for yourselves.'

¹⁰"But while they were on their way to buy the oil, the bridegroom arrived. The virgins who were ready went in with him to the wedding banquet. And the door was shut.

¹¹"Later the others also came. 'Lord, Lord,' they said, 'open the door for us!'

¹²"But he replied, 'Truly I tell you, I don't know you.'

¹³"Therefore keep watch, because you do not know the day or the hour.

¹⁴"Again, it will be like a man going on a journey, who called his servants and entrusted his wealth to them. ¹⁵To one he gave five bags of gold, to another two bags, and to another one bag,ᵃ each according to his ability. Then he went on his journey. ¹⁶The man who had received five bags of gold went at once and put his money to work and gained five bags more. ¹⁷So also, the one with two bags of gold gained two more. ¹⁸But the man who had received one bag went off, dug a hole in the ground and hid his master's money.

¹⁹"After a long time the master of those servants returned and settled accounts with them. ²⁰The man who had received five bags of gold brought the other five. 'Master,' he said, 'you entrusted me with five bags of gold. See, I have gained five more.'

²¹"His master replied, 'Well done, good and faithful servant! You have been faithful with a few things; I will put you in charge of many things. Come and share your master's happiness!'

²²"The man with two bags of gold also came. 'Master,' he said, 'you entrusted me with two bags of gold; see, I have gained two more.'

²³"His master replied, 'Well done, good and faithful servant! You have been faithful with a few things; I will put you in charge of many things. Come and share your master's happiness!'

²⁴"Then the man who had re-

---

ᵃ 15 Greek *five talents . . . two talents . . . one talent*; also throughout this parable; a talent was worth about 20 years of a day laborer's wage.

ceived one bag of gold came. 'Master,' he said, 'I knew that you are a hard man, harvesting where you have not sown and gathering where you have not scattered seed. ²⁵So I was afraid and went out and hid your gold in the ground. See, here is what belongs to you.'

²⁶"His master replied, 'You wicked, lazy servant! So you knew that I harvest where I have not sown and gather where I have not scattered seed? ²⁷Well then, you should have put my money on deposit with the bankers, so that when I returned I would have received it back with interest.

²⁸"'So take the bag of gold from him and give it to the one who has ten bags. ²⁹For whoever has will be given more, and they will have an abundance. Whoever does not have, even what they have will be taken from them. ³⁰And throw that worthless servant outside, into the darkness, where there will be weeping and gnashing of teeth.'

³¹"When the Son of Man comes in his glory, and all the angels with him, he will sit on his glorious throne. ³²All the nations will be gathered before him, and he will separate the people one from another as a shepherd separates the sheep from the goats. ³³He will put the sheep on his right and the goats on his left.

³⁴"Then the King will say to those on his right, 'Come; you who are blessed by my Father; take your inheritance, the kingdom prepared for you since the creation of the world. ³⁵For I was hungry and you gave me something to eat, I was thirsty and you gave me something to drink, I was a stranger and you invited me in, ³⁶I needed clothes and you clothed me, I was sick and

you looked after me, I was in prison and you came to visit me.'

³⁷"Then the righteous will answer him, 'Lord, when did we see you hungry and feed you, or thirsty and give you something to drink? ³⁸When did we see you a stranger and invite you in, or needing clothes and clothe you? ³⁹When did we see you sick or in prison and go to visit you?'

⁴⁰"The King will reply, 'Truly I tell you, whatever you did for one of the least of these brothers and sisters of mine, you did for me.'

⁴¹"Then he will say to those on his left, 'Depart from me, you who are cursed, into the eternal fire prepared for the devil and his angels. ⁴²For I was hungry and you gave me nothing to eat, I was thirsty and you gave me nothing to drink, ⁴³I was a stranger and you did not invite me in, I needed clothes and you did not clothe me, I was sick and in prison and you did not look after me.'

⁴⁴"They also will answer, 'Lord, when did we see you hungry or thirsty or a stranger or needing clothes or sick or in prison, and did not help you?'

⁴⁵"He will reply, 'Truly I tell you, whatever you did not do for one of the least of these, you did not do for me.'

⁴⁶"Then they will go away to eternal punishment, but the righteous to eternal life."

26 When Jesus had finished saying all these things, he said to his disciples, ²"As you know, the Passover is two days away — and the Son of Man will be handed over to be crucified."

³Then the chief priests and the elders of the people assembled in the palace of the high priest, whose

name was Caiaphas, 4and they schemed to arrest Jesus secretly and kill him. 5 "But not during the festival," they said, "or there may be a riot among the people."

6While Jesus was in Bethany in the home of Simon the Leper, 7a woman came to him with an alabaster jar of very expensive perfume, which she poured on his head as he was reclining at the table.

8When the disciples saw this, they were indignant. "Why this waste?" they asked. 9 "This perfume could have been sold at a high price and the money given to the poor."

10Aware of this, Jesus said to them, "Why are you bothering this woman? She has done a beautiful thing to me. 11The poor you will always have with you,*a* but you will not always have me. 12When she poured this perfume on my body, she did it to prepare me for burial. 13Truly I tell you, wherever this gospel is preached throughout the world, what she has done will also be told, in memory of her."

14Then one of the Twelve—the one called Judas Iscariot—went to the chief priests 15and asked, "What are you willing to give me if I deliver him over to you?" So they counted out for him thirty pieces of silver. 16From then on Judas watched for an opportunity to hand him over.

17On the first day of the Festival of Unleavened Bread, the disciples came to Jesus and asked, "Where do you want us to make preparations for you to eat the Passover?"

18He replied, "Go into the city to a certain man and tell him, 'The Teacher says: My appointed time is near. I am going to celebrate the Passover with my disciples at your house.'" 19So the disciples did as

Jesus had directed them and prepared the Passover.

20When evening came, Jesus was reclining at the table with the Twelve. 21And while they were eating, he said, "Truly I tell you, one of you will betray me."

22They were very sad and began to say to him one after the other, "Surely you don't mean me, Lord?"

23Jesus replied, "The one who has dipped his hand into the bowl with me will betray me. 24The Son of Man will go just as it is written about him. But woe to that man who betrays the Son of Man! It would be better for him if he had not been born."

25Then Judas, the one who would betray him, said, "Surely you don't mean me, Rabbi?"

Jesus answered, "You have said so."

26While they were eating, Jesus took bread, and when he had given thanks, he broke it and gave it to his disciples, saying, "Take and eat; this is my body."

27Then he took a cup, and when he had given thanks, he gave it to them, saying, "Drink from it, all of you. 28This is my blood of the*b* covenant, which is poured out for many for the forgiveness of sins. 29I tell you, I will not drink from this fruit of the vine from now on until that day when I drink it new with you in my Father's kingdom."

30When they had sung a hymn, they went out to the Mount of Olives.

31Then Jesus told them, "This very night you will all fall away on account of me, for it is written:

" 'I will strike the shepherd,
    and the sheep of the flock will
        be scattered.'*c*

*a 11* See Deut. 15:11.    *b 28* Some manuscripts *the new*    *c 31* Zech. 13:7

³²But after I have risen, I will go ahead of you into Galilee."

³³Peter replied, "Even if all fall away on account of you, I never will."

³⁴"Truly I tell you," Jesus answered, "this very night, before the rooster crows, you will disown me three times."

³⁵But Peter declared, "Even if I have to die with you, I will never disown you." And all the other disciples said the same.

³⁶Then Jesus went with his disciples to a place called Gethsemane, and he said to them, "Sit here while I go over there and pray." ³⁷He took Peter and the two sons of Zebedee along with him, and he began to be sorrowful and troubled. ³⁸Then he said to them, "My soul is overwhelmed with sorrow to the point of death. Stay here and keep watch with me."

³⁹Going a little farther, he fell with his face to the ground and prayed, "My Father, if it is possible, may this cup be taken from me. Yet not as I will, but as you will."

⁴⁰Then he returned to his disciples and found them sleeping. "Couldn't you men keep watch with me for one hour?" he asked Peter. ⁴¹"Watch and pray so that you will not fall into temptation. The spirit is willing, but the flesh is weak."

⁴²He went away a second time and prayed, "My Father, if it is not possible for this cup to be taken away unless I drink it, may your will be done."

⁴³When he came back, he again found them sleeping, because their eyes were heavy. ⁴⁴So he left them and went away once more and prayed the third time, saying the same thing.

⁴⁵Then he returned to the disciples and said to them, "Are you still sleeping and resting? Look, the hour has come, and the Son of Man is delivered into the hands of sinners. ⁴⁶Rise! Let us go! Here comes my betrayer!"

⁴⁷While he was still speaking, Judas, one of the Twelve, arrived. With him was a large crowd armed with swords and clubs, sent from the chief priests and the elders of the people. ⁴⁸Now the betrayer had arranged a signal with them: "The one I kiss is the man; arrest him." ⁴⁹Going at once to Jesus, Judas said, "Greetings, Rabbi!" and kissed him.

⁵⁰Jesus replied, "Do what you came for, friend."ᵃ

Then the men stepped forward, seized Jesus and arrested him. ⁵¹With that, one of Jesus' companions reached for his sword, drew it out and struck the servant of the high priest, cutting off his ear.

⁵²"Put your sword back in its place," Jesus said to him, "for all who draw the sword will die by the sword. ⁵³Do you think I cannot call on my Father, and he will at once put at my disposal more than twelve legions of angels? ⁵⁴But how then would the Scriptures be fulfilled that say it must happen in this way?"

⁵⁵In that hour Jesus said to the crowd, "Am I leading a rebellion, that you have come out with swords and clubs to capture me? Every day I sat in the temple courts teaching, and you did not arrest me. ⁵⁶But this has all taken place that the writings of the prophets might be fulfilled." Then all the disciples deserted him and fled.

⁵⁷Those who had arrested Jesus

---

ᵃ 50 Or "Why have you come, friend?"

took him to Caiaphas the high priest, where the teachers of the law and the elders had assembled. 58But Peter followed him at a distance, right up to the courtyard of the high priest. He entered and sat down with the guards to see the outcome.

59The chief priests and the whole Sanhedrin were looking for false evidence against Jesus so that they could put him to death. 60But they did not find any, though many false witnesses came forward.

Finally two came forward 61and declared, "This fellow said, 'I am able to destroy the temple of God and rebuild it in three days.'"

62Then the high priest stood up and said to Jesus, "Are you not going to answer? What is this testimony that these men are bringing against you?" 63But Jesus remained silent.

The high priest said to him, "I charge you under oath by the living God: Tell us if you are the Messiah, the Son of God."

64"You have said so," Jesus replied. "But I say to all of you: From now on you will see the Son of Man sitting at the right hand of the Mighty One and coming on the clouds of heaven."[a]

65Then the high priest tore his clothes and said, "He has spoken blasphemy! Why do we need any more witnesses? Look, now you have heard the blasphemy. 66What do you think?"

"He is worthy of death," they answered.

67Then they spit in his face and struck him with their fists. Others slapped him 68and said, "Prophesy to us, Messiah. Who hit you?"

69Now Peter was sitting out in the courtyard, and a servant girl came

to him. "You also were with Jesus of Galilee," she said.

70But he denied it before them all. "I don't know what you're talking about," he said.

71Then he went out to the gateway, where another servant girl saw him and said to the people there, "This fellow was with Jesus of Nazareth."

72He denied it again, with an oath: "I don't know the man!"

73After a little while, those standing there went up to Peter and said, "Surely you are one of them; your accent gives you away."

74Then he began to call down curses, and he swore to them, "I don't know the man!"

Immediately a rooster crowed. 75Then Peter remembered the word Jesus had spoken: "Before the rooster crows, you will disown me three times." And he went outside and wept bitterly.

27 Early in the morning, all the chief priests and the elders of the people made their plans how to have Jesus executed. 2So they bound him, led him away and handed him over to Pilate the governor.

3When Judas, who had betrayed him, saw that Jesus was condemned, he was seized with remorse and returned the thirty pieces of silver to the chief priests and the elders. 4"I have sinned," he said, "for I have betrayed innocent blood."

"What is that to us?" they replied. "That's your responsibility."

5So Judas threw the money into the temple and left. Then he went away and hanged himself.

6The chief priests picked up the coins and said, "It is against the law to put this into the treasury, since it is blood money." 7So they de-

---

[a] 64 See Psalm 110:1; Daniel 7:13.

cided to use the money to buy the potter's field as a burial place for foreigners. [8]That is why it has been called the Field of Blood to this day. [9]Then what was spoken by Jeremiah the prophet was fulfilled: "They took the thirty pieces of silver, the price set on him by the people of Israel, [10]and they used them to buy the potter's field, as the Lord commanded me."[a]

[11]Meanwhile Jesus stood before the governor, and the governor asked him, "Are you the king of the Jews?"

"You have said so," Jesus replied.

[12]When he was accused by the chief priests and the elders, he gave no answer. [13]Then Pilate asked him, "Don't you hear the testimony they are bringing against you?" [14]But Jesus made no reply, not even to a single charge — to the great amazement of the governor.

[15]Now it was the governor's custom at the festival to release a prisoner chosen by the crowd. [16]At that time they had a well-known prisoner whose name was Jesus[b] Barabbas. [17]So when the crowd had gathered, Pilate asked them, "Which one do you want me to release to you: Jesus Barabbas, or Jesus who is called the Messiah?" [18]For he knew it was out of self-interest that they had handed Jesus over to him.

[19]While Pilate was sitting on the judge's seat, his wife sent him this message: "Don't have anything to do with that innocent man, for I have suffered a great deal today in a dream because of him."

[20]But the chief priests and the elders persuaded the crowd to ask for Barabbas and to have Jesus executed.

[21]"Which of the two do you want me to release to you?" asked the governor.

"Barabbas," they answered.

[22]"What shall I do, then, with Jesus who is called the Messiah?" Pilate asked.

They all answered, "Crucify him!"

[23]"Why? What crime has he committed?" asked Pilate.

But they shouted all the louder, "Crucify him!"

[24]When Pilate saw that he was getting nowhere, but that instead an uproar was starting, he took water and washed his hands in front of the crowd. "I am innocent of this man's blood," he said. "It is your responsibility!"

[25]All the people answered, "His blood is on us and on our children!"

[26]Then he released Barabbas to them. But he had Jesus flogged, and handed him over to be crucified.

[27]Then the governor's soldiers took Jesus into the Praetorium and gathered the whole company of soldiers around him. [28]They stripped him and put a scarlet robe on him, [29]and then twisted together a crown of thorns and set it on his head. They put a staff in his right hand. Then they knelt in front of him and mocked him. "Hail, king of the Jews!" they said. [30]They spit on him, and took the staff and struck him on the head again and again. [31]After they had mocked him, they took off the robe and put his own clothes on him. Then they led him away to crucify him.

[32]As they were going out, they met a man from Cyrene, named Simon, and they forced him to carry

[a] 10 See Zech. 11:12,13; Jer. 19:1-13; 32:6-9.    [b] 16 Many manuscripts do not have Jesus; also in verse 17.

the cross. 33They came to a place called Golgotha (which means "the place of the skull"). 34There they offered Jesus wine to drink, mixed with gall; but after tasting it, he refused to drink it. 35When they had crucified him, they divided up his clothes by casting lots. 36And sitting down, they kept watch over him there. 37Above his head they placed the written charge against him: THIS IS JESUS, THE KING OF THE JEWS.

38Two rebels were crucified with him, one on his right and one on his left. 39Those who passed by hurled insults at him, shaking their heads 40and saying, "You who are going to destroy the temple and build it in three days, save yourself! Come down from the cross, if you are the Son of God!" 41In the same way the chief priests, the teachers of the law and the elders mocked him. 42"He saved others," they said, "but he can't save himself! He's the king of Israel! Let him come down now from the cross, and we will believe in him. 43He trusts in God. Let God rescue him now if he wants him, for he said, 'I am the Son of God.'" 44In the same way the rebels who were crucified with him also heaped insults on him.

45From noon until three in the afternoon darkness came over all the land. 46About three in the afternoon Jesus cried out in a loud voice, *"Eli, Eli,a lema sabachthani?"* (which means "My God, my God, why have you forsaken me?").b

47When some of those standing there heard this, they said, "He's calling Elijah."

48Immediately one of them ran and got a sponge. He filled it with wine vinegar, put it on a staff, and offered it to Jesus to drink. 49The rest said, "Now leave him alone. Let's see if Elijah comes to save him."

50And when Jesus had cried out again in a loud voice, he gave up his spirit.

51At that moment the curtain of the temple was torn in two from top to bottom. The earth shook, the rocks split 52and the tombs broke open. The bodies of many holy people who had died were raised to life. 53They came out of the tombs after Jesus' resurrection andc went into the holy city and appeared to many people.

54When the centurion and those with him who were guarding Jesus saw the earthquake and all that had happened, they were terrified, and exclaimed, "Surely he was the Son of God!"

55Many women were there, watching from a distance. They had followed Jesus from Galilee to care for his needs. 56Among them were Mary Magdalene, Mary the mother of James and Joseph,d and the mother of Zebedee's sons.

57As evening approached, there came a rich man from Arimathea, named Joseph, who had himself become a disciple of Jesus. 58Going to Pilate, he asked for Jesus' body, and Pilate ordered that it be given to him. 59Joseph took the body, wrapped it in a clean linen cloth, 60and placed it in his own new tomb that he had cut out of the rock. He rolled a big stone in front of the entrance to the tomb and went away. 61Mary Magdalene and the other Mary were sitting there opposite the tomb.

---

a 46 Some manuscripts *Eloi, Eloi*     b 46 Psalm 22:1     c 53 Or *tombs, and after Jesus' resurrection they*     d 56 Greek *Joses,* a variant of *Joseph*

62The next day, the one after Preparation Day, the chief priests and the Pharisees went to Pilate. 63"Sir," they said, "we remember that while he was still alive that deceiver said, 'After three days I will rise again.' 64So give the order for the tomb to be made secure until the third day. Otherwise, his disciples may come and steal the body and tell the people that he has been raised from the dead. This last deception will be worse than the first."

65"Take a guard," Pilate answered. "Go, make the tomb as secure as you know how." 66So they went and made the tomb secure by putting a seal on the stone and posting the guard.

28 After the Sabbath, at dawn on the first day of the week, Mary Magdalene and the other Mary went to look at the tomb.

2There was a violent earthquake, for an angel of the Lord came down from heaven and, going to the tomb, rolled back the stone and sat on it. 3His appearance was like lightning, and his clothes were white as snow. 4The guards were so afraid of him that they shook and became like dead men.

5The angel said to the women, "Do not be afraid, for I know that you are looking for Jesus, who was crucified. 6He is not here; he has risen, just as he said. Come and see the place where he lay. 7Then go quickly and tell his disciples: 'He has risen from the dead and is going ahead of you into Galilee. There you will see him.' Now I have told you."

8So the women hurried away from the tomb, afraid yet filled with joy, and ran to tell his disciples. 9Suddenly Jesus met them. "Greetings," he said. They came to him, clasped his feet and worshiped him. 10Then Jesus said to them, "Do not be afraid. Go and tell my brothers to go to Galilee; there they will see me."

11While the women were on their way, some of the guards went into the city and reported to the chief priests everything that had happened. 12When the chief priests had met with the elders and devised a plan, they gave the soldiers a large sum of money, 13telling them, "You are to say, 'His disciples came during the night and stole him away while we were asleep.' 14If this report gets to the governor, we will satisfy him and keep you out of trouble." 15So the soldiers took the money and did as they were instructed. And this story has been widely circulated among the Jews to this very day.

16Then the eleven disciples went to Galilee, to the mountain where Jesus had told them to go. 17When they saw him, they worshiped him; but some doubted. 18Then Jesus came to them and said, "All authority in heaven and on earth has been given to me. 19Therefore go and make disciples of all nations, baptizing them in the name of the Father and of the Son and of the Holy Spirit, 20and teaching them to obey everything I have commanded you. And surely I am with you always, to the very end of the age."

# MARK

Mark appears to be written for an audience in Rome. A Roman centurion's declaration near the end of the book—*Surely this man was the Son of God!*—models the witness to Jesus this gospel calls for.

The opening half of this fast-moving drama keys on the question: *Who do you say I am?* An episode at the end of the first half shows Jesus healing a blind man in two stages, so that he slowly comes to see. In the same way the disciples have only gradually come to recognize who Jesus is. Then in a key moment in the story, between its two halves, Peter confesses that Jesus is the Messiah.

Now the conflict moves out into the open. Jesus has come to introduce a radical new way of life that will undercut existing power relationships. The second half of the drama depicts this in three acts:

: First, Jesus and his disciples travel to Jerusalem.
: Next, Jesus teaches in the temple and clashes with the established leadership.
: In the final act, that leadership executes its plan and has Jesus arrested and crucified, seemingly overturning all he has done. But then God overturns their deed and raises Jesus to life. So Mark's readers are called to be faithful to Jesus, even in suffering, because this is how God continues to overturn the existing order and establish the way of life that Jesus taught.

---

1 The beginning of the good news about Jesus the Messiah,[a] the Son of God,[b] 2 as it is written in Isaiah the prophet:

"I will send my messenger ahead
of you,
who will prepare your way"[c]—
3 "a voice of one calling in the
wilderness,
'Prepare the way for the Lord,
make straight paths for him.'"[d]

4 And so John the Baptist appeared in the wilderness, preaching a baptism of repentance for the forgiveness of sins. 5 The whole Judean countryside and all the people of Jerusalem went out to him. Confessing their sins, they were baptized by him in the Jordan River. 6 John

wore clothing made of camel's hair, with a leather belt around his waist, and he ate locusts and wild honey. 7 And this was his message: "After me comes the one more powerful than I, the straps of whose sandals I am not worthy to stoop down and untie. 8 I baptize you with[e] water, but he will baptize you with[e] the Holy Spirit."

9 At that time Jesus came from Nazareth in Galilee and was baptized by John in the Jordan. 10 Just as Jesus was coming up out of the water, he saw heaven being torn open and the Spirit descending on him like a dove. 11 And a voice came from heaven: "You are my Son, whom I love; with you I am well pleased."

*a 1 Or Jesus Christ. Messiah (Hebrew) and Christ (Greek) both mean Anointed One.* *b 1 Some manuscripts do not have the Son of God.* *c 2 Mal. 3:1* *d 3 Isaiah 40:3* *e 8 Or in*

¹²At once the Spirit sent him out into the wilderness, ¹³and he was in the wilderness forty days, being tempted[a] by Satan. He was with the wild animals, and angels attended him.

¹⁴After John was put in prison, Jesus went into Galilee, proclaiming the good news of God. ¹⁵"The time has come," he said. "The kingdom of God has come near. Repent and believe the good news!"

¹⁶As Jesus walked beside the Sea of Galilee, he saw Simon and his brother Andrew casting a net into the lake, for they were fishermen. ¹⁷"Come, follow me," Jesus said, "and I will send you out to fish for people." ¹⁸At once they left their nets and followed him.

¹⁹When he had gone a little farther, he saw James son of Zebedee and his brother John in a boat, preparing their nets. ²⁰Without delay he called them, and they left their father Zebedee in the boat with the hired men and followed him.

²¹They went to Capernaum, and when the Sabbath came, Jesus went into the synagogue and began to teach. ²²The people were amazed at his teaching, because he taught them as one who had authority, not as the teachers of the law. ²³Just then a man in their synagogue who was possessed by an impure spirit cried out, ²⁴"What do you want with us, Jesus of Nazareth? Have you come to destroy us? I know who you are—the Holy One of God!"

²⁵"Be quiet!" said Jesus sternly. "Come out of him!" ²⁶The impure spirit shook the man violently and came out of him with a shriek.

²⁷The people were all so amazed that they asked each other, "What is this? A new teaching—and with authority! He even gives orders to impure spirits and they obey him." ²⁸News about him spread quickly over the whole region of Galilee.

²⁹As soon as they left the synagogue, they went with James and John to the home of Simon and Andrew. ³⁰Simon's mother-in-law was in bed with a fever, and they immediately told Jesus about her. ³¹So he went to her, took her hand and helped her up. The fever left her and she began to wait on them.

³²That evening after sunset the people brought to Jesus all the sick and demon-possessed. ³³The whole town gathered at the door, ³⁴and Jesus healed many who had various diseases. He also drove out many demons, but he would not let the demons speak because they knew who he was.

³⁵Very early in the morning, while it was still dark, Jesus got up, left the house and went off to a solitary place, where he prayed. ³⁶Simon and his companions went to look for him, ³⁷and when they found him, they exclaimed: "Everyone is looking for you!"

³⁸Jesus replied, "Let us go somewhere else—to the nearby villages—so I can preach there also. That is why I have come." ³⁹So he traveled throughout Galilee, preaching in their synagogues and driving out demons.

⁴⁰A man with leprosy[b] came to him and begged him on his knees, "If you are willing, you can make me clean."

⁴¹Jesus was indignant.[c] He

---

[a] 13 The Greek for *tempted* can also mean *tested*. [b] 40 The Greek word traditionally translated *leprosy* was used for various diseases affecting the skin. [c] 41 Many manuscripts *Jesus was filled with compassion*

reached out his hand and touched the man. "I am willing," he said. "Be clean!" [42]Immediately the leprosy left him and he was cleansed.

[43]Jesus sent him away at once with a strong warning: [44]"See that you don't tell this to anyone. But go, show yourself to the priest and offer the sacrifices that Moses commanded for your cleansing, as a testimony to them." [45]Instead he went out and began to talk freely, spreading the news. As a result, Jesus could no longer enter a town openly but stayed outside in lonely places. Yet the people still came to him from everywhere.

2 A few days later, when Jesus again entered Capernaum, the people heard that he had come home. [2]They gathered in such large numbers that there was no room left, not even outside the door, and he preached the word to them. [3]Some men came, bringing to him a paralyzed man, carried by four of them. [4]Since they could not get him to Jesus because of the crowd, they made an opening in the roof above Jesus by digging through it and then lowered the mat the man was lying on. [5]When Jesus saw their faith, he said to the paralyzed man, "Son, your sins are forgiven."

[6]Now some teachers of the law were sitting there, thinking to themselves, [7]"Why does this fellow talk like that? He's blaspheming! Who can forgive sins but God alone?"

[8]Immediately Jesus knew in his spirit that this was what they were thinking in their hearts, and he said to them, "Why are you thinking these things? [9]Which is easier: to say to this paralyzed man, 'Your sins are forgiven,' or to say, 'Get up, take your mat and walk'? [10]But I want you to know that the Son of Man has authority on earth to forgive sins." So he said to the man, [11]"I tell you, get up, take your mat and go home." [12]He got up, took his mat and walked out in full view of them all. This amazed everyone and they praised God, saying, "We have never seen anything like this!"

[13]Once again Jesus went out beside the lake. A large crowd came to him, and he began to teach them. [14]As he walked along, he saw Levi son of Alphaeus sitting at the tax collector's booth. "Follow me," Jesus told him, and Levi got up and followed him.

[15]While Jesus was having dinner at Levi's house, many tax collectors and sinners were eating with him and his disciples, for there were many who followed him. [16]When the teachers of the law who were Pharisees saw him eating with the sinners and tax collectors, they asked his disciples: "Why does he eat with tax collectors and sinners?"

[17]On hearing this, Jesus said to them, "It is not the healthy who need a doctor, but the sick. I have not come to call the righteous, but sinners."

[18]Now John's disciples and the Pharisees were fasting. Some people came and asked Jesus, "How is it that John's disciples and the disciples of the Pharisees are fasting, but yours are not?"

[19]Jesus answered, "How can the guests of the bridegroom fast while he is with them? They cannot, so long as they have him with them. [20]But the time will come when the bridegroom will be taken from them, and on that day they will fast.

[21]"No one sews a patch of unshrunk cloth on an old garment.

Otherwise, the new piece will pull away from the old, making the tear worse. <sup>22</sup>And no one pours new wine into old wineskins. Otherwise, the wine will burst the skins, and both the wine and the wineskins will be ruined. No, they pour new wine into new wineskins."

<sup>23</sup>One Sabbath Jesus was going through the grainfields, and as his disciples walked along, they began to pick some heads of grain. <sup>24</sup>The Pharisees said to him, "Look, why are they doing what is unlawful on the Sabbath?"

<sup>25</sup>He answered, "Have you never read what David did when he and his companions were hungry and in need? <sup>26</sup>In the days of Abiathar the high priest, he entered the house of God and ate the consecrated bread, which is lawful only for priests to eat. And he also gave some to his companions."

<sup>27</sup>Then he said to them, "The Sabbath was made for man, not man for the Sabbath. <sup>28</sup>So the Son of Man is Lord even of the Sabbath."

3 Another time Jesus went into the synagogue, and a man with a shriveled hand was there. <sup>2</sup>Some of them were looking for a reason to accuse Jesus, so they watched him closely to see if he would heal him on the Sabbath. <sup>3</sup>Jesus said to the man with the shriveled hand, "Stand up in front of everyone."

<sup>4</sup>Then Jesus asked them, "Which is lawful on the Sabbath: to do good or to do evil, to save life or to kill?" But they remained silent.

<sup>5</sup>He looked around at them in anger and, deeply distressed at their stubborn hearts, said to the man, "Stretch out your hand." He stretched it out, and his hand was completely restored. <sup>6</sup>Then the Pharisees went out and began to plot with the Herodians how they might kill Jesus.

<sup>7</sup>Jesus withdrew with his disciples to the lake, and a large crowd from Galilee followed. <sup>8</sup>When they heard about all he was doing, many people came to him from Judea, Jerusalem, Idumea, and the regions across the Jordan and around Tyre and Sidon. <sup>9</sup>Because of the crowd he told his disciples to have a small boat ready for him, to keep the people from crowding him. <sup>10</sup>For he had healed many, so that those with diseases were pushing forward to touch him. <sup>11</sup>Whenever the impure spirits saw him, they fell down before him and cried out, "You are the Son of God." <sup>12</sup>But he gave them strict orders not to tell others about him.

<sup>13</sup>Jesus went up on a mountainside and called to him those he wanted, and they came to him. <sup>14</sup>He appointed twelve[a] that they might be with him and that he might send them out to preach <sup>15</sup>and to have authority to drive out demons. <sup>16</sup>These are the twelve he appointed: Simon (to whom he gave the name Peter), <sup>17</sup>James son of Zebedee and his brother John (to them he gave the name Boanerges, which means "sons of thunder"), <sup>18</sup>Andrew, Philip, Bartholomew, Matthew, Thomas, James son of Alphaeus, Thaddaeus, Simon the Zealot <sup>19</sup>and Judas Iscariot, who betrayed him.

<sup>20</sup>Then Jesus entered a house, and again a crowd gathered, so that he and his disciples were not even able to eat. <sup>21</sup>When his family[b] heard about this, they went to take charge of him, for they said, "He is out of his mind."

<sup>a</sup> 14 Some manuscripts twelve—designating them apostles—     <sup>b</sup> 21 Or his associates

²²And the teachers of the law who came down from Jerusalem said, "He is possessed by Beelzebul! By the prince of demons he is driving out demons."

²³So Jesus called them over to him and began to speak to them in parables: "How can Satan drive out Satan? ²⁴If a kingdom is divided against itself, that kingdom cannot stand. ²⁵If a house is divided against itself, that house cannot stand. ²⁶And if Satan opposes himself and is divided, he cannot stand; his end has come. ²⁷In fact, no one can enter a strong man's house without first tying him up. Then he can plunder the strong man's house. ²⁸Truly I tell you, people can be forgiven all their sins and every slander they utter, ²⁹but whoever blasphemes against the Holy Spirit will never be forgiven; they are guilty of an eternal sin."

³⁰He said this because they were saying, "He has an impure spirit."

³¹Then Jesus' mother and brothers arrived. Standing outside, they sent someone in to call him. ³²A crowd was sitting around him, and they told him, "Your mother and brothers are outside looking for you."

³³"Who are my mother and my brothers?" he asked.

³⁴Then he looked at those seated in a circle around him and said, "Here are my mother and my brothers! ³⁵Whoever does God's will is my brother and sister and mother."

4 Again Jesus began to teach by the lake. The crowd that gathered around him was so large that he got into a boat and sat in it out on the lake, while all the people were along the shore at the water's edge. ²He taught them many things by

parables, and in his teaching said: ³"Listen! A farmer went out to sow his seed. ⁴As he was scattering the seed, some fell along the path, and the birds came and ate it up. ⁵Some fell on rocky places, where it did not have much soil. It sprang up quickly, because the soil was shallow. ⁶But when the sun came up, the plants were scorched, and they withered because they had no root. ⁷Other seed fell among thorns, which grew up and choked the plants, so that they did not bear grain. ⁸Still other seed fell on good soil. It came up, grew and produced a crop, some multiplying thirty, some sixty, some a hundred times."

⁹Then Jesus said, "Whoever has ears to hear, let them hear."

¹⁰When he was alone, the Twelve and the others around him asked him about the parables. ¹¹He told them, "The secret of the kingdom of God has been given to you. But to those on the outside everything is said in parables ¹²so that,

" 'they may be ever seeing but
        never perceiving,
    and ever hearing but never
        understanding;
    otherwise they might turn and
        be forgiven!' ᵃ"

¹³Then Jesus said to them, "Don't you understand this parable? How then will you understand any parable? ¹⁴The farmer sows the word. ¹⁵Some people are like seed along the path, where the word is sown. As soon as they hear it, Satan comes and takes away the word that was sown in them. ¹⁶Others, like seed sown on rocky places, hear the word and at once receive it with joy. ¹⁷But since they have no root, they last only a short time. When

ᵃ 12 Isaiah 6:9,10

trouble or persecution comes because of the word, they quickly fall away. ¹⁸Still others, like seed sown among thorns, hear the word; ¹⁹but the worries of this life, the deceitfulness of wealth and the desires for other things come in and choke the word, making it unfruitful. ²⁰Others, like seed sown on good soil, hear the word, accept it, and produce a crop—some thirty, some sixty, some a hundred times what was sown."

²¹He said to them, "Do you bring in a lamp to put it under a bowl or a bed? Instead, don't you put it on its stand? ²²For whatever is hidden is meant to be disclosed, and whatever is concealed is meant to be brought out into the open. ²³If anyone has ears to hear, let them hear."

²⁴"Consider carefully what you hear," he continued. "With the measure you use, it will be measured to you—and even more. ²⁵Whoever has will be given more; whoever does not have, even what they have will be taken from them."

²⁶He also said, "This is what the kingdom of God is like. A man scatters seed on the ground. ²⁷Night and day, whether he sleeps or gets up, the seed sprouts and grows, though he does not know how. ²⁸All by itself the soil produces grain—first the stalk, then the head, then the full kernel in the head. ²⁹As soon as the grain is ripe, he puts the sickle to it, because the harvest has come."

³⁰Again he said, "What shall we say the kingdom of God is like, or what parable shall we use to describe it? ³¹It is like a mustard seed, which is the smallest of all seeds on earth. ³²Yet when planted, it grows and becomes the largest of all garden plants, with such big branches that the birds can perch in its shade."

³³With many similar parables Jesus spoke the word to them, as much as they could understand. ³⁴He did not say anything to them without using a parable. But when he was alone with his own disciples, he explained everything.

³⁵That day when evening came, he said to his disciples, "Let us go over to the other side." ³⁶Leaving the crowd behind, they took him along, just as he was, in the boat. There were also other boats with him. ³⁷A furious squall came up, and the waves broke over the boat, so that it was nearly swamped. ³⁸Jesus was in the stern, sleeping on a cushion. The disciples woke him and said to him, "Teacher, don't you care if we drown?"

³⁹He got up, rebuked the wind and said to the waves, "Quiet! Be still!" Then the wind died down and it was completely calm.

⁴⁰He said to his disciples, "Why are you so afraid? Do you still have no faith?"

⁴¹They were terrified and asked each other, "Who is this? Even the wind and the waves obey him!"

5 They went across the lake to the region of the Gerasenes.ᵃ ²When Jesus got out of the boat, a man with an impure spirit came from the tombs to meet him. ³This man lived in the tombs, and no one could bind him anymore, not even with a chain. ⁴For he had often been chained hand and foot, but he tore the chains apart and broke the irons on his feet. No one was strong enough to subdue him. ⁵Night and day among the tombs and in the hills he would cry out and cut himself with stones.

---

ᵃ 1 Some manuscripts Gadarenes; other manuscripts Gergesenes

6When he saw Jesus from a distance, he ran and fell on his knees in front of him. 7He shouted at the top of his voice, "What do you want with me, Jesus, Son of the Most High God? In God's name don't torture me!" 8For Jesus had said to him, "Come out of this man, you impure spirit!"

9Then Jesus asked him, "What is your name?"

"My name is Legion," he replied, "for we are many." 10And he begged Jesus again and again not to send them out of the area.

11A large herd of pigs was feeding on the nearby hillside. 12The demons begged Jesus, "Send us among the pigs; allow us to go into them." 13He gave them permission, and the impure spirits came out and went into the pigs. The herd, about two thousand in number, rushed down the steep bank into the lake and were drowned.

14Those tending the pigs ran off and reported this in the town and countryside, and the people went out to see what had happened. 15When they came to Jesus, they saw the man who had been possessed by the legion of demons, sitting there, dressed and in his right mind; and they were afraid. 16Those who had seen it told the people what had happened to the demon-possessed man — and told about the pigs as well. 17Then the people began to plead with Jesus to leave their region.

18As Jesus was getting into the boat, the man who had been demon-possessed begged to go with him. 19Jesus did not let him, but said, "Go home to your own people and tell them how much the Lord has done for you, and how he has had mercy on you." 20So the man went away and began to tell in the Decapolis*a* how much Jesus had done for him. And all the people were amazed.

21When Jesus had again crossed over by boat to the other side of the lake, a large crowd gathered around him while he was by the lake. 22Then one of the synagogue leaders, named Jairus, came, and when he saw Jesus, he fell at his feet. 23He pleaded earnestly with him, "My little daughter is dying. Please come and put your hands on her so that she will be healed and live." 24So Jesus went with him.

A large crowd followed and pressed around him. 25And a woman was there who had been subject to bleeding for twelve years. 26She had suffered a great deal under the care of many doctors and had spent all she had, yet instead of getting better she grew worse. 27When she heard about Jesus, she came up behind him in the crowd and touched his cloak, 28because she thought, "If I just touch his clothes, I will be healed." 29Immediately her bleeding stopped and she felt in her body that she was freed from her suffering.

30At once Jesus realized that power had gone out from him. He turned around in the crowd and asked, "Who touched my clothes?"

31"You see the people crowding against you," his disciples answered, "and yet you can ask, 'Who touched me?'"

32But Jesus kept looking around to see who had done it. 33Then the woman, knowing what had happened to her, came and fell at his feet and, trembling with fear, told him the whole truth. 34He said

*a* 20 That is, the Ten Cities

to her, "Daughter, your faith has healed you. Go in peace and be freed from your suffering."

³⁵While Jesus was still speaking, some people came from the house of Jairus, the synagogue leader. "Your daughter is dead," they said. "Why bother the teacher anymore?"

³⁶Overhearing[a] what they said, Jesus told him, "Don't be afraid; just believe."

³⁷He did not let anyone follow him except Peter, James and John the brother of James. ³⁸When they came to the home of the synagogue leader, Jesus saw a commotion, with people crying and wailing loudly. ³⁹He went in and said to them, "Why all this commotion and wailing? The child is not dead but asleep." ⁴⁰But they laughed at him.

After he put them all out, he took the child's father and mother and the disciples who were with him, and went in where the child was. ⁴¹He took her by the hand and said to her, *"Talitha koum!"* (which means "Little girl, I say to you, get up!"). ⁴²Immediately the girl stood up and began to walk around (she was twelve years old). At this they were completely astonished. ⁴³He gave strict orders not to let anyone know about this, and told them to give her something to eat.

6 Jesus left there and went to his hometown, accompanied by his disciples. ²When the Sabbath came, he began to teach in the synagogue, and many who heard him were amazed.

"Where did this man get these things?" they asked. "What's this wisdom that has been given him? What are these remarkable miracles he is performing? ³Isn't this the carpenter? Isn't this Mary's son and the brother of James, Joseph,[b] Judas and Simon? Aren't his sisters here with us?" And they took offense at him.

⁴Jesus said to them, "A prophet is not without honor except in his own town, among his relatives and in his own home." ⁵He could not do any miracles there, except lay his hands on a few sick people and heal them. ⁶He was amazed at their lack of faith.

Then Jesus went around teaching from village to village. ⁷Calling the Twelve to him, he began to send them out two by two and gave them authority over impure spirits.

⁸These were his instructions: "Take nothing for the journey except a staff—no bread, no bag, no money in your belts. ⁹Wear sandals but not an extra shirt. ¹⁰Whenever you enter a house, stay there until you leave that town. ¹¹And if any place will not welcome you or listen to you, leave that place and shake the dust off your feet as a testimony against them."

¹²They went out and preached that people should repent. ¹³They drove out many demons and anointed many sick people with oil and healed them.

¹⁴King Herod heard about this, for Jesus' name had become well known. Some were saying,[c] "John the Baptist has been raised from the dead, and that is why miraculous powers are at work in him."

¹⁵Others said, "He is Elijah."

And still others claimed, "He is a prophet, like one of the prophets of long ago."

¹⁶But when Herod heard this, he

---

[a] 36 Or *Ignoring*    [b] 3 Greek *Joses*, a variant of *Joseph*    [c] 14 Some early manuscripts *He was saying*

said, "John, whom I beheaded, has been raised from the dead!"

[17] For Herod himself had given orders to have John arrested, and he had him bound and put in prison. He did this because of Herodias, his brother Philip's wife, whom he had married. [18] For John had been saying to Herod, "It is not lawful for you to have your brother's wife." [19] So Herodias nursed a grudge against John and wanted to kill him. But she was not able to, [20] because Herod feared John and protected him, knowing him to be a righteous and holy man. When Herod heard John, he was greatly puzzled[a]; yet he liked to listen to him.

[21] Finally the opportune time came. On his birthday Herod gave a banquet for his high officials and military commanders and the leading men of Galilee. [22] When the daughter of[b] Herodias came in and danced, she pleased Herod and his dinner guests.

The king said to the girl, "Ask me for anything you want, and I'll give it to you." [23] And he promised her with an oath, "Whatever you ask I will give you, up to half my kingdom."

[24] She went out and said to her mother, "What shall I ask for?"

"The head of John the Baptist," she answered.

[25] At once the girl hurried in to the king with the request: "I want you to give me right now the head of John the Baptist on a platter."

[26] The king was greatly distressed, but because of his oaths and his dinner guests, he did not want to refuse her. [27] So he immediately sent an executioner with orders to bring John's head. The man went, beheaded John in the prison, [28] and brought back his head on a platter. He presented it to the girl, and she gave it to her mother. [29] On hearing of this, John's disciples came and took his body and laid it in a tomb.

[30] The apostles gathered around Jesus and reported to him all they had done and taught. [31] Then, because so many people were coming and going that they did not even have a chance to eat, he said to them, "Come with me by yourselves to a quiet place and get some rest."

[32] So they went away by themselves in a boat to a solitary place. [33] But many who saw them leaving recognized them and ran on foot from all the towns and got there ahead of them. [34] When Jesus landed and saw a large crowd, he had compassion on them, because they were like sheep without a shepherd. So he began teaching them many things.

[35] By this time it was late in the day, so his disciples came to him. "This is a remote place," they said, "and it's already very late. [36] Send the people away so that they can go to the surrounding countryside and villages and buy themselves something to eat."

[37] But he answered, "You give them something to eat."

They said to him, "That would take more than half a year's wages[c]! Are we to go and spend that much on bread and give it to them to eat?"

[38] "How many loaves do you have?" he asked. "Go and see."

When they found out, they said, "Five—and two fish."

[39] Then Jesus directed them to have all the people sit down in groups on the green grass. [40] So they

[a] 20 Some early manuscripts *he did many things*  [b] 22 Some early manuscripts *When his daughter*  [c] 37 Greek *take two hundred denarii*

sat down in groups of hundreds and fifties. [41]Taking the five loaves and the two fish and looking up to heaven, he gave thanks and broke the loaves. Then he gave them to his disciples to distribute to the people. He also divided the two fish among them all. [42]They all ate and were satisfied, [43]and the disciples picked up twelve basketfuls of broken pieces of bread and fish. [44]The number of the men who had eaten was five thousand.

[45]Immediately Jesus made his disciples get into the boat and go on ahead of him to Bethsaida, while he dismissed the crowd. [46]After leaving them, he went up on a mountainside to pray.

[47]Later that night, the boat was in the middle of the lake, and he was alone on land. [48]He saw the disciples straining at the oars, because the wind was against them. Shortly before dawn he went out to them, walking on the lake. He was about to pass by them, [49]but when they saw him walking on the lake, they thought he was a ghost. They cried out, [50]because they all saw him and were terrified.

Immediately he spoke to them and said, "Take courage! It is I. Don't be afraid." [51]Then he climbed into the boat with them, and the wind died down. They were completely amazed, [52]for they had not understood about the loaves; their hearts were hardened.

[53]When they had crossed over, they landed at Gennesaret and anchored there. [54]As soon as they got out of the boat, people recognized Jesus. [55]They ran throughout that whole region and carried the sick on mats to wherever they heard he was.

[56]And wherever he went — into villages, towns or countryside — they placed the sick in the marketplaces. They begged him to let them touch even the edge of his cloak, and all who touched it were healed.

7 The Pharisees and some of the teachers of the law who had come from Jerusalem gathered around Jesus [2]and saw some of his disciples eating food with hands that were defiled, that is, unwashed. [3](The Pharisees and all the Jews do not eat unless they give their hands a ceremonial washing, holding to the tradition of the elders. [4]When they come from the marketplace they do not eat unless they wash. And they observe many other traditions, such as the washing of cups, pitchers and kettles.[a])

[5]So the Pharisees and teachers of the law asked Jesus, "Why don't your disciples live according to the tradition of the elders instead of eating their food with defiled hands?"

[6]He replied, "Isaiah was right when he prophesied about you hypocrites; as it is written:

> "'These people honor me with
>      their lips,
>   but their hearts are far from
>      me.
> [7]They worship me in vain;
>   their teachings are merely
>      human rules.'[b]

[8]You have let go of the commands of God and are holding on to human traditions."

[9]And he continued, "You have a fine way of setting aside the commands of God in order to observe[c] your own traditions! [10]For Moses said, 'Honor your father and mother,'[d] and, 'Anyone who curses their

---

[a] 4 Some early manuscripts *pitchers, kettles and dining couches*    [b] 6,7 Isaiah 29:13    [c] 9 Some manuscripts *set up*    [d] 10 Exodus 20:12; Deut. 5:16

father or mother is to be put to death.[a] 11But you say that if anyone declares that what might have been used to help their father or mother is Corban (that is, devoted to God)— 12then you no longer let them do anything for their father or mother. 13Thus you nullify the word of God by your tradition that you have handed down. And you do many things like that."

14Again Jesus called the crowd to him and said, "Listen to me, everyone, and understand this. 15Nothing outside a person can defile them by going into them. Rather, it is what comes out of a person that defiles them." [16]b

17After he had left the crowd and entered the house, his disciples asked him about this parable. 18"Are you so dull?" he asked. "Don't you see that nothing that enters a person from the outside can defile them? 19For it doesn't go into their heart but into their stomach, and then out of the body." (In saying this, Jesus declared all foods clean.)

20He went on: "What comes out of a person is what defiles them. 21For it is from within, out of a person's heart, that evil thoughts come— sexual immorality, theft, murder, 22adultery, greed, malice, deceit, lewdness, envy, slander, arrogance and folly. 23All these evils come from inside and defile a person."

24Jesus left that place and went to the vicinity of Tyre.c He entered a house and did not want anyone to know it; yet he could not keep his presence secret. 25In fact, as soon as she heard about him, a woman whose little daughter was possessed by an impure spirit came

and fell at his feet. 26The woman was a Greek, born in Syrian Phoenicia. She begged Jesus to drive the demon out of her daughter.

27"First let the children eat all they want," he told her, "for it is not right to take the children's bread and toss it to the dogs."

28"Lord," she replied, "even the dogs under the table eat the children's crumbs."

29Then he told her, "For such a reply, you may go; the demon has left your daughter."

30She went home and found her child lying on the bed, and the demon gone.

31Then Jesus left the vicinity of Tyre and went through Sidon, down to the Sea of Galilee and into the region of the Decapolis.d 32There some people brought to him a man who was deaf and could hardly talk, and they begged Jesus to place his hand on him.

33After he took him aside, away from the crowd, Jesus put his fingers into the man's ears. Then he spit and touched the man's tongue. 34He looked up to heaven and with a deep sigh said to him, *"Ephphatha!"* (which means "Be opened!"). 35At this, the man's ears were opened, his tongue was loosened and he began to speak plainly.

36Jesus commanded them not to tell anyone. But the more he did so, the more they kept talking about it. 37People were overwhelmed with amazement. "He has done everything well," they said. "He even makes the deaf hear and the mute speak."

8 During those days another large crowd gathered. Since they had nothing to eat, Jesus called his

---

a 10 Exodus 21:17; Lev. 20:9    b 16 Some manuscripts include here the words of 4:23.
c 24 Many early manuscripts *Tyre and Sidon*    d 31 That is, the Ten Cities

disciples to him and said, ²"I have compassion for these people; they have already been with me three days and have nothing to eat. ³If I send them home hungry, they will collapse on the way, because some of them have come a long distance."

⁴His disciples answered, "But where in this remote place can anyone get enough bread to feed them?"

⁵"How many loaves do you have?" Jesus asked.

"Seven," they replied.

⁶He told the crowd to sit down on the ground. When he had taken the seven loaves and given thanks, he broke them and gave them to his disciples to distribute to the people, and they did so. ⁷They had a few small fish as well; he gave thanks for them also and told the disciples to distribute them. ⁸The people ate and were satisfied. Afterward the disciples picked up seven basketfuls of broken pieces that were left over. ⁹About four thousand were present. After he had sent them away, ¹⁰he got into the boat with his disciples and went to the region of Dalmanutha.

¹¹The Pharisees came and began to question Jesus. To test him, they asked him for a sign from heaven. ¹²He sighed deeply and said, "Why does this generation ask for a sign? Truly I tell you, no sign will be given to it." ¹³Then he left them, got back into the boat and crossed to the other side.

¹⁴The disciples had forgotten to bring bread, except for one loaf they had with them in the boat. ¹⁵"Be careful," Jesus warned them. "Watch out for the yeast of the Pharisees and that of Herod."

¹⁶They discussed this with one another and said, "It is because we have no bread."

¹⁷Aware of their discussion, Jesus asked them: "Why are you talking about having no bread? Do you still not see or understand? Are your hearts hardened? ¹⁸Do you have eyes but fail to see, and ears but fail to hear? And don't you remember? ¹⁹When I broke the five loaves for the five thousand, how many basketfuls of pieces did you pick up?"

"Twelve," they replied.

²⁰"And when I broke the seven loaves for the four thousand, how many basketfuls of pieces did you pick up?"

They answered, "Seven."

²¹He said to them, "Do you still not understand?"

²²They came to Bethsaida, and some people brought a blind man and begged Jesus to touch him. ²³He took the blind man by the hand and led him outside the village. When he had spit on the man's eyes and put his hands on him, Jesus asked, "Do you see anything?"

²⁴He looked up and said, "I see people; they look like trees walking around."

²⁵Once more Jesus put his hands on the man's eyes. Then his eyes were opened, his sight was restored, and he saw everything clearly. ²⁶Jesus sent him home, saying, "Don't even go into[a] the village."

²⁷Jesus and his disciples went on to the villages around Caesarea Philippi. On the way he asked them, "Who do people say I am?"

²⁸They replied, "Some say John the Baptist; others say Elijah; and still others, one of the prophets."

²⁹"But what about you?" he asked. "Who do you say I am?"

---

ᵃ 26 Some manuscripts *go and tell anyone in*

Peter answered, "You are the Messiah."

30 Jesus warned them not to tell anyone about him.

31 He then began to teach them that the Son of Man must suffer many things and be rejected by the elders, the chief priests and the teachers of the law, and that he must be killed and after three days rise again. 32 He spoke plainly about this, and Peter took him aside and began to rebuke him.

33 But when Jesus turned and looked at his disciples, he rebuked Peter. "Get behind me, Satan!" he said. "You do not have in mind the concerns of God, but merely human concerns."

34 Then he called the crowd to him along with his disciples and said: "Whoever wants to be my disciple must deny themselves and take up their cross and follow me. 35 For whoever wants to save their life[a] will lose it, but whoever loses their life for me and for the gospel will save it. 36 What good is it for someone to gain the whole world, yet forfeit their soul? 37 Or what can anyone give in exchange for their soul? 38 If anyone is ashamed of me and my words in this adulterous and sinful generation, the Son of Man will be ashamed of them when he comes in his Father's glory with the holy angels.

9 And he said to them, "Truly I tell you, some who are standing here will not taste death before they see that the kingdom of God has come with power."

2 After six days Jesus took Peter, James and John with him and led them up a high mountain, where they were all alone. There he was transfigured before them. 3 His clothes became dazzling white, whiter than anyone in the world could bleach them. 4 And there appeared before them Elijah and Moses, who were talking with Jesus.

5 Peter said to Jesus, "Rabbi, it is good for us to be here. Let us put up three shelters — one for you, one for Moses and one for Elijah." 6 (He did not know what to say, they were so frightened.)

7 Then a cloud appeared and covered them, and a voice came from the cloud: "This is my Son, whom I love. Listen to him!"

8 Suddenly, when they looked around, they no longer saw anyone with them except Jesus.

9 As they were coming down the mountain, Jesus gave them orders not to tell anyone what they had seen until the Son of Man had risen from the dead. 10 They kept the matter to themselves, discussing what "rising from the dead" meant.

11 And they asked him, "Why do the teachers of the law say that Elijah must come first?"

12 Jesus replied, "To be sure, Elijah does come first, and restores all things. Why then is it written that the Son of Man must suffer much and be rejected? 13 But I tell you, Elijah has come, and they have done to him everything they wished, just as it is written about him."

14 When they came to the other disciples, they saw a large crowd around them and the teachers of the law arguing with them. 15 As soon as all the people saw Jesus, they were overwhelmed with wonder and ran to greet him.

16 "What are you arguing with them about?" he asked.

17 A man in the crowd answered,

---

a 35 The Greek word means either *life* or *soul*; also in verses 36 and 37.

"Teacher, I brought you my son, who is possessed by a spirit that has robbed him of speech. [18]Whenever it seizes him, it throws him to the ground. He foams at the mouth, gnashes his teeth and becomes rigid. I asked your disciples to drive out the spirit, but they could not."

[19]"You unbelieving generation," Jesus replied, "how long shall I stay with you? How long shall I put up with you? Bring the boy to me."

[20]So they brought him. When the spirit saw Jesus, it immediately threw the boy into a convulsion. He fell to the ground and rolled around, foaming at the mouth.

[21]Jesus asked the boy's father, "How long has he been like this?"

"From childhood," he answered. [22]"It has often thrown him into fire or water to kill him. But if you can do anything, take pity on us and help us."

[23]"'If you can'?" said Jesus. "Everything is possible for one who believes."

[24]Immediately the boy's father exclaimed, "I do believe; help me overcome my unbelief!"

[25]When Jesus saw that a crowd was running to the scene, he rebuked the impure spirit. "You deaf and mute spirit," he said, "I command you, come out of him and never enter him again."

[26]The spirit shrieked, convulsed him violently and came out. The boy looked so much like a corpse that many said, "He's dead." [27]But Jesus took him by the hand and lifted him to his feet, and he stood up.

[28]After Jesus had gone indoors, his disciples asked him privately, "Why couldn't we drive it out?"

[29]He replied, "This kind can come out only by prayer.ᵃ"

[30]They left that place and passed through Galilee. Jesus did not want anyone to know where they were, [31]because he was teaching his disciples. He said to them, "The Son of Man is going to be delivered into the hands of men. They will kill him, and after three days he will rise." [32]But they did not understand what he meant and were afraid to ask him about it.

[33]They came to Capernaum. When he was in the house, he asked them, "What were you arguing about on the road?" [34]But they kept quiet because on the way they had argued about who was the greatest.

[35]Sitting down, Jesus called the Twelve and said, "Anyone who wants to be first must be the very last, and the servant of all."

[36]He took a little child whom he placed among them. Taking the child in his arms, he said to them, [37]"Whoever welcomes one of these little children in my name welcomes me; and whoever welcomes me does not welcome me but the one who sent me."

[38]"Teacher," said John, "we saw someone driving out demons in your name and we told him to stop, because he was not one of us."

[39]"Do not stop him," Jesus said. "For no one who does a miracle in my name can in the next moment say anything bad about me, [40]for whoever is not against us is for us. [41]Truly I tell you, anyone who gives you a cup of water in my name because you belong to the Messiah will certainly not lose their reward.

[42]"If anyone causes one of these little ones—those who believe in me—to stumble, it would be better for them if a large millstone were hung around their neck and

---

ᵃ 29 Some manuscripts *prayer and fasting*

they were thrown into the sea. ⁴³If your hand causes you to stumble, cut it off. It is better for you to enter life maimed than with two hands to go into hell, where the fire never goes out. [⁴⁴]ᵃ ⁴⁵And if your foot causes you to stumble, cut it off. It is better for you to enter life crippled than to have two feet and be thrown into hell. [⁴⁶]ᵃ ⁴⁷And if your eye causes you to stumble, pluck it out. It is better for you to enter the kingdom of God with one eye than to have two eyes and be thrown into hell, ⁴⁸where

" 'the worms that eat them do not die,
   and the fire is not quenched.'ᵇ

⁴⁹Everyone will be salted with fire.

⁵⁰"Salt is good, but if it loses its saltiness, how can you make it salty again? Have salt among yourselves, and be at peace with each other."

**10** Jesus then left that place and went into the region of Judea and across the Jordan. Again crowds of people came to him, and as was his custom, he taught them.

²Some Pharisees came and tested him by asking, "Is it lawful for a man to divorce his wife?"

³"What did Moses command you?" he replied.

⁴They said, "Moses permitted a man to write a certificate of divorce and send her away."

⁵"It was because your hearts were hard that Moses wrote you this law," Jesus replied. ⁶"But at the beginning of creation God 'made them male and female.'ᶜ ⁷'For this reason a man will leave his father and mother and be united to his wife,ᵈ ⁸and the two will become

one flesh.'ᵉ So they are no longer two, but one flesh. ⁹Therefore what God has joined together, let no one separate."

¹⁰When they were in the house again, the disciples asked Jesus about this. ¹¹He answered, "Anyone who divorces his wife and marries another woman commits adultery against her. ¹²And if she divorces her husband and marries another man, she commits adultery."

¹³People were bringing little children to Jesus for him to place his hands on them, but the disciples rebuked them. ¹⁴When Jesus saw this, he was indignant. He said to them, "Let the little children come to me, and do not hinder them, for the kingdom of God belongs to such as these. ¹⁵Truly I tell you, anyone who will not receive the kingdom of God like a little child will never enter it." ¹⁶And he took the children in his arms, placed his hands on them and blessed them.

¹⁷As Jesus started on his way, a man ran up to him and fell on his knees before him. "Good teacher," he asked, "what must I do to inherit eternal life?"

¹⁸"Why do you call me good?" Jesus answered. "No one is good — except God alone. ¹⁹You know the commandments: 'You shall not murder, you shall not commit adultery, you shall not steal, you shall not give false testimony, you shall not defraud, honor your father and mother.'ᶠ"

²⁰"Teacher," he declared, "all these I have kept since I was a boy."

²¹Jesus looked at him and loved him. "One thing you lack," he said. "Go, sell everything you have and

---

ᵃ 44,46 Some manuscripts include here the words of verse 48.    ᵇ 48 Isaiah 66:24    ᶜ 6 Gen.
1:27    ᵈ 7 Some early manuscripts do not have and be united to his wife.    ᵉ 8 Gen. 2:24
ᶠ 19 Exodus 20:12-16; Deut. 5:16-20

give to the poor, and you will have treasure in heaven. Then come, follow me."

²²At this the man's face fell. He went away sad, because he had great wealth.

²³Jesus looked around and said to his disciples, "How hard it is for the rich to enter the kingdom of God!"

²⁴The disciples were amazed at his words. But Jesus said again, "Children, how hard it isᵃ to enter the kingdom of God! ²⁵It is easier for a camel to go through the eye of a needle than for someone who is rich to enter the kingdom of God."

²⁶The disciples were even more amazed, and said to each other, "Who then can be saved?"

²⁷Jesus looked at them and said, "With man this is impossible, but not with God; all things are possible with God."

²⁸Then Peter spoke up, "We have left everything to follow you!"

²⁹"Truly I tell you," Jesus replied, "no one who has left home or brothers or sisters or mother or father or children or fields for me and the gospel ³⁰will fail to receive a hundred times as much in this present age: homes, brothers, sisters, mothers, children and fields — along with persecutions — and in the age to come eternal life. ³¹But many who are first will be last, and the last first."

³²They were on their way up to Jerusalem, with Jesus leading the way, and the disciples were astonished, while those who followed were afraid. Again he took the Twelve aside and told them what was going to happen to him. ³³"We are going up to Jerusalem," he said, "and the Son of Man will be delivered over to the chief priests and the teachers of the law. They will condemn him to death and will hand him over to the Gentiles, ³⁴who will mock him and spit on him, flog him and kill him. Three days later he will rise."

³⁵Then James and John, the sons of Zebedee, came to him. "Teacher," they said, "we want you to do for us whatever we ask."

³⁶"What do you want me to do for you?" he asked.

³⁷They replied, "Let one of us sit at your right and the other at your left in your glory."

³⁸"You don't know what you are asking," Jesus said. "Can you drink the cup I drink or be baptized with the baptism I am baptized with?"

³⁹"We can," they answered.

Jesus said to them, "You will drink the cup I drink and be baptized with the baptism I am baptized with, ⁴⁰but to sit at my right or left is not for me to grant. These places belong to those for whom they have been prepared."

⁴¹When the ten heard about this, they became indignant with James and John. ⁴²Jesus called them together and said, "You know that those who are regarded as rulers of the Gentiles lord it over them, and their high officials exercise authority over them. ⁴³Not so with you. Instead, whoever wants to become great among you must be your servant, ⁴⁴and whoever wants to be first must be slave of all. ⁴⁵For even the Son of Man did not come to be served, but to serve, and to give his life as a ransom for many."

⁴⁶Then they came to Jericho. As Jesus and his disciples, together with a large crowd, were leaving the city, a blind man, Bartimaeus (which means "son of Timaeus"), was sitting by the roadside begging.

ᵃ 24 Some manuscripts *is for those who trust in riches*

⁴⁷When he heard that it was Jesus of Nazareth, he began to shout, "Jesus, Son of David, have mercy on me!"

⁴⁸Many rebuked him and told him to be quiet, but he shouted all the more, "Son of David, have mercy on me!"

⁴⁹Jesus stopped and said, "Call him."

So they called to the blind man, "Cheer up! On your feet! He's calling you." ⁵⁰Throwing his cloak aside, he jumped to his feet and came to Jesus.

⁵¹"What do you want me to do for you?" Jesus asked him.

The blind man said, "Rabbi, I want to see."

⁵²"Go," said Jesus, "your faith has healed you." Immediately he received his sight and followed Jesus along the road.

11 As they approached Jerusalem and came to Bethphage and Bethany at the Mount of Olives, Jesus sent two of his disciples, ²saying to them, "Go to the village ahead of you, and just as you enter it, you will find a colt tied there, which no one has ever ridden. Untie it and bring it here. ³If anyone asks you, 'Why are you doing this?' say, 'The Lord needs it and will send it back here shortly.'"

⁴They went and found a colt outside in the street, tied at a doorway. As they untied it, ⁵some people standing there asked, "What are you doing, untying that colt?" ⁶They answered as Jesus had told them to, and the people let them go. ⁷When they brought the colt to Jesus and threw their cloaks over it, he sat on it. ⁸Many people spread their cloaks on the road, while others spread branches they had cut in the fields. ⁹Those who went ahead and those who followed shouted,

"Hosanna!ᵃ"

"Blessed is he who comes in the name of the Lord!"ᵇ

¹⁰"Blessed is the coming kingdom of our father David!"

"Hosanna in the highest heaven!"

¹¹Jesus entered Jerusalem and went into the temple courts. He looked around at everything, but since it was already late, he went out to Bethany with the Twelve.

¹²The next day as they were leaving Bethany, Jesus was hungry. ¹³Seeing in the distance a fig tree in leaf, he went to find out if it had any fruit. When he reached it, he found nothing but leaves, because it was not the season for figs. ¹⁴Then he said to the tree, "May no one ever eat fruit from you again." And his disciples heard him say it.

¹⁵On reaching Jerusalem, Jesus entered the temple courts and began driving out those who were buying and selling there. He overturned the tables of the money changers and the benches of those selling doves, ¹⁶and would not allow anyone to carry merchandise through the temple courts. ¹⁷And as he taught them, he said, "Is it not written: 'My house will be called a house of prayer for all nations'ᶜ? But you have made it 'a den of robbers.'ᵈ"

¹⁸The chief priests and the teachers of the law heard this and began looking for a way to kill him, for they feared him, because the whole crowd was amazed at his teaching.

---

ᵃ 9 A Hebrew expression meaning "Save!" which became an exclamation of praise; also in verse 10    ᵇ 9 Psalm 118:25,26    ᶜ 17 Isaiah 56:7    ᵈ 17 Jer. 7:11

¹⁹When evening came, Jesus and his disciples[a] went out of the city.

²⁰In the morning, as they went along, they saw the fig tree withered from the roots. ²¹Peter remembered and said to Jesus, "Rabbi, look! The fig tree you cursed has withered!"

²²"Have faith in God," Jesus answered. ²³"Truly[b] I tell you, if anyone says to this mountain, 'Go, throw yourself into the sea,' and does not doubt in their heart but believes that what they say will happen, it will be done for them. ²⁴Therefore I tell you, whatever you ask for in prayer, believe that you have received it, and it will be yours. ²⁵And when you stand praying, if you hold anything against anyone, forgive them, so that your Father in heaven may forgive you your sins." [26][c]

²⁷They arrived again in Jerusalem, and while Jesus was walking in the temple courts, the chief priests, the teachers of the law and the elders came to him. ²⁸"By what authority are you doing these things?" they asked. "And who gave you authority to do this?"

²⁹Jesus replied, "I will ask you one question. Answer me, and I will tell you by what authority I am doing these things. ³⁰John's baptism—was it from heaven, or of human origin? Tell me!"

³¹They discussed it among themselves and said, "If we say, 'From heaven,' he will ask, 'Then why didn't you believe him?' ³²But if we say, 'Of human origin' . . ." (They feared the people, for everyone held that John really was a prophet.)

³³So they answered Jesus, "We don't know."

Jesus said, "Neither will I tell you by what authority I am doing these things."

12 Jesus then began to speak to them in parables: "A man planted a vineyard. He put a wall around it, dug a pit for the winepress and built a watchtower. Then he rented the vineyard to some farmers and moved to another place. ²At harvest time he sent a servant to the tenants to collect from them some of the fruit of the vineyard. ³But they seized him, beat him and sent him away empty-handed. ⁴Then he sent another servant to them; they struck this man on the head and treated him shamefully. ⁵He sent still another, and that one they killed. He sent many others; some of them they beat, others they killed.

⁶"He had one left to send, a son, whom he loved. He sent him last of all, saying, 'They will respect my son.'

⁷"But the tenants said to one another, 'This is the heir. Come, let's kill him, and the inheritance will be ours.' ⁸So they took him and killed him, and threw him out of the vineyard.

⁹"What then will the owner of the vineyard do? He will come and kill those tenants and give the vineyard to others. ¹⁰Haven't you read this passage of Scripture:

"'The stone the builders rejected
    has become the cornerstone;
¹¹ the Lord has done this,
    and it is marvelous in our
        eyes'[d]?"

¹²Then the chief priests, the teachers of the law and the elders looked for a way to arrest him be-

---

[a] 19 Some early manuscripts *came, Jesus in God," Jesus answered,* ²³*"truly*    [b] 22,23 Some early manuscripts *"If you have faith in God," Jesus answered,* ²³*"truly*    [c] 26 Some manuscripts include here words similar to Matt. 6:15.    [d] 11 Psalm 118:22,23

cause they knew he had spoken the parable against them. But they were afraid of the crowd; so they left him and went away.

¹³Later they sent some of the Pharisees and Herodians to Jesus to catch him in his words. ¹⁴They came to him and said, "Teacher, we know that you are a man of integrity. You aren't swayed by others, because you pay no attention to who they are; but you teach the way of God in accordance with the truth. Is it right to pay the imperial tax*ᵃ* to Caesar or not? ¹⁵Should we pay or shouldn't we?"

But Jesus knew their hypocrisy. "Why are you trying to trap me?" he asked. "Bring me a denarius and let me look at it." ¹⁶They brought the coin, and he asked them, "Whose image is this? And whose inscription?"

"Caesar's," they replied.

¹⁷Then Jesus said to them, "Give back to Caesar what is Caesar's and to God what is God's."

And they were amazed at him.

¹⁸Then the Sadducees, who say there is no resurrection, came to him with a question. ¹⁹"Teacher," they said, "Moses wrote for us that if a man's brother dies and leaves a wife but no children, the man must marry the widow and raise up offspring for his brother. ²⁰Now there were seven brothers. The first one married and died without leaving any children. ²¹The second one married the widow, but he also died, leaving no child. It was the same with the third. ²²In fact, none of the seven left any children. Last of all, the woman died too. ²³At the resurrection*ᵇ* whose wife will she

be, since the seven were married to her?"

²⁴Jesus replied, "Are you not in error because you do not know the Scriptures or the power of God? ²⁵When the dead rise, they will neither marry nor be given in marriage; they will be like the angels in heaven. ²⁶Now about the dead rising—have you not read in the Book of Moses, in the account of the burning bush, how God said to him, 'I am the God of Abraham, the God of Isaac, and the God of Jacob'*ᶜ*? ²⁷He is not the God of the dead, but of the living. You are badly mistaken!"

²⁸One of the teachers of the law came and heard them debating. Noticing that Jesus had given them a good answer, he asked him, "Of all the commandments, which is the most important?"

²⁹"The most important one," answered Jesus, "is this: 'Hear, O Israel: The Lord our God, the Lord is one.*ᵈ* ³⁰Love the Lord your God with all your heart and with all your soul and with all your mind and with all your strength.'*ᵉ* ³¹The second is this: 'Love your neighbor as yourself.'*ᶠ* There is no commandment greater than these."

³²"Well said, teacher," the man replied. "You are right in saying that God is one and there is no other but him. ³³To love him with all your heart, with all your understanding and with all your strength, and to love your neighbor as yourself is more important than all burnt offerings and sacrifices."

³⁴When Jesus saw that he had answered wisely, he said to him, "You are not far from the kingdom

---

*ᵃ 14* A special tax levied on subject peoples, not on Roman citizens    *ᵇ 23* Some manuscripts *resurrection, when people rise from the dead,*    *ᶜ 26* Exodus 3:6    *ᵈ 29* Or *The Lord our God is one Lord*    *ᵉ 30* Deut. 6:4,5    *ᶠ 31* Lev. 19:18

of God." And from then on no one dared ask him any more questions.

[35] While Jesus was teaching in the temple courts, he asked, "Why do the teachers of the law say that the Messiah is the son of David? [36] David himself, speaking by the Holy Spirit, declared:

> "'The Lord said to my Lord:
>    "Sit at my right hand
> until I put your enemies
>    under your feet."' [a]

[37] David himself calls him 'Lord.' How then can he be his son?"

The large crowd listened to him with delight.

[38] As he taught, Jesus said, "Watch out for the teachers of the law. They like to walk around in flowing robes and be greeted with respect in the marketplaces, [39] and have the most important seats in the synagogues and the places of honor at banquets. [40] They devour widows' houses and for a show make lengthy prayers. These men will be punished most severely."

[41] Jesus sat down opposite the place where the offerings were put and watched the crowd putting their money into the temple treasury. Many rich people threw in large amounts. [42] But a poor widow came and put in two very small copper coins, worth only a few cents.

[43] Calling his disciples to him, Jesus said, "Truly I tell you, this poor widow has put more into the treasury than all the others. [44] They all gave out of their wealth; but she, out of her poverty, put in everything—all she had to live on."

13 As Jesus was leaving the temple, one of his disciples said to him, "Look, Teacher! What massive stones! What magnificent buildings!"

[2] "Do you see all these great buildings?" replied Jesus. "Not one stone here will be left on another; every one will be thrown down."

[3] As Jesus was sitting on the Mount of Olives opposite the temple, Peter, James, John and Andrew asked him privately, [4] "Tell us, when will these things happen? And what will be the sign that they are all about to be fulfilled?"

[5] Jesus said to them: "Watch out that no one deceives you. [6] Many will come in my name, claiming, 'I am he,' and will deceive many. [7] When you hear of wars and rumors of wars, do not be alarmed. Such things must happen, but the end is still to come. [8] Nation will rise against nation, and kingdom against kingdom. There will be earthquakes in various places, and famines. These are the beginning of birth pains.

[9] "You must be on your guard. You will be handed over to the local councils and flogged in the synagogues. On account of me you will stand before governors and kings as witnesses to them. [10] And the gospel must first be preached to all nations. [11] Whenever you are arrested and brought to trial, do not worry beforehand about what to say. Just say whatever is given you at the time, for it is not you speaking, but the Holy Spirit.

[12] "Brother will betray brother to death, and a father his child. Children will rebel against their parents and have them put to death. [13] Everyone will hate you because of me, but the one who stands firm to the end will be saved.

[14] "When you see 'the abomina-

---

[a] 36 Psalm 110:1

tion that causes desolation'[a] standing where it[b] does not belong—then let the reader understand—then let those who are in Judea flee to the mountains. 15Let no one on the housetop go down or enter the house to take anything out. 16Let no one in the field go back to get their cloak. 17How dreadful it will be in those days for pregnant women and nursing mothers! 18Pray that this will not take place in winter, 19because those will be days of distress unequaled from the beginning, when God created the world, until now—and never to be equaled again.

20"If the Lord had not cut short those days, no one would survive. But for the sake of the elect, whom he has chosen, he has shortened them. 21At that time if anyone says to you, 'Look, here is the Messiah!' or, 'Look, there he is!' do not believe it. 22For false messiahs and false prophets will appear and perform signs and wonders to deceive, if possible, even the elect. 23So be on your guard; I have told you everything ahead of time.

24"But in those days, following that distress,

> "'the sun will be darkened,
>     and the moon will not give its
>         light;
> 25the stars will fall from the sky,
>     and the heavenly bodies will
>         be shaken.'[c]

26"At that time people will see the Son of Man coming in clouds with great power and glory. 27And he will send his angels and gather his elect from the four winds, from the ends of the earth to the ends of the heavens.

28"Now learn this lesson from the fig tree: As soon as its twigs get tender and its leaves come out, you know that summer is near. 29Even so, when you see these things happening, you know that it[b] is near, right at the door. 30Truly I tell you, this generation will certainly not pass away until all these things have happened. 31Heaven and earth will pass away, but my words will never pass away.

32"But about that day or hour no one knows, not even the angels in heaven, nor the Son, but only the Father. 33Be on guard! Be alert[d]! You do not know when that time will come. 34It's like a man going away: He leaves his house and puts his servants in charge, each with their assigned task, and tells the one at the door to keep watch.

35"Therefore keep watch because you do not know when the owner of the house will come back—whether in the evening, or at midnight, or when the rooster crows, or at dawn. 36If he comes suddenly, do not let him find you sleeping. 37What I say to you, I say to everyone: 'Watch!'"

14 Now the Passover and the Festival of Unleavened Bread were only two days away, and the chief priests and the teachers of the law were scheming to arrest Jesus secretly and kill him. 2"But not during the festival," they said, "or the people may riot."

3While he was in Bethany, reclining at the table in the home of Simon the Leper, a woman came with an alabaster jar of very expensive perfume, made of pure nard. She broke the jar and poured the perfume on his head.

---

[a] 14 Daniel 9:27; 11:31; 12:11    [b] 14,29 Or he    [c] 25 Isaiah 13:10; 34:4    [d] 33 Some manuscripts alert and pray

⁴Some of those present were saying indignantly to one another, "Why this waste of perfume? ⁵It could have been sold for more than a year's wages[a] and the money given to the poor." And they rebuked her harshly.

⁶"Leave her alone," said Jesus. "Why are you bothering her? She has done a beautiful thing to me. ⁷The poor you will always have with you,[b] and you can help them any time you want. But you will not always have me. ⁸She did what she could. She poured perfume on my body beforehand to prepare for my burial. ⁹Truly I tell you, wherever the gospel is preached throughout the world, what she has done will also be told, in memory of her."

¹⁰Then Judas Iscariot, one of the Twelve, went to the chief priests to betray Jesus to them. ¹¹They were delighted to hear this and promised to give him money. So he watched for an opportunity to hand him over.

¹²On the first day of the Festival of Unleavened Bread, when it was customary to sacrifice the Passover lamb, Jesus' disciples asked him, "Where do you want us to go and make preparations for you to eat the Passover?"

¹³So he sent two of his disciples, telling them, "Go into the city, and a man carrying a jar of water will meet you. Follow him. ¹⁴Say to the owner of the house he enters, 'The Teacher asks: Where is my guest room, where I may eat the Passover with my disciples?' ¹⁵He will show you a large room upstairs, furnished and ready. Make preparations for us there."

¹⁶The disciples left, went into the city and found things just as Jesus had told them. So they prepared the Passover.

¹⁷When evening came, Jesus arrived with the Twelve. ¹⁸While they were reclining at the table eating, he said, "Truly I tell you, one of you will betray me—one who is eating with me."

¹⁹They were saddened, and one by one they said to him, "Surely you don't mean me?"

²⁰"It is one of the Twelve," he replied, "one who dips bread into the bowl with me. ²¹The Son of Man will go just as it is written about him. But woe to that man who betrays the Son of Man! It would be better for him if he had not been born."

²²While they were eating, Jesus took bread, and when he had given thanks, he broke it and gave it to his disciples, saying, "Take it; this is my body."

²³Then he took a cup, and when he had given thanks, he gave it to them, and they all drank from it.

²⁴"This is my blood of the[c] covenant, which is poured out for many," he said to them. ²⁵"Truly I tell you, I will not drink again from the fruit of the vine until that day when I drink it new in the kingdom of God."

²⁶When they had sung a hymn, they went out to the Mount of Olives.

²⁷"You will all fall away," Jesus told them, "for it is written:

" 'I will strike the shepherd,
    and the sheep will be
      scattered.'[d]

²⁸But after I have risen, I will go ahead of you into Galilee."

²⁹Peter declared, "Even if all fall away, I will not."

---

[a] 5 Greek *than three hundred denarii*   [b] 7 See Deut. 15:11.   [c] 24 Some manuscripts *the new*
[d] 27 Zech. 13:7

30 "Truly I tell you," Jesus answered, "today—yes, tonight—before the rooster crows twice[a] you yourself will disown me three times."

31 But Peter insisted emphatically, "Even if I have to die with you, I will never disown you." And all the others said the same.

32 They went to a place called Gethsemane, and Jesus said to his disciples, "Sit here while I pray." 33 He took Peter, James and John along with him, and he began to be deeply distressed and troubled. 34 "My soul is overwhelmed with sorrow to the point of death," he said to them. "Stay here and keep watch."

35 Going a little farther, he fell to the ground and prayed that if possible the hour might pass from him. 36 "Abba,[b] Father," he said, "everything is possible for you. Take this cup from me. Yet not what I will, but what you will."

37 Then he returned to his disciples and found them sleeping. "Simon," he said to Peter, "are you asleep? Couldn't you keep watch for one hour? 38 Watch and pray so that you will not fall into temptation. The spirit is willing, but the flesh is weak."

39 Once more he went away and prayed the same thing. 40 When he came back, he again found them sleeping, because their eyes were heavy. They did not know what to say to him.

41 Returning the third time, he said to them, "Are you still sleeping and resting? Enough! The hour has come. Look, the Son of Man is delivered into the hands of sinners. 42 Rise! Let us go! Here comes my betrayer!"

43 Just as he was speaking, Judas, one of the Twelve, appeared. With him was a crowd armed with swords and clubs, sent from the chief priests, the teachers of the law, and the elders.

44 Now the betrayer had arranged a signal with them: "The one I kiss is the man; arrest him and lead him away under guard." 45 Going at once to Jesus, Judas said, "Rabbi!" and kissed him. 46 The men seized Jesus and arrested him. 47 Then one of those standing near drew his sword and struck the servant of the high priest, cutting off his ear.

48 "Am I leading a rebellion," said Jesus, "that you have come out with swords and clubs to capture me? 49 Every day I was with you, teaching in the temple courts, and you did not arrest me. But the Scriptures must be fulfilled." 50 Then everyone deserted him and fled.

51 A young man, wearing nothing but a linen garment, was following Jesus. When they seized him, 52 he fled naked, leaving his garment behind.

53 They took Jesus to the high priest, and all the chief priests, the elders and the teachers of the law came together. 54 Peter followed him at a distance, right into the courtyard of the high priest. There he sat with the guards and warmed himself at the fire.

55 The chief priests and the whole Sanhedrin were looking for evidence against Jesus so that they could put him to death, but they did not find any. 56 Many testified falsely against him, but their statements did not agree.

57 Then some stood up and gave this false testimony against him: 58 "We heard him say, 'I will destroy this temple made with human hands and in three days will build another,

---

[a] 30 Some early manuscripts do not have twice.      [b] 36 Aramaic for father

not made with hands.' " <sup>59</sup>Yet even then their testimony did not agree.

<sup>60</sup>Then the high priest stood up before them and asked Jesus, "Are you not going to answer? What is this testimony that these men are bringing against you?" <sup>61</sup>But Jesus remained silent and gave no answer.

Again the high priest asked him, "Are you the Messiah, the Son of the Blessed One?"

<sup>62</sup>"I am," said Jesus. "And you will see the Son of Man sitting at the right hand of the Mighty One and coming on the clouds of heaven."

<sup>63</sup>The high priest tore his clothes. "Why do we need any more witnesses?" he asked. <sup>64</sup>"You have heard the blasphemy. What do you think?"

They all condemned him as worthy of death. <sup>65</sup>Then some began to spit at him; they blindfolded him, struck him with their fists, and said, "Prophesy!" And the guards took him and beat him.

<sup>66</sup>While Peter was below in the courtyard, one of the servant girls of the high priest came by. <sup>67</sup>When she saw Peter warming himself, she looked closely at him.

"You also were with that Nazarene, Jesus," she said.

<sup>68</sup>But he denied it. "I don't know or understand what you're talking about," he said, and went out into the entryway.[a]

<sup>69</sup>When the servant girl saw him there, she said again to those standing around, "This fellow is one of them." <sup>70</sup>Again he denied it.

After a little while, those standing near said to Peter, "Surely you are one of them, for you are a Galilean."

<sup>71</sup>He began to call down curses, and he swore to them, "I don't know this man you're talking about."

<sup>72</sup>Immediately the rooster crowed the second time.[b] Then Peter remembered the word Jesus had spoken to him: "Before the rooster crows twice[c] you will disown me three times." And he broke down and wept.

## 15

Very early in the morning, the chief priests, with the elders, the teachers of the law and the whole Sanhedrin, made their plans. So they bound Jesus, led him away and handed him over to Pilate.

<sup>2</sup>"Are you the king of the Jews?" asked Pilate.

"You have said so," Jesus replied.

<sup>3</sup>The chief priests accused him of many things. <sup>4</sup>So again Pilate asked him, "Aren't you going to answer? See how many things they are accusing you of."

<sup>5</sup>But Jesus still made no reply, and Pilate was amazed.

<sup>6</sup>Now it was the custom at the festival to release a prisoner whom the people requested. <sup>7</sup>A man called Barabbas was in prison with the insurrectionists who had committed murder in the uprising. <sup>8</sup>The crowd came up and asked Pilate to do for them what he usually did.

<sup>9</sup>"Do you want me to release to you the king of the Jews?" asked Pilate, <sup>10</sup>knowing it was out of self-interest that the chief priests had handed Jesus over to him. <sup>11</sup>But the chief priests stirred up the crowd to have Pilate release Barabbas instead.

<sup>12</sup>"What shall I do, then, with the one you call the king of the Jews?" Pilate asked them.

<sup>13</sup>"Crucify him!" they shouted.

<sup>14</sup>"Why? What crime has he committed?" asked Pilate.

But they shouted all the louder, "Crucify him!"

---

<sup>a</sup> 68 Some early manuscripts *entryway and the rooster crowed*     <sup>b</sup> 72 Some early manuscripts do not have *the second time.*     <sup>c</sup> 72 Some early manuscripts do not have *twice.*

¹⁵Wanting to satisfy the crowd, Pilate released Barabbas to them. He had Jesus flogged, and handed him over to be crucified.

¹⁶The soldiers led Jesus away into the palace (that is, the Praetorium) and called together the whole company of soldiers. ¹⁷They put a purple robe on him, then twisted together a crown of thorns and set it on him. ¹⁸And they began to call out to him, "Hail, king of the Jews!" ¹⁹Again and again they struck him on the head with a staff and spit on him. Falling on their knees, they paid homage to him. ²⁰And when they had mocked him, they took off the purple robe and put his own clothes on him. Then they led him out to crucify him.

²¹A certain man from Cyrene, Simon, the father of Alexander and Rufus, was passing by on his way in from the country, and they forced him to carry the cross. ²²They brought Jesus to the place called Golgotha (which means "the place of the skull"). ²³Then they offered him wine mixed with myrrh, but he did not take it. ²⁴And they crucified him. Dividing up his clothes, they cast lots to see what each would get.

²⁵It was nine in the morning when they crucified him. ²⁶The written notice of the charge against him read: THE KING OF THE JEWS.

²⁷They crucified two rebels with him, one on his right and one on his left. [²⁸] ᵃ ²⁹Those who passed by hurled insults at him, shaking their heads and saying, "So! You who are going to destroy the temple and build it in three days, ³⁰come down from the cross and save yourself!" ³¹In the same way the chief priests and the teachers of the law mocked him among themselves. "He saved others," they said, "but he can't save himself! ³²Let this Messiah, this king of Israel, come down now from the cross, that we may see and believe." Those crucified with him also heaped insults on him.

³³At noon, darkness came over the whole land until three in the afternoon. ³⁴And at three in the afternoon Jesus cried out in a loud voice, *"Eloi, Eloi, lema sabachthani?"* (which means "My God, my God, why have you forsaken me?").ᵇ

³⁵When some of those standing near heard this, they said, "Listen, he's calling Elijah."

³⁶Someone ran, filled a sponge with wine vinegar, put it on a staff, and offered it to Jesus to drink. "Now leave him alone. Let's see if Elijah comes to take him down," he said.

³⁷With a loud cry, Jesus breathed his last.

³⁸The curtain of the temple was torn in two from top to bottom. ³⁹And when the centurion, who stood there in front of Jesus, saw how he died,ᶜ he said, "Surely this man was the Son of God!"

⁴⁰Some women were watching from a distance. Among them were Mary Magdalene, Mary the mother of James the younger and of Joseph,ᵈ and Salome. ⁴¹In Galilee these women had followed him and cared for his needs. Many other women who had come up with him to Jerusalem were also there.

⁴²It was Preparation Day (that is, the day before the Sabbath). So as evening approached, ⁴³Joseph of Arimathea, a prominent member of the Council, who was himself waiting

---

ᵃ 28 Some manuscripts include here words similar to Luke 22:37.   ᵇ 34 Psalm 22:1
ᶜ 39 Some manuscripts *saw that he died with such a cry*   ᵈ 40 Greek *Joses*, a variant of *Joseph*; also in verse 47

for the kingdom of God, went boldly to Pilate and asked for Jesus' body. [44]Pilate was surprised to hear that he was already dead. Summoning the centurion, he asked him if Jesus had already died. [45]When he learned from the centurion that it was so, he gave the body to Joseph. [46]So Joseph bought some linen cloth, took down the body, wrapped it in the linen, and placed it in a tomb cut out of rock. Then he rolled a stone against the entrance of the tomb. [47]Mary Magdalene and Mary the mother of Joseph saw where he was laid.

16 When the Sabbath was over, Mary Magdalene, Mary the mother of James, and Salome bought spices so that they might go to anoint Jesus' body. [2]Very early on the first day of the week, just after sunrise, they were on their way to the tomb [3]and they asked each other, "Who will roll the stone away from the entrance of the tomb?"

[4]But when they looked up, they saw that the stone, which was very large, had been rolled away. [5]As they entered the tomb, they saw a young man dressed in a white robe sitting on the right side, and they were alarmed.

[6]"Don't be alarmed," he said. "You are looking for Jesus the Nazarene, who was crucified. He has risen! He is not here. See the place where they laid him. [7]But go, tell his disciples and Peter, 'He is going ahead of you into Galilee. There you will see him, just as he told you.'"

[8]Trembling and bewildered, the women went out and fled from the tomb. They said nothing to anyone, because they were afraid.[a]

[The earliest manuscripts and some other ancient witnesses do not have verses 9–20.]

[9]When Jesus rose early on the first day of the week, he appeared first to Mary Magdalene, out of whom he had driven seven demons. [10]She went and told those who had been with him and who were mourning and weeping. [11]When they heard that Jesus was alive and that she had seen him, they did not believe it.

[12]Afterward Jesus appeared in a different form to two of them while they were walking in the country. [13]These returned and reported it to the rest; but they did not believe them either.

[14]Later Jesus appeared to the Eleven as they were eating; he rebuked them for their lack of faith and their stubborn refusal to believe those who had seen him after he had risen.

[15]He said to them, "Go into all the world and preach the gospel to all creation. [16]Whoever believes and is baptized will be saved, but whoever does not believe will be condemned. [17]And these signs will accompany those who believe: In my name they will drive out demons; they will speak in new tongues; [18]they will pick up snakes with their hands; and when they drink deadly poison, it will not hurt them at all; they will place their hands on sick people, and they will get well."

[19]After the Lord Jesus had spoken to them, he was taken up into heaven and he sat at the right hand of God. [20]Then the disciples went out and preached everywhere, and the Lord worked with them and confirmed his word by the signs that accompanied it.

[a] 8 Some manuscripts have the following ending between verses 8 and 9, and one manuscript has it after verse 8 (omitting verses 9-20): Then they quickly reported all these instructions to those around Peter. After this, Jesus himself also sent out through them from east to west the sacred and imperishable proclamation of eternal salvation. Amen.

# LUKE

The books of Luke and Acts are two volumes of a single work (see p. 148 for a more detailed introduction to Acts). Together they tell the story of how God first invited the people of Israel, and then all nations, to follow Jesus. In the first volume, the movement is toward Jerusalem, the center of Jewish national life. In the second, the movement is from Jerusalem to other nations, closing with Paul proclaiming the kingdom of God in Rome, the capital of the empire.

Luke addresses his history to *most excellent Theophilus*, most likely a Roman official. His volumes are stocked with details from sources Luke had available: letters, speeches, songs, travel accounts, trial transcripts and biographical anecdotes. Luke's purpose is to show the fulfillment of God's plan to bring his light to the world through Israel. The earliest Jesus-followers take up this calling by announcing Jesus' victory over sin and death to all the nations.

The first volume, Luke's telling of the story of Jesus, has three main sections:

: First, Jesus ministers in Galilee, the northern area of the land of Israel.

: Next, he takes a long journey to Jerusalem, during which he welcomes people into the way of God's reign and challenges Israel's current understanding of the kingdom.

: Third, Luke tells how Jesus gives his life in Jerusalem and then rises from the dead to be revealed as Israel's King and the world's true Lord.

---

1 Many have undertaken to draw up an account of the things that have been fulfilled[a] among us, ²just as they were handed down to us by those who from the first were eyewitnesses and servants of the word. ³With this in mind, since I myself have carefully investigated everything from the beginning, I too decided to write an orderly account for you, most excellent Theophilus, ⁴so that you may know the certainty of the things you have been taught.

⁵In the time of Herod king of Judea there was a priest named Zechariah, who belonged to the priestly division of Abijah; his wife Elizabeth was also a descendant of Aaron. ⁶Both of them were righteous in the sight of God, observing all the Lord's commands and decrees blamelessly. ⁷But they were childless because Elizabeth was not able to conceive, and they were both very old.

⁸Once when Zechariah's division was on duty and he was serving as priest before God, ⁹he was chosen by lot, according to the custom of the priesthood, to go into the temple of the Lord and burn incense. ¹⁰And when the time for the burning of incense came, all the assembled worshipers were praying outside.

¹¹Then an angel of the Lord ap-

---

*a 1 Or been surely believed*

peared to him, standing at the right side of the altar of incense. ¹²When Zechariah saw him, he was startled and was gripped with fear. ¹³But the angel said to him: "Do not be afraid, Zechariah; your prayer has been heard. Your wife Elizabeth will bear you a son, and you are to call him John. ¹⁴He will be a joy and delight to you, and many will rejoice because of his birth, ¹⁵for he will be great in the sight of the Lord. He is never to take wine or other fermented drink, and he will be filled with the Holy Spirit even before he is born. ¹⁶He will bring back many of the people of Israel to the Lord their God. ¹⁷And he will go on before the Lord, in the spirit and power of Elijah, to turn the hearts of the parents to their children and the disobedient to the wisdom of the righteous — to make ready a people prepared for the Lord."

¹⁸Zechariah asked the angel, "How can I be sure of this? I am an old man and my wife is well along in years."

¹⁹The angel said to him, "I am Gabriel. I stand in the presence of God, and I have been sent to speak to you and to tell you this good news. ²⁰And now you will be silent and not able to speak until the day this happens, because you did not believe my words, which will come true at their appointed time."

²¹Meanwhile, the people were waiting for Zechariah and wondering why he stayed so long in the temple. ²²When he came out, he could not speak to them. They realized he had seen a vision in the temple, for he kept making signs to them but remained unable to speak.

²³When his time of service was completed, he returned home. ²⁴After this his wife Elizabeth became pregnant and for five months remained in seclusion. ²⁵"The Lord has done this for me," she said. "In these days he has shown his favor and taken away my disgrace among the people."

²⁶In the sixth month of Elizabeth's pregnancy, God sent the angel Gabriel to Nazareth, a town in Galilee, ²⁷to a virgin pledged to be married to a man named Joseph, a descendant of David. The virgin's name was Mary. ²⁸The angel went to her and said, "Greetings, you who are highly favored! The Lord is with you."

²⁹Mary was greatly troubled at his words and wondered what kind of greeting this might be. ³⁰But the angel said to her, "Do not be afraid, Mary; you have found favor with God. ³¹You will conceive and give birth to a son, and you are to call him Jesus. ³²He will be great and will be called the Son of the Most High. The Lord God will give him the throne of his father David, ³³and he will reign over Jacob's descendants forever; his kingdom will never end."

³⁴"How will this be," Mary asked the angel, "since I am a virgin?"

³⁵The angel answered, "The Holy Spirit will come on you, and the power of the Most High will overshadow you. So the holy one to be born will be called*a* the Son of God. ³⁶Even Elizabeth your relative is going to have a child in her old age, and she who was said to be unable to conceive is in her sixth month. ³⁷For no word from God will ever fail."

³⁸"I am the Lord's servant," Mary

---

*a 35* Or *So the child to be born will be called holy,*

answered. "May your word to me be fulfilled." Then the angel left her.

39 At that time Mary got ready and hurried to a town in the hill country of Judea, 40 where she entered Zechariah's home and greeted Elizabeth. 41 When Elizabeth heard Mary's greeting, the baby leaped in her womb, and Elizabeth was filled with the Holy Spirit. 42 In a loud voice she exclaimed: "Blessed are you among women, and blessed is the child you will bear! 43 But why am I so favored, that the mother of my Lord should come to me? 44 As soon as the sound of your greeting reached my ears, the baby in my womb leaped for joy. 45 Blessed is she who has believed that the Lord would fulfill his promises to her!"

46 And Mary said:

"My soul glorifies the Lord
47    and my spirit rejoices in God
          my Savior,
48 for he has been mindful
       of the humble state of his
          servant.
    From now on all generations will
          call me blessed,
49    for the Mighty One has done
          great things for me —
       holy is his name.
50 His mercy extends to those who
       fear him,
    from generation to generation.
51 He has performed mighty deeds
       with his arm;
    he has scattered those who
       are proud in their inmost
       thoughts.
52 He has brought down rulers
       from their thrones
    but has lifted up the humble.
53 He has filled the hungry with
       good things
    but has sent the rich away
       empty.
54 He has helped his servant Israel,

remembering to be merciful
55 to Abraham and his descendants
       forever,
    just as he promised our
       ancestors."

56 Mary stayed with Elizabeth for about three months and then returned home.

57 When it was time for Elizabeth to have her baby, she gave birth to a son. 58 Her neighbors and relatives heard that the Lord had shown her great mercy, and they shared her joy.

59 On the eighth day they came to circumcise the child, and they were going to name him after his father Zechariah, 60 but his mother spoke up and said, "No! He is to be called John."

61 They said to her, "There is no one among your relatives who has that name."

62 Then they made signs to his father, to find out what he would like to name the child. 63 He asked for a writing tablet, and to everyone's astonishment he wrote, "His name is John." 64 Immediately his mouth was opened and his tongue set free, and he began to speak, praising God. 65 All the neighbors were filled with awe, and throughout the hill country of Judea people were talking about all these things. 66 Everyone who heard this wondered about it, asking, "What then is this child going to be?" For the Lord's hand was with him.

67 His father Zechariah was filled with the Holy Spirit and prophesied:

68 "Praise be to the Lord, the God
       of Israel,
    because he has come to his
       people and redeemed
       them.

[69] He has raised up a horn[a] of
       salvation for us
    in the house of his servant
       David
[70] (as he said through his holy
       prophets of long ago),
[71] salvation from our enemies
    and from the hand of all who
       hate us—
[72] to show mercy to our ancestors
    and to remember his holy
       covenant,
[73]    the oath he swore to our father
       Abraham:
[74] to rescue us from the hand of our
       enemies,
    and to enable us to serve him
       without fear
[75]    in holiness and righteousness
       before him all our days.

[76] And you, my child, will be called
       a prophet of the Most High;
    for you will go on before the
       Lord to prepare the way
       for him,
[77] to give his people the knowledge
       of salvation
    through the forgiveness of
       their sins,
[78] because of the tender mercy of
       our God,
    by which the rising sun will
       come to us from heaven
[79] to shine on those living in
       darkness
    and in the shadow of death,
    to guide our feet into the path of
       peace."

[80] And the child grew and became
strong in spirit[b]; and he lived in the
wilderness until he appeared publicly to Israel.

2 In those days Caesar Augustus
  issued a decree that a census

should be taken of the entire Roman world. [2] (This was the first
census that took place while[c] Qui-
rinius was governor of Syria.) [3] And
everyone went to their own town to
register.

[4] So Joseph also went up from
the town of Nazareth in Galilee to
Judea, to Bethlehem the town of
David, because he belonged to the
house and line of David. [5] He went
there to register with Mary, who
was pledged to be married to him
and was expecting a child. [6] While
they were there, the time came for
the baby to be born, [7] and she gave
birth to her firstborn, a son. She
wrapped him in cloths and placed
him in a manger, because there was
no guest room available for them.

[8] And there were shepherds living out in the fields nearby, keeping
watch over their flocks at night. [9] An
angel of the Lord appeared to them,
and the glory of the Lord shone
around them, and they were terrified. [10] But the angel said to them,
"Do not be afraid. I bring you good
news that will cause great joy for
all the people. [11] Today in the town
of David a Savior has been born to
you; he is the Messiah, the Lord.
[12] This will be a sign to you: You will
find a baby wrapped in cloths and
lying in a manger."

[13] Suddenly a great company of
the heavenly host appeared with
the angel, praising God and saying,

[14] "Glory to God in the highest
       heaven,
    and on earth peace to those on
       whom his favor rests."

[15] When the angels had left them
and gone into heaven, the shep-

---

[a] 69 *Horn* here symbolizes a strong king.    [b] 80 Or *in the Spirit*    [c] 2 Or *This census took place before*

herds said to one another, "Let's go to Bethlehem and see this thing that has happened, which the Lord has told us about."

16So they hurried off and found Mary and Joseph, and the baby, who was lying in the manger. 17When they had seen him, they spread the word concerning what had been told them about this child, 18and all who heard it were amazed at what the shepherds said to them. 19But Mary treasured up all these things and pondered them in her heart. 20The shepherds returned, glorifying and praising God for all the things they had heard and seen, which were just as they had been told.

21On the eighth day, when it was time to circumcise the child, he was named Jesus, the name the angel had given him before he was conceived.

22When the time came for the purification rites required by the Law of Moses, Joseph and Mary took him to Jerusalem to present him to the Lord 23(as it is written in the Law of the Lord, "Every firstborn male is to be consecrated to the Lord"a), 24and to offer a sacrifice in keeping with what is said in the Law of the Lord: "a pair of doves or two young pigeons."b

25Now there was a man in Jerusalem called Simeon, who was righteous and devout. He was waiting for the consolation of Israel, and the Holy Spirit was on him. 26It had been revealed to him by the Holy Spirit that he would not die before he had seen the Lord's Messiah. 27Moved by the Spirit, he went into the temple courts. When the parents brought in the child Jesus to do

for him what the custom of the Law required, 28Simeon took him in his arms and praised God, saying:

29 "Sovereign Lord, as you have promised,
  you may now dismissc your servant in peace.
30For my eyes have seen your salvation,
31  which you have prepared in the sight of all nations:
32a light for revelation to the Gentiles,
  and the glory of your people Israel."

33The child's father and mother marveled at what was said about him. 34Then Simeon blessed them and said to Mary, his mother: "This child is destined to cause the falling and rising of many in Israel, and to be a sign that will be spoken against, 35so that the thoughts of many hearts will be revealed. And a sword will pierce your own soul too."

36There was also a prophet, Anna, the daughter of Penuel, of the tribe of Asher. She was very old; she had lived with her husband seven years after her marriage, 37and then was a widow until she was eighty-four.d She never left the temple but worshiped night and day, fasting and praying. 38Coming up to them at that very moment, she gave thanks to God and spoke about the child to all who were looking forward to the redemption of Jerusalem.

39When Joseph and Mary had done everything required by the Law of the Lord, they returned to Galilee to their own town of Nazareth. 40And the child grew and became strong; he was filled with

a 23 Exodus 13:2,12    b 24 Lev. 12:8    c 29 Or promised, / now dismiss    d 37 Or then had been a widow for eighty-four years.

wisdom, and the grace of God was on him.

⁴¹Every year Jesus' parents went to Jerusalem for the Festival of the Passover. ⁴²When he was twelve years old, they went up to the festival, according to the custom. ⁴³After the festival was over, while his parents were returning home, the boy Jesus stayed behind in Jerusalem, but they were unaware of it. ⁴⁴Thinking he was in their company, they traveled on for a day. Then they began looking for him among their relatives and friends. ⁴⁵When they did not find him, they went back to Jerusalem to look for him. ⁴⁶After three days they found him in the temple courts, sitting among the teachers, listening to them and asking them questions. ⁴⁷Everyone who heard him was amazed at his understanding and his answers. ⁴⁸When his parents saw him, they were astonished. His mother said to him, "Son, why have you treated us like this? Your father and I have been anxiously searching for you."

⁴⁹"Why were you searching for me?" he asked. "Didn't you know I had to be in my Father's house?"ᵃ ⁵⁰But they did not understand what he was saying to them.

⁵¹Then he went down to Nazareth with them and was obedient to them. But his mother treasured all these things in her heart. ⁵²And Jesus grew in wisdom and stature, and in favor with God and man.

3 In the fifteenth year of the reign of Tiberius Caesar—when Pontius Pilate was governor of Judea, Herod tetrarch of Galilee, his brother Philip tetrarch of Iturea and Traconitis, and Lysanias tetrarch of Abilene— ²during the high-priesthood of Annas and Caiaphas,

the word of God came to John son of Zechariah in the wilderness. ³He went into all the country around the Jordan, preaching a baptism of repentance for the forgiveness of sins. ⁴As it is written in the book of the words of Isaiah the prophet:

"A voice of one calling in the
    wilderness,
'Prepare the way for the Lord,
    make straight paths for him.
⁵ Every valley shall be filled in,
    every mountain and hill made
        low.
The crooked roads shall become
    straight,
    the rough ways smooth.
⁶ And all people will see God's
    salvation.' "ᵇ

⁷John said to the crowds coming out to be baptized by him, "You brood of vipers! Who warned you to flee from the coming wrath? ⁸Produce fruit in keeping with repentance. And do not begin to say to yourselves, 'We have Abraham as our father.' For I tell you that out of these stones God can raise up children for Abraham. ⁹The ax is already at the root of the trees, and every tree that does not produce good fruit will be cut down and thrown into the fire."

¹⁰"What should we do then?" the crowd asked.

¹¹John answered, "Anyone who has two shirts should share with the one who has none, and anyone who has food should do the same."

¹²Even tax collectors came to be baptized. "Teacher," they asked, "what should we do?"

¹³"Don't collect any more than you are required to," he told them.

¹⁴Then some soldiers asked him, "And what should we do?"

---

ᵃ 49 Or be about my Father's business     ᵇ 6 Isaiah 40:3-5

He replied, "Don't extort money and don't accuse people falsely—be content with your pay."

15The people were waiting expectantly and were all wondering in their hearts if John might possibly be the Messiah. 16John answered them all, "I baptize you with[a] water. But one who is more powerful than I will come, the straps of whose sandals I am not worthy to untie. He will baptize you with[a] the Holy Spirit and fire. 17His winnowing fork is in his hand to clear his threshing floor and to gather the wheat into his barn, but he will burn up the chaff with unquenchable fire." 18And with many other words John exhorted the people and proclaimed the good news to them.

19But when John rebuked Herod the tetrarch because of his marriage to Herodias, his brother's wife, and all the other evil things he had done, 20Herod added this to them all: He locked John up in prison.

21When all the people were being baptized, Jesus was baptized too. And as he was praying, heaven was opened 22and the Holy Spirit descended on him in bodily form like a dove. And a voice came from heaven: "You are my Son, whom I love; with you I am well pleased."

23Now Jesus himself was about thirty years old when he began his ministry. He was the son, so it was thought, of Joseph,

the son of Heli, 24the son of Matthat,

the son of Levi, the son of Melki,

the son of Jannai, the son of Joseph,

25the son of Mattathias, the son of Amos,

the son of Nahum, the son of Esli,

the son of Naggai, 26the son of Maath,

the son of Mattathias, the son of Semein,

the son of Josek, the son of Joda,

27the son of Joanan, the son of Rhesa,

the son of Zerubbabel, the son of Shealtiel,

the son of Neri, 28the son of Melki,

the son of Addi, the son of Cosam,

the son of Elmadam, the son of Er,

29the son of Joshua, the son of Eliezer,

the son of Jorim, the son of Matthat,

the son of Levi, 30the son of Simeon,

the son of Judah, the son of Joseph,

the son of Jonam, the son of Eliakim,

31the son of Melea, the son of Menna,

the son of Mattatha, the son of Nathan,

the son of David, 32the son of Jesse,

the son of Obed, the son of Boaz,

the son of Salmon,[b] the son of Nahshon,

33the son of Amminadab, the son of Ram,[c]

the son of Hezron, the son of Perez,

---

a 16 Or in    b 32 Some early manuscripts Sala of Admin, the son of Arni; other manuscripts vary widely.    c 33 Some manuscripts Amminadab, the son the son of Judah, ³⁴the son of Jacob,

the son of Isaac, the son of Abraham,

the son of Terah, the son of Nahor,

³⁵the son of Serug, the son of Reu,

the son of Peleg, the son of Eber,

the son of Shelah, ³⁶the son of Cainan,

the son of Arphaxad, the son of Shem,

the son of Noah, the son of Lamech,

³⁷the son of Methuselah, the son of Enoch,

the son of Jared, the son of Mahalalel,

the son of Kenan, ³⁸the son of Enosh,

the son of Seth, the son of Adam,

the son of God.

4 Jesus, full of the Holy Spirit, left the Jordan and was led by the Spirit into the wilderness, ²where for forty days he was tempted*a* by the devil. He ate nothing during those days, and at the end of them he was hungry.

³The devil said to him, "If you are the Son of God, tell this stone to become bread."

⁴Jesus answered, "It is written: 'Man shall not live on bread alone.'*b*"

⁵The devil led him up to a high place and showed him in an instant all the kingdoms of the world. ⁶And he said to him, "I will give you all their authority and splendor; it has been given to me, and I can give it to anyone I want

to. ⁷If you worship me, it will all be yours."

⁸Jesus answered, "It is written: 'Worship the Lord your God and serve him only.'*c*"

⁹The devil led him to Jerusalem and had him stand on the highest point of the temple. "If you are the Son of God," he said, "throw yourself down from here. ¹⁰For it is written:

"'He will command his angels concerning you
    to guard you carefully;
¹¹they will lift you up in their hands,
    so that you will not strike your foot against a stone.'*d*"

¹²Jesus answered, "It is said: 'Do not put the Lord your God to the test.'*e*"

¹³When the devil had finished all this tempting, he left him until an opportune time.

¹⁴Jesus returned to Galilee in the power of the Spirit, and news about him spread through the whole countryside. ¹⁵He was teaching in their synagogues, and everyone praised him.

¹⁶He went to Nazareth, where he had been brought up, and on the Sabbath day he went into the synagogue, as was his custom. He stood up to read, ¹⁷and the scroll of the prophet Isaiah was handed to him. Unrolling it, he found the place where it is written:

¹⁸"The Spirit of the Lord is on me, because he has anointed me to proclaim good news to the poor.

---

*a* 2 The Greek for *tempted* can also mean *tested*.    *b* 4 Deut. 8:3    *c* 8 Deut. 6:13
*d* 11 Psalm 91:11,12    *e* 12 Deut. 6:16

He has sent me to proclaim
>> freedom for the prisoners
and recovery of sight for the
>> blind,
to set the oppressed free,
19    to proclaim the year of the
>> Lord's favor."[a]

20Then he rolled up the scroll, gave it back to the attendant and sat down. The eyes of everyone in the synagogue were fastened on him. 21He began by saying to them, "Today this scripture is fulfilled in your hearing."

22All spoke well of him and were amazed at the gracious words that came from his lips. "Isn't this Joseph's son?" they asked.

23Jesus said to them, "Surely you will quote this proverb to me: 'Physician, heal yourself!' And you will tell me, 'Do here in your hometown what we have heard that you did in Capernaum.'"

24"Truly I tell you," he continued, "no prophet is accepted in his hometown. 25I assure you that there were many widows in Israel in Elijah's time, when the sky was shut for three and a half years and there was a severe famine throughout the land. 26Yet Elijah was not sent to any of them, but to a widow in Zarephath in the region of Sidon. 27And there were many in Israel with leprosy[b] in the time of Elisha the prophet, yet not one of them was cleansed—only Naaman the Syrian."

28All the people in the synagogue were furious when they heard this. 29They got up, drove him out of the town, and took him to the brow of the hill on which the town was built, in order to throw him off the cliff. 30But he walked right through the crowd and went on his way.

31Then he went down to Capernaum, a town in Galilee, and on the Sabbath he taught the people. 32They were amazed at his teaching, because his words had authority.

33In the synagogue there was a man possessed by a demon, an impure spirit. He cried out at the top of his voice, 34"Go away! What do you want with us, Jesus of Nazareth? Have you come to destroy us? I know who you are—the Holy One of God!"

35"Be quiet!" Jesus said sternly. "Come out of him!" Then the demon threw the man down before them all and came out without injuring him.

36All the people were amazed and said to each other, "What words these are! With authority and power he gives orders to impure spirits and they come out!" 37And the news about him spread throughout the surrounding area.

38Jesus left the synagogue and went to the home of Simon. Now Simon's mother-in-law was suffering from a high fever, and they asked Jesus to help her. 39So he bent over her and rebuked the fever, and it left her. She got up at once and began to wait on them.

40At sunset, the people brought to Jesus all who had various kinds of sickness, and laying his hands on each one, he healed them. 41Moreover, demons came out of many people, shouting, "You are the Son of God!" But he rebuked them and would not allow them to speak, because they knew he was the Messiah.

---

a 19 Isaiah 61:1,2 (see Septuagint); Isaiah 58:6    b 27 The Greek word traditionally translated *leprosy* was used for various diseases affecting the skin.

42At daybreak, Jesus went out to a solitary place. The people were looking for him and when they came to where he was, they tried to keep him from leaving them. 43But he said, "I must proclaim the good news of the kingdom of God to the other towns also, because that is why I was sent." 44And he kept on preaching in the synagogues of Judea.

5 One day as Jesus was standing by the Lake of Gennesaret,a the people were crowding around him and listening to the word of God. 2He saw at the water's edge two boats, left there by the fishermen, who were washing their nets. 3He got into one of the boats, the one belonging to Simon, and asked him to put out a little from shore. Then he sat down and taught the people from the boat.

4When he had finished speaking, he said to Simon, "Put out into deep water, and let down the nets for a catch."

5Simon answered, "Master, we've worked hard all night and haven't caught anything. But because you say so, I will let down the nets."

6When they had done so, they caught such a large number of fish that their nets began to break. 7So they signaled their partners in the other boat to come and help them, and they came and filled both boats so full that they began to sink.

8When Simon Peter saw this, he fell at Jesus' knees and said, "Go away from me, Lord; I am a sinful man!" 9For he and all his companions were astonished at the catch of fish they had taken, 10and so were James and John, the sons of Zebedee, Simon's partners.

Then Jesus said to Simon, "Don't be afraid; from now on you will fish for people." 11So they pulled their boats up on shore, left everything and followed him.

12While Jesus was in one of the towns, a man came along who was covered with leprosy.b When he saw Jesus, he fell with his face to the ground and begged him, "Lord, if you are willing, you can make me clean."

13Jesus reached out his hand and touched the man. "I am willing," he said. "Be clean!" And immediately the leprosy left him.

14Then Jesus ordered him, "Don't tell anyone, but go, show yourself to the priest and offer the sacrifices that Moses commanded for your cleansing, as a testimony to them."

15Yet the news about him spread all the more, so that crowds of people came to hear him and to be healed of their sicknesses. 16But Jesus often withdrew to lonely places and prayed.

17One day Jesus was teaching, and Pharisees and teachers of the law were sitting there. They had come from every village of Galilee and from Judea and Jerusalem. And the power of the Lord was with Jesus to heal the sick. 18Some men came carrying a paralyzed man on a mat and tried to take him into the house to lay him before Jesus. 19When they could not find a way to do this because of the crowd, they went up on the roof and lowered him on his mat through the tiles into the middle of the crowd, right in front of Jesus.

20When Jesus saw their faith, he said, "Friend, your sins are forgiven."

a 1 That is, the Sea of Galilee   b 12 The Greek word traditionally translated leprosy was used for various diseases affecting the skin.

²¹The Pharisees and the teachers of the law began thinking to themselves, "Who is this fellow who speaks blasphemy? Who can forgive sins but God alone?"

²²Jesus knew what they were thinking and asked, "Why are you thinking these things in your hearts? ²³Which is easier: to say, 'Your sins are forgiven,' or to say, 'Get up and walk'? ²⁴But I want you to know that the Son of Man has authority on earth to forgive sins." So he said to the paralyzed man, "I tell you, get up, take your mat and go home." ²⁵Immediately he stood up in front of them, took what he had been lying on and went home praising God. ²⁶Everyone was amazed and gave praise to God. They were filled with awe and said, "We have seen remarkable things today."

²⁷After this, Jesus went out and saw a tax collector by the name of Levi sitting at his tax booth. "Follow me," Jesus said to him, ²⁸and Levi got up, left everything and followed him.

²⁹Then Levi held a great banquet for Jesus at his house, and a large crowd of tax collectors and others were eating with them. ³⁰But the Pharisees and the teachers of the law who belonged to their sect complained to his disciples, "Why do you eat and drink with tax collectors and sinners?"

³¹Jesus answered them, "It is not the healthy who need a doctor, but the sick. ³²I have not come to call the righteous, but sinners to repentance."

³³They said to him, "John's disciples often fast and pray, and so do the disciples of the Pharisees, but yours go on eating and drinking."

³⁴Jesus answered, "Can you make the friends of the bridegroom fast while he is with them? ³⁵But the time will come when the bridegroom will be taken from them; in those days they will fast."

³⁶He told them this parable: "No one tears a piece out of a new garment to patch an old one. Otherwise, they will have torn the new garment, and the patch from the new will not match the old. ³⁷And no one pours new wine into old wineskins. Otherwise, the new wine will burst the skins; the wine will run out and the wineskins will be ruined. ³⁸No, new wine must be poured into new wineskins. ³⁹And no one after drinking old wine wants the new, for they say, 'The old is better.'"

6 One Sabbath Jesus was going through the grainfields, and his disciples began to pick some heads of grain, rub them in their hands and eat the kernels. ²Some of the Pharisees asked, "Why are you doing what is unlawful on the Sabbath?"

³Jesus answered them, "Have you never read what David did when he and his companions were hungry? ⁴He entered the house of God, and taking the consecrated bread, he ate what is lawful only for priests to eat. And he also gave some to his companions." ⁵Then Jesus said to them, "The Son of Man is Lord of the Sabbath."

⁶On another Sabbath he went into the synagogue and was teaching, and a man was there whose right hand was shriveled. ⁷The Pharisees and the teachers of the law were looking for a reason to accuse Jesus, so they watched him closely to see if he would heal on the Sabbath. ⁸But Jesus knew what they were thinking and said to the man with the shriveled hand, "Get

up and stand in front of everyone." So he got up and stood there.

⁹Then Jesus said to them, "I ask you, which is lawful on the Sabbath: to do good or to do evil, to save life or to destroy it?"

¹⁰He looked around at them all, and then said to the man, "Stretch out your hand." He did so, and his hand was completely restored. ¹¹But the Pharisees and the teachers of the law were furious and began to discuss with one another what they might do to Jesus.

¹²One of those days Jesus went out to a mountainside to pray, and spent the night praying to God. ¹³When morning came, he called his disciples to him and chose twelve of them, whom he also designated apostles: ¹⁴Simon (whom he named Peter), his brother Andrew, James, John, Philip, Bartholomew, ¹⁵Matthew, Thomas, James son of Alphaeus, Simon who was called the Zealot, ¹⁶Judas son of James, and Judas Iscariot, who became a traitor.

¹⁷He went down with them and stood on a level place. A large crowd of his disciples was there and a great number of people from all over Judea, from Jerusalem, and from the coastal region around Tyre and Sidon, ¹⁸who had come to hear him and to be healed of their diseases. Those troubled by impure spirits were cured, ¹⁹and the people all tried to touch him, because power was coming from him and healing them all.

²⁰Looking at his disciples, he said:

"Blessed are you who are poor,
    for yours is the kingdom of
        God.
²¹Blessed are you who hunger
    now,
        for you will be satisfied.
Blessed are you who weep now,
    for you will laugh.
²²Blessed are you when people
    hate you,
    when they exclude you and
        insult you
    and reject your name as evil,
        because of the Son of Man.

²³"Rejoice in that day and leap for joy, because great is your reward in heaven. For that is how their ancestors treated the prophets.

²⁴"But woe to you who are rich,
    for you have already received
        your comfort.
²⁵Woe to you who are well fed now,
    for you will go hungry.
Woe to you who laugh now,
    for you will mourn and weep.
²⁶Woe to you when everyone
        speaks well of you,
    for that is how their ancestors
        treated the false prophets.

²⁷"But to you who are listening I say: Love your enemies, do good to those who hate you, ²⁸bless those who curse you, pray for those who mistreat you. ²⁹If someone slaps you on one cheek, turn to them the other also. If someone takes your coat, do not withhold your shirt from them. ³⁰Give to everyone who asks you, and if anyone takes what belongs to you, do not demand it back. ³¹Do to others as you would have them do to you.

³²"If you love those who love you, what credit is that to you? Even sinners love those who love them. ³³And if you do good to those who are good to you, what credit is that to you? Even sinners do that. ³⁴And if you lend to those from whom you expect repayment, what credit is that to you? Even sinners lend to sinners, expecting to be repaid in

full. 35But love your enemies, do good to them, and lend to them without expecting to get anything back. Then your reward will be great, and you will be children of the Most High, because he is kind to the ungrateful and wicked. 36Be merciful, just as your Father is merciful.

37"Do not judge, and you will not be judged. Do not condemn, and you will not be condemned. Forgive, and you will be forgiven. 38Give, and it will be given to you. A good measure, pressed down, shaken together and running over, will be poured into your lap. For with the measure you use, it will be measured to you."

39He also told them this parable: "Can the blind lead the blind? Will they not both fall into a pit? 40The student is not above the teacher, but everyone who is fully trained will be like their teacher.

41"Why do you look at the speck of sawdust in your brother's eye and pay no attention to the plank in your own eye? 42How can you say to your brother, 'Brother, let me take the speck out of your eye,' when you yourself fail to see the plank in your own eye? You hypocrite, first take the plank out of your eye, and then you will see clearly to remove the speck from your brother's eye.

43"No good tree bears bad fruit, nor does a bad tree bear good fruit. 44Each tree is recognized by its own fruit. People do not pick figs from thornbushes, or grapes from briers. 45A good man brings good things out of the good stored up in his heart, and an evil man brings evil things out of the evil stored up in his heart. For the mouth speaks what the heart is full of.

46"Why do you call me, 'Lord, Lord,' and do not do what I say? 47As for everyone who comes to me and hears my words and puts them into practice, I will show you what they are like. 48They are like a man building a house, who dug down deep and laid the foundation on rock. When a flood came, the torrent struck that house but could not shake it, because it was well built. 49But the one who hears my words and does not put them into practice is like a man who built a house on the ground without a foundation. The moment the torrent struck that house, it collapsed and its destruction was complete."

7 When Jesus had finished saying all this to the people who were listening, he entered Capernaum. 2There a centurion's servant, whom his master valued highly, was sick and about to die. 3The centurion heard of Jesus and sent some elders of the Jews to him, asking him to come and heal his servant. 4When they came to Jesus, they pleaded earnestly with him, "This man deserves to have you do this, 5because he loves our nation and has built our synagogue." 6So Jesus went with them.

He was not far from the house when the centurion sent friends to say to him: "Lord, don't trouble yourself, for I do not deserve to have you come under my roof. 7That is why I did not even consider myself worthy to come to you. But say the word, and my servant will be healed. 8For I myself am a man under authority, with soldiers under me. I tell this one, 'Go,' and he goes; and that one, 'Come,' and he comes. I say to my servant, 'Do this,' and he does it."

9When Jesus heard this, he was amazed at him, and turning to the crowd following him, he said, "I tell you, I have not found such great faith even in Israel." ¹⁰Then the men who had been sent returned to the house and found the servant well.

¹¹Soon afterward, Jesus went to a town called Nain, and his disciples and a large crowd went along with him. ¹²As he approached the town gate, a dead person was being carried out—the only son of his mother, and she was a widow. And a large crowd from the town was with her. ¹³When the Lord saw her, his heart went out to her and he said, "Don't cry."

¹⁴Then he went up and touched the bier they were carrying him on, and the bearers stood still. He said, "Young man, I say to you, get up!" ¹⁵The dead man sat up and began to talk, and Jesus gave him back to his mother.

¹⁶They were all filled with awe and praised God. "A great prophet has appeared among us," they said. "God has come to help his people." ¹⁷This news about Jesus spread throughout Judea and the surrounding country.

¹⁸John's disciples told him about all these things. Calling two of them, ¹⁹he sent them to the Lord to ask, "Are you the one who is to come, or should we expect someone else?"

²⁰When the men came to Jesus, they said, "John the Baptist sent us to you to ask, 'Are you the one who is to come, or should we expect someone else?'"

²¹At that very time Jesus cured many who had diseases, sicknesses and evil spirits, and gave sight to many who were blind. ²²So he replied to the messengers, "Go back and report to John what you have seen and heard: The blind receive sight, the lame walk, those who have leprosy[a] are cleansed, the deaf hear, the dead are raised, and the good news is proclaimed to the poor. ²³Blessed is anyone who does not stumble on account of me."

²⁴After John's messengers left, Jesus began to speak to the crowd about John: "What did you go out into the wilderness to see? A reed swayed by the wind? ²⁵If not, what did you go out to see? A man dressed in fine clothes? No, those who wear expensive clothes and indulge in luxury are in palaces. ²⁶But what did you go out to see? A prophet? Yes, I tell you, and more than a prophet. ²⁷This is the one about whom it is written:

" 'I will send my messenger
    ahead of you,
  who will prepare your way
    before you.'[b]

²⁸I tell you, among those born of women there is no one greater than John; yet the one who is least in the kingdom of God is greater than he."

²⁹(All the people, even the tax collectors, when they heard Jesus' words, acknowledged that God's way was right, because they had been baptized by John. ³⁰But the Pharisees and the experts in the law rejected God's purpose for themselves, because they had not been baptized by John.)

³¹Jesus went on to say, "To what, then, can I compare the people of this generation? What are they like? ³²They are like children sitting in

<hr>

a 22 The Greek word traditionally translated *leprosy* was used for various diseases affecting the skin.  b 27 Mal. 3:1

the marketplace and calling out to each other:

"'We played the pipe for you,
    and you did not dance;
we sang a dirge,
    and you did not cry.'

33For John the Baptist came neither eating bread nor drinking wine, and you say, 'He has a demon.' 34The Son of Man came eating and drinking, and you say, 'Here is a glutton and a drunkard, a friend of tax collectors and sinners.' 35But wisdom is proved right by all her children."

36When one of the Pharisees invited Jesus to have dinner with him, he went to the Pharisee's house and reclined at the table. 37A woman in that town who lived a sinful life learned that Jesus was eating at the Pharisee's house, so she came there with an alabaster jar of perfume. 38As she stood behind him at his feet weeping, she began to wet his feet with her tears. Then she wiped them with her hair, kissed them and poured perfume on them.

39When the Pharisee who had invited him saw this, he said to himself, "If this man were a prophet, he would know who is touching him and what kind of woman she is—that she is a sinner."

40Jesus answered him, "Simon, I have something to tell you."

"Tell me, teacher," he said.

41"Two people owed money to a certain moneylender. One owed him five hundred denarii,a and the other fifty. 42Neither of them had the money to pay him back, so he forgave the debts of both. Now which of them will love him more?"

43Simon replied, "I suppose the one who had the bigger debt forgiven."

"You have judged correctly," Jesus said.

44Then he turned toward the woman and said to Simon, "Do you see this woman? I came into your house. You did not give me any water for my feet, but she wet my feet with her tears and wiped them with her hair. 45You did not give me a kiss, but this woman, from the time I entered, has not stopped kissing my feet. 46You did not put oil on my head, but she has poured perfume on my feet. 47Therefore, I tell you, her many sins have been forgiven—as her great love has shown. But whoever has been forgiven little loves little."

48Then Jesus said to her, "Your sins are forgiven."

49The other guests began to say among themselves, "Who is this who even forgives sins?"

50Jesus said to the woman, "Your faith has saved you; go in peace."

8 After this, Jesus traveled about from one town and village to another, proclaiming the good news of the kingdom of God. The Twelve were with him, 2and also some women who had been cured of evil spirits and diseases: Mary (called Magdalene) from whom seven demons had come out; 3Joanna the wife of Chuza, the manager of Herod's household; Susanna; and many others. These women were helping to support them out of their own means.

4While a large crowd was gathering and people were coming to Jesus from town after town, he told this parable: 5"A farmer went out to sow his seed. As he was scattering the seed, some fell along the path; it

---

a 41 A denarius was the usual daily wage of a day laborer (see Matt. 20:2).

was trampled on, and the birds ate it up. [6]Some fell on rocky ground, and when it came up, the plants withered because they had no moisture. [7]Other seed fell among thorns, which grew up with it and choked the plants. [8]Still other seed fell on good soil. It came up and yielded a crop, a hundred times more than was sown."

When he said this, he called out, "Whoever has ears to hear, let them hear."

[9]His disciples asked him what this parable meant. [10]He said, "The knowledge of the secrets of the kingdom of God has been given to you, but to others I speak in parables, so that,

> " 'though seeing, they may not
> see;
> though hearing, they may not
> understand.'[a]

[11]"This is the meaning of the parable: The seed is the word of God. [12]Those along the path are the ones who hear, and then the devil comes and takes away the word from their hearts, so that they may not believe and be saved. [13]Those on the rocky ground are the ones who receive the word with joy when they hear it, but they have no root. They believe for a while, but in the time of testing they fall away. [14]The seed that fell among thorns stands for those who hear, but as they go on their way they are choked by life's worries, riches and pleasures, and they do not mature. [15]But the seed on good soil stands for those with a noble and good heart, who hear the word, retain it, and by persevering produce a crop.

[16]"No one lights a lamp and hides it in a clay jar or puts it under a bed. Instead, they put it on a stand, so that those who come in can see the light. [17]For there is nothing hidden that will not be disclosed, and nothing concealed that will not be known or brought out into the open. [18]Therefore consider carefully how you listen. Whoever has will be given more; whoever does not have, even what they think they have will be taken from them."

[19]Now Jesus' mother and brothers came to see him, but they were not able to get near him because of the crowd. [20]Someone told him, "Your mother and brothers are standing outside, wanting to see you."

[21]He replied, "My mother and brothers are those who hear God's word and put it into practice."

[22]One day Jesus said to his disciples, "Let us go over to the other side of the lake." So they got into a boat and set out. [23]As they sailed, he fell asleep. A squall came down on the lake, so that the boat was being swamped, and they were in great danger.

[24]The disciples went and woke him, saying, "Master, Master, we're going to drown!"

He got up and rebuked the wind and the raging waters; the storm subsided, and all was calm. [25]"Where is your faith?" he asked his disciples.

In fear and amazement they asked one another, "Who is this? He commands even the winds and the water, and they obey him."

[26]They sailed to the region of the Gerasenes,[b] which is across the lake from Galilee. [27]When Jesus stepped ashore, he was met by a demon-possessed man from the

---

[a] 10 Isaiah 6:9    [b] 26 Some manuscripts *Gadarenes*; other manuscripts *Gergesenes*; also in verse 37

town. For a long time this man had not worn clothes or lived in a house, but had lived in the tombs. ²⁸When he saw Jesus, he cried out and fell at his feet, shouting at the top of his voice, "What do you want with me, Jesus, Son of the Most High God? I beg you, don't torture me!" ²⁹For Jesus had commanded the impure spirit to come out of the man. Many times it had seized him, and though he was chained hand and foot and kept under guard, he had broken his chains and had been driven by the demon into solitary places.

³⁰Jesus asked him, "What is your name?"

"Legion," he replied, because many demons had gone into him. ³¹And they begged Jesus repeatedly not to order them to go into the Abyss.

³²A large herd of pigs was feeding there on the hillside. The demons begged Jesus to let them go into the pigs, and he gave them permission. ³³When the demons came out of the man, they went into the pigs, and the herd rushed down the steep bank into the lake and was drowned.

³⁴When those tending the pigs saw what had happened, they ran off and reported this in the town and countryside, ³⁵and the people went out to see what had happened. When they came to Jesus, they found the man from whom the demons had gone out, sitting at Jesus' feet, dressed and in his right mind; and they were afraid. ³⁶Those who had seen it told the people how the demon-possessed man had been cured. ³⁷Then all the people of the region of the Gerasenes asked Jesus to leave them, because they were overcome with fear. So he got into the boat and left.

³⁸The man from whom the demons had gone out begged to go with him, but Jesus sent him away, saying, ³⁹"Return home and tell how much God has done for you." So the man went away and told all over town how much Jesus had done for him.

⁴⁰Now when Jesus returned, a crowd welcomed him, for they were all expecting him. ⁴¹Then a man named Jairus, a synagogue leader, came and fell at Jesus' feet, pleading with him to come to his house ⁴²because his only daughter, a girl of about twelve, was dying.

As Jesus was on his way, the crowds almost crushed him. ⁴³And a woman was there who had been subject to bleeding for twelve years,ᵃ but no one could heal her. ⁴⁴She came up behind him and touched the edge of his cloak, and immediately her bleeding stopped.

⁴⁵"Who touched me?" Jesus asked.

When they all denied it, Peter said, "Master, the people are crowding and pressing against you."

⁴⁶But Jesus said, "Someone touched me; I know that power has gone out from me."

⁴⁷Then the woman, seeing that she could not go unnoticed, came trembling and fell at his feet. In the presence of all the people, she told why she had touched him and how she had been instantly healed. ⁴⁸Then he said to her, "Daughter, your faith has healed you. Go in peace."

⁴⁹While Jesus was still speaking, someone came from the house of Jairus, the synagogue leader. "Your

ᵃ 43 Many manuscripts *years, and she had spent all she had on doctors* daughter is dead," he said. "Don't bother the teacher anymore."

50 Hearing this, Jesus said to Jairus, "Don't be afraid; just believe, and she will be healed."

51 When he arrived at the house of Jairus, he did not let anyone go in with him except Peter, John and James, and the child's father and mother. 52 Meanwhile, all the people were wailing and mourning for her. "Stop wailing," Jesus said. "She is not dead but asleep."

53 They laughed at him, knowing that she was dead. 54 But he took her by the hand and said, "My child, get up!" 55 Her spirit returned, and at once she stood up. Then Jesus told them to give her something to eat. 56 Her parents were astonished, but he ordered them not to tell anyone what had happened.

9 When Jesus had called the Twelve together, he gave them power and authority to drive out all demons and to cure diseases, 2 and he sent them out to proclaim the kingdom of God and to heal the sick. 3 He told them: "Take nothing for the journey—no staff, no bag, no bread, no money, no extra shirt. 4 Whatever house you enter, stay there until you leave that town. 5 If people do not welcome you, leave their town and shake the dust off your feet as a testimony against them." 6 So they set out and went from village to village, proclaiming the good news and healing people everywhere.

7 Now Herod the tetrarch heard about all that was going on. And he was perplexed because some were saying that John had been raised from the dead, 8 others that Elijah had appeared, and still others that one of the prophets of long ago had come back to life. 9 But Herod said,

"I beheaded John. Who, then, is this I hear such things about?" And he tried to see him.

10 When the apostles returned, they reported to Jesus what they had done. Then he took them with him and they withdrew by themselves to a town called Bethsaida, 11 but the crowds learned about it and followed him. He welcomed them and spoke to them about the kingdom of God, and healed those who needed healing.

12 Late in the afternoon the Twelve came to him and said, "Send the crowd away so they can go to the surrounding villages and countryside and find food and lodging, because we are in a remote place here."

13 He replied, "You give them something to eat."

They answered, "We have only five loaves of bread and two fish—unless we go and buy food for all this crowd." 14 (About five thousand men were there.)

But he said to his disciples, "Have them sit down in groups of about fifty each." 15 The disciples did so, and everyone sat down. 16 Taking the five loaves and the two fish and looking up to heaven, he gave thanks and broke them. Then he gave them to the disciples to distribute to the people. 17 They all ate and were satisfied, and the disciples picked up twelve basketfuls of broken pieces that were left over.

18 Once when Jesus was praying in private and his disciples were with him, he asked them, "Who do the crowds say I am?"

19 They replied, "Some say John the Baptist; others say Elijah; and still others, that one of the prophets of long ago has come back to life."

20 "But what about you?" he asked. "Who do you say I am?"

Peter answered, "God's Messiah."

21 Jesus strictly warned them not to tell this to anyone. 22 And he said, "The Son of Man must suffer many things and be rejected by the elders, the chief priests and the teachers of the law, and he must be killed and on the third day be raised to life."

23 Then he said to them all: "Whoever wants to be my disciple must deny themselves and take up their cross daily and follow me. 24 For whoever wants to save their life will lose it, but whoever loses their life for me will save it. 25 What good is it for someone to gain the whole world, and yet lose or forfeit their very self? 26 Whoever is ashamed of me and my words, the Son of Man will be ashamed of them when he comes in his glory and in the glory of the Father and of the holy angels.

27 "Truly I tell you, some who are standing here will not taste death before they see the kingdom of God."

28 About eight days after Jesus said this, he took Peter, John and James with him and went up onto a mountain to pray. 29 As he was praying, the appearance of his face changed, and his clothes became as bright as a flash of lightning. 30 Two men, Moses and Elijah, appeared in glorious splendor, talking with Jesus. 31 They spoke about his departure,a which he was about to bring to fulfillment at Jerusalem. 32 Peter and his companions were very sleepy, but when they became fully awake, they saw his glory and the two men standing with him. 33 As the men were leaving Jesus,

Peter said to him, "Master, it is good for us to be here. Let us put up three shelters — one for you, one for Moses and one for Elijah." (He did not know what he was saying.)

34 While he was speaking, a cloud appeared and covered them, and they were afraid as they entered the cloud. 35 A voice came from the cloud, saying, "This is my Son, whom I have chosen; listen to him." 36 When the voice had spoken, they found that Jesus was alone. The disciples kept this to themselves and did not tell anyone at that time what they had seen.

37 The next day, when they came down from the mountain, a large crowd met him. 38 A man in the crowd called out, "Teacher, I beg you to look at my son, for he is my only child. 39 A spirit seizes him and he suddenly screams; it throws him into convulsions so that he foams at the mouth. It scarcely ever leaves him and is destroying him. 40 I begged your disciples to drive it out, but they could not."

41 "You unbelieving and perverse generation," Jesus replied, "how long shall I stay with you and put up with you? Bring your son here."

42 Even while the boy was coming, the demon threw him to the ground in a convulsion. But Jesus rebuked the impure spirit, healed the boy and gave him back to his father. 43 And they were all amazed at the greatness of God.

While everyone was marveling at all that Jesus did, he said to his disciples, 44 "Listen carefully to what I am about to tell you: The Son of Man is going to be delivered into the hands of men." 45 But they did not understand what this meant. It was hidden from them, so that

a 31 Greek exodus

they did not grasp it, and they were afraid to ask him about it.

⁴⁶An argument started among the disciples as to which of them would be the greatest. ⁴⁷Jesus, knowing their thoughts, took a little child and had him stand beside him. ⁴⁸Then he said to them, "Whoever welcomes this little child in my name welcomes me; and whoever welcomes me welcomes the one who sent me. For it is the one who is least among you all who is the greatest."

⁴⁹"Master," said John, "we saw someone driving out demons in your name and we tried to stop him, because he is not one of us."

⁵⁰"Do not stop him," Jesus said, "for whoever is not against you is for you."

⁵¹As the time approached for him to be taken up to heaven, Jesus resolutely set out for Jerusalem. ⁵²And he sent messengers on ahead, who went into a Samaritan village to get things ready for him; ⁵³but the people there did not welcome him, because he was heading for Jerusalem. ⁵⁴When the disciples James and John saw this, they asked, "Lord, do you want us to call fire down from heaven to destroy them*a*?" ⁵⁵But Jesus turned and rebuked them. ⁵⁶Then he and his disciples went to another village.

⁵⁷As they were walking along the road, a man said to him, "I will follow you wherever you go."

⁵⁸Jesus replied, "Foxes have dens and birds have nests, but the Son of Man has no place to lay his head."

⁵⁹He said to another man, "Follow me."

But he replied, "Lord, first let me go and bury my father."

⁶⁰Jesus said to him, "Let the dead bury their own dead, but you go and proclaim the kingdom of God."

⁶¹Still another said, "I will follow you, Lord; but first let me go back and say goodbye to my family."

⁶²Jesus replied, "No one who puts a hand to the plow and looks back is fit for service in the kingdom of God."

10 After this the Lord appointed seventy-two*b* others and sent them two by two ahead of him to every town and place where he was about to go. ²He told them, "The harvest is plentiful, but the workers are few. Ask the Lord of the harvest, therefore, to send out workers into his harvest field. ³Go! I am sending you out like lambs among wolves. ⁴Do not take a purse or bag or sandals; and do not greet anyone on the road.

⁵"When you enter a house, first say, 'Peace to this house.' ⁶If someone who promotes peace is there, your peace will rest on them; if not, it will return to you. ⁷Stay there, eating and drinking whatever they give you, for the worker deserves his wages. Do not move around from house to house.

⁸"When you enter a town and are welcomed, eat what is offered to you. ⁹Heal the sick who are there and tell them, 'The kingdom of God has come near to you.' ¹⁰But when you enter a town and are not welcomed, go into its streets and say, ¹¹'Even the dust of your town we wipe from our feet as a warning to you. Yet be sure of this: the kingdom of God has come near.' ¹²I tell you, it will be more bearable on that day for Sodom than for that town.

¹³"Woe to you, Chorazin! Woe to

*a 54* Some manuscripts *them, just as Elijah did*     *b 1* Some manuscripts *seventy*; also in verse 17 you, Bethsaida! For if the miracles that were performed in you had been performed in Tyre and Sidon, they would have repented long ago, sitting in sackcloth and ashes. [14] But it will be more bearable for Tyre and Sidon at the judgment than for you. [15] And you, Capernaum, will you be lifted to the heavens? No, you will go down to Hades.[a]

[16] "Whoever listens to you listens to me; whoever rejects you rejects me; but whoever rejects me rejects him who sent me."

[17] The seventy-two returned with joy and said, "Lord, even the demons submit to us in your name."

[18] He replied, "I saw Satan fall like lightning from heaven. [19] I have given you authority to trample on snakes and scorpions and to overcome all the power of the enemy; nothing will harm you. [20] However, do not rejoice that the spirits submit to you, but rejoice that your names are written in heaven."

[21] At that time Jesus, full of joy through the Holy Spirit, said, "I praise you, Father, Lord of heaven and earth, because you have hidden these things from the wise and learned, and revealed them to little children. Yes, Father, for this is what you were pleased to do.

[22] "All things have been committed to me by my Father. No one knows who the Son is except the Father, and no one knows who the Father is except the Son and those to whom the Son chooses to reveal him."

[23] Then he turned to his disciples and said privately, "Blessed are the eyes that see what you see. [24] For I tell you that many prophets and kings wanted to see what you see

but did not see it, and to hear what you hear but did not hear it."

[25] On one occasion an expert in the law stood up to test Jesus. "Teacher," he asked, "what must I do to inherit eternal life?"

[26] "What is written in the Law?" he replied. "How do you read it?"

[27] He answered, " 'Love the Lord your God with all your heart and with all your soul and with all your strength and with all your mind'[b]; and, 'Love your neighbor as yourself.'[c]"

[28] "You have answered correctly," Jesus replied. "Do this and you will live."

[29] But he wanted to justify himself, so he asked Jesus, "And who is my neighbor?"

[30] In reply Jesus said: "A man was going down from Jerusalem to Jericho, when he was attacked by robbers. They stripped him of his clothes, beat him and went away, leaving him half dead. [31] A priest happened to be going down the same road, and when he saw the man, he passed by on the other side. [32] So too, a Levite, when he came to the place and saw him, passed by on the other side. [33] But a Samaritan, as he traveled, came where the man was; and when he saw him, he took pity on him. [34] He went to him and bandaged his wounds, pouring on oil and wine. Then he put the man on his own donkey, brought him to an inn and took care of him. [35] The next day he took out two denarii[d] and gave them to the innkeeper. 'Look after him,' he said, 'and when I return, I will reimburse you for any extra expense you may have.'

[36] "Which of these three do you

---

[a] 15 That is, the realm of the dead    [b] 27 Deut. 6:5    [c] 27 Lev. 19:18    [d] 35 A denarius was the usual daily wage of a day laborer (see Matt. 20:2).

think was a neighbor to the man who fell into the hands of robbers?"

37The expert in the law replied, "The one who had mercy on him."

Jesus told him, "Go and do likewise."

38As Jesus and his disciples were on their way, he came to a village where a woman named Martha opened her home to him. 39She had a sister called Mary, who sat at the Lord's feet listening to what he said. 40But Martha was distracted by all the preparations that had to be made. She came to him and asked, "Lord, don't you care that my sister has left me to do the work by myself? Tell her to help me!"

41"Martha, Martha," the Lord answered, "you are worried and upset about many things, 42but few things are needed—or indeed only one.a Mary has chosen what is better, and it will not be taken away from her."

11 One day Jesus was praying in a certain place. When he finished, one of his disciples said to him, "Lord, teach us to pray, just as John taught his disciples."

2He said to them, "When you pray, say:

" 'Father,b
hallowed be your name,
　your kingdom come.c
3Give us each day our daily
　bread.
4Forgive us our sins,
　for we also forgive everyone
　　who sins against us.d
And lead us not into
　temptation.e' "

5Then Jesus said to them, "Suppose you have a friend, and you go to him at midnight and say, 'Friend, lend me three loaves of bread; 6a friend of mine on a journey has come to me, and I have no food to offer him.' 7And suppose the one inside answers, 'Don't bother me. The door is already locked, and my children and I are in bed. I can't get up and give you anything.' 8I tell you, even though he will not get up and give you the bread because of friendship, yet because of your shameless audacityf he will surely get up and give you as much as you need.

9"So I say to you: Ask and it will be given to you; seek and you will find; knock and the door will be opened to you. 10For everyone who asks receives; the one who seeks finds; and to the one who knocks, the door will be opened.

11"Which of you fathers, if your son asks forg a fish, will give him a snake instead? 12Or if he asks for an egg, will give him a scorpion? 13If you then, though you are evil, know how to give good gifts to your children, how much more will your Father in heaven give the Holy Spirit to those who ask him!"

14Jesus was driving out a demon that was mute. When the demon left, the man who had been mute spoke, and the crowd was amazed. 15But some of them said, "By Beelzebul, the prince of demons, he is driving out demons." 16Others tested him by asking for a sign from heaven.

17Jesus knew their thoughts and

a 42 Some manuscripts but only one thing is needed　b 2 Some manuscripts Our Father in heaven　c 2 Some manuscripts come. May your will be done on earth as it is in heaven.　d 4 Greek everyone who is indebted to us　e 4 Some manuscripts temptation, but deliver us from the evil one　f 8 Or yet to preserve his good name　g 11 Some manuscripts for bread, will give him a stone? Or if he asks for said to them: "Any kingdom divided against itself will be ruined, and a house divided against itself will fall. ¹⁸If Satan is divided against himself, how can his kingdom stand? I say this because you claim that I drive out demons by Beelzebul. ¹⁹Now if I drive out demons by Beelzebul, by whom do your followers drive them out? So then, they will be your judges. ²⁰But if I drive out demons by the finger of God, then the kingdom of God has come upon you.

²¹"When a strong man, fully armed, guards his own house, his possessions are safe. ²²But when someone stronger attacks and overpowers him, he takes away the armor in which the man trusted and divides up his plunder.

²³"Whoever is not with me is against me, and whoever does not gather with me scatters.

²⁴"When an impure spirit comes out of a person, it goes through arid places seeking rest and does not find it. Then it says, 'I will return to the house I left.' ²⁵When it arrives, it finds the house swept clean and put in order. ²⁶Then it goes and takes seven other spirits more wicked than itself, and they go in and live there. And the final condition of that person is worse than the first."

²⁷As Jesus was saying these things, a woman in the crowd called out, "Blessed is the mother who gave you birth and nursed you."

²⁸He replied, "Blessed rather are those who hear the word of God and obey it."

²⁹As the crowds increased, Jesus said, "This is a wicked generation. It asks for a sign, but none will be given it except the sign of Jonah. ³⁰For as Jonah was a sign to the Ninevites, so also will the Son of Man be to this generation. ³¹The Queen of the South will rise at the judgment with the people of this generation and condemn them, for she came from the ends of the earth to listen to Solomon's wisdom; and now something greater than Solomon is here. ³²The men of Nineveh will stand up at the judgment with this generation and condemn it, for they repented at the preaching of Jonah; and now something greater than Jonah is here.

³³"No one lights a lamp and puts it in a place where it will be hidden, or under a bowl. Instead they put it on its stand, so that those who come in may see the light. ³⁴Your eye is the lamp of your body. When your eyes are healthy,$^a$ your whole body also is full of light. But when they are unhealthy,$^b$ your body also is full of darkness. ³⁵See to it, then, that the light within you is not darkness. ³⁶Therefore, if your whole body is full of light, and no part of it dark, it will be just as full of light as when a lamp shines its light on you."

³⁷When Jesus had finished speaking, a Pharisee invited him to eat with him; so he went in and reclined at the table. ³⁸But the Pharisee was surprised when he noticed that Jesus did not first wash before the meal.

³⁹Then the Lord said to him, "Now then, you Pharisees clean the outside of the cup and dish, but inside you are full of greed and wickedness. ⁴⁰You foolish people! Did

---

$^a$ 34 The Greek for healthy here implies generous, stingy.

$^b$ 34 The Greek for unhealthy here implies

not the one who made the outside make the inside also? <sup>41</sup>But now as for what is inside you — be generous to the poor, and everything will be clean for you.

<sup>42</sup>"Woe to you Pharisees, because you give God a tenth of your mint, rue and all other kinds of garden herbs, but you neglect justice and the love of God. You should have practiced the latter without leaving the former undone.

<sup>43</sup>"Woe to you Pharisees, because you love the most important seats in the synagogues and respectful greetings in the marketplaces.

<sup>44</sup>"Woe to you, because you are like unmarked graves, which people walk over without knowing it."

<sup>45</sup>One of the experts in the law answered him, "Teacher, when you say these things, you insult us also."

<sup>46</sup>Jesus replied, "And you experts in the law, woe to you, because you load people down with burdens they can hardly carry, and you yourselves will not lift one finger to help them.

<sup>47</sup>"Woe to you, because you build tombs for the prophets, and it was your ancestors who killed them. <sup>48</sup>So you testify that you approve of what your ancestors did; they killed the prophets, and you build their tombs. <sup>49</sup>Because of this, God in his wisdom said, 'I will send them prophets and apostles, some of whom they will kill and others they will persecute.' <sup>50</sup>Therefore this generation will be held responsible for the blood of all the prophets that has been shed since the beginning of the world, <sup>51</sup>from the blood of Abel to the blood of Zechariah, who was killed between the altar and the sanctuary. Yes, I tell you,

this generation will be held responsible for it all.

<sup>52</sup>"Woe to you experts in the law, because you have taken away the key to knowledge. You yourselves have not entered, and you have hindered those who were entering."

<sup>53</sup>When Jesus went outside, the Pharisees and the teachers of the law began to oppose him fiercely and to besiege him with questions, <sup>54</sup>waiting to catch him in something he might say.

**12** Meanwhile, when a crowd of many thousands had gathered, so that they were trampling on one another, Jesus began to speak first to his disciples, saying: "Be<sup>a</sup> on your guard against the yeast of the Pharisees, which is hypocrisy. <sup>2</sup>There is nothing concealed that will not be disclosed, or hidden that will not be made known. <sup>3</sup>What you have said in the dark will be heard in the daylight, and what you have whispered in the ear in the inner rooms will be proclaimed from the roofs.

<sup>4</sup>"I tell you, my friends, do not be afraid of those who kill the body and after that can do no more. <sup>5</sup>But I will show you whom you should fear: Fear him who, after your body has been killed, has authority to throw you into hell. Yes, I tell you, fear him. <sup>6</sup>Are not five sparrows sold for two pennies? Yet not one of them is forgotten by God. <sup>7</sup>Indeed, the very hairs of your head are all numbered. Don't be afraid; you are worth more than many sparrows.

<sup>8</sup>"I tell you, whoever publicly acknowledges me before others, the Son of Man will also acknowledge before the angels of God. <sup>9</sup>But whoever disowns me before others will be disowned before the angels of

---

<sup>a</sup> 1  Or *speak to his disciples, saying: "First of all, be*

God. ¹⁰And everyone who speaks a word against the Son of Man will be forgiven, but anyone who blasphemes against the Holy Spirit will not be forgiven.

¹¹ "When you are brought before synagogues, rulers and authorities, do not worry about how you will defend yourselves or what you will say, ¹²for the Holy Spirit will teach you at that time what you should say."

¹³Someone in the crowd said to him, "Teacher, tell my brother to divide the inheritance with me."

¹⁴Jesus replied, "Man, who appointed me a judge or an arbiter between you?" ¹⁵Then he said to them, "Watch out! Be on your guard against all kinds of greed; life does not consist in an abundance of possessions."

¹⁶And he told them this parable: "The ground of a certain rich man yielded an abundant harvest. ¹⁷He thought to himself, 'What shall I do? I have no place to store my crops.'

¹⁸ "Then he said, 'This is what I'll do. I will tear down my barns and build bigger ones, and there I will store my surplus grain. ¹⁹And I'll say to myself, "You have plenty of grain laid up for many years. Take life easy; eat, drink and be merry." '

²⁰ "But God said to him, 'You fool! This very night your life will be demanded from you. Then who will get what you have prepared for yourself?'

²¹ "This is how it will be with whoever stores up things for themselves but is not rich toward God."

²²Then Jesus said to his disciples: "Therefore I tell you, do not worry about your life, what you will eat; or about your body, what you will wear. ²³For life is more than food, and the body more than clothes. ²⁴Consider the ravens: They do not sow or reap, they have no storeroom or barn; yet God feeds them. And how much more valuable you are than birds! ²⁵Who of you by worrying can add a single hour to your lifeᵃ? ²⁶Since you cannot do this very little thing, why do you worry about the rest?

²⁷ "Consider how the wild flowers grow. They do not labor or spin. Yet I tell you, not even Solomon in all his splendor was dressed like one of these. ²⁸If that is how God clothes the grass of the field, which is here today, and tomorrow is thrown into the fire, how much more will he clothe you — you of little faith! ²⁹And do not set your heart on what you will eat or drink; do not worry about it. ³⁰For the pagan world runs after all such things, and your Father knows that you need them. ³¹But seek his kingdom, and these things will be given to you as well.

³² "Do not be afraid, little flock, for your Father has been pleased to give you the kingdom. ³³Sell your possessions and give to the poor. Provide purses for yourselves that will not wear out, a treasure in heaven that will never fail, where no thief comes near and no moth destroys. ³⁴For where your treasure is, there your heart will be also.

³⁵ "Be dressed ready for service and keep your lamps burning, ³⁶like servants waiting for their master to return from a wedding banquet, so that when he comes and knocks they can immediately open the door for him. ³⁷It will be good for those servants whose master finds them watching when he comes. Truly I tell you, he will dress

ᵃ 25  Or single cubit to your height

himself to serve, will have them recline at the table and will come and wait on them. ³⁸It will be good for those servants whose master finds them ready, even if he comes in the middle of the night or toward daybreak. ³⁹But understand this: If the owner of the house had known at what hour the thief was coming, he would not have let his house be broken into. ⁴⁰You also must be ready, because the Son of Man will come at an hour when you do not expect him."

⁴¹Peter asked, "Lord, are you telling this parable to us, or to everyone?"

⁴²The Lord answered, "Who then is the faithful and wise manager, whom the master puts in charge of his servants to give them their food allowance at the proper time? ⁴³It will be good for that servant whom the master finds doing so when he returns. ⁴⁴Truly I tell you, he will put him in charge of all his possessions. ⁴⁵But suppose the servant says to himself, 'My master is taking a long time in coming,' and he then begins to beat the other servants, both men and women, and to eat and drink and get drunk. ⁴⁶The master of that servant will come on a day when he does not expect him and at an hour he is not aware of. He will cut him to pieces and assign him a place with the unbelievers.

⁴⁷"The servant who knows the master's will and does not get ready or does not do what the master wants will be beaten with many blows. ⁴⁸But the one who does not know and does things deserving punishment will be beaten with few blows. From everyone who has been given much, much will be demanded; and from the one who has

been entrusted with much, much more will be asked.

⁴⁹"I have come to bring fire on the earth, and how I wish it were already kindled! ⁵⁰But I have a baptism to undergo, and what constraint I am under until it is completed! ⁵¹Do you think I came to bring peace on earth? No, I tell you, but division. ⁵²From now on there will be five in one family divided against each other, three against two and two against three. ⁵³They will be divided, father against son and son against father, mother against daughter and daughter against mother, mother-in-law against daughter-in-law and daughter-in-law against mother-in-law."

⁵⁴He said to the crowd: "When you see a cloud rising in the west, immediately you say, 'It's going to rain,' and it does. ⁵⁵And when the south wind blows, you say, 'It's going to be hot,' and it is. ⁵⁶Hypocrites! You know how to interpret the appearance of the earth and the sky. How is it that you don't know how to interpret this present time?

⁵⁷"Why don't you judge for yourselves what is right? ⁵⁸As you are going with your adversary to the magistrate, try hard to be reconciled on the way, or your adversary may drag you off to the judge, and the judge turn you over to the officer, and the officer throw you into prison. ⁵⁹I tell you, you will not get out until you have paid the last penny."

13 Now there were some present at that time who told Jesus about the Galileans whose blood Pilate had mixed with their sacrifices. ²Jesus answered, "Do you think that these Galileans were worse sinners than all the other

Galileans because they suffered this way? [3] I tell you, no! But unless you repent, you too will all perish. [4] Or those eighteen who died when the tower in Siloam fell on them — do you think they were more guilty than all the others living in Jerusalem? [5] I tell you, no! But unless you repent, you too will all perish."

[6] Then he told this parable: "A man had a fig tree growing in his vineyard, and he went to look for fruit on it but did not find any. [7] So he said to the man who took care of the vineyard, 'For three years now I've been coming to look for fruit on this fig tree and haven't found any. Cut it down! Why should it use up the soil?'

[8] " 'Sir,' the man replied, 'leave it alone for one more year, and I'll dig around it and fertilize it. [9] If it bears fruit next year, fine! If not, then cut it down.' "

[10] On a Sabbath Jesus was teaching in one of the synagogues, [11] and a woman was there who had been crippled by a spirit for eighteen years. She was bent over and could not straighten up at all. [12] When Jesus saw her, he called her forward and said to her, "Woman, you are set free from your infirmity." [13] Then he put his hands on her, and immediately she straightened up and praised God.

[14] Indignant because Jesus had healed on the Sabbath, the synagogue leader said to the people, "There are six days for work. So come and be healed on those days, not on the Sabbath."

[15] The Lord answered him, "You hypocrites! Doesn't each of you on the Sabbath untie your ox or donkey from the stall and lead it out to give it water? [16] Then should not this woman, a daughter of Abraham, whom Satan has kept bound for eighteen long years, be set free on the Sabbath day from what bound her?"

[17] When he said this, all his opponents were humiliated, but the people were delighted with all the wonderful things he was doing.

[18] Then Jesus asked, "What is the kingdom of God like? What shall I compare it to? [19] It is like a mustard seed, which a man took and planted in his garden. It grew and became a tree, and the birds perched in its branches."

[20] Again he asked, "What shall I compare the kingdom of God to? [21] It is like yeast that a woman took and mixed into about sixty pounds[a] of flour until it worked all through the dough."

[22] Then Jesus went through the towns and villages, teaching as he made his way to Jerusalem. [23] Someone asked him, "Lord, are only a few people going to be saved?"

He said to them, [24] "Make every effort to enter through the narrow door, because many, I tell you, will try to enter and will not be able to. [25] Once the owner of the house gets up and closes the door, you will stand outside knocking and pleading, 'Sir, open the door for us.'

"But he will answer, 'I don't know you or where you come from.'

[26] "Then you will say, 'We ate and drank with you, and you taught in our streets.'

[27] "But he will reply, 'I don't know you or where you come from. Away from me, all you evildoers!'

[28] "There will be weeping there, and gnashing of teeth, when you see Abraham, Isaac and Jacob and all the prophets in the kingdom of

---

a 21  Or about 27 kilograms

God, but you yourselves thrown out. [29] People will come from east and west and north and south, and will take their places at the feast in the kingdom of God. [30] Indeed there are those who are last who will be first, and first who will be last."

[31] At that time some Pharisees came to Jesus and said to him, "Leave this place and go somewhere else. Herod wants to kill you."

[32] He replied, "Go tell that fox, 'I will keep on driving out demons and healing people today and tomorrow, and on the third day I will reach my goal.' [33] In any case, I must press on today and tomorrow and the next day—for surely no prophet can die outside Jerusalem!

[34] "Jerusalem, Jerusalem, you who kill the prophets and stone those sent to you, how often I have longed to gather your children together, as a hen gathers her chicks under her wings, and you were not willing. [35] Look, your house is left to you desolate. I tell you, you will not see me again until you say, 'Blessed is he who comes in the name of the Lord.'[a]

14 One Sabbath, when Jesus went to eat in the house of a prominent Pharisee, he was being carefully watched. [2] There in front of him was a man suffering from abnormal swelling of his body. [3] Jesus asked the Pharisees and experts in the law, "Is it lawful to heal on the Sabbath or not?" [4] But they remained silent. So taking hold of the man, he healed him and sent him on his way.

[5] Then he asked them, "If one of you has a child[b] or an ox that falls into a well on the Sabbath day, will you not immediately pull it out?" [6] And they had nothing to say.

[7] When he noticed how the guests picked the places of honor at the table, he told them this parable: [8] "When someone invites you to a wedding feast, do not take the place of honor, for a person more distinguished than you may have been invited. [9] If so, the host who invited both of you will come and say to you, 'Give this person your seat.' Then, humiliated, you will have to take the least important place. [10] But when you are invited, take the lowest place, so that when your host comes, he will say to you, 'Friend, move up to a better place.' Then you will be honored in the presence of all the other guests. [11] For all those who exalt themselves will be humbled, and those who humble themselves will be exalted."

[12] Then Jesus said to his host, "When you give a luncheon or dinner, do not invite your friends, your brothers or sisters, your relatives, or your rich neighbors; if you do, they may invite you back and so you will be repaid. [13] But when you give a banquet, invite the poor, the crippled, the lame, the blind, [14] and you will be blessed. Although they cannot repay you, you will be repaid at the resurrection of the righteous."

[15] When one of those at the table with him heard this, he said to Jesus, "Blessed is the one who will eat at the feast in the kingdom of God."

[16] Jesus replied: "A certain man was preparing a great banquet and invited many guests. [17] At the time of the banquet he sent his servant to tell those who had been invited, 'Come, for everything is now ready.'

[18] "But they all alike began to make excuses. The first said, 'I have

---

[a] 35 Psalm 118:26     [b] 5 Some manuscripts *donkey*

just bought a field, and I must go and see it. Please excuse me.'

¹⁹ "Another said, 'I have just bought five yoke of oxen, and I'm on my way to try them out. Please excuse me.'

²⁰ "Still another said, 'I just got married, so I can't come.'

²¹ "The servant came back and reported this to his master. Then the owner of the house became angry and ordered his servant, 'Go out quickly into the streets and alleys of the town and bring in the poor, the crippled, the blind and the lame.'

²² "'Sir,' the servant said, 'what you ordered has been done, but there is still room.'

²³ "Then the master told his servant, 'Go out to the roads and country lanes and compel them to come in, so that my house will be full. ²⁴ I tell you, not one of those who were invited will get a taste of my banquet.'"

²⁵ Large crowds were traveling with Jesus, and turning to them he said: ²⁶ "If anyone comes to me and does not hate father and mother, wife and children, brothers and sisters—yes, even their own life—such a person cannot be my disciple. ²⁷ And whoever does not carry their cross and follow me cannot be my disciple.

²⁸ "Suppose one of you wants to build a tower. Won't you first sit down and estimate the cost to see if you have enough money to complete it? ²⁹ For if you lay the foundation and are not able to finish it, everyone who sees it will ridicule you, ³⁰ saying, 'This person began to build and wasn't able to finish.'

³¹ "Or suppose a king is about to go to war against another king.

Won't he first sit down and consider whether he is able with ten thousand men to oppose the one coming against him with twenty thousand? ³² If he is not able, he will send a delegation while the other is still a long way off and will ask for terms of peace. ³³ In the same way, those of you who do not give up everything you have cannot be my disciples.

³⁴ "Salt is good, but if it loses its saltiness, how can it be made salty again? ³⁵ It is fit neither for the soil nor for the manure pile; it is thrown out.

"Whoever has ears to hear, let them hear."

15 Now the tax collectors and sinners were all gathering around to hear Jesus. ² But the Pharisees and the teachers of the law muttered, "This man welcomes sinners and eats with them."

³ Then Jesus told them this parable: ⁴ "Suppose one of you has a hundred sheep and loses one of them. Doesn't he leave the ninety-nine in the open country and go after the lost sheep until he finds it? ⁵ And when he finds it, he joyfully puts it on his shoulders ⁶ and goes home. Then he calls his friends and neighbors together and says, 'Rejoice with me; I have found my lost sheep.' ⁷ I tell you that in the same way there will be more rejoicing in heaven over one sinner who repents than over ninety-nine righteous persons who do not need to repent.

⁸ "Or suppose a woman has ten silver coins[a] and loses one. Doesn't she light a lamp, sweep the house and search carefully until she finds it? ⁹ And when she finds it, she calls her friends and neighbors together

---

*a 8* Greek *ten drachmas,* each worth about a day's wages

and says, 'Rejoice with me; I have found my lost coin.' ¹⁰In the same way, I tell you, there is rejoicing in the presence of the angels of God over one sinner who repents."

¹¹Jesus continued: "There was a man who had two sons. ¹²The younger one said to his father, 'Father, give me my share of the estate.' So he divided his property between them.

¹³"Not long after that, the younger son got together all he had, set off for a distant country and there squandered his wealth in wild living. ¹⁴After he had spent everything, there was a severe famine in that whole country, and he began to be in need. ¹⁵So he went and hired himself out to a citizen of that country, who sent him to his fields to feed pigs. ¹⁶He longed to fill his stomach with the pods that the pigs were eating, but no one gave him anything.

¹⁷"When he came to his senses, he said, 'How many of my father's hired servants have food to spare, and here I am starving to death! ¹⁸I will set out and go back to my father and say to him: Father, I have sinned against heaven and against you. ¹⁹I am no longer worthy to be called your son; make me like one of your hired servants.' ²⁰So he got up and went to his father.

"But while he was still a long way off, his father saw him and was filled with compassion for him; he ran to his son, threw his arms around him and kissed him.

²¹"The son said to him, 'Father, I have sinned against heaven and against you. I am no longer worthy to be called your son.'

²²"But the father said to his servants, 'Quick! Bring the best robe and put it on him. Put a ring on his finger and sandals on his feet. ²³Bring the fattened calf and kill it. Let's have a feast and celebrate. ²⁴For this son of mine was dead and is alive again; he was lost and is found.' So they began to celebrate.

²⁵"Meanwhile, the older son was in the field. When he came near the house, he heard music and dancing. ²⁶So he called one of the servants and asked him what was going on. ²⁷'Your brother has come,' he replied, 'and your father has killed the fattened calf because he has him back safe and sound.'

²⁸"The older brother became angry and refused to go in. So his father went out and pleaded with him. ²⁹But he answered his father, 'Look! All these years I've been slaving for you and never disobeyed your orders. Yet you never gave me even a young goat so I could celebrate with my friends. ³⁰But when this son of yours who has squandered your property with prostitutes comes home, you kill the fattened calf for him!'

³¹"'My son,' the father said, 'you are always with me, and everything I have is yours. ³²But we had to celebrate and be glad, because this brother of yours was dead and is alive again; he was lost and is found.'"

16 Jesus told his disciples: "There was a rich man whose manager was accused of wasting his possessions. ²So he called him in and asked him, 'What is this I hear about you? Give an account of your management, because you cannot be manager any longer.'

³"The manager said to himself, 'What shall I do now? My master is taking away my job. I'm not strong enough to dig, and I'm ashamed to beg— ⁴I know what I'll do so that,

when I lose my job here, people will welcome me into their houses.'

⁵"So he called in each one of his master's debtors. He asked the first, 'How much do you owe my master?'

⁶"'Nine hundred gallons*ᵃ* of olive oil,' he replied.

"The manager told him, 'Take your bill, sit down quickly, and make it four hundred and fifty.'

⁷"Then he asked the second, 'And how much do you owe?'

"'A thousand bushels*ᵇ* of wheat,' he replied.

"He told him, 'Take your bill and make it eight hundred.'

⁸"The master commended the dishonest manager because he had acted shrewdly. For the people of this world are more shrewd in dealing with their own kind than are the people of the light. ⁹I tell you, use worldly wealth to gain friends for yourselves, so that when it is gone, you will be welcomed into eternal dwellings.

¹⁰"Whoever can be trusted with very little can also be trusted with much, and whoever is dishonest with very little will also be dishonest with much. ¹¹So if you have not been trustworthy in handling worldly wealth, who will trust you with true riches? ¹²And if you have not been trustworthy with someone else's property, who will give you property of your own?

¹³"No one can serve two masters. Either you will hate the one and love the other, or you will be devoted to the one and despise the other. You cannot serve both God and money."

¹⁴The Pharisees, who loved money, heard all this and were sneering at Jesus. ¹⁵He said to them, "You are the ones who justify yourselves in the eyes of others, but God knows your hearts. What people value highly is detestable in God's sight.

¹⁶"The Law and the Prophets were proclaimed until John. Since that time, the good news of the kingdom of God is being preached, and everyone is forcing their way into it. ¹⁷It is easier for heaven and earth to disappear than for the least stroke of a pen to drop out of the Law.

¹⁸"Anyone who divorces his wife and marries another woman commits adultery, and the man who marries a divorced woman commits adultery.

¹⁹"There was a rich man who was dressed in purple and fine linen and lived in luxury every day. ²⁰At his gate was laid a beggar named Lazarus, covered with sores ²¹and longing to eat what fell from the rich man's table. Even the dogs came and licked his sores.

²²"The time came when the beggar died and the angels carried him to Abraham's side. The rich man also died and was buried. ²³In Hades, where he was in torment, he looked up and saw Abraham far away, with Lazarus by his side. ²⁴So he called to him, 'Father Abraham, have pity on me and send Lazarus to dip the tip of his finger in water and cool my tongue, because I am in agony in this fire.'

²⁵"But Abraham replied, 'Son, remember that in your lifetime you received your good things, while Lazarus received bad things, but now he is comforted here and you are in agony. ²⁶And besides all this, between us and you a great chasm has been set in place, so that those who want to go from here to you

---

*ᵃ 6* Or about 3,000 liters    *ᵇ 7* Or about 30 tons

cannot, nor can anyone cross over from there to us.'

27 "He answered, 'Then I beg you, father, send Lazarus to my family, 28 for I have five brothers. Let him warn them, so that they will not also come to this place of torment.'

29 "Abraham replied, 'They have Moses and the Prophets; let them listen to them.'

30 "'No, father Abraham,' he said, 'but if someone from the dead goes to them, they will repent.'

31 "He said to him, 'If they do not listen to Moses and the Prophets, they will not be convinced even if someone rises from the dead.'"

17 Jesus said to his disciples: "Things that cause people to stumble are bound to come, but woe to anyone through whom they come. 2 It would be better for them to be thrown into the sea with a millstone tied around their neck than to cause one of these little ones to stumble. 3 So watch yourselves.

"If your brother or sister[a] sins against you, rebuke them; and if they repent, forgive them. 4 Even if they sin against you seven times in a day and seven times come back to you saying 'I repent,' you must forgive them."

5 The apostles said to the Lord, "Increase our faith!"

6 He replied, "If you have faith as small as a mustard seed, you can say to this mulberry tree, 'Be uprooted and planted in the sea,' and it will obey you.

7 "Suppose one of you has a servant plowing or looking after the sheep. Will he say to the servant when he comes in from the field, 'Come along now and sit down to eat'? 8 Won't he rather say, 'Prepare my supper, get yourself ready and wait on me while I eat and drink; after that you may eat and drink'? 9 Will he thank the servant because he did what he was told to do? 10 So you also, when you have done everything you were told to do, should say, 'We are unworthy servants; we have only done our duty.'"

11 Now on his way to Jerusalem, Jesus traveled along the border between Samaria and Galilee. 12 As he was going into a village, ten men who had leprosy[b] met him. They stood at a distance 13 and called out in a loud voice, "Jesus, Master, have pity on us!"

14 When he saw them, he said, "Go, show yourselves to the priests." And as they went, they were cleansed.

15 One of them, when he saw he was healed, came back, praising God in a loud voice. 16 He threw himself at Jesus' feet and thanked him — and he was a Samaritan.

17 Jesus asked, "Were not all ten cleansed? Where are the other nine? 18 Has no one returned to give praise to God except this foreigner?" 19 Then he said to him, "Rise and go; your faith has made you well."

20 Once, on being asked by the Pharisees when the kingdom of God would come, Jesus replied, "The coming of the kingdom of God is not something that can be observed, 21 nor will people say, 'Here it is,' or 'There it is,' because the kingdom of God is in your midst."[c]

22 Then he said to his disciples, "The time is coming when you will

---

[a] 3 The Greek word for brother or sister (adelphos) refers here to a fellow disciple, whether man or woman.    [b] 12 The Greek word traditionally translated leprosy was used for various diseases affecting the skin.    [c] 21 Or is within you

long to see one of the days of the Son of Man, but you will not see it. ²³People will tell you, 'There he is!' or 'Here he is!' Do not go running off after them. ²⁴For the Son of Man in his day[a] will be like the lightning, which flashes and lights up the sky from one end to the other. ²⁵But first he must suffer many things and be rejected by this generation.

²⁶"Just as it was in the days of Noah, so also will it be in the days of the Son of Man. ²⁷People were eating, drinking, marrying and being given in marriage up to the day Noah entered the ark. Then the flood came and destroyed them all.

²⁸"It was the same in the days of Lot. People were eating and drinking, buying and selling, planting and building. ²⁹But the day Lot left Sodom, fire and sulfur rained down from heaven and destroyed them all.

³⁰"It will be just like this on the day the Son of Man is revealed. ³¹On that day no one who is on the housetop, with possessions inside, should go down to get them. Likewise, no one in the field should go back for anything. ³²Remember Lot's wife! ³³Whoever tries to keep their life will lose it, and whoever loses their life will preserve it. ³⁴I tell you, on that night two people will be in one bed; one will be taken and the other left. ³⁵Two women will be grinding grain together; one will be taken and the other left." [36][b]

³⁷"Where, Lord?" they asked.

He replied, "Where there is a dead body, there the vultures will gather."

**18** Then Jesus told his disciples a parable to show them that they should always pray and not give up. ²He said: "In a certain town there was a judge who neither feared God nor cared what people thought. ³And there was a widow in that town who kept coming to him with the plea, 'Grant me justice against my adversary.'

⁴"For some time he refused. But finally he said to himself, 'Even though I don't fear God or care what people think, ⁵yet because this widow keeps bothering me, I will see that she gets justice, so that she won't eventually come and attack me!'"

⁶And the Lord said, "Listen to what the unjust judge says. ⁷And will not God bring about justice for his chosen ones, who cry out to him day and night? Will he keep putting them off? ⁸I tell you, he will see that they get justice, and quickly. However, when the Son of Man comes, will he find faith on the earth?"

⁹To some who were confident of their own righteousness and looked down on everyone else, Jesus told this parable: ¹⁰"Two men went up to the temple to pray, one a Pharisee and the other a tax collector. ¹¹The Pharisee stood by himself and prayed: 'God, I thank you that I am not like other people — robbers, evildoers, adulterers — or even like this tax collector. ¹²I fast twice a week and give a tenth of all I get.'

¹³"But the tax collector stood at a distance. He would not even look up to heaven, but beat his breast and said, 'God, have mercy on me, a sinner.'

¹⁴"I tell you that this man, rather than the other, went home justified

---

[a] 24 Some manuscripts do not have *in his day*. similar to Matt. 24:40.

[b] 36 Some manuscripts include here words

before God. For all those who exalt themselves will be humbled, and those who humble themselves will be exalted."

¹⁵People were also bringing babies to Jesus for him to place his hands on them. When the disciples saw this, they rebuked them. ¹⁶But Jesus called the children to him and said, "Let the little children come to me, and do not hinder them, for the kingdom of God belongs to such as these. ¹⁷Truly I tell you, anyone who will not receive the kingdom of God like a little child will never enter it."

¹⁸A certain ruler asked him, "Good teacher, what must I do to inherit eternal life?"

¹⁹"Why do you call me good?" Jesus answered. "No one is good — except God alone. ²⁰You know the commandments: 'You shall not commit adultery, you shall not murder, you shall not steal, you shall not give false testimony, honor your father and mother.'ᵃ"

²¹"All these I have kept since I was a boy," he said.

²²When Jesus heard this, he said to him, "You still lack one thing. Sell everything you have and give to the poor, and you will have treasure in heaven. Then come, follow me."

²³When he heard this, he became very sad, because he was very wealthy. ²⁴Jesus looked at him and said, "How hard it is for the rich to enter the kingdom of God! ²⁵Indeed, it is easier for a camel to go through the eye of a needle than for someone who is rich to enter the kingdom of God."

²⁶Those who heard this asked, "Who then can be saved?"

²⁷Jesus replied, "What is impos-sible with man is possible with God."

²⁸Peter said to him, "We have left all we had to follow you!"

²⁹"Truly I tell you," Jesus said to them, "no one who has left home or wife or brothers or sisters or parents or children for the sake of the kingdom of God ³⁰will fail to receive many times as much in this age, and in the age to come eternal life."

³¹Jesus took the Twelve aside and told them, "We are going up to Jerusalem, and everything that is written by the prophets about the Son of Man will be fulfilled. ³²He will be delivered over to the Gentiles. They will mock him, insult him and spit on him; ³³they will flog him and kill him. On the third day he will rise again."

³⁴The disciples did not understand any of this. Its meaning was hidden from them, and they did not know what he was talking about.

³⁵As Jesus approached Jericho, a blind man was sitting by the roadside begging. ³⁶When he heard the crowd going by, he asked what was happening. ³⁷They told him, "Jesus of Nazareth is passing by."

³⁸He called out, "Jesus, Son of David, have mercy on me!"

³⁹Those who led the way rebuked him and told him to be quiet, but he shouted all the more, "Son of David, have mercy on me!"

⁴⁰Jesus stopped and ordered the man to be brought to him. When he came near, Jesus asked him, ⁴¹"What do you want me to do for you?"

"Lord, I want to see," he replied.

⁴²Jesus said to him, "Receive your sight; your faith has healed you." ⁴³Immediately he received

ᵃ 20 Exodus 20:12-16; Deut. 5:16-20

his sight and followed Jesus, praising God. When all the people saw it, they also praised God.

19 Jesus entered Jericho and was passing through. ²A man was there by the name of Zacchaeus; he was a chief tax collector and was wealthy. ³He wanted to see who Jesus was, but because he was short he could not see over the crowd. ⁴So he ran ahead and climbed a sycamore-fig tree to see him, since Jesus was coming that way.

⁵When Jesus reached the spot, he looked up and said to him, "Zacchaeus, come down immediately. I must stay at your house today." ⁶So he came down at once and welcomed him gladly.

⁷All the people saw this and began to mutter, "He has gone to be the guest of a sinner."

⁸But Zacchaeus stood up and said to the Lord, "Look, Lord! Here and now I give half of my possessions to the poor, and if I have cheated anybody out of anything, I will pay back four times the amount."

⁹Jesus said to him, "Today salvation has come to this house, because this man, too, is a son of Abraham. ¹⁰For the Son of Man came to seek and to save the lost."

¹¹While they were listening to this, he went on to tell them a parable, because he was near Jerusalem and the people thought that the kingdom of God was going to appear at once. ¹²He said: "A man of noble birth went to a distant country to have himself appointed king and then to return. ¹³So he called ten of his servants and gave them ten minas.ᵃ 'Put this money to work,' he said, 'until I come back.'

¹⁴"But his subjects hated him and sent a delegation after him to say, 'We don't want this man to be our king.'

¹⁵"He was made king, however, and returned home. Then he sent for the servants to whom he had given the money, in order to find out what they had gained with it.

¹⁶"The first one came and said, 'Sir, your mina has earned ten more.'

¹⁷"'Well done, my good servant!' his master replied. 'Because you have been trustworthy in a very small matter, take charge of ten cities.'

¹⁸"The second came and said, 'Sir, your mina has earned five more.'

¹⁹"His master answered, 'You take charge of five cities.'

²⁰"Then another servant came and said, 'Sir, here is your mina; I have kept it laid away in a piece of cloth. ²¹I was afraid of you, because you are a hard man. You take out what you did not put in and reap what you did not sow.'

²²"His master replied, 'I will judge you by your own words, you wicked servant! You knew, did you, that I am a hard man, taking out what I did not put in, and reaping what I did not sow? ²³Why then didn't you put my money on deposit, so that when I came back, I could have collected it with interest?'

²⁴"Then he said to those standing by, 'Take his mina away from him and give it to the one who has ten minas.'

²⁵"'Sir,' they said, 'he already has ten!'

²⁶"He replied, 'I tell you that to everyone who has, more will be given, but as for the one who has nothing, even what they have will be taken away. ²⁷But those enemies

---

ᵃ 13 A mina was about three months' wages.

of mine who did not want me to be king over them — bring them here and kill them in front of me.' "

28 After Jesus had said this, he went on ahead, going up to Jerusalem. 29 As he approached Bethphage and Bethany at the hill called the Mount of Olives, he sent two of his disciples, saying to them, 30 "Go to the village ahead of you, and as you enter it, you will find a colt tied there, which no one has ever ridden. Untie it and bring it here. 31 If anyone asks you, 'Why are you untying it?' say, 'The Lord needs it.' "

32 Those who were sent ahead went and found it just as he had told them. 33 As they were untying the colt, its owners asked them, "Why are you untying the colt?"

34 They replied, "The Lord needs it."

35 They brought it to Jesus, threw their cloaks on the colt and put Jesus on it. 36 As he went along, people spread their cloaks on the road.

37 When he came near the place where the road goes down the Mount of Olives, the whole crowd of disciples began joyfully to praise God in loud voices for all the miracles they had seen:

38 "Blessed is the king who comes
      in the name of the Lord!"*a*

"Peace in heaven and glory in
      the highest!"

39 Some of the Pharisees in the crowd said to Jesus, "Teacher, rebuke your disciples!"

40 "I tell you," he replied, "if they keep quiet, the stones will cry out."

41 As he approached Jerusalem and saw the city, he wept over it 42 and said, "If you, even you, had only known on this day what would bring you peace — but now it is hidden from your eyes. 43 The days will come upon you when your enemies will build an embankment against you and encircle you and hem you in on every side. 44 They will dash you to the ground, you and the children within your walls. They will not leave one stone on another, because you did not recognize the time of God's coming to you."

45 When Jesus entered the temple courts, he began to drive out those who were selling. 46 "It is written," he said to them, " 'My house will be a house of prayer'*b*; but you have made it 'a den of robbers.'*c*"

47 Every day he was teaching at the temple. But the chief priests, the teachers of the law and the leaders among the people were trying to kill him. 48 Yet they could not find any way to do it, because all the people hung on his words.

20 One day as Jesus was teaching the people in the temple courts and proclaiming the good news, the chief priests and the teachers of the law, together with the elders, came up to him. 2 "Tell us by what authority you are doing these things," they said. "Who gave you this authority?"

3 He replied, "I will also ask you a question. Tell me: 4 John's baptism — was it from heaven, or of human origin?"

5 They discussed it among themselves and said, "If we say, 'From heaven,' he will ask, 'Why didn't you believe him?' 6 But if we say, 'Of human origin,' all the people will stone us, because they are persuaded that John was a prophet."

7 So they answered, "We don't know where it was from."

---

*a 38* Psalm 118:26     *b 46* Isaiah 56:7     *c 46* Jer. 7:11

⁸Jesus said, "Neither will I tell you by what authority I am doing these things."

⁹He went on to tell the people this parable: "A man planted a vineyard, rented it to some farmers and went away for a long time. ¹⁰At harvest time he sent a servant to the tenants so they would give him some of the fruit of the vineyard. But the tenants beat him and sent him away empty-handed. ¹¹He sent another servant, but that one also they beat and treated shamefully and sent away empty-handed. ¹²He sent still a third, and they wounded him and threw him out.

¹³"Then the owner of the vineyard said, 'What shall I do? I will send my son, whom I love; perhaps they will respect him.'

¹⁴"But when the tenants saw him, they talked the matter over. 'This is the heir,' they said. 'Let's kill him, and the inheritance will be ours.' ¹⁵So they threw him out of the vineyard and killed him.

"What then will the owner of the vineyard do to them? ¹⁶He will come and kill those tenants and give the vineyard to others."

When the people heard this, they said, "God forbid!"

¹⁷Jesus looked directly at them and asked, "Then what is the meaning of that which is written:

"'The stone the builders rejected
    has become the cornerstone'ᵃ?

¹⁸Everyone who falls on that stone will be broken to pieces; anyone on whom it falls will be crushed."

¹⁹The teachers of the law and the chief priests looked for a way to arrest him immediately, because they knew he had spoken this parable against them. But they were afraid of the people.

²⁰Keeping a close watch on him, they sent spies, who pretended to be sincere. They hoped to catch Jesus in something he said, so that they might hand him over to the power and authority of the governor. ²¹So the spies questioned him: "Teacher, we know that you speak and teach what is right, and that you do not show partiality but teach the way of God in accordance with the truth. ²²Is it right for us to pay taxes to Caesar or not?"

²³He saw through their duplicity and said to them, ²⁴"Show me a denarius. Whose image and inscription are on it?"

"Caesar's," they replied.

²⁵He said to them, "Then give back to Caesar what is Caesar's, and to God what is God's."

²⁶They were unable to trap him in what he had said there in public. And astonished by his answer, they became silent.

²⁷Some of the Sadducees, who say there is no resurrection, came to Jesus with a question. ²⁸"Teacher," they said, "Moses wrote for us that if a man's brother dies and leaves a wife but no children, the man must marry the widow and raise up offspring for his brother. ²⁹Now there were seven brothers. The first one married a woman and died childless. ³⁰The second ³¹and then the third married her, and in the same way the seven died, leaving no children. ³²Finally, the woman died too. ³³Now then, at the resurrection whose wife will she be, since the seven were married to her?"

³⁴Jesus replied, "The people of this age marry and are given in marriage. ³⁵But those who are con-

ᵃ 17 Psalm 118:22

sidered worthy of taking part in the age to come and in the resurrection from the dead will neither marry nor be given in marriage, ³⁶and they can no longer die; for they are like the angels. They are God's children, since they are children of the resurrection. ³⁷But in the account of the burning bush, even Moses showed that the dead rise, for he calls the Lord 'the God of Abraham, and the God of Isaac, and the God of Jacob.'ᵃ ³⁸He is not the God of the dead, but of the living, for to him all are alive.'

³⁹Some of the teachers of the law responded, "Well said, teacher!" ⁴⁰And no one dared to ask him any more questions.

⁴¹Then Jesus said to them, "Why is it said that the Messiah is the son of David? ⁴²David himself declares in the Book of Psalms:

" 'The Lord said to my Lord:
    "Sit at my right hand
⁴³until I make your enemies
    a footstool for your feet." 'ᵇ

⁴⁴David calls him 'Lord.' How then can he be his son?"

⁴⁵While all the people were listening, Jesus said to his disciples, ⁴⁶"Beware of the teachers of the law. They like to walk around in flowing robes and love to be greeted with respect in the marketplaces and have the most important seats in the synagogues and the places of honor at banquets. ⁴⁷They devour widows' houses and for a show make lengthy prayers. These men will be punished most severely."

21 As Jesus looked up, he saw the rich putting their gifts into the temple treasury. ²He also saw a poor widow put in two very small copper coins. ³"Truly I tell you," he said, "this poor widow has put in more than all the others. ⁴All these people gave their gifts out of their wealth; but she out of her poverty put in all she had to live on."

⁵Some of his disciples were remarking about how the temple was adorned with beautiful stones and with gifts dedicated to God. But Jesus said, ⁶"As for what you see here, the time will come when not one stone will be left on another; every one of them will be thrown down."

⁷"Teacher," they asked, "when will these things happen? And what will be the sign that they are about to take place?"

⁸He replied: "Watch out that you are not deceived. For many will come in my name, claiming, 'I am he,' and, 'The time is near.' Do not follow them. ⁹When you hear of wars and uprisings, do not be frightened. These things must happen first, but the end will not come right away."

¹⁰Then he said to them: "Nation will rise against nation, and kingdom against kingdom. ¹¹There will be great earthquakes, famines and pestilences in various places, and fearful events and great signs from heaven.

¹²"But before all this, they will seize you and persecute you. They will hand you over to synagogues and put you in prison, and you will be brought before kings and governors, and all on account of my name. ¹³And so you will bear testimony to me. ¹⁴But make up your mind not to worry beforehand how you will defend yourselves. ¹⁵For I will give you words and wisdom that none of your adversaries will be able to resist or contradict. ¹⁶You

ᵃ 37 Exodus 3:6    ᵇ 43 Psalm 110:1

will be betrayed even by parents, brothers and sisters, relatives and friends, and they will put some of you to death. <sup>17</sup>Everyone will hate you because of me. <sup>18</sup>But not a hair of your head will perish. <sup>19</sup>Stand firm, and you will win life.

<sup>20</sup>"When you see Jerusalem being surrounded by armies, you will know that its desolation is near. <sup>21</sup>Then let those who are in Judea flee to the mountains, let those in the city get out, and let those in the country not enter the city. <sup>22</sup>For this is the time of punishment in fulfillment of all that has been written. <sup>23</sup>How dreadful it will be in those days for pregnant women and nursing mothers! There will be great distress in the land and wrath against this people. <sup>24</sup>They will fall by the sword and will be taken as prisoners to all the nations. Jerusalem will be trampled on by the Gentiles until the times of the Gentiles are fulfilled.

<sup>25</sup>"There will be signs in the sun, moon and stars. On the earth, nations will be in anguish and perplexity at the roaring and tossing of the sea. <sup>26</sup>People will faint from terror, apprehensive of what is coming on the world, for the heavenly bodies will be shaken. <sup>27</sup>At that time they will see the Son of Man coming in a cloud with power and great glory. <sup>28</sup>When these things begin to take place, stand up and lift up your heads, because your redemption is drawing near."

<sup>29</sup>He told them this parable: "Look at the fig tree and all the trees. <sup>30</sup>When they sprout leaves, you can see for yourselves and know that summer is near. <sup>31</sup>Even so, when you see these things happening, you know that the kingdom of God is near.

<sup>32</sup>"Truly I tell you, this generation will certainly not pass away until all these things have happened. <sup>33</sup>Heaven and earth will pass away, but my words will never pass away.

<sup>34</sup>"Be careful, or your hearts will be weighed down with carousing, drunkenness and the anxieties of life, and that day will close on you suddenly like a trap. <sup>35</sup>For it will come on all those who live on the face of the whole earth. <sup>36</sup>Be always on the watch, and pray that you may be able to escape all that is about to happen, and that you may be able to stand before the Son of Man."

<sup>37</sup>Each day Jesus was teaching at the temple, and each evening he went out to spend the night on the hill called the Mount of Olives, <sup>38</sup>and all the people came early in the morning to hear him at the temple.

22 Now the Festival of Unleavened Bread, called the Passover, was approaching, <sup>2</sup>and the chief priests and the teachers of the law were looking for some way to get rid of Jesus, for they were afraid of the people. <sup>3</sup>Then Satan entered Judas, called Iscariot, one of the Twelve. <sup>4</sup>And Judas went to the chief priests and the officers of the temple guard and discussed with them how he might betray Jesus. <sup>5</sup>They were delighted and agreed to give him money. <sup>6</sup>He consented, and watched for an opportunity to hand Jesus over to them when no crowd was present.

<sup>7</sup>Then came the day of Unleavened Bread on which the Passover lamb had to be sacrificed. <sup>8</sup>Jesus sent Peter and John, saying, "Go and make preparations for us to eat the Passover."

<sup>9</sup>"Where do you want us to prepare for it?" they asked.

[10]He replied, "As you enter the city, a man carrying a jar of water will meet you. Follow him to the house that he enters, [11]and say to the owner of the house, 'The Teacher asks: Where is the guest room, where I may eat the Passover with my disciples?' [12]He will show you a large room upstairs, all furnished. Make preparations there."

[13]They left and found things just as Jesus had told them. So they prepared the Passover.

[14]When the hour came, Jesus and his apostles reclined at the table. [15]And he said to them, "I have eagerly desired to eat this Passover with you before I suffer. [16]For I tell you, I will not eat it again until it finds fulfillment in the kingdom of God."

[17]After taking the cup, he gave thanks and said, "Take this and divide it among you. [18]For I tell you I will not drink again from the fruit of the vine until the kingdom of God comes."

[19]And he took bread, gave thanks and broke it, and gave it to them, saying, "This is my body given for you; do this in remembrance of me."[a]

[20]In the same way, after the supper he took the cup, saying, "This cup is the new covenant in my blood, which is poured out for you.[a] [21]But the hand of him who is going to betray me is with mine on the table. [22]The Son of Man will go as it has been decreed. But woe to that man who betrays him!" [23]They began to question among themselves which of them it might be who would do this.

[24]A dispute also arose among them as to which of them was considered to be greatest. [25]Jesus said to them, "The kings of the Gentiles lord it over them; and those who exercise authority over them call themselves Benefactors. [26]But you are not to be like that. Instead, the greatest among you should be like the youngest, and the one who rules like the one who serves. [27]For who is greater, the one who is at the table or the one who serves? Is it not the one who is at the table? But I am among you as one who serves. [28]You are those who have stood by me in my trials. [29]And I confer on you a kingdom, just as my Father conferred one on me, [30]so that you may eat and drink at my table in my kingdom and sit on thrones, judging the twelve tribes of Israel.

[31]"Simon, Simon, Satan has asked to sift all of you as wheat. [32]But I have prayed for you, Simon, that your faith may not fail. And when you have turned back, strengthen your brothers."

[33]But he replied, "Lord, I am ready to go with you to prison and to death."

[34]Jesus answered, "I tell you, Peter, before the rooster crows today, you will deny three times that you know me."

[35]Then Jesus asked them, "When I sent you without purse, bag or sandals, did you lack anything?"

"Nothing," they answered.

[36]He said to them, "But now if you have a purse, take it, and also a bag; and if you don't have a sword, sell your cloak and buy one. [37]It is written: 'And he was numbered with the transgressors'[b]; and I tell you that this must be fulfilled in me. Yes, what is written about me is reaching its fulfillment."

[38]The disciples said, "See, Lord, here are two swords."

---

a 19,20 Some manuscripts do not have given for you . . . poured out for you.    b 37 Isaiah 53:12

"That's enough!" he replied.

39 Jesus went out as usual to the Mount of Olives, and his disciples followed him. 40 On reaching the place, he said to them, "Pray that you will not fall into temptation." 41 He withdrew about a stone's throw beyond them, knelt down and prayed, 42 "Father, if you are willing, take this cup from me; yet not my will, but yours be done." 43 An angel from heaven appeared to him and strengthened him. 44 And being in anguish, he prayed more earnestly, and his sweat was like drops of blood falling to the ground.*a*

45 When he rose from prayer and went back to the disciples, he found them asleep, exhausted from sorrow. 46 "Why are you sleeping?" he asked them. "Get up and pray so that you will not fall into temptation."

47 While he was still speaking, a crowd came up, and the man who was called Judas, one of the Twelve, was leading them. He approached Jesus to kiss him, 48 but Jesus asked him, "Judas, are you betraying the Son of Man with a kiss?"

49 When Jesus' followers saw what was going to happen, they said, "Lord, should we strike with our swords?" 50 And one of them struck the servant of the high priest, cutting off his right ear.

51 But Jesus answered, "No more of this!" And he touched the man's ear and healed him.

52 Then Jesus said to the chief priests, the officers of the temple guard, and the elders, who had come for him, "Am I leading a rebellion, that you have come with swords and clubs? 53 Every day I was with you in the temple courts,

and you did not lay a hand on me. But this is your hour — when darkness reigns."

54 Then seizing him, they led him away and took him into the house of the high priest. Peter followed at a distance. 55 And when some there had kindled a fire in the middle of the courtyard and had sat down together, Peter sat down with them. 56 A servant girl saw him seated there in the firelight. She looked closely at him and said, "This man was with him."

57 But he denied it. "Woman, I don't know him," he said.

58 A little later someone else saw him and said, "You also are one of them."

"Man, I am not!" Peter replied.

59 About an hour later another asserted, "Certainly this fellow was with him, for he is a Galilean."

60 Peter replied, "Man, I don't know what you're talking about!" Just as he was speaking, the rooster crowed. 61 The Lord turned and looked straight at Peter. Then Peter remembered the word the Lord had spoken to him: "Before the rooster crows today, you will disown me three times." 62 And he went outside and wept bitterly.

63 The men who were guarding Jesus began mocking and beating him. 64 They blindfolded him and demanded, "Prophesy! Who hit you?" 65 And they said many other insulting things to him.

66 At daybreak the council of the elders of the people, both the chief priests and the teachers of the law, met together, and Jesus was led before them. 67 "If you are the Messiah," they said, "tell us."

Jesus answered, "If I tell you, you will not believe me, 68 and if I asked

---

*a 43,44* Many early manuscripts do not have verses 43 and 44.

you, you would not answer. 69But from now on, the Son of Man will be seated at the right hand of the mighty God."

70They all asked, "Are you then the Son of God?"

He replied, "You say that I am."

71Then they said, "Why do we need any more testimony? We have heard it from his own lips."

23 Then the whole assembly rose and led him off to Pilate. 2And they began to accuse him, saying, "We have found this man subverting our nation. He opposes payment of taxes to Caesar and claims to be Messiah, a king."

3So Pilate asked Jesus, "Are you the king of the Jews?"

"You have said so," Jesus replied.

4Then Pilate announced to the chief priests and the crowd, "I find no basis for a charge against this man."

5But they insisted, "He stirs up the people all over Judea by his teaching. He started in Galilee and has come all the way here."

6On hearing this, Pilate asked if the man was a Galilean. 7When he learned that Jesus was under Herod's jurisdiction, he sent him to Herod, who was also in Jerusalem at that time.

8When Herod saw Jesus, he was greatly pleased, because for a long time he had been wanting to see him. From what he had heard about him, he hoped to see him perform a sign of some sort. 9He plied him with many questions, but Jesus gave him no answer. 10The chief priests and the teachers of the law were standing there, vehemently accusing him. 11Then Herod and his soldiers ridiculed and mocked him. Dressing him in an elegant robe, they sent him back to Pilate. 12That day Herod and Pilate became friends—before this they had been enemies.

13Pilate called together the chief priests, the rulers and the people, 14and said to them, "You brought me this man as one who was inciting the people to rebellion. I have examined him in your presence and have found no basis for your charges against him. 15Neither has Herod, for he sent him back to us; as you can see, he has done nothing to deserve death. 16Therefore, I will punish him and then release him." [17]a

18But the whole crowd shouted, "Away with this man! Release Barabbas to us!" 19(Barabbas had been thrown into prison for an insurrection in the city, and for murder.)

20Wanting to release Jesus, Pilate appealed to them again. 21But they kept shouting, "Crucify him! Crucify him!"

22For the third time he spoke to them: "Why? What crime has this man committed? I have found in him no grounds for the death penalty. Therefore I will have him punished and then release him."

23But with loud shouts they insistently demanded that he be crucified, and their shouts prevailed. 24So Pilate decided to grant their demand. 25He released the man who had been thrown into prison for insurrection and murder, the one they asked for, and surrendered Jesus to their will.

26As the soldiers led him away, they seized Simon from Cyrene, who was on his way in from the country, and put the cross on him and made him carry it behind Jesus. 27A large number of people

---

a 17 Some manuscripts include here words similar to Matt. 27:15 and Mark 15:6.

followed him, including women who mourned and wailed for him. [28]Jesus turned and said to them, "Daughters of Jerusalem, do not weep for me; weep for yourselves and for your children. [29]For the time will come when you will say, 'Blessed are the childless women, the wombs that never bore and the breasts that never nursed!' [30]Then

"'they will say to the mountains, "Fall on us!" and to the hills, "Cover us!"'[a]

[31]For if people do these things when the tree is green, what will happen when it is dry?"

[32]Two other men, both criminals, were also led out with him to be executed. [33]When they came to the place called the Skull, they crucified him there, along with the criminals — one on his right, the other on his left. [34]Jesus said, "Father, forgive them, for they do not know what they are doing."[b] And they divided up his clothes by casting lots.

[35]The people stood watching, and the rulers even sneered at him. They said, "He saved others; let him save himself if he is God's Messiah, the Chosen One."

[36]The soldiers also came up and mocked him. They offered him wine vinegar [37]and said, "If you are the king of the Jews, save yourself."

[38]There was a written notice above him, which read: THIS IS THE KING OF THE JEWS.

[39]One of the criminals who hung there hurled insults at him: "Aren't you the Messiah? Save yourself and us!"

[40]But the other criminal rebuked him. "Don't you fear God," he said,

"since you are under the same sentence? [41]We are punished justly, for we are getting what our deeds deserve. But this man has done nothing wrong."

[42]Then he said, "Jesus, remember me when you come into your kingdom.[c]"

[43]Jesus answered him, "Truly I tell you, today you will be with me in paradise."

[44]It was now about noon, and darkness came over the whole land until three in the afternoon, [45]for the sun stopped shining. And the curtain of the temple was torn in two. [46]Jesus called out with a loud voice, "Father, into your hands I commit my spirit."[d] When he had said this, he breathed his last.

[47]The centurion, seeing what had happened, praised God and said, "Surely this was a righteous man." [48]When all the people who had gathered to witness this sight saw what took place, they beat their breasts and went away. [49]But all those who knew him, including the women who had followed him from Galilee, stood at a distance, watching these things.

[50]Now there was a man named Joseph, a member of the Council, a good and upright man, [51]who had not consented to their decision and action. He came from the Judean town of Arimathea, and he himself was waiting for the kingdom of God. [52]Going to Pilate, he asked for Jesus' body. [53]Then he took it down, wrapped it in linen cloth and placed it in a tomb cut in the rock, one in which no one had yet been laid. [54]It was Preparation Day, and the Sabbath was about to begin.

[55]The women who had come

---

[a] 30 Hosea 10:8   [b] 34 Some early manuscripts do not have this sentence.   [c] 42 Some manuscripts *come with your kingly power*   [d] 46 Psalm 31:5

with Jesus from Galilee followed Joseph and saw the tomb and how his body was laid in it. ⁵⁶Then they went home and prepared spices and perfumes. But they rested on the Sabbath in obedience to the commandment.

24 On the first day of the week, very early in the morning, the women took the spices they had prepared and went to the tomb. ²They found the stone rolled away from the tomb, ³but when they entered, they did not find the body of the Lord Jesus. ⁴While they were wondering about this, suddenly two men in clothes that gleamed like lightning stood beside them. ⁵In their fright the women bowed down with their faces to the ground, but the men said to them, "Why do you look for the living among the dead? ⁶He is not here; he has risen! Remember how he told you, while he was still with you in Galilee: ⁷'The Son of Man must be delivered over to the hands of sinners, be crucified and on the third day be raised again.'" ⁸Then they remembered his words.

⁹When they came back from the tomb, they told all these things to the Eleven and to all the others. ¹⁰It was Mary Magdalene, Joanna, Mary the mother of James, and the others with them who told this to the apostles. ¹¹But they did not believe the women, because their words seemed to them like nonsense. ¹²Peter, however, got up and ran to the tomb. Bending over, he saw the strips of linen lying by themselves, and he went away, wondering to himself what had happened.

¹³Now that same day two of them were going to a village called Emmaus, about seven miles[a] from Je-

rusalem. ¹⁴They were talking with each other about everything that had happened. ¹⁵As they talked and discussed these things with each other, Jesus himself came up and walked along with them; ¹⁶but they were kept from recognizing him.

¹⁷He asked them, "What are you discussing together as you walk along?"

They stood still, their faces downcast. ¹⁸One of them, named Cleopas, asked him, "Are you the only one visiting Jerusalem who does not know the things that have happened there in these days?"

¹⁹"What things?" he asked.

"About Jesus of Nazareth," they replied. "He was a prophet, powerful in word and deed before God and all the people. ²⁰The chief priests and our rulers handed him over to be sentenced to death, and they crucified him; ²¹but we had hoped that he was the one who was going to redeem Israel. And what is more, it is the third day since all this took place. ²²In addition, some of our women amazed us. They went to the tomb early this morning ²³but didn't find his body. They came and told us that they had seen a vision of angels, who said he was alive. ²⁴Then some of our companions went to the tomb and found it just as the women had said, but they did not see Jesus."

²⁵He said to them, "How foolish you are, and how slow to believe all that the prophets have spoken! ²⁶Did not the Messiah have to suffer these things and then enter his glory?" ²⁷And beginning with Moses and all the Prophets, he explained to them what was said in all the Scriptures concerning himself.

²⁸As they approached the village

---

a 13 Or about 11 kilometers

to which they were going, Jesus continued on as if he were going farther. ²⁹But they urged him strongly, "Stay with us, for it is nearly evening; the day is almost over." So he went in to stay with them.

³⁰When he was at the table with them, he took bread, gave thanks, broke it and began to give it to them. ³¹Then their eyes were opened and they recognized him, and he disappeared from their sight. ³²They asked each other, "Were not our hearts burning within us while he talked with us on the road and opened the Scriptures to us?"

³³They got up and returned at once to Jerusalem. There they found the Eleven and those with them, assembled together ³⁴and saying, "It is true! The Lord has risen and has appeared to Simon." ³⁵Then the two told what had happened on the way, and how Jesus was recognized by them when he broke the bread.

³⁶While they were still talking about this, Jesus himself stood among them and said to them, "Peace be with you."

³⁷They were startled and frightened, thinking they saw a ghost. ³⁸He said to them, "Why are you troubled, and why do doubts rise in your minds? ³⁹Look at my hands and my feet. It is I myself! Touch me and see; a ghost does not have flesh and bones, as you see I have."

⁴⁰When he had said this, he showed them his hands and feet. ⁴¹And while they still did not believe it because of joy and amazement, he asked them, "Do you have anything here to eat?" ⁴²They gave him a piece of broiled fish, ⁴³and he took it and ate it in their presence.

⁴⁴He said to them, "This is what I told you while I was still with you: Everything must be fulfilled that is written about me in the Law of Moses, the Prophets and the Psalms."

⁴⁵Then he opened their minds so they could understand the Scriptures. ⁴⁶He told them, "This is what is written: The Messiah will suffer and rise from the dead on the third day, ⁴⁷and repentance for the forgiveness of sins will be preached in his name to all nations, beginning at Jerusalem. ⁴⁸You are witnesses of these things. ⁴⁹I am going to send you what my Father has promised; but stay in the city until you have been clothed with power from on high."

⁵⁰When he had led them out to the vicinity of Bethany, he lifted up his hands and blessed them. ⁵¹While he was blessing them, he left them and was taken up into heaven. ⁵²Then they worshiped him and returned to Jerusalem with great joy. ⁵³And they stayed continually at the temple, praising God.

# JOHN

John closes his book by revealing his purpose in writing Jesus' story: *These are written that you may believe that Jesus is the Messiah, the Son of God, and that by believing you may have life in his name.*

John begins his book by echoing words from the Bible's creation story—*In the beginning*—showing his readers that this is a story of a new creation. Just as the first creation was completed in seven days, John uses the number seven to structure his book. For the Jews the number seven represented completeness and wholeness, a finished work of God revealing his purpose for the world.

The story is told in two main parts. The first describes Jesus' public ministry and has seven sections. Each section closes with a report on how people respond to Jesus, either in faith or unbelief. The second part is devoted to the Passover weekend, when Jesus gave his life for the world.

John records seven instances in which Jesus revealed his identity by using the phrase *I am*, the name by which God had revealed himself earlier. Similarly, John records seven miraculous signs that Jesus performed. John's narrative mentions twice that the resurrection of Jesus took place on the *first day of the week*. In this way he confirms that the power of a new creation has broken into our world.

---

1 In the beginning was the Word, and the Word was with God, and the Word was God. ²He was with God in the beginning. ³Through him all things were made; without him nothing was made that has been made. ⁴In him was life, and that life was the light of all mankind. ⁵The light shines in the darkness, and the darkness has not overcome[a] it.

⁶There was a man sent from God whose name was John. ⁷He came as a witness to testify concerning that light, so that through him all might believe. ⁸He himself was not the light; he came only as a witness to the light.

⁹The true light that gives light to everyone was coming into the world. ¹⁰He was in the world, and though the world was made through him, the world did not recognize him. ¹¹He came to that which was his own, but his own did not receive him. ¹²Yet to all who did receive him, to those who believed in his name, he gave the right to become children of God— ¹³children born not of natural descent, nor of human decision or a husband's will, but born of God.

¹⁴The Word became flesh and made his dwelling among us. We have seen his glory, the glory of the one and only Son, who came from the Father, full of grace and truth.

¹⁵(John testified concerning him. He cried out, saying, "This is the one I spoke about when I said, 'He who comes after me has surpassed me because he was before me.'") ¹⁶Out of his fullness we have all received grace in place of grace already given. ¹⁷For the law was given through Moses; grace and

---

a 5 Or *understood*

truth came through Jesus Christ. [18]No one has ever seen God, but the one and only Son, who is himself God and[a] is in closest relationship with the Father, has made him known.

[19]Now this was John's testimony when the Jewish leaders[b] in Jerusalem sent priests and Levites to ask him who he was. [20]He did not fail to confess, but confessed freely, "I am not the Messiah."

[21]They asked him, "Then who are you? Are you Elijah?"

He said, "I am not."

"Are you the Prophet?"

He answered, "No."

[22]Finally they said, "Who are you? Give us an answer to take back to those who sent us. What do you say about yourself?"

[23]John replied in the words of Isaiah the prophet, "I am the voice of one calling in the wilderness, 'Make straight the way for the Lord.'"[c]

[24]Now the Pharisees who had been [25]questioned him, "Why then do you baptize if you are not the Messiah, nor Elijah, nor the Prophet?"

[26]"I baptize with[d] water," John replied, "but among you stands one you do not know. [27]He is the one who comes after me, the straps of whose sandals I am not worthy to untie."

[28]This all happened at Bethany on the other side of the Jordan, where John was baptizing.

[29]The next day John saw Jesus coming toward him and said, "Look, the Lamb of God, who takes away the sin of the world! [30]This is the one I meant when I said, 'A man who comes after me has surpassed me because he was before me.' [31]I myself did not know him, but the reason I came baptizing with water was that he might be revealed to Israel."

[32]Then John gave this testimony: "I saw the Spirit come down from heaven as a dove and remain on him. [33]And I myself did not know him, but the one who sent me to baptize with water told me, 'The man on whom you see the Spirit come down and remain is the one who will baptize with the Holy Spirit.' [34]I have seen and I testify that this is God's Chosen One."[e]

[35]The next day John was there again with two of his disciples. [36]When he saw Jesus passing by, he said, "Look, the Lamb of God!"

[37]When the two disciples heard him say this, they followed Jesus. [38]Turning around, Jesus saw them following and asked, "What do you want?"

They said, "Rabbi" (which means "Teacher"), "where are you staying?"

[39]"Come," he replied, "and you will see."

So they went and saw where he was staying, and they spent that day with him. It was about four in the afternoon.

[40]Andrew, Simon Peter's brother, was one of the two who heard what John had said and who had followed Jesus. [41]The first thing Andrew did was to find his brother Simon and tell him, "We have found the Mes-

---

[a] 18 Some manuscripts *but the only Son, who the Jews (hoi Ioudaioi)* refers here and elsewhere in John's Gospel to those Jewish leaders who opposed Jesus; also in 5:10, 15, 16; 7:1, 11, 13; 9:22; 18:14, 28, 36; 19:7, 12, 31, 38; 20:19.     [b] 19 The Greek term traditionally translated [c] 23 Isaiah 40:3     [d] 26 Or *in*; also in verses 31 and 33 (twice)     [e] 34 See Isaiah 42:1; many manuscripts *is the Son of God*.

siah" (that is, the Christ). ⁴²And he brought him to Jesus.

Jesus looked at him and said, "You are Simon son of John. You will be called Cephas" (which, when translated, is Peterᵃ).

⁴³The next day Jesus decided to leave for Galilee. Finding Philip, he said to him, "Follow me."

⁴⁴Philip, like Andrew and Peter, was from the town of Bethsaida. ⁴⁵Philip found Nathanael and told him, "We have found the one Moses wrote about in the Law, and about whom the prophets also wrote—Jesus of Nazareth, the son of Joseph."

⁴⁶"Nazareth! Can anything good come from there?" Nathanael asked.

"Come and see," said Philip.

⁴⁷When Jesus saw Nathanael approaching, he said of him, "Here truly is an Israelite in whom there is no deceit."

⁴⁸"How do you know me?" Nathanael asked.

Jesus answered, "I saw you while you were still under the fig tree before Philip called you."

⁴⁹Then Nathanael declared, "Rabbi, you are the Son of God; you are the king of Israel."

⁵⁰Jesus said, "You believeᵇ because I told you I saw you under the fig tree. You will see greater things than that." ⁵¹He then added, "Very truly I tell you,ᶜ you° will see 'heaven open, and the angels of God ascending and descending on'ᵈ the Son of Man."

2 On the third day a wedding took place at Cana in Galilee. Jesus' mother was there, ²and Jesus and his disciples had also been invited

to the wedding. ³When the wine was gone, Jesus' mother said to him, "They have no more wine."

⁴"Woman,ᵉ why do you involve me?" Jesus replied. "My hour has not yet come."

⁵His mother said to the servants, "Do whatever he tells you."

⁶Nearby stood six stone water jars, the kind used by the Jews for ceremonial washing, each holding from twenty to thirty gallons.ᶠ

⁷Jesus said to the servants, "Fill the jars with water"; so they filled them to the brim.

⁸Then he told them, "Now draw some out and take it to the master of the banquet."

They did so, ⁹and the master of the banquet tasted the water that had been turned into wine. He did not realize where it had come from, though the servants who had drawn the water knew. Then he called the bridegroom aside ¹⁰and said, "Everyone brings out the choice wine first and then the cheaper wine after the guests have had too much to drink; but you have saved the best till now."

¹¹What Jesus did here in Cana of Galilee was the first of the signs through which he revealed his glory; and his disciples believed in him.

¹²After this he went down to Capernaum with his mother and brothers and his disciples. There they stayed for a few days.

¹³When it was almost time for the Jewish Passover, Jesus went up to Jerusalem. ¹⁴In the temple courts he found people selling cattle, sheep and doves, and others sitting

---

ᵃ 42 *Cephas* (Aramaic) and *Peter* (Greek) both mean *rock.*     ᵇ 50 Or *Do you believe . . . ?*     ᶜ 51 The Greek is plural.     ᵈ 51 Gen. 28:12     ᵉ 4 The Greek for *Woman* does not denote any disrespect.     ᶠ 6 Or *from about 75 to about 115 liters* at tables exchanging money. 15So he made a whip out of cords, and drove all from the temple courts, both sheep and cattle; he scattered the coins of the money changers and overturned their tables. 16To those who sold doves he said, "Get these out of here! Stop turning my Father's house into a market!" 17His disciples remembered that it is written: "Zeal for your house will consume me."*a*

18The Jews then responded to him, "What sign can you show us to prove your authority to do all this?"

19Jesus answered them, "Destroy this temple, and I will raise it again in three days."

20They replied, "It has taken forty-six years to build this temple, and you are going to raise it in three days?" 21But the temple he had spoken of was his body. 22After he was raised from the dead, his disciples recalled what he had said. Then they believed the scripture and the words that Jesus had spoken.

23Now while he was in Jerusalem at the Passover Festival, many people saw the signs he was performing and believed in his name.*b* 24But Jesus would not entrust himself to them, for he knew all people. 25He did not need any testimony about mankind, for he knew what was in each person.

3 Now there was a Pharisee, a man named Nicodemus who was a member of the Jewish ruling council. 2He came to Jesus at night and said, "Rabbi, we know that you are a teacher who has come from God. For no one could perform the signs you are doing if God were not with him."

3Jesus replied, "Very truly I tell you, no one can see the kingdom of God unless they are born again.*c*"

4"How can someone be born when they are old?" Nicodemus asked. "Surely they cannot enter a second time into their mother's womb to be born!"

5Jesus answered, "Very truly I tell you, no one can enter the kingdom of God unless they are born of water and the Spirit. 6Flesh gives birth to flesh, but the Spirit*d* gives birth to spirit. 7You should not be surprised at my saying, 'You*e* must be born again.' 8The wind blows wherever it pleases. You hear its sound, but you cannot tell where it comes from or where it is going. So it is with everyone born of the Spirit."*f*

9"How can this be?" Nicodemus asked.

10"You are Israel's teacher," said Jesus, "and do you not understand these things? 11Very truly I tell you, we speak of what we know, and we testify to what we have seen, but still you people do not accept our testimony. 12I have spoken to you of earthly things and you do not believe; how then will you believe if I speak of heavenly things? 13No one has ever gone into heaven except the one who came from heaven—the Son of Man.*g* 14Just as Moses lifted up the snake in the wilderness, the Son of Man must be lifted up,*h* 15that everyone who believes may have eternal life in him."*i*

16For God so loved the world that he gave his one and only Son, that whoever believes in him shall not perish but have eternal life. 17For God did not send his Son into the world

---

*a* 17 Psalm 69:9    *b* 23 Or *in him*    *c* 3 The Greek for *again* also means *from above*; also in verse 7.    *d* 6 Or *but spirit*    *e* 7 The Greek is plural.    *f* 8 The Greek for *Spirit* is the same as that for *wind*.    *g* 13 Some manuscripts *Man, who is in heaven*    *h* 14 The Greek for *lifted up* also means *exalted*.    *i* 15 Some interpreters end the quotation with verse 21.

to condemn the world, but to save the world through him. 18Whoever believes in him is not condemned, but whoever does not believe stands condemned already because they have not believed in the name of God's one and only Son. 19This is the verdict: Light has come into the world, but people loved darkness instead of light because their deeds were evil. 20Everyone who does evil hates the light, and will not come into the light for fear that their deeds will be exposed. 21But whoever lives by the truth comes into the light, so that it may be seen plainly that what they have done has been done in the sight of God.

22After this, Jesus and his disciples went out into the Judean countryside, where he spent some time with them, and baptized. 23Now John also was baptizing at Aenon near Salim, because there was plenty of water, and people were coming and being baptized. 24(This was before John was put in prison.) 25An argument developed between some of John's disciples and a certain Jew over the matter of ceremonial washing. 26They came to John and said to him, "Rabbi, that man who was with you on the other side of the Jordan—the one you testified about—look, he is baptizing, and everyone is going to him."

27To this John replied, "A person can receive only what is given them from heaven. 28You yourselves can testify that I said, 'I am not the Messiah but am sent ahead of him.' 29The bride belongs to the bridegroom. The friend who attends the bridegroom waits and listens for him, and is full of joy when he hears the bridegroom's voice. That joy is

mine, and it is now complete. 30He must become greater; I must become less."a

31The one who comes from above is above all; the one who is from the earth belongs to the earth, and speaks as one from the earth. The one who comes from heaven is above all. 32He testifies to what he has seen and heard, but no one accepts his testimony. 33Whoever has accepted it has certified that God is truthful. 34For the one whom God has sent speaks the words of God, for Godb gives the Spirit without limit. 35The Father loves the Son and has placed everything in his hands. 36Whoever believes in the Son has eternal life, but whoever rejects the Son will not see life, for God's wrath remains on them.

4 Now Jesus learned that the Pharisees had heard that he was gaining and baptizing more disciples than John— 2although in fact it was not Jesus who baptized, but his disciples. 3So he left Judea and went back once more to Galilee.

4Now he had to go through Samaria. 5So he came to a town in Samaria called Sychar, near the plot of ground Jacob had given to his son Joseph. 6Jacob's well was there, and Jesus, tired as he was from the journey, sat down by the well. It was about noon.

7When a Samaritan woman came to draw water, Jesus said to her, "Will you give me a drink?" 8(His disciples had gone into the town to buy food.)

9The Samaritan woman said to him, "You are a Jew and I am a Samaritan woman. How can you ask me for a drink?" (For Jews do not associate with Samaritans.c)

a 30 Some interpreters end the quotation with verse 36.    b 34 Greek he    c 9 Or do not use dishes Samaritans have used

¹⁰Jesus answered her, "If you knew the gift of God and who it is that asks you for a drink, you would have asked him and he would have given you living water."

¹¹"Sir," the woman said, "you have nothing to draw with and the well is deep. Where can you get this living water? ¹²Are you greater than our father Jacob, who gave us the well and drank from it himself, as did also his sons and his livestock?"

¹³Jesus answered, "Everyone who drinks this water will be thirsty again, ¹⁴but whoever drinks the water I give them will never thirst. Indeed, the water I give them will become in them a spring of water welling up to eternal life."

¹⁵The woman said to him, "Sir, give me this water so that I won't get thirsty and have to keep coming here to draw water."

¹⁶He told her, "Go, call your husband and come back."

¹⁷"I have no husband," she replied.

Jesus said to her, "You are right when you say you have no husband. ¹⁸The fact is, you have had five husbands, and the man you now have is not your husband. What you have just said is quite true."

¹⁹"Sir," the woman said, "I can see that you are a prophet. ²⁰Our ancestors worshiped on this mountain, but you Jews claim that the place where we must worship is in Jerusalem."

²¹"Woman," Jesus replied, "believe me, a time is coming when you will worship the Father neither on this mountain nor in Jerusalem. ²²You Samaritans worship what you do not know; we worship what we do know, for salvation is from the Jews. ²³Yet a time is coming and has now come when the true worshipers will worship the Father in the Spirit and in truth, for they are the kind of worshipers the Father seeks. ²⁴God is spirit, and his worshipers must worship in the Spirit and in truth."

²⁵The woman said, "I know that Messiah" (called Christ) "is coming. When he comes, he will explain everything to us."

²⁶Then Jesus declared, "I, the one speaking to you—I am he."

²⁷Just then his disciples returned and were surprised to find him talking with a woman. But no one asked, "What do you want?" or "Why are you talking with her?"

²⁸Then, leaving her water jar, the woman went back to the town and said to the people, ²⁹"Come, see a man who told me everything I ever did. Could this be the Messiah?" ³⁰They came out of the town and made their way toward him.

³¹Meanwhile his disciples urged him, "Rabbi, eat something."

³²But he said to them, "I have food to eat that you know nothing about."

³³Then his disciples said to each other, "Could someone have brought him food?"

³⁴"My food," said Jesus, "is to do the will of him who sent me and to finish his work. ³⁵Don't you have a saying, 'It's still four months until harvest'? I tell you, open your eyes and look at the fields! They are ripe for harvest. ³⁶Even now the one who reaps draws a wage and harvests a crop for eternal life, so that the sower and the reaper may be glad together. ³⁷Thus the saying 'One sows and another reaps' is true. ³⁸I sent you to reap what you have not worked for. Others have done the hard work, and you have reaped the benefits of their labor."

39 Many of the Samaritans from that town believed in him because of the woman's testimony, "He told me everything I ever did." 40 So when the Samaritans came to him, they urged him to stay with them, and he stayed two days. 41 And because of his words many more became believers.

42 They said to the woman, "We no longer believe just because of what you said; now we have heard for ourselves, and we know that this man really is the Savior of the world."

43 After the two days he left for Galilee. 44 (Now Jesus himself had pointed out that a prophet has no honor in his own country.) 45 When he arrived in Galilee, the Galileans welcomed him. They had seen all that he had done in Jerusalem at the Passover Festival, for they also had been there.

46 Once more he visited Cana in Galilee, where he had turned the water into wine. And there was a certain royal official whose son lay sick at Capernaum. 47 When this man heard that Jesus had arrived in Galilee from Judea, he went to him and begged him to come and heal his son, who was close to death.

48 "Unless you people see signs and wonders," Jesus told him, "you will never believe."

49 The royal official said, "Sir, come down before my child dies."

50 "Go," Jesus replied, "your son will live."

The man took Jesus at his word and departed. 51 While he was still on the way, his servants met him with the news that his boy was living. 52 When he inquired as to the time when his son got better, they said to him, "Yesterday, at one in the afternoon, the fever left him."

53 Then the father realized that this was the exact time at which Jesus had said to him, "Your son will live." So he and his whole household believed.

54 This was the second sign Jesus performed after coming from Judea to Galilee.

5 Some time later, Jesus went up to Jerusalem for one of the Jewish festivals. 2 Now there is in Jerusalem near the Sheep Gate a pool, which in Aramaic is called Bethesda[a] and which is surrounded by five covered colonnades. 3 Here a great number of disabled people used to lie — the blind, the lame, the paralyzed. [4] b 5 One who was there had been an invalid for thirty-eight years. 6 When Jesus saw him lying there and learned that he had been in this condition for a long time, he asked him, "Do you want to get well?"

7 "Sir," the invalid replied, "I have no one to help me into the pool when the water is stirred. While I am trying to get in, someone else goes down ahead of me."

8 Then Jesus said to him, "Get up! Pick up your mat and walk." 9 At once the man was cured; he picked up his mat and walked.

The day on which this took place was a Sabbath, 10 and so the Jewish leaders said to the man who had been healed, "It is the Sabbath; the law forbids you to carry your mat."

11 But he replied, "The man who

---

a 2 Some manuscripts *Bethzatha*; other manuscripts *Bethsaida*    b 3,4 Some manuscripts include here, wholly or in part, *paralyzed — and they waited for the moving of the waters. 4 From time to time an angel of the Lord would come down and stir up the waters. The first one into the pool after each such disturbance would be cured of whatever disease they had.*

made me well said to me, 'Pick up your mat and walk.'"

12 So they asked him, "Who is this fellow who told you to pick it up and walk?"

13 The man who was healed had no idea who it was, for Jesus had slipped away into the crowd that was there.

14 Later Jesus found him at the temple and said to him, "See, you are well again. Stop sinning or something worse may happen to you." 15 The man went away and told the Jewish leaders that it was Jesus who had made him well.

16 So, because Jesus was doing these things on the Sabbath, the Jewish leaders began to persecute him. 17 In his defense Jesus said to them, "My Father is always at his work to this very day, and I too am working." 18 For this reason they tried all the more to kill him; not only was he breaking the Sabbath, but he was even calling God his own Father, making himself equal with God.

19 Jesus gave them this answer: "Very truly I tell you, the Son can do nothing by himself; he can do only what he sees his Father doing, because whatever the Father does the Son also does. 20 For the Father loves the Son and shows him all he does. Yes, and he will show him even greater works than these, so that you will be amazed. 21 For just as the Father raises the dead and gives them life, even so the Son gives life to whom he is pleased to give it. 22 Moreover, the Father judges no one, but has entrusted all judgment to the Son, 23 that all may honor the Son just as they honor the Father. Whoever does not honor the Son does not honor the Father, who sent him.

24 "Very truly I tell you, whoever hears my word and believes him who sent me has eternal life and will not be judged but has crossed over from death to life. 25 Very truly I tell you, a time is coming and has now come when the dead will hear the voice of the Son of God and those who hear will live. 26 For as the Father has life in himself, so he has granted the Son also to have life in himself. 27 And he has given him authority to judge because he is the Son of Man.

28 "Do not be amazed at this, for a time is coming when all who are in their graves will hear his voice 29 and come out — those who have done what is good will rise to live, and those who have done what is evil will rise to be condemned. 30 By myself I can do nothing; I judge only as I hear, and my judgment is just, for I seek not to please myself but him who sent me.

31 "If I testify about myself, my testimony is not true. 32 There is another who testifies in my favor, and I know that his testimony about me is true.

33 "You have sent to John and he has testified to the truth. 34 Not that I accept human testimony; but I mention it that you may be saved. 35 John was a lamp that burned and gave light, and you chose for a time to enjoy his light.

36 "I have testimony weightier than that of John. For the works that the Father has given me to finish — the very works that I am doing — testify that the Father has sent me. 37 And the Father who sent me has himself testified concerning me. You have never heard his voice nor seen his form, 38 nor does his word dwell in you, for you do not believe the one he sent. 39 You

study[a] the Scriptures diligently because you think that in them you have eternal life. These are the very Scriptures that testify about me, [40]yet you refuse to come to me to have life.

[41]"I do not accept glory from human beings, [42]but I know you. I know that you do not have the love of God in your hearts. [43]I have come in my Father's name, and you do not accept me; but if someone else comes in his own name, you will accept him. [44]How can you believe since you accept glory from one another but do not seek the glory that comes from the only God[b]?

[45]"But do not think I will accuse you before the Father. Your accuser is Moses, on whom your hopes are set. [46]If you believed Moses, you would believe me, for he wrote about me. [47]But since you do not believe what he wrote, how are you going to believe what I say?"

6 Some time after this, Jesus crossed to the far shore of the Sea of Galilee (that is, the Sea of Tiberias), [2]and a great crowd of people followed him because they saw the signs he had performed by healing the sick. [3]Then Jesus went up on a mountainside and sat down with his disciples. [4]The Jewish Passover Festival was near.

[5]When Jesus looked up and saw a great crowd coming toward him, he said to Philip, "Where shall we buy bread for these people to eat?" [6]He asked this only to test him, for he already had in mind what he was going to do.

[7]Philip answered him, "It would take more than half a year's wages[c] to buy enough bread for each one to have a bite!"

[8]Another of his disciples, Andrew, Simon Peter's brother, spoke up, [9]"Here is a boy with five small barley loaves and two small fish, but how far will they go among so many?"

[10]Jesus said, "Have the people sit down." There was plenty of grass in that place, and they sat down (about five thousand men were there). [11]Jesus then took the loaves, gave thanks, and distributed to those who were seated as much as they wanted. He did the same with the fish.

[12]When they had all had enough to eat, he said to his disciples, "Gather the pieces that are left over. Let nothing be wasted." [13]So they gathered them and filled twelve baskets with the pieces of the five barley loaves left over by those who had eaten.

[14]After the people saw the sign Jesus performed, they began to say, "Surely this is the Prophet who is to come into the world." [15]Jesus, knowing that they intended to come and make him king by force, withdrew again to a mountain by himself.

[16]When evening came, his disciples went down to the lake, [17]where they got into a boat and set off across the lake for Capernaum. By now it was dark, and Jesus had not yet joined them. [18]A strong wind was blowing and the waters grew rough. [19]When they had rowed about three or four miles,[d] they saw Jesus approaching the boat, walking on the water; and they were frightened. [20]But he said to them, "It is I; don't be afraid." [21]Then

---

[a] 39 Or [39]Study    [b] 44 Some early manuscripts the Only One    [c] 7 Greek take two hundred denarii    [d] 19 Or about 5 or 6 kilometers

they were willing to take him into the boat, and immediately the boat reached the shore where they were heading.

²²The next day the crowd that had stayed on the opposite shore of the lake realized that only one boat had been there, and that Jesus had not entered it with his disciples, but that they had gone away alone. ²³Then some boats from Tiberias landed near the place where the people had eaten the bread after the Lord had given thanks. ²⁴Once the crowd realized that neither Jesus nor his disciples were there, they got into the boats and went to Capernaum in search of Jesus.

²⁵When they found him on the other side of the lake, they asked him, "Rabbi, when did you get here?"

²⁶Jesus answered, "Very truly I tell you, you are looking for me, not because you saw the signs I performed but because you ate the loaves and had your fill. ²⁷Do not work for food that spoils, but for food that endures to eternal life, which the Son of Man will give you. For on him God the Father has placed his seal of approval."

²⁸Then they asked him, "What must we do to do the works God requires?"

²⁹Jesus answered, "The work of God is this: to believe in the one he has sent."

³⁰So they asked him, "What sign then will you give that we may see it and believe you? What will you do? ³¹Our ancestors ate the manna in the wilderness; as it is written: 'He gave them bread from heaven to eat.'[a]

³²Jesus said to them, "Very truly I tell you, it is not Moses who has given you the bread from heaven, but it is my Father who gives you the true bread from heaven. ³³For the bread of God is the bread that comes down from heaven and gives life to the world."

³⁴"Sir," they said, "always give us this bread."

³⁵Then Jesus declared, "I am the bread of life. Whoever comes to me will never go hungry, and whoever believes in me will never be thirsty. ³⁶But as I told you, you have seen me and still you do not believe. ³⁷All those the Father gives me will come to me, and whoever comes to me I will never drive away. ³⁸For I have come down from heaven not to do my will but to do the will of him who sent me. ³⁹And this is the will of him who sent me, that I shall lose none of all those he has given me, but raise them up at the last day. ⁴⁰For my Father's will is that everyone who looks to the Son and believes in him shall have eternal life, and I will raise them up at the last day."

⁴¹At this the Jews there began to grumble about him because he said, "I am the bread that came down from heaven." ⁴²They said, "Is this not Jesus, the son of Joseph, whose father and mother we know? How can he now say, 'I came down from heaven'?"

⁴³"Stop grumbling among yourselves," Jesus answered. ⁴⁴"No one can come to me unless the Father who sent me draws them, and I will raise them up at the last day. ⁴⁵It is written in the Prophets: 'They will all be taught by God.'[b] Everyone who has heard the Father and learned from him comes to me. ⁴⁶No one has seen the Father except the one who is from God; only he has seen the Father. ⁴⁷Very truly

---

[a] 31 Exodus 16:4; Neh. 9:15; Psalm 78:24,25   [b] 45 Isaiah 54:13

I tell you, the one who believes has eternal life. 48I am the bread of life. 49Your ancestors ate the manna in the wilderness, yet they died. 50But here is the bread that comes down from heaven, which anyone may eat and not die. 51I am the living bread that came down from heaven. Whoever eats this bread will live forever. This bread is my flesh, which I will give for the life of the world."

52Then the Jews began to argue sharply among themselves, "How can this man give us his flesh to eat?"

53Jesus said to them, "Very truly I tell you, unless you eat the flesh of the Son of Man and drink his blood, you have no life in you. 54Whoever eats my flesh and drinks my blood has eternal life, and I will raise them up at the last day. 55For my flesh is real food and my blood is real drink. 56Whoever eats my flesh and drinks my blood remains in me, and I in them. 57Just as the living Father sent me and I live because of the Father, so the one who feeds on me will live because of me. 58This is the bread that came down from heaven. Your ancestors ate manna and died, but whoever feeds on this bread will live forever." 59He said this while teaching in the synagogue in Capernaum.

60On hearing it, many of his disciples said, "This is a hard teaching. Who can accept it?"

61Aware that his disciples were grumbling about this, Jesus said to them, "Does this offend you? 62Then what if you see the Son of Man ascend to where he was before! 63The Spirit gives life; the flesh counts for nothing. The words I have spoken to you—they are full of the Spirit[a]

and life. 64Yet there are some of you who do not believe." For Jesus had known from the beginning which of them did not believe and who would betray him. 65He went on to say, "This is why I told you that no one can come to me unless the Father has enabled them."

66From this time many of his disciples turned back and no longer followed him.

67"You do not want to leave too, do you?" Jesus asked the Twelve.

68Simon Peter answered him, "Lord, to whom shall we go? You have the words of eternal life. 69We have come to believe and to know that you are the Holy One of God."

70Then Jesus replied, "Have I not chosen you, the Twelve? Yet one of you is a devil!" 71(He meant Judas, the son of Simon Iscariot, who, though one of the Twelve, was later to betray him.)

7 After this, Jesus went around in Galilee. He did not want[b] to go about in Judea because the Jewish leaders there were looking for a way to kill him. 2But when the Jewish Festival of Tabernacles was near, 3Jesus' brothers said to him, "Leave Galilee and go to Judea, so that your disciples there may see the works you do. 4No one who wants to become a public figure acts in secret. Since you are doing these things, show yourself to the world." 5For even his own brothers did not believe in him.

6Therefore Jesus told them, "My time is not yet here; for you any time will do. 7The world cannot hate you, but it hates me because I testify that its works are evil. 8You go up to this festival. I am not[c] going up to this fes-

a 63 Or are Spirit; or are spirit    b 1 Some manuscripts not have authority    c 8 Some manuscripts not yet tival, because my time has not yet fully come." [9] After he had said this, he stayed in Galilee.

[10] However, after his brothers had left for the festival, he went also, not publicly, but in secret. [11] Now at the festival the Jewish leaders were watching for Jesus and asking, "Where is he?"

[12] Among the crowds there was widespread whispering about him. Some said, "He is a good man."

Others replied, "No, he deceives the people." [13] But no one would say anything publicly about him for fear of the leaders.

[14] Not until halfway through the festival did Jesus go up to the temple courts and begin to teach. [15] The Jews there were amazed and asked, "How did this man get such learning without having been taught?"

[16] Jesus answered, "My teaching is not my own. It comes from the one who sent me. [17] Anyone who chooses to do the will of God will find out whether my teaching comes from God or whether I speak on my own. [18] Whoever speaks on their own does so to gain personal glory, but he who seeks the glory of the one who sent him is a man of truth; there is nothing false about him. [19] Has not Moses given you the law? Yet not one of you keeps the law. Why are you trying to kill me?"

[20] "You are demon-possessed," the crowd answered. "Who is trying to kill you?"

[21] Jesus said to them, "I did one miracle, and you are all amazed. [22] Yet, because Moses gave you circumcision (though actually it did not come from Moses, but from the patriarchs), you circumcise a boy on the Sabbath. [23] Now if a boy can be circumcised on the Sabbath so that the law of Moses may not be broken, why are you angry with me for healing a man's whole body on the Sabbath? [24] Stop judging by mere appearances, but instead judge correctly."

[25] At that point some of the people of Jerusalem began to ask, "Isn't this the man they are trying to kill? [26] Here he is, speaking publicly, and they are not saying a word to him. Have the authorities really concluded that he is the Messiah? [27] But we know where this man is from; when the Messiah comes, no one will know where he is from."

[28] Then Jesus, still teaching in the temple courts, cried out, "Yes, you know me, and you know where I am from. I am not here on my own authority, but he who sent me is true. You do not know him, [29] but I know him because I am from him and he sent me."

[30] At this they tried to seize him, but no one laid a hand on him, because his hour had not yet come. [31] Still, many in the crowd believed in him. They said, "When the Messiah comes, will he perform more signs than this man?"

[32] The Pharisees heard the crowd whispering such things about him. Then the chief priests and the Pharisees sent temple guards to arrest him.

[33] Jesus said, "I am with you for only a short time, and then I am going to the one who sent me. [34] You will look for me, but you will not find me; and where I am, you cannot come."

[35] The Jews said to one another, "Where does this man intend to go that we cannot find him? Will he go where our people live scattered among the Greeks, and teach the Greeks? [36] What did he mean when he said, 'You will look for me, but

you will not find me,' and 'Where I am, you cannot come'?"

37On the last and greatest day of the festival, Jesus stood and said in a loud voice, "Let anyone who is thirsty come to me and drink. 38Whoever believes in me, as Scripture has said, rivers of living water will flow from within them."*a* 39By this he meant the Spirit, whom those who believed in him were later to receive. Up to that time the Spirit had not been given, since Jesus had not yet been glorified.

40On hearing his words, some of the people said, "Surely this man is the Prophet."

41Others said, "He is the Messiah."

Still others asked, "How can the Messiah come from Galilee? 42Does not Scripture say that the Messiah will come from David's descendants and from Bethlehem, the town where David lived?" 43Thus the people were divided because of Jesus. 44Some wanted to seize him, but no one laid a hand on him.

45Finally the temple guards went back to the chief priests and the Pharisees, who asked them, "Why didn't you bring him in?"

46"No one ever spoke the way this man does," the guards replied.

47"You mean he has deceived you also?" the Pharisees retorted. 48"Have any of the rulers or of the Pharisees believed in him? 49No! But this mob that knows nothing of the law — there is a curse on them."

50Nicodemus, who had gone to Jesus earlier and who was one of their own number, asked, 51"Does our law condemn a man without first hearing him to find out what he has been doing?"

52They replied, "Are you from Galilee, too? Look into it, and you will find that a prophet does not come out of Galilee."

---

[The earliest manuscripts and many other ancient witnesses do not have John 7:53 — 8:11. A few manuscripts include these verses, wholly or in part, after John 7:36, John 21:25, Luke 21:38 or Luke 24:53.]

8 53Then they all went home, 1but Jesus went to the Mount of Olives.

2At dawn he appeared again in the temple courts, where all the people gathered around him, and he sat down to teach them. 3The teachers of the law and the Pharisees brought in a woman caught in adultery. They made her stand before the group 4and said to Jesus, "Teacher, this woman was caught in the act of adultery. 5In the Law Moses commanded us to stone such women. Now what do you say?" 6They were using this question as a trap, in order to have a basis for accusing him.

But Jesus bent down and started to write on the ground with his finger. 7When they kept on questioning him, he straightened up and said to them, "Let any one of you who is without sin be the first to throw a stone at her." 8Again he stooped down and wrote on the ground.

9At this, those who heard began to go away one at a time, the older ones first, until only Jesus was left, with the woman still standing there. 10Jesus straightened up and asked her, "Woman, where are they? Has no one condemned you?"

11"No one, sir," she said.

"Then neither do I condemn you," Jesus declared. "Go now and leave your life of sin."

---

*a 37,38 Or me. And let anyone drink 38who believes in me." As Scripture has said, "Out of him (or them) will flow rivers of living water."*

¹²When Jesus spoke again to the people, he said, "I am the light of the world. Whoever follows me will never walk in darkness, but will have the light of life."

¹³The Pharisees challenged him, "Here you are, appearing as your own witness; your testimony is not valid."

¹⁴Jesus answered, "Even if I testify on my own behalf, my testimony is valid, for I know where I am going. But you have no idea where I come from or where I am going. ¹⁵You judge by human standards; I pass judgment on no one. ¹⁶But if I do judge, my decisions are true, because I am not alone. I stand with the Father, who sent me. ¹⁷In your own Law it is written that the testimony of two witnesses is true. ¹⁸I am one who testifies for myself; my other witness is the Father, who sent me."

¹⁹Then they asked him, "Where is your father?"

"You do not know me or my Father," Jesus replied. "If you knew me, you would know my Father also." ²⁰He spoke these words while teaching in the temple courts near the place where the offerings were put. Yet no one seized him, because his hour had not yet come.

²¹Once more Jesus said to them, "I am going away, and you will look for me, and you will die in your sin. Where I go, you cannot come."

²²This made the Jews ask, "Will he kill himself? Is that why he says, 'Where I go, you cannot come'?"

²³But he continued, "You are from below; I am from above. You are of this world; I am not of this world. ²⁴I told you that you would die in your sins; if you do not believe that I am he, you will indeed die in your sins."

²⁵"Who are you?" they asked.

"Just what I have been telling you from the beginning," Jesus replied. ²⁶"I have much to say in judgment of you. But he who sent me is trustworthy, and what I have heard from him I tell the world."

²⁷They did not understand that he was telling them about his Father. ²⁸So Jesus said, "When you have lifted up[a] the Son of Man, then you will know that I am he and that I do nothing on my own but speak just what the Father has taught me. ²⁹The one who sent me is with me; he has not left me alone, for I always do what pleases him." ³⁰Even as he spoke, many believed in him.

³¹To the Jews who had believed him, Jesus said, "If you hold to my teaching, you are really my disciples. ³²Then you will know the truth, and the truth will set you free."

³³They answered him, "We are Abraham's descendants and have never been slaves of anyone. How can you say that we shall be set free?"

³⁴Jesus replied, "Very truly I tell you, everyone who sins is a slave to sin. ³⁵Now a slave has no permanent place in the family, but a son belongs to it forever. ³⁶So if the Son sets you free, you will be free indeed. ³⁷I know that you are Abraham's descendants. Yet you are looking for a way to kill me, because you have no room for my word. ³⁸I am telling you what I have seen in the Father's presence, and you are doing what you have heard from your father.[b]"

---

[a] 28 The Greek for *lifted up* also means *exalted*. *heard from the Father.*

[b] 38 Or *presence. Therefore do what you have*

³⁹"Abraham is our father," they answered.

"If you were Abraham's children," said Jesus, "then you would*ᵃ* do what Abraham did. ⁴⁰As it is, you are looking for a way to kill me, a man who has told you the truth that I heard from God. Abraham did not do such things. ⁴¹You are doing the works of your own father."

"We are not illegitimate children," they protested. "The only Father we have is God himself."

⁴²Jesus said to them, "If God were your Father, you would love me, for I have come here from God. I have not come on my own; God sent me. ⁴³Why is my language not clear to you? Because you are unable to hear what I say. ⁴⁴You belong to your father, the devil, and you want to carry out your father's desires. He was a murderer from the beginning, not holding to the truth, for there is no truth in him. When he lies, he speaks his native language, for he is a liar and the father of lies. ⁴⁵Yet because I tell the truth, you do not believe me! ⁴⁶Can any of you prove me guilty of sin? If I am telling the truth, why don't you believe me? ⁴⁷Whoever belongs to God hears what God says. The reason you do not hear is that you do not belong to God."

⁴⁸The Jews answered him, "Aren't we right in saying that you are a Samaritan and demon-possessed?"

⁴⁹"I am not possessed by a demon," said Jesus, "but I honor my Father and you dishonor me. ⁵⁰I am not seeking glory for myself; but there is one who seeks it, and he is the judge. ⁵¹Very truly I tell you, whoever obeys my word will never see death."

⁵²At this they exclaimed, "Now we know that you are demon-possessed! Abraham died and so did the prophets, yet you say that whoever obeys your word will never taste death. ⁵³Are you greater than our father Abraham? He died, and so did the prophets. Who do you think you are?"

⁵⁴Jesus replied, "If I glorify myself, my glory means nothing. My Father, whom you claim as your God, is the one who glorifies me. ⁵⁵Though you do not know him, I know him. If I said I did not, I would be a liar like you, but I do know him and obey his word. ⁵⁶Your father Abraham rejoiced at the thought of seeing my day; he saw it and was glad."

⁵⁷"You are not yet fifty years old," they said to him, "and you have seen Abraham!"

⁵⁸"Very truly I tell you," Jesus answered, "before Abraham was born, I am!" ⁵⁹At this, they picked up stones to stone him, but Jesus hid himself, slipping away from the temple grounds.

9 As he went along, he saw a man blind from birth. ²His disciples asked him, "Rabbi, who sinned, this man or his parents, that he was born blind?"

³"Neither this man nor his parents sinned," said Jesus, "but this happened so that the works of God might be displayed in him. ⁴As long as it is day, we must do the works of him who sent me. Night is coming, when no one can work. ⁵While I am in the world, I am the light of the world.

⁶After saying this, he spit on the ground, made some mud with the saliva, and put it on the man's eyes. ⁷"Go," he told him, "wash in the

---

*ᵃ 39* Some early manuscripts *"If you are Abraham's children," said Jesus, "then*

Pool of Siloam" (this word means "Sent"). So the man went and washed, and came home seeing.

8 His neighbors and those who had formerly seen him begging asked, "Isn't this the same man who used to sit and beg?" 9 Some claimed that he was.

Others said, "No, he only looks like him."

But he himself insisted, "I am the man."

10 "How then were your eyes opened?" they asked.

11 He replied, "The man they call Jesus made some mud and put it on my eyes. He told me to go to Siloam and wash. So I went and washed, and then I could see."

12 "Where is this man?" they asked him.

"I don't know," he said.

13 They brought to the Pharisees the man who had been blind. 14 Now the day on which Jesus had made the mud and opened the man's eyes was a Sabbath. 15 Therefore the Pharisees also asked him how he had received his sight. "He put mud on my eyes," the man replied, "and I washed, and now I see."

16 Some of the Pharisees said, "This man is not from God, for he does not keep the Sabbath."

But others asked, "How can a sinner perform such signs?" So they were divided.

17 Then they turned again to the blind man, "What have you to say about him? It was your eyes he opened."

The man replied, "He is a prophet."

18 They still did not believe that he had been blind and had received his sight until they sent for the man's parents. 19 "Is this your son?" they asked. "Is this the one you say was born blind? How is it that now he can see?"

20 "We know he is our son," the parents answered, "and we know he was born blind. 21 But how he can see now, or who opened his eyes, we don't know. Ask him. He is of age; he will speak for himself." 22 His parents said this because they were afraid of the Jewish leaders, who already had decided that anyone who acknowledged that Jesus was the Messiah would be put out of the synagogue. 23 That was why his parents said, "He is of age; ask him."

24 A second time they summoned the man who had been blind. "Give glory to God by telling the truth," they said. "We know this man is a sinner."

25 He replied, "Whether he is a sinner or not, I don't know. One thing I do know. I was blind but now I see!"

26 Then they asked him, "What did he do to you? How did he open your eyes?"

27 He answered, "I have told you already and you did not listen. Why do you want to hear it again? Do you want to become his disciples too?"

28 Then they hurled insults at him and said, "You are this fellow's disciple! We are disciples of Moses! 29 We know that God spoke to Moses, but as for this fellow, we don't even know where he comes from."

30 The man answered, "Now that is remarkable! You don't know where he comes from, yet he opened my eyes. 31 We know that God does not listen to sinners. He listens to the godly person who does his will. 32 Nobody has ever heard of opening the eyes of a man born blind. 33 If this man were not from God, he could do nothing."

34 To this they replied, "You were

steeped in sin at birth; how dare you lecture us!" And they threw him out.

<sup>35</sup>Jesus heard that they had thrown him out, and when he found him, he said, "Do you believe in the Son of Man?"

<sup>36</sup>"Who is he, sir?" the man asked. "Tell me so that I may believe in him."

<sup>37</sup>Jesus said, "You have now seen him; in fact, he is the one speaking with you."

<sup>38</sup>Then the man said, "Lord, I believe," and he worshiped him.

<sup>39</sup>Jesus said,[a] "For judgment I have come into this world, so that the blind will see and those who see will become blind."

<sup>40</sup>Some Pharisees who were with him heard him say this and asked, "What? Are we blind too?"

<sup>41</sup>Jesus said, "If you were blind, you would not be guilty of sin; but now that you claim you can see, your guilt remains.

**10** "Very truly I tell you Pharisees, anyone who does not enter the sheep pen by the gate, but climbs in by some other way, is a thief and a robber. <sup>2</sup>The one who enters by the gate is the shepherd of the sheep. <sup>3</sup>The gatekeeper opens the gate for him, and the sheep listen to his voice. He calls his own sheep by name and leads them out. <sup>4</sup>When he has brought out all his own, he goes on ahead of them, and his sheep follow him because they know his voice. <sup>5</sup>But they will never follow a stranger; in fact, they will run away from him because they do not recognize a stranger's voice." <sup>6</sup>Jesus used this figure of speech, but the Pharisees did not understand what he was telling them.

<sup>7</sup>Therefore Jesus said again, "Very truly I tell you, I am the gate for the sheep. <sup>8</sup>All who have come before me are thieves and robbers, but the sheep have not listened to them. <sup>9</sup>I am the gate; whoever enters through me will be saved.[b] They will come in and go out, and find pasture. <sup>10</sup>The thief comes only to steal and kill and destroy; I have come that they may have life, and have it to the full.

<sup>11</sup>"I am the good shepherd. The good shepherd lays down his life for the sheep. <sup>12</sup>The hired hand is not the shepherd and does not own the sheep. So when he sees the wolf coming, he abandons the sheep and runs away. Then the wolf attacks the flock and scatters it. <sup>13</sup>The man runs away because he is a hired hand and cares nothing for the sheep.

<sup>14</sup>"I am the good shepherd; I know my sheep and my sheep know me — <sup>15</sup>just as the Father knows me and I know the Father — and I lay down my life for the sheep. <sup>16</sup>I have other sheep that are not of this sheep pen. I must bring them also. They too will listen to my voice, and there shall be one flock and one shepherd. <sup>17</sup>The reason my Father loves me is that I lay down my life — only to take it up again. <sup>18</sup>No one takes it from me, but I lay it down of my own accord. I have authority to lay it down and authority to take it up again. This command I received from my Father."

<sup>19</sup>The Jews who heard these words were again divided. <sup>20</sup>Many of them said, "He is demon-possessed and raving mad. Why listen to him?"

<sup>21</sup>But others said, "These are not the sayings of a man possessed by a

---

[a] 38,39 Some early manuscripts do not have *Then the man said . . .*, *39Jesus said.*    [b] 9 Or *kept safe*

demon. Can a demon open the eyes of the blind?"

22 Then came the Festival of Dedication[a] at Jerusalem. It was winter, 23 and Jesus was in the temple courts walking in Solomon's Colonnade. 24 The Jews who were there gathered around him, saying, "How long will you keep us in suspense? If you are the Messiah, tell us plainly."

25 Jesus answered, "I did tell you, but you do not believe. The works I do in my Father's name testify about me, 26 but you do not believe because you are not my sheep. 27 My sheep listen to my voice; I know them, and they follow me. 28 I give them eternal life, and they shall never perish; no one will snatch them out of my hand. 29 My Father, who has given them to me, is greater than all[b]; no one can snatch them out of my Father's hand. 30 I and the Father are one."

31 Again his Jewish opponents picked up stones to stone him, 32 but Jesus said to them, "I have shown you many good works from the Father. For which of these do you stone me?"

33 "We are not stoning you for any good work," they replied, "but for blasphemy, because you, a mere man, claim to be God."

34 Jesus answered them, "Is it not written in your Law, 'I have said you are "gods"'[c]? 35 If he called them 'gods,' to whom the word of God came—and Scripture cannot be set aside— 36 what about the one whom the Father set apart as his very own and sent into the world? Why then do you accuse me of blasphemy because I said, 'I am God's Son'? 37 Do not believe me unless I

do the works of my Father. 38 But if I do them, even though you do not believe me, believe the works, that you may know and understand that the Father is in me, and I in the Father." 39 Again they tried to seize him, but he escaped their grasp.

40 Then Jesus went back across the Jordan to the place where John had been baptizing in the early days. There he stayed, 41 and many people came to him. They said, "Though John never performed a sign, all that John said about this man was true." 42 And in that place many believed in Jesus.

11 Now a man named Lazarus was sick. He was from Bethany, the village of Mary and her sister Martha. 2 (This Mary, whose brother Lazarus now lay sick, was the same one who poured perfume on the Lord and wiped his feet with her hair.) 3 So the sisters sent word to Jesus, "Lord, the one you love is sick."

4 When he heard this, Jesus said, "This sickness will not end in death. No, it is for God's glory so that God's Son may be glorified through it." 5 Now Jesus loved Martha and her sister and Lazarus. 6 So when he heard that Lazarus was sick, he stayed where he was two more days, 7 and then he said to his disciples, "Let us go back to Judea."

8 "But Rabbi," they said, "a short while ago the Jews there tried to stone you, and yet you are going back?"

9 Jesus answered, "Are there not twelve hours of daylight? Anyone who walks in the daytime will not stumble, for they see by this world's light. 10 It is when a person walks at

---

[a] 22 That is, Hanukkah    [b] 29 Many early manuscripts *What my Father has given me is greater than all*    [c] 34 Psalm 82:6

night that they stumble, for they have no light."

11 After he had said this, he went on to tell them, "Our friend Lazarus has fallen asleep; but I am going there to wake him up."

12 His disciples replied, "Lord, if he sleeps, he will get better." 13 Jesus had been speaking of his death, but his disciples thought he meant natural sleep.

14 So then he told them plainly, "Lazarus is dead, 15 and for your sake I am glad I was not there, so that you may believe. But let us go to him."

16 Then Thomas (also known as Didymus*a*) said to the rest of the disciples, "Let us also go, that we may die with him."

17 On his arrival, Jesus found that Lazarus had already been in the tomb for four days. 18 Now Bethany was less than two miles*b* from Jerusalem, 19 and many Jews had come to Martha and Mary to comfort them in the loss of their brother. 20 When Martha heard that Jesus was coming, she went out to meet him, but Mary stayed at home.

21 "Lord," Martha said to Jesus, "if you had been here, my brother would not have died. 22 But I know that even now God will give you whatever you ask."

23 Jesus said to her, "Your brother will rise again."

24 Martha answered, "I know he will rise again in the resurrection at the last day."

25 Jesus said to her, "I am the resurrection and the life. The one who believes in me will live, even though they die; 26 and whoever lives by believing in me will never die. Do you believe this?"

27 "Yes, Lord," she replied, "I believe that you are the Messiah, the Son of God, who is to come into the world."

28 After she had said this, she went back and called her sister Mary aside. "The Teacher is here," she said, "and is asking for you." 29 When Mary heard this, she got up quickly and went to him. 30 Now Jesus had not yet entered the village, but was still at the place where Martha had met him. 31 When the Jews who had been with Mary in the house, comforting her, noticed how quickly she got up and went out, they followed her, supposing she was going to the tomb to mourn there.

32 When Mary reached the place where Jesus was and saw him, she fell at his feet and said, "Lord, if you had been here, my brother would not have died."

33 When Jesus saw her weeping, and the Jews who had come along with her also weeping, he was deeply moved in spirit and troubled. 34 "Where have you laid him?" he asked.

"Come and see, Lord," they replied.

35 Jesus wept.

36 Then the Jews said, "See how he loved him!"

37 But some of them said, "Could not he who opened the eyes of the blind man have kept this man from dying?"

38 Jesus, once more deeply moved, came to the tomb. It was a cave with a stone laid across the entrance. 39 "Take away the stone," he said.

"But, Lord," said Martha, the sister of the dead man, "by this time there is a bad odor, for he has been there four days."

40 Then Jesus said, "Did I not tell

---

*a 16* Thomas (Aramaic) and *Didymus* (Greek) both mean *twin.*     *b 18* Or about 3 kilometers you that if you believe, you will see the glory of God?"

⁴¹So they took away the stone. Then Jesus looked up and said, "Father, I thank you that you have heard me. ⁴²I knew that you always hear me, but I said this for the benefit of the people standing here, that they may believe that you sent me."

⁴³When he had said this, Jesus called in a loud voice, "Lazarus, come out!" ⁴⁴The dead man came out, his hands and feet wrapped with strips of linen, and a cloth around his face.

Jesus said to them, "Take off the grave clothes and let him go."

⁴⁵Therefore many of the Jews who had come to visit Mary, and had seen what Jesus did, believed in him. ⁴⁶But some of them went to the Pharisees and told them what Jesus had done. ⁴⁷Then the chief priests and the Pharisees called a meeting of the Sanhedrin.

"What are we accomplishing?" they asked. "Here is this man performing many signs. ⁴⁸If we let him go on like this, everyone will believe in him, and then the Romans will come and take away both our temple and our nation."

⁴⁹Then one of them, named Caiaphas, who was high priest that year, spoke up, "You know nothing at all! ⁵⁰You do not realize that it is better for you that one man die for the people than that the whole nation perish."

⁵¹He did not say this on his own, but as high priest that year he prophesied that Jesus would die for the Jewish nation, ⁵²and not only for that nation but also for the scattered children of God, to bring them together and make them one. ⁵³So

from that day on they plotted to take his life.

⁵⁴Therefore Jesus no longer moved about publicly among the people of Judea. Instead he withdrew to a region near the wilderness, to a village called Ephraim, where he stayed with his disciples.

⁵⁵When it was almost time for the Jewish Passover, many went up from the country to Jerusalem for their ceremonial cleansing before the Passover. ⁵⁶They kept looking for Jesus, and as they stood in the temple courts they asked one another, "What do you think? Isn't he coming to the festival at all?" ⁵⁷But the chief priests and the Pharisees had given orders that anyone who found out where Jesus was should report it so that they might arrest him.

12 Six days before the Passover, Jesus came to Bethany, where Lazarus lived, whom Jesus had raised from the dead. ²Here a dinner was given in Jesus' honor. Martha served, while Lazarus was among those reclining at the table with him. ³Then Mary took about a pint[a] of pure nard, an expensive perfume; she poured it on Jesus' feet and wiped his feet with her hair. And the house was filled with the fragrance of the perfume.

⁴But one of his disciples, Judas Iscariot, who was later to betray him, objected, ⁵"Why wasn't this perfume sold and the money given to the poor? It was worth a year's wages.[b]" ⁶He did not say this because he cared about the poor but because he was a thief; as keeper of the money bag, he used to help himself to what was put into it.

⁷"Leave her alone," Jesus replied. "It was intended that she should

---

[a] 3 Or about 0.5 liter     [b] 5 Greek *three hundred denarii*

save this perfume for the day of my burial. [8]You will always have the poor among you,[a] but you will not always have me."

[9]Meanwhile a large crowd of Jews found out that Jesus was there and came, not only because of him but also to see Lazarus, whom he had raised from the dead. [10]So the chief priests made plans to kill Lazarus as well, [11]for on account of him many of the Jews were going over to Jesus and believing in him.

[12]The next day the great crowd that had come for the festival heard that Jesus was on his way to Jerusalem. [13]They took palm branches and went out to meet him, shouting,

"Hosanna!"[b]

"Blessed is he who comes in the name of the Lord!"[c]

"Blessed is the king of Israel!"

[14]Jesus found a young donkey and sat on it, as it is written:

[15] "Do not be afraid, Daughter Zion;
    see, your king is coming,
    seated on a donkey's colt."[d]

[16]At first his disciples did not understand all this. Only after Jesus was glorified did they realize that these things had been written about him and that these things had been done to him.

[17]Now the crowd that was with him when he called Lazarus from the tomb and raised him from the dead continued to spread the word. [18]Many people, because they had heard that he had performed this sign, went out to meet him. [19]So

the Pharisees said to one another, "See, this is getting us nowhere. Look how the whole world has gone after him!"

[20]Now there were some Greeks among those who went up to worship at the festival. [21]They came to Philip, who was from Bethsaida in Galilee, with a request. "Sir," they said, "we would like to see Jesus." [22]Philip went to tell Andrew; Andrew and Philip in turn told Jesus.

[23]Jesus replied, "The hour has come for the Son of Man to be glorified. [24]Very truly I tell you, unless a kernel of wheat falls to the ground and dies, it remains only a single seed. But if it dies, it produces many seeds. [25]Anyone who loves their life will lose it, while anyone who hates their life in this world will keep it for eternal life. [26]Whoever serves me must follow me; and where I am, my servant also will be. My Father will honor the one who serves me.

[27]"Now my soul is troubled, and what shall I say? 'Father, save me from this hour'? No, it was for this very reason I came to this hour. [28]Father, glorify your name!"

Then a voice came from heaven, "I have glorified it, and will glorify it again." [29]The crowd that was there and heard it said it had thundered; others said an angel had spoken to him.

[30]Jesus said, "This voice was for your benefit, not mine. [31]Now is the time for judgment on this world; now the prince of this world will be driven out. [32]And I, when I am lifted up[e] from the earth, will draw all people to myself." [33]He said this to show the kind of death he was going to die.

---

[a] 8 See Deut. 15:11.    [b] 13 A Hebrew expression meaning "Save!" which became an exclamation of praise    [c] 13 Psalm 118:25,26    [d] 15 Zech. 9:9    [e] 32 The Greek for *lifted up* also means *exalted*.

34The crowd spoke up, "We have heard from the Law that the Messiah will remain forever, so how can you say, 'The Son of Man must be lifted up'? Who is this 'Son of Man'?"

35Then Jesus told them, "You are going to have the light just a little while longer. Walk while you have the light, before darkness overtakes you. Whoever walks in the dark does not know where they are going. 36Believe in the light while you have the light, so that you may become children of light." When he had finished speaking, Jesus left and hid himself from them.

37Even after Jesus had performed so many signs in their presence, they still would not believe in him. 38This was to fulfill the word of Isaiah the prophet:

"Lord, who has believed our
        message
    and to whom has the arm of
        the Lord been revealed?"[a]

39For this reason they could not believe, because, as Isaiah says elsewhere:

40"He has blinded their eyes
    and hardened their hearts,
so they can neither see with their
        eyes,
    nor understand with their
        hearts,
    nor turn — and I would heal
        them."[b]

41Isaiah said this because he saw Jesus' glory and spoke about him.

42Yet at the same time many even among the leaders believed in him. But because of the Pharisees they would not openly acknowledge their faith for fear they would be put out of the synagogue; 43for they loved human praise more than praise from God.

44Then Jesus cried out, "Whoever believes in me does not believe in me only, but in the one who sent me. 45The one who looks at me is seeing the one who sent me. 46I have come into the world as a light, so that no one who believes in me should stay in darkness.

47"If anyone hears my words but does not keep them, I do not judge that person. For I did not come to judge the world, but to save the world. 48There is a judge for the one who rejects me and does not accept my words; the very words I have spoken will condemn them at the last day. 49For I did not speak on my own, but the Father who sent me commanded me to say all that I have spoken. 50I know that his command leads to eternal life. So whatever I say is just what the Father has told me to say."

13 It was just before the Passover Festival. Jesus knew that the hour had come for him to leave this world and go to the Father. Having loved his own who were in the world, he loved them to the end.

2The evening meal was in progress, and the devil had already prompted Judas, the son of Simon Iscariot, to betray Jesus. 3Jesus knew that the Father had put all things under his power, and that he had come from God and was returning to God; 4so he got up from the meal, took off his outer clothing, and wrapped a towel around his waist. 5After that, he poured water into a basin and began to wash his disciples' feet, drying them with the towel that was wrapped around him.

a 38 Isaiah 53:1    b 40 Isaiah 6:10

⁶He came to Simon Peter, who said to him, "Lord, are you going to wash my feet?"

⁷Jesus replied, "You do not realize now what I am doing, but later you will understand."

⁸"No," said Peter, "you shall never wash my feet."

Jesus answered, "Unless I wash you, you have no part with me."

⁹"Then, Lord," Simon Peter replied, "not just my feet but my hands and my head as well!"

¹⁰Jesus answered, "Those who have had a bath need only to wash their feet; their whole body is clean. And you are clean, though not every one of you." ¹¹For he knew who was going to betray him, and that was why he said not every one was clean.

¹²When he had finished washing their feet, he put on his clothes and returned to his place. "Do you understand what I have done for you?" he asked them. ¹³"You call me 'Teacher' and 'Lord,' and rightly so, for that is what I am. ¹⁴Now that I, your Lord and Teacher, have washed your feet, you also should wash one another's feet. ¹⁵I have set you an example that you should do as I have done for you. ¹⁶Very truly I tell you, no servant is greater than his master, nor is a messenger greater than the one who sent him. ¹⁷Now that you know these things, you will be blessed if you do them.

¹⁸"I am not referring to all of you; I know those I have chosen. But this is to fulfill this passage of Scripture: 'He who shared my bread has turnedᵃ against me.'ᵇ

¹⁹"I am telling you now before it happens, so that when it does happen you will believe that I am who I

am. ²⁰Very truly I tell you, whoever accepts anyone I send accepts me; and whoever accepts me accepts the one who sent me."

²¹After he had said this, Jesus was troubled in spirit and testified, "Very truly I tell you, one of you is going to betray me."

²²His disciples stared at one another, at a loss to know which of them he meant. ²³One of them, the disciple whom Jesus loved, was reclining next to him. ²⁴Simon Peter motioned to this disciple and said, "Ask him which one he means."

²⁵Leaning back against Jesus, he asked him, "Lord, who is it?"

²⁶Jesus answered, "It is the one to whom I will give this piece of bread when I have dipped it in the dish." Then, dipping the piece of bread, he gave it to Judas, the son of Simon Iscariot. ²⁷As soon as Judas took the bread, Satan entered into him.

So Jesus told him, "What you are about to do, do quickly." ²⁸But no one at the meal understood why Jesus said this to him. ²⁹Since Judas had charge of the money, some thought Jesus was telling him to buy what was needed for the festival, or to give something to the poor. ³⁰As soon as Judas had taken the bread, he went out. And it was night.

³¹When he was gone, Jesus said, "Now the Son of Man is glorified and God is glorified in him. ³²If God is glorified in him,ᶜ God will glorify the Son in himself, and will glorify him at once.

³³"My children, I will be with you only a little longer. You will look for me, and just as I told the Jews, so I tell you now: Where I am going, you cannot come.

³⁴"A new command I give you:

ᵃ 18 Greek *has lifted up his heel*    ᵇ 18 Psalm 41:9    ᶜ 32 Many early manuscripts do not have *If God is glorified in him.*

Love one another. As I have loved you, so you must love one another. ³⁵By this everyone will know that you are my disciples, if you love one another."

³⁶Simon Peter asked him, "Lord, where are you going?"

Jesus replied, "Where I am going, you cannot follow now, but you will follow later."

³⁷Peter asked, "Lord, why can't I follow you now? I will lay down my life for you."

³⁸Then Jesus answered, "Will you really lay down your life for me? Very truly I tell you, before the rooster crows, you will disown me three times!

14 "Do not let your hearts be troubled. You believe in God[a]; believe also in me. ²My Father's house has many rooms; if that were not so, would I have told you that I am going there to prepare a place for you? ³And if I go and prepare a place for you, I will come back and take you to be with me that you also may be where I am. ⁴You know the way to the place where I am going."

⁵Thomas said to him, "Lord, we don't know where you are going, so how can we know the way?"

⁶Jesus answered, "I am the way and the truth and the life. No one comes to the Father except through me. ⁷If you really know me, you will know[b] my Father as well. From now on, you do know him and have seen him."

⁸Philip said, "Lord, show us the Father and that will be enough for us."

⁹Jesus answered: "Don't you know me, Philip, even after I have been among you such a long time? Anyone who has seen me has seen

the Father. How can you say, 'Show us the Father'? ¹⁰Don't you believe that I am in the Father, and that the Father is in me? The words I say to you I do not speak on my own authority. Rather, it is the Father, living in me, who is doing his work. ¹¹Believe me when I say that I am in the Father and the Father is in me; or at least believe on the evidence of the works themselves. ¹²Very truly I tell you, whoever believes in me will do the works I have been doing, and they will do even greater things than these, because I am going to the Father. ¹³And I will do whatever you ask in my name, so that the Father may be glorified in the Son. ¹⁴You may ask me for anything in my name, and I will do it.

¹⁵"If you love me, keep my commands. ¹⁶And I will ask the Father, and he will give you another advocate to help you and be with you forever— ¹⁷the Spirit of truth. The world cannot accept him, because it neither sees him nor knows him. But you know him, for he lives with you and will be[c] in you. ¹⁸I will not leave you as orphans; I will come to you. ¹⁹Before long, the world will not see me anymore, but you will see me. Because I live, you also will live. ²⁰On that day you will realize that I am in my Father, and you are in me, and I am in you. ²¹Whoever has my commands and keeps them is the one who loves me. The one who loves me will be loved by my Father, and I too will love them and show myself to them."

²²Then Judas (not Judas Iscariot) said, "But, Lord, why do you intend to show yourself to us and not to the world?"

²³Jesus replied, "Anyone who

---

[a] 1  Or *Believe in God*    [b] 7  Some manuscripts *If you really knew me, you would know*
[c] 17  Some early manuscripts *and is*

loves me will obey my teaching. My Father will love them, and we will come to them and make our home with them. 24 Anyone who does not love me will not obey my teaching. These words you hear are not my own; they belong to the Father who sent me.

25 "All this I have spoken while still with you. 26 But the Advocate, the Holy Spirit, whom the Father will send in my name, will teach you all things and will remind you of everything I have said to you. 27 Peace I leave with you; my peace I give you. I do not give to you as the world gives. Do not let your hearts be troubled and do not be afraid.

28 "You heard me say, 'I am going away and I am coming back to you.' If you loved me, you would be glad that I am going to the Father, for the Father is greater than I. 29 I have told you now before it happens, so that when it does happen you will believe. 30 I will not say much more to you, for the prince of this world is coming. He has no hold over me, 31 but he comes so that the world may learn that I love the Father and do exactly what my Father has commanded me.

"Come now; let us leave.

15 "I am the true vine, and my Father is the gardener. 2 He cuts off every branch in me that bears no fruit, while every branch that does bear fruit he prunes[a] so that it will be even more fruitful. 3 You are already clean because of the word I have spoken to you. 4 Remain in me, as I also remain in you. No branch can bear fruit by itself; it must remain in the vine. Neither can you bear fruit unless you remain in me.

5 "I am the vine; you are the branches. If you remain in me and

I in you, you will bear much fruit; apart from me you can do nothing. 6 If you do not remain in me, you are like a branch that is thrown away and withers; such branches are picked up, thrown into the fire and burned. 7 If you remain in me and my words remain in you, ask whatever you wish, and it will be done for you. 8 This is to my Father's glory, that you bear much fruit, showing yourselves to be my disciples.

9 "As the Father has loved me, so have I loved you. Now remain in my love. 10 If you keep my commands, you will remain in my love, just as I have kept my Father's commands and remain in his love. 11 I have told you this so that my joy may be in you and that your joy may be complete. 12 My command is this: Love each other as I have loved you. 13 Greater love has no one than this: to lay down one's life for one's friends. 14 You are my friends if you do what I command. 15 I no longer call you servants, because a servant does not know his master's business. Instead, I have called you friends, for everything that I learned from my Father I have made known to you. 16 You did not choose me, but I chose you and appointed you so that you might go and bear fruit—fruit that will last—and so that whatever you ask in my name the Father will give you. 17 This is my command: Love each other.

18 "If the world hates you, keep in mind that it hated me first. 19 If you belonged to the world, it would love you as its own. As it is, you do not belong to the world, but I have chosen you out of the world. That is why the world hates you. 20 Remember what I told you: 'A servant is not greater than his master.'[b] If

---

_a 2_ The Greek for _he prunes_ also means _he cleans._     _b 20_ John 13:16

they persecuted me, they will persecute you also. If they obeyed my teaching, they will obey yours also. <sup>21</sup>They will treat you this way because of my name, for they do not know the one who sent me. <sup>22</sup>If I had not come and spoken to them, they would not be guilty of sin; but now they have no excuse for their sin. <sup>23</sup>Whoever hates me hates my Father as well. <sup>24</sup>If I had not done among them the works no one else did, they would not be guilty of sin. As it is, they have seen, and yet they have hated both me and my Father. <sup>25</sup>But this is to fulfill what is written in their Law: 'They hated me without reason.'<sup>a</sup>

<sup>26</sup>"When the Advocate comes, whom I will send to you from the Father — the Spirit of truth who goes out from the Father — he will testify about me. <sup>27</sup>And you also must testify, for you have been with me from the beginning.

16 "All this I have told you so that you will not fall away. <sup>2</sup>They will put you out of the synagogue; in fact, the time is coming when anyone who kills you will think they are offering a service to God. <sup>3</sup>They will do such things because they have not known the Father or me. <sup>4</sup>I have told you this, so that when their time comes you will remember that I warned you about them. I did not tell you this from the beginning because I was with you, <sup>5</sup>but now I am going to him who sent me. None of you asks me, 'Where are you going?' <sup>6</sup>Rather, you are filled with grief because I have said these things. <sup>7</sup>But very truly I tell you, it is for your good that I am going away. Unless I go away, the Advocate will not come to you; but if I go, I will send him to you. <sup>8</sup>When he comes,

he will prove the world to be in the wrong about sin and righteousness and judgment; <sup>9</sup>about sin, because people do not believe in me; <sup>10</sup>about righteousness, because I am going to the Father, where you can see me no longer; <sup>11</sup>and about judgment, because the prince of this world now stands condemned.

<sup>12</sup>"I have much more to say to you, more than you can now bear. <sup>13</sup>But when he, the Spirit of truth, comes, he will guide you into all the truth. He will not speak on his own; he will speak only what he hears, and he will tell you what is yet to come. <sup>14</sup>He will glorify me because it is from me that he will receive what he will make known to you. <sup>15</sup>All that belongs to the Father is mine. That is why I said the Spirit will receive from me what he will make known to you."

<sup>16</sup>Jesus went on to say, "In a little while you will see me no more, and then after a little while you will see me."

<sup>17</sup>At this, some of his disciples said to one another, "What does he mean by saying, 'In a little while you will see me no more, and then after a little while you will see me,' and 'Because I am going to the Father'?" <sup>18</sup>They kept asking, "What does he mean by 'a little while'? We don't understand what he is saying."

<sup>19</sup>Jesus saw that they wanted to ask him about this, so he said to them, "Are you asking one another what I meant when I said, 'In a little while you will see me no more, and then after a little while you will see me'? <sup>20</sup>Very truly I tell you, you will weep and mourn while the world rejoices. You will grieve, but your grief will turn to joy. <sup>21</sup>A woman giving birth to a child has pain because her

<sup>a</sup> 25 Psalms 35:19; 69:4

time has come; but when her baby is born she forgets the anguish because of her joy that a child is born into the world. ²²So with you: Now is your time of grief, but I will see you again and you will rejoice, and no one will take away your joy. ²³In that day you will no longer ask me anything. Very truly I tell you, my Father will give you whatever you ask in my name. ²⁴Until now you have not asked for anything in my name. Ask and you will receive, and your joy will be complete.

²⁵"Though I have been speaking figuratively, a time is coming when I will no longer use this kind of language but will tell you plainly about my Father. ²⁶In that day you will ask in my name. I am not saying that I will ask the Father on your behalf. ²⁷No, the Father himself loves you because you have loved me and have believed that I came from God. ²⁸I came from the Father and entered the world; now I am leaving the world and going back to the Father."

²⁹Then Jesus' disciples said, "Now you are speaking clearly and without figures of speech. ³⁰Now we can see that you know all things and that you do not even need to have anyone ask you questions. This makes us believe that you came from God."

³¹"Do you now believe?" Jesus replied. ³²"A time is coming and in fact has come when you will be scattered, each to your own home. You will leave me all alone. Yet I am not alone, for my Father is with me.

³³"I have told you these things, so that in me you may have peace. In this world you will have trouble. But take heart! I have overcome the world."

**17** After Jesus said this, he looked toward heaven and prayed:

"Father, the hour has come. Glorify your Son, that your Son may glorify you. ²For you granted him authority over all people that he might give eternal life to all those you have given him. ³Now this is eternal life: that they know you, the only true God, and Jesus Christ, whom you have sent. ⁴I have brought you glory on earth by finishing the work you gave me to do. ⁵And now, Father, glorify me in your presence with the glory I had with you before the world began.

⁶"I have revealed you[a] to those whom you gave me out of the world. They were yours; you gave them to me and they have obeyed your word. ⁷Now they know that everything you have given me comes from you. ⁸For I gave them the words you gave me and they accepted them. They knew with certainty that I came from you, and they believed that you sent me. ⁹I pray for them. I am not praying for the world, but for those you have given me, for they are yours. ¹⁰All I have is yours, and all you have is mine. And glory has come to me through them. ¹¹I will remain in the world no longer, but they are still in the world, and I am coming to you. Holy Father, protect them by the power of[b] your name, the name you gave me, so that they may be one as we are one. ¹²While I was with them, I protected them and kept them safe by[c] that name you gave me. None

---

[a] 6 Greek *your name*　　[b] 11 Or *Father, keep them faithful to*　　[c] 12 Or *kept them faithful to*

has been lost except the one doomed to destruction so that Scripture would be fulfilled.

¹³"I am coming to you now, but I say these things while I am still in the world, so that they may have the full measure of my joy within them. ¹⁴I have given them your word and the world has hated them, for they are not of the world any more than I am of the world. ¹⁵My prayer is not that you take them out of the world but that you protect them from the evil one. ¹⁶They are not of the world, even as I am not of it. ¹⁷Sanctify them by[a] the truth; your word is truth. ¹⁸As you sent me into the world, I have sent them into the world. ¹⁹For them I sanctify myself, that they too may be truly sanctified.

²⁰"My prayer is not for them alone. I pray also for those who will believe in me through their message, ²¹that all of them may be one, Father, just as you are in me and I am in you. May they also be in us so that the world may believe that you have sent me. ²²I have given them the glory that you gave me, that they may be one as we are one — ²³I in them and you in me — so that they may be brought to complete unity. Then the world will know that you sent me and have loved them even as you have loved me.

²⁴"Father, I want those you have given me to be with me where I am, and to see my glory, the glory you have given me because you loved me before the creation of the world.

²⁵"Righteous Father, though the world does not know you, I know you, and they know that you have sent me. ²⁶I have made you[b] known to them, and will continue to make you known in order that the love you have for me may be in them and that I myself may be in them."

18 When he had finished praying, Jesus left with his disciples and crossed the Kidron Valley. On the other side there was a garden, and he and his disciples went into it.

²Now Judas, who betrayed him, knew the place, because Jesus had often met there with his disciples. ³So Judas came to the garden, guiding a detachment of soldiers and some officials from the chief priests and the Pharisees. They were carrying torches, lanterns and weapons.

⁴Jesus, knowing all that was going to happen to him, went out and asked them, "Who is it you want?"

⁵"Jesus of Nazareth," they replied.

"I am he," Jesus said. (And Judas the traitor was standing there with them.) ⁶When Jesus said, "I am he," they drew back and fell to the ground.

⁷Again he asked them, "Who is it you want?"

"Jesus of Nazareth," they said.

⁸Jesus answered, "I told you that I am he. If you are looking for me, then let these men go." ⁹This happened so that the words he had spoken would be fulfilled: "I have not lost one of those you gave me."[c]

¹⁰Then Simon Peter, who had a sword, drew it and struck the high priest's servant, cutting off his right ear. (The servant's name was Malchus.)

¹¹Jesus commanded Peter, "Put

your sword away! Shall I not drink the cup the Father has given me?"

¹²Then the detachment of soldiers with its commander and the Jewish officials arrested Jesus. They bound him ¹³and brought him first to Annas, who was the father-in-law of Caiaphas, the high priest that year. ¹⁴Caiaphas was the one who had advised the Jewish leaders that it would be good if one man died for the people.

¹⁵Simon Peter and another disciple were following Jesus. Because this disciple was known to the high priest, he went with Jesus into the high priest's courtyard, ¹⁶but Peter had to wait outside at the door. The other disciple, who was known to the high priest, came back, spoke to the servant girl on duty there and brought Peter in.

¹⁷"You aren't one of this man's disciples too, are you?" she asked Peter.

He replied, "I am not."

¹⁸It was cold, and the servants and officials stood around a fire they had made to keep warm. Peter also was standing with them, warming himself.

¹⁹Meanwhile, the high priest questioned Jesus about his disciples and his teaching.

²⁰"I have spoken openly to the world," Jesus replied. "I always taught in synagogues or at the temple, where all the Jews come together. I said nothing in secret. ²¹Why question me? Ask those who heard me. Surely they know what I said."

²²When Jesus said this, one of the officials nearby slapped him in the face. "Is this the way you answer the high priest?" he demanded.

²³"If I said something wrong," Jesus replied, "testify as to what is wrong. But if I spoke the truth, why

did you strike me?" ²⁴Then Annas sent him bound to Caiaphas the high priest.

²⁵Meanwhile, Simon Peter was still standing there warming himself. So they asked him, "You aren't one of his disciples too, are you?"

He denied it, saying, "I am not."

²⁶One of the high priest's servants, a relative of the man whose ear Peter had cut off, challenged him, "Didn't I see you with him in the garden?" ²⁷Again Peter denied it, and at that moment a rooster began to crow.

²⁸Then the Jewish leaders took Jesus from Caiaphas to the palace of the Roman governor. By now it was early morning, and to avoid ceremonial uncleanness they did not enter the palace, because they wanted to be able to eat the Passover. ²⁹So Pilate came out to them and asked, "What charges are you bringing against this man?"

³⁰"If he were not a criminal," they replied, "we would not have handed him over to you."

³¹Pilate said, "Take him yourselves and judge him by your own law."

"But we have no right to execute anyone," they objected. ³²This took place to fulfill what Jesus had said about the kind of death he was going to die.

³³Pilate then went back inside the palace, summoned Jesus and asked him, "Are you the king of the Jews?"

³⁴"Is that your own idea," Jesus asked, "or did others talk to you about me?"

³⁵"Am I a Jew?" Pilate replied. "Your own people and chief priests handed you over to me. What is it you have done?"

³⁶Jesus said, "My kingdom is not

of this world. If it were, my servants would fight to prevent my arrest by the Jewish leaders. But now my kingdom is from another place."

37 "You are a king, then!" said Pilate.

Jesus answered, "You say that I am a king. In fact, the reason I was born and came into the world is to testify to the truth. Everyone on the side of truth listens to me."

38 "What is truth?" retorted Pilate. With this he went out again to the Jews gathered there and said, "I find no basis for a charge against him. 39 But it is your custom for me to release to you one prisoner at the time of the Passover. Do you want me to release 'the king of the Jews'?"

40 They shouted back, "No, not him! Give us Barabbas!" Now Barabbas had taken part in an uprising.

19 Then Pilate took Jesus and had him flogged. 2 The soldiers twisted together a crown of thorns and put it on his head. They clothed him in a purple robe 3 and went up to him again and again, saying, "Hail, king of the Jews!" And they slapped him in the face.

4 Once more Pilate came out and said to the Jews gathered there, "Look, I am bringing him out to you to let you know that I find no basis for a charge against him." 5 When Jesus came out wearing the crown of thorns and the purple robe, Pilate said to them, "Here is the man!"

6 As soon as the chief priests and their officials saw him, they shouted, "Crucify! Crucify!"

But Pilate answered, "You take him and crucify him. As for me, I find no basis for a charge against him."

7 The Jewish leaders insisted, "We have a law, and according to that law he must die, because he claimed to be the Son of God."

8 When Pilate heard this, he was even more afraid, 9 and he went back inside the palace. "Where do you come from?" he asked Jesus, but Jesus gave him no answer. 10 "Do you refuse to speak to me?" Pilate said. "Don't you realize I have power either to free you or to crucify you?"

11 Jesus answered, "You would have no power over me if it were not given to you from above. Therefore the one who handed me over to you is guilty of a greater sin."

12 From then on, Pilate tried to set Jesus free, but the Jewish leaders kept shouting, "If you let this man go, you are no friend of Caesar. Anyone who claims to be a king opposes Caesar."

13 When Pilate heard this, he brought Jesus out and sat down on the judge's seat at a place known as the Stone Pavement (which in Aramaic is Gabbatha). 14 It was the day of Preparation of the Passover; it was about noon.

"Here is your king," Pilate said to the Jews.

15 But they shouted, "Take him away! Take him away! Crucify him!"

"Shall I crucify your king?" Pilate asked.

"We have no king but Caesar," the chief priests answered.

16 Finally Pilate handed him over to them to be crucified.

So the soldiers took charge of Jesus. 17 Carrying his own cross, he went out to the place of the Skull (which in Aramaic is called Golgotha). 18 There they crucified him, and with him two others—one on each side and Jesus in the middle.

19 Pilate had a notice prepared

and fastened to the cross. It read: JESUS OF NAZARETH, THE KING OF THE JEWS. ²⁰Many of the Jews read this sign, for the place where Jesus was crucified was near the city, and the sign was written in Aramaic, Latin and Greek. ²¹The chief priests of the Jews protested to Pilate, "Do not write 'The King of the Jews,' but that this man claimed to be king of the Jews."

²²Pilate answered, "What I have written, I have written."

²³When the soldiers crucified Jesus, they took his clothes, dividing them into four shares, one for each of them, with the undergarment remaining. This garment was seamless, woven in one piece from top to bottom.

²⁴"Let's not tear it," they said to one another. "Let's decide by lot who will get it."

This happened that the scripture might be fulfilled that said,

"They divided my clothes among them
    and cast lots for my garment."*a*

So this is what the soldiers did.

²⁵Near the cross of Jesus stood his mother, his mother's sister, Mary the wife of Clopas, and Mary Magdalene. ²⁶When Jesus saw his mother there, and the disciple whom he loved standing nearby, he said to her, "Woman,*b* here is your son," ²⁷and to the disciple, "Here is your mother." From that time on, this disciple took her into his home.

²⁸Later, knowing that everything had now been finished, and so that Scripture would be fulfilled, Jesus said, "I am thirsty." ²⁹A jar of wine vinegar was there, so they soaked a sponge in it, put the sponge on a stalk of the hyssop plant, and lifted it to Jesus' lips. ³⁰When he had received the drink, Jesus said, "It is finished." With that, he bowed his head and gave up his spirit.

³¹Now it was the day of Preparation, and the next day was to be a special Sabbath. Because the Jewish leaders did not want the bodies left on the crosses during the Sabbath, they asked Pilate to have the legs broken and the bodies taken down. ³²The soldiers therefore came and broke the legs of the first man who had been crucified with Jesus, and then those of the other. ³³But when they came to Jesus and found that he was already dead, they did not break his legs. ³⁴Instead, one of the soldiers pierced Jesus' side with a spear, bringing a sudden flow of blood and water. ³⁵The man who saw it has given testimony, and his testimony is true. He knows that he tells the truth, and he testifies so that you also may believe. ³⁶These things happened so that the scripture would be fulfilled: "Not one of his bones will be broken,*c* ³⁷and, as another scripture says, "They will look on the one they have pierced."*d*

³⁸Later, Joseph of Arimathea asked Pilate for the body of Jesus. Now Joseph was a disciple of Jesus, but secretly because he feared the Jewish leaders. With Pilate's permission, he came and took the body away. ³⁹He was accompanied by Nicodemus, the man who earlier had visited Jesus at night. Nicodemus brought a mixture of myrrh and aloes, about seventy-five pounds.*e* ⁴⁰Taking Jesus' body, the two of them wrapped it, with the spices, in strips of linen. This was in

---

*a 24* Psalm 22:18    *b 26* The Greek for *Woman* does not denote any disrespect.
*c 36* Exodus 12:46; Num. 9:12; Psalm 34:20    *d 37* Zech. 12:10    *e 39* Or about 34 kilograms

accordance with Jewish burial customs. 41At the place where Jesus was crucified, there was a garden, and in the garden a new tomb, in which no one had ever been laid. 42Because it was the Jewish day of Preparation and since the tomb was nearby, they laid Jesus there.

20 Early on the first day of the week, while it was still dark, Mary Magdalene went to the tomb and saw that the stone had been removed from the entrance. 2So she came running to Simon Peter and the other disciple, the one Jesus loved, and said, "They have taken the Lord out of the tomb, and we don't know where they have put him!"

3So Peter and the other disciple started for the tomb. 4Both were running, but the other disciple outran Peter and reached the tomb first. 5He bent over and looked in at the strips of linen lying there but did not go in. 6Then Simon Peter came along behind him and went straight into the tomb. He saw the strips of linen lying there, 7as well as the cloth that had been wrapped around Jesus' head. The cloth was still lying in its place, separate from the linen. 8Finally the other disciple, who had reached the tomb first, also went inside. He saw and believed. 9(They still did not understand from Scripture that Jesus had to rise from the dead.) 10Then the disciples went back to where they were staying.

11Now Mary stood outside the tomb crying. As she wept, she bent over to look into the tomb 12and saw two angels in white, seated where Jesus' body had been, one at the head and the other at the foot.

13They asked her, "Woman, why are you crying?"

"They have taken my Lord away," she said, "and I don't know where they have put him." 14At this, she turned around and saw Jesus standing there, but she did not realize that it was Jesus.

15He asked her, "Woman, why are you crying? Who is it you are looking for?"

Thinking he was the gardener, she said, "Sir, if you have carried him away, tell me where you have put him, and I will get him."

16Jesus said to her, "Mary."

She turned toward him and cried out in Aramaic, "Rabboni!" (which means "Teacher").

17Jesus said, "Do not hold on to me, for I have not yet ascended to the Father. Go instead to my brothers and tell them, 'I am ascending to my Father and your Father, to my God and your God.'"

18Mary Magdalene went to the disciples with the news: "I have seen the Lord!" And she told them that he had said these things to her.

19On the evening of that first day of the week, when the disciples were together, with the doors locked for fear of the Jewish leaders, Jesus came and stood among them and said, "Peace be with you!" 20After he said this, he showed them his hands and side. The disciples were overjoyed when they saw the Lord.

21Again Jesus said, "Peace be with you! As the Father has sent me, I am sending you." 22And with that he breathed on them and said, "Receive the Holy Spirit. 23If you forgive anyone's sins, their sins are forgiven; if you do not forgive them, they are not forgiven."

24Now Thomas (also known as Didymus[a]), one of the Twelve, was not with the disciples when Jesus

---

[a] 24 Thomas (Aramaic) and Didymus (Greek) both mean twin.

came. ²⁵So the other disciples told him, "We have seen the Lord!"

But he said to them, "Unless I see the nail marks in his hands and put my finger where the nails were, and put my hand into his side, I will not believe."

²⁶A week later his disciples were in the house again, and Thomas was with them. Though the doors were locked, Jesus came and stood among them and said, "Peace be with you!" ²⁷Then he said to Thomas, "Put your finger here; see my hands. Reach out your hand and put it into my side. Stop doubting and believe."

²⁸Thomas said to him, "My Lord and my God!"

²⁹Then Jesus told him, "Because you have seen me, you have believed; blessed are those who have not seen and yet have believed."

³⁰Jesus performed many other signs in the presence of his disciples, which are not recorded in this book. ³¹But these are written that you may believe[a] that Jesus is the Messiah, the Son of God, and that by believing you may have life in his name.

21 Afterward Jesus appeared again to his disciples, by the Sea of Galilee.[b] It happened this way: ²Simon Peter, Thomas (also known as Didymus[c]), Nathanael from Cana in Galilee, the sons of Zebedee, and two other disciples were together. ³"I'm going out to fish," Simon Peter told them, and they said, "We'll go with you." So they went out and got into the boat, but that night they caught nothing.

⁴Early in the morning, Jesus stood on the shore, but the disciples did not realize that it was Jesus.

⁵He called out to them, "Friends, haven't you any fish?"

"No," they answered.

⁶He said, "Throw your net on the right side of the boat and you will find some." When they did, they were unable to haul the net in because of the large number of fish.

⁷Then the disciple whom Jesus loved said to Peter, "It is the Lord!" As soon as Simon Peter heard him say, "It is the Lord," he wrapped his outer garment around him (for he had taken it off) and jumped into the water. ⁸The other disciples followed in the boat, towing the net full of fish, for they were not far from shore, about a hundred yards.[d] ⁹When they landed, they saw a fire of burning coals there with fish on it, and some bread.

¹⁰Jesus said to them, "Bring some of the fish you have just caught." ¹¹So Simon Peter climbed back into the boat and dragged the net ashore. It was full of large fish, 153, but even with so many the net was not torn. ¹²Jesus said to them, "Come and have breakfast." None of the disciples dared ask him, "Who are you?" They knew it was the Lord. ¹³Jesus came, took the bread and gave it to them, and did the same with the fish. ¹⁴This was now the third time Jesus appeared to his disciples after he was raised from the dead.

¹⁵When they had finished eating, Jesus said to Simon Peter, "Simon son of John, do you love me more than these?"

"Yes, Lord," he said, "you know that I love you."

Jesus said, "Feed my lambs."

---

a 31 Or *may continue to believe*　　b 1 Greek *Tiberias*　　c 2 *Thomas* (Aramaic) and *Didymus* (Greek) both mean *twin*.　　d 8 Or about 90 meters

¹⁶Again Jesus said, "Simon son of John, do you love me?"

He answered, "Yes, Lord, you know that I love you."

Jesus said, "Take care of my sheep."

¹⁷The third time he said to him, "Simon son of John, do you love me?"

Peter was hurt because Jesus asked him the third time, "Do you love me?" He said, "Lord, you know all things; you know that I love you."

Jesus said, "Feed my sheep. ¹⁸Very truly I tell you, when you were younger you dressed yourself and went where you wanted; but when you are old you will stretch out your hands, and someone else will dress you and lead you where you do not want to go." ¹⁹Jesus said this to indicate the kind of death by which Peter would glorify God. Then he said to him, "Follow me!"

²⁰Peter turned and saw that the disciple whom Jesus loved was following them. (This was the one who had leaned back against Jesus at the supper and had said, "Lord, who is going to betray you?") ²¹When Peter saw him, he asked, "Lord, what about him?"

²²Jesus answered, "If I want him to remain alive until I return, what is that to you? You must follow me." ²³Because of this, the rumor spread among the believers that this disciple would not die. But Jesus did not say that he would not die; he only said, "If I want him to remain alive until I return, what is that to you?"

²⁴This is the disciple who testifies to these things and who wrote them down. We know that his testimony is true.

²⁵Jesus did many other things as well. If every one of them were written down, I suppose that even the whole world would not have room for the books that would be written.

# ACTS

Luke's second volume is known as the book of Acts (see p. 69 for the Invitation to Luke-Acts, and for more detailed information on the Gospel of Luke). The six parts of the book of Acts each describe a new phase in the expansion of the Messiah-following movement outward from Jerusalem. These sections are all marked by variations on the phrase *the word of God continued to spread and flourish*:

: First, the church is established in Jerusalem and becomes Greek-speaking, allowing it to spread its message throughout the empire.
: Next, the movement expands into the rest of Palestine.
: Third, Gentiles are included in the gathering of Jesus-followers alongside Jews.
: Fourth, messengers are sent west into the Roman province of Asia.
: Fifth, these messengers enter Europe.
: In the sixth and final phase, the movement reaches the capital city of Rome and into the highest levels of society; God's kingdom is thus announced to all nations.

1 In my former book, Theophilus, I wrote about all that Jesus began to do and to teach ²until the day he was taken up to heaven, after giving instructions through the Holy Spirit to the apostles he had chosen. ³After his suffering, he presented himself to them and gave many convincing proofs that he was alive. He appeared to them over a period of forty days and spoke about the kingdom of God. ⁴On one occasion, while he was eating with them, he gave them this command: "Do not leave Jerusalem, but wait for the gift my Father promised, which you have heard me speak about. ⁵For John baptized with[a] water, but in a few days you will be baptized with[a] the Holy Spirit."

⁶Then they gathered around him and asked him, "Lord, are you at this time going to restore the kingdom to Israel?"

⁷He said to them: "It is not for you to know the times or dates the Father has set by his own authority. ⁸But you will receive power when the Holy Spirit comes on you; and you will be my witnesses in Jerusalem, and in all Judea and Samaria, and to the ends of the earth."

⁹After he said this, he was taken up before their very eyes, and a cloud hid him from their sight.

¹⁰They were looking intently up into the sky as he was going, when suddenly two men dressed in white stood beside them. ¹¹"Men of Galilee," they said, "why do you stand here looking into the sky? This same Jesus, who has been taken from you into heaven, will come back in the same way you have seen him go into heaven."

¹²Then the apostles returned to Jerusalem from the hill called the Mount of Olives, a Sabbath day's walk[b] from the city. ¹³When they arrived, they went upstairs to the room where they were staying. Those present were Peter, John,

---

[a] 5 Or *in*   [b] 12 That is, about 5/8 mile or about 1 kilometer

James and Andrew; Philip and Thomas, Bartholomew and Matthew; James son of Alphaeus and Simon the Zealot, and Judas son of James. [14] They all joined together constantly in prayer, along with the women and Mary the mother of Jesus, and with his brothers.

[15] In those days Peter stood up among the believers (a group numbering about a hundred and twenty) [16] and said, "Brothers and sisters,[a] the Scripture had to be fulfilled in which the Holy Spirit spoke long ago through David concerning Judas, who served as guide for those who arrested Jesus. [17] He was one of our number and shared in our ministry."

[18] (With the payment he received for his wickedness, Judas bought a field; there he fell headlong, his body burst open and all his intestines spilled out. [19] Everyone in Jerusalem heard about this, so they called that field in their language Akeldama, that is, Field of Blood.)

[20] "For," said Peter, "it is written in the Book of Psalms:

"'May his place be deserted;
    let there be no one to dwell
        in it,'[b]

and,

"'May another take his place of
    leadership.'[c]

[21] Therefore it is necessary to choose one of the men who have been with us the whole time the Lord Jesus was living among us, [22] beginning from John's baptism to the time when Jesus was taken up from us. For one of these must become a witness with us of his resurrection."

[23] So they nominated two men: Joseph called Barsabbas (also known as Justus) and Matthias. [24] Then they prayed, "Lord, you know everyone's heart. Show us which of these two you have chosen [25] to take over this apostolic ministry, which Judas left to go where he belongs." [26] Then they cast lots, and the lot fell to Matthias; so he was added to the eleven apostles.

2 When the day of Pentecost came, they were all together in one place. [2] Suddenly a sound like the blowing of a violent wind came from heaven and filled the whole house where they were sitting. [3] They saw what seemed to be tongues of fire that separated and came to rest on each of them. [4] All of them were filled with the Holy Spirit and began to speak in other tongues[d] as the Spirit enabled them.

[5] Now there were staying in Jerusalem God-fearing Jews from every nation under heaven. [6] When they heard this sound, a crowd came together in bewilderment, because each one heard their own language being spoken. [7] Utterly amazed, they asked: "Aren't all these who are speaking Galileans? [8] Then how is it that each of us hears them in our native language? [9] Parthians, Medes and Elamites; residents of Mesopotamia, Judea and Cappadocia, Pontus and Asia,[e] [10] Phrygia and Pamphylia, Egypt and the parts of Libya near Cyrene; visitors from Rome [11] (both Jews and converts to Judaism); Cretans and Arabs—we hear them declaring the wonders of God

---

[a] 16  The Greek word for *brothers and sisters* (*adelphoi*) refers here to believers, both men and women, as part of God's family; also in 6:3; 11:29; 12:17; 16:40; 18:18, 27; 21:7, 17; 28:14, 15.
[b] 20  Psalm 69:25    [c] 20  Psalm 109:8    [d] 4  Or *languages*; also in verse 11    [e] 9  That is, the Roman province by that name

in our own tongues!" [12] Amazed and perplexed, they asked one another, "What does this mean?"

[13] Some, however, made fun of them and said, "They have had too much wine."

[14] Then Peter stood up with the Eleven, raised his voice and addressed the crowd: "Fellow Jews and all of you who live in Jerusalem, let me explain this to you; listen carefully to what I say. [15] These people are not drunk, as you suppose. It's only nine in the morning! [16] No, this is what was spoken by the prophet Joel:

[17] "'In the last days, God says,
    I will pour out my Spirit on all people.
  Your sons and daughters will prophesy,
    your young men will see visions,
    your old men will dream dreams.
[18] Even on my servants, both men and women,
    I will pour out my Spirit in those days,
    and they will prophesy.
[19] I will show wonders in the heavens above
    and signs on the earth below,
    blood and fire and billows of smoke.
[20] The sun will be turned to darkness
    and the moon to blood
    before the coming of the great and glorious day of the Lord.
[21] And everyone who calls
    on the name of the Lord will be saved.'[a]

[22] "Fellow Israelites, listen to this: Jesus of Nazareth was a man accredited by God to you by miracles, wonders and signs, which God did among you through him, as you yourselves know. [23] This man was handed over to you by God's deliberate plan and foreknowledge; and you, with the help of wicked men,[b] put him to death by nailing him to the cross. [24] But God raised him from the dead, freeing him from the agony of death, because it was impossible for death to keep its hold on him. [25] David said about him:

  "'I saw the Lord always before me.
    Because he is at my right hand,
    I will not be shaken.
[26] Therefore my heart is glad and my tongue rejoices;
    my body also will rest in hope,
[27] because you will not abandon me to the realm of the dead,
    you will not let your holy one see decay.
[28] You have made known to me the paths of life;
    you will fill me with joy in your presence.'[c]

[29] "Fellow Israelites, I can tell you confidently that the patriarch David died and was buried, and his tomb is here to this day. [30] But he was a prophet and knew that God had promised him on oath that he would place one of his descendants on his throne. [31] Seeing what was to come, he spoke of the resurrection of the Messiah, that he was not abandoned to the realm of the dead, nor did his body see decay. [32] God has raised this Jesus to life, and we are all witnesses of it. [33] Exalted to the right hand of God, he has re-

---

[a] 21 Joel 2:28-32   [b] 23 Or of those not having the law (that is, Gentiles)   [c] 28 Psalm 16:8-11
(see Septuagint)

ceived from the Father the promised Holy Spirit and has poured out what you now see and hear. [34] For David did not ascend to heaven, and yet he said,

" 'The Lord said to my Lord:
    "Sit at my right hand
[35] until I make your enemies
    a footstool for your feet." ' [a]

[36] "Therefore let all Israel be assured of this: God has made this Jesus, whom you crucified, both Lord and Messiah."

[37] When the people heard this, they were cut to the heart and said to Peter and the other apostles, "Brothers, what shall we do?"

[38] Peter replied, "Repent and be baptized, every one of you, in the name of Jesus Christ for the forgiveness of your sins. And you will receive the gift of the Holy Spirit. [39] The promise is for you and your children and for all who are far off—for all whom the Lord our God will call."

[40] With many other words he warned them; and he pleaded with them, "Save yourselves from this corrupt generation." [41] Those who accepted his message were baptized, and about three thousand were added to their number that day.

[42] They devoted themselves to the apostles' teaching and to fellowship, to the breaking of bread and to prayer. [43] Everyone was filled with awe at the many wonders and signs performed by the apostles. [44] All the believers were together and had everything in common. [45] They sold property and possessions to give to anyone who had need. [46] Every day they continued to meet together in the temple courts. They broke bread

in their homes and ate together with glad and sincere hearts, [47] praising God and enjoying the favor of all the people. And the Lord added to their number daily those who were being saved.

3 One day Peter and John were going up to the temple at the time of prayer—at three in the afternoon. [2] Now a man who was lame from birth was being carried to the temple gate called Beautiful, where he was put every day to beg from those going into the temple courts. [3] When he saw Peter and John about to enter, he asked them for money. [4] Peter looked straight at him, as did John. Then Peter said, "Look at us!" [5] So the man gave them his attention, expecting to get something from them.

[6] Then Peter said, "Silver or gold I do not have, but what I do have I give you. In the name of Jesus Christ of Nazareth, walk." [7] Taking him by the right hand, he helped him up, and instantly the man's feet and ankles became strong. [8] He jumped to his feet and began to walk. Then he went with them into the temple courts, walking and jumping, and praising God. [9] When all the people saw him walking and praising God, [10] they recognized him as the same man who used to sit begging at the temple gate called Beautiful, and they were filled with wonder and amazement at what had happened to him.

[11] While the man held on to Peter and John, all the people were astonished and came running to them in the place called Solomon's Colonnade. [12] When Peter saw this, he said to them: "Fellow Israelites, why does this surprise you? Why do you stare at us as if by our own

[a] 35 Psalm 110:1

power or godliness we had made this man walk? [13] The God of Abraham, Isaac and Jacob, the God of our fathers, has glorified his servant Jesus. You handed him over to be killed, and you disowned him before Pilate, though he had decided to let him go. [14] You disowned the Holy and Righteous One and asked that a murderer be released to you. [15] You killed the author of life, but God raised him from the dead. We are witnesses of this. [16] By faith in the name of Jesus, this man whom you see and know was made strong. It is Jesus' name and the faith that comes through him that has completely healed him, as you can all see.

[17] "Now, fellow Israelites, I know that you acted in ignorance, as did your leaders. [18] But this is how God fulfilled what he had foretold through all the prophets, saying that his Messiah would suffer. [19] Repent, then, and turn to God, so that your sins may be wiped out, that times of refreshing may come from the Lord, [20] and that he may send the Messiah, who has been appointed for you—even Jesus. [21] Heaven must receive him until the time comes for God to restore everything, as he promised long ago through his holy prophets. [22] For Moses said, 'The Lord your God will raise up for you a prophet like me from among your own people; you must listen to everything he tells you. [23] Anyone who does not listen to him will be completely cut off from their people.'[a]

[24] "Indeed, beginning with Samuel, all the prophets who have spoken have foretold these days. [25] And you are heirs of the prophets and of the covenant God made with your fathers. He said to Abraham, 'Through your offspring all peoples on earth will be blessed.'[b] [26] When God raised up his servant, he sent him first to you to bless you by turning each of you from your wicked ways."

4 The priests and the captain of the temple guard and the Sadducees came up to Peter and John while they were speaking to the people. [2] They were greatly disturbed because the apostles were teaching the people, proclaiming in Jesus the resurrection of the dead. [3] They seized Peter and John and, because it was evening, they put them in jail until the next day. [4] But many who heard the message believed; so the number of men who believed grew to about five thousand.

[5] The next day the rulers, the elders and the teachers of the law met in Jerusalem. [6] Annas the high priest was there, and so were Caiaphas, John, Alexander and others of the high priest's family. [7] They had Peter and John brought before them and began to question them: "By what power or what name did you do this?"

[8] Then Peter, filled with the Holy Spirit, said to them: "Rulers and elders of the people! [9] If we are being called to account today for an act of kindness shown to a man who was lame and are being asked how he was healed, [10] then know this, you and all the people of Israel: It is by the name of Jesus Christ of Nazareth, whom you crucified but whom God raised from the dead, that this man stands before you healed. [11] Jesus is

"'the stone you builders rejected, which has become the cornerstone.'[c]

---

[a] 23 Deut. 18:15,18,19     [b] 25 Gen. 22:18; 26:4     [c] 11 Psalm 118:22

¹²Salvation is found in no one else, for there is no other name under heaven given to mankind by which we must be saved."

¹³When they saw the courage of Peter and John and realized that they were unschooled, ordinary men, they were astonished and they took note that these men had been with Jesus. ¹⁴But since they could see the man who had been healed standing there with them, there was nothing they could say. ¹⁵So they ordered them to withdraw from the Sanhedrin and then conferred together. ¹⁶"What are we going to do with these men?" they asked. "Everyone living in Jerusalem knows they have performed a notable sign, and we cannot deny it. ¹⁷But to stop this thing from spreading any further among the people, we must warn them to speak no longer to anyone in this name."

¹⁸Then they called them in again and commanded them not to speak or teach at all in the name of Jesus. ¹⁹But Peter and John replied, "Which is right in God's eyes: to listen to you, or to him? You be the judges! ²⁰As for us, we cannot help speaking about what we have seen and heard."

²¹After further threats they let them go. They could not decide how to punish them, because all the people were praising God for what had happened. ²²For the man who was miraculously healed was over forty years old.

²³On their release, Peter and John went back to their own people and reported all that the chief priests and the elders had said to them. ²⁴When they heard this, they raised their voices together in prayer to God. "Sovereign Lord," they said,

"you made the heavens and the earth and the sea, and everything in them. ²⁵You spoke by the Holy Spirit through the mouth of your servant, our father David:

" 'Why do the nations rage
        and the peoples plot in vain?
²⁶The kings of the earth rise up
        and the rulers band together
    against the Lord
        and against his anointed
            one.ᵃᵇ

²⁷Indeed Herod and Pontius Pilate met together with the Gentiles and the people of Israel in this city to conspire against your holy servant Jesus, whom you anointed. ²⁸They did what your power and will had decided beforehand should happen. ²⁹Now, Lord, consider their threats and enable your servants to speak your word with great boldness. ³⁰Stretch out your hand to heal and perform signs and wonders through the name of your holy servant Jesus."

³¹After they prayed, the place where they were meeting was shaken. And they were all filled with the Holy Spirit and spoke the word of God boldly.

³²All the believers were one in heart and mind. No one claimed that any of their possessions was their own, but they shared everything they had. ³³With great power the apostles continued to testify to the resurrection of the Lord Jesus. And God's grace was so powerfully at work in them all ³⁴that there were no needy persons among them. For from time to time those who owned land or houses sold them, brought the money from the sales ³⁵and put it at the apostles' feet, and it was distributed to anyone who had need.

ᵃ 26  That is, Messiah or Christ    ᵇ 26  Psalm 2:1,2

³⁶Joseph, a Levite from Cyprus, whom the apostles called Barnabas (which means "son of encouragement"), ³⁷sold a field he owned and brought the money and put it at the apostles' feet.

5 Now a man named Ananias, together with his wife Sapphira, also sold a piece of property. ²With his wife's full knowledge he kept back part of the money for himself, but brought the rest and put it at the apostles' feet.

³Then Peter said, "Ananias, how is it that Satan has so filled your heart that you have lied to the Holy Spirit and have kept for yourself some of the money you received for the land? ⁴Didn't it belong to you before it was sold? And after it was sold, wasn't the money at your disposal? What made you think of doing such a thing? You have not lied just to human beings but to God."

⁵When Ananias heard this, he fell down and died. And great fear seized all who heard what had happened. ⁶Then some young men came forward, wrapped up his body, and carried him out and buried him.

⁷About three hours later his wife came in, not knowing what had happened. ⁸Peter asked her, "Tell me, is this the price you and Ananias got for the land?"

"Yes," she said, "that is the price."

⁹Peter said to her, "How could you conspire to test the Spirit of the Lord? Listen! The feet of the men who buried your husband are at the door, and they will carry you out also."

¹⁰At that moment she fell down at his feet and died. Then the young men came in and, finding her dead, carried her out and buried her beside her husband. ¹¹Great fear seized the whole church and all who heard about these events.

¹²The apostles performed many signs and wonders among the people. And all the believers used to meet together in Solomon's Colonnade. ¹³No one else dared join them, even though they were highly regarded by the people. ¹⁴Nevertheless, more and more men and women believed in the Lord and were added to their number. ¹⁵As a result, people brought the sick into the streets and laid them on beds and mats so that at least Peter's shadow might fall on some of them as he passed by. ¹⁶Crowds gathered also from the towns around Jerusalem, bringing their sick and those tormented by impure spirits, and all of them were healed.

¹⁷Then the high priest and all his associates, who were members of the party of the Sadducees, were filled with jealousy. ¹⁸They arrested the apostles and put them in the public jail. ¹⁹But during the night an angel of the Lord opened the doors of the jail and brought them out. ²⁰"Go, stand in the temple courts," he said, "and tell the people all about this new life."

²¹At daybreak they entered the temple courts, as they had been told, and began to teach the people.

When the high priest and his associates arrived, they called together the Sanhedrin—the full assembly of the elders of Israel—and sent to the jail for the apostles. ²²But on arriving at the jail, the officers did not find them there. So they went back and reported, ²³"We found the jail securely locked, with the guards standing at the doors; but when we opened them, we found no one inside." ²⁴On hearing this report, the captain of the temple guard and the chief priests were at a loss, wondering what this might lead to.

25Then someone came and said, "Look! The men you put in jail are standing in the temple courts teaching the people." 26At that, the captain went with his officers and brought the apostles. They did not use force, because they feared that the people would stone them.

27The apostles were brought in and made to appear before the Sanhedrin to be questioned by the high priest. 28"We gave you strict orders not to teach in this name," he said. "Yet you have filled Jerusalem with your teaching and are determined to make us guilty of this man's blood."

29Peter and the other apostles replied: "We must obey God rather than human beings! 30The God of our ancestors raised Jesus from the dead—whom you killed by hanging him on a cross. 31God exalted him to his own right hand as Prince and Savior that he might bring Israel to repentance and forgive their sins. 32We are witnesses of these things, and so is the Holy Spirit, whom God has given to those who obey him."

33When they heard this, they were furious and wanted to put them to death. 34But a Pharisee named Gamaliel, a teacher of the law, who was honored by all the people, stood up in the Sanhedrin and ordered that the men be put outside for a little while. 35Then he addressed the Sanhedrin: "Men of Israel, consider carefully what you intend to do to these men. 36Some time ago Theudas appeared, claiming to be somebody, and about four hundred men rallied to him. He was killed, all his followers were dispersed, and it all came to nothing. 37After him, Judas the Galilean appeared in the days of the census and led a band of people in revolt. He too was killed, and all his followers were scattered. 38Therefore, in the present case I advise you: Leave these men alone! Let them go! For if their purpose or activity is of human origin, it will fail. 39But if it is from God, you will not be able to stop these men; you will only find yourselves fighting against God."

40His speech persuaded them. They called the apostles in and had them flogged. Then they ordered them not to speak in the name of Jesus, and let them go.

41The apostles left the Sanhedrin, rejoicing because they had been counted worthy of suffering disgrace for the Name. 42Day after day, in the temple courts and from house to house, they never stopped teaching and proclaiming the good news that Jesus is the Messiah.

6 In those days when the number of disciples was increasing, the Hellenistic Jews[a] among them complained against the Hebraic Jews because their widows were being overlooked in the daily distribution of food. 2So the Twelve gathered all the disciples together and said, "It would not be right for us to neglect the ministry of the word of God in order to wait on tables. 3Brothers and sisters, choose seven men from among you who are known to be full of the Spirit and wisdom. We will turn this responsibility over to them 4and will give our attention to prayer and the ministry of the word."

5This proposal pleased the whole group. They chose Stephen, a man full of faith and of the Holy Spirit;

---

a 1 That is, Jews who had adopted the Greek language and culture also Philip, Procorus, Nicanor, Timon, Parmenas, and Nicolas from Antioch, a convert to Judaism. [6]They presented these men to the apostles, who prayed and laid their hands on them.

[7]So the word of God spread. The number of disciples in Jerusalem increased rapidly, and a large number of priests became obedient to the faith.

[8]Now Stephen, a man full of God's grace and power, performed great wonders and signs among the people. [9]Opposition arose, however, from members of the Synagogue of the Freedmen (as it was called) — Jews of Cyrene and Alexandria as well as the provinces of Cilicia and Asia — who began to argue with Stephen. [10]But they could not stand up against the wisdom the Spirit gave him as he spoke.

[11]Then they secretly persuaded some men to say, "We have heard Stephen speak blasphemous words against Moses and against God."

[12]So they stirred up the people and the elders and the teachers of the law. They seized Stephen and brought him before the Sanhedrin. [13]They produced false witnesses, who testified, "This fellow never stops speaking against this holy place and against the law. [14]For we have heard him say that this Jesus of Nazareth will destroy this place and change the customs Moses handed down to us."

[15]All who were sitting in the Sanhedrin looked intently at Stephen, and they saw that his face was like the face of an angel.

7 Then the high priest asked Stephen, "Are these charges true?"
[2]To this he replied: "Brothers and fathers, listen to me! The God of glory appeared to our father Abraham while he was still in Mesopotamia, before he lived in Harran. [3]'Leave your country and your people,' God said, 'and go to the land I will show you.'[a]

[4]"So he left the land of the Chaldeans and settled in Harran. After the death of his father, God sent him to this land where you are now living. [5]He gave him no inheritance here, not even enough ground to set his foot on. But God promised him that he and his descendants after him would possess the land, even though at that time Abraham had no child. [6]God spoke to him in this way: 'For four hundred years your descendants will be strangers in a country not their own, and they will be enslaved and mistreated. [7]But I will punish the nation they serve as slaves,' God said, 'and afterward they will come out of that country and worship me in this place.'[b] [8]Then he gave Abraham the covenant of circumcision. And Abraham became the father of Isaac and circumcised him eight days after his birth. Later Isaac became the father of Jacob, and Jacob became the father of the twelve patriarchs.

[9]"Because the patriarchs were jealous of Joseph, they sold him as a slave into Egypt. But God was with him [10]and rescued him from all his troubles. He gave Joseph wisdom and enabled him to gain the goodwill of Pharaoh king of Egypt. So Pharaoh made him ruler over Egypt and all his palace.

[11]"Then a famine struck all Egypt and Canaan, bringing great suffering, and our ancestors could not find food. [12]When Jacob heard that there was grain in Egypt, he sent

---

[a] 3 Gen. 12:1     [b] 7 Gen. 15:13,14

our forefathers on their first visit. 13On their second visit, Joseph told his brothers who he was, and Pharaoh learned about Joseph's family. 14After this, Joseph sent for his father Jacob and his whole family, seventy-five in all. 15Then Jacob went down to Egypt, where he and our ancestors died. 16Their bodies were brought back to Shechem and placed in the tomb that Abraham had bought from the sons of Hamor at Shechem for a certain sum of money.

17"As the time drew near for God to fulfill his promise to Abraham, the number of our people in Egypt had greatly increased. 18Then 'a new king, to whom Joseph meant nothing, came to power in Egypt.'*a* 19He dealt treacherously with our people and oppressed our ancestors by forcing them to throw out their newborn babies so that they would die.

20"At that time Moses was born, and he was no ordinary child.*b* For three months he was cared for by his family. 21When he was placed outside, Pharaoh's daughter took him and brought him up as her own son. 22Moses was educated in all the wisdom of the Egyptians and was powerful in speech and action.

23"When Moses was forty years old, he decided to visit his own people, the Israelites. 24He saw one of them being mistreated by an Egyptian, so he went to his defense and avenged him by killing the Egyptian. 25Moses thought that his own people would realize that God was using him to rescue them, but they did not. 26The next day Moses came upon two Israelites who were fighting. He tried to reconcile them by

saying, 'Men, you are brothers; why do you want to hurt each other?'

27"But the man who was mistreating the other pushed Moses aside and said, 'Who made you ruler and judge over us? 28Are you thinking of killing me as you killed the Egyptian yesterday?'*c* 29When Moses heard this, he fled to Midian, where he settled as a foreigner and had two sons.

30"After forty years had passed, an angel appeared to Moses in the flames of a burning bush in the desert near Mount Sinai. 31When he saw this, he was amazed at the sight. As he went over to get a closer look, he heard the Lord say: 32'I am the God of your fathers, the God of Abraham, Isaac and Jacob.'*d* Moses trembled with fear and did not dare to look.

33"Then the Lord said to him, 'Take off your sandals, for the place where you are standing is holy ground. 34I have indeed seen the oppression of my people in Egypt. I have heard their groaning and have come down to set them free. Now come, I will send you back to Egypt.'*e*

35"This is the same Moses they had rejected with the words, 'Who made you ruler and judge?' He was sent to be their ruler and deliverer by God himself, through the angel who appeared to him in the bush. 36He led them out of Egypt and performed wonders and signs in Egypt, at the Red Sea and for forty years in the wilderness.

37"This is the Moses who told the Israelites, 'God will raise up for you a prophet like me from your own people.'*f* 38He was in the assembly in the wilderness, with the

*a 18* Exodus 1:8    *b 20 Or was fair in the sight of God*    *c 28* Exodus 2:14    *d 32* Exodus 3:6
*e 34* Exodus 3:5,7,8,10    *f 37* Deut. 18:15

angel who spoke to him on Mount Sinai, and with our ancestors; and he received living words to pass on to us.

39 "But our ancestors refused to obey him. Instead, they rejected him and in their hearts turned back to Egypt. 40 They told Aaron, 'Make us gods who will go before us. As for this fellow Moses who led us out of Egypt—we don't know what has happened to him!'[a] 41 That was the time they made an idol in the form of a calf. They brought sacrifices to it and reveled in what their own hands had made. 42 But God turned away from them and gave them over to the worship of the sun, moon and stars. This agrees with what is written in the book of the prophets:

" 'Did you bring me sacrifices
      and offerings
   forty years in the wilderness,
      people of Israel?
43 You have taken up the tabernacle
      of Molek
   and the star of your god
      Rephan,
   the idols you made to worship.
Therefore I will send you into
   exile'[b] beyond Babylon.

44 "Our ancestors had the tabernacle of the covenant law with them in the wilderness. It had been made as God directed Moses, according to the pattern he had seen. 45 After receiving the tabernacle, our ancestors under Joshua brought it with them when they took the land from the nations God drove out before them. It remained in the land until the time of David, 46 who enjoyed God's favor and asked that he might provide a dwelling place for the God of Jacob.[c] 47 But it was Solomon who built a house for him.

48 "However, the Most High does not live in houses made by human hands. As the prophet says:

49 " 'Heaven is my throne,
      and the earth is my footstool.
   What kind of house will you
      build for me?
         says the Lord.
      Or where will my resting place
         be?
50 Has not my hand made all these
      things?'[d]

51 "You stiff-necked people! Your hearts and ears are still uncircumcised. You are just like your ancestors: You always resist the Holy Spirit! 52 Was there ever a prophet your ancestors did not persecute? They even killed those who predicted the coming of the Righteous One. And now you have betrayed and murdered him— 53 you who have received the law that was given through angels but have not obeyed it."

54 When the members of the Sanhedrin heard this, they were furious and gnashed their teeth at him. 55 But Stephen, full of the Holy Spirit, looked up to heaven and saw the glory of God, and Jesus standing at the right hand of God. 56 "Look," he said, "I see heaven open and the Son of Man standing at the right hand of God."

57 At this they covered their ears and, yelling at the top of their voices, they all rushed at him, 58 dragged him out of the city and began to stone him. Meanwhile, the witnesses laid their coats at the feet of a young man named Saul.

59 While they were stoning him,

---

[a] 40 Exodus 32:1    [b] 43 Amos 5:25-27 (see Septuagint)    [c] 46 Some early manuscripts the house of Jacob    [d] 50 Isaiah 66:1,2

Stephen prayed, "Lord Jesus, receive my spirit." 60Then he fell on his knees and cried out, "Lord, do not hold this sin against them." When he had said this, he fell asleep.

8 And Saul approved of their killing him.

On that day a great persecution broke out against the church in Jerusalem, and all except the apostles were scattered throughout Judea and Samaria. 2Godly men buried Stephen and mourned deeply for him. 3But Saul began to destroy the church. Going from house to house, he dragged off both men and women and put them in prison.

4Those who had been scattered preached the word wherever they went. 5Philip went down to a city in Samaria and proclaimed the Messiah there. 6When the crowds heard Philip and saw the signs he performed, they all paid close attention to what he said. 7For with shrieks, impure spirits came out of many, and many who were paralyzed or lame were healed. 8So there was great joy in that city.

9Now for some time a man named Simon had practiced sorcery in the city and amazed all the people of Samaria. He boasted that he was someone great, 10and all the people, both high and low, gave him their attention and exclaimed, "This man is rightly called the Great Power of God." 11They followed him because he had amazed them for a long time with his sorcery. 12But when they believed Philip as he proclaimed the good news of the kingdom of God and the name of Jesus Christ, they were baptized, both men and women. 13Simon himself believed and was baptized. And he followed Philip everywhere, astonished by the great signs and miracles he saw.

14When the apostles in Jerusalem heard that Samaria had accepted the word of God, they sent Peter and John to Samaria. 15When they arrived, they prayed for the new believers there that they might receive the Holy Spirit, 16because the Holy Spirit had not yet come on any of them; they had simply been baptized in the name of the Lord Jesus. 17Then Peter and John placed their hands on them, and they received the Holy Spirit.

18When Simon saw that the Spirit was given at the laying on of the apostles' hands, he offered them money 19and said, "Give me also this ability so that everyone on whom I lay my hands may receive the Holy Spirit."

20Peter answered: "May your money perish with you, because you thought you could buy the gift of God with money! 21You have no part or share in this ministry, because your heart is not right before God. 22Repent of this wickedness and pray to the Lord in the hope that he may forgive you for having such a thought in your heart. 23For I see that you are full of bitterness and captive to sin."

24Then Simon answered, "Pray to the Lord for me so that nothing you have said may happen to me."

25After they had further proclaimed the word of the Lord and testified about Jesus, Peter and John returned to Jerusalem, preaching the gospel in many Samaritan villages.

26Now an angel of the Lord said to Philip, "Go south to the road—the desert road—that goes down from Jerusalem to Gaza." 27So he started out, and on his way he met an Ethiopian[a] eunuch, an important official in charge of all the treasury of the Kandake (which means "queen of the Ethiopians"). This man had gone to Jerusalem to worship, 28 and on his way home was sitting in his chariot reading the Book of Isaiah the prophet. 29 The Spirit told Philip, "Go to that chariot and stay near it."

30 Then Philip ran up to the chariot and heard the man reading Isaiah the prophet. "Do you understand what you are reading?" Philip asked.

31 "How can I," he said, "unless someone explains it to me?" So he invited Philip to come up and sit with him.

32 This is the passage of Scripture the eunuch was reading:

"He was led like a sheep to the
    slaughter,
and as a lamb before its
    shearer is silent,
so he did not open his mouth.
33 In his humiliation he was
    deprived of justice.
Who can speak of his
    descendants?
For his life was taken from the
    earth."[b]

34 The eunuch asked Philip, "Tell me, please, who is the prophet talking about, himself or someone else?" 35 Then Philip began with that very passage of Scripture and told him the good news about Jesus.

36 As they traveled along the road, they came to some water and the eunuch said, "Look, here is water. What can stand in the way of my being baptized?" [37][c] 38 And he gave orders to stop the chariot.

Then both Philip and the eunuch went down into the water and Philip baptized him. 39 When they came up out of the water, the Spirit of the Lord suddenly took Philip away, and the eunuch did not see him again, but went on his way rejoicing. 40 Philip, however, appeared at Azotus and traveled about, preaching the gospel in all the towns until he reached Caesarea.

9 Meanwhile, Saul was still breathing out murderous threats against the Lord's disciples. He went to the high priest 2 and asked him for letters to the synagogues in Damascus, so that if he found any there who belonged to the Way, whether men or women, he might take them as prisoners to Jerusalem. 3 As he neared Damascus on his journey, suddenly a light from heaven flashed around him. 4 He fell to the ground and heard a voice say to him, "Saul, Saul, why do you persecute me?"

5 "Who are you, Lord?" Saul asked.

"I am Jesus, whom you are persecuting," he replied. 6 "Now get up and go into the city, and you will be told what you must do."

7 The men traveling with Saul stood there speechless; they heard the sound but did not see anyone. 8 Saul got up from the ground, but when he opened his eyes he could see nothing. So they led him by the hand into Damascus. 9 For three days he was blind, and did not eat or drink anything.

10 In Damascus there was a disciple named Ananias. The Lord called to him in a vision, "Ananias!"

"Yes, Lord," he answered.

---

[a] 27 That is, from the southern Nile region    [b] 33 Isaiah 53:7,8 (see Septuagint)    [c] 37 Some manuscripts include here *Philip said, "If you believe with all your heart, you may." The eunuch answered, "I believe that Jesus Christ is the Son of God."*

¹¹The Lord told him, "Go to the house of Judas on Straight Street and ask for a man from Tarsus named Saul, for he is praying. ¹²In a vision he has seen a man named Ananias come and place his hands on him to restore his sight."

¹³"Lord," Ananias answered, "I have heard many reports about this man and all the harm he has done to your holy people in Jerusalem. ¹⁴And he has come here with authority from the chief priests to arrest all who call on your name."

¹⁵But the Lord said to Ananias, "Go! This man is my chosen instrument to proclaim my name to the Gentiles and their kings and to the people of Israel. ¹⁶I will show him how much he must suffer for my name."

¹⁷Then Ananias went to the house and entered it. Placing his hands on Saul, he said, "Brother Saul, the Lord—Jesus, who appeared to you on the road as you were coming here—has sent me so that you may see again and be filled with the Holy Spirit." ¹⁸Immediately, something like scales fell from Saul's eyes, and he could see again. He got up and was baptized, ¹⁹and after taking some food, he regained his strength.

Saul spent several days with the disciples in Damascus. ²⁰At once he began to preach in the synagogues that Jesus is the Son of God. ²¹All those who heard him were astonished and asked, "Isn't he the man who raised havoc in Jerusalem among those who call on this name? And hasn't he come here to take them as prisoners to the chief priests?" ²²Yet Saul grew more and more powerful and baffled the Jews living in Damascus by proving that Jesus is the Messiah.

²³After many days had gone by, there was a conspiracy among the Jews to kill him, ²⁴but Saul learned of their plan. Day and night they kept close watch on the city gates in order to kill him. ²⁵But his followers took him by night and lowered him in a basket through an opening in the wall.

²⁶When he came to Jerusalem, he tried to join the disciples, but they were all afraid of him, not believing that he really was a disciple. ²⁷But Barnabas took him and brought him to the apostles. He told them how Saul on his journey had seen the Lord and that the Lord had spoken to him, and how in Damascus he had preached fearlessly in the name of Jesus. ²⁸So Saul stayed with them and moved about freely in Jerusalem, speaking boldly in the name of the Lord. ²⁹He talked and debated with the Hellenistic Jews,[a] but they tried to kill him. ³⁰When the believers learned of this, they took him down to Caesarea and sent him off to Tarsus.

³¹Then the church throughout Judea, Galilee and Samaria enjoyed a time of peace and was strengthened. Living in the fear of the Lord and encouraged by the Holy Spirit, it increased in numbers.

³²As Peter traveled about the country, he went to visit the Lord's people who lived in Lydda. ³³There he found a man named Aeneas, who was paralyzed and had been bedridden for eight years. ³⁴"Aeneas," Peter said to him, "Jesus Christ heals you. Get up and roll up your mat." Immediately Aeneas got up. ³⁵All those who lived in Lydda and

---

[a] 29 That is, Jews who had adopted the Greek language and culture

Sharon saw him and turned to the Lord.

³⁶In Joppa there was a disciple named Tabitha (in Greek her name is Dorcas); she was always doing good and helping the poor. ³⁷About that time she became sick and died, and her body was washed and placed in an upstairs room. ³⁸Lydda was near Joppa; so when the disciples heard that Peter was in Lydda, they sent two men to him and urged him, "Please come at once!"

³⁹Peter went with them, and when he arrived he was taken upstairs to the room. All the widows stood around him, crying and showing him the robes and other clothing that Dorcas had made while she was still with them.

⁴⁰Peter sent them all out of the room; then he got down on his knees and prayed. Turning toward the dead woman, he said, "Tabitha, get up." She opened her eyes, and seeing Peter she sat up. ⁴¹He took her by the hand and helped her to her feet. Then he called for the believers, especially the widows, and presented her to them alive. ⁴²This became known all over Joppa, and many people believed in the Lord. ⁴³Peter stayed in Joppa for some time with a tanner named Simon.

**10** At Caesarea there was a man named Cornelius, a centurion in what was known as the Italian Regiment. ²He and all his family were devout and God-fearing; he gave generously to those in need and prayed to God regularly. ³One day at about three in the afternoon he had a vision. He distinctly saw an angel of God, who came to him and said, "Cornelius!"

⁴Cornelius stared at him in fear. "What is it, Lord?" he asked.

The angel answered, "Your prayers and gifts to the poor have come up as a memorial offering before God. ⁵Now send men to Joppa to bring back a man named Simon who is called Peter. ⁶He is staying with Simon the tanner, whose house is by the sea."

⁷When the angel who spoke to him had gone, Cornelius called two of his servants and a devout soldier who was one of his attendants. ⁸He told them everything that had happened and sent them to Joppa.

⁹About noon the following day as they were on their journey and approaching the city, Peter went up on the roof to pray. ¹⁰He became hungry and wanted something to eat, and while the meal was being prepared, he fell into a trance. ¹¹He saw heaven opened and something like a large sheet being let down to earth by its four corners. ¹²It contained all kinds of four-footed animals, as well as reptiles and birds. ¹³Then a voice told him, "Get up, Peter. Kill and eat."

¹⁴"Surely not, Lord!" Peter replied. "I have never eaten anything impure or unclean."

¹⁵The voice spoke to him a second time, "Do not call anything impure that God has made clean."

¹⁶This happened three times, and immediately the sheet was taken back to heaven.

¹⁷While Peter was wondering about the meaning of the vision, the men sent by Cornelius found out where Simon's house was and stopped at the gate. ¹⁸They called out, asking if Simon who was known as Peter was staying there.

¹⁹While Peter was still thinking about the vision, the Spirit said to him, "Simon, three*ᵃ* men are

---

*ᵃ 19* One early manuscript *two*; other manuscripts do not have the number.

looking for you. ²⁰So get up and go downstairs. Do not hesitate to go with them, for I have sent them."

²¹Peter went down and said to the men, "I'm the one you're looking for. Why have you come?"

²²The men replied, "We have come from Cornelius the centurion. He is a righteous and God-fearing man, who is respected by all the Jewish people. A holy angel told him to ask you to come to his house so that he could hear what you have to say." ²³Then Peter invited the men into the house to be his guests.

The next day Peter started out with them, and some of the believers from Joppa went along. ²⁴The following day he arrived in Caesarea. Cornelius was expecting them and had called together his relatives and close friends. ²⁵As Peter entered the house, Cornelius met him and fell at his feet in reverence. ²⁶But Peter made him get up. "Stand up," he said, "I am only a man myself."

²⁷While talking with him, Peter went inside and found a large gathering of people. ²⁸He said to them: "You are well aware that it is against our law for a Jew to associate with or visit a Gentile. But God has shown me that I should not call anyone impure or unclean. ²⁹So when I was sent for, I came without raising any objection. May I ask why you sent for me?"

³⁰Cornelius answered: "Three days ago I was in my house praying at this hour, at three in the afternoon. Suddenly a man in shining clothes stood before me ³¹and said, 'Cornelius, God has heard your prayer and remembered your gifts to the poor. ³²Send to Joppa for Simon who is called Peter. He is a guest in the home of Simon the tanner, who lives by the sea.' ³³So I sent for you immediately, and it was good of you to come. Now we are all here in the presence of God to listen to everything the Lord has commanded you to tell us."

³⁴Then Peter began to speak: "I now realize how true it is that God does not show favoritism ³⁵but accepts from every nation the one who fears him and does what is right. ³⁶You know the message God sent to the people of Israel, announcing the good news of peace through Jesus Christ, who is Lord of all. ³⁷You know what has happened throughout the province of Judea, beginning in Galilee after the baptism that John preached— ³⁸how God anointed Jesus of Nazareth with the Holy Spirit and power, and how he went around doing good and healing all who were under the power of the devil, because God was with him.

³⁹"We are witnesses of everything he did in the country of the Jews and in Jerusalem. They killed him by hanging him on a cross, ⁴⁰but God raised him from the dead on the third day and caused him to be seen. ⁴¹He was not seen by all the people, but by witnesses whom God had already chosen—by us who ate and drank with him after he rose from the dead. ⁴²He commanded us to preach to the people and to testify that he is the one whom God appointed as judge of the living and the dead. ⁴³All the prophets testify about him that everyone who believes in him receives forgiveness of sins through his name."

⁴⁴While Peter was still speaking these words, the Holy Spirit came on all who heard the message. ⁴⁵The circumcised believers who had come with Peter were astonished

that the gift of the Holy Spirit had been poured out even on Gentiles. [46] For they heard them speaking in tongues[a] and praising God.

Then Peter said, [47] "Surely no one can stand in the way of their being baptized with water. They have received the Holy Spirit just as we have." [48] So he ordered that they be baptized in the name of Jesus Christ. Then they asked Peter to stay with them for a few days.

11 The apostles and the believers throughout Judea heard that the Gentiles also had received the word of God. [2] So when Peter went up to Jerusalem, the circumcised believers criticized him [3] and said, "You went into the house of uncircumcised men and ate with them."

[4] Starting from the beginning, Peter told them the whole story: [5] "I was in the city of Joppa praying, and in a trance I saw a vision. I saw something like a large sheet being let down from heaven by its four corners, and it came down to where I was. [6] I looked into it and saw fourfooted animals of the earth, wild beasts, reptiles and birds. [7] Then I heard a voice telling me, 'Get up, Peter. Kill and eat.'

[8] "I replied, 'Surely not, Lord! Nothing impure or unclean has ever entered my mouth.'

[9] "The voice spoke from heaven a second time, 'Do not call anything impure that God has made clean.' [10] This happened three times, and then it was all pulled up to heaven again.

[11] "Right then three men who had been sent to me from Caesarea stopped at the house where I was staying. [12] The Spirit told me to have no hesitation about going with them. These six brothers also went

with me, and we entered the man's house. [13] He told us how he had seen an angel appear in his house and say, 'Send to Joppa for Simon who is called Peter. [14] He will bring you a message through which you and all your household will be saved.'

[15] "As I began to speak, the Holy Spirit came on them as he had come on us at the beginning. [16] Then I remembered what the Lord had said: 'John baptized with[b] water, but you will be baptized with[b] the Holy Spirit.' [17] So if God gave them the same gift he gave us who believed in the Lord Jesus Christ, who was I to think that I could stand in God's way?"

[18] When they heard this, they had no further objections and praised God, saying, "So then, even to Gentiles God has granted repentance that leads to life."

[19] Now those who had been scattered by the persecution that broke out when Stephen was killed traveled as far as Phoenicia, Cyprus and Antioch, spreading the word only among Jews. [20] Some of them, however, men from Cyprus and Cyrene, went to Antioch and began to speak to Greeks also, telling them the good news about the Lord Jesus. [21] The Lord's hand was with them, and a great number of people believed and turned to the Lord.

[22] News of this reached the church in Jerusalem, and they sent Barnabas to Antioch. [23] When he arrived and saw what the grace of God had done, he was glad and encouraged them all to remain true to the Lord with all their hearts. [24] He was a good man, full of the Holy Spirit and faith, and a great number of people were brought to the Lord.

[25] Then Barnabas went to Tar-

---

[a] 46 Or other languages    [b] 16 Or in

sus to look for Saul, 26and when he found him, he brought him to Antioch. So for a whole year Barnabas and Saul met with the church and taught great numbers of people. The disciples were called Christians first at Antioch.

27During this time some prophets came down from Jerusalem to Antioch. 28One of them, named Agabus, stood up and through the Spirit predicted that a severe famine would spread over the entire Roman world. (This happened during the reign of Claudius.) 29The disciples, as each one was able, decided to provide help for the brothers and sisters living in Judea. 30This they did, sending their gift to the elders by Barnabas and Saul.

12 It was about this time that King Herod arrested some who belonged to the church, intending to persecute them. 2He had James, the brother of John, put to death with the sword. 3When he saw that this met with approval among the Jews, he proceeded to seize Peter also. This happened during the Festival of Unleavened Bread. 4After arresting him, he put him in prison, handing him over to be guarded by four squads of four soldiers each. Herod intended to bring him out for public trial after the Passover.

5So Peter was kept in prison, but the church was earnestly praying to God for him.

6The night before Herod was to bring him to trial, Peter was sleeping between two soldiers, bound with two chains, and sentries stood guard at the entrance. 7Suddenly an angel of the Lord appeared and a light shone in the cell. He struck Peter on the side and woke him up. "Quick, get up!" he said, and the chains fell off Peter's wrists.

8Then the angel said to him, "Put on your clothes and sandals." And Peter did so. "Wrap your cloak around you and follow me," the angel told him. 9Peter followed him out of the prison, but he had no idea that what the angel was doing was really happening; he thought he was seeing a vision. 10They passed the first and second guards and came to the iron gate leading to the city. It opened for them by itself, and they went through it. When they had walked the length of one street, suddenly the angel left him.

11Then Peter came to himself and said, "Now I know without a doubt that the Lord has sent his angel and rescued me from Herod's clutches and from everything the Jewish people were hoping would happen."

12When this had dawned on him, he went to the house of Mary the mother of John, also called Mark, where many people had gathered and were praying. 13Peter knocked at the outer entrance, and a servant named Rhoda came to answer the door. 14When she recognized Peter's voice, she was so overjoyed she ran back without opening it and exclaimed, "Peter is at the door!"

15"You're out of your mind," they told her. When she kept insisting that it was so, they said, "It must be his angel."

16But Peter kept on knocking, and when they opened the door and saw him, they were astonished. 17Peter motioned with his hand for them to be quiet and described how the Lord had brought him out of prison. "Tell James and the other brothers and sisters about this," he said, and then he left for another place.

18In the morning, there was no small commotion among the soldiers as to what had become of Peter. [19]After Herod had a thorough search made for him and did not find him, he cross-examined the guards and ordered that they be executed.

Then Herod went from Judea to Caesarea and stayed there. [20]He had been quarreling with the people of Tyre and Sidon; they now joined together and sought an audience with him. After securing the support of Blastus, a trusted personal servant of the king, they asked for peace, because they depended on the king's country for their food supply.

[21]On the appointed day Herod, wearing his royal robes, sat on his throne and delivered a public address to the people. [22]They shouted, "This is the voice of a god, not of a man." [23]Immediately, because Herod did not give praise to God, an angel of the Lord struck him down, and he was eaten by worms and died.

[24]But the word of God continued to spread and flourish.

[25]When Barnabas and Saul had finished their mission, they returned from[a] Jerusalem, taking with them John, also called Mark.

13 [1]Now in the church at Antioch there were prophets and teachers: Barnabas, Simeon called Niger, Lucius of Cyrene, Manaen (who had been brought up with Herod the tetrarch) and Saul. [2]While they were worshiping the Lord and fasting, the Holy Spirit said, "Set apart for me Barnabas and Saul for the work to which I have called them." [3]So after they had fasted and prayed, they placed their hands on them and sent them off.

[4]The two of them, sent on their way by the Holy Spirit, went down to Seleucia and sailed from there to Cyprus. [5]When they arrived at Salamis, they proclaimed the word of God in the Jewish synagogues. John was with them as their helper.

[6]They traveled through the whole island until they came to Paphos. There they met a Jewish sorcerer and false prophet named Bar-Jesus, [7]who was an attendant of the proconsul, Sergius Paulus. The proconsul, an intelligent man, sent for Barnabas and Saul because he wanted to hear the word of God. [8]But Elymas the sorcerer (for that is what his name means) opposed them and tried to turn the proconsul from the faith. [9]Then Saul, who was also called Paul, filled with the Holy Spirit, looked straight at Elymas and said, [10]"You are a child of the devil and an enemy of everything that is right! You are full of all kinds of deceit and trickery. Will you never stop perverting the right ways of the Lord? [11]Now the hand of the Lord is against you. You are going to be blind for a time, not even able to see the light of the sun."

Immediately mist and darkness came over him, and he groped about, seeking someone to lead him by the hand. [12]When the proconsul saw what had happened, he believed, for he was amazed at the teaching about the Lord.

[13]From Paphos, Paul and his companions sailed to Perga in Pamphylia, where John left them to return to Jerusalem. [14]From Perga they went on to Pisidian Antioch. On the Sabbath they entered the synagogue and sat down. [15]After the reading from the Law and the Prophets, the leaders of the synagogue sent word

[a] 25 Some manuscripts *to*

to them, saying, "Brothers, if you have a word of exhortation for the people, please speak."

¹⁶Standing up, Paul motioned with his hand and said: "Fellow Israelites and you Gentiles who worship God, listen to me! ¹⁷The God of the people of Israel chose our ancestors; he made the people prosper during their stay in Egypt; with mighty power he led them out of that country; ¹⁸for about forty years he endured their conduct*a* in the wilderness; ¹⁹and he overthrew seven nations in Canaan, giving their land to his people as their inheritance. ²⁰All this took about 450 years.

"After this, God gave them judges until the time of Samuel the prophet. ²¹Then the people asked for a king, and he gave them Saul son of Kish, of the tribe of Benjamin, who ruled forty years. ²²After removing Saul, he made David their king. God testified concerning him: 'I have found David son of Jesse, a man after my own heart; he will do everything I want him to do.'

²³"From this man's descendants God has brought to Israel the Savior Jesus, as he promised. ²⁴Before the coming of Jesus, John preached repentance and baptism to all the people of Israel. ²⁵As John was completing his work, he said: 'Who do you suppose I am? I am not the one you are looking for. But there is one coming after me whose sandals I am not worthy to untie.'

²⁶"Fellow children of Abraham and you God-fearing Gentiles, it is to us that this message of salvation has been sent. ²⁷The people of Jerusalem and their rulers did not recognize Jesus, yet in condemn-

ing him they fulfilled the words of the prophets that are read every Sabbath. ²⁸Though they found no proper ground for a death sentence, they asked Pilate to have him executed. ²⁹When they had carried out all that was written about him, they took him down from the cross and laid him in a tomb. ³⁰But God raised him from the dead, ³¹and for many days he was seen by those who had traveled with him from Galilee to Jerusalem. They are now his witnesses to our people.

³²"We tell you the good news: What God promised our ancestors ³³he has fulfilled for us, their children, by raising up Jesus. As it is written in the second Psalm:

" 'You are my son;
    today I have become your
        father.'*b*

³⁴God raised him from the dead so that he will never be subject to decay. As God has said,

" 'I will give you the holy and
    sure blessings promised to
        David.'*c*

³⁵So it is also stated elsewhere:

" 'You will not let your holy one
    see decay.'*d*

³⁶"Now when David had served God's purpose in his own generation, he fell asleep; he was buried with his ancestors and his body decayed. ³⁷But the one whom God raised from the dead did not see decay.

³⁸"Therefore, my friends, I want you to know that through Jesus the forgiveness of sins is proclaimed to you. ³⁹Through him everyone who believes is set free from every sin,

---

*a* 18 Some manuscripts *he cared for them*    *b* 33 Psalm 2:7    *c* 34 Isaiah 55:3
*d* 35 Psalm 16:10 (see Septuagint)

a justification you were not able to obtain under the law of Moses. ⁴⁰Take care that what the prophets have said does not happen to you:

⁴¹ " 'Look, you scoffers,
      wonder and perish,
   for I am going to do something in
      your days
      that you would never believe,
      even if someone told you.'ᵃ

⁴²As Paul and Barnabas were leaving the synagogue, the people invited them to speak further about these things on the next Sabbath. ⁴³When the congregation was dismissed, many of the Jews and devout converts to Judaism followed Paul and Barnabas, who talked with them and urged them to continue in the grace of God.

⁴⁴On the next Sabbath almost the whole city gathered to hear the word of the Lord. ⁴⁵When the Jews saw the crowds, they were filled with jealousy. They began to contradict what Paul was saying and heaped abuse on him.

⁴⁶Then Paul and Barnabas answered them boldly: "We had to speak the word of God to you first. Since you reject it and do not consider yourselves worthy of eternal life, we now turn to the Gentiles. ⁴⁷For this is what the Lord has commanded us:

" 'I have made youᵇ a light for the
      Gentiles,
   that youᵇ may bring salvation
      to the ends of the earth.'ᶜ

⁴⁸When the Gentiles heard this, they were glad and honored the word of the Lord; and all who were appointed for eternal life believed.

⁴⁹The word of the Lord spread through the whole region. ⁵⁰But the Jewish leaders incited the God-fearing women of high standing and the leading men of the city. They stirred up persecution against Paul and Barnabas, and expelled them from their region. ⁵¹So they shook the dust off their feet as a warning to them and went to Iconium. ⁵²And the disciples were filled with joy and with the Holy Spirit.

14 At Iconium Paul and Barnabas went as usual into the Jewish synagogue. There they spoke so effectively that a great number of Jews and Greeks believed. ²But the Jews who refused to believe stirred up the other Gentiles and poisoned their minds against the brothers. ³So Paul and Barnabas spent considerable time there, speaking boldly for the Lord, who confirmed the message of his grace by enabling them to perform signs and wonders. ⁴The people of the city were divided; some sided with the Jews, others with the apostles. ⁵There was a plot afoot among both Gentiles and Jews, together with their leaders, to mistreat them and stone them. ⁶But they found out about it and fled to the Lycaonian cities of Lystra and Derbe and to the surrounding country, ⁷where they continued to preach the gospel.

⁸In Lystra there sat a man who was lame. He had been that way from birth and had never walked. ⁹He listened to Paul as he was speaking. Paul looked directly at him, saw that he had faith to be healed ¹⁰and called out, "Stand up on your feet!" At that, the man jumped up and began to walk.

¹¹When the crowd saw what Paul had done, they shouted in the Lycaonian language, "The gods have come down to us in human form!"

---

ᵃ 41 Hab. 1:5    ᵇ 47 The Greek is singular.    ᶜ 47 Isaiah 49:6

¹²Barnabas they called Zeus, and Paul they called Hermes because he was the chief speaker. ¹³The priest of Zeus, whose temple was just outside the city, brought bulls and wreaths to the city gates because he and the crowd wanted to offer sacrifices to them.

¹⁴But when the apostles Barnabas and Paul heard of this, they tore their clothes and rushed out into the crowd, shouting: ¹⁵"Friends, why are you doing this? We too are only human, like you. We are bringing you good news, telling you to turn from these worthless things to the living God, who made the heavens and the earth and the sea and everything in them. ¹⁶In the past, he let all nations go their own way. ¹⁷Yet he has not left himself without testimony: He has shown kindness by giving you rain from heaven and crops in their seasons; he provides you with plenty of food and fills your hearts with joy." ¹⁸Even with these words, they had difficulty keeping the crowd from sacrificing to them.

¹⁹Then some Jews came from Antioch and Iconium and won the crowd over. They stoned Paul and dragged him outside the city, thinking he was dead. ²⁰But after the disciples had gathered around him, he got up and went back into the city. The next day he and Barnabas left for Derbe.

²¹They preached the gospel in that city and won a large number of disciples. Then they returned to Lystra, Iconium and Antioch, ²²strengthening the disciples and encouraging them to remain true to the faith. "We must go through many hardships to enter the kingdom of God," they said. ²³Paul

and Barnabas appointed elders[a] for them in each church and, with prayer and fasting, committed them to the Lord, in whom they had put their trust. ²⁴After going through Pisidia, they came into Pamphylia, ²⁵and when they had preached the word in Perga, they went down to Attalia.

²⁶From Attalia they sailed back to Antioch, where they had been committed to the grace of God for the work they had now completed. ²⁷On arriving there, they gathered the church together and reported all that God had done through them and how he had opened a door of faith to the Gentiles. ²⁸And they stayed there a long time with the disciples.

15 Certain people came down from Judea to Antioch and were teaching the believers: "Unless you are circumcised, according to the custom taught by Moses, you cannot be saved." ²This brought Paul and Barnabas into sharp dispute and debate with them. So Paul and Barnabas were appointed, along with some other believers, to go up to Jerusalem to see the apostles and elders about this question. ³The church sent them on their way, and as they traveled through Phoenicia and Samaria, they told how the Gentiles had been converted. This news made all the believers very glad. ⁴When they came to Jerusalem, they were welcomed by the church and the apostles and elders, to whom they reported everything God had done through them.

⁵Then some of the believers who belonged to the party of the Pharisees stood up and said, "The Gen-

---

*a 23 Or Barnabas ordained elders; or Barnabas had elders elected* tiles must be circumcised and required to keep the law of Moses."

<sup>6</sup>The apostles and elders met to consider this question. <sup>7</sup>After much discussion, Peter got up and addressed them: "Brothers, you know that some time ago God made a choice among you that the Gentiles might hear from my lips the message of the gospel and believe. <sup>8</sup>God, who knows the heart, showed that he accepted them by giving the Holy Spirit to them, just as he did to us. <sup>9</sup>He did not discriminate between us and them, for he purified their hearts by faith. <sup>10</sup>Now then, why do you try to test God by putting on the necks of Gentiles a yoke that neither we nor our ancestors have been able to bear? <sup>11</sup>No! We believe it is through the grace of our Lord Jesus that we are saved, just as they are."

<sup>12</sup>The whole assembly became silent as they listened to Barnabas and Paul telling about the signs and wonders God had done among the Gentiles through them. <sup>13</sup>When they finished, James spoke up. "Brothers," he said, "listen to me. <sup>14</sup>Simon[a] has described to us how God first intervened to choose a people for his name from the Gentiles. <sup>15</sup>The words of the prophets are in agreement with this, as it is written:

<sup>16</sup> "'After this I will return
        and rebuild David's fallen
        tent.
    Its ruins I will rebuild,
        and I will restore it,
<sup>17</sup> that the rest of mankind may
        seek the Lord,
        even all the Gentiles who bear
        my name,

says the Lord, who does these
        things'[b] —
<sup>18</sup> things known from long ago.[c]

<sup>19</sup> "It is my judgment, therefore, that we should not make it difficult for the Gentiles who are turning to God. <sup>20</sup>Instead we should write to them, telling them to abstain from food polluted by idols, from sexual immorality, from the meat of strangled animals and from blood. <sup>21</sup>For the law of Moses has been preached in every city from the earliest times and is read in the synagogues on every Sabbath."

<sup>22</sup>Then the apostles and elders, with the whole church, decided to choose some of their own men and send them to Antioch with Paul and Barnabas. They chose Judas (called Barsabbas) and Silas, men who were leaders among the believers. <sup>23</sup>With them they sent the following letter:

The apostles and elders, your brothers,

To the Gentile believers in Antioch, Syria and Cilicia:

Greetings.

<sup>24</sup>We have heard that some went out from us without our authorization and disturbed you, troubling your minds by what they said. <sup>25</sup>So we all agreed to choose some men and send them to you with our dear friends Barnabas and Paul— <sup>26</sup>men who have risked their lives for the name of our Lord Jesus Christ. <sup>27</sup>Therefore we are sending Judas and Silas to confirm by word of mouth what we are writing. <sup>28</sup>It seemed good

---

[a] 14 Greek *Simeon*, a variant of *Simon*; that is, Peter    [b] 17 Amos 9:11,12 (see Septuagint)
[c] 17,18 Some manuscripts *things'* — / <sup>18</sup>*the Lord's work is known to him from long ago*

to the Holy Spirit and to us not to burden you with anything beyond the following requirements: ²⁹You are to abstain from food sacrificed to idols, from blood, from the meat of strangled animals and from sexual immorality. You will do well to avoid these things.

Farewell.

³⁰So the men were sent off and went down to Antioch, where they gathered the church together and delivered the letter. ³¹The people read it and were glad for its encouraging message. ³²Judas and Silas, who themselves were prophets, said much to encourage and strengthen the believers. ³³After spending some time there, they were sent off by the believers with the blessing of peace to return to those who had sent them. [³⁴] ª ³⁵But Paul and Barnabas remained in Antioch, where they and many others taught and preached the word of the Lord.

³⁶Some time later Paul said to Barnabas, "Let us go back and visit the believers in all the towns where we preached the word of the Lord and see how they are doing." ³⁷Barnabas wanted to take John, also called Mark, with them, ³⁸but Paul did not think it wise to take him, because he had deserted them in Pamphylia and had not continued with them in the work. ³⁹They had such a sharp disagreement that they parted company. Barnabas took Mark and sailed for Cyprus, ⁴⁰but Paul chose Silas and left, commended by the believers to the grace of the Lord. ⁴¹He went through Syria and Cilicia, strengthening the churches.

16 Paul came to Derbe and then to Lystra, where a disciple named Timothy lived, whose mother was Jewish and a believer but whose father was a Greek. ²The believers at Lystra and Iconium spoke well of him. ³Paul wanted to take him along on the journey, so he circumcised him because of the Jews who lived in that area, for they all knew that his father was a Greek. ⁴As they traveled from town to town, they delivered the decisions reached by the apostles and elders in Jerusalem for the people to obey. ⁵So the churches were strengthened in the faith and grew daily in numbers.

⁶Paul and his companions traveled throughout the region of Phrygia and Galatia, having been kept by the Holy Spirit from preaching the word in the province of Asia. ⁷When they came to the border of Mysia, they tried to enter Bithynia, but the Spirit of Jesus would not allow them to. ⁸So they passed by Mysia and went down to Troas. ⁹During the night Paul had a vision of a man of Macedonia standing and begging him, "Come over to Macedonia and help us." ¹⁰After Paul had seen the vision, we got ready at once to leave for Macedonia, concluding that God had called us to preach the gospel to them.

¹¹From Troas we put out to sea and sailed straight for Samothrace, and the next day we went on to Neapolis. ¹²From there we traveled to Philippi, a Roman colony and the leading city of that district ᵇ of Macedonia. And we stayed there several days.

¹³On the Sabbath we went outside the city gate to the river, where we

---

ª 34 Some manuscripts include here *But Silas decided to remain there.*   ᵇ 12 The text and meaning of the Greek for *the leading city of that district* are uncertain.

expected to find a place of prayer. We sat down and began to speak to the women who had gathered there. ¹⁴One of those listening was a woman from the city of Thyatira named Lydia, a dealer in purple cloth. She was a worshiper of God. The Lord opened her heart to respond to Paul's message. ¹⁵When she and the members of her household were baptized, she invited us to her home. "If you consider me a believer in the Lord," she said, "come and stay at my house." And she persuaded us.

¹⁶Once when we were going to the place of prayer, we were met by a female slave who had a spirit by which she predicted the future. She earned a great deal of money for her owners by fortune-telling. ¹⁷She followed Paul and the rest of us, shouting, "These men are servants of the Most High God, who are telling you the way to be saved." ¹⁸She kept this up for many days. Finally Paul became so annoyed that he turned around and said to the spirit, "In the name of Jesus Christ I command you to come out of her!" At that moment the spirit left her.

¹⁹When her owners realized that their hope of making money was gone, they seized Paul and Silas and dragged them into the marketplace to face the authorities. ²⁰They brought them before the magistrates and said, "These men are Jews, and are throwing our city into an uproar ²¹by advocating customs unlawful for us Romans to accept or practice."

²²The crowd joined in the attack against Paul and Silas, and the magistrates ordered them to be stripped and beaten with rods. ²³After they had been severely flogged, they were thrown into prison, and the jailer was commanded to guard them carefully. ²⁴When he received these orders, he put them in the inner cell and fastened their feet in the stocks.

²⁵About midnight Paul and Silas were praying and singing hymns to God, and the other prisoners were listening to them. ²⁶Suddenly there was such a violent earthquake that the foundations of the prison were shaken. At once all the prison doors flew open, and everyone's chains came loose. ²⁷The jailer woke up, and when he saw the prison doors open, he drew his sword and was about to kill himself because he thought the prisoners had escaped. ²⁸But Paul shouted, "Don't harm yourself! We are all here!"

²⁹The jailer called for lights, rushed in and fell trembling before Paul and Silas. ³⁰He then brought them out and asked, "Sirs, what must I do to be saved?"

³¹They replied, "Believe in the Lord Jesus, and you will be saved—you and your household." ³²Then they spoke the word of the Lord to him and to all the others in his house. ³³At that hour of the night the jailer took them and washed their wounds; then immediately he and all his household were baptized. ³⁴The jailer brought them into his house and set a meal before them; he was filled with joy because he had come to believe in God—he and his whole household.

³⁵When it was daylight, the magistrates sent their officers to the jailer with the order: "Release those men." ³⁶The jailer told Paul, "The magistrates have ordered that you and Silas be released. Now you can leave. Go in peace."

³⁷But Paul said to the officers: "They beat us publicly without a tri-

al, even though we are Roman citizens, and threw us into prison. And now do they want to get rid of us quietly? No! Let them come themselves and escort us out."

38 The officers reported this to the magistrates, and when they heard that Paul and Silas were Roman citizens, they were alarmed. 39 They came to appease them and escorted them from the prison, requesting them to leave the city. 40 After Paul and Silas came out of the prison, they went to Lydia's house, where they met with the brothers and sisters and encouraged them. Then they left.

17 When Paul and his companions had passed through Amphipolis and Apollonia, they came to Thessalonica, where there was a Jewish synagogue. 2 As was his custom, Paul went into the synagogue, and on three Sabbath days he reasoned with them from the Scriptures, 3 explaining and proving that the Messiah had to suffer and rise from the dead. "This Jesus I am proclaiming to you is the Messiah," he said. 4 Some of the Jews were persuaded and joined Paul and Silas, as did a large number of God-fearing Greeks and quite a few prominent women.

5 But other Jews were jealous; so they rounded up some bad characters from the marketplace, formed a mob and started a riot in the city. They rushed to Jason's house in search of Paul and Silas in order to bring them out to the crowd.[a] 6 But when they did not find them, they dragged Jason and some other believers before the city officials, shouting: "These men who have caused trouble all over the world have now come here, 7 and Jason

has welcomed them into his house. They are all defying Caesar's decrees, saying that there is another king, one called Jesus." 8 When they heard this, the crowd and the city officials were thrown into turmoil. 9 Then they made Jason and the others post bond and let them go.

10 As soon as it was night, the believers sent Paul and Silas away to Berea. On arriving there, they went to the Jewish synagogue. 11 Now the Berean Jews were of more noble character than those in Thessalonica, for they received the message with great eagerness and examined the Scriptures every day to see if what Paul said was true. 12 As a result, many of them believed, as did also a number of prominent Greek women and many Greek men.

13 But when the Jews in Thessalonica learned that Paul was preaching the word of God at Berea, some of them went there too, agitating the crowds and stirring them up. 14 The believers immediately sent Paul to the coast, but Silas and Timothy stayed at Berea. 15 Those who escorted Paul brought him to Athens and then left with instructions for Silas and Timothy to join him as soon as possible.

16 While Paul was waiting for them in Athens, he was greatly distressed to see that the city was full of idols. 17 So he reasoned in the synagogue with both Jews and God-fearing Greeks, as well as in the marketplace day by day with those who happened to be there. 18 A group of Epicurean and Stoic philosophers began to debate with him. Some of them asked, "What is this babbler trying to say?" Others remarked, "He seems to be advocating foreign gods." They said this because Paul

a 5 Or the assembly of the people

was preaching the good news about Jesus and the resurrection. [19]Then they took him and brought him to a meeting of the Areopagus, where they said to him, "May we know what this new teaching is that you are presenting? [20]You are bringing some strange ideas to our ears, and we would like to know what they mean." [21](All the Athenians and the foreigners who lived there spent their time doing nothing but talking about and listening to the latest ideas.)

[22]Paul then stood up in the meeting of the Areopagus and said: "People of Athens! I see that in every way you are very religious. [23]For as I walked around and looked carefully at your objects of worship, I even found an altar with this inscription: TO AN UNKNOWN GOD. So you are ignorant of the very thing you worship—and this is what I am going to proclaim to you.

[24]"The God who made the world and everything in it is the Lord of heaven and earth and does not live in temples built by human hands. [25]And he is not served by human hands, as if he needed anything. Rather, he himself gives everyone life and breath and everything else. [26]From one man he made all the nations, that they should inhabit the whole earth; and he marked out their appointed times in history and the boundaries of their lands. [27]God did this so that they would seek him and perhaps reach out for him and find him, though he is not far from any one of us. [28]'For in him we live and move and have our being.'[a] As some of your own poets have said, 'We are his offspring.'[b]

[29]"Therefore since we are God's offspring, we should not think that the divine being is like gold or silver or stone—an image made by human design and skill. [30]In the past God overlooked such ignorance, but now he commands all people everywhere to repent. [31]For he has set a day when he will judge the world with justice by the man he has appointed. He has given proof of this to everyone by raising him from the dead."

[32]When they heard about the resurrection of the dead, some of them sneered, but others said, "We want to hear you again on this subject." [33]At that, Paul left the Council. [34]Some of the people became followers of Paul and believed. Among them was Dionysius, a member of the Areopagus, also a woman named Damaris, and a number of others.

18 After this, Paul left Athens and went to Corinth. [2]There he met a Jew named Aquila, a native of Pontus, who had recently come from Italy with his wife Priscilla, because Claudius had ordered all Jews to leave Rome. Paul went to see them, [3]and because he was a tentmaker as they were, he stayed and worked with them. [4]Every Sabbath he reasoned in the synagogue, trying to persuade Jews and Greeks.

[5]When Silas and Timothy came from Macedonia, Paul devoted himself exclusively to preaching, testifying to the Jews that Jesus was the Messiah. [6]But when they opposed Paul and became abusive, he shook out his clothes in protest and said to them, "Your blood be on your own heads! I am innocent of it. From now on I will go to the Gentiles."

[7]Then Paul left the synagogue and went next door to the house of

_____

[a] 28 From the Cretan philosopher Epimenides    [b] 28 From the Cilician Stoic philosopher Aratus

Titius Justus, a worshiper of God. [8]Crispus, the synagogue leader, and his entire household believed in the Lord; and many of the Corinthians who heard Paul believed and were baptized.

[9]One night the Lord spoke to Paul in a vision: "Do not be afraid; keep on speaking, do not be silent. [10]For I am with you, and no one is going to attack and harm you, because I have many people in this city." [11]So Paul stayed in Corinth for a year and a half, teaching them the word of God.

[12]While Gallio was proconsul of Achaia, the Jews of Corinth made a united attack on Paul and brought him to the place of judgment. [13]"This man," they charged, "is persuading the people to worship God in ways contrary to the law."

[14]Just as Paul was about to speak, Gallio said to them, "If you Jews were making a complaint about some misdemeanor or serious crime, it would be reasonable for me to listen to you. [15]But since it involves questions about words and names and your own law—settle the matter yourselves. I will not be a judge of such things." [16]So he drove them off. [17]Then the crowd there turned on Sosthenes the synagogue leader and beat him in front of the proconsul; and Gallio showed no concern whatever.

[18]Paul stayed on in Corinth for some time. Then he left the brothers and sisters and sailed for Syria, accompanied by Priscilla and Aquila. Before he sailed, he had his hair cut off at Cenchreae because of a vow he had taken. [19]They arrived at Ephesus, where Paul left Priscilla and Aquila. He himself went into the synagogue and reasoned with

the Jews. [20]When they asked him to spend more time with them, he declined. [21]But as he left, he promised, "I will come back if it is God's will." Then he set sail from Ephesus. [22]When he landed at Caesarea, he went up to Jerusalem and greeted the church and then went down to Antioch.

[23]After spending some time in Antioch, Paul set out from there and traveled from place to place throughout the region of Galatia and Phrygia, strengthening all the disciples.

[24]Meanwhile a Jew named Apollos, a native of Alexandria, came to Ephesus. He was a learned man, with a thorough knowledge of the Scriptures. [25]He had been instructed in the way of the Lord, and he spoke with great fervor[a] and taught about Jesus accurately, though he knew only the baptism of John. [26]He began to speak boldly in the synagogue. When Priscilla and Aquila heard him, they invited him to their home and explained to him the way of God more adequately.

[27]When Apollos wanted to go to Achaia, the brothers and sisters encouraged him and wrote to the disciples there to welcome him. When he arrived, he was a great help to those who by grace had believed. [28]For he vigorously refuted his Jewish opponents in public debate, proving from the Scriptures that Jesus was the Messiah.

19 While Apollos was at Corinth, Paul took the road through the interior and arrived at Ephesus. There he found some disciples [2]and asked them, "Did you receive the Holy Spirit when[b] you believed?"

They answered, "No, we have

---

[a] 25 Or with fervor in the Spirit    [b] 2 Or after

not even heard that there is a Holy Spirit."

3 So Paul asked, "Then what baptism did you receive?"

"John's baptism," they replied.

4 Paul said, "John's baptism was a baptism of repentance. He told the people to believe in the one coming after him, that is, in Jesus." 5 On hearing this, they were baptized in the name of the Lord Jesus. 6 When Paul placed his hands on them, the Holy Spirit came on them, and they spoke in tongues[a] and prophesied. 7 There were about twelve men in all.

8 Paul entered the synagogue and spoke boldly there for three months, arguing persuasively about the kingdom of God. 9 But some of them became obstinate; they refused to believe and publicly maligned the Way. So Paul left them. He took the disciples with him and had discussions daily in the lecture hall of Tyrannus. 10 This went on for two years, so that all the Jews and Greeks who lived in the province of Asia heard the word of the Lord.

11 God did extraordinary miracles through Paul, 12 so that even handkerchiefs and aprons that had touched him were taken to the sick, and their illnesses were cured and the evil spirits left them.

13 Some Jews who went around driving out evil spirits tried to invoke the name of the Lord Jesus over those who were demon-possessed. They would say, "In the name of the Jesus whom Paul preaches, I command you to come out." 14 Seven sons of Sceva, a Jewish chief priest, were doing this. 15 One day the evil spirit answered them, "Jesus I know, and Paul I know about, but who are you?" 16 Then the man who had the evil spirit jumped on them and overpowered them all. He gave them such a beating that they ran out of the house naked and bleeding.

17 When this became known to the Jews and Greeks living in Ephesus, they were all seized with fear, and the name of the Lord Jesus was held in high honor. 18 Many of those who believed now came and openly confessed what they had done. 19 A number who had practiced sorcery brought their scrolls together and burned them publicly. When they calculated the value of the scrolls, the total came to fifty thousand drachmas.[b] 20 In this way the word of the Lord spread widely and grew in power.

21 After all this had happened, Paul decided[c] to go to Jerusalem, passing through Macedonia and Achaia. "After I have been there," he said, "I must visit Rome also." 22 He sent two of his helpers, Timothy and Erastus, to Macedonia, while he stayed in the province of Asia a little longer.

23 About that time there arose a great disturbance about the Way. 24 A silversmith named Demetrius, who made silver shrines of Artemis, brought in a lot of business for the craftsmen there. 25 He called them together, along with the workers in related trades, and said: "You know, my friends, that we receive a good income from this business. 26 And you see and hear how this fellow Paul has convinced and led astray large numbers of people here in Ephesus and in practically the whole province of Asia. He says

---

[a] 6 Or *other languages*    [b] 19 A drachma was a silver coin worth about a day's wages.
[c] 21 Or *decided in the Spirit*

that gods made by human hands are no gods at all. ²⁷There is danger not only that our trade will lose its good name, but also that the temple of the great goddess Artemis will be discredited; and the goddess herself, who is worshiped throughout the province of Asia and the world, will be robbed of her divine majesty."

²⁸When they heard this, they were furious and began shouting: "Great is Artemis of the Ephesians!" ²⁹Soon the whole city was in an uproar. The people seized Gaius and Aristarchus, Paul's traveling companions from Macedonia, and all of them rushed into the theater together. ³⁰Paul wanted to appear before the crowd, but the disciples would not let him. ³¹Even some of the officials of the province, friends of Paul, sent him a message begging him not to venture into the theater.

³²The assembly was in confusion: Some were shouting one thing, some another. Most of the people did not even know why they were there. ³³The Jews in the crowd pushed Alexander to the front, and they shouted instructions to him. He motioned for silence in order to make a defense before the people. ³⁴But when they realized he was a Jew, they all shouted in unison for about two hours: "Great is Artemis of the Ephesians!"

³⁵The city clerk quieted the crowd and said: "Fellow Ephesians, doesn't all the world know that the city of Ephesus is the guardian of the temple of the great Artemis and of her image, which fell from heaven? ³⁶Therefore, since these facts are undeniable, you ought to calm down and not do anything rash. ³⁷You have brought these men here, though they have neither robbed temples nor blasphemed our goddess. ³⁸If, then, Demetrius and his fellow craftsmen have a grievance against anybody, the courts are open and there are proconsuls. They can press charges. ³⁹If there is anything further you want to bring up, it must be settled in a legal assembly. ⁴⁰As it is, we are in danger of being charged with rioting because of what happened today. In that case we would not be able to account for this commotion, since there is no reason for it." ⁴¹After he had said this, he dismissed the assembly.

20 When the uproar had ended, Paul sent for the disciples and, after encouraging them, said goodbye and set out for Macedonia. ²He traveled through that area, speaking many words of encouragement to the people, and finally arrived in Greece, ³where he stayed three months. Because some Jews had plotted against him just as he was about to sail for Syria, he decided to go back through Macedonia. ⁴He was accompanied by Sopater son of Pyrrhus from Berea, Aristarchus and Secundus from Thessalonica, Gaius from Derbe, Timothy also, and Tychicus and Trophimus from the province of Asia. ⁵These men went on ahead and waited for us at Troas. ⁶But we sailed from Philippi after the Festival of Unleavened Bread, and five days later joined the others at Troas, where we stayed seven days.

⁷On the first day of the week we came together to break bread. Paul spoke to the people and, because he intended to leave the next day, kept on talking until midnight. ⁸There were many lamps in the upstairs room where we were meeting. ⁹Seated in a window was a young

man named Eutychus, who was sinking into a deep sleep as Paul talked on and on. When he was sound asleep, he fell to the ground from the third story and was picked up dead. ¹⁰Paul went down, threw himself on the young man and put his arms around him. "Don't be alarmed," he said. "He's alive!" ¹¹Then he went upstairs again and broke bread and ate. After talking until daylight, he left. ¹²The people took the young man home alive and were greatly comforted.

¹³We went on ahead to the ship and sailed for Assos, where we were going to take Paul aboard. He had made this arrangement because he was going there on foot. ¹⁴When he met us at Assos, we took him aboard and went on to Mitylene. ¹⁵The next day we set sail from there and arrived off Chios. The day after that we crossed over to Samos, and on the following day arrived at Miletus. ¹⁶Paul had decided to sail past Ephesus to avoid spending time in the province of Asia, for he was in a hurry to reach Jerusalem, if possible, by the day of Pentecost.

¹⁷From Miletus, Paul sent to Ephesus for the elders of the church. ¹⁸When they arrived, he said to them: "You know how I lived the whole time I was with you, from the first day I came into the province of Asia. ¹⁹I served the Lord with great humility and with tears and in the midst of severe testing by the plots of my Jewish opponents. ²⁰You know that I have not hesitated to preach anything that would be helpful to you but have taught you publicly and from house to house. ²¹I have declared to both Jews and Greeks that they must turn to God

in repentance and have faith in our Lord Jesus.

²²"And now, compelled by the Spirit, I am going to Jerusalem, not knowing what will happen to me there. ²³I only know that in every city the Holy Spirit warns me that prison and hardships are facing me. ²⁴However, I consider my life worth nothing to me; my only aim is to finish the race and complete the task the Lord Jesus has given me — the task of testifying to the good news of God's grace.

²⁵"Now I know that none of you among whom I have gone about preaching the kingdom will ever see me again. ²⁶Therefore, I declare to you today that I am innocent of the blood of any of you. ²⁷For I have not hesitated to proclaim to you the whole will of God. ²⁸Keep watch over yourselves and all the flock of which the Holy Spirit has made you overseers. Be shepherds of the church of God,ᵃ which he bought with his own blood.ᵇ ²⁹I know that after I leave, savage wolves will come in among you and will not spare the flock. ³⁰Even from your own number men will arise and distort the truth in order to draw away disciples after them. ³¹So be on your guard! Remember that for three years I never stopped warning each of you night and day with tears.

³²"Now I commit you to God and to the word of his grace, which can build you up and give you an inheritance among all those who are sanctified. ³³I have not coveted anyone's silver or gold or clothing. ³⁴You yourselves know that these hands of mine have supplied my own needs and the needs of my companions. ³⁵In everything I did, I showed you

---

ᵃ 28 Many manuscripts *of the Lord*    ᵇ 28 Or *with the blood of his own Son*.

that by this kind of hard work we must help the weak, remembering the words the Lord Jesus himself said: 'It is more blessed to give than to receive.'"

36When Paul had finished speaking, he knelt down with all of them and prayed. 37They all wept as they embraced him and kissed him. 38What grieved them most was his statement that they would never see his face again. Then they accompanied him to the ship.

21 After we had torn ourselves away from them, we put out to sea and sailed straight to Kos. The next day we went to Rhodes and from there to Patara. 2We found a ship crossing over to Phoenicia, went on board and set sail. 3After sighting Cyprus and passing to the south of it, we sailed on to Syria. We landed at Tyre, where our ship was to unload its cargo. 4We sought out the disciples there and stayed with them seven days. Through the Spirit they urged Paul not to go on to Jerusalem. 5When it was time to leave, we left and continued on our way. All of them, including wives and children, accompanied us out of the city, and there on the beach we knelt to pray. 6After saying goodbye to each other, we went aboard the ship, and they returned home.

7We continued our voyage from Tyre and landed at Ptolemais, where we greeted the brothers and sisters and stayed with them for a day. 8Leaving the next day, we reached Caesarea and stayed at the house of Philip the evangelist, one of the Seven. 9He had four unmarried daughters who prophesied.

10After we had been there a number of days, a prophet named Agabus came down from Judea. 11Coming over to us, he took Paul's belt, tied his own hands and feet with it and said, "The Holy Spirit says, 'In this way the Jewish leaders in Jerusalem will bind the owner of this belt and will hand him over to the Gentiles.'"

12When we heard this, we and the people there pleaded with Paul not to go up to Jerusalem. 13Then Paul answered, "Why are you weeping and breaking my heart? I am ready not only to be bound, but also to die in Jerusalem for the name of the Lord Jesus." 14When he would not be dissuaded, we gave up and said, "The Lord's will be done."

15After this, we started on our way up to Jerusalem. 16Some of the disciples from Caesarea accompanied us and brought us to the home of Mnason, where we were to stay. He was a man from Cyprus and one of the early disciples.

17When we arrived at Jerusalem, the brothers and sisters received us warmly. 18The next day Paul and the rest of us went to see James, and all the elders were present. 19Paul greeted them and reported in detail what God had done among the Gentiles through his ministry.

20When they heard this, they praised God. Then they said to Paul: "You see, brother, how many thousands of Jews have believed, and all of them are zealous for the law. 21They have been informed that you teach all the Jews who live among the Gentiles to turn away from Moses, telling them not to circumcise their children or live according to our customs. 22What shall we do? They will certainly hear that you have come, 23so do what we tell you. There are four men with us who have made a vow. 24Take these men, join in their purification rites and pay their expenses, so that they can have their heads shaved. Then everyone will know there is no truth in these reports about you, but that you yourself are living in obedience to the law. 25 As for the Gentile believers, we have written to them our decision that they should abstain from food sacrificed to idols, from blood, from the meat of strangled animals and from sexual immorality."

26 The next day Paul took the men and purified himself along with them. Then he went to the temple to give notice of the date when the days of purification would end and the offering would be made for each of them.

27 When the seven days were nearly over, some Jews from the province of Asia saw Paul at the temple. They stirred up the whole crowd and seized him, 28 shouting, "Fellow Israelites, help us! This is the man who teaches everyone everywhere against our people and our law and this place. And besides, he has brought Greeks into the temple and defiled this holy place." 29 (They had previously seen Trophimus the Ephesian in the city with Paul and assumed that Paul had brought him into the temple.)

30 The whole city was aroused, and the people came running from all directions. Seizing Paul, they dragged him from the temple, and immediately the gates were shut. 31 While they were trying to kill him, news reached the commander of the Roman troops that the whole city of Jerusalem was in an uproar. 32 He at once took some officers and soldiers and ran down to the crowd. When the rioters saw the commander and his soldiers, they stopped beating Paul.

33 The commander came up and arrested him and ordered him to be bound with two chains. Then he asked who he was and what he had done. 34 Some in the crowd shouted one thing and some another, and since the commander could not get at the truth because of the uproar, he ordered that Paul be taken into the barracks. 35 When Paul reached the steps, the violence of the mob was so great he had to be carried by the soldiers. 36 The crowd that followed kept shouting, "Get rid of him!"

37 As the soldiers were about to take Paul into the barracks, he asked the commander, "May I say something to you?"

"Do you speak Greek?" he replied. 38 "Aren't you the Egyptian who started a revolt and led four thousand terrorists out into the wilderness some time ago?"

39 Paul answered, "I am a Jew, from Tarsus in Cilicia, a citizen of no ordinary city. Please let me speak to the people."

40 After receiving the commander's permission, Paul stood on the steps and motioned to the crowd. When they were all silent, he said to them in Aramaic[a]: 22 1 "Brothers and fathers, listen now to my defense."

2 When they heard him speak to them in Aramaic, they became very quiet.

Then Paul said: 3 "I am a Jew, born in Tarsus of Cilicia, but brought up in this city. I studied under Gamaliel and was thoroughly trained in the law of our ancestors. I was just as zealous for God as any of you are today. 4 I persecuted the followers of this Way to their death, arresting both men and women and throwing

a 40 Or possibly Hebrew; also in 22:2

them into prison, 5as the high priest and all the Council can themselves testify. I even obtained letters from them to their associates in Damascus, and went there to bring these people as prisoners to Jerusalem to be punished.

6"About noon as I came near Damascus, suddenly a bright light from heaven flashed around me. 7I fell to the ground and heard a voice say to me, 'Saul! Saul! Why do you persecute me?'

8" 'Who are you, Lord?' I asked.

" 'I am Jesus of Nazareth, whom you are persecuting,' he replied. 9My companions saw the light, but they did not understand the voice of him who was speaking to me.

10" 'What shall I do, Lord?' I asked.

" 'Get up,' the Lord said, 'and go into Damascus. There you will be told all that you have been assigned to do.' 11My companions led me by the hand into Damascus, because the brilliance of the light had blinded me.

12"A man named Ananias came to see me. He was a devout observer of the law and highly respected by all the Jews living there. 13He stood beside me and said, 'Brother Saul, receive your sight!' And at that very moment I was able to see him.

14"Then he said: 'The God of our ancestors has chosen you to know his will and to see the Righteous One and to hear words from his mouth. 15You will be his witness to all people of what you have seen and heard. 16And now what are you waiting for? Get up, be baptized and wash your sins away, calling on his name.'

17"When I returned to Jerusalem and was praying at the temple, I fell into a trance 18and saw the Lord speaking to me. 'Quick!' he said. 'Leave Jerusalem immediately, because the people here will not accept your testimony about me.'

19" 'Lord,' I replied, 'these people know that I went from one synagogue to another to imprison and beat those who believe in you. 20And when the blood of your martyr$^a$ Stephen was shed, I stood there giving my approval and guarding the clothes of those who were killing him.'

21"Then the Lord said to me, 'Go; I will send you far away to the Gentiles.' "

22The crowd listened to Paul until he said this. Then they raised their voices and shouted, "Rid the earth of him! He's not fit to live!"

23As they were shouting and throwing off their cloaks and flinging dust into the air, 24the commander ordered that Paul be taken into the barracks. He directed that he be flogged and interrogated in order to find out why the people were shouting at him like this. 25As they stretched him out to flog him, Paul said to the centurion standing there, "Is it legal for you to flog a Roman citizen who hasn't even been found guilty?"

26When the centurion heard this, he went to the commander and reported it. "What are you going to do?" he asked. "This man is a Roman citizen."

27The commander went to Paul and asked, "Tell me, are you a Roman citizen?"

"Yes, I am," he answered.

28Then the commander said, "I had to pay a lot of money for my citizenship."

---

$^a$ 20 Or witness

"But I was born a citizen," Paul replied.

²⁹Those who were about to interrogate him withdrew immediately. The commander himself was alarmed when he realized that he had put Paul, a Roman citizen, in chains.

³⁰The commander wanted to find out exactly why Paul was being accused by the Jews. So the next day he released him and ordered the chief priests and all the members of the Sanhedrin to assemble. Then he brought Paul and had him stand before them.

23 Paul looked straight at the Sanhedrin and said, "My brothers, I have fulfilled my duty to God in all good conscience to this day." ²At this the high priest Ananias ordered those standing near Paul to strike him on the mouth. ³Then Paul said to him, "God will strike you, you whitewashed wall! You sit there to judge me according to the law, yet you yourself violate the law by commanding that I be struck!"

⁴Those who were standing near Paul said, "How dare you insult God's high priest!"

⁵Paul replied, "Brothers, I did not realize that he was the high priest; for it is written: 'Do not speak evil about the ruler of your people.'ᵃ"

⁶Then Paul, knowing that some of them were Sadducees and the others Pharisees, called out in the Sanhedrin, "My brothers, I am a Pharisee, descended from Pharisees. I stand on trial because of the hope of the resurrection of the dead." ⁷When he said this, a dispute broke out between the Pharisees and the Sadducees, and the assembly was divided. ⁸(The Sadducees say that there is no resurrection, and that

there are neither angels nor spirits, but the Pharisees believe all these things.)

⁹There was a great uproar, and some of the teachers of the law who were Pharisees stood up and argued vigorously. "We find nothing wrong with this man," they said. "What if a spirit or an angel has spoken to him?" ¹⁰The dispute became so violent that the commander was afraid Paul would be torn to pieces by them. He ordered the troops to go down and take him away from them by force and bring him into the barracks.

¹¹The following night the Lord stood near Paul and said, "Take courage! As you have testified about me in Jerusalem, so you must also testify in Rome."

¹²The next morning some Jews formed a conspiracy and bound themselves with an oath not to eat or drink until they had killed Paul. ¹³More than forty men were involved in this plot. ¹⁴They went to the chief priests and the elders and said, "We have taken a solemn oath not to eat anything until we have killed Paul. ¹⁵Now then, you and the Sanhedrin petition the commander to bring him before you on the pretext of wanting more accurate information about his case. We are ready to kill him before he gets here."

¹⁶But when the son of Paul's sister heard of this plot, he went into the barracks and told Paul.

¹⁷Then Paul called one of the centurions and said, "Take this young man to the commander; he has something to tell him." ¹⁸So he took him to the commander.

The centurion said, "Paul, the prisoner, sent for me and asked

ᵃ 5 Exodus 22:28

me to bring this young man to you because he has something to tell you."

¹⁹The commander took the young man by the hand, drew him aside and asked, "What is it you want to tell me?"

²⁰He said: "Some Jews have agreed to ask you to bring Paul before the Sanhedrin tomorrow on the pretext of wanting more accurate information about him. ²¹Don't give in to them, because more than forty of them are waiting in ambush for him. They have taken an oath not to eat or drink until they have killed him. They are ready now, waiting for your consent to their request."

²²The commander dismissed the young man with this warning: "Don't tell anyone that you have reported this to me."

²³Then he called two of his centurions and ordered them, "Get ready a detachment of two hundred soldiers, seventy horsemen and two hundred spearmen*a* to go to Caesarea at nine tonight. ²⁴Provide horses for Paul so that he may be taken safely to Governor Felix."

²⁵He wrote a letter as follows:

²⁶Claudius Lysias,

To His Excellency, Governor Felix:

Greetings.

²⁷This man was seized by the Jews and they were about to kill him, but I came with my troops and rescued him, for I had learned that he is a Roman citizen. ²⁸I wanted to know why they were accusing him, so I brought him to their Sanhedrin. ²⁹I found that the accu-

sation had to do with questions about their law, but there was no charge against him that deserved death or imprisonment. ³⁰When I was informed of a plot to carry out against the man, I sent him to you at once. I also ordered his accusers to present to you their case against him.

³¹So the soldiers, carrying out their orders, took Paul with them during the night and brought him as far as Antipatris. ³²The next day they let the cavalry go on with him, while they returned to the barracks. ³³When the cavalry arrived in Caesarea, they delivered the letter to the governor and handed Paul over to him. ³⁴The governor read the letter and asked what province he was from. Learning that he was from Cilicia, ³⁵he said, "I will hear your case when your accusers get here." Then he ordered that Paul be kept under guard in Herod's palace.

24 Five days later the high priest Ananias went down to Caesarea with some of the elders and a lawyer named Tertullus, and they brought their charges against Paul before the governor. ²When Paul was called in, Tertullus presented his case before Felix: "We have enjoyed a long period of peace under you, and your foresight has brought about reforms in this nation. ³Everywhere and in every way, most excellent Felix, we acknowledge this with profound gratitude. ⁴But in order not to weary you further, I would request that you be kind enough to hear us briefly.

⁵"We have found this man to be a troublemaker, stirring up riots among the Jews all over the world.

---

*a* 23 The meaning of the Greek for this word is uncertain.

He is a ringleader of the Nazarene sect [6]and even tried to desecrate the temple; so we seized him. [7]a [8]By examining him yourself you will be able to learn the truth about all these charges we are bringing against him."

[9]The other Jews joined in the accusation, asserting that these things were true.

[10]When the governor motioned for him to speak, Paul replied: "I know that for a number of years you have been a judge over this nation; so I gladly make my defense. [11]You can easily verify that no more than twelve days ago I went up to Jerusalem to worship. [12]My accusers did not find me arguing with anyone at the temple, or stirring up a crowd in the synagogues or anywhere else in the city. [13]And they cannot prove to you the charges they are now making against me. [14]However, I admit that I worship the God of our ancestors as a follower of the Way, which they call a sect. I believe everything that is in accordance with the Law and that is written in the Prophets, [15]and I have the same hope in God as these men themselves have, that there will be a resurrection of both the righteous and the wicked. [16]So I strive always to keep my conscience clear before God and man.

[17]"After an absence of several years, I came to Jerusalem to bring my people gifts for the poor and to present offerings. [18]I was ceremonially clean when they found me in the temple courts doing this. There was no crowd with me, nor was I involved in any disturbance. [19]But there are some Jews from the province of Asia, who ought to be here before you and bring charges if they have anything against me. [20]Or these who are here should state what crime they found in me when I stood before the Sanhedrin— [21]unless it was this one thing I shouted as I stood in their presence: 'It is concerning the resurrection of the dead that I am on trial before you today.'"

[22]Then Felix, who was well acquainted with the Way, adjourned the proceedings. "When Lysias the commander comes," he said, "I will decide your case." [23]He ordered the centurion to keep Paul under guard but to give him some freedom and permit his friends to take care of his needs.

[24]Several days later Felix came with his wife Drusilla, who was Jewish. He sent for Paul and listened to him as he spoke about faith in Christ Jesus. [25]As Paul talked about righteousness, self-control and the judgment to come, Felix was afraid and said, "That's enough for now! You may leave. When I find it convenient, I will send for you." [26]At the same time he was hoping that Paul would offer him a bribe, so he sent for him frequently and talked with him.

[27]When two years had passed, Felix was succeeded by Porcius Festus, but because Felix wanted to grant a favor to the Jews, he left Paul in prison.

25 Three days after arriving in the province, Festus went up from Caesarea to Jerusalem, [2]where the chief priests and the Jewish leaders appeared before him and presented the charges against Paul. [3]They requested Festus, as a favor to them,

---

a 6-8 Some manuscripts include here *him, and we would have judged him in accordance with our law.* [7]*But the commander Lysias came and took him from us with much violence,* [8]*ordering his accusers to come before you.*

to have Paul transferred to Jerusalem, for they were preparing an ambush to kill him along the way. 7 Festus answered, "Paul is being held at Caesarea, and I myself am going there soon. 5 Let some of your leaders come with me, and if the man has done anything wrong, they can press charges against him there."

6 After spending eight or ten days with them, Festus went down to Caesarea. The next day he convened the court and ordered that Paul be brought before him. 7 When Paul came in, the Jews who had come down from Jerusalem stood around him. They brought many serious charges against him, but they could not prove them.

8 Then Paul made his defense: "I have done nothing wrong against the Jewish law or against the temple or against Caesar."

9 Festus, wishing to do the Jews a favor, said to Paul, "Are you willing to go up to Jerusalem and stand trial before me there on these charges?"

10 Paul answered: "I am now standing before Caesar's court, where I ought to be tried. I have not done any wrong to the Jews, as you yourself know very well. 11 If, however, I am guilty of doing anything deserving death, I do not refuse to die. But if the charges brought against me by these Jews are not true, no one has the right to hand me over to them. I appeal to Caesar!"

12 After Festus had conferred with his council, he declared: "You have appealed to Caesar. To Caesar you will go!"

13 A few days later King Agrippa and Bernice arrived at Caesarea to pay their respects to Festus. 14 Since they were spending many days there, Festus discussed Paul's case with the king. He said: "There is a man here whom Felix left as a prisoner. 15 When I went to Jerusalem, the chief priests and the elders of the Jews brought charges against him and asked that he be condemned.

16 "I told them that it is not the Roman custom to hand over anyone before they have faced their accusers and have had an opportunity to defend themselves against the charges. 17 When they came here with me, I did not delay the case, but convened the court the next day and ordered the man to be brought in. 18 When his accusers got up to speak, they did not charge him with any of the crimes I had expected. 19 Instead, they had some points of dispute with him about their own religion and about a dead man named Jesus who Paul claimed was alive. 20 I was at a loss how to investigate such matters; so I asked if he would be willing to go to Jerusalem and stand trial there on these charges. 21 But when Paul made his appeal to be held over for the Emperor's decision, I ordered him held until I could send him to Caesar."

22 Then Agrippa said to Festus, "I would like to hear this man myself."

He replied, "Tomorrow you will hear him."

23 The next day Agrippa and Bernice came with great pomp and entered the audience room with the high-ranking military officers and the prominent men of the city. At the command of Festus, Paul was brought in. 24 Festus said: "King Agrippa, and all who are present with us, you see this man! The whole Jewish community has petitioned me about him in Jerusalem and here in Caesarea, shouting that

he ought not to live any longer. 25I found he had done nothing deserving of death, but because he made his appeal to the Emperor I decided to send him to Rome. 26But I have nothing definite to write to His Majesty about him. Therefore I have brought him before all of you, and especially before you, King Agrippa, so that as a result of this investigation I may have something to write. 27For I think it is unreasonable to send a prisoner on to Rome without specifying the charges against him."

26 Then Agrippa said to Paul, "You have permission to speak for yourself."

So Paul motioned with his hand and began his defense: 2"King Agrippa, I consider myself fortunate to stand before you today as I make my defense against all the accusations of the Jews, 3and especially so because you are well acquainted with all the Jewish customs and controversies. Therefore, I beg you to listen to me patiently.

4"The Jewish people all know the way I have lived ever since I was a child, from the beginning of my life in my own country, and also in Jerusalem. 5They have known me for a long time and can testify, if they are willing, that I conformed to the strictest sect of our religion, living as a Pharisee. 6And now it is because of my hope in what God has promised our ancestors that I am on trial today. 7This is the promise our twelve tribes are hoping to see fulfilled as they earnestly serve God day and night. King Agrippa, it is because of this hope that these Jews are accusing me. 8Why should any of you consider it incredible that God raises the dead?

9"I too was convinced that I ought to do all that was possible to oppose the name of Jesus of Nazareth. 10And that is just what I did in Jerusalem. On the authority of the chief priests I put many of the Lord's people in prison, and when they were put to death, I cast my vote against them. 11Many a time I went from one synagogue to another to have them punished, and I tried to force them to blaspheme. I was so obsessed with persecuting them that I even hunted them down in foreign cities.

12"On one of these journeys I was going to Damascus with the authority and commission of the chief priests. 13About noon, King Agrippa, as I was on the road, I saw a light from heaven, brighter than the sun, blazing around me and my companions. 14We all fell to the ground, and I heard a voice saying to me in Aramaic,ᵃ 'Saul, Saul, why do you persecute me? It is hard for you to kick against the goads.'

15"Then I asked, 'Who are you, Lord?'

"'I am Jesus, whom you are persecuting,' the Lord replied. 16'Now get up and stand on your feet. I have appeared to you to appoint you as a servant and as a witness of what you have seen and will see of me. 17I will rescue you from your own people and from the Gentiles. I am sending you to them 18to open their eyes and turn them from darkness to light, and from the power of Satan to God, so that they may receive forgiveness of sins and a place among those who are sanctified by faith in me.'

19"So then, King Agrippa, I was not disobedient to the vision from heaven. 20First to those in Damas-

ᵃ 14 Or Hebrew

cus, then to those in Jerusalem and in all Judea, and then to the Gentiles, I preached that they should repent and turn to God and demonstrate their repentance by their deeds. 21That is why some Jews seized me in the temple courts and tried to kill me. 22But God has helped me to this very day; so I stand here and testify to small and great alike. I am saying nothing beyond what the prophets and Moses said would happen— 23that the Messiah would suffer and, as the first to rise from the dead, would bring the message of light to his own people and to the Gentiles."

24At this point Festus interrupted Paul's defense. "You are out of your mind, Paul!" he shouted. "Your great learning is driving you insane."

25"I am not insane, most excellent Festus," Paul replied. "What I am saying is true and reasonable. 26The king is familiar with these things, and I can speak freely to him. I am convinced that none of this has escaped his notice, because it was not done in a corner. 27King Agrippa, do you believe the prophets? I know you do."

28Then Agrippa said to Paul, "Do you think that in such a short time you can persuade me to be a Christian?"

29Paul replied, "Short time or long—I pray to God that not only you but all who are listening to me today may become what I am, except for these chains."

30The king rose, and with him the governor and Bernice and those sitting with them. 31After they left the room, they began saying to one another, "This man is not doing any-

thing that deserves death or imprisonment."

32Agrippa said to Festus, "This man could have been set free if he had not appealed to Caesar."

27 When it was decided that we would sail for Italy, Paul and some other prisoners were handed over to a centurion named Julius, who belonged to the Imperial Regiment. 2We boarded a ship from Adramyttium about to sail for ports along the coast of the province of Asia, and we put out to sea. Aristarchus, a Macedonian from Thessalonica, was with us.

3The next day we landed at Sidon; and Julius, in kindness to Paul, allowed him to go to his friends so they might provide for his needs. 4From there we put out to sea again and passed to the lee of Cyprus because the winds were against us. 5When we had sailed across the open sea off the coast of Cilicia and Pamphylia, we landed at Myra in Lycia. 6There the centurion found an Alexandrian ship sailing for Italy and put us on board. 7We made slow headway for many days and had difficulty arriving off Cnidus. When the wind did not allow us to hold our course, we sailed to the lee of Crete, opposite Salmone. 8We moved along the coast with difficulty and came to a place called Fair Havens, near the town of Lasea.

9Much time had been lost, and sailing had already become dangerous because by now it was after the Day of Atonement.*a* So Paul warned them, 10"Men, I can see that our voyage is going to be disastrous and bring great loss to ship and cargo, and to our own lives also." 11But the centurion, instead of listening to what Paul said, followed the ad-

---

*a* 9 That is, Yom Kippur

vice of the pilot and of the owner of the ship. [12]Since the harbor was unsuitable to winter in, the majority decided that we should sail on, hoping to reach Phoenix and winter there. This was a harbor in Crete, facing both southwest and northwest.

[13]When a gentle south wind began to blow, they saw their opportunity; so they weighed anchor and sailed along the shore of Crete. [14]Before very long, a wind of hurricane force, called the Northeaster, swept down from the island. [15]The ship was caught by the storm and could not head into the wind; so we gave way to it and were driven along. [16]As we passed to the lee of a small island called Cauda, we were hardly able to make the lifeboat secure, [17]so the men hoisted it aboard. Then they passed ropes under the ship itself to hold it together. Because they were afraid they would run aground on the sandbars of Syrtis, they lowered the sea anchor[a] and let the ship be driven along. [18]We took such a violent battering from the storm that the next day they began to throw the cargo overboard. [19]On the third day, they threw the ship's tackle overboard with their own hands. [20]When neither sun nor stars appeared for many days and the storm continued raging, we finally gave up all hope of being saved.

[21]After they had gone a long time without food, Paul stood up before them and said: "Men, you should have taken my advice not to sail from Crete; then you would have spared yourselves this damage and loss. [22]But now I urge you to keep up your courage, because not one

of you will be lost; only the ship will be destroyed. [23]Last night an angel of the God to whom I belong and whom I serve stood beside me [24]and said, 'Do not be afraid, Paul. You must stand trial before Caesar; and God has graciously given you the lives of all who sail with you.' [25]So keep up your courage, men, for I have faith in God that it will happen just as he told me. [26]Nevertheless, we must run aground on some island."

[27]On the fourteenth night we were still being driven across the Adriatic[b] Sea, when about midnight the sailors sensed they were approaching land. [28]They took soundings and found that the water was a hundred and twenty feet[c] deep. A short time later they took soundings again and found it was ninety feet[d] deep. [29]Fearing that we would be dashed against the rocks, they dropped four anchors from the stern and prayed for daylight. [30]In an attempt to escape from the ship, the sailors let the lifeboat down into the sea, pretending they were going to lower some anchors from the bow. [31]Then Paul said to the centurion and the soldiers, "Unless these men stay with the ship, you cannot be saved." [32]So the soldiers cut the ropes that held the lifeboat and let it drift away.

[33]Just before dawn Paul urged them all to eat. "For the last fourteen days," he said, "you have been in constant suspense and have gone without food—you haven't eaten anything. [34]Now I urge you to take some food. You need it to survive. Not one of you will lose a single hair from his head." [35]After he said this, he took some bread and gave

---

[a] 17 Or *the sails*    [b] 27 In ancient times the name referred to an area extending well south of Italy.    [c] 28 Or about 37 meters    [d] 28 Or about 27 meters

thanks to God in front of them all. Then he broke it and began to eat. ³⁶They were all encouraged and ate some food themselves. ³⁷Altogether there were 276 of us on board. ³⁸When they had eaten as much as they wanted, they lightened the ship by throwing the grain into the sea.

³⁹When daylight came, they did not recognize the land, but they saw a bay with a sandy beach, where they decided to run the ship aground if they could. ⁴⁰Cutting loose the anchors, they left them in the sea and at the same time untied the ropes that held the rudders. Then they hoisted the foresail to the wind and made for the beach. ⁴¹But the ship struck a sandbar and ran aground. The bow stuck fast and would not move, and the stern was broken to pieces by the pounding of the surf.

⁴²The soldiers planned to kill the prisoners to prevent any of them from swimming away and escaping. ⁴³But the centurion wanted to spare Paul's life and kept them from carrying out their plan. He ordered those who could swim to jump overboard first and get to land. ⁴⁴The rest were to get there on planks or on other pieces of the ship. In this way everyone reached land safely.

28 Once safely on shore, we found out that the island was called Malta. ²The islanders showed us unusual kindness. They built a fire and welcomed us all because it was raining and cold. ³Paul gathered a pile of brushwood and, as he put it on the fire, a viper, driven out by the heat, fastened itself on his hand. ⁴When the islanders saw the snake hanging from his hand, they said to each other, "This man must be a murderer; for though he escaped from the sea, the goddess Justice has not allowed him to live." ⁵But Paul shook the snake off into the fire and suffered no ill effects. ⁶The people expected him to swell up or suddenly fall dead; but after waiting a long time and seeing nothing unusual happen to him, they changed their minds and said he was a god.

⁷There was an estate nearby that belonged to Publius, the chief official of the island. He welcomed us to his home and showed us generous hospitality for three days. ⁸His father was sick in bed, suffering from fever and dysentery. Paul went in to see him and, after prayer, placed his hands on him and healed him. ⁹When this had happened, the rest of the sick on the island came and were cured. ¹⁰They honored us in many ways; and when we were ready to sail, they furnished us with the supplies we needed.

¹¹After three months we put out to sea in a ship that had wintered in the island — it was an Alexandrian ship with the figurehead of the twin gods Castor and Pollux. ¹²We put in at Syracuse and stayed there three days. ¹³From there we set sail and arrived at Rhegium. The next day the south wind came up, and on the following day we reached Puteoli. ¹⁴There we found some brothers and sisters who invited us to spend a week with them. And so we came to Rome. ¹⁵The brothers and sisters there had heard that we were coming, and they traveled as far as the Forum of Appius and the Three Taverns to meet us. At the sight of these people Paul thanked God and was encouraged. ¹⁶When we got to Rome, Paul was allowed to live by himself, with a soldier to guard him.

¹⁷Three days later he called to-

gether the local Jewish leaders. When they had assembled, Paul said to them: "My brothers, although I have done nothing against our people or against the customs of our ancestors, I was arrested in Jerusalem and handed over to the Romans. ¹⁸They examined me and wanted to release me, because I was not guilty of any crime deserving death. ¹⁹The Jews objected, so I was compelled to make an appeal to Caesar. I certainly did not intend to bring any charge against my own people. ²⁰For this reason I have asked to see you and talk with you. It is because of the hope of Israel that I am bound with this chain."

²¹They replied, "We have not received any letters from Judea concerning you, and none of our people who have come from there has reported or said anything bad about you. ²²But we want to hear what your views are, for we know that people everywhere are talking against this sect."

²³They arranged to meet Paul on a certain day, and came in even larger numbers to the place where he was staying. He witnessed to them from morning till evening, explaining about the kingdom of God, and from the Law of Moses and from the Prophets he tried to persuade them about Jesus. ²⁴Some

were convinced by what he said, but others would not believe. ²⁵They disagreed among themselves and began to leave after Paul had made this final statement: "The Holy Spirit spoke the truth to your ancestors when he said through Isaiah the prophet:

²⁶ " 'Go to this people and say,
  "You will be ever hearing but
      never understanding;
    you will be ever seeing but
      never perceiving."
²⁷For this people's heart has
      become calloused;
  they hardly hear with their
      ears,
  and they have closed their
      eyes.
Otherwise they might see with
      their eyes,
  hear with their ears,
  understand with their hearts
  and turn, and I would heal
      them.'ᵃ

²⁸"Therefore I want you to know that God's salvation has been sent to the Gentiles, and they will listen!" [29]ᵇ

³⁰For two whole years Paul stayed there in his own rented house and welcomed all who came to see him. ³¹He proclaimed the kingdom of God and taught about the Lord Jesus Christ—with all boldness and without hindrance!

---

ᵃ 27 Isaiah 6:9,10 (see Septuagint)    ᵇ 29 Some manuscripts include here After he said this, the Jews left, arguing vigorously among themselves.

# ROMANS

Addressing the believers in Rome, Paul writes what is most likely the meatiest missionary fundraising letter ever written. To Jesus-followers living directly under the shadow of Caesar, he is appealing for help to bring the gospel to the western part of the empire. As an apostle, Paul has been set apart to make the royal announcement about the Lordship of Jesus. God's plan for the world has been revealed through a descendant of king David—Jesus the Messiah. This message demonstrates that God has been faithful to his covenant with Israel.

The flow of the letter follows the pattern of the ancient Jewish story of slavery and rescue. Humanity is in exile due to the entrance of sin and death into the world. Even the Jewish law could not defeat death and bring life. But God has come to rescue both Jews and Gentiles through the death and resurrection of Jesus. A new worldwide family is being created. Baptism into Jesus breaks the power of evil and brings freedom. The Holy Spirit leads the way into this new life that will be complete in a new inheritance—a redeemed creation.

Although many in Israel had failed to believe in the Messiah, this ended up bringing life to the rest of the world. The offer of life through Jesus remains for all, however, and in the end God's mercy will triumph over judgment. The closing emphasis is on the practical shape of a redeemed humanity's new way of life.

1 Paul, a servant of Christ Jesus, called to be an apostle and set apart for the gospel of God — [2]the gospel he promised beforehand through his prophets in the Holy Scriptures [3]regarding his Son, who as to his earthly life[a] was a descendant of David, [4]and who through the Spirit of holiness was appointed the Son of God in power[b] by his resurrection from the dead: Jesus Christ our Lord. [5]Through him we received grace and apostleship to call all the Gentiles to the obedience that comes from[c] faith for his name's sake. [6]And you also are among those Gentiles who are called to belong to Jesus Christ.

[7]To all in Rome who are loved by God and called to be his holy people:

Grace and peace to you from God our Father and from the Lord Jesus Christ.

[8]First, I thank my God through Jesus Christ for all of you, because your faith is being reported all over the world. [9]God, whom I serve in my spirit in preaching the gospel of his Son, is my witness how constantly I remember you [10]in my prayers at all times; and I pray that now at last by God's will the way may be opened for me to come to you.

[11]I long to see you so that I may impart to you some spiritual gift to make you strong— [12]that is, that you and I may be mutually encour-

[a] 3 Or who according to the flesh    [b] 4 Or was declared with power to be the Son of God
[c] 5 Or that is

aged by each other's faith. [13] I do not want you to be unaware, brothers and sisters,[a] that I planned many times to come to you (but have been prevented from doing so until now) in order that I might have a harvest among you, just as I have had among the other Gentiles.

[14] I am obligated both to Greeks and non-Greeks, both to the wise and the foolish. [15] That is why I am so eager to preach the gospel also to you who are in Rome.

[16] For I am not ashamed of the gospel, because it is the power of God that brings salvation to everyone who believes: first to the Jew, then to the Gentile. [17] For in the gospel the righteousness of God is revealed—a righteousness that is by faith from first to last,[b] just as it is written: "The righteous will live by faith."[c]

[18] The wrath of God is being revealed from heaven against all the godlessness and wickedness of people, who suppress the truth by their wickedness, [19] since what may be known about God is plain to them, because God has made it plain to them. [20] For since the creation of the world God's invisible qualities—his eternal power and divine nature—have been clearly seen, being understood from what has been made, so that people are without excuse.

[21] For although they knew God, they neither glorified him as God nor gave thanks to him, but their thinking became futile and their foolish hearts were darkened. [22] Although they claimed to be wise, they became fools [23] and exchanged the glory of the immortal God for images made to look like a mortal human being and birds and animals and reptiles.

[24] Therefore God gave them over in the sinful desires of their hearts to sexual impurity for the degrading of their bodies with one another. [25] They exchanged the truth about God for a lie, and worshiped and served created things rather than the Creator—who is forever praised. Amen.

[26] Because of this, God gave them over to shameful lusts. Even their women exchanged natural sexual relations for unnatural ones. [27] In the same way the men also abandoned natural relations with women and were inflamed with lust for one another. Men committed shameful acts with other men, and received in themselves the due penalty for their error.

[28] Furthermore, just as they did not think it worthwhile to retain the knowledge of God, so God gave them over to a depraved mind, so that they do what ought not to be done. [29] They have become filled with every kind of wickedness, evil, greed and depravity. They are full of envy, murder, strife, deceit and malice. They are gossips, [30] slanderers, God-haters, insolent, arrogant and boastful; they invent ways of doing evil; they disobey their parents; [31] they have no understanding, no fidelity, no love, no mercy. [32] Although they know God's righteous decree that those who do such things deserve death, they not only continue to do these very things but also approve of those who practice them.

---

*a 13* The Greek word for *brothers and sisters* (*adelphoi*) refers here to believers, both men and women, as part of God's family; also in 7:1, 4; 8:12, 29; 10:1; 11:25; 12:1; 15:14, 30; 16:14, 17.
*b 17* Or *is from faith to faith*   *c 17* Hab. 2:4

2 You, therefore, have no excuse, you who pass judgment on someone else, for at whatever point you judge another, you are condemning yourself, because you who pass judgment do the same things. ²Now we know that God's judgment against those who do such things is based on truth. ³So when you, a mere human being, pass judgment on them and yet do the same things, do you think you will escape God's judgment? ⁴Or do you show contempt for the riches of his kindness, forbearance and patience, not realizing that God's kindness is intended to lead you to repentance?

⁵But because of your stubbornness and your unrepentant heart, you are storing up wrath against yourself for the day of God's wrath, when his righteous judgment will be revealed. ⁶God "will repay each person according to what they have done."[a] ⁷To those who by persistence in doing good seek glory, honor and immortality, he will give eternal life. ⁸But for those who are self-seeking and who reject the truth and follow evil, there will be wrath and anger. ⁹There will be trouble and distress for every human being who does evil: first for the Jew, then for the Gentile; ¹⁰but glory, honor and peace for everyone who does good: first for the Jew, then for the Gentile. ¹¹For God does not show favoritism.

¹²All who sin apart from the law will also perish apart from the law, and all who sin under the law will be judged by the law. ¹³For it is not those who hear the law who are righteous in God's sight, but it is those who obey the law who will be declared righteous. ¹⁴(In-deed, when Gentiles, who do not have the law, do by nature things required by the law, they are a law for themselves, even though they do not have the law. ¹⁵They show that the requirements of the law are written on their hearts, their consciences also bearing witness, and their thoughts sometimes accusing them and at other times even defending them.) ¹⁶This will take place on the day when God judges people's secrets through Jesus Christ, as my gospel declares.

¹⁷Now you, if you call yourself a Jew; if you rely on the law and boast in God; ¹⁸if you know his will and approve of what is superior because you are instructed by the law; ¹⁹if you are convinced that you are a guide for the blind, a light for those who are in the dark, ²⁰an instructor of the foolish, a teacher of little children, because you have in the law the embodiment of knowledge and truth — ²¹you, then, who teach others, do you not teach yourself? You who preach against stealing, do you steal? ²²You who say that people should not commit adultery, do you commit adultery? You who abhor idols, do you rob temples? ²³You who boast in the law, do you dishonor God by breaking the law? ²⁴As it is written: "God's name is blasphemed among the Gentiles because of you."[b]

²⁵Circumcision has value if you observe the law, but if you break the law, you have become as though you had not been circumcised. ²⁶So then, if those who are not circumcised keep the law's requirements, will they not be regarded as though they were circumcised? ²⁷The one who is not circumcised physically and yet obeys the law will condemn

---

[a] 6 Psalm 62:12; Prov. 24:12    [b] 24 Isaiah 52:5 (see Septuagint); Ezek. 36:20,22

you who, even though you have the[a] written code and circumcision, are a lawbreaker.

28 A person is not a Jew who is one only outwardly, nor is circumcision merely outward and physical. 29 No, a person is a Jew who is one inwardly; and circumcision is circumcision of the heart, by the Spirit, not by the written code. Such a person's praise is not from other people, but from God.

3 What advantage, then, is there in being a Jew, or what value is there in circumcision? 2 Much in every way! First of all, the Jews have been entrusted with the very words of God.

3 What if some were unfaithful? Will their unfaithfulness nullify God's faithfulness? 4 Not at all! Let God be true, and every human being a liar. As it is written:

"So that you may be proved right
    when you speak
and prevail when you judge."[b]

5 But if our unrighteousness brings out God's righteousness more clearly, what shall we say? That God is unjust in bringing his wrath on us? (I am using a human argument.) 6 Certainly not! If that were so, how could God judge the world? 7 Someone might argue, "If my falsehood enhances God's truthfulness and so increases his glory, why am I still condemned as a sinner?" 8 Why not say — as some slanderously claim that we say — "Let us do evil that good may result"? Their condemnation is just!

9 What shall we conclude then? Do we have any advantage? Not at all! For we have already made the

charge that Jews and Gentiles alike are all under the power of sin. 10 As it is written:

"There is no one righteous, not
    even one;
11    there is no one who
        understands;
    there is no one who seeks God.
12 All have turned away,
    they have together become
        worthless;
there is no one who does good,
    not even one."[c]

13 "Their throats are open graves;
    their tongues practice
        deceit."[d]

"The poison of vipers is on their
    lips."[e]

14    "Their mouths are full of
        cursing and bitterness."[f]

15 "Their feet are swift to shed
        blood;
16    ruin and misery mark their
        ways,
17 and the way of peace they do not
        know."[g]

18    "There is no fear of God before
        their eyes."[h]

19 Now we know that whatever the law says, it says to those who are under the law, so that every mouth may be silenced and the whole world held accountable to God. 20 Therefore no one will be declared righteous in God's sight by the works of the law; rather, through the law we become conscious of our sin.

21 But now apart from the law the righteousness of God has been made known, to which the Law and the Prophets testify. 22 This righteousness is given through faith in[i] Jesus Christ to all who believe.

---

a 27 Or who, by means of a    b 4 Psalm 51:4    c 12 Psalms 14:1-3; 53:1-3; Eccles. 7:20
d 13 Psalm 5:9    e 13 Psalm 140:3    f 14 Psalm 10:7 (see Septuagint)    g 17 Isaiah 59:7,8
h 18 Psalm 36:1    i 22 Or through the faithfulness of

There is no difference between Jew and Gentile, 23for all have sinned and fall short of the glory of God, 24and all are justified freely by his grace through the redemption that came by Christ Jesus. 25God presented Christ as a sacrifice of atonement,*a* through the shedding of his blood — to be received by faith. He did this to demonstrate his righteousness, because in his forbearance he had left the sins committed beforehand unpunished — 26he did it to demonstrate his righteousness at the present time, so as to be just and the one who justifies those who have faith in Jesus.

27Where, then, is boasting? It is excluded. Because of what law? The law that requires works? No, because of the law that requires faith. 28For we maintain that a person is justified by faith apart from the works of the law. 29Or is God the God of Jews only? Is he not the God of Gentiles too? Yes, of Gentiles too, 30since there is only one God, who will justify the circumcised by faith and the uncircumcised through that same faith. 31Do we, then, nullify the law by this faith? Not at all! Rather, we uphold the law.

4 What then shall we say that Abraham, our forefather according to the flesh, discovered in this matter? 2If, in fact, Abraham was justified by works, he had something to boast about — but not before God. 3What does Scripture say? "Abraham believed God, and it was credited to him as righteousness."*b*

4Now to the one who works, wages are not credited as a gift but as an obligation. 5However, to the one who does not work but trusts God who justifies the ungodly, their faith is credited as righteousness. 6David says the same thing when he speaks of the blessedness of the one to whom God credits righteousness apart from works:

7 "Blessed are those
        whose transgressions are
            forgiven,
        whose sins are covered.
8 Blessed is the one
        whose sin the Lord will never
            count against them."*c*

9Is this blessedness only for the circumcised, or also for the uncircumcised? We have been saying that Abraham's faith was credited to him as righteousness. 10Under what circumstances was it credited? Was it after he was circumcised, or before? It was not after, but before! 11And he received circumcision as a sign, a seal of the righteousness that he had by faith while he was still uncircumcised. So then, he is the father of all who believe but have not been circumcised, in order that righteousness might be credited to them. 12And he is then also the father of the circumcised who not only are circumcised but who also follow in the footsteps of the faith that our father Abraham had before he was circumcised.

13It was not through the law that Abraham and his offspring received the promise that he would be heir of the world, but through the righteousness that comes by faith. 14For if those who depend on the law are heirs, faith means nothing and the promise is worthless, 15because the law brings wrath.

---

*a 25* The Greek for *sacrifice of atonement* refers to the atonement cover on the ark of the covenant (see Lev. 16:15,16).      *b 3* Gen. 15:6; also in verse 22      *c 8* Psalm 32:1,2

And where there is no law there is no transgression.

¹⁶Therefore, the promise comes by faith, so that it may be by grace and may be guaranteed to all Abraham's offspring—not only to those who are of the law but also to those who have the faith of Abraham. He is the father of us all. ¹⁷As it is written: "I have made you a father of many nations."ᵃ He is our father in the sight of God, in whom he believed—the God who gives life to the dead and calls into being things that were not.

¹⁸Against all hope, Abraham in hope believed and so became the father of many nations, just as it had been said to him, "So shall your offspring be."ᵇ ¹⁹Without weakening in his faith, he faced the fact that his body was as good as dead—since he was about a hundred years old—and that Sarah's womb was also dead. ²⁰Yet he did not waver through unbelief regarding the promise of God, but was strengthened in his faith and gave glory to God, ²¹being fully persuaded that God had power to do what he had promised. ²²This is why "it was credited to him as righteousness." ²³The words "it was credited to him" were written not for him alone, ²⁴but also for us, to whom God will credit righteousness—for us who believe in him who raised Jesus our Lord from the dead. ²⁵He was delivered over to death for our sins and was raised to life for our justification.

5 Therefore, since we have been justified through faith, weᶜ have peace with God through our Lord Jesus Christ, ²through whom we have gained access by faith into this grace in which we now stand. And weᵈ boast in the hope of the glory of God. ³Not only so, but weᵈ also glory in our sufferings, because we know that suffering produces perseverance; ⁴perseverance, character; and character, hope. ⁵And hope does not put us to shame, because God's love has been poured out into our hearts through the Holy Spirit, who has been given to us.

⁶You see, at just the right time, when we were still powerless, Christ died for the ungodly. ⁷Very rarely will anyone die for a righteous person, though for a good person someone might possibly dare to die. ⁸But God demonstrates his own love for us in this: While we were still sinners, Christ died for us.

⁹Since we have now been justified by his blood, how much more shall we be saved from God's wrath through him! ¹⁰For if, while we were God's enemies, we were reconciled to him through the death of his Son, how much more, having been reconciled, shall we be saved through his life! ¹¹Not only is this so, but we also boast in God through our Lord Jesus Christ, through whom we have now received reconciliation.

¹²Therefore, just as sin entered the world through one man, and death through sin, and in this way death came to all people, because all sinned—

¹³To be sure, sin was in the world before the law was given, but sin is not charged against anyone's account where there is no law. ¹⁴Nevertheless, death reigned from the time of Adam to the time of Moses, even over those who did not sin by breaking a command, as did Adam, who is a pattern of the one to come.

ᵃ 17 Gen. 17:5   ᵇ 18 Gen. 15:5   ᶜ 1 Many manuscripts let us   ᵈ 2,3 Or let us

15 But the gift is not like the trespass. For if the many died by the trespass of the one man, how much more did God's grace and the gift that came by the grace of the one man, Jesus Christ, overflow to the many! 16 Nor can the gift of God be compared with the result of one man's sin: The judgment followed one sin and brought condemnation, but the gift followed many trespasses and brought justification. 17 For if, by the trespass of the one man, death reigned through that one man, how much more will those who receive God's abundant provision of grace and of the gift of righteousness reign in life through the one man, Jesus Christ!

18 Consequently, just as one trespass resulted in condemnation for all people, so also one righteous act resulted in justification and life for all people. 19 For just as through the disobedience of the one man the many were made sinners, so also through the obedience of the one man the many will be made righteous.

20 The law was brought in so that the trespass might increase. But where sin increased, grace increased all the more, 21 so that, just as sin reigned in death, so also grace might reign through righteousness to bring eternal life through Jesus Christ our Lord.

6 What shall we say, then? Shall we go on sinning so that grace may increase? 2 By no means! We are those who have died to sin; how can we live in it any longer? 3 Or don't you know that all of us who were baptized into Christ Jesus were baptized into his death? 4 We were therefore buried with him through baptism into death in order that, just as Christ was raised from the dead through the glory of the Father, we too may live a new life.

5 For if we have been united with him in a death like his, we will certainly also be united with him in a resurrection like his. 6 For we know that our old self was crucified with him so that the body ruled by sin might be done away with,[a] that we should no longer be slaves to sin — 7 because anyone who has died has been set free from sin.

8 Now if we died with Christ, we believe that we will also live with him. 9 For we know that since Christ was raised from the dead, he cannot die again; death no longer has mastery over him. 10 The death he died, he died to sin once for all; but the life he lives, he lives to God.

11 In the same way, count yourselves dead to sin but alive to God in Christ Jesus. 12 Therefore do not let sin reign in your mortal body so that you obey its evil desires. 13 Do not offer any part of yourself to sin as an instrument of wickedness, but rather offer yourselves to God as those who have been brought from death to life; and offer every part of yourself to him as an instrument of righteousness. 14 For sin shall no longer be your master, because you are not under the law, but under grace.

15 What then? Shall we sin because we are not under the law but under grace? By no means! 16 Don't you know that when you offer yourselves to someone as obedient slaves, you are slaves of the one you obey — whether you are slaves to sin, which leads to death, or to obedience, which leads to righteousness? 17 But thanks be to God that,

_a 6  Or_ be rendered powerless

though you used to be slaves to sin, you have come to obey from your heart the pattern of teaching that has now claimed your allegiance. [18]You have been set free from sin and have become slaves to righteousness.

[19]I am using an example from everyday life because of your human limitations. Just as you used to offer yourselves as slaves to impurity and to ever-increasing wickedness, so now offer yourselves as slaves to righteousness leading to holiness. [20]When you were slaves to sin, you were free from the control of righteousness. [21]What benefit did you reap at that time from the things you are now ashamed of? Those things result in death! [22]But now that you have been set free from sin and have become slaves of God, the benefit you reap leads to holiness, and the result is eternal life. [23]For the wages of sin is death, but the gift of God is eternal life in[a] Christ Jesus our Lord.

7 Do you not know, brothers and sisters—for I am speaking to those who know the law—that the law has authority over someone only as long as that person lives? [2]For example, by law a married woman is bound to her husband as long as he is alive, but if her husband dies, she is released from the law that binds her to him. [3]So then, if she has sexual relations with another man while her husband is still alive, she is called an adulteress. But if her husband dies, she is released from that law and is not an adulteress if she marries another man.

[4]So, my brothers and sisters, you also died to the law through the body of Christ, that you might belong to another, to him who was raised from the dead, in order that we might bear fruit for God. [5]For when we were in the realm of the flesh,[b] the sinful passions aroused by the law were at work in us, so that we bore fruit for death. [6]But now, by dying to what once bound us, we have been released from the law so that we serve in the new way of the Spirit, and not in the old way of the written code.

[7]What shall we say, then? Is the law sinful? Certainly not! Nevertheless, I would not have known what sin was had it not been for the law. For I would not have known what coveting really was if the law had not said, "You shall not covet."[c] [8]But sin, seizing the opportunity afforded by the commandment, produced in me every kind of coveting. For apart from the law, sin was dead. [9]Once I was alive apart from the law; but when the commandment came, sin sprang to life and I died. [10]I found that the very commandment that was intended to bring life actually brought death. [11]For sin, seizing the opportunity afforded by the commandment, deceived me, and through the commandment put me to death. [12]So then, the law is holy, and the commandment is holy, righteous and good.

[13]Did that which is good, then, become death to me? By no means! Nevertheless, in order that sin might be recognized as sin, it used what is good to bring about my death, so that through the com-

---

[a] 23 Or *through*   [b] 5 In contexts like this, the Greek word for *flesh (sarx)* refers to the sinful state of human beings, often presented as a power in opposition to the Spirit.
[c] 7 Exodus 20:17; Deut. 5:21

mandment sin might become utterly sinful.

¹⁴We know that the law is spiritual; but I am unspiritual, sold as a slave to sin. ¹⁵I do not understand what I do. For what I want to do I do not do, but what I hate I do. ¹⁶And if I do what I do not want to do, I agree that the law is good. ¹⁷As it is, it is no longer I myself who do it, but it is sin living in me. ¹⁸For I know that good itself does not dwell in me, that is, in my sinful nature.*a* For I have the desire to do what is good, but I cannot carry it out. ¹⁹For I do not do the good I want to do, but the evil I do not want to do—this I keep on doing. ²⁰Now if I do what I do not want to do, it is no longer I who do it, but it is sin living in me that does it.

²¹So I find this law at work: Although I want to do good, evil is right there with me. ²²For in my inner being I delight in God's law; ²³but I see another law at work in me, waging war against the law of my mind and making me a prisoner of the law of sin at work within me. ²⁴What a wretched man I am! Who will rescue me from this body that is subject to death? ²⁵Thanks be to God, who delivers me through Jesus Christ our Lord!

So then, I myself in my mind am a slave to God's law, but in my sinful nature*b* a slave to the law of sin.

**8** Therefore, there is now no condemnation for those who are in Christ Jesus, ²because through Christ Jesus the law of the Spirit who gives life has set you*c* free from the law of sin and death. ³For

what the law was powerless to do because it was weakened by the flesh,*d* God did by sending his own Son in the likeness of sinful flesh to be a sin offering.*e* And so he condemned sin in the flesh, ⁴in order that the righteous requirement of the law might be fully met in us, who do not live according to the flesh but according to the Spirit.

⁵Those who live according to the flesh have their minds set on what the flesh desires; but those who live in accordance with the Spirit have their minds set on what the Spirit desires. ⁶The mind governed by the flesh is death, but the mind governed by the Spirit is life and peace. ⁷The mind governed by the flesh is hostile to God; it does not submit to God's law, nor can it do so. ⁸Those who are in the realm of the flesh cannot please God.

⁹You, however, are not in the realm of the flesh but are in the realm of the Spirit, if indeed the Spirit of God lives in you. And if anyone does not have the Spirit of Christ, they do not belong to Christ. ¹⁰But if Christ is in you, then even though your body is subject to death because of sin, the Spirit gives life*f* because of righteousness. ¹¹And if the Spirit of him who raised Jesus from the dead is living in you, he who raised Christ from the dead will also give life to your mortal bodies because of*g* his Spirit who lives in you.

¹²Therefore, brothers and sisters, we have an obligation—but it is not to the flesh, to live according to it. ¹³For if you live according to the

*a 18* Or *my flesh*    *b 25* Or *in the flesh*    *c 2* The Greek is singular; some manuscripts *me*
*d 3* In contexts like this, the Greek word for *flesh* (*sarx*) refers to the sinful state of human beings, often presented as a power in opposition to the Spirit; also in verses 4-13.    *e 3* Or *flesh, for sin*
*f 10* Or *you, your body is dead because of sin, yet your spirit is alive*    *g 11* Some manuscripts *bodies through*

flesh, you will die; but if by the Spirit you put to death the misdeeds of the body, you will live.

¹⁴For those who are led by the Spirit of God are the children of God. ¹⁵The Spirit you received does not make you slaves, so that you live in fear again; rather, the Spirit you received brought about your adoption to sonship.*ᵃ* And by him we cry, "*Abba,ᵇ* Father." ¹⁶The Spirit himself testifies with our spirit that we are God's children. ¹⁷Now if we are children, then we are heirs—heirs of God and co-heirs with Christ, if indeed we share in his sufferings in order that we may also share in his glory.

¹⁸I consider that our present sufferings are not worth comparing with the glory that will be revealed in us. ¹⁹For the creation waits in eager expectation for the children of God to be revealed. ²⁰For the creation was subjected to frustration, not by its own choice, but by the will of the one who subjected it, in hope ²¹thatᶜ the creation itself will be liberated from its bondage to decay and brought into the freedom and glory of the children of God.

²²We know that the whole creation has been groaning as in the pains of childbirth right up to the present time. ²³Not only so, but we ourselves, who have the firstfruits of the Spirit, groan inwardly as we wait eagerly for our adoption to sonship, the redemption of our bodies. ²⁴For in this hope we were saved. But hope that is seen is no hope at all. Who hopes for what

they already have? ²⁵But if we hope for what we do not yet have, we wait for it patiently.

²⁶In the same way, the Spirit helps us in our weakness. We do not know what we ought to pray for, but the Spirit himself intercedes for us through wordless groans. ²⁷And he who searches our hearts knows the mind of the Spirit, because the Spirit intercedes for God's people in accordance with the will of God.

²⁸And we know that in all things God works for the good of those who love him, whoᵈ have been called according to his purpose. ²⁹For those God foreknew he also predestined to be conformed to the image of his Son, that he might be the firstborn among many brothers and sisters. ³⁰And those he predestined, he also called; those he called, he also justified; those he justified, he also glorified.

³¹What, then, shall we say in response to these things? If God is for us, who can be against us? ³²He who did not spare his own Son, but gave him up for us all—how will he not also, along with him, graciously give us all things? ³³Who will bring any charge against those whom God has chosen? It is God who justifies. ³⁴Who then is the one who condemns? No one. Christ Jesus who died—more than that, who was raised to life—is at the right hand of God and is also interceding for us. ³⁵Who shall separate us from the love of Christ? Shall trouble or hardship or persecution or famine or nakedness or danger or sword? ³⁶As it is written:

---

*ᵃ 15* The Greek word for *adoption to sonship* is a term referring to the full legal standing of an adopted male heir in Roman culture; also in verse 23.    *ᵇ 15* Aramaic for *father*    *ᶜ 20,21* Or *subjected it in hope. ²¹For*    *ᵈ 28* Or *that all things work together for good to those who love God, who; or that in all things God works together with those who love him to bring about what is good—with those who*

"For your sake we face death all
day long;
we are considered as sheep to
be slaughtered."[a]

37No, in all these things we are
more than conquerors through
him who loved us. 38For I am convinced that neither death nor life,
neither angels nor demons,[b] neither the present nor the future,
nor any powers, 39neither height
nor depth, nor anything else in all
creation, will be able to separate
us from the love of God that is in
Christ Jesus our Lord.

9 I speak the truth in Christ—I am
not lying, my conscience confirms it through the Holy Spirit—
2I have great sorrow and unceasing
anguish in my heart. 3For I could
wish that I myself were cursed and
cut off from Christ for the sake of
my people, those of my own race,
4the people of Israel. Theirs is the
adoption to sonship; theirs the divine glory, the covenants, the receiving of the law, the temple worship and the promises. 5Theirs are
the patriarchs, and from them is
traced the human ancestry of the
Messiah, who is God over all, forever praised![c] Amen.

6It is not as though God's word
had failed. For not all who are descended from Israel are Israel. 7Nor
because they are his descendants
are they all Abraham's children.
On the contrary, "It is through Isaac
that your offspring will be reckoned."[d] 8In other words, it is not
the children by physical descent
who are God's children, but it is the
children of the promise who are

regarded as Abraham's offspring.
9For this was how the promise was
stated: "At the appointed time I
will return, and Sarah will have a
son."[e]

10Not only that, but Rebekah's
children were conceived at the
same time by our father Isaac. 11Yet,
before the twins were born or had
done anything good or bad—in order that God's purpose in election
might stand: 12not by works but
by him who calls—she was told,
"The older will serve the younger."[f]
13Just as it is written: "Jacob I loved,
but Esau I hated."[g]

14What then shall we say? Is God
unjust? Not at all! 15For he says to
Moses,

"I will have mercy on whom I
have mercy,
and I will have compassion
on whom I have
compassion."[h]

16It does not, therefore, depend
on human desire or effort, but on
God's mercy. 17For Scripture says
to Pharaoh: "I raised you up for this
very purpose, that I might display
my power in you and that my name
might be proclaimed in all the
earth."[i] 18Therefore God has mercy
on whom he wants to have mercy,
and he hardens whom he wants to
harden.

19One of you will say to me:
"Then why does God still blame
us? For who is able to resist his
will?" 20But who are you, a human
being, to talk back to God? "Shall
what is formed say to the one who
formed it, 'Why did you make me
like this?'"[j] 21Does not the potter

a 36 Psalm 44:22    b 38 Or nor heavenly rulers
praised! Or Messiah. God who is over all be forever praised!    c 5 Or Messiah, who is over all. God be forever praised! Or Messiah. God who is over all be forever praised!    d 7 Gen. 21:12    e 9 Gen. 18:10,14
f 12 Gen. 25:23    g 13 Mal. 1:2,3    h 15 Exodus 33:19    i 17 Exodus 9:16    j 20 Isaiah 29:16;
45:9

have the right to make out of the same lump of clay some pottery for special purposes and some for common use?

²²What if God, although choosing to show his wrath and make his power known, bore with great patience the objects of his wrath—prepared for destruction? ²³What if he did this to make the riches of his glory known to the objects of his mercy, whom he prepared in advance for glory— ²⁴even us, whom he also called, not only from the Jews but also from the Gentiles? ²⁵As he says in Hosea:

"I will call them 'my people' who
    are not my people;
and I will call her 'my loved
    one' who is not my loved
    one,"[a]

²⁶and,

"In the very place where it was
    said to them,
    'You are not my people,'
there they will be called
    'children of the living
    God.'"[b]

²⁷Isaiah cries out concerning Israel:

"Though the number of the
    Israelites be like the sand
    by the sea,
only the remnant will be
    saved.

²⁸For the Lord will carry out
his sentence on earth with
    speed and finality."[c]

²⁹It is just as Isaiah said previously:

"Unless the Lord Almighty
    had left us descendants,

we would have become like
    Sodom,
we would have been like
    Gomorrah."[d]

³⁰What then shall we say? That the Gentiles, who did not pursue righteousness, have obtained it, a righteousness that is by faith; ³¹but the people of Israel, who pursued the law as the way of righteousness, have not attained their goal. ³²Why not? Because they pursued it not by faith but as if it were by works. They stumbled over the stumbling stone. ³³As it is written:

"See, I lay in Zion a stone that
    causes people to stumble
    and a rock that makes them
    fall,
and the one who believes in
    him will never be put to
    shame."[e]

**10** Brothers and sisters, my heart's desire and prayer to God for the Israelites is that they may be saved. ²For I can testify about them that they are zealous for God, but their zeal is not based on knowledge. ³Since they did not know the righteousness of God and sought to establish their own, they did not submit to God's righteousness. ⁴Christ is the culmination of the law so that there may be righteousness for everyone who believes.

⁵Moses writes this about the righteousness that is by the law: "The person who does these things will live by them."[f] ⁶But the righteousness that is by faith says: "Do not say in your heart, 'Who will ascend into heaven?'"[g] (that is, to bring Christ down) ⁷"or 'Who will descend into the deep?'"[h]

---

[a] 25 Hosea 2:23    [b] 26 Hosea 1:10    [c] 28 Isaiah 10:22,23 (see Septuagint)    [d] 29 Isaiah 1:9
[e] 33 Isaiah 8:14; 28:16    [f] 5 Lev. 18:5    [g] 6 Deut. 30:12    [h] 7 Deut. 30:13

(that is, to bring Christ up from the dead). ⁸But what does it say? "The word is near you; it is in your mouth and in your heart,"ᵃ that is, the message concerning faith that we proclaim: ⁹If you declare with your mouth, "Jesus is Lord," and believe in your heart that God raised him from the dead, you will be saved. ¹⁰For it is with your heart that you believe and are justified, and it is with your mouth that you profess your faith and are saved. ¹¹As Scripture says, "Anyone who believes in him will never be put to shame."ᵇ ¹²For there is no difference between Jew and Gentile—the same Lord is Lord of all and richly blesses all who call on him, ¹³for, "Everyone who calls on the name of the Lord will be saved."ᶜ

¹⁴How, then, can they call on the one they have not believed in? And how can they believe in the one of whom they have not heard? And how can they hear without someone preaching to them? ¹⁵And how can anyone preach unless they are sent? As it is written: "How beautiful are the feet of those who bring good news!"ᵈ

¹⁶But not all the Israelites accepted the good news. For Isaiah says, "Lord, who has believed our message?"ᵉ ¹⁷Consequently, faith comes from hearing the message, and the message is heard through the word about Christ. ¹⁸But I ask: Did they not hear? Of course they did:

"Their voice has gone out into all the earth,
    their words to the ends of the world."ᶠ

¹⁹Again I ask: Did Israel not understand? First, Moses says,

"I will make you envious by
    those who are not a
    nation;
I will make you angry by
    a nation that has no
    understanding."ᵍ

²⁰And Isaiah boldly says,

"I was found by those who did
    not seek me;
I revealed myself to those who
    did not ask for me."ʰ

²¹But concerning Israel he says,

"All day long I have held out my
    hands
to a disobedient and obstinate
    people."ⁱ

**11** I ask then: Did God reject his people? By no means! I am an Israelite myself, a descendant of Abraham, from the tribe of Benjamin. ²God did not reject his people, whom he foreknew. Don't you know what Scripture says in the passage about Elijah— how he appealed to God against Israel: ³"Lord, they have killed your prophets and torn down your altars; I am the only one left, and they are trying to kill me"ʲ? ⁴And what was God's answer to him? "I have reserved for myself seven thousand who have not bowed the knee to Baal."ᵏ ⁵So too, at the present time there is a remnant chosen by grace. ⁶And if by grace, then it cannot be based on works; if it were, grace would no longer be grace.

⁷What then? What the people of Israel sought so earnestly they did not obtain. The elect among them

---

ᵃ 8 Deut. 30:14    ᵇ 11 Isaiah 28:16 (see Septuagint)    ᶜ 13 Joel 2:32    ᵈ 15 Isaiah 52:7
ᵉ 16 Isaiah 53:1    ᶠ 18 Psalm 19:4    ᵍ 19 Deut. 32:21    ʰ 20 Isaiah 65:1    ⁱ 21 Isaiah 65:2
ʲ 3 1 Kings 19:10,14    ᵏ 4 1 Kings 19:18

did, but the others were hardened, [8]as it is written:

> "God gave them a spirit of
> stupor,
> eyes that could not see
> and ears that could not hear,
> to this very day."[a]

[9]And David says:

> "May their table become a snare
> and a trap,
> a stumbling block and a
> retribution for them.
> [10]May their eyes be darkened so
> they cannot see,
> and their backs be bent
> forever."[b]

[11]Again I ask: Did they stumble so as to fall beyond recovery? Not at all! Rather, because of their transgression, salvation has come to the Gentiles to make Israel envious. [12]But if their transgression means riches for the world, and their loss means riches for the Gentiles, how much greater riches will their full inclusion bring!

[13]I am talking to you Gentiles. Inasmuch as I am the apostle to the Gentiles, I take pride in my ministry [14]in the hope that I may somehow arouse my own people to envy and save some of them. [15]For if their rejection brought reconciliation to the world, what will their acceptance be but life from the dead? [16]If the part of the dough offered as firstfruits is holy, then the whole batch is holy; if the root is holy, so are the branches.

[17]If some of the branches have been broken off, and you, though a wild olive shoot, have been grafted in among the others and now share in the nourishing sap from the olive root, [18]do not consider yourself to be superior to those other branches. If you do, consider this: You do not support the root, but the root supports you. [19]You will say then, "Branches were broken off so that I could be grafted in." [20]Granted. But they were broken off because of unbelief, and you stand by faith. Do not be arrogant, but tremble. [21]For if God did not spare the natural branches, he will not spare you either.

[22]Consider therefore the kindness and sternness of God: sternness to those who fell, but kindness to you, provided that you continue in his kindness. Otherwise, you also will be cut off. [23]And if they do not persist in unbelief, they will be grafted in, for God is able to graft them in again. [24]After all, if you were cut out of an olive tree that is wild by nature, and contrary to nature were grafted into a cultivated olive tree, how much more readily will these, the natural branches, be grafted into their own olive tree!

[25]I do not want you to be ignorant of this mystery, brothers and sisters, so that you may not be conceited: Israel has experienced a hardening in part until the full number of the Gentiles has come in, [26]and in this way[c] all Israel will be saved. As it is written:

> "The deliverer will come from
> Zion;
> he will turn godlessness away
> from Jacob.
> [27]And this is[d] my covenant with
> them
> when I take away their sins."[e]

[28]As far as the gospel is concerned, they are enemies for your

---

[a] 8 Deut. 29:4; Isaiah 29:10　　[b] 10 Psalm 69:22,23　　[c] 26 Or and so　　[d] 27 Or will be
[e] 27 Isaiah 59:20,21; 27:9 (see Septuagint); Jer. 31:33,34

sake; but as far as election is concerned, they are loved on account of the patriarchs, [29] for God's gifts and his call are irrevocable. [30] Just as you who were at one time disobedient to God have now received mercy as a result of their disobedience, [31] so they too have now become disobedient in order that they too may now[a] receive mercy as a result of God's mercy to you. [32] For God has bound everyone over to disobedience so that he may have mercy on them all.

[33] Oh, the depth of the riches of the
        wisdom and[b] knowledge
        of God!
    How unsearchable his
        judgments,
    and his paths beyond tracing
        out!
[34] "Who has known the mind of the
        Lord?
    Or who has been his
        counselor?"[c]
[35] "Who has ever given to God,
    that God should repay them?"[d]
[36] For from him and through him
        and for him are all things.
    To him be the glory forever!
        Amen.

12 Therefore, I urge you, brothers and sisters, in view of God's mercy, to offer your bodies as a living sacrifice, holy and pleasing to God — this is your true and proper worship. [2] Do not conform to the pattern of this world, but be transformed by the renewing of your mind. Then you will be able to test and approve what God's will is — his good, pleasing and perfect will.

[3] For by the grace given me I say to every one of you: Do not think of yourself more highly than you ought, but rather think of yourself with sober judgment, in accordance with the faith God has distributed to each of you. [4] For just as each of us has one body with many members, and these members do not all have the same function, [5] so in Christ we, though many, form one body, and each member belongs to all the others. [6] We have different gifts, according to the grace given to each of us. If your gift is prophesying, then prophesy in accordance with your[e] faith; [7] if it is serving, then serve; if it is teaching, then teach; [8] if it is to encourage, then give encouragement; if it is giving, then give generously; if it is to lead,[f] do it diligently; if it is to show mercy, do it cheerfully.

[9] Love must be sincere. Hate what is evil; cling to what is good. [10] Be devoted to one another in love. Honor one another above yourselves. [11] Never be lacking in zeal, but keep your spiritual fervor, serving the Lord. [12] Be joyful in hope, patient in affliction, faithful in prayer. [13] Share with the Lord's people who are in need. Practice hospitality.

[14] Bless those who persecute you; bless and do not curse. [15] Rejoice with those who rejoice; mourn with those who mourn. [16] Live in harmony with one another. Do not be proud, but be willing to associate with people of low position.[g] Do not be conceited.

[17] Do not repay anyone evil for evil. Be careful to do what is right in the eyes of everyone. [18] If it is possible, as far as it depends on you, live at peace with everyone. [19] Do

---

[a] 31 Some manuscripts do not have *now*.   [b] 33 Or *riches and the wisdom and the*
[c] 34 Isaiah 40:13   [d] 35 Job 41:11   [e] 6 Or *the*   [f] 8 Or *to provide for others*   [g] 16 Or *willing to do menial work*

not take revenge, my dear friends, but leave room for God's wrath, for it is written: "It is mine to avenge; I will repay,"[a] says the Lord. 20 On the contrary:

"If your enemy is hungry, feed
    him;
    if he is thirsty, give him
        something to drink.
In doing this, you will heap
    burning coals on his
        head."[b]

21 Do not be overcome by evil, but overcome evil with good.

13 Let everyone be subject to the governing authorities, for there is no authority except that which God has established. The authorities that exist have been established by God. 2 Consequently, whoever rebels against the authority is rebelling against what God has instituted, and those who do so will bring judgment on themselves. 3 For rulers hold no terror for those who do right, but for those who do wrong. Do you want to be free from fear of the one in authority? Then do what is right and you will be commended. 4 For the one in authority is God's servant for your good. But if you do wrong, be afraid, for rulers do not bear the sword for no reason. They are God's servants, agents of wrath to bring punishment on the wrongdoer. 5 Therefore, it is necessary to submit to the authorities, not only because of possible punishment but also as a matter of conscience.

6 This is also why you pay taxes, for the authorities are God's servants, who give their full time to governing. 7 Give to everyone what

you owe them: If you owe taxes, pay taxes; if revenue, then revenue; if respect, then respect; if honor, then honor.

8 Let no debt remain outstanding, except the continuing debt to love one another, for whoever loves others has fulfilled the law. 9 The commandments, "You shall not commit adultery," "You shall not murder," "You shall not steal," "You shall not covet,"[c] and whatever other command there may be, are summed up in this one command: "Love your neighbor as yourself."[d] 10 Love does no harm to a neighbor. Therefore love is the fulfillment of the law.

11 And do this, understanding the present time: The hour has already come for you to wake up from your slumber, because our salvation is nearer now than when we first believed. 12 The night is nearly over; the day is almost here. So let us put aside the deeds of darkness and put on the armor of light. 13 Let us behave decently, as in the daytime, not in carousing and drunkenness, not in sexual immorality and debauchery, not in dissension and jealousy. 14 Rather, clothe yourselves with the Lord Jesus Christ, and do not think about how to gratify the desires of the flesh.[e]

14 Accept the one whose faith is weak, without quarreling over disputable matters. 2 One person's faith allows them to eat anything, but another, whose faith is weak, eats only vegetables. 3 The one who eats everything must not treat with contempt the one who does not, and the one who does not eat everything must not judge the one who

---

[a] 19 Deut. 32:35    [b] 20 Prov. 25:21,22    [c] 9 Exodus 20:13-15,17; Deut. 5:17-19,21
[d] 9 Lev. 19:18    [e] 14 In contexts like this, the Greek word for *flesh* (*sarx*) refers to the sinful state of human beings, often presented as a power in opposition to the Spirit.

does, for God has accepted them. [4]Who are you to judge someone else's servant? To their own master, servants stand or fall. And they will stand, for the Lord is able to make them stand.

[5]One person considers one day more sacred than another; another considers every day alike. Each of them should be fully convinced in their own mind. [6]Whoever regards one day as special does so to the Lord. Whoever eats meat does so to the Lord, for they give thanks to God; and whoever abstains does so to the Lord and gives thanks to God. [7]For none of us lives for ourselves alone, and none of us dies for ourselves alone. [8]If we live, we live for the Lord; and if we die, we die for the Lord. So, whether we live or die, we belong to the Lord. [9]For this very reason, Christ died and returned to life so that he might be the Lord of both the dead and the living.

[10]You, then, why do you judge your brother or sister[a]? Or why do you treat them with contempt? For we will all stand before God's judgment seat. [11]It is written:

"'As surely as I live,' says the Lord,
'every knee will bow before me;
    every tongue will acknowledge God.'"[b]

[12]So then, each of us will give an account of ourselves to God.

[13]Therefore let us stop passing judgment on one another. Instead, make up your mind not to put any stumbling block or obstacle in the way of a brother or sister. [14]I am convinced, being fully persuaded in the Lord Jesus, that nothing is unclean in itself. But if anyone regards something as unclean, then for that person it is unclean. [15]If your brother or sister is distressed because of what you eat, you are no longer acting in love. Do not by your eating destroy someone for whom Christ died. [16]Therefore do not let what you know is good be spoken of as evil. [17]For the kingdom of God is not a matter of eating and drinking, but of righteousness, peace and joy in the Holy Spirit, [18]because anyone who serves Christ in this way is pleasing to God and receives human approval.

[19]Let us therefore make every effort to do what leads to peace and to mutual edification. [20]Do not destroy the work of God for the sake of food. All food is clean, but it is wrong for a person to eat anything that causes someone else to stumble. [21]It is better not to eat meat or drink wine or to do anything else that will cause your brother or sister to fall.

[22]So whatever you believe about these things keep between yourself and God. Blessed is the one who does not condemn himself by what he approves. [23]But whoever has doubts is condemned if they eat, because their eating is not from faith; and everything that does not come from faith is sin.[c]

15 We who are strong ought to bear with the failings of the weak and not to please ourselves. [2]Each of us should please our neighbors for their good, to build them up. [3]For even Christ did not please himself but, as it is written: "The insults of those who insult you have

---

[a] 10 The Greek word for brother or sister (adelphos) refers here to a believer, whether man or woman, as part of God's family; also in verses 13, 15 and 21.   [b] 11 Isaiah 45:23   [c] 23 Some manuscripts place 16:25-27 here; others after 15:33.

fallen on me."[a] [4]For everything that was written in the past was written to teach us, so that through the endurance taught in the Scriptures and the encouragement they provide we might have hope.

[5]May the God who gives endurance and encouragement give you the same attitude of mind toward each other that Christ Jesus had, [6]so that with one mind and one voice you may glorify the God and Father of our Lord Jesus Christ.

[7]Accept one another, then, just as Christ accepted you, in order to bring praise to God. [8]For I tell you that Christ has become a servant of the Jews[b] on behalf of God's truth, so that the promises made to the patriarchs might be confirmed [9]and, moreover, that the Gentiles might glorify God for his mercy. As it is written:

> "Therefore I will praise you
>      among the Gentiles;
>   I will sing the praises of your
>      name."[c]

[10]Again, it says,

> "Rejoice, you Gentiles, with his
>      people."[d]

[11]And again,

> "Praise the Lord, all you
>      Gentiles;
>   let all the peoples extol him."[e]

[12]And again, Isaiah says,

> "The Root of Jesse will spring up,
>      one who will arise to rule over
>      the nations;
>   in him the Gentiles will
>      hope."[f]

[13]May the God of hope fill you with all joy and peace as you trust in him, so that you may overflow with hope by the power of the Holy Spirit.

[14]I myself am convinced, my brothers and sisters, that you yourselves are full of goodness, filled with knowledge and competent to instruct one another. [15]Yet I have written you quite boldly on some points to remind you of them again, because of the grace God gave me [16]to be a minister of Christ Jesus to the Gentiles. He gave me the priestly duty of proclaiming the gospel of God, so that the Gentiles might become an offering acceptable to God, sanctified by the Holy Spirit.

[17]Therefore I glory in Christ Jesus in my service to God. [18]I will not venture to speak of anything except what Christ has accomplished through me in leading the Gentiles to obey God by what I have said and done — [19]by the power of signs and wonders, through the power of the Spirit of God. So from Jerusalem all the way around to Illyricum, I have fully proclaimed the gospel of Christ. [20]It has always been my ambition to preach the gospel where Christ was not known, so that I would not be building on someone else's foundation. [21]Rather, as it is written:

> "Those who were not told about
>      him will see,
>   and those who have not heard
>      will understand."[g]

[22]This is why I have often been hindered from coming to you.

[23]But now that there is no more place for me to work in these regions, and since I have been longing for many years to visit you, [24]I

---

[a] 3 Psalm 69:9    [b] 8 Greek *circumcision*    [c] 9 2 Samuel 22:50; Psalm 18:49    [d] 10 Deut. 32:43
[e] 11 Psalm 117:1    [f] 12 Isaiah 11:10 (see Septuagint)    [g] 21 Isaiah 52:15 (see Septuagint)

plan to do so when I go to Spain. I hope to see you while passing through and to have you assist me on my journey there, after I have enjoyed your company for a while. ²⁵Now, however, I am on my way to Jerusalem in the service of the Lord's people there. ²⁶For Macedonia and Achaia were pleased to make a contribution for the poor among the Lord's people in Jerusalem. ²⁷They were pleased to do it, and indeed they owe it to them. For if the Gentiles have shared in the Jews' spiritual blessings, they owe it to the Jews to share with them their material blessings. ²⁸So after I have completed this task and have made sure that they have received this contribution, I will go to Spain and visit you on the way. ²⁹I know that when I come to you, I will come in the full measure of the blessing of Christ.

³⁰I urge you, brothers and sisters, by our Lord Jesus Christ and by the love of the Spirit, to join me in my struggle by praying to God for me. ³¹Pray that I may be kept safe from the unbelievers in Judea and that the contribution I take to Jerusalem may be favorably received by the Lord's people there, ³²so that I may come to you with joy, by God's will, and in your company be refreshed. ³³The God of peace be with you all. Amen.

**16** I commend to you our sister Phoebe, a deacon[a,b] of the church in Cenchreae. ²I ask you to receive her in the Lord in a way worthy of his people and to give her any help she may need from you, for she has been the benefactor of many people, including me.

³Greet Priscilla[c] and Aquila, my co-workers in Christ Jesus. ⁴They risked their lives for me. Not only I but all the churches of the Gentiles are grateful to them.

⁵Greet also the church that meets at their house.

Greet my dear friend Epenetus, who was the first convert to Christ in the province of Asia.

⁶Greet Mary, who worked very hard for you.

⁷Greet Andronicus and Junia, my fellow Jews who have been in prison with me. They are outstanding among[d] the apostles, and they were in Christ before I was.

⁸Greet Ampliatus, my dear friend in the Lord.

⁹Greet Urbanus, our co-worker in Christ, and my dear friend Stachys.

¹⁰Greet Apelles, whose fidelity to Christ has stood the test.

Greet those who belong to the household of Aristobulus.

¹¹Greet Herodion, my fellow Jew.

Greet those in the household of Narcissus who are in the Lord.

¹²Greet Tryphena and Tryphosa, those women who work hard in the Lord.

Greet my dear friend Persis, another woman who has worked very hard in the Lord.

¹³Greet Rufus, chosen in the Lord, and his mother, who has been a mother to me, too.

¹⁴Greet Asyncritus, Phlegon, Hermes, Patrobas, Hermas and the other brothers and sisters with them.

¹⁵Greet Philologus, Julia, Nereus

---

*a 1* Or *servant*    *b 1* The word *deacon* refers here to a Christian designated to serve with the overseers/elders of the church in a variety of ways; similarly in Phil. 1:1 and 1 Tim. 3:8,12.
*c 3* Greek *Prisca*, a variant of *Priscilla*    *d 7* Or *are esteemed by*

and his sister, and Olympas and all the Lord's people who are with them.

16 Greet one another with a holy kiss.

All the churches of Christ send greetings.

17 I urge you, brothers and sisters, to watch out for those who cause divisions and put obstacles in your way that are contrary to the teaching you have learned. Keep away from them. 18 For such people are not serving our Lord Christ, but their own appetites. By smooth talk and flattery they deceive the minds of naive people. 19 Everyone has heard about your obedience, so I rejoice because of you; but I want you to be wise about what is good, and innocent about what is evil.

20 The God of peace will soon crush Satan under your feet.

The grace of our Lord Jesus be with you.

21 Timothy, my co-worker, sends his greetings to you, as do Lucius, Jason and Sosipater, my fellow Jews.

22 I, Tertius, who wrote down this letter, greet you in the Lord.

23 Gaius, whose hospitality I and the whole church here enjoy, sends you his greetings.

Erastus, who is the city's director of public works, and our brother Quartus send you their greetings. [24] a

25 Now to him who is able to establish you in accordance with my gospel, the message I proclaim about Jesus Christ, in keeping with the revelation of the mystery hidden for long ages past, 26 but now revealed and made known through the prophetic writings by the command of the eternal God, so that all the Gentiles might come to the obedience that comes from b faith — 27 to the only wise God be glory forever through Jesus Christ! Amen.

---

a 24 Some manuscripts include here May the grace of our Lord Jesus Christ be with all of you. Amen.    b 26 Or that is

# 1 CORINTHIANS

The book of Acts describes how Paul brought the royal news about Jesus the Messiah to Macedonia (northern Greece), but then had to flee to Achaia (southern Greece) for his own safety. He visited the city of Corinth there, a wealthy and cosmopolitan commercial center. Many people became believers, so he stayed for a year and a half to teach them.

After he left, the Corinthians wrote to Paul (in a letter we no longer have) with some key questions. The Corinthians had adopted the common Greek idea that physical things are bad, so they wanted to free the human spirit from the body. This affected the way they saw such things as marriage, attendance at ceremonial meals for pagan gods, and even the resurrection of Jesus. In the letter we know as 1 Corinthians Paul addresses all of these concerns, as well as questions about worship.

Paul writes that *this world in its present form is passing away*, but the Corinthians can give themselves *fully to the work of the Lord* since their *labor in the Lord is not in vain*. The coming resurrection of the dead, and the new world that will accompany it, will show the value of all their current efforts. Paul's practical advice for how to consistently embody the new life of God's kingdom during a particular scene in the biblical drama gives us great insight as we seek to take up our roles today.

---

1 Paul, called to be an apostle of Christ Jesus by the will of God, and our brother Sosthenes,

2 To the church of God in Corinth, to those sanctified in Christ Jesus and called to be his holy people, together with all those everywhere who call on the name of our Lord Jesus Christ — their Lord and ours:

3 Grace and *peace* to you from God our *Father* and the Lord Jesus *Christ*.

4 I always thank my God for you because of his grace given you in Christ Jesus. 5 For in him you have been enriched in every way — with all kinds of speech and with all knowledge — 6 God thus confirming our testimony about Christ among you. 7 Therefore you do not lack any spiritual gift as you eagerly wait for our Lord Jesus Christ to be revealed. 8 He will also keep you firm to the end, so that you will be blameless on the day of our Lord Jesus Christ. 9 God is faithful, who has called you into fellowship with his Son, Jesus Christ our Lord.

10 I appeal to you, brothers and sisters,[a] in the name of our Lord Jesus Christ, that all of you agree with one another in what you say and that there be no divisions among you, but that you be perfectly united in mind and thought. 11 My brothers and sisters, some from Chloe's household have informed me that there are quarrels among you. 12 What I mean is this: One of you says, "I follow Paul"; another, "I follow Apollos"; another,

---

a 10 The Greek word for *brothers and sisters* (*adelphoi*) refers here to believers, both men and women, as part of God's family; also in verses 11 and 26; and in 2:1; 3:1; 4:6; 6:8; 7:24, 29; 10:1; 11:33; 12:1; 14:6, 20, 26, 39; 15:1, 6, 50, 58; 16:15, 20.

"I follow Cephas[a]"; still another, "I follow Christ."

¹³Is Christ divided? Was Paul crucified for you? Were you baptized in the name of Paul? ¹⁴I thank God that I did not baptize any of you except Crispus and Gaius, ¹⁵so no one can say that you were baptized in my name. ¹⁶(Yes, I also baptized the household of Stephanas; beyond that, I don't remember if I baptized anyone else.) ¹⁷For Christ did not send me to baptize, but to preach the gospel—not with wisdom and eloquence, lest the cross of Christ be emptied of its power.

¹⁸For the message of the cross is foolishness to those who are perishing, but to us who are being saved it is the power of God. ¹⁹For it is written:

"I will destroy the wisdom of the
    wise;
the intelligence of the
    intelligent I will
    frustrate."[b]

²⁰Where is the wise person? Where is the teacher of the law? Where is the philosopher of this age? Has not God made foolish the wisdom of the world? ²¹For since in the wisdom of God the world through its wisdom did not know him, God was pleased through the foolishness of what was preached to save those who believe. ²²Jews demand signs and Greeks look for wisdom, ²³but we preach Christ crucified: a stumbling block to Jews and foolishness to Gentiles, ²⁴but to those whom God has called, both Jews and Greeks, Christ the power of God and the wisdom of God. ²⁵For the foolishness of God is wiser than human wisdom, and

the weakness of God is stronger than human strength.

²⁶Brothers and sisters, think of what you were when you were called. Not many of you were wise by human standards; not many were influential; not many were of noble birth. ²⁷But God chose the foolish things of the world to shame the wise; God chose the weak things of the world to shame the strong. ²⁸God chose the lowly things of this world and the despised things—and the things that are not—to nullify the things that are, ²⁹so that no one may boast before him. ³⁰It is because of him that you are in Christ Jesus, who has become for us wisdom from God—that is, our righteousness, holiness and redemption. ³¹Therefore, as it is written: "Let the one who boasts boast in the Lord."[c]

2 And so it was with me, brothers and sisters. When I came to you, I did not come with eloquence or human wisdom as I proclaimed to you the testimony about God.[d] ²For I resolved to know nothing while I was with you except Jesus Christ and him crucified. ³I came to you in weakness with great fear and trembling. ⁴My message and my preaching were not with wise and persuasive words, but with a demonstration of the Spirit's power, ⁵so that your faith might not rest on human wisdom, but on God's power.

⁶We do, however, speak a message of wisdom among the mature, but not the wisdom of this age or of the rulers of this age, who are coming to nothing. ⁷No, we declare God's wisdom, a mystery that has been hidden and that God destined for our glory before time be-

---

[a] 12 That is, Peter    [b] 19 Isaiah 29:14    [c] 31 Jer. 9:24    [d] 1 Some manuscripts *proclaimed to you God's mystery*

gan. [8]None of the rulers of this age understood it, for if they had, they would not have crucified the Lord of glory. [9]However, as it is written:

"What no eye has seen,
    what no ear has heard,
    and what no human mind has
        conceived"[a]—
    the things God has prepared
        for those who love him—

[10]these are the things God has revealed to us by his Spirit.

The Spirit searches all things, even the deep things of God. [11]For who knows a person's thoughts except their own spirit within them? In the same way no one knows the thoughts of God except the Spirit of God. [12]What we have received is not the spirit of the world, but the Spirit who is from God, so that we may understand what God has freely given us. [13]This is what we speak, not in words taught us by human wisdom but in words taught by the Spirit, explaining spiritual realities with Spirit-taught words.[b] [14]The person without the Spirit does not accept the things that come from the Spirit of God but considers them foolishness, and cannot understand them because they are discerned only through the Spirit. [15]The person with the Spirit makes judgments about all things, but such a person is not subject to merely human judgments, [16]for,

"Who has known the mind of the
        Lord
    so as to instruct him?"[c]

But we have the mind of Christ.

3 Brothers and sisters, I could not address you as people who live by the Spirit but as people who are still worldly—mere infants in Christ. [2]I gave you milk, not solid food, for you were not yet ready for it. Indeed, you are still not ready. [3]You are still worldly. For since there is jealousy and quarreling among you, are you not worldly? Are you not acting like mere humans? [4]For when one says, "I follow Paul," and another, "I follow Apollos," are you not mere human beings?

[5]What, after all, is Apollos? And what is Paul? Only servants, through whom you came to believe—as the Lord has assigned to each his task. [6]I planted the seed, Apollos watered it, but God has been making it grow. [7]So neither the one who plants nor the one who waters is anything, but only God, who makes things grow. [8]The one who plants and the one who waters have one purpose, and they will each be rewarded according to their own labor. [9]For we are co-workers in God's service; you are God's field, God's building.

[10]By the grace God has given me, I laid a foundation as a wise builder, and someone else is building on it. But each one should build with care. [11]For no one can lay any foundation other than the one already laid, which is Jesus Christ. [12]If anyone builds on this foundation using gold, silver, costly stones, wood, hay or straw, [13]their work will be shown for what it is, because the Day will bring it to light. It will be revealed with fire, and the fire will test the quality of each person's work. [14]If what has been built survives, the builder will receive a reward. [15]If it is burned up, the builder will suffer loss but yet will be saved—

[a] 9 Isaiah 64:4    [b] 13 Or Spirit, interpreting spiritual truths to those who are spiritual
[c] 16 Isaiah 40:13

even though only as one escaping through the flames.

¹⁶Don't you know that you yourselves are God's temple and that God's Spirit dwells in your midst? ¹⁷If anyone destroys God's temple, God will destroy that person; for God's temple is sacred, and you together are that temple.

¹⁸Do not deceive yourselves. If any of you think you are wise by the standards of this age, you should become "fools" so that you may become wise. ¹⁹For the wisdom of this world is foolishness in God's sight. As it is written: "He catches the wise in their craftiness"ᵃ; ²⁰and again, "The Lord knows that the thoughts of the wise are futile."ᵇ ²¹So then, no more boasting about human leaders! All things are yours, ²²whether Paul or Apollos or Cephasᶜ or the world or life or death or the present or the future—all are yours, ²³and you are of Christ, and Christ is of God.

4 This, then, is how you ought to regard us: as servants of Christ and as those entrusted with the mysteries God has revealed. ²Now it is required that those who have been given a trust must prove faithful. ³I care very little if I am judged by you or by any human court; indeed, I do not even judge myself. ⁴My conscience is clear, but that does not make me innocent. It is the Lord who judges me. ⁵Therefore judge nothing before the appointed time; wait until the Lord comes. He will bring to light what is hidden in darkness and will expose the motives of the heart. At that time each will receive their praise from God.

⁶Now, brothers and sisters, I have applied these things to myself and Apollos for your benefit, so that you may learn from us the meaning of the saying, "Do not go beyond what is written." Then you will not be puffed up in being a follower of one of us over against the other. ⁷For who makes you different from anyone else? What do you have that you did not receive? And if you did receive it, why do you boast as though you did not?

⁸Already you have all you want! Already you have become rich! You have begun to reign—and that without us! How I wish that you really had begun to reign so that we also might reign with you! ⁹For it seems to me that God has put us apostles on display at the end of the procession, like those condemned to die in the arena. We have been made a spectacle to the whole universe, to angels as well as to human beings. ¹⁰We are fools for Christ, but you are so wise in Christ! We are weak, but you are strong! You are honored, we are dishonored! ¹¹To this very hour we go hungry and thirsty, we are in rags, we are brutally treated, we are homeless. ¹²We work hard with our own hands. When we are cursed, we bless; when we are persecuted, we endure it; ¹³when we are slandered, we answer kindly. We have become the scum of the earth, the garbage of the world—right up to this moment.

¹⁴I am writing this not to shame you but to warn you as my dear children. ¹⁵Even if you had ten thousand guardians in Christ, you do not have many fathers, for in Christ Jesus I became your father through the gospel. ¹⁶Therefore I urge you to imitate me. ¹⁷For this reason I have sent to you Timothy, my son whom I love, who is faithful in the

---

ᵃ 19 Job 5:13    ᵇ 20 Psalm 94:11    ᶜ 22 That is, Peter

Lord. He will remind you of my way of life in Christ Jesus, which agrees with what I teach everywhere in every church.

18 Some of you have become arrogant, as if I were not coming to you. 19 But I will come to you very soon, if the Lord is willing, and then I will find out not only how these arrogant people are talking, but what power they have. 20 For the kingdom of God is not a matter of talk but of power. 21 What do you prefer? Shall I come to you with a rod of discipline, or shall I come in love and with a gentle spirit?

5 It is actually reported that there is sexual immorality among you, and of a kind that even pagans do not tolerate: A man is sleeping with his father's wife. 2 And you are proud! Shouldn't you rather have gone into mourning and have put out of your fellowship the man who has been doing this? 3 For my part, even though I am not physically present, I am with you in spirit. As one who is present with you in this way, I have already passed judgment in the name of our Lord Jesus on the one who has been doing this. 4 So when you are assembled and I am with you in spirit, and the power of our Lord Jesus is present, 5 hand this man over to Satan for the destruction of the flesh,[a,b] so that his spirit may be saved on the day of the Lord.

6 Your boasting is not good. Don't you know that a little yeast leavens the whole batch of dough? 7 Get rid of the old yeast, so that you may be a new unleavened batch—as you really are. For Christ, our Passover lamb, has been sacrificed. 8 Therefore let us keep the Festival, not with the old bread leavened with malice and wickedness, but with the unleavened bread of sincerity and truth.

9 I wrote to you in my letter not to associate with sexually immoral people— 10 not at all meaning the people of this world who are immoral, or the greedy and swindlers, or idolaters. In that case you would have to leave this world. 11 But now I am writing to you that you must not associate with anyone who claims to be a brother or sister[c] but is sexually immoral or greedy, an idolater or slanderer, a drunkard or swindler. Do not even eat with such people.

12 What business is it of mine to judge those outside the church? Are you not to judge those inside? 13 God will judge those outside. "Expel the wicked person from among you."[d]

6 If any of you has a dispute with another, do you dare to take it before the ungodly for judgment instead of before the Lord's people? 2 Or do you not know that the Lord's people will judge the world? And if you are to judge the world, are you not competent to judge trivial cases? 3 Do you not know that we will judge angels? How much more the things of this life! 4 Therefore, if you have disputes about such matters, do you ask for a ruling from those whose way of life is scorned in the church? 5 I say this to shame you. Is it possible that there is nobody

---

[a] 5 In contexts like this, the Greek word for *flesh* (*sarx*) refers to the sinful state of human beings, often presented as a power in opposition to the Spirit.    [b] 5 Or *of his body*    [c] 11 The Greek word for *brother or sister* (*adelphos*) refers to a believer, whether man or woman, as part of God's family; also in 8:11, 13.    [d] 13 Deut. 13:5; 17:7; 19:19; 21:21; 22:21,24; 24:7

among you wise enough to judge a dispute between believers? 6But instead, one brother takes another to court—and this in front of unbelievers!

7The very fact that you have lawsuits among you means you have been completely defeated already. Why not rather be wronged? Why not rather be cheated? 8Instead, you yourselves cheat and do wrong, and you do this to your brothers and sisters. 9Or do you not know that wrongdoers will not inherit the kingdom of God? Do not be deceived: Neither the sexually immoral nor idolaters nor adulterers nor men who have sex with men*a* nor thieves nor the greedy nor drunkards nor slanderers nor swindlers will inherit the kingdom of God. 11And that is what some of you were. But you were washed, you were sanctified, you were justified in the name of the Lord Jesus Christ and by the Spirit of our God.

12"I have the right to do anything," you say—but not everything is beneficial. "I have the right to do anything"—but I will not be mastered by anything. 13You say, "Food for the stomach and the stomach for food, and God will destroy them both." The body, however, is not meant for sexual immorality but for the Lord, and the Lord for the body. 14By his power God raised the Lord from the dead, and he will raise us also. 15Do you not know that your bodies are members of Christ himself? Shall I then take the members of Christ and unite them with a prostitute? Never! 16Do you not know that he who unites himself with a prostitute is one with her in body? For it is said, "The two will become one flesh."*b* 17But whoever is united with the Lord is one with him in spirit.*c*

18Flee from sexual immorality. All other sins a person commits are outside the body, but whoever sins sexually, sins against their own body. 19Do you not know that your bodies are temples of the Holy Spirit, who is in you, whom you have received from God? You are not your own; 20you were bought at a price. Therefore honor God with your bodies.

7 Now for the matters you wrote about: "It is good for a man not to have sexual relations with a woman." 2But since sexual immorality is occurring, each man should have sexual relations with his own wife, and each woman with her own husband. 3The husband should fulfill his marital duty to his wife, and likewise the wife to her husband. 4The wife does not have authority over her own body but yields it to her husband. In the same way, the husband does not have authority over his own body but yields it to his wife. 5Do not deprive each other except perhaps by mutual consent and for a time, so that you may devote yourselves to prayer. Then come together again so that Satan will not tempt you because of your lack of self-control. 6I say this as a concession, not as a command. 7I wish that all of you were as I am. But each of you has your own gift from God; one has this gift, another has that.

8Now to the unmarried*d* and the

---

*a* 9 The words *men who have sex with men* translate two Greek words that refer to the passive and active participants in homosexual acts.    *b* 16 Gen. 2:24    *c* 17 Or *in the Spirit*
*d* 8 Or *widowers*

widows I say: It is good for them to stay unmarried, as I do. 9 But if they cannot control themselves, they should marry, for it is better to marry than to burn with passion.

10 To the married I give this command (not I, but the Lord): A wife must not separate from her husband. 11 But if she does, she must remain unmarried or else be reconciled to her husband. And a husband must not divorce his wife.

12 To the rest I say this (I, not the Lord): If any brother has a wife who is not a believer and she is willing to live with him, he must not divorce her. 13 And if a woman has a husband who is not a believer and he is willing to live with her, she must not divorce him. 14 For the unbelieving husband has been sanctified through his wife, and the unbelieving wife has been sanctified through her believing husband. Otherwise your children would be unclean, but as it is, they are holy.

15 But if the unbeliever leaves, let it be so. The brother or the sister is not bound in such circumstances; God has called us to live in peace. 16 How do you know, wife, whether you will save your husband? Or, how do you know, husband, whether you will save your wife?

17 Nevertheless, each person should live as a believer in whatever situation the Lord has assigned to them, just as God has called them. This is the rule I lay down in all the churches. 18 Was a man already circumcised when he was called? He should not become uncircumcised. Was a man uncircumcised when he was called? He should not be circumcised. 19 Circumcision is nothing and uncircumcision is nothing. Keeping God's commands is what counts. 20 Each person should remain in the situation they were in when God called them.

21 Were you a slave when you were called? Don't let it trouble you — although if you can gain your freedom, do so. 22 For the one who was a slave when called to faith in the Lord is the Lord's freed person; similarly, the one who was free when called is Christ's slave. 23 You were bought at a price; do not become slaves of human beings. 24 Brothers and sisters, each person, as responsible to God, should remain in the situation they were in when God called them.

25 Now about virgins: I have no command from the Lord, but I give a judgment as one who by the Lord's mercy is trustworthy. 26 Because of the present crisis, I think that it is good for a man to remain as he is. 27 Are you pledged to a woman? Do not seek to be released. Are you free from such a commitment? Do not look for a wife. 28 But if you do marry, you have not sinned; and if a virgin marries, she has not sinned. But those who marry will face many troubles in this life, and I want to spare you this.

29 What I mean, brothers and sisters, is that the time is short. From now on those who have wives should live as if they do not; 30 those who mourn, as if they did not; those who are happy, as if they were not; those who buy something, as if it were not theirs to keep; 31 those who use the things of the world, as if not engrossed in them. For this world in its present form is passing away.

32 I would like you to be free from concern. An unmarried man is concerned about the Lord's affairs — how he can please the Lord. 33 But

a married man is concerned about the affairs of this world—how he can please his wife— [34] and his interests are divided. An unmarried woman or virgin is concerned about the Lord's affairs: Her aim is to be devoted to the Lord in both body and spirit. But a married woman is concerned about the affairs of this world—how she can please her husband. [35] I am saying this for your own good, not to restrict you, but that you may live in a right way in undivided devotion to the Lord.

[36] If anyone is worried that he might not be acting honorably toward the virgin he is engaged to, and if his passions are too strong[a] and he feels he ought to marry, he should do as he wants. He is not sinning. They should get married. [37] But the man who has settled the matter in his own mind, who is under no compulsion but has control over his own will, and who has made up his mind not to marry the virgin—this man also does the right thing. [38] So then, he who marries the virgin does right, but he who does not marry her does better.[b]

[39] A woman is bound to her husband as long as he lives. But if her husband dies, she is free to marry anyone she wishes, but he must belong to the Lord. [40] In my judgment, she is happier if she stays as she is—and I think that I too have the Spirit of God.

[8] Now about food sacrificed to idols: We know that "We all possess knowledge." But knowledge puffs up while love builds up. [2] Those who think they know something do not yet know as they ought to know. [3] But whoever loves God is known by God.[c]

[4] So then, about eating food sacrificed to idols: We know that "An idol is nothing at all in the world" and that "There is no God but one." [5] For even if there are so-called gods, whether in heaven or on earth (as indeed there are many "gods" and many "lords"), [6] yet for us there is but one God, the Father, from whom all things came and for whom we live; and there is but one Lord, Jesus Christ, through whom all things came and through whom we live.

[7] But not everyone possesses this knowledge. Some people are still so accustomed to idols that when they eat sacrificial food they think of it as having been sacrificed to a god, and since their conscience is weak, it is defiled. [8] But food does not bring us near to God; we are no worse if we do not eat, and no better if we do.

[9] Be careful, however, that the exercise of your rights does not become a stumbling block to the weak. [10] For if someone with a weak conscience sees you, with all your knowledge, eating in an idol's temple, won't that person be emboldened to eat what is sacrificed

---

[a] 36 Or *if she is getting beyond the usual age for marriage*     [b] 36-38 Or *36If anyone thinks he is not treating his daughter properly, and if she is getting along in years (or if her passions are too strong), and he feels she ought to marry, he should do as he wants. He is not sinning. He should let her get married. 37But the man who has settled the matter in his own mind, who is under no compulsion but has control over his own will, and who has made up his mind to keep the virgin unmarried—this man also does the right thing. 38So then, he who gives his virgin in marriage does right, but he who does not give her in marriage does better.*     [c] 2,3 An early manuscript and another ancient witness *think they have knowledge do not yet know as they ought to know. 3But whoever loves truly knows.*

to idols? ¹¹So this weak brother or sister, for whom Christ died, is destroyed by your knowledge. ¹²When you sin against them in this way and wound their weak conscience, you sin against Christ. ¹³Therefore, if what I eat causes my brother or sister to fall into sin, I will never eat meat again, so that I will not cause them to fall.

9 Am I not free? Am I not an apostle? Have I not seen Jesus our Lord? Are you not the result of my work in the Lord? ²Even though I may not be an apostle to others, surely I am to you! For you are the seal of my apostleship in the Lord.

³This is my defense to those who sit in judgment on me. ⁴Don't we have the right to food and drink? ⁵Don't we have the right to take a believing wife along with us, as do the other apostles and the Lord's brothers and Cephas*a*? ⁶Or is it only I and Barnabas who lack the right to not work for a living?

⁷Who serves as a soldier at his own expense? Who plants a vineyard and does not eat its grapes? Who tends a flock and does not drink the milk? ⁸Do I say this merely on human authority? Doesn't the Law say the same thing? ⁹For it is written in the Law of Moses: "Do not muzzle an ox while it is treading out the grain."*b* Is it about oxen that God is concerned? ¹⁰Surely he says this for us, doesn't he? Yes, this was written for us, because whoever plows and threshes should be able to do so in the hope of sharing in the harvest. ¹¹If we have sown spiritual seed among you, is it too much if we reap a material harvest from you? ¹²If others have this right of support from you, shouldn't we have it all the more?

But we did not use this right. On the contrary, we put up with anything rather than hinder the gospel of Christ.

¹³Don't you know that those who serve in the temple get their food from the temple, and that those who serve at the altar share in what is offered on the altar? ¹⁴In the same way, the Lord has commanded that those who preach the gospel should receive their living from the gospel.

¹⁵But I have not used any of these rights. And I am not writing this in the hope that you will do such things for me, for I would rather die than allow anyone to deprive me of this boast. ¹⁶For when I preach the gospel, I cannot boast, since I am compelled to preach. Woe to me if I do not preach the gospel! ¹⁷If I preach voluntarily, I have a reward; if not voluntarily, I am simply discharging the trust committed to me. ¹⁸What then is my reward? Just this: that in preaching the gospel I may offer it free of charge, and so not make full use of my rights as a preacher of the gospel.

¹⁹Though I am free and belong to no one, I have made myself a slave to everyone, to win as many as possible. ²⁰To the Jews I became like a Jew, to win the Jews. To those under the law I became like one under the law (though I myself am not under the law), so as to win those under the law. ²¹To those not having the law I became like one not having the law (though I am not free from God's law but am under Christ's law), so as to win those not having the law. ²²To the weak I became weak, to win the weak. I have become all things to all people so that by all possible means I might save

*a* 5 That is, Peter    *b* 9 Deut. 25:4

some. 23I do all this for the sake of the gospel, that I may share in its blessings.

24Do you not know that in a race all the runners run, but only one gets the prize? Run in such a way as to get the prize. 25Everyone who competes in the games goes into strict training. They do it to get a crown that will not last, but we do it to get a crown that will last forever. 26Therefore I do not run like someone running aimlessly; I do not fight like a boxer beating the air. 27No, I strike a blow to my body and make it my slave so that after I have preached to others, I myself will not be disqualified for the prize.

10 For I do not want you to be ignorant of the fact, brothers and sisters, that our ancestors were all under the cloud and that they all passed through the sea. 2They were all baptized into Moses in the cloud and in the sea. 3They all ate the same spiritual food 4and drank the same spiritual drink; for they drank from the spiritual rock that accompanied them, and that rock was Christ. 5Nevertheless, God was not pleased with most of them; their bodies were scattered in the wilderness.

6Now these things occurred as examples to keep us from setting our hearts on evil things as they did. 7Do not be idolaters, as some of them were; as it is written: "The people sat down to eat and drink and got up to indulge in revelry."a 8We should not commit sexual immorality, as some of them did—and in one day twenty-three thousand of them died. 9We should not test Christ,b as some of them did—and were killed by snakes.

10And do not grumble, as some of them did—and were killed by the destroying angel.

11These things happened to them as examples and were written down as warnings for us, on whom the culmination of the ages has come. 12So, if you think you are standing firm, be careful that you don't fall! 13No temptationc has overtaken you except what is common to mankind. And God is faithful; he will not let you be temptedc beyond what you can bear. But when you are tempted,c he will also provide a way out so that you can endure it.

14Therefore, my dear friends, flee from idolatry. 15I speak to sensible people; judge for yourselves what I say. 16Is not the cup of thanksgiving for which we give thanks a participation in the blood of Christ? And is not the bread that we break a participation in the body of Christ? 17Because there is one loaf, we, who are many, are one body, for we all share the one loaf.

18Consider the people of Israel: Do not those who eat the sacrifices participate in the altar? 19Do I mean then that food sacrificed to an idol is anything, or that an idol is anything? 20No, but the sacrifices of pagans are offered to demons, not to God, and I do not want you to be participants with demons. 21You cannot drink the cup of the Lord and the cup of demons too; you cannot have a part in both the Lord's table and the table of demons. 22Are we trying to arouse the Lord's jealousy? Are we stronger than he?

23"I have the right to do anything," you say—but not everything is beneficial. "I have the right

---

a 7 Exodus 32:6    b 9 Some manuscripts test the Lord    c 13 The Greek for temptation and tempted can also mean testing and tested.

to do anything"—but not everything is constructive. ²⁴No one should seek their own good, but the good of others.

²⁵Eat anything sold in the meat market without raising questions of conscience, ²⁶for, "The earth is the Lord's, and everything in it."ᵃ

²⁷If an unbeliever invites you to a meal and you want to go, eat whatever is put before you without raising questions of conscience. ²⁸But if someone says to you, "This has been offered in sacrifice," then do not eat it, both for the sake of the one who told you and for the sake of conscience. ²⁹I am referring to the other person's conscience, not yours. For why is my freedom being judged by another's conscience? ³⁰If I take part in the meal with thankfulness, why am I denounced because of something I thank God for?

³¹So whether you eat or drink or whatever you do, do it all for the glory of God. ³²Do not cause anyone to stumble, whether Jews, Greeks or the church of God— ³³even as I try to please everyone in every way. For I am not seeking my own good but the good of many, so that they may

11 be saved. ¹Follow my example, as I follow the example of Christ.

²I praise you for remembering me in everything and for holding to the traditions just as I passed them on to you. ³But I want you to realize that the head of every man is Christ, and the head of the woman is man,ᵇ and the head of Christ

is God. ⁴Every man who prays or prophesies with his head covered dishonors his head. ⁵But every woman who prays or prophesies with her head uncovered dishonors her head—it is the same as having her head shaved. ⁶For if a woman does not cover her head, she might as well have her hair cut off; but if it is a disgrace for a woman to have her hair cut off or her head shaved, then she should cover her head.

⁷A man ought not to cover his head,ᶜ since he is the image and glory of God; but woman is the glory of man. ⁸For man did not come from woman, but woman from man; ⁹neither was man created for woman, but woman for man. ¹⁰It is for this reason that a woman ought to have authority over her ownᵈ head, because of the angels. ¹¹Nevertheless, in the Lord woman is not independent of man, nor is man independent of woman. ¹²For as woman came from man, so also man is born of woman. But everything comes from God.

¹³Judge for yourselves: Is it proper for a woman to pray to God with her head uncovered? ¹⁴Does not the very nature of things teach you that if a man has long hair, it is a disgrace to him, ¹⁵but that if a woman has long hair, it is her glory? For long hair is given to her as a covering. ¹⁶If anyone wants to be contentious about this, we have no other practice—nor do the churches of God.

¹⁷In the following directives I have no praise for you, for your

---

ᵃ 26 Psalm 24:1    ᵇ 3 Or of the wife is her husband    ᶜ 4-7 Or ⁴Every man who prays or prophesies with long hair dishonors his head. ⁵But every woman who prays or prophesies with no covering of hair dishonors her head—she is just like one of the "shorn women." ⁶If a woman has no covering, let her be for now with short hair; but since it is a disgrace for a woman to have her hair shorn or shaved, she should grow it again. ⁷A man ought not to have long hair    ᵈ 10 Or have a sign of authority on her meetings do more harm than good. <sup>18</sup>In the first place, I hear that when you come together as a church, there are divisions among you, and to some extent I believe it. <sup>19</sup>No doubt there have to be differences among you to show which of you have God's approval. <sup>20</sup>So then, when you come together, it is not the Lord's Supper you eat, <sup>21</sup>for when you are eating, some of you go ahead with your own private suppers. As a result, one person remains hungry and another gets drunk. <sup>22</sup>Don't you have homes to eat and drink in? Or do you despise the church of God by humiliating those who have nothing? What shall I say to you? Shall I praise you? Certainly not in this matter!

<sup>23</sup>For I received from the Lord what I also passed on to you: The Lord Jesus, on the night he was betrayed, took bread, <sup>24</sup>and when he had given thanks, he broke it and said, "This is my body, which is for you; do this in remembrance of me." <sup>25</sup>In the same way, after supper he took the cup, saying, "This cup is the new covenant in my blood; do this, whenever you drink it, in remembrance of me." <sup>26</sup>For whenever you eat this bread and drink this cup, you proclaim the Lord's death until he comes.

<sup>27</sup>So then, whoever eats the bread or drinks the cup of the Lord in an unworthy manner will be guilty of sinning against the body and blood of the Lord. <sup>28</sup>Everyone ought to examine themselves before they eat of the bread and drink from the cup. <sup>29</sup>For those who eat and drink without discerning the body of Christ eat and drink judgment on themselves. <sup>30</sup>That is why many among you are weak and sick, and a number of you have fallen asleep.

<sup>31</sup>But if we were more discerning with regard to ourselves, we would not come under such judgment. <sup>32</sup>Nevertheless, when we are judged in this way by the Lord, we are being disciplined so that we will not be finally condemned with the world.

<sup>33</sup>So then, my brothers and sisters, when you gather to eat, you should all eat together. <sup>34</sup>Anyone who is hungry should eat something at home, so that when you meet together it may not result in judgment.

And when I come I will give further directions.

12 Now about the gifts of the Spirit, brothers and sisters, I do not want you to be uninformed. <sup>2</sup>You know that when you were pagans, somehow or other you were influenced and led astray to mute idols. <sup>3</sup>Therefore I want you to know that no one who is speaking by the Spirit of God says, "Jesus be cursed," and no one can say, "Jesus is Lord," except by the Holy Spirit.

<sup>4</sup>There are different kinds of gifts, but the same Spirit distributes them. <sup>5</sup>There are different kinds of service, but the same Lord. <sup>6</sup>There are different kinds of working, but in all of them and in everyone it is the same God at work.

<sup>7</sup>Now to each one the manifestation of the Spirit is given for the common good. <sup>8</sup>To one there is given through the Spirit a message of wisdom, to another a message of knowledge by means of the same Spirit, <sup>9</sup>to another faith by the same Spirit, to another gifts of healing by that one Spirit, <sup>10</sup>to another miraculous powers, to another prophecy, to another distinguishing between spirits, to another speaking in dif-

ferent kinds of tongues,[a] and to still another the interpretation of tongues.[a] [11] All these are the work of one and the same Spirit, and he distributes them to each one, just as he determines.

[12] Just as a body, though one, has many parts, but all its many parts form one body, so it is with Christ. [13] For we were all baptized by[b] one Spirit so as to form one body—whether Jews or Gentiles, slave or free—and we were all given the one Spirit to drink. [14] Even so the body is not made up of one part but of many.

[15] Now if the foot should say, "Because I am not a hand, I do not belong to the body," it would not for that reason stop being part of the body. [16] And if the ear should say, "Because I am not an eye, I do not belong to the body," it would not for that reason stop being part of the body. [17] If the whole body were an eye, where would the sense of hearing be? If the whole body were an ear, where would the sense of smell be? [18] But in fact God has placed the parts in the body, every one of them, just as he wanted them to be. [19] If they were all one part, where would the body be? [20] As it is, there are many parts, but one body.

[21] The eye cannot say to the hand, "I don't need you!" And the head cannot say to the feet, "I don't need you!" [22] On the contrary, those parts of the body that seem to be weaker are indispensable, [23] and the parts that we think are less honorable we treat with special honor. And the parts that are unpresentable are treated with special modesty, [24] while our presentable parts need no special treatment. But

God has put the body together, giving greater honor to the parts that lacked it, [25] so that there should be no division in the body, but that its parts should have equal concern for each other. [26] If one part suffers, every part suffers with it; if one part is honored, every part rejoices with it.

[27] Now you are the body of Christ, and each one of you is a part of it. [28] And God has placed in the church first of all apostles, second prophets, third teachers, then miracles, then gifts of healing, of helping, of guidance, and of different kinds of tongues. [29] Are all apostles? Are all prophets? Are all teachers? Do all work miracles? [30] Do all have gifts of healing? Do all speak in tongues[c]? Do all interpret? [31] Now eagerly desire the greater gifts.

And yet I will show you the most excellent way.

13 If I speak in the tongues[d] of men or of angels, but do not have love, I am only a resounding gong or a clanging cymbal. [2] If I have the gift of prophecy and can fathom all mysteries and all knowledge, and if I have a faith that can move mountains, but do not have love, I am nothing. [3] If I give all I possess to the poor and give over my body to hardship that I may boast,[e] but do not have love, I gain nothing.

[4] Love is patient, love is kind. It does not envy, it does not boast, it is not proud. [5] It does not dishonor others, it is not self-seeking, it is not easily angered, it keeps no record of wrongs. [6] Love does not delight in evil but rejoices with the truth. [7] It always protects, always trusts, always hopes, always perseveres.

---

a 10 Or languages; also in verse 28    b 13 Or with; or in    c 30 Or other languages
d 1 Or languages    e 3 Some manuscripts body to the flames

8Love never fails. But where there are prophecies, they will cease; where there are tongues, they will be stilled; where there is knowledge, it will pass away. 9For we know in part and we prophesy in part, 10but when completeness comes, what is in part disappears. 11When I was a child, I talked like a child, I thought like a child, I reasoned like a child. When I became a man, I put the ways of childhood behind me. 12For now we see only a reflection as in a mirror; then we shall see face to face. Now I know in part; then I shall know fully, even as I am fully known.

13And now these three remain: faith, hope and love. But the greatest of these is love.

14 Follow the way of love and eagerly desire gifts of the Spirit, especially prophecy. 2For anyone who speaks in a tongue*a* does not speak to people but to God. Indeed, no one understands them; they utter mysteries by the Spirit. 3But the one who prophesies speaks to people for their strengthening, encouraging and comfort. 4Anyone who speaks in a tongue edifies themselves, but the one who prophesies edifies the church. 5I would like every one of you to speak in tongues,*b* but I would rather have you prophesy. The one who prophesies is greater than the one who speaks in tongues,*b* unless someone interprets, so that the church may be edified.

6Now, brothers and sisters, if I come to you and speak in tongues, what good will I be to you, unless I bring you some revelation or knowledge or prophecy or word of instruction? 7Even in the case of lifeless things that make sounds, such as the pipe or harp, how will anyone know what tune is being played unless there is a distinction in the notes? 8Again, if the trumpet does not sound a clear call, who will get ready for battle? 9So it is with you. Unless you speak intelligible words with your tongue, how will anyone know what you are saying? You will just be speaking into the air. 10Undoubtedly there are all sorts of languages in the world, yet none of them is without meaning. 11If then I do not grasp the meaning of what someone is saying, I am a foreigner to the speaker, and the speaker is a foreigner to me. 12So it is with you. Since you are eager for gifts of the Spirit, try to excel in those that build up the church.

13For this reason the one who speaks in a tongue should pray that they may interpret what they say. 14For if I pray in a tongue, my spirit prays, but my mind is unfruitful. 15So what shall I do? I will pray with my spirit, but I will also pray with my understanding; I will sing with my spirit, but I will also sing with my understanding. 16Otherwise when you are praising God in the Spirit, how can someone else, who is now put in the position of an inquirer,*c* say "Amen" to your thanksgiving, since they do not know what you are saying? 17You are giving thanks well enough, but no one else is edified.

18I thank God that I speak in tongues more than all of you. 19But in the church I would rather speak five intelligible words to instruct others than ten thousand words in a tongue.

---

*a 2* Or *in another language*; also in verses 4, 13, 14, 19, 26 and 27    *b 5* Or *in other languages*; also in verses 6, 18, 22, 23 and 39    *c 16* The Greek word for *inquirer* is a technical term for someone not fully initiated into a religion; also in verses 23 and 24.

20Brothers and sisters, stop thinking like children. In regard to evil be infants, but in your thinking be adults. 21In the Law it is written:

"With other tongues
    and through the lips of
        foreigners
I will speak to this people,
    but even then they will not
        listen to me,
            says the Lord."a

22Tongues, then, are a sign, not for believers but for unbelievers; prophecy, however, is not for unbelievers but for believers. 23So if the whole church comes together and everyone speaks in tongues, and inquirers or unbelievers come in, will they not say that you are out of your mind? 24But if an unbeliever or an inquirer comes in while everyone is prophesying, they are convicted of sin and are brought under judgment by all, 25as the secrets of their hearts are laid bare. So they will fall down and worship God, exclaiming, "God is really among you!"

26What then shall we say, brothers and sisters? When you come together, each of you has a hymn, or a word of instruction, a revelation, a tongue or an interpretation. Everything must be done so that the church may be built up. 27If anyone speaks in a tongue, two — or at the most three — should speak, one at a time, and someone must interpret. 28If there is no interpreter, the speaker should keep quiet in the church and speak to himself and to God.

29Two or three prophets should speak, and the others should weigh carefully what is said. 30And if a revelation comes to someone who is sitting down, the first speaker should stop. 31For you can all prophesy in turn so that everyone may be instructed and encouraged. 32The spirits of prophets are subject to the control of prophets. 33For God is not a God of disorder but of peace — as in all the congregations of the Lord's people.

34Womenb should remain silent in the churches. They are not allowed to speak, but must be in submission, as the law says. 35If they want to inquire about something, they should ask their own husbands at home; for it is disgraceful for a woman to speak in the church.c

36Or did the word of God originate with you? Or are you the only people it has reached? 37If anyone thinks they are a prophet or otherwise gifted by the Spirit, let them acknowledge that what I am writing to you is the Lord's command. 38But if anyone ignores this, they will themselves be ignored.d

39Therefore, my brothers and sisters, be eager to prophesy, and do not forbid speaking in tongues. 40But everything should be done in a fitting and orderly way.

15 Now, brothers and sisters, I want to remind you of the gospel I preached to you, which you received and on which you have taken your stand. 2By this gospel you are saved, if you hold firmly to the word I preached to you. Otherwise, you have believed in vain.

3For what I received I passed on to you as of first importancee: that Christ died for our sins according to the Scriptures, 4that he was bur-

---

a 21 Isaiah 28:11,12    b 33,34 Or peace. As in all the congregations of the Lord's people, 34women
c 34,35 In a few manuscripts these verses come after verse 40.    d 38 Some manuscripts But anyone who is ignorant of this will be ignorant    e 3 Or you at the first

ied, that he was raised on the third day according to the Scriptures, ⁵and that he appeared to Cephas,ᵃ and then to the Twelve. ⁶After that, he appeared to more than five hundred of the brothers and sisters at the same time, most of whom are still living, though some have fallen asleep. ⁷Then he appeared to James, then to all the apostles, ⁸and last of all he appeared to me also, as to one abnormally born.

⁹For I am the least of the apostles and do not even deserve to be called an apostle, because I persecuted the church of God. ¹⁰But by the grace of God I am what I am, and his grace to me was not without effect. No, I worked harder than all of them — yet not I, but the grace of God that was with me. ¹¹Whether, then, it is I or they, this is what we preach, and this is what you believed.

¹²But if it is preached that Christ has been raised from the dead, how can some of you say that there is no resurrection of the dead? ¹³If there is no resurrection of the dead, then not even Christ has been raised. ¹⁴And if Christ has not been raised, our preaching is useless and so is your faith. ¹⁵More than that, we are then found to be false witnesses about God, for we have testified about God that he raised Christ from the dead. But he did not raise him if in fact the dead are not raised. ¹⁶For if the dead are not raised, then Christ has not been raised either. ¹⁷And if Christ has not been raised, your faith is futile; you are still in your sins. ¹⁸Then those also who have fallen asleep in Christ are lost. ¹⁹If only for this life we have hope in Christ, we are of all people most to be pitied.

²⁰But Christ has indeed been raised from the dead, the firstfruits of those who have fallen asleep. ²¹For since death came through a man, the resurrection of the dead comes also through a man. ²²For as in Adam all die, so in Christ all will be made alive. ²³But each in turn: Christ, the firstfruits; then, when he comes, those who belong to him. ²⁴Then the end will come, when he hands over the kingdom to God the Father after he has destroyed all dominion, authority and power. ²⁵For he must reign until he has put all his enemies under his feet. ²⁶The last enemy to be destroyed is death. ²⁷For he "has put everything under his feet."ᵇ Now when it says that "everything" has been put under him, it is clear that this does not include God himself, who put everything under Christ. ²⁸When he has done this, then the Son himself will be made subject to him who put everything under him, so that God may be all in all.

²⁹Now if there is no resurrection, what will those do who are baptized for the dead? If the dead are not raised at all, why are people baptized for them? ³⁰And as for us, why do we endanger ourselves every hour? ³¹I face death every day — yes, just as surely as I boast about you in Christ Jesus our Lord. ³²If I fought wild beasts in Ephesus with no more than human hopes, what have I gained? If the dead are not raised,

"Let us eat and drink,
    for tomorrow we die."ᶜ

³³Do not be misled: "Bad company corrupts good character."ᵈ ³⁴Come back to your senses as you ought, and stop sinning; for there are

---

ᵃ 5 That is, Peter    ᵇ 27 Psalm 8:6    ᶜ 32 Isaiah 22:13    ᵈ 33 From the Greek poet Menander some who are ignorant of God—I say this to your shame.

35 But someone will ask, "How are the dead raised? With what kind of body will they come?" 36 How foolish! What you sow does not come to life unless it dies. 37 When you sow, you do not plant the body that will be, but just a seed, perhaps of wheat or of something else. 38 But God gives it a body as he has determined, and to each kind of seed he gives its own body. 39 Not all flesh is the same: People have one kind of flesh, animals have another, birds another and fish another. 40 There are also heavenly bodies and there are earthly bodies; but the splendor of the heavenly bodies is one kind, and the splendor of the earthly bodies is another. 41 The sun has one kind of splendor, the moon another and the stars another; and star differs from star in splendor.

42 So will it be with the resurrection of the dead. The body that is sown is perishable, it is raised imperishable; 43 it is sown in dishonor, it is raised in glory; it is sown in weakness, it is raised in power; 44 it is sown a natural body, it is raised a spiritual body.

If there is a natural body, there is also a spiritual body. 45 So it is written: "The first man Adam became a living being"[a]; the last Adam, a life-giving spirit. 46 The spiritual did not come first, but the natural, and after that the spiritual. 47 The first man was of the dust of the earth; the second man is of heaven. 48 As was the earthly man, so are those who are of the earth; and as is the heavenly man, so also are those who are of heaven. 49 And just as we have borne the image of the earthly man, so shall we[b] bear the image of the heavenly man.

50 I declare to you, brothers and sisters, that flesh and blood cannot inherit the kingdom of God, nor does the perishable inherit the imperishable. 51 Listen, I tell you a mystery: We will not all sleep, but we will all be changed— 52 in a flash, in the twinkling of an eye, at the last trumpet. For the trumpet will sound, the dead will be raised imperishable, and we will be changed. 53 For the perishable must clothe itself with the imperishable, and the mortal with immortality. 54 When the perishable has been clothed with the imperishable, and the mortal with immortality, then the saying that is written will come true: "Death has been swallowed up in victory."[c]

55 "Where, O death, is your victory?
     Where, O death, is your
          sting?"[d]

56 The sting of death is sin, and the power of sin is the law. 57 But thanks be to God! He gives us the victory through our Lord Jesus Christ.

58 Therefore, my dear brothers and sisters, stand firm. Let nothing move you. Always give yourselves fully to the work of the Lord, because you know that your labor in the Lord is not in vain.

16 Now about the collection for the Lord's people: Do what I told the Galatian churches to do. 2 On the first day of every week, each one of you should set aside a sum of money in keeping with your income, saving it up, so that when I come no collections will have to be made. 3 Then, when I arrive, I will give letters of introduction to the

[a] 45 Gen. 2:7   [b] 49 Some early manuscripts so let us   [c] 54 Isaiah 25:8   [d] 55 Hosea 13:14

men you approve and send them with your gift to Jerusalem. ⁴If it seems advisable for me to go also, they will accompany me.

⁵After I go through Macedonia, I will come to you — for I will be going through Macedonia. ⁶Perhaps I will stay with you for a while, or even spend the winter, so that you can help me on my journey, wherever I go. ⁷For I do not want to see you now and make only a passing visit; I hope to spend some time with you, if the Lord permits. ⁸But I will stay on at Ephesus until Pentecost, ⁹because a great door for effective work has opened to me, and there are many who oppose me.

¹⁰When Timothy comes, see to it that he has nothing to fear while he is with you, for he is carrying on the work of the Lord, just as I am. ¹¹No one, then, should treat him with contempt. Send him on his way in peace so that he may return to me. I am expecting him along with the brothers.

¹²Now about our brother Apollos: I strongly urged him to go to you with the brothers. He was quite unwilling to go now, but he will go when he has the opportunity.

¹³Be on your guard; stand firm in the faith; be courageous; be strong. ¹⁴Do everything in love.

¹⁵You know that the household of Stephanas were the first converts in Achaia, and they have devoted themselves to the service of the Lord's people. I urge you, brothers and sisters, ¹⁶to submit to such people and to everyone who joins in the work and labors at it. ¹⁷I was glad when Stephanas, Fortunatus and Achaicus arrived, because they have supplied what was lacking from you. ¹⁸For they refreshed my spirit and yours also. Such men deserve recognition.

¹⁹The churches in the province of Asia send you greetings. Aquila and Priscilla[a] greet you warmly in the Lord, and so does the church that meets at their house. ²⁰All the brothers and sisters here send you greetings. Greet one another with a holy kiss.

²¹I, Paul, write this greeting in my own hand.

²²If anyone does not love the Lord, let that person be cursed! Come, Lord[b]!

²³The grace of the Lord Jesus be with you.

²⁴My love to all of you in Christ Jesus. Amen.[c]

---

[a] 19 Greek Prisca, a variant of Priscilla    [b] 22 The Greek for Come, Lord reproduces an Aramaic expression (Marana tha) used by early Christians.    [c] 24 Some manuscripts do not have Amen.

# 2 CORINTHIANS

Paul's first letter to the believers in Corinth gives us a glimpse into his deeply personal and tumultuous relationship with this gathering of Jesus-followers. The letter we know as 2 Corinthians further reveals the triumphs and struggles that result when life in the present age meets up with the in-breaking reality of God's kingdom. Here we see Paul working to repair relationships, explain various changes in travel plans, make practical arrangements for collecting a gift for the struggling believers in Jerusalem, and directly confront challenges to his own leadership by the self-proclaimed "super-apostles."

In the four main parts of the letter, each introduced by a reference to a place, Paul envisions himself in different locations, recalling or anticipating his relationship with the Corinthians. The single theme running through these sections is that God will comfort us in all our troubles, and we will offer this comfort to each other. This models the life of Jesus himself, who suffered first and then was comforted. Like the crucified Messiah, we are weak, yet we live in God's power.

In the final section, however, Paul feels he has no choice but to make the Corinthians uncomfortable, to help them face their present condition. But he ends the letter hopefully, calling on them to rejoice in God's grace, love and fellowship.

1 Paul, an apostle of Christ Jesus by the will of God, and Timothy our brother,

To the church of God in Corinth, together with all his holy people throughout Achaia:

2 Grace and peace to you from God our Father and the Lord Jesus Christ.

3 Praise be to the God and Father of our Lord Jesus Christ, the Father of compassion and the God of all comfort, 4 who comforts us in all our troubles, so that we can comfort those in any trouble with the comfort we ourselves receive from God. 5 For just as we share abundantly in the sufferings of Christ, so also our comfort abounds through Christ. 6 If we are distressed, it is for your comfort and salvation; if we are comforted, it is for your comfort, which produces in you patient endurance of the same sufferings we suffer. 7 And our hope for you is firm, because we know that just as you share in our sufferings, so also you share in our comfort.

8 We do not want you to be uninformed, brothers and sisters,[a] about the troubles we experienced in the province of Asia. We were under great pressure, far beyond our ability to endure, so that we despaired of life itself. 9 Indeed, we felt we had received the sentence of death. But this happened that we might not rely on ourselves but on God, who raises the dead. 10 He has delivered us from such a deadly peril, and he will deliver us again. On him we

---

[a] 8 The Greek word for *brothers and sisters* (*adelphoi*) refers here to believers, both men and women, as part of God's family; also in 8:1; 13:11.

have set our hope that he will continue to deliver us, [11] as you help us by your prayers. Then many will give thanks on our behalf for the gracious favor granted us in answer to the prayers of many.

[12] Now this is our boast: Our conscience testifies that we have conducted ourselves in the world, and especially in our relations with you, with integrity and godly sincerity. We have done so, relying not on worldly wisdom but on God's grace. [13] For we do not write you anything you cannot read or understand. And I hope that, [14] as you have understood us in part, you will come to understand fully that you can boast of us just as we will boast of you in the day of the Lord Jesus.

[15] Because I was confident of this, I wanted to visit you first so that you might benefit twice. [16] I wanted to visit you on my way to Macedonia and to come back to you from Macedonia, and then to have you send me on my way to Judea. [17] Was I fickle when I intended to do this? Or do I make my plans in a worldly manner so that in the same breath I say both "Yes, yes" and "No, no"?

[18] But as surely as God is faithful, our message to you is not "Yes" and "No." [19] For the Son of God, Jesus Christ, who was preached among you by us—by me and Silas[b] and Timothy—was not "Yes" and "No," but in him it has always been "Yes." [20] For no matter how many promises God has made, they are "Yes" in Christ. And so through him the "Amen" is spoken by us to the glory of God. [21] Now it is God who makes both us and you stand firm in Christ. He anointed us, [22] set his seal of ownership on us, and put

his Spirit in our hearts as a deposit, guaranteeing what is to come.

[23] I call God as my witness—and I stake my life on it—that it was in order to spare you that I did not return to Corinth. [24] Not that we lord it over your faith, but we work with you for your joy, because it is by faith 2 you stand firm. [1] So I made up my mind that I would not make another painful visit to you. [2] For if I grieve you, who is left to make me glad but you whom I have grieved? [3] I wrote as I did, so that when I came I would not be distressed by those who should have made me rejoice. I had confidence in all of you, that you would all share my joy. [4] For I wrote you out of great distress and anguish of heart and with many tears, not to grieve you but to let you know the depth of my love for you.

[5] If anyone has caused grief, he has not so much grieved me as he has grieved all of you to some extent—not to put it too severely. [6] The punishment inflicted on him by the majority is sufficient. [7] Now instead, you ought to forgive and comfort him, so that he will not be overwhelmed by excessive sorrow. [8] I urge you, therefore, to reaffirm your love for him. [9] Another reason I wrote you was to see if you would stand the test and be obedient in everything. [10] Anyone you forgive, I also forgive. And what I have forgiven—if there was anything to forgive—I have forgiven in the sight of Christ for your sake, [11] in order that Satan might not outwit us. For we are not unaware of his schemes.

[12] Now when I went to Troas to preach the gospel of Christ and found that the Lord had opened a

---

door for me, [13] I still had no peace of mind, because I did not find my brother Titus there. So I said goodbye to them and went on to Macedonia.

[14] But thanks be to God, who always leads us as captives in Christ's triumphal procession and uses us to spread the aroma of the knowledge of him everywhere. [15] For we are to God the pleasing aroma of Christ among those who are being saved and those who are perishing. [16] To the one we are an aroma that brings death; to the other, an aroma that brings life. And who is equal to such a task? [17] Unlike so many, we do not peddle the word of God for profit. On the contrary, in Christ we speak before God with sincerity, as those sent from God.

3 Are we beginning to commend ourselves again? Or do we need, like some people, letters of recommendation to you or from you? [2] You yourselves are our letter, written on our hearts, known and read by everyone. [3] You show that you are a letter from Christ, the result of our ministry, written not with ink but with the Spirit of the living God, not on tablets of stone but on tablets of human hearts.

[4] Such confidence we have through Christ before God. [5] Not that we are competent in ourselves to claim anything for ourselves, but our competence comes from God. [6] He has made us competent as ministers of a new covenant—not of the letter but of the Spirit; for the letter kills, but the Spirit gives life.

[7] Now if the ministry that brought death, which was engraved in letters on stone, came with glory, so that the Israelites could not look steadily at the face of Moses be-cause of its glory, transitory though it was, [8] will not the ministry of the Spirit be even more glorious? [9] If the ministry that brought condemnation was glorious, how much more glorious is the ministry that brings righteousness! [10] For what was glorious has no glory now in comparison with the surpassing glory. [11] And if what was transitory came with glory, how much greater is the glory of that which lasts!

[12] Therefore, since we have such a hope, we are very bold. [13] We are not like Moses, who would put a veil over his face to prevent the Israelites from seeing the end of what was passing away. [14] But their minds were made dull, for to this day the same veil remains when the old covenant is read. It has not been removed, because only in Christ is it taken away. [15] Even to this day when Moses is read, a veil covers their hearts. [16] But whenever anyone turns to the Lord, the veil is taken away. [17] Now the Lord is the Spirit, and where the Spirit of the Lord is, there is freedom. [18] And we all, who with unveiled faces contemplate[a] the Lord's glory, are being transformed into his image with ever-increasing glory, which comes from the Lord, who is the Spirit.

4 Therefore, since through God's mercy we have this ministry, we do not lose heart. [2] Rather, we have renounced secret and shameful ways; we do not use deception, nor do we distort the word of God. On the contrary, by setting forth the truth plainly we commend ourselves to everyone's conscience in the sight of God. [3] And even if our gospel is veiled, it is veiled to those who are perishing. [4] The god of this age has blinded the minds of unbe-

a 18 Or reflect

lievers, so that they cannot see the light of the gospel that displays the glory of Christ, who is the image of God. ⁵For what we preach is not ourselves, but Jesus Christ as Lord, and ourselves as your servants for Jesus' sake. ⁶For God, who said, "Let light shine out of darkness,"ᵃ made his light shine in our hearts to give us the light of the knowledge of God's glory displayed in the face of Christ.

⁷But we have this treasure in jars of clay to show that this all-surpassing power is from God and not from us. ⁸We are hard pressed on every side, but not crushed; perplexed, but not in despair; ⁹persecuted, but not abandoned; struck down, but not destroyed. ¹⁰We always carry around in our body the death of Jesus, so that the life of Jesus may also be revealed in our body. ¹¹For we who are alive are always being given over to death for Jesus' sake, so that his life may also be revealed in our mortal body. ¹²So then, death is at work in us, but life is at work in you.

¹³It is written: "I believed; therefore I have spoken."ᵇ Since we have that same spirit ofᶜ faith, we also believe and therefore speak, ¹⁴because we know that the one who raised the Lord Jesus from the dead will also raise us with Jesus and present us with you to himself. ¹⁵All this is for your benefit, so that the grace that is reaching more and more people may cause thanksgiving to overflow to the glory of God.

¹⁶Therefore we do not lose heart. Though outwardly we are wasting away, yet inwardly we are being renewed day by day. ¹⁷For our light and momentary troubles are achieving for us an eternal glory that far outweighs them all. ¹⁸So we fix our eyes not on what is seen, but on what is unseen, since what is seen is temporary, but what is unseen is eternal.

5 For we know that if the earthly tent we live in is destroyed, we have a building from God, an eternal house in heaven, not built by human hands. ²Meanwhile we groan, longing to be clothed instead with our heavenly dwelling, ³because when we are clothed, we will not be found naked. ⁴For while we are in this tent, we groan and are burdened, because we do not wish to be unclothed but to be clothed instead with our heavenly dwelling, so that what is mortal may be swallowed up by life. ⁵Now the one who has fashioned us for this very purpose is God, who has given us the Spirit as a deposit, guaranteeing what is to come.

⁶Therefore we are always confident and know that as long as we are at home in the body we are away from the Lord. ⁷For we live by faith, not by sight. ⁸We are confident, I say, and would prefer to be away from the body and at home with the Lord. ⁹So we make it our goal to please him, whether we are at home in the body or away from it. ¹⁰For we must all appear before the judgment seat of Christ, so that each of us may receive what is due us for the things done while in the body, whether good or bad.

¹¹Since, then, we know what it is to fear the Lord, we try to persuade others. What we are is plain to God, and I hope it is also plain to your conscience. ¹²We are not trying to commend ourselves to you again, but are giving you an opportunity to take pride in us, so that you can

---

ᵃ 6 Gen. 1:3    ᵇ 13 Psalm 116:10 (see Septuagint)    ᶜ 13 Or Spirit-given answer those who take pride in what is seen rather than in what is in the heart. 13 If we are "out of our mind," as some say, it is for God; if we are in our right mind, it is for you. 14 For Christ's love compels us, because we are convinced that one died for all, and therefore all died. 15 And he died for all, that those who live should no longer live for themselves but for him who died for them and was raised again.

16 So from now on we regard no one from a worldly point of view. Though we once regarded Christ in this way, we do so no longer. 17 Therefore, if anyone is in Christ, the new creation has come:[a] The old has gone, the new is here! 18 All this is from God, who reconciled us to himself through Christ and gave us the ministry of reconciliation: 19 that God was reconciling the world to himself in Christ, not counting people's sins against them. And he has committed to us the message of reconciliation. 20 We are therefore Christ's ambassadors, as though God were making his appeal through us. We implore you on Christ's behalf: Be reconciled to God. 21 God made him who had no sin to be sin[b] for us, so that in him we might become the righteousness of God.

6 As God's co-workers we urge you not to receive God's grace in vain. 2 For he says,

"In the time of my favor I heard you,
   and in the day of salvation I helped you."[c]

I tell you, now is the time of God's favor, now is the day of salvation.

3 We put no stumbling block in anyone's path, so that our ministry will not be discredited. 4 Rather, as servants of God we commend ourselves in every way: in great endurance; in troubles, hardships and distresses; 5 in beatings, imprisonments and riots; in hard work, sleepless nights and hunger; 6 in purity, understanding, patience and kindness; in the Holy Spirit and in sincere love; 7 in truthful speech and in the power of God; with weapons of righteousness in the right hand and in the left; 8 through glory and dishonor, bad report and good report; genuine, yet regarded as impostors; 9 known, yet regarded as unknown; dying, and yet we live on; beaten, and yet not killed; 10 sorrowful, yet always rejoicing; poor, yet making many rich; having nothing, and yet possessing everything.

11 We have spoken freely to you, Corinthians, and opened wide our hearts to you. 12 We are not withholding our affection from you, but you are withholding yours from us. 13 As a fair exchange—I speak as to my children—open wide your hearts also.

14 Do not be yoked together with unbelievers. For what do righteousness and wickedness have in common? Or what fellowship can light have with darkness? 15 What harmony is there between Christ and Belial[d]? Or what does a believer have in common with an unbeliever? 16 What agreement is there between the temple of God and idols? For we are the temple of the living God. As God has said:

"I will live with them
   and walk among them,

---

a 17 Or Christ, that person is a new creation.   b 21 Or be a sin offering   c 2 Isaiah 49:8
d 15 Greek Beliar, a variant of Belial

and I will be their God,
and they will be my people."[a]

[17] Therefore,

"Come out from them
and be separate,
            says the Lord.
Touch no unclean thing,
and I will receive you."[b]

[18] And,

"I will be a Father to you,
and you will be my sons and
daughters,
            says the Lord Almighty."[c]

7 Therefore, since we have these promises, dear friends, let us purify ourselves from everything that contaminates body and spirit, perfecting holiness out of reverence for God.

[2] Make room for us in your hearts. We have wronged no one, we have corrupted no one, we have exploited no one. [3] I do not say this to condemn you; I have said before that you have such a place in our hearts that we would live or die with you. [4] I have spoken to you with great frankness; I take great pride in you. I am greatly encouraged; in all our troubles my joy knows no bounds.

[5] For when we came into Macedonia, we had no rest, but we were harassed at every turn—conflicts on the outside, fears within. [6] But God, who comforts the downcast, comforted us by the coming of Titus, [7] and not only by his coming but also by the comfort you had given him. He told us about your longing for me, your deep sorrow, your ardent concern for me, so that my joy was greater than ever.

[8] Even if I caused you sorrow by my letter, I do not regret it. Though I did regret it—I see that my letter hurt you, but only for a little while— [9] yet now I am happy, not because you were made sorry, but because your sorrow led you to repentance. For you became sorrowful as God intended and so were not harmed in any way by us. [10] Godly sorrow brings repentance that leads to salvation and leaves no regret, but worldly sorrow brings death. [11] See what this godly sorrow has produced in you: what earnestness, what eagerness to clear yourselves, what indignation, what alarm, what longing, what concern, what readiness to see justice done. At every point you have proved yourselves to be innocent in this matter. [12] So even though I wrote to you, it was neither on account of the one who did the wrong nor on account of the injured party, but rather that before God you could see for yourselves how devoted to us you are. [13] By all this we are encouraged.

In addition to our own encouragement, we were especially delighted to see how happy Titus was, because his spirit has been refreshed by all of you. [14] I had boasted to him about you, and you have not embarrassed me. But just as everything we said to you was true, so our boasting about you to Titus has proved to be true as well. [15] And his affection for you is all the greater when he remembers that you were all obedient, receiving him with fear and trembling. [16] I am glad I can have complete confidence in you.

---

*a 16* Lev. 26:12; Jer. 32:38; Ezek. 37:27    *b 17* Isaiah 52:11; Ezek. 20:34,41    *c 18* 2 Samuel 7:14; 7:8

8 And now, brothers and sisters, we want you to know about the grace that God has given the Macedonian churches. [2] In the midst of a very severe trial, their overflowing joy and their extreme poverty welled up in rich generosity. [3] For I testify that they gave as much as they were able, and even beyond their ability. Entirely on their own, [4] they urgently pleaded with us for the privilege of sharing in this service to the Lord's people. [5] And they exceeded our expectations: They gave themselves first of all to the Lord, and then by the will of God also to us. [6] So we urged Titus, just as he had earlier made a beginning, to bring also to completion this act of grace on your part. [7] But since you excel in everything — in faith, in speech, in knowledge, in complete earnestness and in the love we have kindled in you[a] — see that you also excel in this grace of giving.

[8] I am not commanding you, but I want to test the sincerity of your love by comparing it with the earnestness of others. [9] For you know the grace of our Lord Jesus Christ, that though he was rich, yet for your sake he became poor, so that you through his poverty might become rich.

[10] And here is my judgment about what is best for you in this matter. Last year you were the first not only to give but also to have the desire to do so. [11] Now finish the work, so that your eager willingness to do it may be matched by your completion of it, according to your means. [12] For if the willingness is there, the gift is acceptable according to what one has, not according to what one does not have.

[13] Our desire is not that others might be relieved while you are hard pressed, but that there might be equality. [14] At the present time your plenty will supply what they need, so that in turn their plenty will supply what you need. The goal is equality, [15] as it is written: "The one who gathered much did not have too much, and the one who gathered little did not have too little."[b]

[16] Thanks be to God, who put into the heart of Titus the same concern I have for you. [17] For Titus not only welcomed our appeal, but he is coming to you with much enthusiasm and on his own initiative. [18] And we are sending along with him the brother who is praised by all the churches for his service to the gospel. [19] What is more, he was chosen by the churches to accompany us as we carry the offering, which we administer in order to honor the Lord himself and to show our eagerness to help. [20] We want to avoid any criticism of the way we administer this liberal gift. [21] For we are taking pains to do what is right, not only in the eyes of the Lord but also in the eyes of man.

[22] In addition, we are sending with them our brother who has often proved to us in many ways that he is zealous, and now even more so because of his great confidence in you. [23] As for Titus, he is my partner and co-worker among you; as for our brothers, they are representatives of the churches and an honor to Christ. [24] Therefore show these men the proof of your love and the reason for our pride in you, so that the churches can see it.

9 There is no need for me to write to you about this service to the Lord's people. [2] For I know your

---

a 7 Some manuscripts *and in your love for us*    b 15 Exodus 16:18

eagerness to help, and I have been boasting about it to the Macedonians, telling them that since last year you in Achaia were ready to give; and your enthusiasm has stirred most of them to action. ³But I am sending the brothers in order that our boasting about you in this matter should not prove hollow, but that you may be ready, as I said you would be. ⁴For if any Macedonians come with me and find you unprepared, we—not to say anything about you—would be ashamed of having been so confident. ⁵So I thought it necessary to urge the brothers to visit you in advance and finish the arrangements for the generous gift you had promised. Then it will be ready as a generous gift, not as one grudgingly given.

⁶Remember this: Whoever sows sparingly will also reap sparingly, and whoever sows generously will also reap generously. ⁷Each of you should give what you have decided in your heart to give, not reluctantly or under compulsion, for God loves a cheerful giver. ⁸And God is able to bless you abundantly, so that in all things at all times, having all that you need, you will abound in every good work. ⁹As it is written:

"They have freely scattered their
    gifts to the poor;
  their righteousness endures
    forever."[a]

¹⁰Now he who supplies seed to the sower and bread for food will also supply and increase your store of seed and will enlarge the harvest of your righteousness. ¹¹You will be enriched in every way so that you can be generous on every occasion, and through us your generosity will result in thanksgiving to God.

¹²This service that you perform is not only supplying the needs of the Lord's people but is also overflowing in many expressions of thanks to God. ¹³Because of the service by which you have proved yourselves, others will praise God for the obedience that accompanies your confession of the gospel of Christ, and for your generosity in sharing with them and with everyone else. ¹⁴And in their prayers for you their hearts will go out to you, because of the surpassing grace God has given you. ¹⁵Thanks be to God for his indescribable gift!

10 By the humility and gentleness of Christ, I appeal to you—I, Paul, who am "timid" when face to face with you, but "bold" toward you when away! ²I beg you that when I come I may not have to be as bold as I expect to be toward some people who think that we live by the standards of this world. ³For though we live in the world, we do not wage war as the world does. ⁴The weapons we fight with are not the weapons of the world. On the contrary, they have divine power to demolish strongholds. ⁵We demolish arguments and every pretension that sets itself up against the knowledge of God, and we take captive every thought to make it obedient to Christ. ⁶And we will be ready to punish every act of disobedience, once your obedience is complete.

⁷You are judging by appearances.[b] If anyone is confident that they belong to Christ, they should consider again that we belong to Christ just as much as they do. ⁸So even if I boast somewhat freely about the authority the Lord gave us for

---

[a] 9 Psalm 112:9     [b] 7 Or *Look at the obvious facts*

building you up rather than tearing you down, I will not be ashamed of it. 9I do not want to seem to be trying to frighten you with my letters. 10For some say, "His letters are weighty and forceful, but in person he is unimpressive and his speaking amounts to nothing." 11Such people should realize that what we are in our letters when we are absent, we will be in our actions when we are present.

12We do not dare to classify or compare ourselves with some who commend themselves. When they measure themselves by themselves and compare themselves with themselves, they are not wise. 13We, however, will not boast beyond proper limits, but will confine our boasting to the sphere of service God himself has assigned to us, a sphere that also includes you. 14We are not going too far in our boasting, as would be the case if we had not come to you, for we did get as far as you with the gospel of Christ. 15Neither do we go beyond our limits by boasting of work done by others. Our hope is that, as your faith continues to grow, our sphere of activity among you will greatly expand, 16so that we can preach the gospel in the regions beyond you. For we do not want to boast about work already done in someone else's territory. 17But, "Let the one who boasts boast in the Lord."ᵃ 18For it is not the one who commends himself who is approved, but the one whom the Lord commends.

11 I hope you will put up with me in a little foolishness. Yes, please put up with me! 2I am jealous for you with a godly jealousy. I promised you to one husband,

to Christ, so that I might present you as a pure virgin to him. 3But I am afraid that just as Eve was deceived by the serpent's cunning, your minds may somehow be led astray from your sincere and pure devotion to Christ. 4For if someone comes to you and preaches a Jesus other than the Jesus we preached, or if you receive a different spirit from the Spirit you received, or a different gospel from the one you accepted, you put up with it easily enough.

5I do not think I am in the least inferior to those "super-apostles."ᵇ 6I may indeed be untrained as a speaker, but I do have knowledge. We have made this perfectly clear to you in every way. 7Was it a sin for me to lower myself in order to elevate you by preaching the gospel of God to you free of charge? 8I robbed other churches by receiving support from them so as to serve you. 9And when I was with you and needed something, I was not a burden to anyone, for the brothers who came from Macedonia supplied what I needed. I have kept myself from being a burden to you in any way, and will continue to do so. 10As surely as the truth of Christ is in me, nobody in the regions of Achaia will stop this boasting of mine. 11Why? Because I do not love you? God knows I do!

12And I will keep on doing what I am doing in order to cut the ground from under those who want an opportunity to be considered equal with us in the things they boast about. 13For such people are false apostles, deceitful workers, masquerading as apostles of Christ. 14And no wonder, for Satan himself masquerades as an angel of

ᵃ 17 Jer. 9:24   ᵇ 5 Or to the most eminent apostles

light. ¹⁵It is not surprising, then, if his servants also masquerade as servants of righteousness. Their end will be what their actions deserve.

¹⁶I repeat: Let no one take me for a fool. But if you do, then tolerate me just as you would a fool, so that I may do a little boasting. ¹⁷In this self-confident boasting I am not talking as the Lord would, but as a fool. ¹⁸Since many are boasting in the way the world does, I too will boast. ¹⁹You gladly put up with fools since you are so wise! ²⁰In fact, you even put up with anyone who enslaves you or exploits you or takes advantage of you or puts on airs or slaps you in the face. ²¹To my shame I admit that we were too weak for that!

Whatever anyone else dares to boast about—I am speaking as a fool—I also dare to boast about. ²²Are they Hebrews? So am I. Are they Israelites? So am I. Are they Abraham's descendants? So am I. ²³Are they servants of Christ? (I am out of my mind to talk like this.) I am more. I have worked much harder, been in prison more frequently, been flogged more severely, and been exposed to death again and again. ²⁴Five times I received from the Jews the forty lashes minus one. ²⁵Three times I was beaten with rods, once I was pelted with stones, three times I was shipwrecked, I spent a night and a day in the open sea, ²⁶I have been constantly on the move. I have been in danger from rivers, in danger from bandits, in danger from my fellow Jews, in danger from Gentiles; in danger in the city, in danger in the country, in danger at sea; and in danger from false believers. ²⁷I have labored and toiled and have often

gone without sleep; I have known hunger and thirst and have often gone without food; I have been cold and naked. ²⁸Besides everything else, I face daily the pressure of my concern for all the churches. ²⁹Who is weak, and I do not feel weak? Who is led into sin, and I do not inwardly burn?

³⁰If I must boast, I will boast of the things that show my weakness. ³¹The God and Father of the Lord Jesus, who is to be praised forever, knows that I am not lying. ³²In Damascus the governor under King Aretas had the city of the Damascenes guarded in order to arrest me. ³³But I was lowered in a basket from a window in the wall and slipped through his hands.

12 I must go on boasting. Although there is nothing to be gained, I will go on to visions and revelations from the Lord. ²I know a man in Christ who fourteen years ago was caught up to the third heaven. Whether it was in the body or out of the body I do not know—God knows. ³And I know that this man—whether in the body or apart from the body I do not know, but God knows— ⁴was caught up to paradise and heard inexpressible things, things that no one is permitted to tell. ⁵I will boast about a man like that, but I will not boast about myself, except about my weaknesses. ⁶Even if I should choose to boast, I would not be a fool, because I would be speaking the truth. But I refrain, so no one will think more of me than is warranted by what I do or say, ⁷or because of these surpassingly great revelations. Therefore, in order to keep me from becoming conceited, I was given a thorn in my flesh, a messenger of Satan, to torment me. ⁸Three times

I pleaded with the Lord to take it away from me. ⁹But he said to me, "My grace is sufficient for you, for my power is made perfect in weakness." Therefore I will boast all the more gladly about my weaknesses, so that Christ's power may rest on me. ¹⁰That is why, for Christ's sake, I delight in weaknesses, in insults, in hardships, in persecutions, in difficulties. For when I am weak, then I am strong.

¹¹I have made a fool of myself, but you drove me to it. I ought to have been commended by you, for I am not in the least inferior to the "super-apostles,"[a] even though I am nothing. ¹²I persevered in demonstrating among you the marks of a true apostle, including signs, wonders and miracles. ¹³How were you inferior to the other churches, except that I was never a burden to you? Forgive me this wrong!

¹⁴Now I am ready to visit you for the third time, and I will not be a burden to you, because what I want is not your possessions but you. After all, children should not have to save up for their parents, but parents for their children. ¹⁵So I will very gladly spend for you everything I have and expend myself as well. If I love you more, will you love me less? ¹⁶Be that as it may, I have not been a burden to you. Yet, crafty fellow that I am, I caught you by trickery! ¹⁷Did I exploit you through any of the men I sent to you? ¹⁸I urged Titus to go to you and I sent our brother with him. Titus did not exploit you, did he? Did we not walk in the same footsteps by the same Spirit?

¹⁹Have you been thinking all along that we have been defending ourselves to you? We have been speaking in the sight of God as those in Christ; and everything we do, dear friends, is for your strengthening. ²⁰For I am afraid that when I come I may not find you as I want you to be, and you may not find me as you want me to be. I fear that there may be discord, jealousy, fits of rage, selfish ambition, slander, gossip, arrogance and disorder. ²¹I am afraid that when I come again my God will humble me before you, and I will be grieved over many who have sinned earlier and have not repented of the impurity, sexual sin and debauchery in which they have indulged.

13 This will be my third visit to you. "Every matter must be established by the testimony of two or three witnesses."[b] ²I already gave you a warning when I was with you the second time. I now repeat it while absent: On my return I will not spare those who sinned earlier or any of the others, ³since you are demanding proof that Christ is speaking through me. He is not weak in dealing with you, but is powerful among you. ⁴For to be sure, he was crucified in weakness, yet he lives by God's power. Likewise, we are weak in him, yet by God's power we will live with him in our dealing with you.

⁵Examine yourselves to see whether you are in the faith; test yourselves. Do you not realize that Christ Jesus is in you—unless, of course, you fail the test? ⁶And I trust that you will discover that we have not failed the test. ⁷Now we pray to God that you will not do anything wrong—not so that people will see that we have stood the test but so that you will do what is right even though we may seem to

---

a 11 Or *the most eminent apostles*    b 1 Deut. 19:15

have failed. <sup>8</sup>For we cannot do anything against the truth, but only for the truth. <sup>9</sup>We are glad whenever we are weak but you are strong; and our prayer is that you may be fully restored. <sup>10</sup>This is why I write these things when I am absent, that when I come I may not have to be harsh in my use of authority — the authority the Lord gave me for building you up, not for tearing you down.

<sup>11</sup>Finally, brothers and sisters, rejoice! Strive for full restoration, encourage one another, be of one mind, live in peace. And the God of love and peace will be with you.

<sup>12</sup>Greet one another with a holy kiss. <sup>13</sup>All God's people here send their greetings.

<sup>14</sup>May the grace of the Lord Jesus Christ, and the love of God, and the fellowship of the Holy Spirit be with you all.

# GALATIANS

Galatia was a Roman province in central Asia Minor. Paul traveled here on each of the three journeys he made to spread the message about Jesus. The Galatians received both Paul and his gospel announcement warmly. But later some people Paul calls *agitators* came and challenged Paul's leadership as well as the foundation of his teaching. So Paul wrote to answer the threat to his status as an apostle and to reaffirm the core message that faith in the Messiah is the basis of membership in God's new community.

Paul doesn't open his letter by appealing to the apostles in Jerusalem. Instead, he insists that *the gospel I preached is not of human origin . . . rather, I received it by revelation from Jesus Christ.* Paul is compelled to share this revelation, and he notes that the other apostles support him.

Paul then proceeds to his main argument, which is that Gentiles who have become followers of Jesus do not need to be circumcised. The new worldwide family which had been promised to Abraham is created by faith in Messiah Jesus, not by keeping the Jewish law (Torah). The biblical story had been pointing to this all along.

But if following Torah is not the basis of the gospel, won't there be anarchy? Paul answers by describing what Spirit-empowered life looks like in the community of Messiah-followers. Paul closes by emphasizing the main theme of his letter once more: *Neither circumcision nor uncircumcision means anything; what counts is the new creation.*

---

1 Paul, an apostle — sent not from men nor by a man, but by Jesus Christ and God the Father, who raised him from the dead — ²and all the brothers and sisters[a] with me,

To the churches in Galatia:

³Grace and peace to you from God our Father and the Lord Jesus Christ, ⁴who gave himself for our sins to rescue us from the present evil age, according to the will of our God and Father, ⁵to whom be glory for ever and ever. Amen.

⁶I am astonished that you are so quickly deserting the one who called you to live in the grace of Christ and are turning to a different gospel — ⁷which is really no gospel at all. Evidently some people are throwing you into confusion and are trying to pervert the gospel of Christ. ⁸But even if we or an angel from heaven should preach a gospel other than the one we preached to you, let them be under God's curse! ⁹As we have already said, so now I say again: If anybody is preaching to you a gospel other than what you accepted, let them be under God's curse!

¹⁰Am I now trying to win the approval of human beings, or of God? Or am I trying to please people? If I were still trying to please people, I would not be a servant of Christ.

¹¹I want you to know, broth-

---

*a 2 The Greek word for brothers and sisters (adelphoi) refers here to believers, both men and women, as part of God's family; also in verse 11; and in 3:15; 4:12, 28, 31; 5:11, 13; 6:1, 18.*

ers and sisters, that the gospel I preached is not of human origin. ¹²I did not receive it from any man, nor was I taught it; rather, I received it by revelation from Jesus Christ.

¹³For you have heard of my previous way of life in Judaism, how intensely I persecuted the church of God and tried to destroy it. ¹⁴I was advancing in Judaism beyond many of my own age among my people and was extremely zealous for the traditions of my fathers. ¹⁵But when God, who set me apart from my mother's womb and called me by his grace, was pleased ¹⁶to reveal his Son in me so that I might preach him among the Gentiles, my immediate response was not to consult any human being. ¹⁷I did not go up to Jerusalem to see those who were apostles before I was, but I went into Arabia. Later I returned to Damascus.

¹⁸Then after three years, I went up to Jerusalem to get acquainted with Cephas[a] and stayed with him fifteen days. ¹⁹I saw none of the other apostles — only James, the Lord's brother. ²⁰I assure you before God that what I am writing you is no lie.

²¹Then I went to Syria and Cilicia. ²²I was personally unknown to the churches of Judea that are in Christ. ²³They only heard the report: "The man who formerly persecuted us is now preaching the faith he once tried to destroy." ²⁴And they praised God because of me.

2 Then after fourteen years, I went up again to Jerusalem, this time with Barnabas. I took Titus along also. ²I went in response to a revelation and, meeting privately with those esteemed as leaders, I presented to them the gospel that I preach among the Gentiles. I wanted to be sure I was not running and had not been running my race in vain. ³Yet not even Titus, who was with me, was compelled to be circumcised, even though he was a Greek. ⁴This matter arose because some false believers had infiltrated our ranks to spy on the freedom we have in Christ Jesus and to make us slaves. ⁵We did not give in to them for a moment, so that the truth of the gospel might be preserved for you.

⁶As for those who were held in high esteem — whatever they were makes no difference to me; God does not show favoritism — they added nothing to my message. ⁷On the contrary, they recognized that I had been entrusted with the task of preaching the gospel to the uncircumcised,[b] just as Peter had been to the circumcised.[c] ⁸For God, who was at work in Peter as an apostle to the circumcised, was also at work in me as an apostle to the Gentiles. ⁹James, Cephas[d] and John, those esteemed as pillars, gave me and Barnabas the right hand of fellowship when they recognized the grace given to me. They agreed that we should go to the Gentiles, and they to the circumcised. ¹⁰All they asked was that we should continue to remember the poor, the very thing I had been eager to do all along.

¹¹When Cephas came to Antioch, I opposed him to his face, because he stood condemned. ¹²For before certain men came from James, he used to eat with the Gentiles. But when they arrived, he began to draw back and separate himself

---

[a] 18 That is, Peter    [b] 7 That is, Gentiles    [c] 7 That is, Jews; also in verses 8 and 9    [d] 9 That is, Peter; also in verses 11 and 14

from the Gentiles because he was afraid of those who belonged to the circumcision group. ¹³The other Jews joined him in his hypocrisy, so that by their hypocrisy even Barnabas was led astray.

¹⁴When I saw that they were not acting in line with the truth of the gospel, I said to Cephas in front of them all, "You are a Jew, yet you live like a Gentile and not like a Jew. How is it, then, that you force Gentiles to follow Jewish customs?

¹⁵"We who are Jews by birth and not sinful ¹⁶know that a person is not justified by the works of the law, but by faith in Jesus Christ. So we, too, have put our faith in Christ Jesus that we may be justified by faith in[a] Christ and not by the works of the law, because by the works of the law no one will be justified.

¹⁷"But if, in seeking to be justified in Christ, we Jews find ourselves also among the sinners, doesn't that mean that Christ promotes sin? Absolutely not! ¹⁸If I rebuild what I destroyed, then I really would be a lawbreaker.

¹⁹"For through the law I died to the law so that I might live for God. ²⁰I have been crucified with Christ and I no longer live, but Christ lives in me. The life I now live in the body, I live by faith in the Son of God, who loved me and gave himself for me. ²¹I do not set aside the grace of God, for if righteousness could be gained through the law, Christ died for nothing!"[b]

3 You foolish Galatians! Who has bewitched you? Before your very eyes Jesus Christ was clearly portrayed as crucified. ²I would like to learn just one thing from you: Did you receive the Spirit by the works of the law, or by believing what you heard? ³Are you so foolish? After beginning by means of the Spirit, are you now trying to finish by means of the flesh?[c] ⁴Have you experienced[d] so much in vain—if it really was in vain? ⁵So again I ask, does God give you his Spirit and work miracles among you by the works of the law, or by your believing what you heard? ⁶So also Abraham "believed God, and it was credited to him as righteousness."[e]

⁷Understand, then, that those who have faith are children of Abraham. ⁸Scripture foresaw that God would justify the Gentiles by faith, and announced the gospel in advance to Abraham: "All nations will be blessed through you."[f] ⁹So those who rely on faith are blessed along with Abraham, the man of faith.

¹⁰For all who rely on the works of the law are under a curse, as it is written: "Cursed is everyone who does not continue to do everything written in the Book of the Law."[g] ¹¹Clearly no one who relies on the law is justified before God, because "the righteous will live by faith."[h] ¹²The law is not based on faith; on the contrary, it says, "The person who does these things will live by them."[i] ¹³Christ redeemed us from the curse of the law by becoming a curse for us, for it is written: "Cursed is everyone who is hung on a pole."[j] ¹⁴He redeemed us in order

---

[a] 16  Or *but through the faithfulness of . . . justified on the basis of the faithfulness of*     [b] 21  Some interpreters end the quotation after verse 14.     [c] 3  In contexts like this, the Greek word for *flesh (sarx)* refers to the sinful state of human beings, often presented as a power in opposition to the Spirit.     [d] 4  Or *suffered*     [e] 6  Gen. 15:6     [f] 8  Gen. 12:3; 18:18; 22:18     [g] 10  Deut. 27:26     [h] 11  Hab. 2:4     [i] 12  Lev. 18:5     [j] 13  Deut. 21:23

that the blessing given to Abraham might come to the Gentiles through Christ Jesus, so that by faith we might receive the promise of the Spirit.

[15] Brothers and sisters, let me take an example from everyday life. Just as no one can set aside or add to a human covenant that has been duly established, so it is in this case. [16] The promises were spoken to Abraham and to his seed. Scripture does not say "and to seeds," meaning many people, but "and to your seed,"[a] meaning one person, who is Christ. [17] What I mean is this: The law, introduced 430 years later, does not set aside the covenant previously established by God and thus do away with the promise. [18] For if the inheritance depends on the law, then it no longer depends on the promise; but God in his grace gave it to Abraham through a promise.

[19] Why, then, was the law given at all? It was added because of transgressions until the Seed to whom the promise referred had come. The law was given through angels and entrusted to a mediator. [20] A mediator, however, implies more than one party; but God is one.

[21] Is the law, therefore, opposed to the promises of God? Absolutely not! For if a law had been given that could impart life, then righteousness would certainly have come by the law. [22] But Scripture has locked up everything under the control of sin, so that what was promised, being given through faith in Jesus Christ, might be given to those who believe.

[23] Before the coming of this faith,[b] we were held in custody under the law, locked up until the faith that was to come would be revealed. [24] So the law was our guardian until Christ came that we might be justified by faith. [25] Now that this faith has come, we are no longer under a guardian.

[26] So in Christ Jesus you are all children of God through faith, [27] for all of you who were baptized into Christ have clothed yourselves with Christ. [28] There is neither Jew nor Gentile, neither slave nor free, nor is there male and female, for you are all one in Christ Jesus. [29] If you belong to Christ, then you are Abraham's seed, and heirs according to the promise.

4 What I am saying is that as long as an heir is underage, he is no different from a slave, although he owns the whole estate. [2] The heir is subject to guardians and trustees until the time set by his father. [3] So also, when we were underage, we were in slavery under the elemental spiritual forces[c] of the world. [4] But when the set time had fully come, God sent his Son, born of a woman, born under the law, [5] to redeem those under the law, that we might receive adoption to sonship.[d] [6] Because you are his sons, God sent the Spirit of his Son into our hearts, the Spirit who calls out, *"Abba,*[e] Father." [7] So you are no longer a slave, but God's child; and since you are his child, God has made you also an heir.

[8] Formerly, when you did not know God, you were slaves to those who by nature are not gods. [9] But

now that you know God — or rather are known by God — how is it that you are turning back to those weak and miserable forces[a]? Do you wish to be enslaved by them all over again? [10] You are observing special days and months and seasons and years! [11] I fear for you, that somehow I have wasted my efforts on you.

[12] I plead with you, brothers and sisters, become like me, for I became like you. You did me no wrong. [13] As you know, it was because of an illness that I first preached the gospel to you, [14] and even though my illness was a trial to you, you did not treat me with contempt or scorn. Instead, you welcomed me as if I were an angel of God, as if I were Christ Jesus himself. [15] Where, then, is your blessing of me now? I can testify that, if you could have done so, you would have torn out your eyes and given them to me. [16] Have I now become your enemy by telling you the truth?

[17] Those people are zealous to win you over, but for no good. What they want is to alienate you from us, so that you may have zeal for them. [18] It is fine to be zealous, provided the purpose is good, and to be so always, not just when I am with you. [19] My dear children, for whom I am again in the pains of childbirth until Christ is formed in you, [20] how I wish I could be with you now and change my tone, because I am perplexed about you!

[21] Tell me, you who want to be under the law, are you not aware of what the law says? [22] For it is written that Abraham had two sons, one by the slave woman and the other by the free woman. [23] His son by the slave woman was born according to the flesh, but his son by the free woman was born as the result of a divine promise.

[24] These things are being taken figuratively: The women represent two covenants. One covenant is from Mount Sinai and bears children who are to be slaves: This is Hagar. [25] Now Hagar stands for Mount Sinai in Arabia and corresponds to the present city of Jerusalem, because she is in slavery with her children. [26] But the Jerusalem that is above is free, and she is our mother. [27] For it is written:

> "Be glad, barren woman,
>     you who never bore a child;
> shout for joy and cry aloud,
>     you who were never in labor;
> because more are the children of
>         the desolate woman
>     than of her who has a
>         husband."[b]

[28] Now you, brothers and sisters, like Isaac, are children of promise. [29] At that time the son born according to the flesh persecuted the son born by the power of the Spirit. It is the same now. [30] But what does Scripture say? "Get rid of the slave woman and her son, for the slave woman's son will never share in the inheritance with the free woman's son."[c] [31] Therefore, brothers and sisters, we are not children of the slave woman, but of the free woman.

5 It is for freedom that Christ has set us free. Stand firm, then, and do not let yourselves be burdened again by a yoke of slavery.

[2] Mark my words! I, Paul, tell you that if you let yourselves be circumcised, Christ will be of no value to you at all. [3] Again I declare to every man who lets himself be circum-

---

[a] 9 Or *principles*   [b] 27 Isaiah 54:1   [c] 30 Gen. 21:10

cised that he is obligated to obey the whole law. ⁴You who are trying to be justified by the law have been alienated from Christ; you have fallen away from grace. ⁵For through the Spirit we eagerly await by faith the righteousness for which we hope. ⁶For in Christ Jesus neither circumcision nor uncircumcision has any value. The only thing that counts is faith expressing itself through love.

⁷You were running a good race. Who cut in on you to keep you from obeying the truth? ⁸That kind of persuasion does not come from the one who calls you. ⁹"A little yeast works through the whole batch of dough." ¹⁰I am confident in the Lord that you will take no other view. The one who is throwing you into confusion, whoever that may be, will have to pay the penalty. ¹¹Brothers and sisters, if I am still preaching circumcision, why am I still being persecuted? In that case the offense of the cross has been abolished. ¹²As for those agitators, I wish they would go the whole way and emasculate themselves!

¹³You, my brothers and sisters, were called to be free. But do not use your freedom to indulge the flesh[a]; rather, serve one another humbly in love. ¹⁴For the entire law is fulfilled in keeping this one command: "Love your neighbor as yourself."[b] ¹⁵If you bite and devour each other, watch out or you will be destroyed by each other.

¹⁶So I say, walk by the Spirit, and you will not gratify the desires of the flesh. ¹⁷For the flesh desires what is contrary to the Spirit, and the Spirit what is contrary to the flesh. They are in conflict with each other, so that you are not to do whatever[c] you want. ¹⁸But if you are led by the Spirit, you are not under the law.

¹⁹The acts of the flesh are obvious: sexual immorality, impurity and debauchery; ²⁰idolatry and witchcraft; hatred, discord, jealousy, fits of rage, selfish ambition, dissensions, factions ²¹and envy; drunkenness, orgies, and the like. I warn you, as I did before, that those who live like this will not inherit the kingdom of God.

²²But the fruit of the Spirit is love, joy, peace, forbearance, kindness, goodness, faithfulness, ²³gentleness and self-control. Against such things there is no law. ²⁴Those who belong to Christ Jesus have crucified the flesh with its passions and desires. ²⁵Since we live by the Spirit, let us keep in step with the Spirit. ²⁶Let us not become conceited, provoking and envying each other.

6 Brothers and sisters, if someone is caught in a sin, you who live by the Spirit should restore that person gently. But watch yourselves, or you also may be tempted. ²Carry each other's burdens, and in this way you will fulfill the law of Christ. ³If anyone thinks they are something when they are not, they deceive themselves. ⁴Each one should test their own actions. Then they can take pride in themselves alone, without comparing themselves to someone else, ⁵for each one should carry their own load. ⁶Nevertheless, the one who receives instruction in the word should share all good things with their instructor.

---

[a] 13 In contexts like this, the Greek word for *flesh* (*sarx*) refers to the sinful state of human beings, often presented as a power in opposition to the Spirit; also in verses 16, 17, 19 and 24; and in 6:8.    [b] 14 Lev. 19:18    [c] 17 Or *you do not do what*

⁷Do not be deceived: God cannot be mocked. A man reaps what he sows. ⁸Whoever sows to please their flesh, from the flesh will reap destruction; whoever sows to please the Spirit, from the Spirit will reap eternal life. ⁹Let us not become weary in doing good, for at the proper time we will reap a harvest if we do not give up. ¹⁰Therefore, as we have opportunity, let us do good to all people, especially to those who belong to the family of believers.

¹¹See what large letters I use as I write to you with my own hand!

¹²Those who want to impress people by means of the flesh are trying to compel you to be circumcised. The only reason they do this is to avoid being persecuted for the cross of Christ. ¹³Not even those who are circumcised keep the law, yet they want you to be circumcised that they may boast about your circumcision in the flesh. ¹⁴May I never boast except in the cross of our Lord Jesus Christ, through which[a] the world has been crucified to me, and I to the world. ¹⁵Neither circumcision nor uncircumcision means anything; what counts is the new creation. ¹⁶Peace and mercy to all who follow this rule — to[b] the Israel of God.

¹⁷From now on, let no one cause me trouble, for I bear on my body the marks of Jesus.

¹⁸The grace of our Lord Jesus Christ be with your spirit, brothers and sisters. Amen.

---

a 14 Or whom    b 16 Or rule and to

# EPHESIANS

Traditionally named Ephesians, this letter may not actually have been written to the believers in Ephesus. Some of the best early copies of the letter don't include the phrase *in Ephesus* in the greeting. While Paul spent two years in Ephesus, this letter appears to address people Paul has never met.

Paul here presents a two-fold pattern, first explaining the new identity believers have in Christ and then bringing out the implications for their new way of life. God has brought everything together under the rule of the Messiah, exalting Jesus above all things. Paul echoes a phrase from Psalm 8—*God placed all things under his feet*—to show that Jesus is the truly human one. Jesus fulfills the original human calling to rule over the creation properly. Jews and Gentiles have been brought together into one body, with Jesus at the head. God is now creating *one new humanity* from all over the world through the reconciling work of the Messiah.

This means Jesus-followers must give up their former way of life and practice purity in daily living and integrity in their relationships. The reciprocal responsibilities of those in and under authority are used as key examples of the new kinds of relationships God is expecting. Paul cautions his readers that they are entering a spiritual battle. They must arm themselves with all the resources God has provided, until the Messiah brings *unity to all things in heaven and on earth.*

---

1 Paul, an apostle of Christ Jesus by the will of God,

To God's holy people in Ephesus,[a] the faithful in Christ Jesus:

²Grace and peace to you from God our Father and the Lord Jesus Christ.

³Praise be to the God and Father of our Lord Jesus Christ, who has blessed us in the heavenly realms with every spiritual blessing in Christ. ⁴For he chose us in him before the creation of the world to be holy and blameless in his sight. In love ⁵he[b] predestined us for adoption to sonship[c] through Jesus Christ, in accordance with his pleasure and will— ⁶to the praise of his glorious grace, which he has freely given us in the One he loves. ⁷In him we have redemption through his blood, the forgiveness of sins, in accordance with the riches of God's grace ⁸that he lavished on us. With all wisdom and understanding, ⁹he[d] made known to us the mystery of his will according to his good pleasure, which he purposed in Christ, ¹⁰to be put into effect when the times reach their fulfillment—to bring unity to all things in heaven and on earth under Christ.

¹¹In him we were also chosen,[e] having been predestined according to the plan of him who works

---

[a] 1 Some early manuscripts do not have *in Ephesus.* [b] 4,5 Or *sight in love.* [sup]5He[/sup] [c] 5 The Greek word for *adoption to sonship* is a legal term referring to the full legal standing of an adopted male heir in Roman culture. [d] 8,9 Or *us with all wisdom and understanding.* [sup]9And[/sup] he [e] 11 Or *were made heirs*

out everything in conformity with the purpose of his will, [12]in order that we, who were the first to put our hope in Christ, might be for the praise of his glory. [13]And you also were included in Christ when you heard the message of truth, the gospel of your salvation. When you believed, you were marked in him with a seal, the promised Holy Spirit, [14]who is a deposit guaranteeing our inheritance until the redemption of those who are God's possession—to the praise of his glory.

[15]For this reason, ever since I heard about your faith in the Lord Jesus and your love for all God's people, [16]I have not stopped giving thanks for you, remembering you in my prayers. [17]I keep asking that the God of our Lord Jesus Christ, the glorious Father, may give you the Spirit[a] of wisdom and revelation, so that you may know him better. [18]I pray that the eyes of your heart may be enlightened in order that you may know the hope to which he has called you, the riches of his glorious inheritance in his holy people, [19]and his incomparably great power for us who believe. That power is the same as the mighty strength [20]he exerted when he raised Christ from the dead and seated him at his right hand in the heavenly realms, [21]far above all rule and authority, power and dominion, and every name that is invoked, not only in the present age but also in the one to come. [22]And God placed all things under his feet and appointed him to be head over everything for the church, [23]which is his body, the fullness of him who fills everything in every way.

2 As for you, you were dead in your transgressions and sins, [2]in which you used to live when you followed the ways of this world and of the ruler of the kingdom of the air, the spirit who is now at work in those who are disobedient. [3]All of us also lived among them at one time, gratifying the cravings of our flesh[b] and following its desires and thoughts. Like the rest, we were by nature deserving of wrath. [4]But because of his great love for us, God, who is rich in mercy, made us alive with Christ even when we were dead in transgressions—it is by grace you have been saved. [5]And God raised us up with Christ and seated us with him in the heavenly realms in Christ Jesus, [7]in order that in the coming ages he might show the incomparable riches of his grace, expressed in his kindness to us in Christ Jesus. [8]For it is by grace you have been saved, through faith—and this is not from yourselves, it is the gift of God— [9]not by works, so that no one can boast. [10]For we are God's handiwork, created in Christ Jesus to do good works, which God prepared in advance for us to do.

[11]Therefore, remember that formerly you who are Gentiles by birth and called "uncircumcised" by those who call themselves "the circumcision" (which is done in the body by human hands)— [12]remember that at that time you were separate from Christ, excluded from citizenship in Israel and foreigners to the covenants of the promise, without hope and without God in the world. [13]But now in Christ Jesus you who once were far away have been brought near by the blood of Christ.

---

*a* 17 Or *a spirit*   *b* 3 In contexts like this, the Greek word for *flesh* (*sarx*) refers to the sinful state of human beings, often presented as a power in opposition to the Spirit.

¹⁴For he himself is our peace, who has made the two groups one and has destroyed the barrier, the dividing wall of hostility, ¹⁵by setting aside in his flesh the law with its commands and regulations. His purpose was to create in himself one new humanity out of the two, thus making peace, ¹⁶and in one body to reconcile both of them to God through the cross, by which he put to death their hostility. ¹⁷He came and preached peace to you who were far away and peace to those who were near. ¹⁸For through him we both have access to the Father by one Spirit.

¹⁹Consequently, you are no longer foreigners and strangers, but fellow citizens with God's people and also members of his household, ²⁰built on the foundation of the apostles and prophets, with Christ Jesus himself as the chief cornerstone. ²¹In him the whole building is joined together and rises to become a holy temple in the Lord. ²²And in him you too are being built together to become a dwelling in which God lives by his Spirit.

3 For this reason I, Paul, the prisoner of Christ Jesus for the sake of you Gentiles — ²Surely you have heard about the administration of God's grace that was given to me for you, ³that is, the mystery made known to me by revelation, as I have already written briefly. ⁴In reading this, then, you will be able to understand my insight into the mystery of Christ, ⁵which was not made known to people in other generations as it has now been revealed by the Spirit to God's holy apostles and prophets. ⁶This mystery is that through

the gospel the Gentiles are heirs together with Israel, members together of one body, and sharers together in the promise in Christ Jesus.

⁷I became a servant of this gospel by the gift of God's grace given me through the working of his power. ⁸Although I am less than the least of all the Lord's people, this grace was given me: to preach to the Gentiles the boundless riches of Christ, ⁹and to make plain to everyone the administration of this mystery, which for ages past was kept hidden in God, who created all things. ¹⁰His intent was that now, through the church, the manifold wisdom of God should be made known to the rulers and authorities in the heavenly realms, ¹¹according to his eternal purpose that he accomplished in Christ Jesus our Lord. ¹²In him and through faith in him we may approach God with freedom and confidence. ¹³I ask you, therefore, not to be discouraged because of my sufferings for you, which are your glory.

¹⁴For this reason I kneel before the Father, ¹⁵from whom every family[a] in heaven and on earth derives its name. ¹⁶I pray that out of his glorious riches he may strengthen you with power through his Spirit in your inner being, ¹⁷so that Christ may dwell in your hearts through faith. And I pray that you, being rooted and established in love, ¹⁸may have power, together with all the Lord's holy people, to grasp how wide and long and high and deep is the love of Christ, ¹⁹and to know this love that surpasses knowledge — that you may be filled to the measure of all the fullness of God.

²⁰Now to him who is able to do immeasurably more than all we ask

---

a 15 The Greek for *family* (*patria*) is derived from the Greek for *father* (*pater*).

or imagine, according to his power that is at work within us, ²¹to him be glory in the church and in Christ Jesus throughout all generations, for ever and ever! Amen.

4 As a prisoner for the Lord, then, I urge you to live a life worthy of the calling you have received. ²Be completely humble and gentle; be patient, bearing with one another in love. ³Make every effort to keep the unity of the Spirit through the bond of peace. ⁴There is one body and one Spirit, just as you were called to one hope when you were called; ⁵one Lord, one faith, one baptism; ⁶one God and Father of all, who is over all and through all and in all.

⁷But to each one of us grace has been given as Christ apportioned it. ⁸This is why it ᵃ says:

"When he ascended on high,
  he took many captives
  and gave gifts to his people."ᵇ

⁹(What does "he ascended" mean except that he also descended to the lower, earthly regionsᶜ? ¹⁰He who descended is the very one who ascended higher than all the heavens, in order to fill the whole universe.) ¹¹So Christ himself gave the apostles, the prophets, the evangelists, the pastors and teachers, ¹²to equip his people for works of service, so that the body of Christ may be built up ¹³until we all reach unity in the faith and in the knowledge of the Son of God and become mature, attaining to the whole measure of the fullness of Christ.

¹⁴Then we will no longer be infants, tossed back and forth by the waves, and blown here and there by every wind of teaching and by the cunning and craftiness of people in their deceitful scheming. ¹⁵Instead, speaking the truth in love, we will grow to become in every respect the mature body of him who is the head, that is, Christ. ¹⁶From him the whole body, joined and held together by every supporting ligament, grows and builds itself up in love, as each part does its work.

¹⁷So I tell you this, and insist on it in the Lord, that you must no longer live as the Gentiles do, in the futility of their thinking. ¹⁸They are darkened in their understanding and separated from the life of God because of the ignorance that is in them due to the hardening of their hearts. ¹⁹Having lost all sensitivity, they have given themselves over to sensuality so as to indulge in every kind of impurity, and they are full of greed.

²⁰That, however, is not the way of life you learned ²¹when you heard about Christ and were taught in him in accordance with the truth that is in Jesus. ²²You were taught, with regard to your former way of life, to put off your old self, which is being corrupted by its deceitful desires; ²³to be made new in the attitude of your minds; ²⁴and to put on the new self, created to be like God in true righteousness and holiness.

²⁵Therefore each of you must put off falsehood and speak truthfully to your neighbor, for we are all members of one body. ²⁶"In your anger do not sin"ᵈ: Do not let the sun go down while you are still angry, ²⁷and do not give the devil a foothold. ²⁸Anyone who has been stealing must steal no longer, but

---

ᵃ 8 Or God     ᵇ 8 Psalm 68:18     ᶜ 9 Or the depths of the earth     ᵈ 26 Psalm 4:4 (see Septuagint) must work, doing something useful with their own hands, that they may have something to share with those in need.

²⁹Do not let any unwholesome talk come out of your mouths, but only what is helpful for building others up according to their needs, that it may benefit those who listen. ³⁰And do not grieve the Holy Spirit of God, with whom you were sealed for the day of redemption. ³¹Get rid of all bitterness, rage and anger, brawling and slander, along with every form of malice. ³²Be kind and compassionate to one another, forgiving each other, just as in Christ

5 God forgave you. ¹Follow God's example, therefore, as dearly loved children ²and walk in the way of love, just as Christ loved us and gave himself up for us as a fragrant offering and sacrifice to God.

³But among you there must not be even a hint of sexual immorality, or of any kind of impurity, or of greed, because these are improper for God's holy people. ⁴Nor should there be obscenity, foolish talk or coarse joking, which are out of place, but rather thanksgiving. ⁵For of this you can be sure: No immoral, impure or greedy person— such a person is an idolater— has any inheritance in the kingdom of Christ and of God.ᵃ ⁶Let no one deceive you with empty words, for because of such things God's wrath comes on those who are disobedient. ⁷Therefore do not be partners with them.

⁸For you were once darkness, but now you are light in the Lord. Live as children of light ⁹(for the fruit of the light consists in all goodness, righteousness and truth) ¹⁰and find

out what pleases the Lord. ¹¹Have nothing to do with the fruitless deeds of darkness, but rather expose them. ¹²It is shameful even to mention what the disobedient do in secret. ¹³But everything exposed by the light becomes visible—and everything that is illuminated becomes a light. ¹⁴This is why it is said:

"Wake up, sleeper,
    rise from the dead,
    and Christ will shine on you."

¹⁵Be very careful, then, how you live—not as unwise but as wise, ¹⁶making the most of every opportunity, because the days are evil. ¹⁷Therefore do not be foolish, but understand what the Lord's will is. ¹⁸Do not get drunk on wine, which leads to debauchery. Instead, be filled with the Spirit, ¹⁹speaking to one another with psalms, hymns, and songs from the Spirit. Sing and make music from your heart to the Lord, ²⁰always giving thanks to God the Father for everything, in the name of our Lord Jesus Christ.

²¹Submit to one another out of reverence for Christ.

²²Wives, submit yourselves to your own husbands as you do to the Lord. ²³For the husband is the head of the wife as Christ is the head of the church, his body, of which he is the Savior. ²⁴Now as the church submits to Christ, so also wives should submit to their husbands in everything.

²⁵Husbands, love your wives, just as Christ loved the church and gave himself up for her ²⁶to make her holy, cleansingᵇ her by the washing with water through the word, ²⁷and to present her to himself as a radiant church, without stain or

ᵃ 5 Or kingdom of the Messiah and God    ᵇ 26 Or having cleansed wrinkle or any other blemish, but holy and blameless. <sup>28</sup>In this same way, husbands ought to love their wives as their own bodies. He who loves his wife loves himself. <sup>29</sup>After all, no one ever hated their own body, but they feed and care for their body, just as Christ does the church— <sup>30</sup>for we are members of his body. <sup>31</sup>"For this reason a man will leave his father and mother and be united to his wife, and the two will become one flesh."[a] <sup>32</sup>This is a profound mystery—but I am talking about Christ and the church. <sup>33</sup>However, each one of you also must love his wife as he loves himself, and the wife must respect her husband.

6 Children, obey your parents in the Lord, for this is right. <sup>2</sup>"Honor your father and mother"—which is the first commandment with a promise— <sup>3</sup>"so that it may go well with you and that you may enjoy long life on the earth."[b]

<sup>4</sup>Fathers,[c] do not exasperate your children; instead, bring them up in the training and instruction of the Lord.

<sup>5</sup>Slaves, obey your earthly masters with respect and fear, and with sincerity of heart, just as you would obey Christ. <sup>6</sup>Obey them not only to win their favor when their eye is on you, but as slaves of Christ, doing the will of God from your heart. <sup>7</sup>Serve wholeheartedly, as if you were serving the Lord, not people, <sup>8</sup>because you know that the Lord will reward each one for whatever good they do, whether they are slave or free.

<sup>9</sup>And masters, treat your slaves in the same way. Do not threaten them, since you know that he who is both their Master and yours is in

heaven, and there is no favoritism with him.

<sup>10</sup>Finally, be strong in the Lord and in his mighty power. <sup>11</sup>Put on the full armor of God, so that you can take your stand against the devil's schemes. <sup>12</sup>For our struggle is not against flesh and blood, but against the rulers, against the authorities, against the powers of this dark world and against the spiritual forces of evil in the heavenly realms. <sup>13</sup>Therefore put on the full armor of God, so that when the day of evil comes, you may be able to stand your ground, and after you have done everything, to stand. <sup>14</sup>Stand firm then, with the belt of truth buckled around your waist, with the breastplate of righteousness in place, <sup>15</sup>and with your feet fitted with the readiness that comes from the gospel of peace. <sup>16</sup>In addition to all this, take up the shield of faith, with which you can extinguish all the flaming arrows of the evil one. <sup>17</sup>Take the helmet of salvation and the sword of the Spirit, which is the word of God.

<sup>18</sup>And pray in the Spirit on all occasions with all kinds of prayers and requests. With this in mind, be alert and always keep on praying for all the Lord's people. <sup>19</sup>Pray also for me, that whenever I speak, words may be given me so that I will fearlessly make known the mystery of the gospel, <sup>20</sup>for which I am an ambassador in chains. Pray that I may declare it fearlessly, as I should.

<sup>21</sup>Tychicus, the dear brother and faithful servant in the Lord, will tell you everything, so that you also may know how I am and what I am

---

<sup>a</sup> 31 Gen. 2:24    <sup>b</sup> 3 Deut. 5:16    <sup>c</sup> 4 Or Parents

doing. [22] I am sending him to you for this very purpose, that you may know how we are, and that he may encourage you.

[23] Peace to the brothers and sisters,[a] and love with faith from God the Father and the Lord Jesus Christ. [24] Grace to all who love our Lord Jesus Christ with an undying love.[b]

---

[a] 23 The Greek word for *brothers and sisters (adelphoi)* refers here to believers, both men and women, as part of God's family.　[b] 24 Or *Grace and immortality to all who love our Lord Jesus Christ.*

# PHILIPPIANS

On his second journey to bring the gospel to the Gentile world, the apostle Paul helped start a church in the city of Philippi (see pp. 171-173), a colony of retired Roman soldiers. The Philippians became Paul's friends and supporters for the rest of his life. When they heard that he was in Rome as a prisoner, they collected money to assist him and sent it with one of their members, a man named Epaphroditus. Later Paul sent him back with a letter to thank the Philippians for their friendship and support.

Paul knows the Philippians were experiencing a lot of opposition, so he appeals to his own life as an example of how to respond to hardship with joy. *Throughout the whole palace guard*—that is, right in the center of Caesar's realm—Paul is boldly making the royal announcement that Jesus is Lord. Paul's desire is that the Philippians will gain the same confidence and *dare all the more to proclaim the gospel without fear.*

In an amazing hymn, Paul urges the Philippians to have the servant attitude that Jesus had. He did not grasp his high position but humbled himself even to the point of death—all for the sake of others. This is the new way to be human that is revealed in God's kingdom. Our citizenship is in God's realm and so we eagerly await the Savior's return to us. Then he will transform our lowly bodies to become like his glorious resurrected body.

---

1 Paul and Timothy, servants of Christ Jesus,

To all God's holy people in Christ Jesus at Philippi, together with the overseers and deacons[a]:

2 Grace and peace to you from God our Father and the Lord Jesus Christ.

3 I thank my God every time I remember you. 4 In all my prayers for all of you, I always pray with joy 5 because of your partnership in the gospel from the first day until now, 6 being confident of this, that he who began a good work in you will carry it on to completion until the day of Christ Jesus.

7 It is right for me to feel this way about all of you, since I have you in my heart and, whether I am in chains or defending and confirming the gospel, all of you share in God's grace with me. 8 God can testify how I long for all of you with the affection of Christ Jesus.

9 And this is my prayer: that your love may abound more and more in knowledge and depth of insight, 10 so that you may be able to discern what is best and may be pure and blameless for the day of Christ, 11 filled with the fruit of righteousness that comes through Jesus Christ — to the glory and praise of God.

12 Now I want you to know, brothers and sisters,[b] that what has hap-

---

[a] 1 The word *deacons* refers here to Christians designated to serve with the overseers/elders of the church in a variety of ways; similarly in Romans 16:1 and 1 Tim. 3:8,12.    [b] 12 The Greek word for *brothers and sisters* (*adelphoi*) refers here to believers, both men and women, as part of God's family; also in verse 14; and in 3:1, 13, 17; 4:1, 8, 21.

pened to me has actually served to advance the gospel. ¹³As a result, it has become clear throughout the whole palace guard[a] and to everyone else that I am in chains for Christ. ¹⁴And because of my chains, most of the brothers and sisters have become confident in the Lord and dare all the more to proclaim the gospel without fear.

¹⁵It is true that some preach Christ out of envy and rivalry, but others out of goodwill. ¹⁶The latter do so out of love, knowing that I am put here for the defense of the gospel. ¹⁷The former preach Christ out of selfish ambition, not sincerely, supposing that they can stir up trouble for me while I am in chains. ¹⁸But what does it matter? The important thing is that in every way, whether from false motives or true, Christ is preached. And because of this I rejoice.

Yes, and I will continue to rejoice, ¹⁹for I know that through your prayers and God's provision of the Spirit of Jesus Christ what has happened to me will turn out for my deliverance.[b] ²⁰I eagerly expect and hope that I will in no way be ashamed, but will have sufficient courage so that now as always Christ will be exalted in my body, whether by life or by death. ²¹For to me, to live is Christ and to die is gain. ²²If I am to go on living in the body, this will mean fruitful labor for me. Yet what shall I choose? I do not know! ²³I am torn between the two: I desire to depart and be with Christ, which is better by far; ²⁴but it is more necessary for you that I remain in the body. ²⁵Convinced of this, I know that I will remain, and I will continue with all of you for your progress and joy in the faith, ²⁶so that through my being with you again your boasting in Christ Jesus will abound on account of me.

²⁷Whatever happens, conduct yourselves in a manner worthy of the gospel of Christ. Then, whether I come and see you or only hear about you in my absence, I will know that you stand firm in the one Spirit,[c] striving together as one for the faith of the gospel ²⁸without being frightened in any way by those who oppose you. This is a sign to them that they will be destroyed, but that you will be saved—and that by God. ²⁹For it has been granted to you on behalf of Christ not only to believe in him, but also to suffer for him, ³⁰since you are going through the same struggle you saw I had, and now hear that I still have.

**2** Therefore if you have any encouragement from being united with Christ, if any comfort from his love, if any common sharing in the Spirit, if any tenderness and compassion, ²then make my joy complete by being like-minded, having the same love, being one in spirit and of one mind. ³Do nothing out of selfish ambition or vain conceit. Rather, in humility value others above yourselves, ⁴not looking to your own interests but each of you to the interests of the others.

⁵In your relationships with one another, have the same mindset as Christ Jesus:

⁶Who, being in very nature[d] God,
    did not consider equality with
        God something to be used
            to his own advantage;

---

[a] 13 Or *whole palace*     [b] 19 Or *vindication; or salvation*     [c] 27 Or *in one spirit*     [d] 6 Or *in the form of*

7 rather, he made himself nothing
  by taking the very nature[a] of a
    servant,
  being made in human
    likeness.
8 And being found in appearance
    as a man,
  he humbled himself
  by becoming obedient to
    death—
    even death on a cross!

9 Therefore God exalted him to
    the highest place
  and gave him the name that is
    above every name,
10 that at the name of Jesus every
    knee should bow,
  in heaven and on earth and
    under the earth,
11 and every tongue acknowledge
    that Jesus Christ is Lord,
  to the glory of God the Father.

12 Therefore, my dear friends, as you have always obeyed—not only in my presence, but now much more in my absence—continue to work out your salvation with fear and trembling, 13 for it is God who works in you to will and to act in order to fulfill his good purpose.

14 Do everything without grumbling or arguing, 15 so that you may become blameless and pure, "children of God without fault in a warped and crooked generation."[b] Then you will shine among them like stars in the sky 16 as you hold firmly to the word of life. And then I will be able to boast on the day of Christ that I did not run or labor in vain. 17 But even if I am being poured out like a drink offering on the sacrifice and service coming from your faith, I am glad and rejoice with all of you. 18 So you too should be glad and rejoice with me.

19 I hope in the Lord Jesus to send Timothy to you soon, that I also may be cheered when I receive news about you. 20 I have no one else like him, who will show genuine concern for your welfare. 21 For everyone looks out for their own interests, not those of Jesus Christ. 22 But you know that Timothy has proved himself, because as a son with his father he has served with me in the work of the gospel. 23 I hope, therefore, to send him as soon as I see how things go with me. 24 And I am confident in the Lord that I myself will come soon.

25 But I think it is necessary to send back to you Epaphroditus, my brother, co-worker and fellow soldier, who is also your messenger, whom you sent to take care of my needs. 26 For he longs for all of you and is distressed because you heard he was ill. 27 Indeed he was ill, and almost died. But God had mercy on him, and not on him only but also on me, to spare me sorrow upon sorrow. 28 Therefore I am all the more eager to send him, so that when you see him again you may be glad and I may have less anxiety. 29 So then, welcome him in the Lord with great joy, and honor people like him, 30 because he almost died for the work of Christ. He risked his life to make up for the help you yourselves could not give me.

3 Further, my brothers and sisters, rejoice in the Lord! It is no trouble for me to write the same things to you again, and it is a safeguard for you. 2 Watch out for those dogs, those evildoers, those mutilators of the flesh. 3 For it is we who are the circumcision, we who serve God by

---

[a] 7 Or *the form*   [b] 15 Deut. 32:5

his Spirit, who boast in Christ Jesus, and who put no confidence in the flesh— [4]though I myself have reasons for such confidence.

If someone else thinks they have reasons to put confidence in the flesh, I have more: [5]circumcised on the eighth day, of the people of Israel, of the tribe of Benjamin, a Hebrew of Hebrews; in regard to the law, a Pharisee; [6]as for zeal, persecuting the church; as for righteousness based on the law, faultless.

[7]But whatever were gains to me I now consider loss for the sake of Christ. [8]What is more, I consider everything a loss because of the surpassing worth of knowing Christ Jesus my Lord, for whose sake I have lost all things. I consider them garbage, that I may gain Christ [9]and be found in him, not having a righteousness of my own that comes from the law, but that which is through faith in[a] Christ— the righteousness that comes from God on the basis of faith. [10]I want to know Christ—yes, to know the power of his resurrection and participation in his sufferings, becoming like him in his death, [11]and so, somehow, attaining to the resurrection from the dead.

[12]Not that I have already obtained all this, or have already arrived at my goal, but I press on to take hold of that for which Christ Jesus took hold of me. [13]Brothers and sisters, I do not consider myself yet to have taken hold of it. But one thing I do: Forgetting what is behind and straining toward what is ahead, [14]I press on toward the goal to win the prize for which God has called me heavenward in Christ Jesus.

[15]All of us, then, who are mature should take such a view of things.

And if on some point you think differently, that too God will make clear to you. [16]Only let us live up to what we have already attained.

[17]Join together in following my example, brothers and sisters, and just as you have us as a model, keep your eyes on those who live as we do. [18]For, as I have often told you before and now tell you again even with tears, many live as enemies of the cross of Christ. [19]Their destiny is destruction, their god is their stomach, and their glory is in their shame. Their mind is set on earthly things. [20]But our citizenship is in heaven. And we eagerly await a Savior from there, the Lord Jesus Christ, [21]who, by the power that enables him to bring everything under his control, will transform our lowly bodies so that they will be like his glorious body.

4 Therefore, my brothers and sisters, you whom I love and long for, my joy and crown, stand firm in the Lord in this way, dear friends!

[2]I plead with Euodia and I plead with Syntyche to be of the same mind in the Lord. [3]Yes, and I ask you, my true companion, help these women since they have contended at my side in the cause of the gospel, along with Clement and the rest of my co-workers, whose names are in the book of life.

[4]Rejoice in the Lord always. I will say it again: Rejoice! [5]Let your gentleness be evident to all. The Lord is near. [6]Do not be anxious about anything, but in every situation, by prayer and petition, with thanksgiving, present your requests to God. [7]And the peace of God, which transcends all understanding, will guard your hearts and your minds in Christ Jesus.

[a] 9 Or *through the faithfulness of*

8Finally, brothers and sisters, whatever is true, whatever is noble, whatever is right, whatever is pure, whatever is lovely, whatever is admirable—if anything is excellent or praiseworthy—think about such things. 9Whatever you have learned or received or heard from me, or seen in me—put it into practice. And the God of peace will be with you.

10I rejoiced greatly in the Lord that at last you renewed your concern for me. Indeed, you were concerned, but you had no opportunity to show it. 11I am not saying this because I am in need, for I have learned to be content whatever the circumstances. 12I know what it is to be in need, and I know what it is to have plenty. I have learned the secret of being content in any and every situation, whether well fed or hungry, whether living in plenty or in want. 13I can do all this through him who gives me strength.

14Yet it was good of you to share in my troubles. 15Moreover, as you Philippians know, in the early days of your acquaintance with the gospel, when I set out from Macedonia, not one church shared with me in the matter of giving and receiving, except you only; 16for even when I was in Thessalonica, you sent me aid more than once when I was in need. 17Not that I desire your gifts; what I desire is that more be credited to your account. 18I have received full payment and have more than enough. I am amply supplied, now that I have received from Epaphroditus the gifts you sent. They are a fragrant offering, an acceptable sacrifice, pleasing to God. 19And my God will meet all your needs according to the riches of his glory in Christ Jesus.

20To our God and Father be glory for ever and ever. Amen.

21Greet all God's people in Christ Jesus. The brothers and sisters who are with me send greetings. 22All God's people here send you greetings, especially those who belong to Caesar's household.

23The grace of the Lord Jesus Christ be with your spirit. Amen.[a]

a 23 Some manuscripts do not have Amen.

# COLOSSIANS

While Paul was in prison in Rome, awaiting his upcoming trial before Caesar, one of the letters he wrote was to the gathering of believers in the city of Colossae. Paul had never met them, but they knew who he was and respected his leadership. Paul had worked with a man named Epaphras when he was in Ephesus. Epaphras was originally from Colossae, about 100 miles to the east. Paul sent him to bring the good news about Jesus to his city and to two other nearby cities, Laodicea and Hierapolis. Epaphras was later arrested and brought to Rome as a prisoner himself. Paul learned from him what was happening in those cities.

The Colossians were mostly Gentiles, but like the Galatians they were being pressured to follow the Jewish law and were adding extra rules and false teachings to the faith. Some of them were priding themselves on having visions and getting secret spiritual knowledge. So Paul wrote them a letter to say, "When you've got Jesus the Messiah, you've got it all!"

Paul emphasizes that all things in heaven and earth were created by the Son and were reconciled to God by the Son's death on the cross. Christ possesses the fullness of God's being. Since the Colossians have been brought into the new kingdom of light, they can live their faith to the fullest. They are to *put on the new self*, awaiting the time the Messiah will appear openly, revealing his glory.

---

1 Paul, an apostle of Christ Jesus by the will of God, and Timothy our brother,

2 To God's holy people in Colossae, the faithful brothers and sisters[a] in Christ:

Grace and peace to you from God our Father.[b]

3 We always thank God, the Father of our Lord Jesus Christ, when we pray for you, 4 because we have heard of your faith in Christ Jesus and of the love you have for all God's people— 5 the faith and love that spring from the hope stored up for you in heaven and about which you have already heard in the true message of the gospel[c] that has come to you. In the same way, the gospel is bearing fruit and growing throughout the whole world—just as it has been doing among you since the day you heard it and truly understood God's grace. 7 You learned it from Epaphras, our dear fellow servant,[c] who is a faithful minister of Christ on our[d] behalf, 8 and who also told us of your love in the Spirit.

9 For this reason, since the day we heard about you, we have not stopped praying for you. We continually ask God to fill you with the knowledge of his will through all the wisdom and understanding that the Spirit gives,[e] 10 so that you may live a life worthy of the Lord and please him in every way:

---

[a] 2 The Greek word for *brothers and sisters* (*adelphoi*) refers here to believers, both men and women, as part of God's family; also in 4:15.   [b] 2 Some manuscripts *Father and the Lord Jesus Christ*   [c] 7 Or *slave*   [d] 7 Some manuscripts *your*   [e] 9 Or *all spiritual wisdom and understanding*

bearing fruit in every good work, growing in the knowledge of God, ¹¹being strengthened with all power according to his glorious might so that you may have great endurance and patience, ¹²and giving joyful thanks to the Father, who has qualified you[a] to share in the inheritance of his holy people in the kingdom of light. ¹³For he has rescued us from the dominion of darkness and brought us into the kingdom of the Son he loves, ¹⁴in whom we have redemption, the forgiveness of sins.

¹⁵The Son is the image of the invisible God, the firstborn over all creation. ¹⁶For in him all things were created: things in heaven and on earth, visible and invisible, whether thrones or powers or rulers or authorities; all things have been created through him and for him. ¹⁷He is before all things, and in him all things hold together. ¹⁸And he is the head of the body, the church; he is the beginning and the firstborn from among the dead, so that in everything he might have the supremacy. ¹⁹For God was pleased to have all his fullness dwell in him, ²⁰and through him to reconcile to himself all things, whether things on earth or things in heaven, by making peace through his blood, shed on the cross.

²¹Once you were alienated from God and were enemies in your minds because of[b] your evil behavior. ²²But now he has reconciled you by Christ's physical body through death to present you holy in his sight, without blemish and free from accusation— ²³if you continue in your faith, established and firm, and do not move from the hope held out in the gospel. This is the gospel that you heard and that has been proclaimed to every creature under heaven, and of which I, Paul, have become a servant.

²⁴Now I rejoice in what I am suffering for you, and I fill up in my flesh what is still lacking in regard to Christ's afflictions, for the sake of his body, which is the church. ²⁵I have become its servant by the commission God gave me to present to you the word of God in its fullness— ²⁶the mystery that has been kept hidden for ages and generations, but is now disclosed to the Lord's people. ²⁷To them God has chosen to make known among the Gentiles the glorious riches of this mystery, which is Christ in you, the hope of glory.

²⁸He is the one we proclaim, admonishing and teaching everyone with all wisdom, so that we may present everyone fully mature in Christ. ²⁹To this end I strenuously contend with all the energy Christ so powerfully works in me.

2 I want you to know how hard I am contending for you and for those at Laodicea, and for all who have not met me personally. ²My goal is that they may be encouraged in heart and united in love, so that they may have the full riches of complete understanding, in order that they may know the mystery of God, namely, Christ, ³in whom are hidden all the treasures of wisdom and knowledge. ⁴I tell you this so that no one may deceive you by fine-sounding arguments. ⁵For though I am absent from you in body, I am present with you in spirit and delight to see how disciplined you are and how firm your faith in Christ is.

⁶So then, just as you received

---

*a 12* Some manuscripts *us*   *b 21* Or *minds, as shown by*

Christ Jesus as Lord, continue to live your lives in him, [7]rooted and built up in him, strengthened in the faith as you were taught, and overflowing with thankfulness.

[8]See to it that no one takes you captive through hollow and deceptive philosophy, which depends on human tradition and the elemental spiritual forces[a] of this world rather than on Christ.

[9]For in Christ all the fullness of the Deity lives in bodily form, [10]and in Christ you have been brought to fullness. He is the head over every power and authority. [11]In him you were also circumcised with a circumcision not performed by human hands. Your whole self ruled by the flesh[b] was put off when you were circumcised by[c] Christ, [12]having been buried with him in baptism, in which you were also raised with him through your faith in the working of God, who raised him from the dead.

[13]When you were dead in your sins and in the uncircumcision of your flesh, God made you[d] alive with Christ. He forgave us all our sins, [14]having canceled the charge of our legal indebtedness, which stood against us and condemned us; he has taken it away, nailing it to the cross. [15]And having disarmed the powers and authorities, he made a public spectacle of them, triumphing over them by the cross.[e]

[16]Therefore do not let anyone judge you by what you eat or drink, or with regard to a religious festival, a New Moon celebration or a Sabbath day. [17]These are a shadow of the things that were to come; the reality, however, is found in Christ. [18]Do not let anyone who delights in false humility and the worship of angels disqualify you. Such a person also goes into great detail about what they have seen; they are puffed up with idle notions by their unspiritual mind. [19]They have lost connection with the head, from whom the whole body, supported and held together by its ligaments and sinews, grows as God causes it to grow.

[20]Since you died with Christ to the elemental spiritual forces of this world, why, as though you still belonged to the world, do you submit to its rules: [21]"Do not handle! Do not taste! Do not touch!"? [22]These rules, which have to do with things that are all destined to perish with use, are based on merely human commands and teachings. [23]Such regulations indeed have an appearance of wisdom, with their self-imposed worship, their false humility and their harsh treatment of the body, but they lack any value in restraining sensual indulgence.

3 Since, then, you have been raised with Christ, set your hearts on things above, where Christ is, seated at the right hand of God. [2]Set your minds on things above, not on earthly things. [3]For you died, and your life is now hidden with Christ in God. [4]When Christ, who is your[f] life, appears, then you also will appear with him in glory.

[5]Put to death, therefore, whatever belongs to your earthly nature: sexual immorality, impurity, lust, evil desires and greed, which

---

[a] 8  Or *the basic principles*; also in verse 20    [b] 11  In contexts like this, the Greek word for *flesh* (*sarx*) refers to the sinful state of human beings, often presented as a power in opposition to the Spirit; also in verse 13.    [c] 11  Or *put off in the circumcision of*    [d] 13  Some manuscripts *us*    [e] 15  Or *them in him*    [f] 4  Some manuscripts *our*

is idolatry. 6Because of these, the wrath of God is coming.*a* 7You used to walk in these ways, in the life you once lived. 8But now you must also rid yourselves of all such things as these: anger, rage, malice, slander, and filthy language from your lips. 9Do not lie to each other, since you have taken off your old self with its practices 10and have put on the new self, which is being renewed in knowledge in the image of its Creator. 11Here there is no Gentile or Jew, circumcised or uncircumcised, barbarian, Scythian, slave or free, but Christ is all, and is in all.

12Therefore, as God's chosen people, holy and dearly loved, clothe yourselves with compassion, kindness, humility, gentleness and patience. 13Bear with each other and forgive one another if any of you has a grievance against someone. Forgive as the Lord forgave you. 14And over all these virtues put on love, which binds them all together in perfect unity.

15Let the peace of Christ rule in your hearts, since as members of one body you were called to peace. And be thankful. 16Let the message of Christ dwell among you richly as you teach and admonish one another with all wisdom through psalms, hymns, and songs from the Spirit, singing to God with gratitude in your hearts. 17And whatever you do, whether in word or deed, do it all in the name of the Lord Jesus, giving thanks to God the Father through him.

18Wives, submit yourselves to your husbands, as is fitting in the Lord.

19Husbands, love your wives and do not be harsh with them.

20Children, obey your parents in everything, for this pleases the Lord.

21Fathers,*b* do not embitter your children, or they will become discouraged.

22Slaves, obey your earthly masters in everything; and do it, not only when their eye is on you and to curry their favor, but with sincerity of heart and reverence for the Lord. 23Whatever you do, work at it with all your heart, as working for the Lord, not for human masters, 24since you know that you will receive an inheritance from the Lord as a reward. It is the Lord Christ you are serving. 25Anyone who does wrong will be repaid for their wrongs, and there is no favoritism.

4 Masters, provide your slaves with what is right and fair, because you know that you also have a Master in heaven.

2Devote yourselves to prayer, being watchful and thankful. 3And pray for us, too, that God may open a door for our message, so that we may proclaim the mystery of Christ, for which I am in chains. 4Pray that I may proclaim it clearly, as I should. 5Be wise in the way you act toward outsiders; make the most of every opportunity. 6Let your conversation be always full of grace, seasoned with salt, so that you may know how to answer everyone.

7Tychicus will tell you all the news about me. He is a dear brother, a faithful minister and fellow servant*c* in the Lord. 8I am sending him to you for the express purpose that you may know about our*d* circumstances and that he may encourage your hearts. 9He is coming

---

*a 6* Some early manuscripts *coming on those who are disobedient*      *b 21* Or *Parents*
*c 7* Or *slave;* also in verse 12      *d 8* Some manuscripts *that he may know about your*

with Onesimus, our faithful and dear brother, who is one of you. They will tell you everything that is happening here.

[10] My fellow prisoner Aristarchus sends you his greetings, as does Mark, the cousin of Barnabas. (You have received instructions about him; if he comes to you, welcome him.) [11] Jesus, who is called Justus, also sends greetings. These are the only Jews[a] among my co-workers for the kingdom of God, and they have proved a comfort to me. [12] Epaphras, who is one of you and a servant of Christ Jesus, sends greetings. He is always wrestling in prayer for you, that you may stand firm in all the will of God, mature and fully assured. [13] I vouch for him that he is working hard for you and for those at Laodicea and Hierapolis. [14] Our dear friend Luke, the doctor, and Demas send greetings. [15] Give my greetings to the brothers and sisters at Laodicea, and to Nympha and the church in her house.

[16] After this letter has been read to you, see that it is also read in the church of the Laodiceans and that you in turn read the letter from Laodicea.

[17] Tell Archippus: "See to it that you complete the ministry you have received in the Lord."

[18] I, Paul, write this greeting in my own hand. Remember my chains. Grace be with you.

---

[a] 11 Greek *only ones of the circumcision group*

# 1 THESSALONIANS

Around AD 51, Paul, Silas and Timothy brought the message about Jesus the Messiah to the city of Thessalonica. Many people became believers, but there was a riot when Paul and Silas were accused of *defying Caesar's decrees, saying that there is another king, one called Jesus* (see p. 173). They narrowly escaped with their lives and had to flee.

A little later Paul became concerned that the believers in Thessalonica might fall away from the faith due to the opposition they were facing. So he sent Timothy to encourage them (as a Greek he could make the trip more safely). When Timothy returned to Achaia with the welcome news that the Thessalonians had remained faithful, Paul wrote to express his joy.

In this short letter, Paul first recalls his time in Thessalonica and gives thanks for their continuing faith, despite trials and challenges. He teaches them to avoid sexual immorality, to love one another sincerely, and to work hard to earn their own living.

Paul then addresses a key pastoral question: What is the Christian hope for those who have died? He explains that believers who die before the royal appearance of the Messiah are not lost, but will surely be raised from the dead when he comes. He reminds the Thessalonians that Jesus will appear suddenly and unexpectedly. They should therefore live in such a way that they would be unashamed to greet him. Throughout the letter Paul's basic message is, "Keep up the good work!"

---

1 Paul, Silas[a] and Timothy,

To the church of the Thessalonians in God the Father and the Lord Jesus Christ:

Grace and peace to you.

2 We always thank God for all of you and continually mention you in our prayers. 3 We remember before our God and Father your work produced by faith, your labor prompted by love, and your endurance inspired by hope in our Lord Jesus Christ.

4 For we know, brothers and sisters[b] loved by God, that he has chosen you, 5 because our gospel came to you not simply with words but also with power, with the Holy Spirit and deep conviction. You know how we lived among you for your sake. 6 You became imitators of us and of the Lord, for you welcomed the message in the midst of severe suffering with the joy given by the Holy Spirit. 7 And so you became a model to all the believers in Macedonia and Achaia. 8 The Lord's message rang out from you not only in Macedonia and Achaia—your faith in God has become known everywhere. Therefore we do not need to say anything about it, 9 for they themselves report what kind of reception you gave us. They tell how you turned to God from

---

a *1* Greek *Silvanus,* a variant of *Silas*    b *4* The Greek word for *brothers and sisters (adelphoi)* refers here to believers, both men and women, as part of God's family; also in 2:1, 9, 14, 17; 3:7; 4:1, 10, 13; 5:1, 4, 12, 14, 25, 27.

idols to serve the living and true God, [10] and to wait for his Son from heaven, whom he raised from the dead — Jesus, who rescues us from the coming wrath.

2 You know, brothers and sisters, that our visit to you was not without results. [2] We had previously suffered and been treated outrageously in Philippi, as you know, but with the help of our God we dared to tell you his gospel in the face of strong opposition. [3] For the appeal we make does not spring from error or impure motives, nor are we trying to trick you. [4] On the contrary, we speak as those approved by God to be entrusted with the gospel. We are not trying to please people but God, who tests our hearts. [5] You know we never used flattery, nor did we put on a mask to cover up greed — God is our witness. [6] We were not looking for praise from people, not from you or anyone else, even though as apostles of Christ we could have asserted our authority. [7] Instead, we were like young children[a] among you.

Just as a nursing mother cares for her children, [8] so we cared for you. Because we loved you so much, we were delighted to share with you not only the gospel of God but our lives as well. [9] Surely you remember, brothers and sisters, our toil and hardship; we worked night and day in order not to be a burden to anyone while we preached the gospel of God to you. [10] You are witnesses, and so is God, of how holy, righteous and blameless we were among you who believed. [11] For you know that we dealt with each of you as a father deals with his own children, [12] encouraging, comforting and urging you to live lives worthy

of God, who calls you into his kingdom and glory.

[13] And we also thank God continually because, when you received the word of God, which you heard from us, you accepted it not as a human word, but as it actually is, the word of God, which is indeed at work in you who believe. [14] For you, brothers and sisters, became imitators of God's churches in Judea, which are in Christ Jesus: You suffered from your own people the same things those churches suffered from the Jews [15] who killed the Lord Jesus and the prophets and also drove us out. They displease God and are hostile to everyone [16] in their effort to keep us from speaking to the Gentiles so that they may be saved. In this way they always heap up their sins to the limit. The wrath of God has come upon them at last.[b]

[17] But, brothers and sisters, when we were orphaned by being separated from you for a short time (in person, not in thought), out of our intense longing we made every effort to see you. [18] For we wanted to come to you — certainly I, Paul, did, again and again — but Satan blocked our way. [19] For what is our hope, our joy, or the crown in which we will glory in the presence of our Lord Jesus when he comes? Is it not you? [20] Indeed, you are our glory and joy.

3 So when we could stand it no longer, we thought it best to be left by ourselves in Athens. [2] We sent Timothy, who is our brother and co-worker in God's service in spreading the gospel of Christ, to strengthen and encourage you in your faith, [3] so that no one would be unsettled by these trials. For

---

[a] 7 Some manuscripts *were gentle*     [b] 16 Or *them fully*

you know quite well that we are destined for them. [4]In fact, when we were with you, we kept telling you that we would be persecuted. And it turned out that way, as you well know. [5]For this reason, when I could stand it no longer, I sent to find out about your faith. I was afraid that in some way the tempter had tempted you and that our labors might have been in vain.

[6]But Timothy has just now come to us from you and has brought good news about your faith and love. He has told us that you always have pleasant memories of us and that you long to see us, just as we also long to see you. [7]Therefore, brothers and sisters, in all our distress and persecution we were encouraged about you because of your faith. [8]For now we really live, since you are standing firm in the Lord. [9]How can we thank God enough for you in return for all the joy we have in the presence of our God because of you? [10]Night and day we pray most earnestly that we may see you again and supply what is lacking in your faith.

[11]Now may our God and Father himself and our Lord Jesus clear the way for us to come to you. [12]May the Lord make your love increase and overflow for each other and for everyone else, just as ours does for you. [13]May he strengthen your hearts so that you will be blameless and holy in the presence of our God and Father when our Lord Jesus comes with all his holy ones.

4 As for other matters, brothers and sisters, we instructed you how to live in order to please God, as in fact you are living. Now we ask you and urge you in the Lord Jesus to do this more and more. [2]For you know what instructions we gave you by the authority of the Lord Jesus.

[3]It is God's will that you should be sanctified: that you should avoid sexual immorality; [4]that each of you should learn to control your own body*a* in a way that is holy and honorable, [5]not in passionate lust like the pagans, who do not know God; [6]and that in this matter no one should wrong or take advantage of a brother or sister.*b* The Lord will punish all those who commit such sins, as we told you and warned you before. [7]For God did not call us to be impure, but to live a holy life. [8]Therefore, anyone who rejects this instruction does not reject a human being but God, the very God who gives you his Holy Spirit.

[9]Now about your love for one another we do not need to write to you, for you yourselves have been taught by God to love each other. [10]And in fact, you do love all of God's family throughout Macedonia. Yet we urge you, brothers and sisters, to do so more and more, [11]and to make it your ambition to lead a quiet life: You should mind your own business and work with your hands, just as we told you, [12]so that your daily life may win the respect of outsiders and so that you will not be dependent on anybody.

[13]Brothers and sisters, we do not want you to be uninformed about those who sleep in death, so that you do not grieve like the rest of mankind, who have no hope. [14]For we believe that Jesus died and rose again, and so we believe that God

*a 4*   Or *learn to live with your own wife;* or *learn to acquire a wife*     *b 6*   The Greek word for *brother or sister (adelphos)* refers here to a believer, whether man or woman, as part of God's family.

will bring with Jesus those who have fallen asleep in him. ¹⁵According to the Lord's word, we tell you that we who are still alive, who are left until the coming of the Lord, will certainly not precede those who have fallen asleep. ¹⁶For the Lord himself will come down from heaven, with a loud command, with the voice of the archangel and with the trumpet call of God, and the dead in Christ will rise first. ¹⁷After that, we who are still alive and are left will be caught up together with them in the clouds to meet the Lord in the air. And so we will be with the Lord forever. ¹⁸Therefore encourage one another with these words.

5 Now, brothers and sisters, about times and dates we do not need to write to you, ²for you know very well that the day of the Lord will come like a thief in the night. ³While people are saying, "Peace and safety," destruction will come on them suddenly, as labor pains on a pregnant woman, and they will not escape.

⁴But you, brothers and sisters, are not in darkness so that this day should surprise you like a thief. ⁵You are all children of the light and children of the day. We do not belong to the night or to the darkness. ⁶So then, let us not be like others, who are asleep, but let us be awake and sober. ⁷For those who sleep, sleep at night, and those who get drunk, get drunk at night. ⁸But since we belong to the day, let us be sober, putting on faith and love as a breastplate, and the hope of salvation as a helmet. ⁹For God did not appoint us to suffer wrath but to receive salvation through our

Lord Jesus Christ. ¹⁰He died for us so that, whether we are awake or asleep, we may live together with him. ¹¹Therefore encourage one another and build each other up, just as in fact you are doing.

¹²Now we ask you, brothers and sisters, to acknowledge those who work hard among you, who care for you in the Lord and who admonish you. ¹³Hold them in the highest regard in love because of their work. Live in peace with each other. ¹⁴And we urge you, brothers and sisters, warn those who are idle and disruptive, encourage the disheartened, help the weak, be patient with everyone. ¹⁵Make sure that nobody pays back wrong for wrong, but always strive to do what is good for each other and for everyone else.

¹⁶Rejoice always, ¹⁷pray continually, ¹⁸give thanks in all circumstances; for this is God's will for you in Christ Jesus.

¹⁹Do not quench the Spirit. ²⁰Do not treat prophecies with contempt ²¹but test them all; hold on to what is good, ²²reject every kind of evil.

²³May God himself, the God of peace, sanctify you through and through. May your whole spirit, soul and body be kept blameless at the coming of our Lord Jesus Christ. ²⁴The one who calls you is faithful, and he will do it.

²⁵Brothers and sisters, pray for us. ²⁶Greet all God's people with a holy kiss. ²⁷I charge you before the Lord to have this letter read to all the brothers and sisters.

²⁸The grace of our Lord Jesus Christ be with you.

# 2 THESSALONIANS

Apparently only shortly after writing his first letter to the Thessalonians, Paul had to write again to correct a false report that he had said the day of the Lord had already come. The *day of the Lord* was a phrase from the Hebrew prophets to describe God's key victory over every opponent, when his faithful ones would be rewarded. The Thessalonians' concern seems to have been not that the day had come and gone and they had missed it, but that it was now present. That would mean nothing more was to be expected from God in terms of setting things right. Since they continued to suffer persecutions, this was a depressing prospect.

Even before he contradicts this false report, Paul reassures the Thessalonians that God will indeed pay back all those who were troubling them. He reminds them of the details he had discussed with them in person of how the day of the Lord would arrive. He then repeats some instruction from his earlier letter, urging them not to be idle but to work hard and earn their own livings.

At the end of the letter, most of which would have been written by a scribe, Paul adds a greeting in his own handwriting. He wants them to know for sure this teaching is really coming from him!

---

## 1 Paul, Silas*a* and Timothy,

To the church of the Thessalonians in God our Father and the Lord Jesus Christ:

2 Grace and peace to you from God the Father and the Lord Jesus Christ.

3 We ought always to thank God for you, brothers and sisters,*b* and rightly so, because your faith is growing more and more, and the love all of you have for one another is increasing. 4 Therefore, among God's churches we boast about your perseverance and faith in all the persecutions and trials you are enduring.

5 All this is evidence that God's judgment is right, and as a result you will be counted worthy of the kingdom of God, for which you are suffering. 6 God is just: He will pay back trouble to those who trouble you 7 and give relief to you who are troubled, and to us as well. This will happen when the Lord Jesus is revealed from heaven in blazing fire with his powerful angels. 8 He will punish those who do not know God and do not obey the gospel of our Lord Jesus. 9 They will be punished with everlasting destruction and shut out from the presence of the Lord and from the glory of his might 10 on the day he comes to be glorified in his holy people and to be marveled at among all those who have believed. This includes you, because you believed our testimony to you.

11 With this in mind, we constantly pray for you, that our God may make you worthy of his calling, and

---

*a 1* Greek *Silvanus*, a variant of *Silas* refers here to believers, both men and women, as part of God's family; also in 2:1, 13, 15; 3:1, 6, 13.   *b 3* The Greek word for *brothers and sisters* (*adelphoi*) that by his power he may bring to fruition your every desire for goodness and your every deed prompted by faith. ¹²We pray this so that the name of our Lord Jesus may be glorified in you, and you in him, according to the grace of our God and the Lord Jesus Christ.[a]

2 Concerning the coming of our Lord Jesus Christ and our being gathered to him, we ask you, brothers and sisters, ²not to become easily unsettled or alarmed by the teaching allegedly from us — whether by a prophecy or by word of mouth or by letter — asserting that the day of the Lord has already come. ³Don't let anyone deceive you in any way, for that day will not come until the rebellion occurs and the man of lawlessness[b] is revealed, the man doomed to destruction. ⁴He will oppose and will exalt himself over everything that is called God or is worshiped, so that he sets himself up in God's temple, proclaiming himself to be God.

⁵Don't you remember that when I was with you I used to tell you these things? ⁶And now you know what is holding him back, so that he may be revealed at the proper time. ⁷For the secret power of lawlessness is already at work; but the one who now holds it back will continue to do so till he is taken out of the way. ⁸And then the lawless one will be revealed, whom the Lord Jesus will overthrow with the breath of his mouth and destroy by the splendor of his coming. ⁹The coming of the lawless one will be in accordance with how Satan works. He will use all sorts of displays of power through signs and wonders that serve the lie, ¹⁰and all the ways

that wickedness deceives those who are perishing. They perish because they refused to love the truth and so be saved. ¹¹For this reason God sends them a powerful delusion so that they will believe the lie ¹²and so that all will be condemned who have not believed the truth but have delighted in wickedness.

¹³But we ought always to thank God for you, brothers and sisters loved by the Lord, because God chose you as firstfruits[c] to be saved through the sanctifying work of the Spirit and through belief in the truth. ¹⁴He called you to this through our gospel, that you might share in the glory of our Lord Jesus Christ.

¹⁵So then, brothers and sisters, stand firm and hold fast to the teachings[d] we passed on to you, whether by word of mouth or by letter.

¹⁶May our Lord Jesus Christ himself and God our Father, who loved us and by his grace gave us eternal encouragement and good hope, ¹⁷encourage your hearts and strengthen you in every good deed and word.

3 As for other matters, brothers and sisters, pray for us that the message of the Lord may spread rapidly and be honored, just as it was with you. ²And pray that we may be delivered from wicked and evil people, for not everyone has faith. ³But the Lord is faithful, and he will strengthen you and protect you from the evil one. ⁴We have confidence in the Lord that you are doing and will continue to do the things we command. ⁵May the Lord direct your hearts into God's love and Christ's perseverance.

---

[a] 12 Or God and Lord, Jesus Christ     [b] 3 Some manuscripts sin     [c] 13 Some manuscripts because from the beginning God chose you     [d] 15 Or traditions

⁶In the name of the Lord Jesus Christ, we command you, brothers and sisters, to keep away from every believer who is idle and disruptive and does not live according to the teaching[a] you received from us. ⁷For you yourselves know how you ought to follow our example. We were not idle when we were with you, ⁸nor did we eat anyone's food without paying for it. On the contrary, we worked night and day, laboring and toiling so that we would not be a burden to any of you. ⁹We did this, not because we do not have the right to such help, but in order to offer ourselves as a model for you to imitate. ¹⁰For even when we were with you, we gave you this rule: "The one who is unwilling to work shall not eat."

¹¹We hear that some among you are idle and disruptive. They are not busy; they are busybodies.

¹²Such people we command and urge in the Lord Jesus Christ to settle down and earn the food they eat. ¹³And as for you, brothers and sisters, never tire of doing what is good.

¹⁴Take special note of anyone who does not obey our instruction in this letter. Do not associate with them, in order that they may feel ashamed. ¹⁵Yet do not regard them as an enemy, but warn them as you would a fellow believer.

¹⁶Now may the Lord of peace himself give you peace at all times and in every way. The Lord be with all of you.

¹⁷I, Paul, write this greeting in my own hand, which is the distinguishing mark in all my letters. This is how I write. ¹⁸The grace of our Lord Jesus Christ be with you all.

_a 6 Or tradition_

# 1 TIMOTHY

After Paul was released from prison in Rome, he discovered that leaders in the Ephesian church had distorted the genuine message they had first heard from Paul himself. They had misapplied certain Jewish practices and borrowed some others from the philosophies of the day. They restricted certain foods, forbade marriage and stressed controversial speculations as the path to spiritual progress. At the same time, they tolerated immoral behavior. So Paul sent his co-worker Timothy to Ephesus and wrote him a letter, which he was expected to share with the church. He hoped it would give Timothy the power and influence to set things in order until Paul could get to Ephesus himself.

Paul's focus is on what true leadership in the church looks like. This would help the Ephesians reject those who weren't qualified and replace them with those who were. Paul includes a special warning toward the end of his letter about the dangers of greed, which seemed to be at the root of their problems.

Throughout the letter Paul uses the phrase *Christ Jesus*—that is, Messiah Jesus—which emphasizes the kingly rule of Jesus. This helped remind the church that Jesus is their real leader and is the clearest model of authentic leadership.

---

1 Paul, an apostle of Christ Jesus by the command of God our Savior and of Christ Jesus our hope,

² To Timothy my true son in the faith:

Grace, mercy and peace from God the Father and Christ Jesus our Lord.

³ As I urged you when I went into Macedonia, stay there in Ephesus so that you may command certain people not to teach false doctrines any longer ⁴ or to devote themselves to myths and endless genealogies. Such things promote controversial speculations rather than advancing God's work—which is by faith. ⁵ The goal of this command is love, which comes from a pure heart and a good conscience and a sincere faith. ⁶ Some have departed from these and have turned to meaningless talk. ⁷ They want to be teachers of the law, but they do not know what they are talking about or what they so confidently affirm.

⁸ We know that the law is good if one uses it properly. ⁹ We also know that the law is made not for the righteous but for lawbreakers and rebels, the ungodly and sinful, the unholy and irreligious, for those who kill their fathers or mothers, for murderers, ¹⁰ for the sexually immoral, for those practicing homosexuality, for slave traders and liars and perjurers—and for whatever else is contrary to the sound doctrine ¹¹ that conforms to the gospel concerning the glory of the blessed God, which he entrusted to me.

¹² I thank Christ Jesus our Lord, who has given me strength, that he considered me trustworthy, appointing me to his service. ¹³ Even though I was once a blasphemer and a persecutor and a violent

man, I was shown mercy because I acted in ignorance and unbelief. [14]The grace of our Lord was poured out on me abundantly, along with the faith and love that are in Christ Jesus.

[15]Here is a trustworthy saying that deserves full acceptance: Christ Jesus came into the world to save sinners — of whom I am the worst. [16]But for that very reason I was shown mercy so that in me, the worst of sinners, Christ Jesus might display his immense patience as an example for those who would believe in him and receive eternal life. [17]Now to the King eternal, immortal, invisible, the only God, be honor and glory for ever and ever. Amen.

[18]Timothy, my son, I am giving you this command in keeping with the prophecies once made about you, so that by recalling them you may fight the battle well, [19]holding on to faith and a good conscience, which some have rejected and so have suffered shipwreck with regard to the faith. [20]Among them are Hymenaeus and Alexander, whom I have handed over to Satan to be taught not to blaspheme.

2 I urge, then, first of all, that petitions, prayers, intercession and thanksgiving be made for all people — [2]for kings and all those in authority, that we may live peaceful and quiet lives in all godliness and holiness. [3]This is good, and pleases God our Savior, [4]who wants all people to be saved and to come to a knowledge of the truth. [5]For there is one God and one mediator between God and mankind, the man Christ Jesus, [6]who gave himself as a ransom for all people. This has

now been witnessed to at the proper time. [7]And for this purpose I was appointed a herald and an apostle — I am telling the truth, I am not lying — and a true and faithful teacher of the Gentiles.

[8]Therefore I want the men everywhere to pray, lifting up holy hands without anger or disputing. [9]I also want the women to dress modestly, with decency and propriety, adorning themselves, not with elaborate hairstyles or gold or pearls or expensive clothes, [10]but with good deeds, appropriate for women who profess to worship God.

[11]A woman[a] should learn in quietness and full submission. [12]I do not permit a woman to teach or to assume authority over a man;[b] she must be quiet. [13]For Adam was formed first, then Eve. [14]And Adam was not the one deceived; it was the woman who was deceived and became a sinner. [15]But women[c] will be saved through childbearing — if they continue in faith, love and holiness with propriety.

3 Here is a trustworthy saying: Whoever aspires to be an overseer desires a noble task. [2]Now the overseer is to be above reproach, faithful to his wife, temperate, self-controlled, respectable, hospitable, able to teach, [3]not given to drunkenness, not violent but gentle, not quarrelsome, not a lover of money. [4]He must manage his own family well and see that his children obey him, and he must do so in a manner worthy of full[d] respect. [5](If anyone does not know how to manage his own family, how can he take care of God's church?) [6]He must not be a recent convert, or he may become conceited and fall under the same

---

[a] 11 Or *wife*; also in verse 12    [b] 12 Or *over her husband*    [c] 15 Greek *she*    [d] 4 Or *him with proper*

judgment as the devil. [7]He must also have a good reputation with outsiders, so that he will not fall into disgrace and into the devil's trap.

[8]In the same way, deacons[a] are to be worthy of respect, sincere, not indulging in much wine, and not pursuing dishonest gain. [9]They must keep hold of the deep truths of the faith with a clear conscience. [10]They must first be tested; and then if there is nothing against them, let them serve as deacons.

[11]In the same way, the women[b] are to be worthy of respect, not malicious talkers but temperate and trustworthy in everything.

[12]A deacon must be faithful to his wife and must manage his children and his household well. [13]Those who have served well gain an excellent standing and great assurance in their faith in Christ Jesus.

[14]Although I hope to come to you soon, I am writing you these instructions so that, [15]if I am delayed, you will know how people ought to conduct themselves in God's household, which is the church of the living God, the pillar and foundation of the truth. [16]Beyond all question, the mystery from which true godliness springs is great:

He appeared in the flesh,
    was vindicated by the Spirit,[c]
was seen by angels,
    was preached among the
        nations,
was believed on in the world,
    was taken up in glory.

4 The Spirit clearly says that in later times some will abandon the faith and follow deceiving spirits and things taught by demons. [2]Such teachings come through hypocritical liars, whose consciences have been seared as with a hot iron. [3]They forbid people to marry and order them to abstain from certain foods, which God created to be received with thanksgiving by those who believe and who know the truth. [4]For everything God created is good, and nothing is to be rejected if it is received with thanksgiving, [5]because it is consecrated by the word of God and prayer.

[6]If you point these things out to the brothers and sisters,[d] you will be a good minister of Christ Jesus, nourished on the truths of the faith and of the good teaching that you have followed. [7]Have nothing to do with godless myths and old wives' tales; rather, train yourself to be godly. [8]For physical training is of some value, but godliness has value for all things, holding promise for both the present life and the life to come. [9]This is a trustworthy saying that deserves full acceptance. [10]That is why we labor and strive, because we have put our hope in the living God, who is the Savior of all people, and especially of those who believe.

[11]Command and teach these things. [12]Don't let anyone look down on you because you are young, but set an example for the believers in speech, in conduct, in love, in faith and in purity. [13]Until I come, devote yourself to the public reading of Scripture, to preaching

[a] 8  The word *deacons* refers here to Christians designated to serve with the overseers/ elders of the church in a variety of ways; similarly in verse 12; and in Romans 16:1 and Phil. 1:1.    [b] 11  Possibly deacons' wives or women who are deacons    [c] 16  Or *vindicated in spirit*
[d] 6  The Greek word for *brothers and sisters* (*adelphoi*) refers here to believers, both men and women, as part of God's family.

and to teaching. ¹⁴Do not neglect your gift, which was given you through prophecy when the body of elders laid their hands on you.

¹⁵Be diligent in these matters; give yourself wholly to them, so that everyone may see your progress. ¹⁶Watch your life and doctrine closely. Persevere in them, because if you do, you will save both yourself and your hearers.

5 Do not rebuke an older man harshly, but exhort him as if he were your father. Treat younger men as brothers, ²older women as mothers, and younger women as sisters, with absolute purity.

³Give proper recognition to those widows who are really in need. ⁴But if a widow has children or grandchildren, these should learn first of all to put their religion into practice by caring for their own family and so repaying their parents and grandparents, for this is pleasing to God. ⁵The widow who is really in need and left all alone puts her hope in God and continues night and day to pray and to ask God for help. ⁶But the widow who lives for pleasure is dead even while she lives. ⁷Give the people these instructions, so that no one may be open to blame. ⁸Anyone who does not provide for their relatives, and especially for their own household, has denied the faith and is worse than an unbeliever.

⁹No widow may be put on the list of widows unless she is over sixty, has been faithful to her husband, ¹⁰and is well known for her good deeds, such as bringing up children, showing hospitality, washing the feet of the Lord's people, helping those in trouble and devoting herself to all kinds of good deeds.

¹¹As for younger widows, do not put them on such a list. For when their sensual desires overcome their dedication to Christ, they want to marry. ¹²Thus they bring judgment on themselves, because they have broken their first pledge. ¹³Besides, they get into the habit of being idle and going about from house to house. And not only do they become idlers, but also busybodies who talk nonsense, saying things they ought not to. ¹⁴So I counsel younger widows to marry, to have children, to manage their homes and to give the enemy no opportunity for slander. ¹⁵Some have in fact already turned away to follow Satan.

¹⁶If any woman who is a believer has widows in her care, she should continue to help them and not let the church be burdened with them, so that the church can help those widows who are really in need.

¹⁷The elders who direct the affairs of the church well are worthy of double honor, especially those whose work is preaching and teaching. ¹⁸For Scripture says, "Do not muzzle an ox while it is treading out the grain,"ᵃ and "The worker deserves his wages."ᵇ ¹⁹Do not entertain an accusation against an elder unless it is brought by two or three witnesses. ²⁰But those elders who are sinning you are to reprove before everyone, so that the others may take warning. ²¹I charge you, in the sight of God and Christ Jesus and the elect angels, to keep these instructions without partiality, and to do nothing out of favoritism.

²²Do not be hasty in the laying on of hands, and do not share in

---

ᵃ 18 Deut. 25:4    ᵇ 18 Luke 10:7

the sins of others. Keep yourself pure.

²³Stop drinking only water, and use a little wine because of your stomach and your frequent illnesses.

²⁴The sins of some are obvious, reaching the place of judgment ahead of them; the sins of others trail behind them. ²⁵In the same way, good deeds are obvious, and even those that are not obvious cannot remain hidden forever.

6 All who are under the yoke of slavery should consider their masters worthy of full respect, so that God's name and our teaching may not be slandered. ²Those who have believing masters should not show them disrespect just because they are fellow believers. Instead, they should serve them even better because their masters are dear to them as fellow believers and are devoted to the welfareª of their slaves.

These are the things you are to teach and insist on. ³If anyone teaches otherwise and does not agree to the sound instruction of our Lord Jesus Christ and to godly teaching, ⁴they are conceited and understand nothing. They have an unhealthy interest in controversies and quarrels about words that result in envy, strife, malicious talk, evil suspicions ⁵and constant friction between people of corrupt mind, who have been robbed of the truth and who think that godliness is a means to financial gain.

⁶But godliness with contentment is great gain. ⁷For we brought nothing into the world, and we can take nothing out of it. ⁸But if we have food and clothing, we will be content with that. ⁹Those who want to get rich fall into temptation and a trap and into many foolish and harmful desires that plunge people into ruin and destruction. ¹⁰For the love of money is a root of all kinds of evil. Some people, eager for money, have wandered from the faith and pierced themselves with many griefs.

¹¹But you, man of God, flee from all this, and pursue righteousness, godliness, faith, love, endurance and gentleness. ¹²Fight the good fight of the faith. Take hold of the eternal life to which you were called when you made your good confession in the presence of many witnesses. ¹³In the sight of God, who gives life to everything, and of Christ Jesus, who while testifying before Pontius Pilate made the good confession, I charge you ¹⁴to keep this command without spot or blame until the appearing of our Lord Jesus Christ, ¹⁵which God will bring about in his own time—God, the blessed and only Ruler, the King of kings and Lord of lords, ¹⁶who alone is immortal and who lives in unapproachable light, whom no one has seen or can see. To him be honor and might forever. Amen.

¹⁷Command those who are rich in this present world not to be arrogant nor to put their hope in wealth, which is so uncertain, but to put their hope in God, who richly provides us with everything for our enjoyment. ¹⁸Command them to do good, to be rich in good deeds, and to be generous and willing to share. ¹⁹In this way they will lay up treasure for themselves as a firm foundation for the coming age, so

---

ª 2 Or *and benefit from the service*

that they may take hold of the life that is truly life.

<sup>20</sup>Timothy, guard what has been entrusted to your care. Turn away from godless chatter and the op-posing ideas of what is falsely called knowledge, <sup>21</sup>which some have professed and in so doing have departed from the faith.

Grace be with you all.

# 2 TIMOTHY

Paul left his co-worker Timothy in the city of Ephesus to deal with some renegade leaders in the church there. When Timothy struggled, however, Paul went back to Ephesus. Once there, Paul suffered a *great deal of harm* from Alexander, one of these leaders, and he was once again imprisoned and taken to Rome. He expected that this time he would be tried and executed. Paul wrote to Timothy to ask him to come to Rome quickly.

Things in Ephesus had not gone as Paul or Timothy expected. Paul had ordered both Alexander and Hymenaeus to step down from leadership, but they were continuing to oppose Paul. Others had joined them, and they were still misdirecting people into a corrupted version of the faith that stressed debate and dissension rather than purity and obedience. Timothy was discouraged and intimidated. Paul's letter includes challenges to stay faithful to the true message—even if this meant suffering or death. Paul reminds Timothy that in the days before the open appearance of Jesus as king, there will be lots of trouble. False teachers, treacherous and insincere people, persecutions and more will all challenge the faithfulness of God's people.

Paul urges Timothy to remember the gospel message: *Jesus Christ, raised from the dead, descended from David.* He points out that the sacred writings Timothy has known since he was a child are God-breathed, and will help him continue in doing good work.

---

1 Paul, an apostle of Christ Jesus by the will of God, in keeping with the promise of life that is in Christ Jesus,

2 To Timothy, my dear son:

Grace, mercy and peace from God the Father and Christ Jesus our Lord.

3 I thank God, whom I serve, as my ancestors did, with a clear conscience, as night and day I constantly remember you in my prayers. 4 Recalling your tears, I long to see you, so that I may be filled with joy. 5 I am reminded of your sincere faith, which first lived in your grandmother Lois and in your mother Eunice and, I am persuaded, now lives in you also.

6 For this reason I remind you to fan into flame the gift of God, which is in you through the laying on of my hands. 7 For the Spirit God gave us does not make us timid, but gives us power, love and self-discipline. 8 So do not be ashamed of the testimony about our Lord or of me his prisoner. Rather, join with me in suffering for the gospel, by the power of God. 9 He has saved us and called us to a holy life—not because of anything we have done but because of his own purpose and grace. This grace was given us in Christ Jesus before the beginning of time, 10 but it has now been revealed through the appearing of our Savior, Christ Jesus, who has destroyed death and has brought life and immortality to light through the gospel. 11 And of this gospel I was appointed a herald and an apostle and a teacher. 12 That is why I am suffering as I am.

Yet this is no cause for shame, because I know whom I have believed, and am convinced that he is able to guard what I have entrusted to him until that day.

[13]What you heard from me, keep as the pattern of sound teaching, with faith and love in Christ Jesus. [14]Guard the good deposit that was entrusted to you—guard it with the help of the Holy Spirit who lives in us.

[15]You know that everyone in the province of Asia has deserted me, including Phygelus and Hermogenes. [16]May the Lord show mercy to the household of Onesiphorus, because he often refreshed me and was not ashamed of my chains. [17]On the contrary, when he was in Rome, he searched hard for me until he found me. [18]May the Lord grant that he will find mercy from the Lord on that day! You know very well in how many ways he helped me in Ephesus.

2 You then, my son, be strong in the grace that is in Christ Jesus. [2]And the things you have heard me say in the presence of many witnesses entrust to reliable people who will also be qualified to teach others. [3]Join with me in suffering, like a good soldier of Christ Jesus. [4]No one serving as a soldier gets entangled in civilian affairs, but rather tries to please his commanding officer. [5]Similarly, anyone who competes as an athlete does not receive the victor's crown except by competing according to the rules. [6]The hardworking farmer should be the first to receive a share of the crops. [7]Reflect on what I am saying, for the Lord will give you insight into all this.

[8]Remember Jesus Christ, raised from the dead, descended from David. This is my gospel, [9]for which I am suffering even to the point of being chained like a criminal. But God's word is not chained. [10]Therefore I endure everything for the sake of the elect, that they too may obtain the salvation that is in Christ Jesus, with eternal glory.

[11]Here is a trustworthy saying:

If we died with him,
    we will also live with him;
[12]if we endure,
    we will also reign with him.
If we disown him,
    he will also disown us;
[13]if we are faithless,
    he remains faithful,
    for he cannot disown himself.

[14]Keep reminding God's people of these things. Warn them before God against quarreling about words; it is of no value, and only ruins those who listen. [15]Do your best to present yourself to God as one approved, a worker who does not need to be ashamed and who correctly handles the word of truth. [16]Avoid godless chatter, because those who indulge in it will become more and more ungodly. [17]Their teaching will spread like gangrene. Among them are Hymenaeus and Philetus, [18]who have departed from the truth. They say that the resurrection has already taken place, and they destroy the faith of some. [19]Nevertheless, God's solid foundation stands firm, sealed with this inscription: "The Lord knows those who are his," and, "Everyone who confesses the name of the Lord must turn away from wickedness."

[20]In a large house there are articles not only of gold and silver, but also of wood and clay; some are for special purposes and some for

common use. 21 Those who cleanse themselves from the latter will be instruments for special purposes, made holy, useful to the Master and prepared to do any good work.

22 Flee the evil desires of youth and pursue righteousness, faith, love and peace, along with those who call on the Lord out of a pure heart. 23 Don't have anything to do with foolish and stupid arguments, because you know they produce quarrels. 24 And the Lord's servant must not be quarrelsome but must be kind to everyone, able to teach, not resentful. 25 Opponents must be gently instructed, in the hope that God will grant them repentance leading them to a knowledge of the truth, 26 and that they will come to their senses and escape from the trap of the devil, who has taken them captive to do his will.

3 But mark this: There will be terrible times in the last days. 2 People will be lovers of themselves, lovers of money, boastful, proud, abusive, disobedient to their parents, ungrateful, unholy, 3 without love, unforgiving, slanderous, without self-control, brutal, not lovers of the good, 4 treacherous, rash, conceited, lovers of pleasure rather than lovers of God — 5 having a form of godliness but denying its power. Have nothing to do with such people.

6 They are the kind who worm their way into homes and gain control over gullible women, who are loaded down with sins and are swayed by all kinds of evil desires, 7 always learning but never able to come to a knowledge of the truth. 8 Just as Jannes and Jambres opposed Moses, so also these teachers oppose the truth. They are men

of depraved minds, who, as far as the faith is concerned, are rejected. 9 But they will not get very far because, as in the case of those men, their folly will be clear to everyone.

10 You, however, know all about my teaching, my way of life, my purpose, faith, patience, love, endurance, 11 persecutions, sufferings — what kinds of things happened to me in Antioch, Iconium and Lystra, the persecutions I endured. Yet the Lord rescued me from all of them. 12 In fact, everyone who wants to live a godly life in Christ Jesus will be persecuted, 13 while evildoers and impostors will go from bad to worse, deceiving and being deceived. 14 But as for you, continue in what you have learned and have become convinced of, because you know those from whom you learned it, 15 and how from infancy you have known the Holy Scriptures, which are able to make you wise for salvation through faith in Christ Jesus. 16 All Scripture is God-breathed and is useful for teaching, rebuking, correcting and training in righteousness, 17 so that the servant of God[a] may be thoroughly equipped for every good work.

4 In the presence of God and of Christ Jesus, who will judge the living and the dead, and in view of his appearing and his kingdom, I give you this charge: 2 Preach the word; be prepared in season and out of season; correct, rebuke and encourage — with great patience and careful instruction. 3 For the time will come when people will not put up with sound doctrine. Instead, to suit their own desires, they will gather around them a great number

a 17 Or that you, a man of God,

of teachers to say what their itching ears want to hear. [4]They will turn their ears away from the truth and turn aside to myths. [5]But you, keep your head in all situations, endure hardship, do the work of an evangelist, discharge all the duties of your ministry.

[6]For I am already being poured out like a drink offering, and the time for my departure is near. [7]I have fought the good fight, I have finished the race, I have kept the faith. [8]Now there is in store for me the crown of righteousness, which the Lord, the righteous Judge, will award to me on that day—and not only to me, but also to all who have longed for his appearing.

[9]Do your best to come to me quickly, [10]for Demas, because he loved this world, has deserted me and has gone to Thessalonica. Crescens has gone to Galatia, and Titus to Dalmatia. [11]Only Luke is with me. Get Mark and bring him with you, because he is helpful to me in my ministry. [12]I sent Tychicus to Ephesus. [13]When you come, bring the cloak that I left with Car-

pus at Troas, and my scrolls, especially the parchments.

[14]Alexander the metalworker did me a great deal of harm. The Lord will repay him for what he has done. [15]You too should be on your guard against him, because he strongly opposed our message.

[16]At my first defense, no one came to my support, but everyone deserted me. May it not be held against them. [17]But the Lord stood at my side and gave me strength, so that through me the message might be fully proclaimed and all the Gentiles might hear it. And I was delivered from the lion's mouth. [18]The Lord will rescue me from every evil attack and will bring me safely to his heavenly kingdom. To him be glory for ever and ever. Amen.

[19]Greet Priscilla[a] and Aquila and the household of Onesiphorus. [20]Erastus stayed in Corinth, and I left Trophimus sick in Miletus. [21]Do your best to get here before winter. Eubulus greets you, and so do Pudens, Linus, Claudia and all the brothers and sisters.[b]

[22]The Lord be with your spirit. Grace be with you all.

---

[a] 19  Greek *Prisca*, a variant of *Priscilla*    [b] 21  The Greek word for *brothers and sisters* (*adelphoi*) refers here to believers, both men and women, as part of God's family.

# TITUS

After the apostle Paul was released from prison in Rome, he discovered that renegade leaders were preying on the people of the church he had founded in Ephesus. He therefore left his long-time co-worker Timothy in that city with a letter authorizing him to replace these leaders and restore order. A similar situation on the island of Crete required Paul to commission another long-time co-worker, Titus, to act as his representative there.

Paul's letter is addressed to Titus, but it is meant for the larger church as well. He confers his own authority on Titus and instructs him to appoint godly leaders. Paul's description of the false teaching matches that in Ephesus: a combination of selective Jewish observances (such as being circumcised and abstaining from certain foods) and the pursuit of controversial speculations. However, the teaching didn't help people live purer lives. Paul tells the community that *the grace of God has appeared that offers salvation to all people*. It is the true message about Jesus that helps God's people live a new kind of life.

Paul reveals his plan to spend the winter in Nicopolis, a city on the west coast of Macedonia. It would provide an excellent jumping-off point for bringing the gospel to the western part of the empire. He trusts that Titus will help restore order in Crete so he can accompany Paul on this new venture.

1 Paul, a servant of God and an apostle of Jesus Christ to further the faith of God's elect and their knowledge of the truth that leads to godliness — ²in the hope of eternal life, which God, who does not lie, promised before the beginning of time, ³and which now at his appointed season he has brought to light through the preaching entrusted to me by the command of God our Savior,

⁴To Titus, my true son in our common faith:

Grace and peace from God the Father and Christ Jesus our Savior.

⁵The reason I left you in Crete was that you might put in order what was left unfinished and ap-

point[a] elders in every town, as I directed you. ⁶An elder must be blameless, faithful to his wife, a man whose children believe[b] and are not open to the charge of being wild and disobedient. ⁷Since an overseer manages God's household, he must be blameless—not overbearing, not quick-tempered, not given to drunkenness, not violent, not pursuing dishonest gain. ⁸Rather, he must be hospitable, one who loves what is good, who is self-controlled, upright, holy and disciplined. ⁹He must hold firmly to the trustworthy message as it has been taught, so that he can encourage others by sound doctrine and refute those who oppose it.

¹⁰For there are many rebellious people, full of meaningless talk

---

[a] 5 Or *ordain*    [b] 6 Or *children are trustworthy*

and deception, especially those of the circumcision group. [11]They must be silenced, because they are disrupting whole households by teaching things they ought not to teach—and that for the sake of dishonest gain. [12]One of Crete's own prophets has said it: "Cretans are always liars, evil brutes, lazy gluttons."[a] [13]This saying is true. Therefore rebuke them sharply, so that they will be sound in the faith [14]and will pay no attention to Jewish myths or to the merely human commands of those who reject the truth. [15]To the pure, all things are pure, but to those who are corrupted and do not believe, nothing is pure. In fact, both their minds and consciences are corrupted. [16]They claim to know God, but by their actions they deny him. They are detestable, disobedient and unfit for doing anything good.

2 You, however, must teach what is appropriate to sound doctrine. [2]Teach the older men to be temperate, worthy of respect, self-controlled, and sound in faith, in love and in endurance.

[3]Likewise, teach the older women to be reverent in the way they live, not to be slanderers or addicted to much wine, but to teach what is good. [4]Then they can urge the younger women to love their husbands and children, [5]to be self-controlled and pure, to be busy at home, to be kind, and to be subject to their husbands, so that no one will malign the word of God.

[6]Similarly, encourage the young men to be self-controlled. [7]In everything set them an example by doing what is good. In your teaching show integrity, seriousness [8]and soundness of speech that can-

not be condemned, so that those who oppose you may be ashamed because they have nothing bad to say about us.

[9]Teach slaves to be subject to their masters in everything, to try to please them, not to talk back to them, [10]and not to steal from them, but to show that they can be fully trusted, so that in every way they will make the teaching about God our Savior attractive.

[11]For the grace of God has appeared that offers salvation to all people. [12]It teaches us to say "No" to ungodliness and worldly passions, and to live self-controlled, upright and godly lives in this present age, [13]while we wait for the blessed hope—the appearing of the glory of our great God and Savior, Jesus Christ, [14]who gave himself for us to redeem us from all wickedness and to purify for himself a people that are his very own, eager to do what is good.

[15]These, then, are the things you should teach. Encourage and rebuke with all authority. Do not let anyone despise you.

3 Remind the people to be subject to rulers and authorities, to be obedient, to be ready to do whatever is good, [2]to slander no one, to be peaceable and considerate, and always to be gentle toward everyone.

[3]At one time we too were foolish, disobedient, deceived and enslaved by all kinds of passions and pleasures. We lived in malice and envy, being hated and hating one another. [4]But when the kindness and love of God our Savior appeared, [5]he saved us, not because of righteous things we had done, but because of his mercy. He saved us through the washing of rebirth

---

[a] 12 From the Cretan philosopher Epimenides

and renewal by the Holy Spirit, [6]whom he poured out on us generously through Jesus Christ our Savior, [7]so that, having been justified by his grace, we might become heirs having the hope of eternal life. [8]This is a trustworthy saying. And I want you to stress these things, so that those who have trusted in God may be careful to devote themselves to doing what is good. These things are excellent and profitable for everyone.

[9]But avoid foolish controversies and genealogies and arguments and quarrels about the law, because these are unprofitable and useless. [10]Warn a divisive person once, and then warn them a second time. After that, have nothing to do with them. [11]You may be sure that such people are warped and sinful; they are self-condemned.

[12]As soon as I send Artemas or Tychicus to you, do your best to come to me at Nicopolis, because I have decided to winter there. [13]Do everything you can to help Zenas the lawyer and Apollos on their way and see that they have everything they need. [14]Our people must learn to devote themselves to doing what is good, in order to provide for urgent needs and not live unproductive lives.

[15]Everyone with me sends you greetings. Greet those who love us in the faith.

Grace be with you all.

# PHILEMON

One of the people Paul chose to deliver the letters we know as Colossians and Ephesians was a man named Onesimus. Onesimus was originally from Colossae, and would have been known to the people there. But Paul was compelled to write a separate letter for him. This was because Onesimus had been the slave of a wealthy Colossian named Philemon, in whose home the church met. Onesimus had run away, probably robbing Philemon in the process. In Rome he had become a follower of Jesus. He'd been helping Paul in prison, but now Paul needed him to return to Colossae. Paul's hope was that Philemon would not only forgive Onesimus, but welcome him as a brother and no longer a slave.

Paul's brief letter to Philemon stresses the change in Onesimus's life. His name meant *useful* in Greek, and Paul tells Philemon that while he had formerly been *useless* (a servant Philemon couldn't count on), now he could be useful to both of them. Paul doesn't put Philemon under any obligation. His appeal is on the basis of love, and he promises to honor the demands of justice by making restitution himself if necessary.

Most likely Paul's appeal was successful, or this letter would not have been preserved. In the life of Onesimus we have a clear example of the kind of transformation that occurred in thousands of lives as the gospel message spread throughout the Roman Empire.

---

¹Paul, a prisoner of Christ Jesus, and Timothy our brother,

To Philemon our dear friend and fellow worker— ²also to Apphia our sister and Archippus our fellow soldier—and to the church that meets in your home:

³Grace and peace to you*a* from God our Father and the Lord Jesus Christ.

⁴I always thank my God as I remember you in my prayers, ⁵because I hear about your love for all his holy people and your faith in the Lord Jesus. ⁶I pray that your partnership with us in the faith may be effective in deepening your understanding of every good thing we share for the sake of Christ. ⁷Your love has given me great joy and encouragement, because you, brother, have refreshed the hearts of the Lord's people.

⁸Therefore, although in Christ I could be bold and order you to do what you ought to do, ⁹yet I prefer to appeal to you on the basis of love. It is as none other than Paul—an old man and now also a prisoner of Christ Jesus— ¹⁰that I appeal to you for my son Onesimus,*b* who became my son while I was in chains. ¹¹Formerly he was useless to you, but now he has become useful both to you and to me.

¹²I am sending him—who is my very heart—back to you. ¹³I would have liked to keep him with me so that he could take your place in helping me while I am in chains for the gospel. ¹⁴But I did not want to do anything without your consent,

---

*a 3* The Greek is plural; also in verses 22 and 25; elsewhere in this letter "you" is singular.
*b 10* Onesimus means *useful*.

so that any favor you do would not seem forced but would be voluntary. ¹⁵Perhaps the reason he was separated from you for a little while was that you might have him back forever— ¹⁶no longer as a slave, but better than a slave, as a dear brother. He is very dear to me but even dearer to you, both as a fellow man and as a brother in the Lord.

¹⁷So if you consider me a partner, welcome him as you would welcome me. ¹⁸If he has done you any wrong or owes you anything, charge it to me. ¹⁹I, Paul, am writing this with my own hand. I will pay it back—not to mention that you owe me your very self. ²⁰I do wish, brother, that I may have some benefit from you in the Lord; refresh my heart in Christ. ²¹Confident of your obedience, I write to you, knowing that you will do even more than I ask.

²²And one thing more: Prepare a guest room for me, because I hope to be restored to you in answer to your prayers.

²³Epaphras, my fellow prisoner in Christ Jesus, sends you greetings. ²⁴And so do Mark, Aristarchus, Demas and Luke, my fellow workers.

²⁵The grace of the Lord Jesus Christ be with your spirit.

# HEBREWS

Neither the author nor the audience of this book is specifically named, but the book itself reveals its nature and purpose. The recipients are Jesus-believing Jews who are in danger of falling away from the faith. They are likely in Italy, since the author passes on greetings to them from those who are from Italy—probably their friends who are traveling elsewhere. The goal of the whole book is to show the superiority of the final realities God has revealed in the new covenant to the temporary ones of the first covenant. Its readers are encouraged to respond to the threat of persecution by recommitting to the new reality brought by Jesus.

The book alternates between teachings—reviews of Israel's history or the temple worship arrangements—and challenges based on these teachings. There are four teaching-challenge pairs:

: Jesus and the salvation he brings are greater than the angels and the salvation they announced (the law of Moses).
: Jesus is our "apostle" (someone sent by God on a specific mission), and he brings us into a greater rest and promised land than Moses and Joshua brought Israel into.
: Jesus is a more effective high priest than the priests appointed by the law of Moses.
: As God's faithful people have done throughout the ages, we must continue living in light of God's unseen heavenly realities and stepping out in faith. Through the Messiah *we are receiving a kingdom that cannot be shaken.*

---

1 In the past God spoke to our ancestors through the prophets at many times and in various ways, 2but in these last days he has spoken to us by his Son, whom he appointed heir of all things, and through whom also he made the universe. 3The Son is the radiance of God's glory and the exact representation of his being, sustaining all things by his powerful word. After he had provided purification for sins, he sat down at the right hand of the Majesty in heaven. 4So he became as much superior to the angels as the name he has inherited is superior to theirs.

5For to which of the angels did God ever say,

"You are my Son;
today I have become your Father"*a*?

Or again,

"I will be his Father,
and he will be my Son"*b*?

6And again, when God brings his firstborn into the world, he says,

"Let all God's angels worship him."*c*

7In speaking of the angels he says,

*a* 5 Psalm 2:7     *b* 5 2 Samuel 7:14; 1 Chron. 17:13     *c* 6 Deut. 32:43 (see Dead Sea Scrolls and Septuagint)

"He makes his angels spirits,
    and his servants flames of
    fire."[a]

[8]But about the Son he says,

"Your throne, O God, will last for
    ever and ever;
    a scepter of justice will be the
    scepter of your kingdom.
[9]You have loved righteousness
    and hated wickedness;
    therefore God, your God,
    has set you above your
    companions
    by anointing you with the oil
    of joy."[b]

[10]He also says,

"In the beginning, Lord, you
    laid the foundations of the
    earth,
    and the heavens are the work
    of your hands.
[11]They will perish, but you
    remain;
    they will all wear out like a
    garment.
[12]You will roll them up like a robe;
    like a garment they will be
    changed.
But you remain the same,
    and your years will never
    end."[c]

[13]To which of the angels did God
ever say,

"Sit at my right hand
    until I make your enemies
    a footstool for your feet"[d]?

[14]Are not all angels ministering
spirits sent to serve those who will
inherit salvation?

2 We must pay the most careful
attention, therefore, to what we
have heard, so that we do not drift

away. [2]For since the message spoken through angels was binding,
and every violation and disobedience received its just punishment,
[3]how shall we escape if we ignore
so great a salvation? This salvation,
which was first announced by the
Lord, was confirmed to us by those
who heard him. [4]God also testified
to it by signs, wonders and various
miracles, and by gifts of the Holy
Spirit distributed according to his
will.

[5]It is not to angels that he has
subjected the world to come, about
which we are speaking. [6]But there
is a place where someone has testified:

"What is mankind that you are
    mindful of them,
    a son of man that you care for
    him?
[7]You made them a little[e] lower
    than the angels;
    you crowned them with glory
    and honor
[8]    and put everything under
    their feet."[f,g]

In putting everything under them,[h]
God left nothing that is not subject
to them.[h] Yet at present we do not
see everything subject to them.[h]
[9]But we do see Jesus, who was
made lower than the angels for a
little while, now crowned with glory and honor because he suffered
death, so that by the grace of God
he might taste death for everyone.

[10]In bringing many sons and
daughters to glory, it was fitting
that God, for whom and through
whom everything exists, should
make the pioneer of their salvation
perfect through what he suffered.

---

[a] 7 Psalm 104:4    [b] 9 Psalm 45:6,7    [c] 12 Psalm 102:25-27    [d] 13 Psalm 110:1    [e] 7 Or them
for a little while    [f] 6-8 Psalm 8:4-6    [g] 7,8 Or 7You made him a little lower than the angels;/
you crowned him with glory and honor/ 6and put everything under his feet."    [h] 8 Or him

¹¹Both the one who makes people holy and those who are made holy are of the same family. So Jesus is not ashamed to call them brothers and sisters.ᵃ ¹²He says,

"I will declare your name to my
    brothers and sisters;
in the assembly I will sing your
    praises."ᵇ

¹³And again,

"I will put my trust in him."ᶜ

And again he says,

"Here am I, and the children
    God has given me."ᵈ

¹⁴Since the children have flesh and blood, he too shared in their humanity so that by his death he might break the power of him who holds the power of death—that is, the devil— ¹⁵and free those who all their lives were held in slavery by their fear of death. ¹⁶For surely it is not angels he helps, but Abraham's descendants. ¹⁷For this reason he had to be made like them,ᵉ fully human in every way, in order that he might become a merciful and faithful high priest in service to God, and that he might make atonement for the sins of the people. ¹⁸Because he himself suffered when he was tempted, he is able to help those who are being tempted.

3 Therefore, holy brothers and sisters, who share in the heavenly calling, fix your thoughts on Jesus, whom we acknowledge as our apostle and high priest. ²He was faithful to the one who appointed him, just as Moses was faithful in

all God's house. ³Jesus has been found worthy of greater honor than Moses, just as the builder of a house has greater honor than the house itself. ⁴For every house is built by someone, but God is the builder of everything. ⁵"Moses was faithful as a servant in all God's house,"ᶠ bearing witness to what would be spoken by God in the future. ⁶But Christ is faithful as the Son over God's house. And we are his house, if indeed we hold firmly to our confidence and the hope in which we glory.

⁷So, as the Holy Spirit says:

"Today, if you hear his voice,
  8   do not harden your hearts
    as you did in the rebellion,
        during the time of testing in
            the wilderness,
⁹where your ancestors tested and
        tried me,
    though for forty years they saw
        what I did.
¹⁰That is why I was angry with that
        generation;
    I said, 'Their hearts are always
        going astray,
    and they have not known my
        ways.'
¹¹ So I declared on oath in my
        anger,
    'They shall never enter my
        rest.' "ᵍ

¹²See to it, brothers and sisters, that none of you has a sinful, unbelieving heart that turns away from the living God. ¹³But encourage one another daily, as long as it is called "Today," so that none of you may be hardened by sin's deceitfulness. ¹⁴We have come to share in Christ,

---

ᵃ 11  The Greek word for *brothers and sisters* (*adelphoi*) refers here to believers, both men and women, as part of God's family; also in verse 12; and in 3:1, 12; 10:19; 13:22.     ᵇ 12  Psalm 22:22
ᶜ 13  Isaiah 8:17     ᵈ 13  Isaiah 8:18     ᵉ 17  Or *like his brothers*     ᶠ 5  Num. 12:7
ᵍ 11  Psalm 95:7-11

if indeed we hold our original conviction firmly to the very end. 15As has just been said:

"Today, if you hear his voice,
    do not harden your hearts
    as you did in the rebellion."[a]

16Who were they who heard and rebelled? Were they not all those Moses led out of Egypt? 17And with whom was he angry for forty years? Was it not with those who sinned, whose bodies perished in the wilderness? 18And to whom did God swear that they would never enter his rest if not to those who disobeyed? 19So we see that they were not able to enter, because of their unbelief.

4 Therefore, since the promise of entering his rest still stands, let us be careful that none of you be found to have fallen short of it. 2For we also have had the good news proclaimed to us, just as they did; but the message they heard was of no value to them, because they did not share the faith of those who obeyed.[b] 3Now we who have believed enter that rest, just as God has said,

"So I declared on oath in my
        anger,
    'They shall never enter my
        rest.'"[c]

And yet his works have been finished since the creation of the world. 4For somewhere he has spoken about the seventh day in these words: "On the seventh day God rested from all his works."[d] 5And again in the passage above he says, "They shall never enter my rest."

6Therefore since it still remains for some to enter that rest, and since those who formerly had the good news proclaimed to them did not go in because of their disobedience, 7God again set a certain day, calling it "Today." This he did when a long time later he spoke through David, as in the passage already quoted:

"Today, if you hear his voice,
    do not harden your hearts."[a]

8For if Joshua had given them rest, God would not have spoken later about another day. 9There remains, then, a Sabbath-rest for the people of God; 10for anyone who enters God's rest also rests from their works,[e] just as God did from his. 11Let us, therefore, make every effort to enter that rest, so that no one will perish by following their example of disobedience.

12For the word of God is alive and active. Sharper than any double-edged sword, it penetrates even to dividing soul and spirit, joints and marrow; it judges the thoughts and attitudes of the heart. 13Nothing in all creation is hidden from God's sight. Everything is uncovered and laid bare before the eyes of him to whom we must give account.

14Therefore, since we have a great high priest who has ascended into heaven,[f] Jesus the Son of God, let us hold firmly to the faith we profess. 15For we do not have a high priest who is unable to empathize with our weaknesses, but we have one who has been tempted in every way, just as we are—yet he did not sin. 16Let us then approach God's throne of grace with confidence,

---

*a 15,7* Psalm 95:7,8    *b 2* Some manuscripts *because those who heard did not combine it with faith*    *c 3* Psalm 95:11; also in verse 5    *d 4* Gen. 2:2    *e 10* Or *labor*    *f 14* Greek *has gone through the heavens* so that we may receive mercy and find grace to help us in our time of need.

5 Every high priest is selected from among the people and is appointed to represent the people in matters related to God, to offer gifts and sacrifices for sins. [2]He is able to deal gently with those who are ignorant and are going astray, since he himself is subject to weakness. [3]This is why he has to offer sacrifices for his own sins, as well as for the sins of the people. [4]And no one takes this honor on himself, but he receives it when called by God, just as Aaron was.

[5]In the same way, Christ did not take on himself the glory of becoming a high priest. But God said to him,

"You are my Son;
    today I have become your
        Father."[a]

[6]And he says in another place,

"You are a priest forever,
    in the order of Melchizedek."[b]

[7]During the days of Jesus' life on earth, he offered up prayers and petitions with fervent cries and tears to the one who could save him from death, and he was heard because of his reverent submission. [8]Son though he was, he learned obedience from what he suffered [9]and, once made perfect, he became the source of eternal salvation for all who obey him [10]and was designated by God to be high priest in the order of Melchizedek.

[11]We have much to say about this, but it is hard to make it clear to you because you no longer try to understand. [12]In fact, though by this time you ought to be teachers, you need someone to teach you the elementary truths of God's word all over again. You need milk, not solid food! [13]Anyone who lives on milk, being still an infant, is not acquainted with the teaching about righteousness. [14]But solid food is for the mature, who by constant use have trained themselves to distinguish good from evil.

6 Therefore let us move beyond the elementary teachings about Christ and be taken forward to maturity, not laying again the foundation of repentance from acts that lead to death,[c] and of faith in God, [2]instruction about cleansing rites,[d] the laying on of hands, the resurrection of the dead, and eternal judgment. [3]And God permitting, we will do so.

[4]It is impossible for those who have once been enlightened, who have tasted the heavenly gift, who have shared in the Holy Spirit, [5]who have tasted the goodness of the word of God and the powers of the coming age [6]and who have fallen[e] away, to be brought back to repentance. To their loss they are crucifying the Son of God all over again and subjecting him to public disgrace. [7]Land that drinks in the rain often falling on it and that produces a crop useful to those for whom it is farmed receives the blessing of God. [8]But land that produces thorns and thistles is worthless and is in danger of being cursed. In the end it will be burned.

[9]Even though we speak like this, dear friends, we are convinced of better things in your case—the things that have to do with salvation. [10]God is not unjust; he will

---

[a] 5 Psalm 2:7    [b] 6 Psalm 110:4    [c] 1 Or *from useless rituals*    [d] 2 Or *about baptisms*
[e] 6 Or *age,* [6]*if they fall*

not forget your work and the love you have shown him as you have helped his people and continue to help them. ¹¹We want each of you to show this same diligence to the very end, so that what you hope for may be fully realized. ¹²We do not want you to become lazy, but to imitate those who through faith and patience inherit what has been promised.

¹³When God made his promise to Abraham, since there was no one greater for him to swear by, he swore by himself, ¹⁴saying, "I will surely bless you and give you many descendants."ᵃ ¹⁵And so after waiting patiently, Abraham received what was promised.

¹⁶People swear by someone greater than themselves, and the oath confirms what is said and puts an end to all argument. ¹⁷Because God wanted to make the unchanging nature of his purpose very clear to the heirs of what was promised, he confirmed it with an oath. ¹⁸God did this so that, by two unchangeable things in which it is impossible for God to lie, we who have fled to take hold of the hope set before us may be greatly encouraged. ¹⁹We have this hope as an anchor for the soul, firm and secure. It enters the inner sanctuary behind the curtain, ²⁰where our forerunner, Jesus, has entered on our behalf. He has become a high priest forever, in the order of Melchizedek.

7 This Melchizedek was king of Salem and priest of God Most High. He met Abraham returning from the defeat of the kings and blessed him, ²and Abraham gave him a tenth of everything. First, the name Melchizedek means "king of righteousness"; then also, "king of Salem" means "king of peace." ³Without father or mother, without genealogy, without beginning of days or end of life, resembling the Son of God, he remains a priest forever.

⁴Just think how great he was: Even the patriarch Abraham gave him a tenth of the plunder! ⁵Now the law requires the descendants of Levi who become priests to collect a tenth from the people — that is, from their fellow Israelites — even though they also are descended from Abraham. ⁶This man, however, did not trace his descent from Levi, yet he collected a tenth from Abraham and blessed him who had the promises. ⁷And without doubt the lesser is blessed by the greater. ⁸In the one case, the tenth is collected by people who die; but in the other case, by him who is declared to be living. ⁹One might even say that Levi, who collects the tenth, paid the tenth through Abraham, ¹⁰because when Melchizedek met Abraham, Levi was still in the body of his ancestor.

¹¹If perfection could have been attained through the Levitical priesthood — and indeed the law given to the people established that priesthood — why was there still need for another priest to come, one in the order of Melchizedek, not in the order of Aaron? ¹²For when the priesthood is changed, the law must be changed also. ¹³He of whom these things are said belonged to a different tribe, and no one from that tribe has ever served at the altar. ¹⁴For it is clear that our Lord descended from Judah, and in regard to that tribe Moses said nothing about priests. ¹⁵And what we have said is even more clear if

ᵃ 14 Gen. 22:17

another priest like Melchizedek appears, ¹⁶one who has become a priest not on the basis of a regulation as to his ancestry but on the basis of the power of an indestructible life. ¹⁷For it is declared:

"You are a priest forever,
    in the order of Melchizedek."ᵃ

¹⁸The former regulation is set aside because it was weak and useless ¹⁹(for the law made nothing perfect), and a better hope is introduced, by which we draw near to God.

²⁰And it was not without an oath! Others became priests without any oath, ²¹but he became a priest with an oath when God said to him:

"The Lord has sworn
    and will not change his mind:
    'You are a priest forever.'"ᵃ

²²Because of this oath, Jesus has become the guarantor of a better covenant.

²³Now there have been many of those priests, since death prevented them from continuing in office; ²⁴but because Jesus lives forever, he has a permanent priesthood. ²⁵Therefore he is able to save completelyᵇ those who come to God through him, because he always lives to intercede for them.

²⁶Such a high priest truly meets our need—one who is holy, blameless, pure, set apart from sinners, exalted above the heavens. ²⁷Unlike the other high priests, he does not need to offer sacrifices day after day, first for his own sins, and then for the sins of the people. He sacrificed for their sins once for all when he offered himself. ²⁸For the law appoints as high priests men

in all their weakness; but the oath, which came after the law, appointed the Son, who has been made perfect forever.

8 Now the main point of what we are saying is this: We do have such a high priest, who sat down at the right hand of the throne of the Majesty in heaven, ²and who serves in the sanctuary, the true tabernacle set up by the Lord, not by a mere human being.

³Every high priest is appointed to offer both gifts and sacrifices, and so it was necessary for this one also to have something to offer. ⁴If he were on earth, he would not be a priest, for there are already priests who offer the gifts prescribed by the law. ⁵They serve at a sanctuary that is a copy and shadow of what is in heaven. This is why Moses was warned when he was about to build the tabernacle: "See to it that you make everything according to the pattern shown you on the mountain."ᶜ ⁶But in fact the ministry Jesus has received is as superior to theirs as the covenant of which he is mediator is superior to the old one, since the new covenant is established on better promises.

⁷For if there had been nothing wrong with that first covenant, no place would have been sought for another. ⁸But God found fault with the people and saidᵈ:

"The days are coming, declares
        the Lord,
    when I will make a new
        covenant
    with the people of Israel
        and with the people of Judah.
⁹It will not be like the covenant
        I made with their ancestors

---

ᵃ 17,21 Psalm 110:4    ᵇ 25 Or forever    ᶜ 5 Exodus 25:40    ᵈ 8 Some manuscripts may be translated fault and said to the people.

when I took them by the hand
to lead them out of Egypt,
because they did not remain
faithful to my covenant,
and I turned away from them,
declares the Lord.

[10] This is the covenant I will
establish with the people
of Israel
after that time, declares the
Lord.
I will put my laws in their minds
and write them on their
hearts.
I will be their God,
and they will be my people.

[11] No longer will they teach their
neighbor,
or say to one another, 'Know
the Lord,'
because they will all know me,
from the least of them to the
greatest.

[12] For I will forgive their
wickedness
and will remember their sins
no more."[a]

[13] By calling this covenant "new,"
he has made the first one obsolete;
and what is obsolete and outdated
will soon disappear.

9 Now the first covenant had regulations for worship and also an
earthly sanctuary. [2] A tabernacle
was set up. In its first room were the
lampstand and the table with its
consecrated bread; this was called
the Holy Place. [3] Behind the second
curtain was a room called the Most
Holy Place, [4] which had the golden
altar of incense and the gold-cov-
ered ark of the covenant. This ark
contained the gold jar of manna,
Aaron's staff that had budded, and
the stone tablets of the covenant.
[5] Above the ark were the cherubim

of the Glory, overshadowing the
atonement cover. But we cannot
discuss these things in detail now.

[6] When everything had been
arranged like this, the priests entered regularly into the outer room
to carry on their ministry. [7] But only
the high priest entered the inner
room, and that only once a year,
and never without blood, which he
offered for himself and for the sins
the people had committed in ignorance. [8] The Holy Spirit was showing by this that the way into the
Most Holy Place had not yet been
disclosed as long as the first tabernacle was still functioning. [9] This
is an illustration for the present
time, indicating that the gifts and
sacrifices being offered were not
able to clear the conscience of the
worshiper. [10] They are only a matter of food and drink and various
ceremonial washings—external
regulations applying until the time
of the new order.

[11] But when Christ came as high
priest of the good things that are
now already here,[b] he went through
the greater and more perfect tabernacle that is not made with human
hands, that is to say, is not a part
of this creation. [12] He did not enter
by means of the blood of goats and
calves; but he entered the Most Holy
Place once for all by his own blood,
thus obtaining[c] eternal redemption. [13] The blood of goats and bulls
and the ashes of a heifer sprinkled
on those who are ceremonially unclean sanctify them so that they
are outwardly clean. [14] How much
more, then, will the blood of Christ,
who through the eternal Spirit offered himself unblemished to God,
cleanse our consciences from acts

---

[a] 12 Jer. 31:31-34   [b] 11 Some early manuscripts *are to come*   [c] 12 Or *blood, having obtained*

that lead to death,[a] so that we may serve the living God!

[15] For this reason Christ is the mediator of a new covenant, that those who are called may receive the promised eternal inheritance—now that he has died as a ransom to set them free from the sins committed under the first covenant.

[16] In the case of a will,[b] it is necessary to prove the death of the one who made it, [17] because a will is in force only when somebody has died; it never takes effect while the one who made it is living. [18] This is why even the first covenant was not put into effect without blood. [19] When Moses had proclaimed every command of the law to all the people, he took the blood of calves, together with water, scarlet wool and branches of hyssop, and sprinkled the scroll and all the people. [20] He said, "This is the blood of the covenant, which God has commanded you to keep."[c] [21] In the same way, he sprinkled with the blood both the tabernacle and everything used in its ceremonies. [22] In fact, the law requires that nearly everything be cleansed with blood, and without the shedding of blood there is no forgiveness.

[23] It was necessary, then, for the copies of the heavenly things to be purified with these sacrifices, but the heavenly things themselves with better sacrifices than these. [24] For Christ did not enter a sanctuary made with human hands that was only a copy of the true one; he entered heaven itself, now to appear for us in God's presence. [25] Nor did he enter heaven to offer himself again and again, the way the high priest enters the Most Holy Place

every year with blood that is not his own. [26] Otherwise Christ would have had to suffer many times since the creation of the world. But he has appeared once for all at the culmination of the ages to do away with sin by the sacrifice of himself. [27] Just as people are destined to die once, and after that to face judgment, [28] so Christ was sacrificed once to take away the sins of many; and he will appear a second time, not to bear sin, but to bring salvation to those who are waiting for him.

10 The law is only a shadow of the good things that are coming—not the realities themselves. For this reason it can never, by the same sacrifices repeated endlessly year after year, make perfect those who draw near to worship. [2] Otherwise, would they not have stopped being offered? For the worshipers would have been cleansed once for all, and would no longer have felt guilty for their sins. [3] But those sacrifices are an annual reminder of sins. [4] It is impossible for the blood of bulls and goats to take away sins.

[5] Therefore, when Christ came into the world, he said:

> "Sacrifice and offering you did
>       not desire,
>   but a body you prepared for
>       me;
> [6] with burnt offerings and sin
>       offerings
>   you were not pleased.
> [7] Then I said, 'Here I am—it is
>       written about me in the
>       scroll—
>   I have come to do your will, my
>       God.'"[d]

---

[a] 14 Or *from useless rituals*    [b] 16 Same Greek word as *covenant*; also in verse 17
[c] 20 Exodus 24:8    [d] 7 Psalm 40:6-8 (see Septuagint)

8First he said, "Sacrifices and offerings, burnt offerings and sin offerings you did not desire, nor were you pleased with them"—though they were offered in accordance with the law. 9Then he said, "Here I am, I have come to do your will." He sets aside the first to establish the second. 10And by that will, we have been made holy through the sacrifice of the body of Jesus Christ once for all.

11Day after day every priest stands and performs his religious duties; again and again he offers the same sacrifices, which can never take away sins. 12But when this priest had offered for all time one sacrifice for sins, he sat down at the right hand of God, 13and since that time he waits for his enemies to be made his footstool. 14For by one sacrifice he has made perfect forever those who are being made holy.

15The Holy Spirit also testifies to us about this. First he says:

16 "This is the covenant I will make
        with them
    after that time, says the Lord.
  I will put my laws in their hearts,
    and I will write them on their
        minds."a

17Then he adds:

  "Their sins and lawless acts
    I will remember no more."b

18And where these have been forgiven, sacrifice for sin is no longer necessary.

19Therefore, brothers and sisters, since we have confidence to enter the Most Holy Place by the blood of Jesus, 20by a new and living way opened for us through the curtain, that is, his body, 21and since we have a great priest over the house of God, 22let us draw near to God with a sincere heart and with the full assurance that faith brings, having our hearts sprinkled to cleanse us from a guilty conscience and having our bodies washed with pure water. 23Let us hold unswervingly to the hope we profess, for he who promised is faithful. 24And let us consider how we may spur one another on toward love and good deeds, 25not giving up meeting together, as some are in the habit of doing, but encouraging one another—and all the more as you see the Day approaching.

26If we deliberately keep on sinning after we have received the knowledge of the truth, no sacrifice for sins is left, 27but only a fearful expectation of judgment and of raging fire that will consume the enemies of God. 28Anyone who rejected the law of Moses died without mercy on the testimony of two or three witnesses. 29How much more severely do you think someone deserves to be punished who has trampled the Son of God underfoot, who has treated as an unholy thing the blood of the covenant that sanctified them, and who has insulted the Spirit of grace? 30For we know him who said, "It is mine to avenge; I will repay,"c and again, "The Lord will judge his people."d 31It is a dreadful thing to fall into the hands of the living God.

32Remember those earlier days after you had received the light, when you endured in a great conflict full of suffering. 33Sometimes you were publicly exposed to insult and persecution; at other times you stood side by side with those who were so treated. 34You suffered

a 16 Jer. 31:33    b 17 Jer. 31:34    c 30 Deut. 32:35    d 30 Deut. 32:36; Psalm 135:14

along with those in prison and joyfully accepted the confiscation of your property, because you knew that you yourselves had better and lasting possessions. 35So do not throw away your confidence; it will be richly rewarded.

36You need to persevere so that when you have done the will of God, you will receive what he has promised. 37For,

"In just a little while,
    he who is coming will come
    and will not delay."[a]

38And,

"But my righteous[b] one will live
    by faith.
And I take no pleasure
    in the one who shrinks back."[c]

39But we do not belong to those who shrink back and are destroyed, but to those who have faith and are saved.

11 Now faith is confidence in what we hope for and assurance about what we do not see. 2This is what the ancients were commended for.

3By faith we understand that the universe was formed at God's command, so that what is seen was not made out of what was visible.

4By faith Abel brought God a better offering than Cain did. By faith he was commended as righteous, when God spoke well of his offerings. And by faith Abel still speaks, even though he is dead.

5By faith Enoch was taken from this life, so that he did not experience death: "He could not be found, because God had taken him away."[d] For before he was taken, he was commended as one who pleased God. 6And without faith it is impossible to please God, because anyone who comes to him must believe that he exists and that he rewards those who earnestly seek him.

7By faith Noah, when warned about things not yet seen, in holy fear built an ark to save his family. By his faith he condemned the world and became heir of the righteousness that is in keeping with faith.

8By faith Abraham, when called to go to a place he would later receive as his inheritance, obeyed and went, even though he did not know where he was going. 9By faith he made his home in the promised land like a stranger in a foreign country; he lived in tents, as did Isaac and Jacob, who were heirs with him of the same promise. 10For he was looking forward to the city with foundations, whose architect and builder is God. 11And by faith even Sarah, who was past childbearing age, was enabled to bear children because she[e] considered him faithful who had made the promise. 12And so from this one man, and he as good as dead, came descendants as numerous as the stars in the sky and as countless as the sand on the seashore.

13All these people were still living by faith when they died. They did not receive the things promised; they only saw them and welcomed them from a distance, admitting that they were foreigners

---

[a] 37 Isaiah 26:20; Hab. 2:3 (see Septuagint)    [b] 38 Some early manuscripts But the righteous    [c] 38 Hab. 2:4    [d] 5 Gen. 5:24    [e] 11 Or By faith Abraham, even though he was too old to have children—and Sarah herself was not able to conceive—was enabled to become a father because he

and strangers on earth. ¹⁴People who say such things show that they are looking for a country of their own. ¹⁵If they had been thinking of the country they had left, they would have had opportunity to return. ¹⁶Instead, they were longing for a better country—a heavenly one. Therefore God is not ashamed to be called their God, for he has prepared a city for them.

¹⁷By faith Abraham, when God tested him, offered Isaac as a sacrifice. He who had embraced the promises was about to sacrifice his one and only son, ¹⁸even though God had said to him, "It is through Isaac that your offspring will be reckoned."ᵃ ¹⁹Abraham reasoned that God could even raise the dead, and so in a manner of speaking he did receive Isaac back from death.

²⁰By faith Isaac blessed Jacob and Esau in regard to their future.

²¹By faith Jacob, when he was dying, blessed each of Joseph's sons, and worshiped as he leaned on the top of his staff.

²²By faith Joseph, when his end was near, spoke about the exodus of the Israelites from Egypt and gave instructions concerning the burial of his bones.

²³By faith Moses' parents hid him for three months after he was born, because they saw he was no ordinary child, and they were not afraid of the king's edict.

²⁴By faith Moses, when he had grown up, refused to be known as the son of Pharaoh's daughter. ²⁵He chose to be mistreated along with the people of God rather than to enjoy the fleeting pleasures of sin. ²⁶He regarded disgrace for the sake of Christ as of greater value than

the treasures of Egypt, because he was looking ahead to his reward. ²⁷By faith he left Egypt, not fearing the king's anger; he persevered because he saw him who is invisible. ²⁸By faith he kept the Passover and the application of blood, so that the destroyer of the firstborn would not touch the firstborn of Israel.

²⁹By faith the people passed through the Red Sea as on dry land; but when the Egyptians tried to do so, they were drowned.

³⁰By faith the walls of Jericho fell, after the army had marched around them for seven days.

³¹By faith the prostitute Rahab, because she welcomed the spies, was not killed with those who were disobedient.ᵇ

³²And what more shall I say? I do not have time to tell about Gideon, Barak, Samson and Jephthah, about David and Samuel and the prophets, ³³who through faith conquered kingdoms, administered justice, and gained what was promised; who shut the mouths of lions, ³⁴quenched the fury of the flames, and escaped the edge of the sword; whose weakness was turned to strength; and who became powerful in battle and routed foreign armies. ³⁵Women received back their dead, raised to life again. There were others who were tortured, refusing to be released so that they might gain an even better resurrection. ³⁶Some faced jeers and flogging, and even chains and imprisonment. ³⁷They were put to death by stoning;ᶜ they were sawed in two; they were killed by the sword. They went about in sheepskins and goatskins, destitute, persecuted and mistreated— ³⁸the world was

<hr>

ᵃ 18 Gen. 21:12   ᵇ 31 Or unbelieving   ᶜ 37 Some early manuscripts stoning; they were put to the test;

not worthy of them. They wandered in deserts and mountains, living in caves and in holes in the ground.

³⁹These were all commended for their faith, yet none of them received what had been promised, ⁴⁰since God had planned something better for us so that only together with us would they be made perfect.

12 Therefore, since we are surrounded by such a great cloud of witnesses, let us throw off everything that hinders and the sin that so easily entangles. And let us run with perseverance the race marked out for us, ²fixing our eyes on Jesus, the pioneer and perfecter of faith. For the joy set before him he endured the cross, scorning its shame, and sat down at the right hand of the throne of God. ³Consider him who endured such opposition from sinners, so that you will not grow weary and lose heart.

⁴In your struggle against sin, you have not yet resisted to the point of shedding your blood. ⁵And have you completely forgotten this word of encouragement that addresses you as a father addresses his son? It says,

"My son, do not make light of the
    Lord's discipline,
  and do not lose heart when he
    rebukes you,
⁶because the Lord disciplines the
    one he loves,
  and he chastens everyone he
    accepts as his son."ᵃ

⁷Endure hardship as discipline; God is treating you as his children. For what children are not disciplined by their father? ⁸If you are not disciplined—and everyone undergoes discipline—then you

are not legitimate, not true sons and daughters at all. ⁹Moreover, we have all had human fathers who disciplined us and we respected them for it. How much more should we submit to the Father of spirits and live! ¹⁰They disciplined us for a little while as they thought best; but God disciplines us for our good, in order that we may share in his holiness. ¹¹No discipline seems pleasant at the time, but painful. Later on, however, it produces a harvest of righteousness and peace for those who have been trained by it.

¹²Therefore, strengthen your feeble arms and weak knees. ¹³"Make level paths for your feet,"ᵇ so that the lame may not be disabled, but rather healed.

¹⁴Make every effort to live in peace with everyone and to be holy; without holiness no one will see the Lord. ¹⁵See to it that no one falls short of the grace of God and that no bitter root grows up to cause trouble and defile many. ¹⁶See that no one is sexually immoral, or is godless like Esau, who for a single meal sold his inheritance rights as the oldest son. ¹⁷Afterward, as you know, when he wanted to inherit this blessing, he was rejected. Even though he sought the blessing with tears, he could not change what he had done.

¹⁸You have not come to a mountain that can be touched and that is burning with fire; to darkness, gloom and storm; ¹⁹to a trumpet blast or to such a voice speaking words that those who heard it begged that no further word be spoken to them, ²⁰because they could not bear what was commanded: "If even an animal touches the moun-

---

ᵃ 5,6 Prov. 3:11,12 (see Septuagint)    ᵇ 13 Prov. 4:26

tain, it must be stoned to death."[a] [21]The sight was so terrifying that Moses said, "I am trembling with fear."[b]

[22]But you have come to Mount Zion, to the city of the living God, the heavenly Jerusalem. You have come to thousands upon thousands of angels in joyful assembly, [23]to the church of the firstborn, whose names are written in heaven. You have come to God, the Judge of all, to the spirits of the righteous made perfect, [24]to Jesus the mediator of a new covenant, and to the sprinkled blood that speaks a better word than the blood of Abel.

[25]See to it that you do not refuse him who speaks. If they did not escape when they refused him who warned them on earth, how much less will we, if we turn away from him who warns us from heaven? [26]At that time his voice shook the earth, but now he has promised, "Once more I will shake not only the earth but also the heavens."[c] [27]The words "once more" indicate the removing of what can be shaken—that is, created things—so that what cannot be shaken may remain.

[28]Therefore, since we are receiving a kingdom that cannot be shaken, let us be thankful, and so worship God acceptably with reverence and awe, [29]for our "God is a consuming fire."[d]

13 Keep on loving one another as brothers and sisters. [2]Do not forget to show hospitality to strangers, for by so doing some people have shown hospitality to angels without knowing it. [3]Continue to remember those in prison as if you were together with them in prison,

and those who are mistreated as if you yourselves were suffering.

[4]Marriage should be honored by all, and the marriage bed kept pure, for God will judge the adulterer and all the sexually immoral. [5]Keep your lives free from the love of money and be content with what you have, because God has said,

> "Never will I leave you;
> never will I forsake you."[e]

[6]So we say with confidence,

> "The Lord is my helper; I will not be afraid.
> What can mere mortals do to me?"[f]

[7]Remember your leaders, who spoke the word of God to you. Consider the outcome of their way of life and imitate their faith. [8]Jesus Christ is the same yesterday and today and forever.

[9]Do not be carried away by all kinds of strange teachings. It is good for our hearts to be strengthened by grace, not by eating ceremonial foods, which is of no benefit to those who do so. [10]We have an altar from which those who minister at the tabernacle have no right to eat.

[11]The high priest carries the blood of animals into the Most Holy Place as a sin offering, but the bodies are burned outside the camp. [12]And so Jesus also suffered outside the city gate to make the people holy through his own blood. [13]Let us, then, go to him outside the camp, bearing the disgrace he bore. [14]For here we do not have an enduring city, but we are looking for the city that is to come.

[15]Through Jesus, therefore, let

[a] 20 Exodus 19:12,13   [b] 21 See Deut. 9:19.   [c] 26 Haggai 2:6   [d] 29 Deut. 4:24   [e] 5 Deut. 31:6   [f] 6 Psalm 118:6,7

us continually offer to God a sacrifice of praise — the fruit of lips that openly profess his name. ¹⁶And do not forget to do good and to share with others, for with such sacrifices God is pleased.

¹⁷Have confidence in your leaders and submit to their authority, because they keep watch over you as those who must give an account. Do this so that their work is a joy, not a burden, for that would be of no benefit to you.

¹⁸Pray for us. We are sure that we have a clear conscience and desire to live honorably in every way. ¹⁹I particularly urge you to pray so that I may be restored to you soon.

²⁰Now may the God of peace, who through the blood of the eternal covenant brought back from the dead our Lord Jesus, that great Shepherd of the sheep, ²¹equip you with everything good for doing his will, and may he work in us what is pleasing to him, through Jesus Christ, to whom be glory for ever and ever. Amen.

²²Brothers and sisters, I urge you to bear with my word of exhortation, for in fact I have written to you quite briefly.

²³I want you to know that our brother Timothy has been released. If he arrives soon, I will come with him to see you.

²⁴Greet all your leaders and all the Lord's people. Those from Italy send you their greetings.

²⁵Grace be with you all.

# JAMES

James, one of the brothers of Jesus, became a leader of the church in Jerusalem after Jesus' death and resurrection. He was respected for the advice he gave and for the wise decisions he helped the community of believers make (see p. 170). At one point he decided to write down some of his best teachings and advice and send them to other Jewish believers in Jesus who were scattered throughout the Roman Empire. What he wrote to them has become known as the book of James.

This book begins like a letter because it's being sent to people at a distance. But it is actually not very much like other letters of the time. It is a collection of short sayings and slightly longer discussions of practical topics. The conversational style, the short, pithy sayings and the interweaving of themes all make this book similar to the wisdom writing found in Proverbs and Ecclesiastes.

Like those wisdom books, James concentrates on questions of daily living in God's good creation. He considers such practical issues as concern for the poor, the responsible use of wealth, control of the tongue, purity of life, unity in the community of Christ-followers, and above all patience and endurance during times of trial. The godly wisdom here remains as valuable a guide to living fully human lives as when James first shared it centuries ago.

---

1 James, a servant of God and of the Lord Jesus Christ,

To the twelve tribes scattered among the nations:

Greetings.

2 Consider it pure joy, my brothers and sisters,[a] whenever you face trials of many kinds, 3 because you know that the testing of your faith produces perseverance. 4 Let perseverance finish its work so that you may be mature and complete, not lacking anything. 5 If any of you lacks wisdom, you should ask God, who gives generously to all without finding fault, and it will be given to you. 6 But when you ask, you must believe and not doubt, because the one who doubts is like a wave of the sea, blown and tossed by the wind. 7 That person should not expect to receive anything from the Lord. 8 Such a person is double-minded and unstable in all they do.

9 Believers in humble circumstances ought to take pride in their high position. 10 But the rich should take pride in their humiliation — since they will pass away like a wild flower. 11 For the sun rises with scorching heat and withers the plant; its blossom falls and its beauty is destroyed. In the same way, the rich will fade away even while they go about their business.

12 Blessed is the one who perseveres under trial because, having stood the test, that person will receive the crown of life that the Lord

---

[a] 2 The Greek word for *brothers and sisters* (*adelphoi*) refers here to believers, both men and women, as part of God's family; also in verses 16 and 19; and in 2:1, 5, 14; 3:10, 12; 4:11; 5:7, 9, 10, 12, 19.

has promised to those who love him.

¹³When tempted, no one should say, "God is tempting me." For God cannot be tempted by evil, nor does he tempt anyone; ¹⁴but each person is tempted when they are dragged away by their own evil desire and enticed. ¹⁵Then, after desire has conceived, it gives birth to sin; and sin, when it is full-grown, gives birth to death.

¹⁶Don't be deceived, my dear brothers and sisters. ¹⁷Every good and perfect gift is from above, coming down from the Father of the heavenly lights, who does not change like shifting shadows. ¹⁸He chose to give us birth through the word of truth, that we might be a kind of firstfruits of all he created.

¹⁹My dear brothers and sisters, take note of this: Everyone should be quick to listen, slow to speak and slow to become angry, ²⁰because human anger does not produce the righteousness that God desires. ²¹Therefore, get rid of all moral filth and the evil that is so prevalent in you, and humbly accept the word planted in you, which can save you.

²²Do not merely listen to the word, and so deceive yourselves. Do what it says. ²³Anyone who listens to the word but does not do what it says is like someone who looks at his face in a mirror ²⁴and, after looking at himself, goes away and immediately forgets what he looks like. ²⁵But whoever looks intently into the perfect law that gives freedom, and continues in it—not forgetting what they have heard, but doing it—they will be blessed in what they do.

²⁶Those who consider themselves religious and yet do not keep a tight rein on their tongues deceive themselves, and their religion is worthless. ²⁷Religion that God our Father accepts as pure and faultless is this: to look after orphans and widows in their distress and to keep oneself from being polluted by the world.

2 My brothers and sisters, believers in our glorious Lord Jesus Christ must not show favoritism. ²Suppose a man comes into your meeting wearing a gold ring and fine clothes, and a poor man in filthy old clothes also comes in. ³If you show special attention to the man wearing fine clothes and say, "Here's a good seat for you," but say to the poor man, "You stand there" or "Sit on the floor by my feet," ⁴have you not discriminated among yourselves and become judges with evil thoughts?

⁵Listen, my dear brothers and sisters: Has not God chosen those who are poor in the eyes of the world to be rich in faith and to inherit the kingdom he promised those who love him? ⁶But you have dishonored the poor. Is it not the rich who are exploiting you? Are they not the ones who are dragging you into court? ⁷Are they not the ones who are blaspheming the noble name of him to whom you belong?

⁸If you really keep the royal law found in Scripture, "Love your neighbor as yourself,"ᵃ you are doing right. ⁹But if you show favoritism, you sin and are convicted by the law as lawbreakers. ¹⁰For whoever keeps the whole law and yet stumbles at just one point is guilty of breaking all of it. ¹¹For he who said, "You shall not commit adultery,"ᵇ also said, "You shall not murder."ᶜ If you do not commit

---

ᵃ 8 Lev. 19:18    ᵇ 11 Exodus 20:14; Deut. 5:18    ᶜ 11 Exodus 20:13; Deut. 5:17

adultery but do commit murder, you have become a lawbreaker.

¹²Speak and act as those who are going to be judged by the law that gives freedom, ¹³because judgment without mercy will be shown to anyone who has not been merciful. Mercy triumphs over judgment.

¹⁴What good is it, my brothers and sisters, if someone claims to have faith but has no deeds? Can such faith save them? ¹⁵Suppose a brother or a sister is without clothes and daily food. ¹⁶If one of you says to them, "Go in peace; keep warm and well fed," but does nothing about their physical needs, what good is it? ¹⁷In the same way, faith by itself, if it is not accompanied by action, is dead.

¹⁸But someone will say, "You have faith; I have deeds."

Show me your faith without deeds, and I will show you my faith by my deeds. ¹⁹You believe that there is one God. Good! Even the demons believe that—and shudder.

²⁰You foolish person, do you want evidence that faith without deeds is useless? ᵃ ²¹Was not our father Abraham considered righteous for what he did when he offered his son Isaac on the altar? ²²You see that his faith and his actions were working together, and his faith was made complete by what he did. ²³And the scripture was fulfilled that says, "Abraham believed God, and it was credited to him as righteousness," ᵇ and he was called God's friend. ²⁴You see that a person is considered righteous by what they do and not by faith alone.

²⁵In the same way, was not even Rahab the prostitute considered righteous for what she did when she gave lodging to the spies and sent them off in a different direction? ²⁶As the body without the spirit is dead, so faith without deeds is dead.

3 Not many of you should become teachers, my fellow believers, because you know that we who teach will be judged more strictly. ²We all stumble in many ways. Anyone who is never at fault in what they say is perfect, able to keep their whole body in check.

³When we put bits into the mouths of horses to make them obey us, we can turn the whole animal. ⁴Or take ships as an example. Although they are so large and are driven by strong winds, they are steered by a very small rudder wherever the pilot wants to go. ⁵Likewise, the tongue is a small part of the body, but it makes great boasts. Consider what a great forest is set on fire by a small spark. ⁶The tongue also is a fire, a world of evil among the parts of the body. It corrupts the whole body, sets the whole course of one's life on fire, and is itself set on fire by hell.

⁷All kinds of animals, birds, reptiles and sea creatures are being tamed and have been tamed by mankind, ⁸but no human being can tame the tongue. It is a restless evil, full of deadly poison.

⁹With the tongue we praise our Lord and Father, and with it we curse human beings, who have been made in God's likeness. ¹⁰Out of the same mouth come praise and cursing. My brothers and sisters, this should not be. ¹¹Can both fresh water and salt water flow from the same spring? ¹²My brothers and sisters, can a fig tree bear

ᵃ 20 Some early manuscripts dead    ᵇ 23 Gen. 15:6

olives, or a grapevine bear figs? Neither can a salt spring produce fresh water.

13 Who is wise and understanding among you? Let them show it by their good life, by deeds done in the humility that comes from wisdom. 14 But if you harbor bitter envy and selfish ambition in your hearts, do not boast about it or deny the truth. 15 Such "wisdom" does not come down from heaven but is earthly, unspiritual, demonic. 16 For where you have envy and selfish ambition, there you find disorder and every evil practice.

17 But the wisdom that comes from heaven is first of all pure; then peace-loving, considerate, submissive, full of mercy and good fruit, impartial and sincere. 18 Peacemakers who sow in peace reap a harvest of righteousness.

4 What causes fights and quarrels among you? Don't they come from your desires that battle within you? 2 You desire but do not have, so you kill. You covet but you cannot get what you want, so you quarrel and fight. You do not have because you do not ask God. 3 When you ask, you do not receive, because you ask with wrong motives, that you may spend what you get on your pleasures.

4 You adulterous people,[a] don't you know that friendship with the world means enmity against God? Therefore, anyone who chooses to be a friend of the world becomes an enemy of God. 5 Or do you think Scripture says without reason that he jealously longs for the spirit he has caused to dwell in us[b]? 6 But he

gives us more grace. That is why Scripture says:

"God opposes the proud
but shows favor to the
humble."[c]

7 Submit yourselves, then, to God. Resist the devil, and he will flee from you. 8 Come near to God and he will come near to you. Wash your hands, you sinners, and purify your hearts, you double-minded. 9 Grieve, mourn and wail. Change your laughter to mourning and your joy to gloom. 10 Humble yourselves before the Lord, and he will lift you up.

11 Brothers and sisters, do not slander one another. Anyone who speaks against a brother or sister[d] or judges them speaks against the law and judges it. When you judge the law, you are not keeping it, but sitting in judgment on it. 12 There is only one Lawgiver and Judge, the one who is able to save and destroy. But you—who are you to judge your neighbor?

13 Now listen, you who say, "Today or tomorrow we will go to this or that city, spend a year there, carry on business and make money." 14 Why, you do not even know what will happen tomorrow. What is your life? You are a mist that appears for a little while and then vanishes. 15 Instead, you ought to say, "If it is the Lord's will, we will live and do this or that." 16 As it is, you boast in your arrogant schemes. All such boasting is evil. 17 If anyone, then, knows the good they ought to do and doesn't do it, it is sin for them.

---

a 4 An allusion to covenant unfaithfulness; see Hosea 3:1.    b 5 Or that the spirit he caused to dwell in us envies intensely; or that the Spirit he caused to dwell in us longs jealously    c 6 Prov. 3:34    d 11 The Greek word for brother or sister (adelphos) refers here to a believer, whether man or woman, as part of God's family.

5 Now listen, you rich people, weep and wail because of the misery that is coming on you. ²Your wealth has rotted, and moths have eaten your clothes. ³Your gold and silver are corroded. Their corrosion will testify against you and eat your flesh like fire. You have hoarded wealth in the last days. ⁴Look! The wages you failed to pay the workers who mowed your fields are crying out against you. The cries of the harvesters have reached the ears of the Lord Almighty. ⁵You have lived on earth in luxury and self-indulgence. You have fattened yourselves in the day of slaughter.ᵃ ⁶You have condemned and murdered the innocent one, who was not opposing you.

⁷Be patient, then, brothers and sisters, until the Lord's coming. See how the farmer waits for the land to yield its valuable crop, patiently waiting for the autumn and spring rains. ⁸You too, be patient and stand firm, because the Lord's coming is near. ⁹Don't grumble against one another, brothers and sisters, or you will be judged. The Judge is standing at the door!

¹⁰Brothers and sisters, as an example of patience in the face of suffering, take the prophets who spoke in the name of the Lord. ¹¹As you know, we count as blessed those who have persevered. You have heard of Job's perseverance and have seen what the Lord final-ly brought about. The Lord is full of compassion and mercy.

¹²Above all, my brothers and sisters, do not swear—not by heaven or by earth or by anything else. All you need to say is a simple "Yes" or "No." Otherwise you will be condemned.

¹³Is anyone among you in trouble? Let them pray. Is anyone happy? Let them sing songs of praise. ¹⁴Is anyone among you sick? Let them call the elders of the church to pray over them and anoint them with oil in the name of the Lord. ¹⁵And the prayer offered in faith will make the sick person well; the Lord will raise them up. If they have sinned, they will be forgiven. ¹⁶Therefore confess your sins to each other and pray for each other so that you may be healed. The prayer of a righteous person is powerful and effective.

¹⁷Elijah was a human being, even as we are. He prayed earnestly that it would not rain, and it did not rain on the land for three and a half years. ¹⁸Again he prayed, and the heavens gave rain, and the earth produced its crops.

¹⁹My brothers and sisters, if one of you should wander from the truth and someone should bring that person back, ²⁰remember this: Whoever turns a sinner from the error of their way will save them from death and cover over a multitude of sins.

ᵃ 5 Or *yourselves as in a day of feasting*

# 1 PETER

The apostle Peter was one of the twelve disciples Jesus appointed and taught during his time on earth. Peter spent the final years of his life and ministry—in the early 60s AD—as a leader of the church in Rome. When he learned that churches in other Roman provinces (all located in what is now Turkey) were experiencing persecution, he wrote to urge them to remain faithful to Jesus. Peter's letter was delivered by Silas, a man who also worked with the apostle Paul (see pp. 170-173). Peter introduces Silas and explains that he helped to compose the letter.

After the opening, the letter has three main sections:

: Peter first tells his readers to *be holy in all you do*. As Gentiles they once lived in ignorance (they did not know the ways of God). But they are now a holy nation, part of God's own people, and are called to a new way of life.

: Peter then explains how this way of life will impress those who might accuse and persecute them without just cause.

: Finally, Peter acknowledges that his readers are suffering for their faith, but he explains that this is only to be expected. The Messiah himself suffered, and believers all over the world are facing the same challenge. The followers of Jesus are waiting for the day God will visit them, and even in their suffering they can show they belong to God.

---

1 Peter, an apostle of Jesus Christ,

To God's elect, exiles scattered throughout the provinces of Pontus, Galatia, Cappadocia, Asia and Bithynia, ²who have been chosen according to the foreknowledge of God the Father, through the sanctifying work of the Spirit, to be obedient to Jesus Christ and sprinkled with his blood:

Grace and peace be yours in abundance.

³Praise be to the God and Father of our Lord Jesus Christ! In his great mercy he has given us new birth into a living hope through the resurrection of Jesus Christ from the dead, ⁴and into an inheritance that can never perish, spoil or fade. This inheritance is kept in heaven for you, ⁵who through faith are shield-ed by God's power until the coming of the salvation that is ready to be revealed in the last time. ⁶In all this you greatly rejoice, though now for a little while you may have had to suffer grief in all kinds of trials. ⁷These have come so that the proven genuineness of your faith—of greater worth than gold, which perishes even though refined by fire—may result in praise, glory and honor when Jesus Christ is revealed. ⁸Though you have not seen him, you love him; and even though you do not see him now, you believe in him and are filled with an inexpressible and glorious joy, ⁹for you are receiving the end result of your faith, the salvation of your souls.

¹⁰Concerning this salvation, the prophets, who spoke of the grace that was to come to you, searched intently and with the greatest care,

[11] trying to find out the time and circumstances to which the Spirit of Christ in them was pointing when he predicted the sufferings of the Messiah and the glories that would follow. [12] It was revealed to them that they were not serving themselves but you, when they spoke of the things that have now been told you by those who have preached the gospel to you by the Holy Spirit sent from heaven. Even angels long to look into these things.

[13] Therefore, with minds that are alert and fully sober, set your hope on the grace to be brought to you when Jesus Christ is revealed at his coming. [14] As obedient children, do not conform to the evil desires you had when you lived in ignorance. [15] But just as he who called you is holy, so be holy in all you do; [16] for it is written: "Be holy, because I am holy."[a]

[17] Since you call on a Father who judges each person's work impartially, live out your time as foreigners here in reverent fear. [18] For you know that it was not with perishable things such as silver or gold that you were redeemed from the empty way of life handed down to you from your ancestors, [19] but with the precious blood of Christ, a lamb without blemish or defect. [20] He was chosen before the creation of the world, but was revealed in these last times for your sake. [21] Through him you believe in God, who raised him from the dead and glorified him, and so your faith and hope are in God.

[22] Now that you have purified yourselves by obeying the truth so that you have sincere love for each other, love one another deeply, from the heart.[b] [23] For you have been born again, not of perishable seed, but of imperishable, through the living and enduring word of God. [24] For,

> "All people are like grass,
>     and all their glory is like the
>         flowers of the field;
> the grass withers and the flowers
>     fall,
> [25]     but the word of the Lord
>         endures forever."[c]

And this is the word that was preached to you.

2 Therefore, rid yourselves of all malice and all deceit, hypocrisy, envy, and slander of every kind. [2] Like newborn babies, crave pure spiritual milk, so that by it you may grow up in your salvation, [3] now that you have tasted that the Lord is good.

[4] As you come to him, the living Stone — rejected by humans but chosen by God and precious to him — [5] you also, like living stones, are being built into a spiritual house[d] to be a holy priesthood, offering spiritual sacrifices acceptable to God through Jesus Christ. [6] For in Scripture it says:

> "See, I lay a stone in Zion,
>     a chosen and precious
>         cornerstone,
> and the one who trusts in him
>     will never be put to shame."[e]

[7] Now to you who believe, this stone is precious. But to those who do not believe,

> "The stone the builders rejected
>     has become the cornerstone,"[f]

[8] and,

---

[a] 16 Lev. 11:44,45; 19:2      [b] 22 Some early manuscripts *from a pure heart*      [c] 25 Isaiah 40:6-8
(see Septuagint)      [d] 5 Or *into a temple of the Spirit*      [e] 6 Isaiah 28:16      [f] 7 Psalm 118:22

"A stone that causes people to
 stumble
and a rock that makes them
 fall."[a]

They stumble because they disobey
the message—which is also what
they were destined for.

9But you are a chosen people,
a royal priesthood, a holy nation,
God's special possession, that you
may declare the praises of him who
called you out of darkness into his
wonderful light. 10Once you were
not a people, but now you are the
people of God; once you had not
received mercy, but now you have
received mercy.

11Dear friends, I urge you, as
foreigners and exiles, to abstain
from sinful desires, which wage
war against your soul. 12Live such
good lives among the pagans that,
though they accuse you of doing
wrong, they may see your good
deeds and glorify God on the day
he visits us.

13Submit yourselves for the Lord's
sake to every human authority:
whether to the emperor, as the supreme authority, 14or to governors,
who are sent by him to punish those
who do wrong and to commend
those who do right. 15For it is God's
will that by doing good you should
silence the ignorant talk of foolish
people. 16Live as free people, but do
not use your freedom as a cover-up
for evil; live as God's slaves. 17Show
proper respect to everyone, love the
family of believers, fear God, honor
the emperor.

18Slaves, in reverent fear of God
submit yourselves to your masters,
not only to those who are good and
considerate, but also to those who
are harsh. 19For it is commendable

if someone bears up under the pain
of unjust suffering because they are
conscious of God. 20But how is it to
your credit if you receive a beating
for doing wrong and endure it? But
if you suffer for doing good and you
endure it, this is commendable before God. 21To this you were called,
because Christ suffered for you,
leaving you an example, that you
should follow in his steps.

22"He committed no sin,
 and no deceit was found in his
 mouth."[b]

23When they hurled their insults at
him, he did not retaliate; when he
suffered, he made no threats. Instead, he entrusted himself to him
who judges justly. 24"He himself
bore our sins" in his body on the
cross, so that we might die to sins
and live for righteousness; "by his
wounds you have been healed."
25For "you were like sheep going
astray,"[c] but now you have returned
to the Shepherd and Overseer of
your souls.

3 Wives, in the same way submit
 yourselves to your own husbands so that, if any of them do not
believe the word, they may be won
over without words by the behavior
of their wives, 2when they see the
purity and reverence of your lives.
3Your beauty should not come from
outward adornment, such as elaborate hairstyles and the wearing of
gold jewelry or fine clothes. 4Rath-
er, it should be that of your inner
self, the unfading beauty of a gentle and quiet spirit, which is of great
worth in God's sight. 5For this is the
way the holy women of the past who
put their hope in God used to adorn
themselves. They submitted themselves to their own husbands, 6like

a 8 Isaiah 8:14    b 22 Isaiah 53:9    c 24,25 Isaiah 53:4,5,6 (see Septuagint)

Sarah, who obeyed Abraham and called him her lord. You are her daughters if you do what is right and do not give way to fear.

⁷Husbands, in the same way be considerate as you live with your wives, and treat them with respect as the weaker partner and as heirs with you of the gracious gift of life, so that nothing will hinder your prayers.

⁸Finally, all of you, be like-minded, be sympathetic, love one another, be compassionate and humble. ⁹Do not repay evil with evil or insult with insult. On the contrary, repay evil with blessing, because to this you were called so that you may inherit a blessing. ¹⁰For,

"Whoever would love life
    and see good days
must keep their tongue from evil
    and their lips from deceitful
        speech.
¹¹They must turn from evil and do
        good;
    they must seek peace and
        pursue it.
¹²For the eyes of the Lord are on
        the righteous
    and his ears are attentive to
        their prayer,
but the face of the Lord is against
        those who do evil."ᵃ

¹³Who is going to harm you if you are eager to do good? ¹⁴But even if you should suffer for what is right, you are blessed. "Do not fear their threatsᵇ; do not be frightened."ᶜ ¹⁵But in your hearts revere Christ as Lord. Always be prepared to give an answer to everyone who asks you to give the reason for the hope that you have. But do this with gentleness and respect, ¹⁶keeping a clear conscience, so that those who speak maliciously against your good behavior in Christ may be ashamed of their slander. ¹⁷For it is better, if it is God's will, to suffer for doing good than for doing evil. ¹⁸For Christ also suffered once for sins, the righteous for the unrighteous, to bring you to God. He was put to death in the body but made alive in the Spirit. ¹⁹After being made alive,ᵈ he went and made proclamation to the imprisoned spirits— ²⁰to those who were disobedient long ago when God waited patiently in the days of Noah while the ark was being built. In it only a few people, eight in all, were saved through water, ²¹and this water symbolizes baptism that now saves you also—not the removal of dirt from the body but the pledge of a clear conscience toward God.ᵉ It saves you by the resurrection of Jesus Christ, ²²who has gone into heaven and is at God's right hand—with angels, authorities and powers in submission to him.

4 Therefore, since Christ suffered in his body, arm yourselves also with the same attitude, because whoever suffers in the body is done with sin. ²As a result, they do not live the rest of their earthly lives for evil human desires, but rather for the will of God. ³For you have spent enough time in the past doing what pagans choose to do—living in debauchery, lust, drunkenness, orgies, carousing and detestable idolatry. ⁴They are surprised that you do not join them in their reckless, wild living, and they heap abuse on you. ⁵But they will have to give account to him who is ready to judge the living and the dead. ⁶For this is

---

ᵃ 12 Psalm 34:12-16    ᵇ 14 Or fear what they fear    ᶜ 14 Isaiah 8:12    ᵈ 18,19 Or but made alive in the spirit, ¹⁹in which also    ᵉ 21 Or but an appeal to God for a clear conscience the reason the gospel was preached even to those who are now dead, so that they might be judged according to human standards in regard to the body, but live according to God in regard to the spirit.

7 The end of all things is near. Therefore be alert and of sober mind so that you may pray. 8 Above all, love each other deeply, because love covers over a multitude of sins. 9 Offer hospitality to one another without grumbling. 10 Each of you should use whatever gift you have received to serve others, as faithful stewards of God's grace in its various forms. 11 If anyone speaks, they should do so as one who speaks the very words of God. If anyone serves, they should do so with the strength God provides, so that in all things God may be praised through Jesus Christ. To him be the glory and the power for ever and ever. Amen.

12 Dear friends, do not be surprised at the fiery ordeal that has come on you to test you, as though something strange were happening to you. 13 But rejoice inasmuch as you participate in the sufferings of Christ, so that you may be overjoyed when his glory is revealed. 14 If you are insulted because of the name of Christ, you are blessed, for the Spirit of glory and of God rests on you. 15 If you suffer, it should not be as a murderer or thief or any other kind of criminal, or even as a meddler. 16 However, if you suffer as a Christian, do not be ashamed, but praise God that you bear that name. 17 For it is time for judgment to begin with God's household; and if it begins with us, what will the outcome be for those who do not obey the gospel of God? 18 And,

"If it is hard for the righteous to be saved,
    what will become of the
        ungodly and the sinner?"[a]

19 So then, those who suffer according to God's will should commit themselves to their faithful Creator and continue to do good.

5 To the elders among you, I appeal as a fellow elder and a witness of Christ's sufferings who also will share in the glory to be revealed: 2 Be shepherds of God's flock that is under your care, watching over them—not because you must, but because you are willing, as God wants you to be; not pursuing dishonest gain, but eager to serve; 3 not lording it over those entrusted to you, but being examples to the flock. 4 And when the Chief Shepherd appears, you will receive the crown of glory that will never fade away.

5 In the same way, you who are younger, submit yourselves to your elders. All of you, clothe yourselves with humility toward one another, because,

"God opposes the proud
    but shows favor to the
        humble."[b]

6 Humble yourselves, therefore, under God's mighty hand, that he may lift you up in due time. 7 Cast all your anxiety on him because he cares for you.

8 Be alert and of sober mind. Your enemy the devil prowls around like a roaring lion looking for someone to devour. 9 Resist him, standing firm in the faith, because you know that the family of believers throughout the world is undergoing the same kind of sufferings.

[a] 18 Prov. 11:31 (see Septuagint)    [b] 5 Prov. 3:34

¹⁰And the God of all grace, who called you to his eternal glory in Christ, after you have suffered a little while, will himself restore you and make you strong, firm and steadfast. ¹¹To him be the power for ever and ever. Amen.

¹²With the help of Silas,ᵃ whom I regard as a faithful brother, I have written to you briefly, encouraging you and testifying that this is the true grace of God. Stand fast in it.

¹³She who is in Babylon, chosen together with you, sends you her greetings, and so does my son Mark. ¹⁴Greet one another with a kiss of love.

Peace to all of you who are in Christ.

---

ᵃ 12  Greek *Silvanus*, a variant of *Silas*

# 2 PETER

Around AD 65 the apostle Peter was imprisoned in Rome by the emperor Nero, and he realized that he would soon be executed. Since he was an eyewitness of the ministry of Jesus, he decided to write another letter to the believers he had written to before, confirming what they had been taught about Jesus. False teachers were proclaiming that, since Jesus hadn't returned already, his return couldn't be expected at all. Because they didn't expect any future judgment, they were living immoral lives. (Peter likely learned about the threat of these teachers from a letter sent by Jude, a brother of Jesus, to warn believers against them. Peter's letter echoes Jude's, but in shorter form. See p. 324.)

Peter answers the false teachers by stressing that he personally saw the glory and majesty of Jesus *on the sacred mountain* (see p. 55). Everyone will see this glory when Jesus returns. In powerful imagery Peter describes the false teachers' destructive effect on the community and the judgment that awaits them. In the final section of his letter, Peter explains that the Messiah's return has been delayed because God wants everyone to repent. Our proper response is to live good lives filled with hope, *since we are looking forward to a new heaven and a new earth, where righteousness dwells.*

---

1 Simon Peter, a servant and apostle of Jesus Christ,

To those who through the righteousness of our God and Savior Jesus Christ have received a faith as precious as ours:

²Grace and peace be yours in abundance through the knowledge of God and of Jesus our Lord.

³His divine power has given us everything we need for a godly life through our knowledge of him who called us by his own glory and goodness. ⁴Through these he has given us his very great and precious promises, so that through them you may participate in the divine nature, having escaped the corruption in the world caused by evil desires.

⁵For this very reason, make every effort to add to your faith goodness; and to goodness, knowledge; ⁶and to knowledge, self-control; and to self-control, perseverance; and to perseverance, godliness; ⁷and to godliness, mutual affection; and to mutual affection, love. ⁸For if you possess these qualities in increasing measure, they will keep you from being ineffective and unproductive in your knowledge of our Lord Jesus Christ. ⁹But whoever does not have them is nearsighted and blind, forgetting that they have been cleansed from their past sins.

¹⁰Therefore, my brothers and sisters,[a] make every effort to confirm your calling and election. For if you do these things, you will never stumble, ¹¹and you will receive a rich welcome into the eternal kingdom of our Lord and Savior Jesus Christ.

[a] 10 The Greek word for *brothers and sisters* (*adelphoi*) refers here to believers, both men and women, as part of God's family.

¹²So I will always remind you of these things, even though you know them and are firmly established in the truth you now have. ¹³I think it is right to refresh your memory as long as I live in the tent of this body, ¹⁴because I know that I will soon put it aside, as our Lord Jesus Christ has made clear to me. ¹⁵And I will make every effort to see that after my departure you will always be able to remember these things.

¹⁶For we did not follow cleverly devised stories when we told you about the coming of our Lord Jesus Christ in power, but we were eyewitnesses of his majesty. ¹⁷He received honor and glory from God the Father when the voice came to him from the Majestic Glory, saying, "This is my Son, whom I love; with him I am well pleased."[a] ¹⁸We ourselves heard this voice that came from heaven when we were with him on the sacred mountain.

¹⁹We also have the prophetic message as something completely reliable, and you will do well to pay attention to it, as to a light shining in a dark place, until the day dawns and the morning stars rise in your hearts. ²⁰Above all, you must understand that no prophecy of Scripture came about by the prophet's own interpretation of things. ²¹For prophecy never had its origin in the human will, but prophets, though human, spoke from God as they were carried along by the Holy Spirit.

2 But there were also false prophets among the people, just as there will be false teachers among you. They will secretly introduce destructive heresies, even denying the sovereign Lord who bought them—bringing swift destruction on themselves. ²Many will follow their depraved conduct and will bring the way of truth into disrepute. ³In their greed these teachers will exploit you with fabricated stories. Their condemnation has long been hanging over them, and their destruction has not been sleeping.

⁴For if God did not spare angels when they sinned, but sent them to hell,[b] putting them in chains of darkness[c] to be held for judgment; ⁵if he did not spare the ancient world when he brought the flood on its ungodly people, but protected Noah, a preacher of righteousness, and seven others; ⁶if he condemned the cities of Sodom and Gomorrah by burning them to ashes, and made them an example of what is going to happen to the ungodly; ⁷and if he rescued Lot, a righteous man, who was distressed by the depraved conduct of the lawless ⁸(for that righteous man, living among them day after day, was tormented in his righteous soul by the lawless deeds he saw and heard)— ⁹if this is so, then the Lord knows how to rescue the godly from trials and to hold the unrighteous for punishment on the day of judgment. ¹⁰This is especially true of those who follow the corrupt desire of the flesh[d] and despise authority.

Bold and arrogant, they are not afraid to heap abuse on celestial beings; ¹¹yet even angels, although they are stronger and more powerful, do not heap abuse on such beings when bringing judgment on

---

[a] 17  Matt. 17:5; Mark 9:7; Luke 9:35    [b] 4  Greek *Tartarus*    [c] 4  Some manuscripts *in gloomy dungeons*    [d] 10  In contexts like this, the Greek word for *flesh* (*sarx*) refers to the sinful state of human beings, often presented as a power in opposition to the Spirit; also in verse 18.

them from[a] the Lord. 12But these people blaspheme in matters they do not understand. They are like unreasoning animals, creatures of instinct, born only to be caught and destroyed, and like animals they too will perish.

13They will be paid back with harm for the harm they have done. Their idea of pleasure is to carouse in broad daylight. They are blots and blemishes, reveling in their pleasures while they feast with you.[b] 14With eyes full of adultery, they never stop sinning; they seduce the unstable; they are experts in greed—an accursed brood! 15They have left the straight way and wandered off to follow the way of Balaam son of Bezer,[c] who loved the wages of wickedness. 16But he was rebuked for his wrongdoing by a donkey—an animal without speech—who spoke with a human voice and restrained the prophet's madness.

17These people are springs without water and mists driven by a storm. Blackest darkness is reserved for them. 18For they mouth empty, boastful words and, by appealing to the lustful desires of the flesh, they entice people who are just escaping from those who live in error. 19They promise them freedom, while they themselves are slaves of depravity—for "people are slaves to whatever has mastered them." 20If they have escaped the corruption of the world by knowing our Lord and Savior Jesus Christ and are again entangled in it and are overcome, they are worse off at the end than they were at the beginning. 21It would have been better for them not to

have known the way of righteousness, than to have known it and then to turn their backs on the sacred command that was passed on to them. 22Of them the proverbs are true: "A dog returns to its vomit,"[d] and, "A sow that is washed returns to her wallowing in the mud."

3 Dear friends, this is now my second letter to you. I have written both of them as reminders to stimulate you to wholesome thinking. 2I want you to recall the words spoken in the past by the holy prophets and the command given by our Lord and Savior through your apostles.

3Above all, you must understand that in the last days scoffers will come, scoffing and following their own evil desires. 4They will say, "Where is this 'coming' he promised? Ever since our ancestors died, everything goes on as it has since the beginning of creation." 5But they deliberately forget that long ago by God's word the heavens came into being and the earth was formed out of water and by water. 6By these waters also the world of that time was deluged and destroyed. 7By the same word the present heavens and earth are reserved for fire, being kept for the day of judgment and destruction of the ungodly.

8But do not forget this one thing, dear friends: With the Lord a day is like a thousand years, and a thousand years are like a day. 9The Lord is not slow in keeping his promise, as some understand slowness. Instead he is patient with you, not wanting anyone to perish, but everyone to come to repentance.

10But the day of the Lord will come like a thief. The heavens will

---

*a* 11 Many manuscripts *beings in the presence of*    *b* 13 Some manuscripts *in their love feasts*
*c* 15 Greek *Bosor*    *d* 22 Prov. 26:11

disappear with a roar; the elements will be destroyed by fire, and the earth and everything done in it will be laid bare.[a]

11 Since everything will be destroyed in this way, what kind of people ought you to be? You ought to live holy and godly lives 12 as you look forward to the day of God and speed its coming.[b] That day will bring about the destruction of the heavens by fire, and the elements will melt in the heat. 13 But in keeping with his promise we are looking forward to a new heaven and a new earth, where righteousness dwells.

14 So then, dear friends, since you are looking forward to this, make every effort to be found spotless, blameless and at peace with him.

15 Bear in mind that our Lord's patience means salvation, just as our dear brother Paul also wrote you with the wisdom that God gave him. 16 He writes the same way in all his letters, speaking in them of these matters. His letters contain some things that are hard to understand, which ignorant and unstable people distort, as they do the other Scriptures, to their own destruction.

17 Therefore, dear friends, since you have been forewarned, be on your guard so that you may not be carried away by the error of the lawless and fall from your secure position. 18 But grow in the grace and knowledge of our Lord and Savior Jesus Christ. To him be glory both now and forever! Amen.

---

[a] 10 Some manuscripts *be burned up*　　[b] 12 Or *as you wait eagerly for the day of God to come*

# 1 JOHN

The letter known as 1 John was sent to a group of believers who were in the midst of an unsettling situation. Some of them had abandoned faith in Jesus the Messiah as it had first been taught to them. They found the proclamation that God had come in a human body impossible to reconcile with the common Greek idea that the flesh is evil and only spirit is good. But despite their denial of the Messiah, their immoral lives and their lack of practical love, they claimed to know God and belong to God. They asserted that their spiritual insight put them above the rest of the group, which they demonstrated by deserting the fellowship. Those left behind were deeply shaken, uncertain about everything they had been taught.

Someone who was close to this community and who had been an eyewitness of Jesus wrote to reassure them of what they had heard *from the beginning*. The author doesn't identify himself, but very likely he was the apostle John. Much of the language is similar to the Gospel of John. The letter testifies to the reality of the Messiah's coming in the flesh, reassuring the believers that they have full access to the truth. It emphasizes godly living and practical caring as the signs of those who genuinely know God.

---

1 That which was from the beginning, which we have heard, which we have seen with our eyes, which we have looked at and our hands have touched—this we proclaim concerning the Word of life. ²The life appeared; we have seen it and testify to it, and we proclaim to you the eternal life, which was with the Father and has appeared to us. ³We proclaim to you what we have seen and heard, so that you also may have fellowship with us. And our fellowship is with the Father and with his Son, Jesus Christ. ⁴We write this to make our*a* joy complete.

⁵This is the message we have heard from him and declare to you: God is light; in him there is no darkness at all. ⁶If we claim to have fellowship with him and yet walk in the darkness, we lie and do not live out the truth. ⁷But if we walk in the light, as he is in the light, we have fellowship with one another, and the blood of Jesus, his Son, purifies us from all*b* sin.

⁸If we claim to be without sin, we deceive ourselves and the truth is not in us. ⁹If we confess our sins, he is faithful and just and will forgive us our sins and purify us from all unrighteousness. ¹⁰If we claim we have not sinned, we make him out to be a liar and his word is not in us.

2 My dear children, I write this to you so that you will not sin. But if anybody does sin, we have an advocate with the Father—Jesus Christ, the Righteous One. ²He is the atoning sacrifice for our sins, and not only for ours but also for the sins of the whole world.

³We know that we have come to know him if we keep his commands. ⁴Whoever says, "I know him," but does not do what he commands is a liar, and the truth is

---

*a* 4 Some manuscripts *your*    *b* 7 Or *every*

not in that person. ⁵But if anyone obeys his word, love for God^a is truly made complete in them. This is how we know we are in him: ⁶Whoever claims to live in him must live as Jesus did.

⁷Dear friends, I am not writing you a new command but an old one, which you have had since the beginning. This old command is the message you have heard. ⁸Yet I am writing you a new command; its truth is seen in him and in you, because the darkness is passing and the true light is already shining.

⁹Anyone who claims to be in the light but hates a brother or sister^b is still in the darkness. ¹⁰Anyone who loves their brother and sister^c lives in the light, and there is nothing in them to make them stumble. ¹¹But anyone who hates a brother or sister is in the darkness and walks around in the darkness. They do not know where they are going, because the darkness has blinded them.

¹²I am writing to you, dear children,
    because your sins have been forgiven on account of his name.
¹³I am writing to you, fathers,
    because you know him who is from the beginning.
I am writing to you, young men,
    because you have overcome the evil one.

¹⁴I write to you, dear children,
    because you know the Father.
I write to you, fathers,
    because you know him who is from the beginning.
I write to you, young men,
    because you are strong,
    and the word of God lives in you,
    and you have overcome the evil one.

¹⁵Do not love the world or anything in the world. If anyone loves the world, love for the Father^d is not in them. ¹⁶For everything in the world—the lust of the flesh, the lust of the eyes, and the pride of life—comes not from the Father but from the world. ¹⁷The world and its desires pass away, but whoever does the will of God lives forever.

¹⁸Dear children, this is the last hour; and as you have heard that the antichrist is coming, even now many antichrists have come. This is how we know it is the last hour. ¹⁹They went out from us, but they did not really belong to us. For if they had belonged to us, they would have remained with us; but their going showed that none of them belonged to us.

²⁰But you have an anointing from the Holy One, and all of you know the truth.^e ²¹I do not write to you because you do not know the truth, but because you do know it and because no lie comes from the truth. ²²Who is the liar? It is whoever denies that Jesus is the Christ. Such a person is the antichrist—denying the Father and the Son. ²³No one who denies the Son has the Father; whoever acknowledges the Son has the Father also.

²⁴As for you, see that what you have heard from the beginning remains in you. If it does, you also

---

^a 5 Or *word, God's love*    ^b 9 The Greek word for *brother or sister* (*adelphos*) refers here to a believer, whether man or woman, as part of God's family; also in verse 11; and in 3:15, 17; 4:20; 5:16.    ^c 10 The Greek word for *brother and sister* (*adelphos*) refers here to a believer, whether man or woman, as part of God's family; also in 3:10; 4:20, 21.    ^d 15 Or *world, the Father's love*    ^e 20 Some manuscripts *and you know all things* will remain in the Son and in the Father. ²⁵And this is what he promised us — eternal life.

²⁶I am writing these things to you about those who are trying to lead you astray. ²⁷As for you, the anointing you received from him remains in you, and you do not need anyone to teach you. But as his anointing teaches you about all things and as that anointing is real, not counterfeit — just as it has taught you, remain in him.

²⁸And now, dear children, continue in him, so that when he appears we may be confident and unashamed before him at his coming.

²⁹If you know that he is righteous, you know that everyone who does what is right has been born of him.

3 See what great love the Father has lavished on us, that we should be called children of God! And that is what we are! The reason the world does not know us is that it did not know him. ²Dear friends, now we are children of God, and what we will be has not yet been made known. But we know that when Christ appears,ᵃ we shall be like him, for we shall see him as he is. ³All who have this hope in him purify themselves, just as he is pure.

⁴Everyone who sins breaks the law; in fact, sin is lawlessness. ⁵But you know that he appeared so that he might take away our sins. And in him is no sin. ⁶No one who lives in him keeps on sinning. No one who continues to sin has either seen him or known him.

⁷Dear children, do not let anyone lead you astray. The one who does what is right is righteous, just as he is righteous. ⁸The one who does what is sinful is of the devil, because the devil has been sinning from the beginning. The reason the Son of God appeared was to destroy the devil's work. ⁹No one who is born of God will continue to sin, because God's seed remains in them; they cannot go on sinning, because they have been born of God. ¹⁰This is how we know who the children of God are and who the children of the devil are: Anyone who does not do what is right is not God's child, nor is anyone who does not love their brother and sister.

¹¹For this is the message you heard from the beginning: We should love one another. ¹²Do not be like Cain, who belonged to the evil one and murdered his brother. And why did he murder him? Because his own actions were evil and his brother's were righteous. ¹³Do not be surprised, my brothers and sisters,ᵇ if the world hates you. ¹⁴We know that we have passed from death to life, because we love each other. Anyone who does not love remains in death. ¹⁵Anyone who hates a brother or sister is a murderer, and you know that no murderer has eternal life residing in him.

¹⁶This is how we know what love is: Jesus Christ laid down his life for us. And we ought to lay down our lives for our brothers and sisters. ¹⁷If anyone has material possessions and sees a brother or sister in need but has no pity on them, how can the love of God be in that person? ¹⁸Dear children, let us not love with words or speech but with actions and in truth.

¹⁹This is how we know that we

---

ᵃ *2* Or *when it is made known*    ᵇ *13* The Greek word for *brothers and sisters (adelphoi)* refers here to believers, both men and women, as part of God's family; also in verse 16.

belong to the truth and how we set our hearts at rest in his presence: 20If our hearts condemn us, we know that God is greater than our hearts, and he knows everything. 21Dear friends, if our hearts do not condemn us, we have confidence before God 22and receive from him anything we ask, because we keep his commands and do what pleases him. 23And this is his command: to believe in the name of his Son, Jesus Christ, and to love one another as he commanded us. 24The one who keeps God's commands lives in him, and he in them. And this is how we know that he lives in us: We know it by the Spirit he gave us.

4 Dear friends, do not believe every spirit, but test the spirits to see whether they are from God, because many false prophets have gone out into the world. 2This is how you can recognize the Spirit of God: Every spirit that acknowledges that Jesus Christ has come in the flesh is from God, 3but every spirit that does not acknowledge Jesus is not from God. This is the spirit of the antichrist, which you have heard is coming and even now is already in the world.

4You, dear children, are from God and have overcome them, because the one who is in you is greater than the one who is in the world. 5They are from the world and therefore speak from the viewpoint of the world, and the world listens to them. 6We are from God, and whoever knows God listens to us; but whoever is not from God does not listen to us. This is how we recognize the Spirita of truth and the spirit of falsehood.

7Dear friends, let us love one another, for love comes from God. Everyone who loves has been born of God and knows God. 8Whoever does not love does not know God, because God is love. 9This is how God showed his love among us: He sent his one and only Son into the world that we might live through him. 10This is love: not that we loved God, but that he loved us and sent his Son as an atoning sacrifice for our sins. 11Dear friends, since God so loved us, we also ought to love one another. 12No one has ever seen God; but if we love one another, God lives in us and his love is made complete in us.

13This is how we know that we live in him and he in us: He has given us of his Spirit. 14And we have seen and testify that the Father has sent his Son to be the Savior of the world. 15If anyone acknowledges that Jesus is the Son of God, God lives in them and they in God. 16And so we know and rely on the love God has for us.

God is love. Whoever lives in love lives in God, and God in them. 17This is how love is made complete among us so that we will have confidence on the day of judgment: In this world we are like Jesus. 18There is no fear in love. But perfect love drives out fear, because fear has to do with punishment. The one who fears is not made perfect in love.

19We love because he first loved us. 20Whoever claims to love God yet hates a brother or sister is a liar. For whoever does not love their brother and sister, whom they have seen, cannot love God, whom they have not seen. 21And he has given us this command: Anyone who loves God must also love their brother and sister.

a 6 Or spirit

5 Everyone who believes that Jesus is the Christ is born of God, and everyone who loves the father loves his child as well. ²This is how we know that we love the children of God: by loving God and carrying out his commands. ³In fact, this is love for God: to keep his commands. And his commands are not burdensome, ⁴for everyone born of God overcomes the world. This is the victory that has overcome the world, even our faith. ⁵Who is it that overcomes the world? Only the one who believes that Jesus is the Son of God.

⁶This is the one who came by water and blood — Jesus Christ. He did not come by water only, but by water and blood. And it is the Spirit who testifies, because the Spirit is the truth. ⁷For there are three that testify: ⁸the[a] Spirit, the water and the blood; and the three are in agreement. ⁹We accept human testimony, but God's testimony is greater because it is the testimony of God, which he has given about his Son. ¹⁰Whoever believes in the Son of God accepts this testimony. Whoever does not believe God has made him out to be a liar, because they have not believed the testimony God has given about his Son. ¹¹And this is the testimony: God has given us eternal life, and this life is in his Son. ¹²Whoever has the Son has life; whoever does not have the Son of God does not have life.

¹³I write these things to you who believe in the name of the Son of God so that you may know that you have eternal life. ¹⁴This is the confidence we have in approaching God: that if we ask anything according to his will, he hears us. ¹⁵And if we know that he hears us — whatever we ask — we know that we have what we asked of him.

¹⁶If you see any brother or sister commit a sin that does not lead to death, you should pray and God will give them life. I refer to those whose sin does not lead to death. There is a sin that leads to death. I am not saying that you should pray about that. ¹⁷All wrongdoing is sin, and there is sin that does not lead to death.

¹⁸We know that anyone born of God does not continue to sin; the One who was born of God keeps them safe, and the evil one cannot harm them. ¹⁹We know that we are children of God, and that the whole world is under the control of the evil one. ²⁰We know also that the Son of God has come and has given us understanding, so that we may know him who is true. And we are in him who is true by being in his Son Jesus Christ. He is the true God and eternal life.

²¹Dear children, keep yourselves from idols.

---

[a] 7,8 Late manuscripts of the Vulgate *testify in heaven: the Father, the Word and the Holy Spirit, and these three are one.* ⁸*And there are three that testify on earth: the* (not found in any Greek manuscript before the fourteenth century)

# 2 JOHN

The same person who wrote 1 John to encourage believers also found it necessary to write to other churches where the false teachers might go to spread their ideas and practices. The letter of 2 John addresses one such gathering, referring to the church as *a lady* and its members as her *children*. The author describes the members of his own community as *the children of your sister*. (This was apparently typical of early followers of Jesus; there is a similar greeting at the end of 1 Peter.) He identifies himself as a church leader by using the title *elder*.

Apparently some people from this church had just come to visit him and he was pleased to learn that they were walking in the truth. He warns the church not to support the false teachers in any way. Despite its brevity, this letter expresses all of the themes that receive deeper development in 1 John.

---

[1] The elder,

To the lady chosen by God and to her children, whom I love in the truth — and not I only, but also all who know the truth — [2] because of the truth, which lives in us and will be with us forever:

[3] Grace, mercy and peace from God the Father and from Jesus Christ, the Father's Son, will be with us in truth and love.

[4] It has given me great joy to find some of your children walking in the truth, just as the Father commanded us. [5] And now, dear lady, I am not writing you a new command but one we have had from the beginning. I ask that we love one another. [6] And this is love: that we walk in obedience to his commands. As you have heard from the beginning, his command is that you walk in love.

[7] I say this because many deceivers, who do not acknowledge Jesus Christ as coming in the flesh, have gone out into the world. Any such person is the deceiver and the antichrist. [8] Watch out that you do not lose what we[a] have worked for, but that you may be rewarded fully. [9] Anyone who runs ahead and does not continue in the teaching of Christ does not have God; whoever continues in the teaching has both the Father and the Son. [10] If anyone comes to you and does not bring this teaching, do not take them into your house or welcome them. [11] Anyone who welcomes them shares in their wicked work.

[12] I have much to write to you, but I do not want to use paper and ink. Instead, I hope to visit you and talk with you face to face, so that our joy may be complete.

[13] The children of your sister, who is chosen by God, send their greetings.

*a 8* Some manuscripts *you*

# 3 JOHN

This letter is a note of thanks and encouragement to an individual named Gaius. John had sent a letter to the church of which Gaius was a member, introducing and commending certain individuals, but a leader named Diotrephes refused to accommodate them. He opposed John's authority to the point of actually expelling anyone who supported the people he had sent. Gaius, however, put these preachers up in his own home, enabling them to carry out their mission. John's gratitude makes it clear that the church should provide a base of operations for traveling preachers who were walking in the truth. John also promises to come soon to set matters right.

---

¹The elder,

To my dear friend Gaius, whom I love in the truth.

²Dear friend, I pray that you may enjoy good health and that all may go well with you, even as your soul is getting along well. ³It gave me great joy when some believers came and testified about your faithfulness to the truth, telling how you continue to walk in it. ⁴I have no greater joy than to hear that my children are walking in the truth.

⁵Dear friend, you are faithful in what you are doing for the brothers and sisters,ᵃ even though they are strangers to you. ⁶They have told the church about your love. Please send them on their way in a manner that honors God. ⁷It was for the sake of the Name that they went out, receiving no help from the pagans. ⁸We ought therefore to show hospitality to such people so that we may work together for the truth.

⁹I wrote to the church, but Diot-rephes, who loves to be first, will not welcome us. ¹⁰So when I come, I will call attention to what he is doing, spreading malicious nonsense about us. Not satisfied with that, he even refuses to welcome other believers. He also stops those who want to do so and puts them out of the church.

¹¹Dear friend, do not imitate what is evil but what is good. Anyone who does what is good is from God. Anyone who does what is evil has not seen God. ¹²Demetrius is well spoken of by everyone — and even by the truth itself. We also speak well of him, and you know that our testimony is true.

¹³I have much to write you, but I do not want to do so with pen and ink. ¹⁴I hope to see you soon, and we will talk face to face.

Peace to you. The friends here send their greetings. Greet the friends there by name.

---

ᵃ 5 The Greek word for *brothers and sisters* (*adelphoi*) refers here to believers, both men and women, as part of God's family.

# JUDE

Jesus had several brothers, two of whom were James and Jude. Much less is known about Jude than James (see p. 302), but he was clearly a church leader, since he wrote to believers with authority in this letter that bears his name. It cannot be determined exactly who was meant to receive the letter, although the references to angels, to Israel's history and to specific writings indicate that Jewish Christians were in view.

Jude addresses the problem of false teachers who have come and are now threatening *the faith that was once for all entrusted to God's holy people*. On the basis of supposedly inspired dreams, they reject authority and pollute their own bodies. Even though they claim to be bringing God's message, they really *follow mere natural instincts and do not have the Spirit*. The believers must actively resist them and cleanse their community by rejecting both the teaching and the example of these ungodly men.

It seems that the apostle Peter received a copy of Jude's letter and wrote a similar one of his own to show that it faithfully presented the teaching of the apostles of the Lord Jesus Christ (see p. 313).

---

¹Jude, a servant of Jesus Christ and a brother of James,

To those who have been called, who are loved in God the Father and kept for[a] Jesus Christ:

²Mercy, peace and love be yours in abundance.

³Dear friends, although I was very eager to write to you about the salvation we share, I felt compelled to write and urge you to contend for the faith that was once for all entrusted to God's holy people. ⁴For certain individuals whose condemnation was written about[b] long ago have secretly slipped in among you. They are ungodly people, who pervert the grace of our God into a license for immorality and deny Jesus Christ our only Sovereign and Lord.

⁵Though you already know all this, I want to remind you that the Lord[c] at one time delivered his people out of Egypt, but later destroyed those who did not believe. ⁶And the angels who did not keep their positions of authority but abandoned their proper dwelling—these he has kept in darkness, bound with everlasting chains for judgment on the great Day. ⁷In a similar way, Sodom and Gomorrah and the surrounding towns gave themselves up to sexual immorality and perversion. They serve as an example of those who suffer the punishment of eternal fire.

⁸In the very same way, on the strength of their dreams these ungodly people pollute their own bodies, reject authority and heap abuse on celestial beings. ⁹But even the archangel Michael, when he was disputing with the devil about the body of Moses, did not himself dare to condemn him for slander but said, "The Lord rebuke

---

*a 1* Or *by;* or *in*     *b 4* Or *individuals who were marked out for condemnation*     *c 5* Some early manuscripts *Jesus* you!"[a] [10]Yet these people slander whatever they do not understand, and the very things they do understand by instinct—as irrational animals do—will destroy them.

[11]Woe to them! They have taken the way of Cain; they have rushed for profit into Balaam's error; they have been destroyed in Korah's rebellion.

[12]These people are blemishes at your love feasts, eating with you without the slightest qualm—shepherds who feed only themselves. They are clouds without rain, blown along by the wind; autumn trees, without fruit and uprooted—twice dead. [13]They are wild waves of the sea, foaming up their shame; wandering stars, for whom blackest darkness has been reserved forever.

[14]Enoch, the seventh from Adam, prophesied about them: "See, the Lord is coming with thousands upon thousands of his holy ones [15]to judge everyone, and to convict all of them of all the ungodly acts they have committed in their ungodliness, and of all the defiant words ungodly sinners have spoken against him."[b] [16]These people are grumblers and faultfinders; they follow their own evil desires; they boast about themselves and flatter others for their own advantage.

[17]But, dear friends, remember what the apostles of our Lord Jesus Christ foretold. [18]They said to you, "In the last times there will be scoffers who will follow their own ungodly desires." [19]These are the people who divide you, who follow mere natural instincts and do not have the Spirit.

[20]But you, dear friends, by building yourselves up in your most holy faith and praying in the Holy Spirit, [21]keep yourselves in God's love as you wait for the mercy of our Lord Jesus Christ to bring you to eternal life.

[22]Be merciful to those who doubt; [23]save others by snatching them from the fire; to others show mercy, mixed with fear—hating even the clothing stained by corrupted flesh.[c]

[24]To him who is able to keep you from stumbling and to present you before his glorious presence without fault and with great joy— [25]to the only God our Savior be glory, majesty, power and authority, through Jesus Christ our Lord, before all ages, now and forevermore! Amen.

---

[a] 9 Jude is alluding to the Jewish *Testament of Moses* (approximately the first century A.D.).
[b] 14,15 From the Jewish *First Book of Enoch* (approximately the first century B.C.)   [c] 22,23 The Greek manuscripts of these verses vary at several points.

# REVELATION

The ancient Roman Empire defended its economic and political control in spiritual terms, calling its gospel the *Pax Romana*, or Roman Peace. While in exile on the island of Patmos, a Jewish Christian prophet named John received a vision showing that the cult of emperor worship would soon become deadly to followers of the Messiah. The book of Revelation (or Apocalypse, meaning *unveiling*) is a warning, circulated to seven cities in the Roman province of Asia Minor. John's main point is to challenge and encourage the believers in the midst of their opposition and persecution.

Revelation is an apocalypse, a literary form well known in John's day. In an apocalypse a visitor from heaven reveals the secrets of the unseen world and the future through vivid symbols. While the symbols may appear strange at first, they become more clear when seen in their first-century setting and in light of other Bible imagery.

John's vision has four main parts, each marked by the phrase *in the Spirit*. After words of warning and encouragement to each of the seven churches, John's visions then center on Jesus—his role in redemption and the judgments he brings to the world. The immoral political and economic forces that rebel against God will be destroyed, and the Messiah will triumph over all his enemies. The vision closes with the promise that God's faithful servants will reign over the new creation.

Revelation also functions as the appropriate conclusion to the entire drama of the Bible. John concludes with images from the garden of Eden, the first story in the Bible. The world will experience a fresh beginning: *He who was seated on the throne said, "I am making everything new!"*

---

1 The revelation from Jesus Christ, which God gave him to show his servants what must soon take place. He made it known by sending his angel to his servant John, ²who testifies to everything he saw — that is, the word of God and the testimony of Jesus Christ. ³Blessed is the one who reads aloud the words of this prophecy, and blessed are those who hear it and take to heart what is written in it, because the time is near.

⁴John,

To the seven churches in the province of Asia:

Grace and peace to you from him who is, and who was, and who is to come, and from the seven spirits*a* before his throne, ⁵and from Jesus Christ, who is the faithful witness, the firstborn from the dead, and the ruler of the kings of the earth.

To him who loves us and has freed us from our sins by his blood, ⁶and has made us to be a kingdom and priests to serve his God and Father — to him be glory and power for ever and ever! Amen.

⁷ "Look, he is coming with the clouds,"*b*
and "every eye will see him,
even those who pierced him";

*a 4* That is, the sevenfold Spirit    *b 7* Daniel 7:13

and all peoples on earth "will
mourn because of him."[a]
   So shall it be! Amen.

[8]"I am the Alpha and the Omega," says the Lord God, "who is, and who was, and who is to come, the Almighty."

[9]I, John, your brother and companion in the suffering and kingdom and patient endurance that are ours in Jesus, was on the island of Patmos because of the word of God and the testimony of Jesus. [10]On the Lord's Day I was in the Spirit, and I heard behind me a loud voice like a trumpet, [11]which said: "Write on a scroll what you see and send it to the seven churches: to Ephesus, Smyrna, Pergamum, Thyatira, Sardis, Philadelphia and Laodicea."

[12]I turned around to see the voice that was speaking to me. And when I turned I saw seven golden lampstands, [13]and among the lampstands was someone like a son of man,[b] dressed in a robe reaching down to his feet and with a golden sash around his chest. [14]The hair on his head was white like wool, as white as snow, and his eyes were like blazing fire. [15]His feet were like bronze glowing in a furnace, and his voice was like the sound of rushing waters. [16]In his right hand he held seven stars, and coming out of his mouth was a sharp, double-edged sword. His face was like the sun shining in all its brilliance.

[17]When I saw him, I fell at his feet as though dead. Then he placed his right hand on me and said: "Do not be afraid. I am the First and the Last. [18]I am the Living One; I was dead, and now look, I am alive for ever and ever! And I hold the keys of death and Hades.

[19]"Write, therefore, what you have seen, what is now and what will take place later. [20]The mystery of the seven stars that you saw in my right hand and of the seven golden lampstands is this: The seven stars are the angels[c] of the seven churches, and the seven lampstands are the seven churches.

2 "To the angel[d] of the church in Ephesus write:

These are the words of him who holds the seven stars in his right hand and walks among the seven golden lampstands. [2]I know your deeds, your hard work and your perseverance. I know that you cannot tolerate wicked people, that you have tested those who claim to be apostles but are not, and have found them false. [3]You have persevered and have endured hardships for my name, and have not grown weary.

[4]Yet I hold this against you: You have forsaken the love you had at first. [5]Consider how far you have fallen! Repent and do the things you did at first. If you do not repent, I will come to you and remove your lampstand from its place. [6]But you have this in your favor: You hate the practices of the Nicolaitans, which I also hate.

[7]Whoever has ears, let them hear what the Spirit says to the churches. To the one who is victorious, I will give the right to eat from the tree of life, which is in the paradise of God.

---

[a] 7 Zech. 12:10    [b] 13 See Daniel 7:13.    [c] 20 Or *messengers*    [d] 1 Or *messenger*; also in
verses 8, 12 and 18

8"To the angel of the church in Smyrna write:

These are the words of him who is the First and the Last, who died and came to life again. 9I know your afflictions and your poverty—yet you are rich! I know about the slander of those who say they are Jews and are not, but are a synagogue of Satan. 10Do not be afraid of what you are about to suffer. I tell you, the devil will put some of you in prison to test you, and you will suffer persecution for ten days. Be faithful, even to the point of death, and I will give you life as your victor's crown.

11Whoever has ears, let them hear what the Spirit says to the churches. The one who is victorious will not be hurt at all by the second death.

12"To the angel of the church in Pergamum write:

These are the words of him who has the sharp, double-edged sword. 13I know where you live—where Satan has his throne. Yet you remain true to my name. You did not renounce your faith in me, not even in the days of Antipas, my faithful witness, who was put to death in your city—where Satan lives.

14Nevertheless, I have a few things against you: There are some among you who hold to the teaching of Balaam, who taught Balak to entice the Israelites to sin so that they ate food sacrificed to idols and committed sexual immorality. 15Likewise, you also have those who hold to the teaching of the Nicolaitans. 16Repent therefore! Otherwise, I will soon come to you and will fight against them with the sword of my mouth.

17Whoever has ears, let them hear what the Spirit says to the churches. To the one who is victorious, I will give some of the hidden manna. I will also give that person a white stone with a new name written on it, known only to the one who receives it.

18"To the angel of the church in Thyatira write:

These are the words of the Son of God, whose eyes are like blazing fire and whose feet are like burnished bronze. 19I know your deeds, your love and faith, your service and perseverance, and that you are now doing more than you did at first.

20Nevertheless, I have this against you: You tolerate that woman Jezebel, who calls herself a prophet. By her teaching she misleads my servants into sexual immorality and the eating of food sacrificed to idols. 21I have given her time to repent of her immorality, but she is unwilling. 22So I will cast her on a bed of suffering, and I will make those who commit adultery with her suffer intensely, unless they repent of her ways. 23I will strike her children dead. Then all the churches will know that I am he who searches hearts and minds, and I will repay each of you according to your deeds.

24Now I say to the rest of you in Thyatira, to you who do not hold to her teaching and have not learned Satan's so-called deep secrets, 'I will not impose any other burden on you, 25except to hold on to what you have until I come.'

26To the one who is victorious and does my will to the end, I will give authority over the nations— 27that one 'will rule them with an iron scepter and will dash them to pieces like pottery'[a]—just as I have received authority from my Father. 28I will also give that one the morning star. 29Whoever has ears, let them hear what the Spirit says to the churches.

3 "To the angel[b] of the church in Sardis write:

These are the words of him who holds the seven spirits[c] of God and the seven stars. I know your deeds; you have a reputation of being alive, but you are dead. 2Wake up! Strengthen what remains and is about to die, for I have found your deeds unfinished in the sight of my God. 3Remember, therefore, what you have received and heard; hold it fast, and repent. But if you do not wake up, I will come like a thief, and you will not know at what time I will come to you.

4Yet you have a few people in Sardis who have not soiled their clothes. They will walk with me, dressed in white, for they are worthy. 5The one who is victorious will, like them, be dressed in white. I will never blot out the name of that person from the book of life, but will acknowledge that name

before my Father and his angels. 6Whoever has ears, let them hear what the Spirit says to the churches.

7"To the angel of the church in Philadelphia write:

These are the words of him who is holy and true, who holds the key of David. What he opens no one can shut, and what he shuts no one can open. 8I know your deeds. See, I have placed before you an open door that no one can shut. I know that you have little strength, yet you have kept my word and have not denied my name. 9I will make those who are of the synagogue of Satan, who claim to be Jews though they are not, but are liars—I will make them come and fall down at your feet and acknowledge that I have loved you. 10Since you have kept my command to endure patiently, I will also keep you from the hour of trial that is going to come on the whole world to test the inhabitants of the earth.

11I am coming soon. Hold on to what you have, so that no one will take your crown. 12The one who is victorious I will make a pillar in the temple of my God. Never again will they leave it. I will write on them the name of my God and the name of the city of my God, the new Jerusalem, which is coming down out of heaven from my God; and I will also write on them my new name. 13Whoever has ears, let them hear what the Spirit says to the churches.

---

a 27 Psalm 2:9    b 1 Or messenger; also in verses 7 and 14    c 1 That is, the sevenfold Spirit

14 "To the angel of the church in Laodicea write:

These are the words of the Amen, the faithful and true witness, the ruler of God's creation. 15 I know your deeds, that you are neither cold nor hot. I wish you were either one or the other! 16 So, because you are lukewarm — neither hot nor cold — I am about to spit you out of my mouth. 17 You say, 'I am rich; I have acquired wealth and do not need a thing.' But you do not realize that you are wretched, pitiful, poor, blind and naked. 18 I counsel you to buy from me gold refined in the fire, so you can become rich; and white clothes to wear, so you can cover your shameful nakedness; and salve to put on your eyes, so you can see.

19 Those whom I love I rebuke and discipline. So be earnest and repent. 20 Here I am! I stand at the door and knock. If anyone hears my voice and opens the door, I will come in and eat with that person, and they with me.

21 To the one who is victorious, I will give the right to sit with me on my throne, just as I was victorious and sat down with my Father on his throne. 22 Whoever has ears, let them hear what the Spirit says to the churches."

4 After this I looked, and there before me was a door standing open in heaven. And the voice I had first heard speaking to me like a trumpet said, "Come up here, and I will show you what must take place after this." 2 At once I was in the Spirit, and there before me was a throne in heaven with someone sitting on it. 3 And the one who sat there had the appearance of jasper and ruby. A rainbow that shone like an emerald encircled the throne. 4 Surrounding the throne were twenty-four other thrones, and seated on them were twenty-four elders. They were dressed in white and had crowns of gold on their heads. 5 From the throne came flashes of lightning, rumblings and peals of thunder. In front of the throne, seven lamps were blazing. These are the seven spirits[a] of God. 6 Also in front of the throne there was what looked like a sea of glass, clear as crystal.

In the center, around the throne, were four living creatures, and they were covered with eyes, in front and in back. 7 The first living creature was like a lion, the second was like an ox, the third had a face like a man, the fourth was like a flying eagle. 8 Each of the four living creatures had six wings and was covered with eyes all around, even under its wings. Day and night they never stop saying:

"'Holy, holy, holy
is the Lord God Almighty,'[b]
who was, and is, and is to come."

9 Whenever the living creatures give glory, honor and thanks to him who sits on the throne and who lives for ever and ever, 10 the twenty-four elders fall down before him who sits on the throne and worship him who lives for ever and ever. They lay their crowns before the throne and say:

---

[a] 5 That is, the sevenfold Spirit　　[b] 8 Isaiah 6:3

11 "You are worthy, our Lord and God,
 to receive glory and honor and power,
 for you created all things,
 and by your will they were created
 and have their being."

5 Then I saw in the right hand of him who sat on the throne a scroll with writing on both sides and sealed with seven seals. 2And I saw a mighty angel proclaiming in a loud voice, "Who is worthy to break the seals and open the scroll?" 3But no one in heaven or on earth or under the earth could open the scroll or even look inside it. 4I wept and wept because no one was found who was worthy to open the scroll or look inside. 5Then one of the elders said to me, "Do not weep! See, the Lion of the tribe of Judah, the Root of David, has triumphed. He is able to open the scroll and its seven seals."

6Then I saw a Lamb, looking as if it had been slain, standing at the center of the throne, encircled by the four living creatures and the elders. The Lamb had seven horns and seven eyes, which are the seven spirits[a] of God sent out into all the earth. 7He went and took the scroll from the right hand of him who sat on the throne. 8And when he had taken it, the four living creatures and the twenty-four elders fell down before the Lamb. Each one had a harp and they were holding golden bowls full of incense, which are the prayers of God's people. 9And they sang a new song, saying:

"You are worthy to take the scroll
 and to open its seals,
 because you were slain,
 and with your blood you purchased for God
 persons from every tribe and language and people and nation.

10 You have made them to be a kingdom and priests to serve our God,
 and they will reign[b] on the earth."

11Then I looked and heard the voice of many angels, numbering thousands upon thousands, and ten thousand times ten thousand. They encircled the throne and the living creatures and the elders. 12In a loud voice they were saying:

"Worthy is the Lamb, who was slain,
 to receive power and wealth and wisdom and strength and honor and glory and praise!"

13Then I heard every creature in heaven and on earth and under the earth and on the sea, and all that is in them, saying:

"To him who sits on the throne and to the Lamb
 be praise and honor and glory and power,
 for ever and ever!"

14The four living creatures said, "Amen," and the elders fell down and worshiped.

6 I watched as the Lamb opened the first of the seven seals. Then I heard one of the four living creatures say in a voice like thunder, "Come!" 2I looked, and there before me was a white horse! Its rider held a bow, and he was given a crown,

a 6 That is, the sevenfold Spirit      b 10 Some manuscripts they reign and he rode out as a conqueror bent on conquest.

³When the Lamb opened the second seal, I heard the second living creature say, "Come!" ⁴Then another horse came out, a fiery red one. Its rider was given power to take peace from the earth and to make people kill each other. To him was given a large sword.

⁵When the Lamb opened the third seal, I heard the third living creature say, "Come!" I looked, and there before me was a black horse! Its rider was holding a pair of scales in his hand. ⁶Then I heard what sounded like a voice among the four living creatures, saying, "Two pounds*a* of wheat for a day's wages,*b* and six pounds*c* of barley for a day's wages,*b* and do not damage the oil and the wine!"

⁷When the Lamb opened the fourth seal, I heard the voice of the fourth living creature say, "Come!" ⁸I looked, and there before me was a pale horse! Its rider was named Death, and Hades was following close behind him. They were given power over a fourth of the earth to kill by sword, famine and plague, and by the wild beasts of the earth.

⁹When he opened the fifth seal, I saw under the altar the souls of those who had been slain because of the word of God and the testimony they had maintained. ¹⁰They called out in a loud voice, "How long, Sovereign Lord, holy and true, until you judge the inhabitants of the earth and avenge our blood?" ¹¹Then each of them was given a white robe, and they were told to wait a little longer, until the full number of their fellow servants,

their brothers and sisters,*d* were killed just as they had been.

¹²I watched as he opened the sixth seal. There was a great earthquake. The sun turned black like sackcloth made of goat hair, the whole moon turned blood red, ¹³and the stars in the sky fell to earth, as figs drop from a fig tree when shaken by a strong wind. ¹⁴The heavens receded like a scroll being rolled up, and every mountain and island was removed from its place.

¹⁵Then the kings of the earth, the princes, the generals, the rich, the mighty, and everyone else, both slave and free, hid in caves and among the rocks of the mountains. ¹⁶They called to the mountains and the rocks, "Fall on us and hide us*e* from the face of him who sits on the throne and from the wrath of the Lamb! ¹⁷For the great day of their*f* wrath has come, and who can withstand it?"

**7** After this I saw four angels standing at the four corners of the earth, holding back the four winds of the earth to prevent any wind from blowing on the land or on the sea or on any tree. ²Then I saw another angel coming up from the east, having the seal of the living God. He called out in a loud voice to the four angels who had been given power to harm the land and the sea: ³"Do not harm the land or the sea or the trees until we put a seal on the foreheads of the servants of our God." ⁴Then I heard the number of those who were sealed: 144,000 from all the tribes of Israel.

⁵From the tribe of Judah 12,000 were sealed,

---

*a 6* Or about 1 kilogram   *b 6* Greek *a denarius*   *c 6* Or about 3 kilograms   *d 11* The Greek word for *brothers and sisters* (*adelphoi*) refers here to believers, both men and women, as part of God's family; also in 12:10; 19:10.   *e 16* See Hosea 10:8.   *f 17* Some manuscripts *his*

from the tribe of Reuben 12,000,
from the tribe of Gad 12,000,
[6] from the tribe of Asher 12,000,
from the tribe of Naphtali 12,000,
from the tribe of Manasseh 12,000,
[7] from the tribe of Simeon 12,000,
from the tribe of Levi 12,000,
from the tribe of Issachar 12,000,
[8] from the tribe of Zebulun 12,000,
from the tribe of Joseph 12,000,
from the tribe of Benjamin 12,000.

[9] After this I looked, and there before me was a great multitude that no one could count, from every nation, tribe, people and language, standing before the throne and before the Lamb. They were wearing white robes and were holding palm branches in their hands. [10] And they cried out in a loud voice:

"Salvation belongs to our God,
who sits on the throne,
and to the Lamb."

[11] All the angels were standing around the throne and around the elders and the four living creatures. They fell down on their faces before the throne and worshiped God, [12] saying:

"Amen!
Praise and glory
and wisdom and thanks and honor
and power and strength
be to our God for ever and ever.
Amen!"

[13] Then one of the elders asked me, "These in white robes—who are they, and where did they come from?"

[14] I answered, "Sir, you know."

And he said, "These are they who have come out of the great tribulation; they have washed their robes and made them white in the blood of the Lamb. [15] Therefore,

"they are before the throne of God
and serve him day and night in his temple;
and he who sits on the throne
will shelter them with his presence.
[16] 'Never again will they hunger;
never again will they thirst.
The sun will not beat down on them,'[a]
nor any scorching heat.
[17] For the Lamb at the center of the throne
will be their shepherd;
'he will lead them to springs of living water.'[a]
'And God will wipe away every tear from their eyes.'[b]

8 When he opened the seventh seal, there was silence in heaven for about half an hour.

[2] And I saw the seven angels who stand before God, and seven trumpets were given to them.

[3] Another angel, who had a golden censer, came and stood at the altar. He was given much incense to offer, with the prayers of all God's people, on the golden altar in front of the throne. [4] The smoke of the incense, together with the prayers of God's people, went up before God from the angel's hand. [5] Then the angel took the censer, filled it with fire from the altar, and hurled it on

---

[a] 16,17 Isaiah 49:10    [b] 17 Isaiah 25:8

the earth; and there came peals of thunder, rumblings, flashes of lightning and an earthquake.

⁶Then the seven angels who had the seven trumpets prepared to sound them.

⁷The first angel sounded his trumpet, and there came hail and fire mixed with blood, and it was hurled down on the earth. A third of the earth was burned up, a third of the trees were burned up, and all the green grass was burned up.

⁸The second angel sounded his trumpet, and something like a huge mountain, all ablaze, was thrown into the sea. A third of the sea turned into blood, ⁹a third of the living creatures in the sea died, and a third of the ships were destroyed.

¹⁰The third angel sounded his trumpet, and a great star, blazing like a torch, fell from the sky on a third of the rivers and on the springs of water— ¹¹the name of the star is Wormwood.ᵃ A third of the waters turned bitter, and many people died from the waters that had become bitter.

¹²The fourth angel sounded his trumpet, and a third of the sun was struck, a third of the moon, and a third of the stars, so that a third of them turned dark. A third of the day was without light, and also a third of the night.

¹³As I watched, I heard an eagle that was flying in midair call out in a loud voice: "Woe! Woe! Woe to the inhabitants of the earth, because of the trumpet blasts about to be sounded by the other three angels!"

**9** The fifth angel sounded his trumpet, and I saw a star that had fallen from the sky to the

earth. The star was given the key to the shaft of the Abyss. ²When he opened the Abyss, smoke rose from it like the smoke from a gigantic furnace. The sun and sky were darkened by the smoke from the Abyss. ³And out of the smoke locusts came down on the earth and were given power like that of scorpions of the earth. ⁴They were told not to harm the grass of the earth or any plant or tree, but only those people who did not have the seal of God on their foreheads. ⁵They were not allowed to kill them but only to torture them for five months. And the agony they suffered was like that of the sting of a scorpion when it strikes. ⁶During those days people will seek death but will not find it; they will long to die, but death will elude them.

⁷The locusts looked like horses prepared for battle. On their heads they wore something like crowns of gold, and their faces resembled human faces. ⁸Their hair was like women's hair, and their teeth were like lions' teeth. ⁹They had breastplates like breastplates of iron, and the sound of their wings was like the thundering of many horses and chariots rushing into battle. ¹⁰They had tails with stingers, like scorpions, and in their tails they had power to torment people for five months. ¹¹They had as king over them the angel of the Abyss, whose name in Hebrew is Abaddon and in Greek is Apollyon (that is, Destroyer).

¹²The first woe is past; two other woes are yet to come.

¹³The sixth angel sounded his trumpet, and I heard a voice coming from the four horns of the golden altar that is before God. ¹⁴It

---

ᵃ 11 Wormwood is a bitter substance.

said to the sixth angel who had the trumpet, "Release the four angels who are bound at the great river Euphrates." 15And the four angels who had been kept ready for this very hour and day and month and year were released to kill a third of mankind. 16The number of the mounted troops was twice ten thousand times ten thousand. I heard their number.

17The horses and riders I saw in my vision looked like this: Their breastplates were fiery red, dark blue, and yellow as sulfur. The heads of the horses resembled the heads of lions, and out of their mouths came fire, smoke and sulfur. 18A third of mankind was killed by the three plagues of fire, smoke and sulfur that came out of their mouths. 19The power of the horses was in their mouths and in their tails; for their tails were like snakes, having heads with which they inflict injury.

20The rest of mankind who were not killed by these plagues still did not repent of the work of their hands; they did not stop worshiping demons, and idols of gold, silver, bronze, stone and wood—idols that cannot see or hear or walk. 21Nor did they repent of their murders, their magic arts, their sexual immorality or their thefts.

10 Then I saw another mighty angel coming down from heaven. He was robed in a cloud, with a rainbow above his head; his face was like the sun, and his legs were like fiery pillars. 2He was holding a little scroll, which lay open in his hand. He planted his right foot on the sea and his left foot on the land, 3and he gave a loud shout like the roar of a lion. When he shouted,

the voices of the seven thunders spoke. 4And when the seven thunders spoke, I was about to write; but I heard a voice from heaven say, "Seal up what the seven thunders have said and do not write it down."

5Then the angel I had seen standing on the sea and on the land raised his right hand to heaven. 6And he swore by him who lives for ever and ever, who created the heavens and all that is in them, the earth and all that is in it, and the sea and all that is in it, and said, "There will be no more delay! 7But in the days when the seventh angel is about to sound his trumpet, the mystery of God will be accomplished, just as he announced to his servants the prophets."

8Then the voice that I had heard from heaven spoke to me once more: "Go, take the scroll that lies open in the hand of the angel who is standing on the sea and on the land."

9So I went to the angel and asked him to give me the little scroll. He said to me, "Take it and eat it. It will turn your stomach sour, but 'in your mouth it will be as sweet as honey.'ᵃ" 10I took the little scroll from the angel's hand and ate it. It tasted as sweet as honey in my mouth, but when I had eaten it, my stomach turned sour. 11Then I was told, "You must prophesy again about many peoples, nations, languages and kings."

11 I was given a reed like a measuring rod and was told, "Go and measure the temple of God and the altar, with its worshipers. 2But exclude the outer court; do not measure it, because it has been given to the Gentiles. They

ᵃ 9 Ezek. 3:3

will trample on the holy city for 42 months. [3] And I will appoint my two witnesses, and they will prophesy for 1,260 days, clothed in sackcloth." [4] They are "the two olive trees" and the two lampstands, and "they stand before the Lord of the earth."[a] [5] If anyone tries to harm them, fire comes from their mouths and devours their enemies. This is how anyone who wants to harm them must die. [6] They have power to shut up the heavens so that it will not rain during the time they are prophesying; and they have power to turn the waters into blood and to strike the earth with every kind of plague as often as they want.

[7] Now when they have finished their testimony, the beast that comes up from the Abyss will attack them, and overpower and kill them. [8] Their bodies will lie in the public square of the great city—which is figuratively called Sodom and Egypt—where also their Lord was crucified. [9] For three and a half days some from every people, tribe, language and nation will gaze on their bodies and refuse them burial. [10] The inhabitants of the earth will gloat over them and will celebrate by sending each other gifts, because these two prophets had tormented those who live on the earth.

[11] But after the three and a half days the breath[b] of life from God entered them, and they stood on their feet, and terror struck those who saw them. [12] Then they heard a loud voice from heaven saying to them, "Come up here." And they went up to heaven in a cloud, while their enemies looked on.

[13] At that very hour there was a severe earthquake and a tenth of the city collapsed. Seven thousand people were killed in the earthquake, and the survivors were terrified and gave glory to the God of heaven.

[14] The second woe has passed; the third woe is coming soon.

[15] The seventh angel sounded his trumpet, and there were loud voices in heaven, which said:

> "The kingdom of the world has become
>     the kingdom of our Lord and of his Messiah,
> and he will reign for ever and ever."

[16] And the twenty-four elders, who were seated on their thrones before God, fell on their faces and worshiped God, [17] saying:

> "We give thanks to you, Lord God Almighty,
>     the One who is and who was,
> because you have taken your great power
>     and have begun to reign.
> [18] The nations were angry,
>     and your wrath has come.
> The time has come for judging the dead,
>     and for rewarding your servants the prophets
> and your people who revere your name,
>     both great and small—
> and for destroying those who destroy the earth."

[19] Then God's temple in heaven was opened, and within his temple was seen the ark of his covenant. And there came flashes of lightning, rumblings, peals of thunder, an earthquake and a severe hailstorm.

---

[a] 4 See Zech. 4:3,11,14.    [b] 11 Or *Spirit* (see Ezek. 37:5,14).

# 12

A great sign appeared in heaven: a woman clothed with the sun, with the moon under her feet and a crown of twelve stars on her head. ²She was pregnant and cried out in pain as she was about to give birth. ³Then another sign appeared in heaven: an enormous red dragon with seven heads and ten horns and seven crowns on its heads. ⁴Its tail swept a third of the stars out of the sky and flung them to the earth. The dragon stood in front of the woman who was about to give birth, so that it might devour her child the moment he was born. ⁵She gave birth to a son, a male child, who "will rule all the nations with an iron scepter."[a] And her child was snatched up to God and to his throne. ⁶The woman fled into the wilderness to a place prepared for her by God, where she might be taken care of for 1,260 days.

⁷Then war broke out in heaven. Michael and his angels fought against the dragon, and the dragon and his angels fought back. ⁸But he was not strong enough, and they lost their place in heaven. ⁹The great dragon was hurled down—that ancient serpent called the devil, or Satan, who leads the whole world astray. He was hurled to the earth, and his angels with him.

¹⁰Then I heard a loud voice in heaven say:

"Now have come the salvation
    and the power
    and the kingdom of our God,
    and the authority of his
        Messiah.
For the accuser of our brothers
        and sisters,
    who accuses them before our
        God day and night,
has been hurled down.
¹¹They triumphed over him
    by the blood of the Lamb
    and by the word of their
        testimony;
they did not love their lives so
        much
    as to shrink from death.
¹²Therefore rejoice, you heavens
    and you who dwell in them!
But woe to the earth and the sea,
    because the devil has gone
        down to you!
He is filled with fury,
    because he knows that his
        time is short."

¹³When the dragon saw that he had been hurled to the earth, he pursued the woman who had given birth to the male child. ¹⁴The woman was given the two wings of a great eagle, so that she might fly to the place prepared for her in the wilderness, where she would be taken care of for a time, times and half a time, out of the serpent's reach. ¹⁵Then from his mouth the serpent spewed water like a river, to overtake the woman and sweep her away with the torrent. ¹⁶But the earth helped the woman by opening its mouth and swallowing the river that the dragon had spewed out of his mouth. ¹⁷Then the dragon was enraged at the woman and went off to wage war against the rest of her offspring—those who keep God's commands and hold fast their testimony about Jesus.

# 13

The dragon[b] stood on the shore of the sea. And I saw a beast coming out of the sea. It had ten horns and seven heads, with ten crowns on its horns, and on each head a blasphemous name. ²The beast I saw resembled a leopard,

---

[a] 5 Psalm 2:9    [b] 1 Some manuscripts *And I*

but had feet like those of a bear and a mouth like that of a lion. The dragon gave the beast his power and his throne and great authority. ³One of the heads of the beast seemed to have had a fatal wound, but the fatal wound had been healed. The whole world was filled with wonder and followed the beast. ⁴People worshiped the dragon because he had given authority to the beast, and they also worshiped the beast and asked, "Who is like the beast? Who can wage war against it?"

⁵The beast was given a mouth to utter proud words and blasphemies and to exercise its authority for forty-two months. ⁶It opened its mouth to blaspheme God, and to slander his name and his dwelling place and those who live in heaven. ⁷It was given power to wage war against God's holy people and to conquer them. And it was given authority over every tribe, people, language and nation. ⁸All inhabitants of the earth will worship the beast—all whose names have not been written in the Lamb's book of life, the Lamb who was slain from the creation of the world.ᵃ

⁹Whoever has ears, let them hear.

¹⁰ "If anyone is to go into captivity,
    into captivity they will go.
If anyone is to be killedᵇ with the
    sword,
  with the sword they will be
    killed."ᶜ

This calls for patient endurance and faithfulness on the part of God's people.

¹¹Then I saw a second beast, coming out of the earth. It had two horns like a lamb, but it spoke like a dragon. ¹²It exercised all the authority of the first beast on its behalf, and made the earth and its inhabitants worship the first beast, whose fatal wound had been healed. ¹³And it performed great signs, even causing fire to come down from heaven to the earth in full view of the people. ¹⁴Because of the signs it was given power to perform on behalf of the first beast, it deceived the inhabitants of the earth. It ordered them to set up an image in honor of the beast who was wounded by the sword and yet lived. ¹⁵The second beast was given power to give breath to the image of the first beast, so that the image could speak and cause all who refused to worship the image to be killed. ¹⁶It also forced all people, great and small, rich and poor, free and slave, to receive a mark on their right hands or on their foreheads, ¹⁷so that they could not buy or sell unless they had the mark, which is the name of the beast or the number of its name.

¹⁸This calls for wisdom. Let the person who has insight calculate the number of the beast, for it is the number of a man.ᵈ That number is 666.

14 Then I looked, and there before me was the Lamb, standing on Mount Zion, and with him 144,000 who had his name and his Father's name written on their foreheads. ²And I heard a sound from heaven like the roar of rushing waters and like a loud peal of thunder. The sound I heard was like that of harpists playing their harps. ³And they sang a new song before the throne and before the four living creatures and the elders. No one

---

ᵃ 8 Or *written from the creation of the world in the book of life belonging to the Lamb who was slain*    ᵇ 10 Some manuscripts *anyone kills*    ᶜ 10 Jer. 15:2    ᵈ 18 Or *is humanity's number* could learn the song except the 144,000 who had been redeemed from the earth. [4]These are those who did not defile themselves with women, for they remained virgins. They follow the Lamb wherever he goes. They were purchased from among mankind and offered as firstfruits to God and the Lamb. [5]No lie was found in their mouths; they are blameless.

[6]Then I saw another angel flying in midair, and he had the eternal gospel to proclaim to those who live on the earth—to every nation, tribe, language and people. [7]He said in a loud voice, "Fear God and give him glory, because the hour of his judgment has come. Worship him who made the heavens, the earth, the sea and the springs of water."

[8]A second angel followed and said, " 'Fallen! Fallen is Babylon the Great,'[a] which made all the nations drink the maddening wine of her adulteries."

[9]A third angel followed them and said in a loud voice: "If anyone worships the beast and its image and receives its mark on their forehead or on their hand, [10]they, too, will drink the wine of God's fury, which has been poured full strength into the cup of his wrath. They will be tormented with burning sulfur in the presence of the holy angels and of the Lamb. [11]And the smoke of their torment will rise for ever and ever. There will be no rest day or night for those who worship the beast and its image, or for anyone who receives the mark of its name." [12]This calls for patient endurance on the part of the people of God who keep his commands and remain faithful to Jesus.

[13]Then I heard a voice from heaven say, "Write this: Blessed are the dead who die in the Lord from now on."

"Yes," says the Spirit, "they will rest from their labor, for their deeds will follow them."

[14]I looked, and there before me was a white cloud, and seated on the cloud was one like a son of man[b] with a crown of gold on his head and a sharp sickle in his hand. [15]Then another angel came out of the temple and called in a loud voice to him who was sitting on the cloud, "Take your sickle and reap, because the time to reap has come, for the harvest of the earth is ripe." [16]So he who was seated on the cloud swung his sickle over the earth, and the earth was harvested.

[17]Another angel came out of the temple in heaven, and he too had a sharp sickle. [18]Still another angel, who had charge of the fire, came from the altar and called in a loud voice to him who had the sharp sickle, "Take your sharp sickle and gather the clusters of grapes from the earth's vine, because its grapes are ripe." [19]The angel swung his sickle on the earth, gathered its grapes and threw them into the great winepress of God's wrath. [20]They were trampled in the winepress outside the city, and blood flowed out of the press, rising as high as the horses' bridles for a distance of 1,600 stadia.[c]

15 I saw in heaven another great and marvelous sign: seven angels with the seven last plagues—last, because with them God's wrath is completed. [2]And I saw what looked like a sea of glass glowing with fire and, standing beside the sea, those who had been

---

[a] 8 Isaiah 21:9   [b] 14 See Daniel 7:13.   [c] 20 That is, about 180 miles or about 300 kilometers

victorious over the beast and its image and over the number of its name. They held harps given them by God [3]and sang the song of God's servant Moses and of the Lamb:

"Great and marvelous are your
    deeds,
    Lord God Almighty.
Just and true are your ways,
    King of the nations.[a]
[4]Who will not fear you, Lord,
    and bring glory to your name?
For you alone are holy.
All nations will come
    and worship before you,
for your righteous acts have
    been revealed."[b]

[5]After this I looked, and I saw in heaven the temple—that is, the tabernacle of the covenant law—and it was opened. [6]Out of the temple came the seven angels with the seven plagues. They were dressed in clean, shining linen and wore golden sashes around their chests. [7]Then one of the four living creatures gave to the seven angels seven golden bowls filled with the wrath of God, who lives for ever and ever. [8]And the temple was filled with smoke from the glory of God and from his power, and no one could enter the temple until the seven plagues of the seven angels were completed.

16 Then I heard a loud voice from the temple saying to the seven angels, "Go, pour out the seven bowls of God's wrath on the earth."

[2]The first angel went and poured out his bowl on the land, and ugly, festering sores broke out on the people who had the mark of the beast and worshiped its image.

[3]The second angel poured out his bowl on the sea, and it turned into blood like that of a dead person, and every living thing in the sea died.

[4]The third angel poured out his bowl on the rivers and springs of water, and they became blood. [5]Then I heard the angel in charge of the waters say:

"You are just in these judgments,
    O Holy One,
    you who are and who were;
[6]for they have shed the blood of
    your holy people and your
    prophets,
    and you have given them
    blood to drink as they
    deserve."

[7]And I heard the altar respond:

"Yes, Lord God Almighty,
    true and just are your
    judgments."

[8]The fourth angel poured out his bowl on the sun, and the sun was allowed to scorch people with fire. [9]They were seared by the intense heat and they cursed the name of God, who had control over these plagues, but they refused to repent and glorify him.

[10]The fifth angel poured out his bowl on the throne of the beast, and its kingdom was plunged into darkness. People gnawed their tongues in agony [11]and cursed the God of heaven because of their pains and their sores, but they refused to repent of what they had done.

[12]The sixth angel poured out his bowl on the great river Euphrates, and its water was dried up to prepare the way for the kings from the East. [13]Then I saw three impure spirits that looked like frogs; they

[a] 3 Some manuscripts ages   [b] 3,4 Phrases in this song are drawn from Psalm 111:2,3; Deut. 32:4; Jer. 10:7; Psalms 86:9; 98:2.

came out of the mouth of the dragon, out of the mouth of the beast and out of the mouth of the false prophet. [14]They are demonic spirits that perform signs, and they go out to the kings of the whole world, to gather them for the battle on the great day of God Almighty.

[15]"Look, I come like a thief! Blessed is the one who stays awake and remains clothed, so as not to go naked and be shamefully exposed."

[16]Then they gathered the kings together to the place that in Hebrew is called Armageddon.

[17]The seventh angel poured out his bowl into the air, and out of the temple came a loud voice from the throne, saying, "It is done!" [18]Then there came flashes of lightning, rumblings, peals of thunder and a severe earthquake. No earthquake like it has ever occurred since mankind has been on earth, so tremendous was the quake. [19]The great city split into three parts, and the cities of the nations collapsed. God remembered Babylon the Great and gave her the cup filled with the wine of the fury of his wrath. [20]Every island fled away and the mountains could not be found. [21]From the sky huge hailstones, each weighing about a hundred pounds,[a] fell on people. And they cursed God on account of the plague of hail, because the plague was so terrible.

17 One of the seven angels who had the seven bowls came and said to me, "Come, I will show you the punishment of the great prostitute, who sits by many waters. [2]With her the kings of the earth committed adultery, and the inhabitants of the earth were intoxicated with the wine of her adulteries."

[3]Then the angel carried me away in the Spirit into a wilderness. There I saw a woman sitting on a scarlet beast that was covered with blasphemous names and had seven heads and ten horns. [4]The woman was dressed in purple and scarlet, and was glittering with gold, precious stones and pearls. She held a golden cup in her hand, filled with abominable things and the filth of her adulteries. [5]The name written on her forehead was a mystery:

BABYLON THE GREAT
THE MOTHER OF PROSTITUTES
AND OF THE ABOMINATIONS
OF THE EARTH.

[6]I saw that the woman was drunk with the blood of God's holy people, the blood of those who bore testimony to Jesus.

When I saw her, I was greatly astonished. [7]Then the angel said to me: "Why are you astonished? I will explain to you the mystery of the woman and of the beast she rides, which has the seven heads and ten horns. [8]The beast, which you saw, once was, now is not, and yet will come up out of the Abyss and go to its destruction. The inhabitants of the earth whose names have not been written in the book of life from the creation of the world will be astonished when they see the beast, because it once was, now is not, and yet will come.

[9]"This calls for a mind with wisdom. The seven heads are seven hills on which the woman sits. [10]They are also seven kings. Five have fallen, one is, the other has not yet come; but when he does come, he must remain for only a little

---

*a 21* Or about 45 kilograms

while. ¹¹The beast who once was, and now is not, is an eighth king. He belongs to the seven and is going to his destruction.

¹²"The ten horns you saw are ten kings who have not yet received a kingdom, but who for one hour will receive authority as kings along with the beast. ¹³They have one purpose and will give their power and authority to the beast. ¹⁴They will wage war against the Lamb, but the Lamb will triumph over them because he is Lord of lords and King of kings—and with him will be his called, chosen and faithful followers."

¹⁵Then the angel said to me, "The waters you saw, where the prostitute sits, are peoples, multitudes, nations and languages. ¹⁶The beast and the ten horns you saw will hate the prostitute. They will bring her to ruin and leave her naked; they will eat her flesh and burn her with fire. ¹⁷For God has put it into their hearts to accomplish his purpose by agreeing to hand over to the beast their royal authority, until God's words are fulfilled. ¹⁸The woman you saw is the great city that rules over the kings of the earth."

18 After this I saw another angel coming down from heaven. He had great authority, and the earth was illuminated by his splendor. ²With a mighty voice he shouted:

"'Fallen! Fallen is Babylon the Great!'ᵃ
    She has become a dwelling for demons
    and a haunt for every impure spirit,
    a haunt for every unclean bird,

a haunt for every unclean and detestable animal.
³For all the nations have drunk the maddening wine of her adulteries.
The kings of the earth committed adultery with her,
    and the merchants of the earth grew rich from her excessive luxuries."

⁴Then I heard another voice from heaven say:

"'Come out of her, my people,'ᵇ
    so that you will not share in her sins,
    so that you will not receive any of her plagues;
⁵for her sins are piled up to heaven,
    and God has remembered her crimes.
⁶Give back to her as she has given;
    pay her back double for what she has done.
    Pour her a double portion from her own cup.
⁷Give her as much torment and grief
    as the glory and luxury she gave herself.
In her heart she boasts,
    'I sit enthroned as queen.
I am not a widow;ᶜ
    I will never mourn.'
⁸Therefore in one day her plagues will overtake her:
    death, mourning and famine.
She will be consumed by fire,
    for mighty is the Lord God who judges her.

⁹"When the kings of the earth who committed adultery with her and shared her luxury see the smoke of her burning, they will

---

ᵃ 2 Isaiah 21:9   ᵇ 4 Jer. 51:45   ᶜ 7 See Isaiah 47:7,8.

weep and mourn over her. ¹⁰Terrified at her torment, they will stand far off and cry:

> "'Woe! Woe to you, great city,
>     you mighty city of Babylon!
> In one hour your doom has
>     come!'

¹¹"The merchants of the earth will weep and mourn over her because no one buys their cargoes anymore— ¹²cargoes of gold, silver, precious stones and pearls; fine linen, purple, silk and scarlet cloth; every sort of citron wood, and articles of every kind made of ivory, costly wood, bronze, iron and marble; ¹³cargoes of cinnamon and spice, of incense, myrrh and frankincense, of wine and olive oil, of fine flour and wheat; cattle and sheep; horses and carriages; and human beings sold as slaves.

¹⁴"They will say, 'The fruit you longed for is gone from you. All your luxury and splendor have vanished, never to be recovered.' ¹⁵The merchants who sold these things and gained their wealth from her will stand far off, terrified at her torment. They will weep and mourn ¹⁶and cry out:

> "'Woe! Woe to you, great city,
>     dressed in fine linen, purple
>     and scarlet,
> and glittering with gold,
>     precious stones and
>     pearls!
> ¹⁷In one hour such great wealth
>     has been brought to ruin!'

"Every sea captain, and all who travel by ship, the sailors, and all who earn their living from the sea, will stand far off. ¹⁸When they see the smoke of her burning, they will exclaim, 'Was there ever a city like this great city?' ¹⁹They will throw dust on their heads, and with weeping and mourning cry out:

> "'Woe! Woe to you, great city,
>     where all who had ships on the
>     sea
> became rich through her
>     wealth!
> In one hour she has been
>     brought to ruin!'

²⁰"Rejoice over her, you heavens!
>     Rejoice, you people of God!
>     Rejoice, apostles and
>     prophets!
> For God has judged her
>     with the judgment she
>     imposed on you."

²¹Then a mighty angel picked up a boulder the size of a large millstone and threw it into the sea, and said:

> "With such violence
>     the great city of Babylon will
>     be thrown down,
>     never to be found again.
> ²²The music of harpists and
>     musicians, pipers and
>     trumpeters,
>     will never be heard in you
>     again.
> No worker of any trade
>     will ever be found in you
>     again.
> The sound of a millstone
>     will never be heard in you
>     again.
> ²³The light of a lamp
>     will never shine in you again.
> The voice of bridegroom and
>     bride
>     will never be heard in you
>     again.
> Your merchants were the world's
>     important people.
> By your magic spell all the
>     nations were led astray.
> ²⁴In her was found the blood of

prophets and of God's holy
people,
of all who have been
slaughtered on the earth."

19 After this I heard what sounded like the roar of a great multitude in heaven shouting:

"Hallelujah!
Salvation and glory and power
belong to our God,
2   for true and just are his
judgments.
He has condemned the great
prostitute
who corrupted the earth by
her adulteries.
He has avenged on her the blood
of his servants."

3 And again they shouted:

"Hallelujah!
The smoke from her goes up for
ever and ever."

4 The twenty-four elders and the
four living creatures fell down and
worshiped God, who was seated on
the throne. And they cried:

"Amen, Hallelujah!"

5 Then a voice came from the
throne, saying:

"Praise our God,
all you his servants,
you who fear him,
both great and small!"

6 Then I heard what sounded like
a great multitude, like the roar of
rushing waters and like loud peals
of thunder, shouting:

"Hallelujah!
For our Lord God Almighty
reigns.
7 Let us rejoice and be glad
and give him glory!

For the wedding of the Lamb has
come,
and his bride has made herself
ready.
8 Fine linen, bright and clean,
was given her to wear."
(Fine linen stands for the righteous
acts of God's holy people.)

9 Then the angel said to me,
"Write this: Blessed are those who
are invited to the wedding supper
of the Lamb!" And he added, "These
are the true words of God."

10 At this I fell at his feet to worship him. But he said to me, "Don't
do that! I am a fellow servant with
you and with your brothers and
sisters who hold to the testimony
of Jesus. Worship God! For it is the
Spirit of prophecy who bears testimony to Jesus."

11 I saw heaven standing open
and there before me was a white
horse, whose rider is called Faithful and True. With justice he judges and wages war. 12 His eyes are
like blazing fire, and on his head
are many crowns. He has a name
written on him that no one knows
but he himself. 13 He is dressed in
a robe dipped in blood, and his
name is the Word of God. 14 The
armies of heaven were following
him, riding on white horses and
dressed in fine linen, white and
clean. 15 Coming out of his mouth
is a sharp sword with which to
strike down the nations. "He will
rule them with an iron scepter."[a]
He treads the winepress of the fury
of the wrath of God Almighty. 16 On
his robe and on his thigh he has
this name written:

KING OF KINGS AND LORD OF LORDS.

a 15 Psalm 2:9

17And I saw an angel standing in the sun, who cried in a loud voice to all the birds flying in midair, "Come, gather together for the great supper of God, 18so that you may eat the flesh of kings, generals, and the mighty, of horses and their riders, and the flesh of all people, free and slave, great and small."

19Then I saw the beast and the kings of the earth and their armies gathered together to wage war against the rider on the horse and his army. 20But the beast was captured, and with it the false prophet who had performed the signs on its behalf. With these signs he had deluded those who had received the mark of the beast and worshiped its image. The two of them were thrown alive into the fiery lake of burning sulfur. 21The rest were killed with the sword coming out of the mouth of the rider on the horse, and all the birds gorged themselves on their flesh.

20 And I saw an angel coming down out of heaven, having the key to the Abyss and holding in his hand a great chain. 2He seized the dragon, that ancient serpent, who is the devil, or Satan, and bound him for a thousand years. 3He threw him into the Abyss, and locked and sealed it over him, to keep him from deceiving the nations anymore until the thousand years were ended. After that, he must be set free for a short time.

4I saw thrones on which were seated those who had been given authority to judge. And I saw the souls of those who had been beheaded because of their testimony about Jesus and because of the word of God. Theya had not worshiped the beast or its image and

had not received its mark on their foreheads or their hands. They came to life and reigned with Christ a thousand years. 5(The rest of the dead did not come to life until the thousand years were ended.) This is the first resurrection. 6Blessed and holy are those who share in the first resurrection. The second death has no power over them, but they will be priests of God and of Christ and will reign with him for a thousand years.

7When the thousand years are over, Satan will be released from his prison 8and will go out to deceive the nations in the four corners of the earth—Gog and Magog—and to gather them for battle. In number they are like the sand on the seashore. 9They marched across the breadth of the earth and surrounded the camp of God's people, the city he loves. But fire came down from heaven and devoured them. 10And the devil, who deceived them, was thrown into the lake of burning sulfur, where the beast and the false prophet had been thrown. They will be tormented day and night for ever and ever.

11Then I saw a great white throne and him who was seated on it. The earth and the heavens fled from his presence, and there was no place for them. 12And I saw the dead, great and small, standing before the throne, and books were opened. Another book was opened, which is the book of life. The dead were judged according to what they had done as recorded in the books. 13The sea gave up the dead that were in it, and death and Hades gave up the dead that were in them, and each person was judged according to what

a 4 Or God; I also saw those who

they had done. ¹⁴Then death and Hades were thrown into the lake of fire. The lake of fire is the second death. ¹⁵Anyone whose name was not found written in the book of life was thrown into the lake of fire.

21 Then I saw "a new heaven and a new earth,"ᵃ for the first heaven and the first earth had passed away, and there was no longer any sea. ²I saw the Holy City, the new Jerusalem, coming down out of heaven from God, prepared as a bride beautifully dressed for her husband. ³And I heard a loud voice from the throne saying, "Look! God's dwelling place is now among the people, and he will dwell with them. They will be his people, and God himself will be with them and be their God. ⁴'He will wipe every tear from their eyes. There will be no more death'ᵇ or mourning or crying or pain, for the old order of things has passed away."

⁵He who was seated on the throne said, "I am making everything new!" Then he said, "Write this down, for these words are trustworthy and true."

⁶He said to me: "It is done. I am the Alpha and the Omega, the Beginning and the End. To the thirsty I will give water without cost from the spring of the water of life. ⁷Those who are victorious will inherit all this, and I will be their God and they will be my children. ⁸But the cowardly, the unbelieving, the vile, the murderers, the sexually immoral, those who practice magic arts, the idolaters and all liars — they will be consigned to the fiery lake of burning sulfur. This is the second death."

⁹One of the seven angels who had the seven bowls full of the seven last plagues came and said to me, "Come, I will show you the bride, the wife of the Lamb." ¹⁰And he carried me away in the Spirit to a mountain great and high, and showed me the Holy City, Jerusalem, coming down out of heaven from God. ¹¹It shone with the glory of God, and its brilliance was like that of a very precious jewel, like a jasper, clear as crystal. ¹²It had a great, high wall with twelve gates, and with twelve angels at the gates. On the gates were written the names of the twelve tribes of Israel. ¹³There were three gates on the east, three on the north, three on the south and three on the west. ¹⁴The wall of the city had twelve foundations, and on them were the names of the twelve apostles of the Lamb.

¹⁵The angel who talked with me had a measuring rod of gold to measure the city, its gates and its walls. ¹⁶The city was laid out like a square, as long as it was wide. He measured the city with the rod and found it to be 12,000 stadiaᶜ in length, and as wide and high as it is long. ¹⁷The angel measured the wall using human measurement, and it was 144 cubitsᵈ thick.ᵉ ¹⁸The wall was made of jasper, and the city of pure gold, as pure as glass. ¹⁹The foundations of the city walls were decorated with every kind of precious stone. The first foundation was jasper, the second sapphire, the third agate, the fourth emerald, ²⁰the fifth onyx, the sixth ruby, the seventh chrysolite, the eighth beryl, the ninth topaz, the tenth turquoise, the eleventh jacinth, and

---

ᵃ *1* Isaiah 65:17   ᵇ *4* Isaiah 25:8   ᶜ *16* That is, about 1,400 miles or about 2,200 kilometers
ᵈ *17* That is, about 200 feet or about 65 meters   ᵉ *17* Or *high*

the twelfth amethyst.$^a$ $^{21}$The twelve gates were twelve pearls, each gate made of a single pearl. The great street of the city was of gold, as pure as transparent glass.

$^{22}$I did not see a temple in the city, because the Lord God Almighty and the Lamb are its temple. $^{23}$The city does not need the sun or the moon to shine on it, for the glory of God gives it light, and the Lamb is its lamp. $^{24}$The nations will walk by its light, and the kings of the earth will bring their splendor into it. $^{25}$On no day will its gates ever be shut, for there will be no night there. $^{26}$The glory and honor of the nations will be brought into it. $^{27}$Nothing impure will ever enter it, nor will anyone who does what is shameful or deceitful, but only those whose names are written in the Lamb's book of life.

22 Then the angel showed me the river of the water of life, as clear as crystal, flowing from the throne of God and of the Lamb $^2$down the middle of the great street of the city. On each side of the river stood the tree of life, bearing twelve crops of fruit, yielding its fruit every month. And the leaves of the tree are for the healing of the nations. $^3$No longer will there be any curse. The throne of God and of the Lamb will be in the city, and his servants will serve him. $^4$They will see his face, and his name will be on their foreheads. $^5$There will be no more night. They will not need the light of a lamp or the light of the sun, for the Lord God will give them light. And they will reign for ever and ever.

$^6$The angel said to me, "These words are trustworthy and true. The Lord, the God who inspires the prophets, sent his angel to show his servants the things that must soon take place."

$^7$"Look, I am coming soon! Blessed is the one who keeps the words of the prophecy written in this scroll."

$^8$I, John, am the one who heard and saw these things. And when I had heard and seen them, I fell down to worship at the feet of the angel who had been showing them to me. $^9$But he said to me, "Don't do that! I am a fellow servant with you and with your fellow prophets and with all who keep the words of this scroll. Worship God!"

$^{10}$Then he told me, "Do not seal up the words of the prophecy of this scroll, because the time is near. $^{11}$Let the one who does wrong continue to do wrong; let the vile person continue to be vile; let the one who does right continue to do right; and let the holy person continue to be holy."

$^{12}$"Look, I am coming soon! My reward is with me, and I will give to each person according to what they have done. $^{13}$I am the Alpha and the Omega, the First and the Last, the Beginning and the End.

$^{14}$"Blessed are those who wash their robes, that they may have the right to the tree of life and may go through the gates into the city. $^{15}$Outside are the dogs, those who practice magic arts, the sexually immoral, the murderers, the idolaters and everyone who loves and practices falsehood.

$^{16}$"I, Jesus, have sent my angel to give you$^b$ this testimony for the

---

$^a$ 20 The precise identification of some of these precious stones is uncertain.     $^b$ 16 The Greek is plural.

churches. I am the Root and the Offspring of David, and the bright Morning Star."

¹⁷The Spirit and the bride say, "Come!" And let the one who hears say, "Come!" Let the one who is thirsty come; and let the one who wishes take the free gift of the water of life.

¹⁸I warn everyone who hears the words of the prophecy of this scroll: If anyone adds anything to them, God will add to that person the plagues described in this scroll. ¹⁹And if anyone takes words away from this scroll of prophecy, God will take away from that person any share in the tree of life and in the Holy City, which are described in this scroll.

²⁰He who testifies to these things says, "Yes, I am coming soon."

Amen. Come, Lord Jesus.

²¹The grace of the Lord Jesus be with God's people. Amen.

A collection of Israel's songs that
**CELEBRATE, LAMENT AND REFLECT
ON VICTORIES AND STRUGGLES,**
together with a gathering of
**ISRAEL'S WISDOM SAYINGS,**
guiding us on our journey
in God's story
**OF OVERCOMING EVIL AND BRINGING
THE NEW CREATION,**

PRESENTED
IN THE BOOKS OF **PSALMS
AND PROVERBS**

# PSALMS

The book of Psalms is a collection of song lyrics. Like many songs, they were first written in response to events in the lives of their authors. Later, the whole community used them in worship. When Israel returned from exile in Babylon many of the songs from over the centuries were collected in the book of Psalms.

The book is structured into five parts marked off by the phrase, *Praise be to the LORD . . . Amen and Amen!* These five "books" remind the reader of the five books of Moses. Like the law, these song lyrics can be read and studied for instruction. Psalm 1 emphasizes such meditation and seems to have been placed first to make this point.

The five books also tell a three-part story of Israel's redemption: monarchy, exile and return. The psalms of King David dominate books one and two. The beginning and ending of book three highlight Israel's exile. The fourth book ends with a plea that God bring the exiled people home. The fifth book declares that God has done just that. Now the reason for the group of praise psalms at the end of the book is apparent: God has been faithful, judging Israel in exile but then bringing the nation home again.

The book of Psalms thus operates at two levels: individually the songs explore a wide variety of honest spiritual responses to God, while the overall collection tells, and celebrates, the work of God in history to save his people.

---

## BOOK I

### *Psalms 1–41*

### Psalm 1

1 Blessed is the one
    who does not walk in step with
        the wicked
    or stand in the way that sinners
        take
    or sit in the company of
        mockers,
2 but whose delight is in the law of
        the LORD,
    and who meditates on his law
        day and night.
3 That person is like a tree planted
        by streams of water,
    which yields its fruit in season
    and whose leaf does not wither —
        whatever they do prospers.

4 Not so the wicked!
    They are like chaff
        that the wind blows away.
5 Therefore the wicked will not
        stand in the judgment,
    nor sinners in the assembly of
        the righteous.

6 For the LORD watches over the
        way of the righteous,
    but the way of the wicked leads
        to destruction.

### Psalm 2

1 Why do the nations conspire[a]
    and the peoples plot in vain?
2 The kings of the earth rise up
    and the rulers band
        together
    against the LORD and against
        his anointed, saying,

a 1 Hebrew; Septuagint *rage*

³ "Let us break their chains
and throw off their shackles."

⁴ The One enthroned in heaven
laughs;
the Lord scoffs at them.

⁵ He rebukes them in his anger
and terrifies them in his
wrath, saying,

⁶ "I have installed my king
on Zion, my holy mountain."

⁷ I will proclaim the LORD's decree:

He said to me, "You are my son;
today I have become your father.

⁸ Ask me,
and I will make the nations
your inheritance,
the ends of the earth your
possession.

⁹ You will break them with a rod of
iron[a];
you will dash them to pieces
like pottery."

¹⁰ Therefore, you kings, be wise;
be warned, you rulers of the
earth.

¹¹ Serve the LORD with fear
and celebrate his rule with
trembling.

¹² Kiss his son, or he will be angry
and your way will lead to your
destruction,
for his wrath can flare up in a
moment.
Blessed are all who take refuge
in him.

## Psalm 3[b]

*A psalm of David. When he fled from his
son Absalom.*

¹ LORD, how many are my foes!
How many rise up against me!

² Many are saying of me,
"God will not deliver him."[c]

³ But you, LORD, are a shield
around me,
my glory, the One who lifts my
head high.

⁴ I call out to the LORD,
and he answers me from his
holy mountain.

⁵ I lie down and sleep;
I wake again, because the
LORD sustains me.

⁶ I will not fear though tens of
thousands
assail me on every side.

⁷ Arise, LORD!
Deliver me, my God!
Strike all my enemies on the
jaw;
break the teeth of the wicked.

⁸ From the LORD comes
deliverance.
May your blessing be on your
people.

## Psalm 4[d]

*For the director of music. With stringed
instruments. A psalm of David.*

¹ Answer me when I call to you,
my righteous God.
Give me relief from my distress;
have mercy on me and hear
my prayer.

² How long will you people turn
my glory into shame?
How long will you love
delusions and seek false
gods[e]?[f]

³ Know that the LORD has set
apart his faithful servant
for himself;

---

[a] 9 Or *will rule them with an iron scepter* (see Septuagint and Syriac)    [b] In Hebrew texts 3:1-8
is numbered 3:2-9.    [c] 2 The Hebrew has *Selah* (a word of uncertain meaning) here and at the
end of verses 4 and 8.    [d] In Hebrew texts 4:1-8 is numbered 4:2-9.    [e] 2 Or *seek lies*    [f] 2 The
Hebrew has *Selah* (a word of uncertain meaning) here and at the end of verse 4.

the LORD hears when I call to
  him.

[4] Tremble and[a] do not sin;
  when you are on your beds,
  search your hearts and be
  silent.
[5] Offer the sacrifices of the
  righteous
  and trust in the LORD.

[6] Many, LORD, are asking, "Who
  will bring us prosperity?"
  Let the light of your face shine
  on us.
[7] Fill my heart with joy
  when their grain and new
  wine abound.

[8] In peace I will lie down and
  sleep,
  for you alone, LORD,
  make me dwell in safety.

## Psalm 5[b]

*For the director of music. For pipes.
A psalm of David.*

[1] Listen to my words, LORD,
  consider my lament.
[2] Hear my cry for help,
  my King and my God,
  for to you I pray.

[3] In the morning, LORD, you hear
  my voice;
  in the morning I lay my
  requests before you
  and wait expectantly.
[4] For you are not a God who is
  pleased with wickedness;
  with you, evil people are not
  welcome.
[5] The arrogant cannot stand
  in your presence.
  You hate all who do wrong;
[6]   you destroy those who tell lies.
  The bloodthirsty and deceitful

you, LORD, detest.
[7] But I, by your great love,
  can come into your house;
  in reverence I bow down
  toward your holy temple.

[8] Lead me, LORD, in your
  righteousness
  because of my enemies —
  make your way straight before
  me.
[9] Not a word from their mouth can
  be trusted;
  their heart is filled with
  malice.
  Their throat is an open grave;
  with their tongues they tell
  lies.
[10] Declare them guilty, O God!
  Let their intrigues be their
  downfall.
  Banish them for their many sins,
  for they have rebelled against
  you.
[11] But let all who take refuge in you
  be glad;
  let them ever sing for joy.
  Spread your protection over
  them,
  that those who love your name
  may rejoice in you.
[12] Surely, LORD, you bless the
  righteous;
  you surround them with your
  favor as with a shield.

## Psalm 6[c]

*For the director of music. With stringed
instruments. According to* sheminith.[d]
*A psalm of David.*

[1] LORD, do not rebuke me in your
  anger
  or discipline me in your wrath.
[2] Have mercy on me, LORD, for I
  am faint;

---

*a* 4 Or *In your anger* (see Septuagint)  *b* In Hebrew texts 5:1-12 is numbered 5:2-13.  *c* In
Hebrew texts 6:1-10 is numbered 6:2-11.  *d* Title: Probably a musical term

heal me, LORD, for my bones
are in agony.
³ My soul is in deep anguish.
How long, LORD, how long?

⁴ Turn, LORD, and deliver me;
save me because of your
unfailing love.
⁵ Among the dead no one
proclaims your name.
Who praises you from the
grave?

⁶ I am worn out from my groaning.

All night long I flood my bed
with weeping
and drench my couch with
tears.
⁷ My eyes grow weak with sorrow;
they fail because of all my foes.

⁸ Away from me, all you who do
evil,
for the LORD has heard my
weeping.
⁹ The LORD has heard my cry for
mercy;
the LORD accepts my prayer.
¹⁰ All my enemies will be
overwhelmed with shame
and anguish;
they will turn back and
suddenly be put to shame.

## Psalm 7 *ᵃ*

*A shiggaionᵇ of David, which he sang to
the LORD concerning Cush, a Benjamite.*

¹ LORD my God, I take refuge in
you;
save and deliver me from all
who pursue me,
² or they will tear me apart like a
lion
and rip me to pieces with no
one to rescue me.

³ LORD my God, if I have done this
and there is guilt on my
hands —
⁴ if I have repaid my ally with evil
or without cause have robbed
my foe —
⁵ then let my enemy pursue and
overtake me;
let him trample my life to the
ground
and make me sleep in the
dust.ᶜ

⁶ Arise, LORD, in your anger;
rise up against the rage of my
enemies.
Awake, my God; decree
justice.
⁷ Let the assembled peoples
gather around you,
while you sit enthroned over
them on high.
⁸ Let the LORD judge the
peoples.
Vindicate me, LORD, according
to my righteousness,
according to my integrity,
O Most High.
⁹ Bring to an end the violence of
the wicked
and make the righteous
secure —
you, the righteous God
who probes minds and hearts.

¹⁰ My shieldᵈ is God Most High,
who saves the upright in heart.
¹¹ God is a righteous judge,
a God who displays his wrath
every day.
¹² If he does not relent,
heᵉ will sharpen his sword;
he will bend and string his
bow.
¹³ He has prepared his deadly
weapons;

---

ᵃ In Hebrew texts 7:1-17 is numbered 7:2-18.   ᵇ Title: Probably a literary or musical term
ᶜ 5 The Hebrew has *Selah* (a word of uncertain meaning) here.   ᵈ 10 Or *sovereign*   ᵉ 12 Or *If
anyone does not repent, / God*

he makes ready his flaming
arrows.

¹⁴ Whoever is pregnant with evil
conceives trouble and gives
birth to disillusionment.
¹⁵ Whoever digs a hole and scoops
it out
falls into the pit they have
made.
¹⁶ The trouble they cause recoils
on them;
their violence comes down on
their own heads.

¹⁷ I will give thanks to the
LORD because of his
righteousness;
I will sing the praises of the
name of the LORD Most
High.

## Psalm 8[a]

*For the director of music. According to
gittith.[b] A psalm of David.*

¹ LORD, our Lord,
how majestic is your name in
all the earth!

You have set your glory
in the heavens.
² Through the praise of children
and infants
you have established a
stronghold against your
enemies,
to silence the foe and the
avenger.
³ When I consider your
heavens,
the work of your fingers,
the moon and the stars,
which you have set in place,

⁴ what is mankind that you are
mindful of them,
human beings that you care
for them?[c]

⁵ You have made them[d] a little
lower than the angels[e]
and crowned them[d] with glory
and honor.
⁶ You made them rulers over the
works of your hands;
you put everything under
their[f] feet:
⁷ all flocks and herds,
and the animals of the wild,
⁸ the birds in the sky,
and the fish in the sea,
all that swim the paths of the
seas.

⁹ LORD, our Lord,
how majestic is your name in
all the earth!

## Psalm 9[g,h]

*For the director of music. To the tune
of "The Death of the Son." A psalm
of David.*

¹ I will give thanks to you, LORD,
with all my heart;
I will tell of all your wonderful
deeds.
² I will be glad and rejoice in you;
I will sing the praises of your
name, O Most High.

³ My enemies turn back;
they stumble and perish
before you.
⁴ For you have upheld my right
and my cause,
sitting enthroned as the
righteous judge.

---

[a] In Hebrew texts 8:1-9 is numbered 8:2-10.   [b] Title: Probably a musical term   [c] 4 Or *what
is a human being that you are mindful of him, / a son of man that you care for him?*   [d] 5 Or *him*
[e] 5 Or *than God*   [f] 6 Or *made him ruler . . . ; / . . . his*   [g] Psalms 9 and 10 may originally have
been a single acrostic poem in which alternating lines began with the successive letters of the
Hebrew alphabet. In the Septuagint they constitute one psalm.   [h] In Hebrew texts 9:1-20 is
numbered 9:2-21.

⁵ You have rebuked the nations
and destroyed the wicked;
you have blotted out their
name for ever and ever.
⁶ Endless ruin has overtaken my
enemies,
you have uprooted their
cities;
even the memory of them has
perished.

⁷ The LORD reigns forever;
he has established his throne
for judgment.
⁸ He rules the world in
righteousness
and judges the peoples with
equity.
⁹ The LORD is a refuge for the
oppressed,
a stronghold in times of
trouble.
¹⁰ Those who know your name
trust in you,
for you, LORD, have never
forsaken those who seek
you.

¹¹ Sing the praises of the LORD,
enthroned in Zion;
proclaim among the nations
what he has done.
¹² For he who avenges blood
remembers;
he does not ignore the cries of
the afflicted.

¹³ LORD, see how my enemies
persecute me!
Have mercy and lift me up
from the gates of death,
¹⁴ that I may declare your praises
in the gates of Daughter Zion,
and there rejoice in your
salvation.

¹⁵ The nations have fallen into the
pit they have dug;
their feet are caught in the net
they have hidden.
¹⁶ The LORD is known by his acts of
justice;
the wicked are ensnared by
the work of their hands.ᵃ

¹⁷ The wicked go down to the
realm of the dead,
all the nations that forget God.
¹⁸ But God will never forget the
needy;
the hope of the afflicted will
never perish.

¹⁹ Arise, LORD, do not let mortals
triumph;
let the nations be judged in
your presence.
²⁰ Strike them with terror, LORD;
let the nations know they are
only mortal.

## Psalm 10ᵇ

¹ Why, LORD, do you stand far off?
Why do you hide yourself in
times of trouble?

² In his arrogance the wicked man
hunts down the weak,
who are caught in the schemes
he devises.
³ He boasts about the cravings of
his heart;
he blesses the greedy and
reviles the LORD.
⁴ In his pride the wicked man
does not seek him;
in all his thoughts there is no
room for God.
⁵ His ways are always prosperous;
your laws are rejected byᶜ him;
he sneers at all his enemies.

ᵃ 16  The Hebrew has *Higgaion* and *Selah* (words of uncertain meaning) here; *Selah* occurs also at the end of verse 20.    ᵇ *Psalms 9 and 10 may originally have been a single acrostic poem in which alternating lines began with the successive letters of the Hebrew alphabet. In the Septuagint they constitute one psalm.*    ᶜ 5  See Septuagint; Hebrew / *they are haughty, and your laws are far from*

6 He says to himself, "Nothing will
    ever shake me."
    He swears, "No one will ever
       do me harm."

7 His mouth is full of lies and
    threats;
    trouble and evil are under his
       tongue.

8 He lies in wait near the villages;
    from ambush he murders the
       innocent.
His eyes watch in secret for his
    victims;

9    like a lion in cover he lies in
       wait.
He lies in wait to catch the
    helpless;
    he catches the helpless and
       drags them off in his net.

10 His victims are crushed, they
    collapse;
    they fall under his strength.

11 He says to himself, "God will
    never notice;
    he covers his face and never
       sees."

12 Arise, Lord! Lift up your hand,
    O God.
    Do not forget the helpless.

13 Why does the wicked man revile
    God?
    Why does he say to himself,
       "He won't call me to account"?

14 But you, God, see the trouble of
    the afflicted;
    you consider their grief and
       take it in hand.
The victims commit themselves
    to you;
    you are the helper of the
       fatherless.

15 Break the arm of the wicked
    man;
    call the evildoer to account for
       his wickedness
    that would not otherwise be
       found out.

16 The Lord is King for ever and
    ever;
    the nations will perish from
       his land.

17 You, Lord, hear the desire of the
    afflicted;
    you encourage them, and you
       listen to their cry,

18 defending the fatherless and the
    oppressed,
    so that mere earthly mortals
       will never again strike terror.

## Psalm 11

*For the director of music. Of David.*

1 In the Lord I take refuge.
    How then can you say to me:
    "Flee like a bird to your
       mountain.

2 For look, the wicked bend their
    bows;
    they set their arrows against
       the strings
to shoot from the shadows
    at the upright in heart.

3 When the foundations are being
    destroyed,
    what can the righteous do?"

4 The Lord is in his holy temple;
    the Lord is on his heavenly
       throne.
He observes everyone on earth;
    his eyes examine them.

5 The Lord examines the
    righteous,
    but the wicked, those who love
       violence,
    he hates with a passion.

6 On the wicked he will rain
    fiery coals and burning
       sulfur;
    a scorching wind will be their
       lot.

7 For the Lord is righteous,
    he loves justice;
    the upright will see his face.

## Psalm 12[a]

*For the director of music. According to sheminith.[b] A psalm of David.*

[1] Help, LORD, for no one is faithful anymore;
  those who are loyal have vanished from the human race.
[2] Everyone lies to their neighbor;
  they flatter with their lips but harbor deception in their hearts.

[3] May the LORD silence all flattering lips
  and every boastful tongue —
[4] those who say,
  "By our tongues we will prevail;
  our own lips will defend us —
  who is lord over us?"

[5] "Because the poor are plundered and the needy groan,
  I will now arise," says the LORD.
  "I will protect them from those who malign them."
[6] And the words of the LORD are flawless,
  like silver purified in a crucible,
  like gold[c] refined seven times.

[7] You, LORD, will keep the needy safe
  and will protect us forever from the wicked,
[8] who freely strut about
  when what is vile is honored by the human race.

## Psalm 13[d]

*For the director of music. A psalm of David.*

[1] How long, LORD? Will you forget me forever?
  How long will you hide your face from me?
[2] How long must I wrestle with my thoughts
  and day after day have sorrow in my heart?
  How long will my enemy triumph over me?

[3] Look on me and answer, LORD my God.
  Give light to my eyes, or I will sleep in death,
[4] and my enemy will say, "I have overcome him,"
  and my foes will rejoice when I fall.

[5] But I trust in your unfailing love;
  my heart rejoices in your salvation.
[6] I will sing the LORD's praise,
  for he has been good to me.

## Psalm 14

*For the director of music. Of David.*

[1] The fool[e] says in his heart,
  "There is no God."
They are corrupt, their deeds are vile;
  there is no one who does good.

[2] The LORD looks down from heaven
  on all mankind
to see if there are any who understand,
  any who seek God.
[3] All have turned away, all have become corrupt;
  there is no one who does good,
  not even one.

[4] Do all these evildoers know nothing?

---

[a] In Hebrew texts 12:1-8 is numbered 12:2-9.   [b] Title: Probably a musical term   [c] 6 Probable reading of the original Hebrew text; Masoretic Text *earth*   [d] In Hebrew texts 13:1-6 is numbered 13:2-6.   [e] 1 The Hebrew words rendered *fool* in Psalms denote one who is morally deficient.

They devour my people as
though eating bread;
   they never call on the LORD.
5 But there they are, overwhelmed
with dread,
   for God is present in the
company of the righteous.
6 You evildoers frustrate the plans
of the poor,
   but the LORD is their refuge.

7 Oh, that salvation for Israel
would come out of Zion!
   When the LORD restores his
people,
   let Jacob rejoice and Israel be
glad!

## Psalm 15

*A psalm of David.*

1 LORD, who may dwell in your
sacred tent?
   Who may live on your holy
mountain?

2 The one whose walk is blameless,
who does what is righteous,
   who speaks the truth from
their heart;
3 whose tongue utters no slander,
who does no wrong to a
neighbor,
   and casts no slur on others;
4 who despises a vile person
but honors those who fear the
LORD;
   who keeps an oath even when it
hurts,
   and does not change their
mind;
5 who lends money to the poor
without interest;
   who does not accept a bribe
against the innocent.

Whoever does these things
will never be shaken.

## Psalm 16

*A miktam*[a] *of David.*

1 Keep me safe, my God,
   for in you I take refuge.

2 I say to the LORD, "You are my
Lord;
   apart from you I have no good
thing."
3 I say of the holy people who are
in the land,
   "They are the noble ones in
whom is all my delight."
4 Those who run after other gods
will suffer more and
more.
   I will not pour out libations of
blood to such gods
   or take up their names on my
lips.

5 LORD, you alone are my portion
and my cup;
   you make my lot secure.
6 The boundary lines have fallen
for me in pleasant places;
   surely I have a delightful
inheritance.
7 I will praise the LORD, who
counsels me;
   even at night my heart
instructs me.
8 I keep my eyes always on the
LORD.
   With him at my right hand, I
will not be shaken.

9 Therefore my heart is glad and
my tongue rejoices;
   my body also will rest secure,
10 because you will not abandon
me to the realm of the
dead,
   nor will you let your faithful[b]
one see decay.
11 You make known to me the path
of life;

---

*a* Title: Probably a literary or musical term    *b* 10 Or *holy*

you will fill me with joy in your
presence,
with eternal pleasures at your
right hand.

## Psalm 17

*A prayer of David.*

1 Hear me, LORD, my plea is just;
listen to my cry.
Hear my prayer—
it does not rise from deceitful
lips.
2 Let my vindication come from
you;
may your eyes see what is right.

3 Though you probe my heart,
though you examine me at
night and test me,
you will find that I have planned
no evil;
my mouth has not transgressed.
4 Though people tried to bribe me,
I have kept myself from the
ways of the violent
through what your lips have
commanded.
5 My steps have held to your paths;
my feet have not stumbled.

6 I call on you, my God, for you
will answer me;
turn your ear to me and hear
my prayer.
7 Show me the wonders of your
great love,
you who save by your right
hand
those who take refuge in you
from their foes.

8 Keep me as the apple of your eye;
hide me in the shadow of your
wings
9 from the wicked who are out to
destroy me,
from my mortal enemies who
surround me.

10 They close up their callous
hearts,
and their mouths speak with
arrogance.
11 They have tracked me down,
they now surround me,
with eyes alert, to throw me to
the ground.
12 They are like a lion hungry for
prey,
like a fierce lion crouching in
cover.

13 Rise up, LORD, confront them,
bring them down;
with your sword rescue me
from the wicked.
14 By your hand save me from such
people, LORD,
from those of this world whose
reward is in this life.
May what you have stored up for
the wicked fill their bellies;
may their children gorge
themselves on it,
and may there be leftovers for
their little ones.

15 As for me, I will be vindicated
and will see your face;
when I awake, I will be
satisfied with seeing your
likeness.

## Psalm 18[a]

*For the director of music. Of David the
servant of the LORD. He sang to the LORD
the words of this song when the LORD
delivered him from the hand of all his
enemies and from the hand of Saul.
He said:*

1 I love you, LORD, my strength.

2 The LORD is my rock, my fortress
and my deliverer;
my God is my rock, in whom I
take refuge,

a In Hebrew texts 18:1-50 is numbered 18:2-51.

my shield[a] and the horn[b] of my
   salvation, my stronghold.

3 I called to the LORD, who is
   worthy of praise,
and I have been saved from my
   enemies.
4 The cords of death entangled
   me;
   the torrents of destruction
      overwhelmed me.
5 The cords of the grave coiled
   around me;
   the snares of death confronted
      me.

6 In my distress I called to the
   LORD;
   I cried to my God for help.
From his temple he heard my
   voice;
   my cry came before him, into
      his ears.
7 The earth trembled and quaked,
   and the foundations of the
      mountains shook;
   they trembled because he was
      angry.
8 Smoke rose from his nostrils;
   consuming fire came from his
      mouth,
   burning coals blazed out of it.
9 He parted the heavens and came
   down;
   dark clouds were under his
      feet.
10 He mounted the cherubim and
   flew;
   he soared on the wings of the
      wind.
11 He made darkness his covering,
   his canopy around him —
   the dark rain clouds of the sky.
12 Out of the brightness of
   his presence clouds
      advanced,

with hailstones and bolts of
   lightning.
13 The LORD thundered from
   heaven;
   the voice of the Most High
      resounded.[c]
14 He shot his arrows and scattered
   the enemy,
   with great bolts of lightning he
      routed them.
15 The valleys of the sea were
   exposed
   and the foundations of the
      earth laid bare
at your rebuke, LORD,
   at the blast of breath from your
      nostrils.

16 He reached down from on high
   and took hold of me;
   he drew me out of deep waters.
17 He rescued me from my
   powerful enemy,
   from my foes, who were too
      strong for me.
18 They confronted me in the day of
   my disaster,
   but the LORD was my support.
19 He brought me out into a
   spacious place;
   he rescued me because he
      delighted in me.

20 The LORD has dealt with
   me according to my
      righteousness;
   according to the cleanness of
      my hands he has rewarded
      me.
21 For I have kept the ways of the
   LORD;
   I am not guilty of turning from
      my God.
22 All his laws are before me;
   I have not turned away from
      his decrees.

---

[a] 2 Or *sovereign*    [b] 2 *Horn* here symbolizes strength.    [c] 13 Some Hebrew manuscripts and
Septuagint (see also 2 Samuel 22:14); most Hebrew manuscripts *resounded, / amid hailstones
and bolts of lightning*

23 I have been blameless before
   him
   and have kept myself from
      sin.
24 The LORD has rewarded
   me according to my
      righteousness,
   according to the cleanness of
      my hands in his sight.

25 To the faithful you show yourself
      faithful,
   to the blameless you show
      yourself blameless,
26 to the pure you show yourself
      pure,
   but to the devious you show
      yourself shrewd.
27 You save the humble
   but bring low those whose
      eyes are haughty.
28 You, LORD, keep my lamp
      burning;
   my God turns my darkness
      into light.
29 With your help I can advance
      against a troop*a*;
   with my God I can scale a wall.

30 As for God, his way is perfect:
   The LORD's word is flawless;
   he shields all who take refuge
      in him.
31 For who is God besides the
      LORD?
   And who is the Rock except
      our God?
32 It is God who arms me with
      strength
   and keeps my way secure.
33 He makes my feet like the feet of
      a deer;
   he causes me to stand on the
      heights.
34 He trains my hands for battle;
   my arms can bend a bow of
      bronze.

35 You make your saving help my
      shield,
   and your right hand sustains
      me;
   your help has made me great.
36 You provide a broad path for my
      feet,
   so that my ankles do not give
      way.

37 I pursued my enemies and
      overtook them;
   I did not turn back till they
      were destroyed.
38 I crushed them so that they
      could not rise;
   they fell beneath my feet.
39 You armed me with strength for
      battle;
   you humbled my adversaries
      before me.
40 You made my enemies turn their
      backs in flight,
   and I destroyed my foes.
41 They cried for help, but there
      was no one to save them —
   to the LORD, but he did not
      answer.
42 I beat them as fine as windblown
      dust;
   I trampled them*b* like mud in
      the streets.

43 You have delivered me from the
      attacks of the people;
   you have made me the head of
      nations.
   People I did not know now serve
      me,
44 foreigners cower before me;
   as soon as they hear of me,
      they obey me.
45 They all lose heart;
   they come trembling from
      their strongholds.
46 The LORD lives! Praise be to my
      Rock!

*a 29* Or *can run through a barricade*    *b 42* Many Hebrew manuscripts, Septuagint, Syriac and
Targum (see also 2 Samuel 22:43); Masoretic Text *I poured them out*

Exalted be God my Savior!
⁴⁷ He is the God who avenges me,
   who subdues nations under
      me,
⁴⁸   who saves me from my
         enemies.
   You exalted me above my foes;
      from a violent man you
         rescued me.
⁴⁹ Therefore I will praise you,
      LORD, among the nations;
   I will sing the praises of your
      name.

⁵⁰ He gives his king great victories;
      he shows unfailing love to his
         anointed,
   to David and to his
      descendants forever.

## Psalm 19ᵃ

*For the director of music. A psalm
of David.*

¹ The heavens declare the glory of
      God;
   the skies proclaim the work of
      his hands.
² Day after day they pour forth
      speech;
   night after night they reveal
      knowledge.
³ They have no speech, they use
      no words;
   no sound is heard from them.
⁴ Yet their voiceᵇ goes out into all
      the earth,
   their words to the ends of the
      world.
   In the heavens God has pitched
      a tent for the sun.
⁵   It is like a bridegroom coming
         out of his chamber,
   like a champion rejoicing to
      run his course.
⁶ It rises at one end of the heavens

and makes its circuit to the
   other;
nothing is deprived of its
   warmth.

⁷ The law of the LORD is perfect,
   refreshing the soul.
The statutes of the LORD are
   trustworthy,
   making wise the simple.
⁸ The precepts of the LORD are
      right,
   giving joy to the heart.
The commands of the LORD are
   radiant,
   giving light to the eyes.
⁹ The fear of the LORD is pure,
   enduring forever.
The decrees of the LORD are
   firm,
   and all of them are righteous.

¹⁰ They are more precious than
      gold,
   than much pure gold;
they are sweeter than honey,
   than honey from the
      honeycomb.
¹¹ By them your servant is warned;
   in keeping them there is great
      reward.
¹² But who can discern their own
      errors?
   Forgive my hidden faults.
¹³ Keep your servant also from
      willful sins;
   may they not rule over me.
Then I will be blameless,
   innocent of great
      transgression.

¹⁴ May these words of my mouth
      and this meditation of my
         heart
   be pleasing in your sight,
   LORD, my Rock and my
      Redeemer.

ᵃ In Hebrew texts 19:1-14 is numbered 19:2-15.   ᵇ 4 Septuagint, Jerome and Syriac; Hebrew
*measuring line*

## Psalm 20[a]

*For the director of music. A psalm of David.*

[1] May the LORD answer you when
    you are in distress;
  may the name of the God of
    Jacob protect you.
[2] May he send you help from the
    sanctuary
  and grant you support from
    Zion.
[3] May he remember all your
    sacrifices
  and accept your burnt
    offerings.[b]
[4] May he give you the desire of
    your heart
  and make all your plans
    succeed.
[5] May we shout for joy over your
    victory
  and lift up our banners in the
    name of our God.

May the LORD grant all your
    requests.

[6] Now this I know:
  The LORD gives victory to his
    anointed.
He answers him from his
    heavenly sanctuary
  with the victorious power of
    his right hand.
[7] Some trust in chariots and some
    in horses,
  but we trust in the name of the
    LORD our God.
[8] They are brought to their knees
    and fall,
  but we rise up and stand
    firm.
[9] LORD, give victory to the king!
  Answer us when we call!

## Psalm 21[c]

*For the director of music. A psalm of David.*

[1] The king rejoices in your
    strength, LORD.
How great is his joy in the
    victories you give!

[2] You have granted him his heart's
    desire
  and have not withheld the
    request of his lips.[b]
[3] You came to greet him with rich
    blessings
  and placed a crown of pure
    gold on his head.
[4] He asked you for life, and you
    gave it to him—
  length of days, for ever and
    ever.
[5] Through the victories you gave,
    his glory is great;
  you have bestowed on him
    splendor and majesty.
[6] Surely you have granted him
    unending blessings
  and made him glad with the
    joy of your presence.
[7] For the king trusts in the LORD;
  through the unfailing love of
    the Most High
  he will not be shaken.

[8] Your hand will lay hold on all
    your enemies;
  your right hand will seize your
    foes.
[9] When you appear for battle,
  you will burn them up as in a
    blazing furnace.
The LORD will swallow them up
    in his wrath,
  and his fire will consume
    them.

---

[a] In Hebrew texts 20:1-9 is numbered 20:2-10.
uncertain meaning) here.   [c] In Hebrew texts 21:1-13 is numbered 21:2-14.
  [b] 3,2 The Hebrew has *Selah* (a word of

¹⁰ You will destroy their
    descendants from the
    earth,
   their posterity from mankind.
¹¹ Though they plot evil against
    you
   and devise wicked schemes,
    they cannot succeed.
¹² You will make them turn their
    backs
   when you aim at them with
    drawn bow.

¹³ Be exalted in your strength, LORD;
   we will sing and praise your
    might.

## Psalm 22[a]

*For the director of music. To the tune
of "The Doe of the Morning." A psalm
of David.*

¹ My God, my God, why have you
    forsaken me?
   Why are you so far from saving
    me,
   so far from my cries of anguish?
² My God, I cry out by day, but you
    do not answer,
   by night, but I find no rest.[b]

³ Yet you are enthroned as the
    Holy One;
   you are the one Israel praises.[c]
⁴ In you our ancestors put their
    trust;
   they trusted and you delivered
    them.
⁵ To you they cried out and were
    saved;
   in you they trusted and were
    not put to shame.

⁶ But I am a worm and not a man,
   scorned by everyone, despised
    by the people.

⁷ All who see me mock me;
   they hurl insults, shaking their
    heads.
⁸ "He trusts in the LORD," they say,
    "let the LORD rescue him.
   Let him deliver him,
    since he delights in him."

⁹ Yet you brought me out of the
    womb;
   you made me trust in you,
    even at my mother's
    breast.
¹⁰ From birth I was cast on you;
   from my mother's womb you
    have been my God.

¹¹ Do not be far from me,
   for trouble is near
   and there is no one to help.

¹² Many bulls surround me;
   strong bulls of Bashan encircle
    me.
¹³ Roaring lions that tear their prey
   open their mouths wide
    against me.
¹⁴ I am poured out like water,
   and all my bones are out of
    joint.
   My heart has turned to wax;
   it has melted within me.
¹⁵ My mouth[d] is dried up like a
    potsherd,
   and my tongue sticks to the
    roof of my mouth;
   you lay me in the dust of
    death.

¹⁶ Dogs surround me,
   a pack of villains encircles me;
   they pierce[e] my hands and my
    feet.
¹⁷ All my bones are on display;
   people stare and gloat over
    me.

---

[a] In Hebrew texts 22:1-31 is numbered 22:2-32.   [b] 2 Or *night, and am not silent*   [c] 3 Or *Yet*
*you are holy, / enthroned on the praises of Israel*   
text; Masoretic Text *strength*   [e] 16 Dead Sea Scrolls and some manuscripts of the Masoretic   [d] 15 Probable reading of the original Hebrew
Text, Septuagint and Syriac; most manuscripts of the Masoretic Text *me, / like a lion*

18 They divide my clothes among
    them
  and cast lots for my garment.

19 But you, LORD, do not be far from
    me.
  You are my strength; come
    quickly to help me.
20 Deliver me from the sword,
  my precious life from the
    power of the dogs.
21 Rescue me from the mouth of
    the lions;
  save me from the horns of the
    wild oxen.

22 I will declare your name to my
    people;
  in the assembly I will praise
    you.
23 You who fear the LORD, praise
    him!
  All you descendants of Jacob,
    honor him!
  Revere him, all you
    descendants of Israel!
24 For he has not despised or
    scorned
  the suffering of the afflicted
    one;
  he has not hidden his face from
    him
  but has listened to his cry for
    help.

25 From you comes the theme of
    my praise in the great
    assembly;
  before those who fear you[a] I
    will fulfill my vows.
26 The poor will eat and be
    satisfied;
  those who seek the LORD will
    praise him —
  may your hearts live forever!

27 All the ends of the earth
  will remember and turn to the
    LORD,

and all the families of the
    nations
  will bow down before him,
28 for dominion belongs to the
    LORD
  and he rules over the nations.

29 All the rich of the earth will feast
    and worship;
  all who go down to the dust
    will kneel before him —
  those who cannot keep
    themselves alive.
30 Posterity will serve him;
  future generations will be told
    about the Lord.
31 They will proclaim his
    righteousness,
  declaring to a people yet
    unborn:
  He has done it!

## Psalm 23

*A psalm of David.*

1 The LORD is my shepherd, I lack
    nothing.
2  He makes me lie down in
    green pastures,
  he leads me beside quiet waters,
3  he refreshes my soul.
  He guides me along the right
    paths
  for his name's sake.
4 Even though I walk
    through the darkest valley,[b]
  I will fear no evil,
  for you are with me;
  your rod and your staff,
    they comfort me.

5 You prepare a table before me
  in the presence of my enemies.
  You anoint my head with oil;
  my cup overflows.
6 Surely your goodness and love
    will follow me
  all the days of my life,

---

*a 25* Hebrew *him*     *b 4* Or *the valley of the shadow of death*

and I will dwell in the house of
    the LORD
    forever.

## Psalm 24

*Of David. A psalm.*

[1] The earth is the LORD's, and
    everything in it,
    the world, and all who live in
        it;
[2] for he founded it on the seas
    and established it on the
        waters.

[3] Who may ascend the mountain
    of the LORD?
    Who may stand in his holy
        place?
[4] The one who has clean hands
    and a pure heart,
    who does not trust in an idol
    or swear by a false god.[a]
[5] They will receive blessing from
    the LORD
    and vindication from God
        their Savior.
[6] Such is the generation of those
    who seek him,
    who seek your face, God of
        Jacob.[b,c]

[7] Lift up your heads, you gates;
    be lifted up, you ancient doors,
    that the King of glory may
        come in.
[8] Who is this King of glory?
    The LORD strong and mighty,
    the LORD mighty in battle.
[9] Lift up your heads, you gates;
    lift them up, you ancient
        doors,
    that the King of glory may
        come in.
[10] Who is he, this King of glory?

The LORD Almighty—
    he is the King of glory.

## Psalm 25[d]

*Of David.*

[1] In you, LORD my God,
    I put my trust.

[2] I trust in you;
    do not let me be put to shame,
    nor let my enemies triumph
        over me.
[3] No one who hopes in you
    will ever be put to shame,
    but shame will come on those
    who are treacherous without
        cause.

[4] Show me your ways, LORD,
    teach me your paths.
[5] Guide me in your truth and
        teach me,
    for you are God my Savior,
    and my hope is in you all day
        long.
[6] Remember, LORD, your great
        mercy and love,
    for they are from of old.
[7] Do not remember the sins of my
        youth
    and my rebellious ways;
    according to your love
        remember me,
    for you, LORD, are good.

[8] Good and upright is the LORD;
    therefore he instructs sinners
        in his ways.
[9] He guides the humble in what is
        right
    and teaches them his way.
[10] All the ways of the LORD are
        loving and faithful
    toward those who keep the
        demands of his covenant.

---

[a] 4 Or *swear falsely*    [b] 6 Two Hebrew manuscripts and Syriac (see also Septuagint); most
Hebrew manuscripts *face, Jacob*    [c] 6 The Hebrew has *Selah* (a word of uncertain meaning)
here and at the end of verse 10.    [d] This psalm is an acrostic poem, the verses of which begin
with the successive letters of the Hebrew alphabet.

11 For the sake of your name, Lord,
        forgive my iniquity, though it
        is great.

12 Who, then, are those who fear
        the Lord?
    He will instruct them in the
        ways they should choose.*a*

13 They will spend their days in
        prosperity,
    and their descendants will
        inherit the land.

14 The Lord confides in those who
        fear him;
    he makes his covenant known
        to them.

15 My eyes are ever on the Lord,
    for only he will release my feet
        from the snare.

16 Turn to me and be gracious to me,
    for I am lonely and afflicted.

17 Relieve the troubles of my heart
    and free me from my anguish.

18 Look on my affliction and my
        distress
    and take away all my sins.

19 See how numerous are my
        enemies
    and how fiercely they hate me!

20 Guard my life and rescue me;
    do not let me be put to shame,
    for I take refuge in you.

21 May integrity and uprightness
        protect me,
    because my hope, Lord,*b* is in
        you.

22 Deliver Israel, O God,
    from all their troubles!

## Psalm 26

*Of David.*

1 Vindicate me, Lord,
    for I have led a blameless life;
  I have trusted in the Lord
    and have not faltered.

2 Test me, Lord, and try me,
    examine my heart and my mind;

3 for I have always been mindful
        of your unfailing love
    and have lived in reliance on
        your faithfulness.

4 I do not sit with the deceitful,
    nor do I associate with
        hypocrites.

5 I abhor the assembly of evildoers
    and refuse to sit with the
        wicked.

6 I wash my hands in innocence,
    and go about your altar, Lord,

7 proclaiming aloud your praise
    and telling of all your
        wonderful deeds.

8 Lord, I love the house where you
        live,
    the place where your glory
        dwells.

9 Do not take away my soul along
        with sinners,
    my life with those who are
        bloodthirsty,

10 in whose hands are wicked
        schemes,
    whose right hands are full of
        bribes.

11 I lead a blameless life;
    deliver me and be merciful to
        me.

12 My feet stand on level ground;
    in the great congregation I will
        praise the Lord.

## Psalm 27

*Of David.*

1 The Lord is my light and my
        salvation—
    whom shall I fear?
  The Lord is the stronghold of
        my life—
    of whom shall I be afraid?

---

*a 12* Or *ways he chooses*     *b 21* Septuagint; Hebrew does not have Lord.

² When the wicked advance
    against me
    to devour[a] me,
it is my enemies and my foes
    who will stumble and fall.
³ Though an army besiege me,
    my heart will not fear;
though war break out against
    me,
    even then I will be confident.

⁴ One thing I ask from the LORD,
    this only do I seek:
that I may dwell in the house of
    the LORD
    all the days of my life,
to gaze on the beauty of the LORD
    and to seek him in his temple.
⁵ For in the day of trouble
    he will keep me safe in his
    dwelling;
he will hide me in the shelter of
    his sacred tent
    and set me high upon a rock.

⁶ Then my head will be exalted
    above the enemies who
    surround me;
at his sacred tent I will sacrifice
    with shouts of joy;
I will sing and make music to
    the LORD.

⁷ Hear my voice when I call, LORD;
    be merciful to me and answer
    me.
⁸ My heart says of you, "Seek his
    face!"
    Your face, LORD, I will seek.
⁹ Do not hide your face from me,
    do not turn your servant away
    in anger;
    you have been my helper.
Do not reject me or forsake me,
    God my Savior.
¹⁰ Though my father and mother
    forsake me,
    the LORD will receive me.

¹¹ Teach me your way, LORD;
    lead me in a straight path
    because of my oppressors.
¹² Do not turn me over to the desire
    of my foes,
for false witnesses rise up
    against me,
    spouting malicious
    accusations.

¹³ I remain confident of this:
    I will see the goodness of the
    LORD
    in the land of the living.
¹⁴ Wait for the LORD;
    be strong and take heart
    and wait for the LORD.

### Psalm 28

*Of David.*

¹ To you, LORD, I call;
    you are my Rock,
    do not turn a deaf ear to me.
For if you remain silent,
    I will be like those who go
    down to the pit.
² Hear my cry for mercy
    as I call to you for help,
as I lift up my hands
    toward your Most Holy Place.

³ Do not drag me away with the
    wicked,
    with those who do evil,
who speak cordially with their
    neighbors
    but harbor malice in their
    hearts.
⁴ Repay them for their deeds
    and for their evil work;
repay them for what their hands
    have done
    and bring back on them what
    they deserve.
⁵ Because they have no regard for
    the deeds of the LORD

---

[a] 2 Or *slander*

and what his hands have done,
he will tear them down
   and never build them up
   again.

6 Praise be to the LORD,
   for he has heard my cry for
    mercy.
7 The LORD is my strength and my
   shield;
   my heart trusts in him, and he
    helps me.
My heart leaps for joy,
   and with my song I praise him.

8 The LORD is the strength of his
   people,
   a fortress of salvation for his
    anointed one.
9 Save your people and bless your
   inheritance;
   be their shepherd and carry
    them forever.

## Psalm 29

*A psalm of David.*

1 Ascribe to the LORD, you
   heavenly beings,
   ascribe to the LORD glory and
    strength.
2 Ascribe to the LORD the glory
   due his name;
   worship the LORD in the
    splendor of his*a* holiness.

3 The voice of the LORD is over the
   waters;
   the God of glory thunders,
   the LORD thunders over the
    mighty waters.
4 The voice of the LORD is
   powerful;
   the voice of the LORD is
    majestic.
5 The voice of the LORD breaks the
   cedars;

the LORD breaks in pieces the
   cedars of Lebanon.
6 He makes Lebanon leap like a
   calf,
   Sirion*b* like a young wild ox.
7 The voice of the LORD strikes
   with flashes of lightning.
8 The voice of the LORD shakes the
   desert;
   the LORD shakes the Desert of
    Kadesh.
9 The voice of the LORD twists the
   oaks*c*
   and strips the forests bare.
And in his temple all cry,
   "Glory!"

10 The LORD sits enthroned over
   the flood;
   the LORD is enthroned as King
    forever.
11 The LORD gives strength to his
   people;
   the LORD blesses his people
    with peace.

## Psalm 30*d*

*A psalm. A song. For the dedication of
the temple.e Of David.*

1 I will exalt you, LORD,
   for you lifted me out of the
    depths
   and did not let my enemies
    gloat over me.
2 LORD my God, I called to you for
   help,
   and you healed me.
3 You, LORD, brought me up from
   the realm of the dead;
   you spared me from going
    down to the pit.

4 Sing the praises of the LORD, you
   his faithful people;
   praise his holy name.

---

*a* 2 Or *LORD with the splendor of*    *b* 6 That is, Mount Hermon    *c* 9 Or *LORD makes the deer give birth*    *d* In Hebrew texts 30:1-12 is numbered 30:2-13.    *e* Title: Or *palace*

⁵ For his anger lasts only a
  moment,
    but his favor lasts a lifetime;
weeping may stay for the night,
    but rejoicing comes in the
  morning.

⁶ When I felt secure, I said,
    "I will never be shaken."
⁷ Lord, when you favored me,
    you made my royal mountain*a*
  stand firm;
but when you hid your face,
    I was dismayed.

⁸ To you, Lord, I called;
    to the Lord I cried for mercy:
⁹ "What is gained if I am silenced,
    if I go down to the pit?
Will the dust praise you?
    Will it proclaim your
  faithfulness?
¹⁰ Hear, Lord, and be merciful to
  me;
    Lord, be my help."

¹¹ You turned my wailing into
  dancing;
    you removed my sackcloth and
  clothed me with joy,
¹² that my heart may sing your
  praises and not be silent.
    Lord my God, I will praise you
  forever.

### Psalm 31*b*

*For the director of music. A psalm
of David.*

¹ In you, Lord, I have taken
  refuge;
    let me never be put to shame;
    deliver me in your
  righteousness.
² Turn your ear to me,
    come quickly to my rescue;
be my rock of refuge,
    a strong fortress to save me.

³ Since you are my rock and my
  fortress,
    for the sake of your name lead
  and guide me.
⁴ Keep me free from the trap that
  is set for me,
    for you are my refuge.
⁵ Into your hands I commit my
  spirit;
    deliver me, Lord, my faithful
  God.

⁶ I hate those who cling to
  worthless idols;
    as for me, I trust in the Lord.
⁷ I will be glad and rejoice in your
  love,
    for you saw my affliction
    and knew the anguish of my
  soul.
⁸ You have not given me into the
  hands of the enemy
    but have set my feet in a
  spacious place.

⁹ Be merciful to me, Lord, for I am
  in distress;
    my eyes grow weak with
  sorrow,
    my soul and body with grief.
¹⁰ My life is consumed by anguish
    and my years by groaning;
my strength fails because of my
  affliction,*c*
    and my bones grow weak.
¹¹ Because of all my enemies,
    I am the utter contempt of my
  neighbors
and an object of dread to my
  closest friends —
    those who see me on the street
  flee from me.
¹² I am forgotten as though I were
  dead;
    I have become like broken
  pottery.
¹³ For I hear many whispering,
    "Terror on every side!"

---

*a* 7 That is, Mount Zion    *b* In Hebrew texts 31:1-24 is numbered 31:2-25.    *c* 10 Or *guilt*

They conspire against me
　　and plot to take my life.

14 But I trust in you, LORD;
　　I say, "You are my God."
15 My times are in your hands;
　　deliver me from the hands of
　　　my enemies,
　　from those who pursue me.
16 Let your face shine on your
　　servant;
　　save me in your unfailing love.
17 Let me not be put to shame,
　　LORD,
　　for I have cried out to you;
　　but let the wicked be put to
　　　shame
　　and be silent in the realm of
　　　the dead.
18 Let their lying lips be silenced,
　　for with pride and contempt
　　they speak arrogantly against
　　　the righteous.

19 How abundant are the good
　　things
　　that you have stored up for
　　　those who fear you,
　　that you bestow in the sight of all,
　　on those who take refuge in
　　　you.
20 In the shelter of your presence
　　you hide them
　　from all human intrigues;
　　you keep them safe in your
　　　dwelling
　　from accusing tongues.
21 Praise be to the LORD,
　　for he showed me the wonders
　　　of his love
　　when I was in a city under
　　　siege.
22 In my alarm I said,
　　"I am cut off from your sight!"
　　Yet you heard my cry for mercy
　　when I called to you for help.

23 Love the LORD, all his faithful
　　people!
　　The LORD preserves those who
　　　are true to him,
　　but the proud he pays back in
　　　full.
24 Be strong and take heart,
　　all you who hope in the LORD.

## Psalm 32

*Of David. A maskil.*[a]

1 Blessed is the one
　　whose transgressions are
　　　forgiven,
　　whose sins are covered.
2 Blessed is the one
　　whose sin the LORD does not
　　　count against them
　　and in whose spirit is no
　　　deceit.

3 When I kept silent,
　　my bones wasted away
　　through my groaning all day
　　　long.
4 For day and night
　　your hand was heavy on me;
　　my strength was sapped
　　　as in the heat of summer.[b]

5 Then I acknowledged my sin to
　　you
　　and did not cover up my
　　　iniquity.
　　I said, "I will confess
　　my transgressions to the
　　　LORD."
　　And you forgave
　　the guilt of my sin.

6 Therefore let all the faithful pray
　　to you
　　while you may be found;
　　surely the rising of the mighty
　　　waters
　　will not reach them.

---

*a* Title: Probably a literary or musical term meaning) here and at the end of verses 5 and 7.　*b 4* The Hebrew has *Selah* (a word of uncertain meaning) here and at the end of verses 5 and 7.

⁷You are my hiding place;
  you will protect me from
    trouble
  and surround me with songs of
    deliverance.

⁸I will instruct you and teach you
    in the way you should go;
  I will counsel you with my
    loving eye on you.
⁹Do not be like the horse or the
    mule,
  which have no understanding
  but must be controlled by bit and
    bridle
  or they will not come to you.
¹⁰Many are the woes of the wicked,
  but the LORD's unfailing love
    surrounds the one who trusts
    in him.

¹¹Rejoice in the LORD and be glad,
    you righteous;
  sing, all you who are upright in
    heart!

## Psalm 33

¹Sing joyfully to the LORD, you
    righteous;
  it is fitting for the upright to
    praise him.
²Praise the LORD with the harp;
  make music to him on the ten-
    stringed lyre.
³Sing to him a new song;
  play skillfully, and shout for
    joy.

⁴For the word of the LORD is right
    and true;
  he is faithful in all he does.
⁵The LORD loves righteousness
    and justice;
  the earth is full of his unfailing
    love.
⁶By the word of the LORD the
  heavens were made,

their starry host by the breath
  of his mouth.
⁷He gathers the waters of the sea
    into jarsᵃ;
  he puts the deep into
    storehouses.
⁸Let all the earth fear the LORD;
  let all the people of the world
    revere him.
⁹For he spoke, and it came to be;
  he commanded, and it stood
    firm.

¹⁰The LORD foils the plans of the
    nations;
  he thwarts the purposes of the
    peoples.
¹¹But the plans of the LORD stand
    firm forever,
  the purposes of his heart
    through all generations.

¹²Blessed is the nation whose God
    is the LORD,
  the people he chose for his
    inheritance.
¹³From heaven the LORD looks
    down
  and sees all mankind;
¹⁴from his dwelling place he
    watches
  all who live on earth—
¹⁵he who forms the hearts of all,
  who considers everything they
    do.

¹⁶No king is saved by the size of his
    army;
  no warrior escapes by his great
    strength.
¹⁷A horse is a vain hope for
    deliverance;
  despite all its great strength it
    cannot save.
¹⁸But the eyes of the LORD are on
    those who fear him,
  on those whose hope is in his
    unfailing love,

---

ᵃ 7 Or *sea as into a heap*

19 to deliver them from death
    and keep them alive in famine.

20 We wait in hope for the LORD;
    he is our help and our shield.
21 In him our hearts rejoice,
    for we trust in his holy name.
22 May your unfailing love be with
        us, LORD,
    even as we put our hope in
        you.

## Psalm 34 *a,b*

*Of David. When he pretended to be
insane before Abimelek, who drove him
away, and he left.*

1 I will extol the LORD at all times;
    his praise will always be on my
        lips.
2 I will glory in the LORD;
    let the afflicted hear and
        rejoice.
3 Glorify the LORD with me;
    let us exalt his name together.

4 I sought the LORD, and he
        answered me;
    he delivered me from all my
        fears.
5 Those who look to him are
        radiant;
    their faces are never covered
        with shame.
6 This poor man called, and the
        LORD heard him;
    he saved him out of all his
        troubles.
7 The angel of the LORD encamps
    around those who fear
        him,
    and he delivers them.

8 Taste and see that the LORD is
        good;
    blessed is the one who takes
        refuge in him.

9 Fear the LORD, you his holy
        people,
    for those who fear him lack
        nothing.
10 The lions may grow weak and
        hungry,
    but those who seek the LORD
        lack no good thing.
11 Come, my children, listen to me;
    I will teach you the fear of the
        LORD.
12 Whoever of you loves life
    and desires to see many good
        days,
13 keep your tongue from evil
    and your lips from telling
        lies.
14 Turn from evil and do good;
    seek peace and pursue it.

15 The eyes of the LORD are on the
        righteous,
    and his ears are attentive to
        their cry;
16 but the face of the LORD is
    against those who do evil,
    to blot out their name from the
        earth.

17 The righteous cry out, and the
        LORD hears them;
    he delivers them from all their
        troubles.
18 The LORD is close to the
        brokenhearted
    and saves those who are
        crushed in spirit.

19 The righteous person may have
        many troubles,
    but the LORD delivers him
        from them all;
20 he protects all his bones,
    not one of them will be broken.

21 Evil will slay the wicked;
    the foes of the righteous will
        be condemned.

---

*a* This psalm is an acrostic poem, the verses of which begin with the successive letters of the
Hebrew alphabet.    *b* In Hebrew texts 34:1-22 is numbered 34:2-23.

²² The LORD will rescue his
    servants;
  no one who takes refuge in
    him will be condemned.

## Psalm 35

*Of David.*

¹ Contend, LORD, with those who
    contend with me;
  fight against those who fight
    against me.
² Take up shield and armor;
  arise and come to my aid.
³ Brandish spear and javelin[a]
    against those who pursue me.
  Say to me,
    "I am your salvation."

⁴ May those who seek my life
    be disgraced and put to
    shame;
  may those who plot my ruin
    be turned back in dismay.
⁵ May they be like chaff before the
    wind,
  with the angel of the LORD
    driving them away;
⁶ may their path be dark and
    slippery,
  with the angel of the LORD
    pursuing them.

⁷ Since they hid their net for me
    without cause
  and without cause dug a pit for
    me,
⁸ may ruin overtake them by
    surprise—
  may the net they hid entangle
    them,
  may they fall into the pit, to
    their ruin.
⁹ Then my soul will rejoice in the
    LORD
  and delight in his salvation.
¹⁰ My whole being will exclaim,

  "Who is like you, LORD?
  You rescue the poor from those
    too strong for them,
  the poor and needy from those
    who rob them."

¹¹ Ruthless witnesses come
    forward;
  they question me on things I
    know nothing about.
¹² They repay me evil for good
  and leave me like one
    bereaved.
¹³ Yet when they were ill, I put on
    sackcloth
  and humbled myself with
    fasting.
  When my prayers returned to me
    unanswered,
¹⁴   I went about mourning
  as though for my friend or
    brother.
  I bowed my head in grief
  as though weeping for my
    mother.
¹⁵ But when I stumbled, they
    gathered in glee;
  assailants gathered against me
  without my knowledge.
  They slandered me without
    ceasing.
¹⁶ Like the ungodly they
    maliciously mocked;[b]
  they gnashed their teeth at me.

¹⁷ How long, Lord, will you look
    on?
  Rescue me from their ravages,
  my precious life from these
    lions.
¹⁸ I will give you thanks in the
    great assembly;
  among the throngs I will
    praise you.
¹⁹ Do not let those gloat over me
  who are my enemies without
    cause;

---

*a 3 Or and block the way*     *b 16 Septuagint; Hebrew may mean Like an ungodly circle of
mockers,*

do not let those who hate me
without reason
maliciously wink the eye.
20 They do not speak peaceably,
but devise false accusations
against those who live quietly
in the land.
21 They sneer at me and say, "Aha!
Aha!
With our own eyes we have
seen it."

22 Lord, you have seen this; do not
be silent.
Do not be far from me, Lord.
23 Awake, and rise to my defense!
Contend for me, my God and
Lord.
24 Vindicate me in your
righteousness, Lord my
God;
do not let them gloat over
me.
25 Do not let them think, "Aha, just
what we wanted!"
or say, "We have swallowed
him up."

26 May all who gloat over my
distress
be put to shame and
confusion;
may all who exalt themselves
over me
be clothed with shame and
disgrace.
27 May those who delight in my
vindication
shout for joy and gladness;
may they always say, "The Lord
be exalted,
who delights in the well-being
of his servant."

28 My tongue will proclaim your
righteousness,
your praises all day long.

## Psalm 36[a]

*For the director of music. Of David the
servant of the Lord.*

1 I have a message from God in my
heart
concerning the sinfulness of
the wicked:[b]
There is no fear of God
before their eyes.

2 In their own eyes they flatter
themselves
too much to detect or hate
their sin.
3 The words of their mouths are
wicked and deceitful;
they fail to act wisely or do
good.
4 Even on their beds they plot
evil;
they commit themselves to a
sinful course
and do not reject what is
wrong.

5 Your love, Lord, reaches to the
heavens,
your faithfulness to the
skies.
6 Your righteousness is like the
highest mountains,
your justice like the great
deep.
You, Lord, preserve both
people and animals.
7 How priceless is your unfailing
love, O God!
People take refuge in the
shadow of your wings.
8 They feast on the abundance of
your house;
you give them drink from your
river of delights.
9 For with you is the fountain of
life;
in your light we see light.

---

a In Hebrew texts 36:1-12 is numbered 36:2-13.
of the wicked / resides in their hearts.

b 1 Or *A message from God: The transgression*

10 Continue your love to those who
know you,
    your righteousness to the
    upright in heart.
11 May the foot of the proud not
come against me,
    nor the hand of the wicked
    drive me away.
12 See how the evildoers lie
fallen—
    thrown down, not able to rise!

## Psalm 37[a]

*Of David.*

1 Do not fret because of those who
are evil
    or be envious of those who do
    wrong;
2 for like the grass they will soon
wither,
    like green plants they will
    soon die away.

3 Trust in the LORD and do good;
    dwell in the land and enjoy
    safe pasture.
4 Take delight in the LORD,
    and he will give you the
    desires of your heart.

5 Commit your way to the LORD;
    trust in him and he will do this:
6 He will make your righteous
reward shine like the
dawn,
    your vindication like the
    noonday sun.

7 Be still before the LORD
    and wait patiently for him;
    do not fret when people succeed
    in their ways,
    when they carry out their
    wicked schemes.

8 Refrain from anger and turn
from wrath;

    do not fret—it leads only to
    evil.
9 For those who are evil will be
destroyed,
    but those who hope in the
    LORD will inherit the
    land.

10 A little while, and the wicked
will be no more;
    though you look for them, they
    will not be found.
11 But the meek will inherit the
land
    and enjoy peace and
    prosperity.

12 The wicked plot against the
righteous
    and gnash their teeth at them;
13 but the Lord laughs at the
wicked,
    for he knows their day is
    coming.

14 The wicked draw the sword
    and bend the bow
to bring down the poor and
needy,
    to slay those whose ways are
    upright.
15 But their swords will pierce their
own hearts,
    and their bows will be broken.

16 Better the little that the
righteous have
    than the wealth of many
    wicked;
17 for the power of the wicked will
be broken,
    but the LORD upholds the
    righteous.

18 The blameless spend their days
under the LORD's care,
    and their inheritance will
    endure forever.

---

[a] This psalm is an acrostic poem, the stanzas of which begin with the successive letters of the
Hebrew alphabet.

19 In times of disaster they will not
    wither;
  in days of famine they will
    enjoy plenty.

20 But the wicked will perish:
  Though the LORD's enemies
    are like the flowers of the
    field,
  they will be consumed, they
    will go up in smoke.

21 The wicked borrow and do not
    repay,
  but the righteous give
    generously;

22 those the LORD blesses will
    inherit the land,
  but those he curses will be
    destroyed.

23 The LORD makes firm the steps
    of the one who delights in him;

24 though he may stumble, he will
    not fall,
  for the LORD upholds him with
    his hand.

25 I was young and now I am old,
  yet I have never seen the
    righteous forsaken
  or their children begging
    bread.

26 They are always generous and
    lend freely;
  their children will be a
    blessing.[a]

27 Turn from evil and do good;
  then you will dwell in the land
    forever.

28 For the LORD loves the just
  and will not forsake his
    faithful ones.

  Wrongdoers will be completely
    destroyed[b];

the offspring of the wicked will
    perish.

29 The righteous will inherit the
    land
  and dwell in it forever.

30 The mouths of the righteous
    utter wisdom,
  and their tongues speak what
    is just.

31 The law of their God is in their
    hearts;
  their feet do not slip.

32 The wicked lie in wait for the
    righteous,
  intent on putting them to
    death;

33 but the LORD will not leave
    them in the power of the
    wicked
  or let them be condemned
    when brought to trial.

34 Hope in the LORD
  and keep his way.
  He will exalt you to inherit the
    land;
  when the wicked are
    destroyed, you will see it.

35 I have seen a wicked and
    ruthless man
  flourishing like a luxuriant
    native tree,

36 but he soon passed away and
    was no more;
  though I looked for him, he
    could not be found.

37 Consider the blameless, observe
    the upright;
  a future awaits those who seek
    peace.[c]

38 But all sinners will be destroyed;
  there will be no future[d] for the
    wicked.

---

[a] 26 Or freely; / the names of their children will be used in blessings (see Gen. 48:20); or freely; / others will see that their children are blessed    [b] 28 See Septuagint; Hebrew They will be protected forever    [c] 37 Or upright; / those who seek peace will have posterity    [d] 38 Or posterity

³⁹ The salvation of the righteous
        comes from the LORD;
    he is their stronghold in time
        of trouble.
⁴⁰ The LORD helps them and
        delivers them;
    he delivers them from the
        wicked and saves them,
    because they take refuge in
        him.

## Psalm 38ᵃ

*A psalm of David. A petition.*

¹ LORD, do not rebuke me in your
        anger
    or discipline me in your
        wrath.
² Your arrows have pierced me,
    and your hand has come down
        on me.
³ Because of your wrath there is
        no health in my body;
    there is no soundness in my
        bones because of my sin.
⁴ My guilt has overwhelmed me
    like a burden too heavy to
        bear.

⁵ My wounds fester and are
        loathsome
    because of my sinful folly.
⁶ I am bowed down and brought
        very low;
    all day long I go about
        mourning.
⁷ My back is filled with searing
        pain;
    there is no health in my body.
⁸ I am feeble and utterly
        crushed;
    I groan in anguish of heart.

⁹ All my longings lie open before
        you, Lord;
    my sighing is not hidden from
        you.

¹⁰ My heart pounds, my strength
        fails me;
    even the light has gone from
        my eyes.
¹¹ My friends and companions
        avoid me because of my
        wounds;
    my neighbors stay far away.
¹² Those who want to kill me set
        their traps,
    those who would harm me talk
        of my ruin;
    all day long they scheme and
        lie.

¹³ I am like the deaf, who cannot
        hear,
    like the mute, who cannot
        speak;
¹⁴ I have become like one who does
        not hear,
    whose mouth can offer no
        reply.
¹⁵ LORD, I wait for you;
    you will answer, Lord my God.
¹⁶ For I said, "Do not let them gloat
    or exalt themselves over me
        when my feet slip."

¹⁷ For I am about to fall,
    and my pain is ever with me.
¹⁸ I confess my iniquity;
    I am troubled by my sin.
¹⁹ Many have become my enemies
        without causeᵇ;
    those who hate me without
        reason are numerous.
²⁰ Those who repay my good with
        evil
    lodge accusations against me,
    though I seek only to do what
        is good.

²¹ LORD, do not forsake me;
    do not be far from me, my God.
²² Come quickly to help me,
    my Lord and my Savior.

---

ᵃ In Hebrew texts 38:1-22 is numbered 38:2-23.
Masoretic Text *my vigorous enemies*      ᵇ 19 One Dead Sea Scrolls manuscript;

## Psalm 39[a]

*For the director of music. For Jeduthun.*
*A psalm of David.*

1 I said, "I will watch my ways
    and keep my tongue from sin;
I will put a muzzle on my mouth
    while in the presence of the
        wicked."
2 So I remained utterly silent,
    not even saying anything
        good.
But my anguish increased;
3     my heart grew hot within me.
While I meditated, the fire
        burned;
    then I spoke with my tongue:

4 "Show me, LORD, my life's end
    and the number of my days;
    let me know how fleeting my
        life is.
5 You have made my days a mere
        handbreadth;
    the span of my years is as
        nothing before you.
Everyone is but a breath,
    even those who seem secure.[b]

6 "Surely everyone goes around
        like a mere phantom;
    in vain they rush about,
        heaping up wealth
    without knowing whose it will
        finally be.

7 "But now, Lord, what do I look
        for?
    My hope is in you.
8 Save me from all my
        transgressions;
    do not make me the scorn of
        fools.
9 I was silent; I would not open my
        mouth,
    for you are the one who has
        done this.

10 Remove your scourge from me;
    I am overcome by the blow of
        your hand.
11 When you rebuke and discipline
        anyone for their sin,
    you consume their wealth like
        a moth—
    surely everyone is but a
        breath.

12 "Hear my prayer, LORD,
    listen to my cry for help;
    do not be deaf to my weeping.
I dwell with you as a foreigner,
    a stranger, as all my ancestors
        were.
13 Look away from me, that I may
        enjoy life again
    before I depart and am no
        more."

## Psalm 40[c]

*For the director of music. Of David.*
*A psalm.*

1 I waited patiently for the LORD;
    he turned to me and heard my
        cry.
2 He lifted me out of the slimy pit,
    out of the mud and mire;
    he set my feet on a rock
    and gave me a firm place to
        stand.
3 He put a new song in my mouth,
    a hymn of praise to our God.
Many will see and fear the LORD
    and put their trust in him.

4 Blessed is the one
    who trusts in the LORD,
    who does not look to the proud,
    to those who turn aside to
        false gods.[d]
5 Many, LORD my God,
    are the wonders you have
        done,

---

[a] In Hebrew texts 39:1-13 is numbered 39:2-14.
uncertain meaning) here and at the end of verse 11.
40:2-18.     [d] 4 Or *to lies*

[b] 5 The Hebrew has *Selah* (a word of
[c] In Hebrew texts 40:1-17 is numbered

the things you planned for
us.
None can compare with you;
were I to speak and tell of your
deeds,
they would be too many to
declare.

⁶ Sacrifice and offering you did
not desire—
but my ears you have
opened[a]—
burnt offerings and sin
offerings[b] you did not
require.
⁷ Then I said, "Here I am, I have
come—
it is written about me in the
scroll.[c]
⁸ I desire to do your will, my
God;
your law is within my heart."

⁹ I proclaim your saving acts in
the great assembly;
I do not seal my lips, Lord,
as you know.
¹⁰ I do not hide your righteousness
in my heart;
I speak of your faithfulness
and your saving help.
I do not conceal your love and
your faithfulness
from the great assembly.

¹¹ Do not withhold your mercy
from me, Lord;
may your love and faithfulness
always protect me.
¹² For troubles without number
surround me;
my sins have overtaken me,
and I cannot see.
They are more than the hairs of
my head,
and my heart fails within me.
¹³ Be pleased to save me, Lord;

come quickly, Lord, to help
me.
¹⁴ May all who want to take my
life
be put to shame and
confusion;
may all who desire my ruin
be turned back in disgrace.
¹⁵ May those who say to me, "Aha!
Aha!"
be appalled at their own
shame.
¹⁶ But may all who seek you
rejoice and be glad in you;
may those who long for your
saving help always say,
"The Lord is great!"

¹⁷ But as for me, I am poor and
needy;
may the Lord think of me.
You are my help and my
deliverer;
you are my God, do not delay.

Psalm 41[d]

*For the director of music. A psalm
of David.*

¹ Blessed are those who have
regard for the weak;
the Lord delivers them in
times of trouble.
² The Lord protects and preserves
them—
they are counted among the
blessed in the land—
he does not give them over to
the desire of their foes.
³ The Lord sustains them on their
sickbed
and restores them from their
bed of illness.

⁴ I said, "Have mercy on me,
Lord;

---

*a 6* Hebrew; some Septuagint manuscripts *but a body you have prepared for me*
*b 6* Or *purification offerings*    *c 7* Or *come / with the scroll written for me*    *d* In Hebrew texts
41:1-13 is numbered 41:2-14.

heal me, for I have sinned
    against you."
⁵ My enemies say of me in
    malice,
    "When will he die and his
        name perish?"
⁶ When one of them comes to see
    me,
    he speaks falsely, while his
        heart gathers slander;
    then he goes out and spreads it
        around.

⁷ All my enemies whisper together
    against me;
    they imagine the worst for me,
        saying,
⁸ "A vile disease has afflicted
    him;
    he will never get up from the
        place where he lies."
⁹ Even my close friend,
    someone I trusted,
    one who shared my bread,
    has turned*ᵃ* against me.

¹⁰ But may you have mercy on me,
    LORD;
    raise me up, that I may repay
        them.
¹¹ I know that you are pleased with
    me,
    for my enemy does not
        triumph over me.
¹² Because of my integrity you
    uphold me
    and set me in your presence
        forever.

¹³ Praise be to the LORD, the God of
    Israel,
    from everlasting to
        everlasting.
        Amen and Amen.

# BOOK II

*Psalms 42 – 72*

## Psalm 42*ᵇ,ᶜ*

*For the director of music. A maskilᵈ of
the Sons of Korah.*

¹ As the deer pants for streams of
    water,
    so my soul pants for you, my
        God.
² My soul thirsts for God, for the
    living God.
    When can I go and meet with
        God?
³ My tears have been my food
    day and night,
    while people say to me all day
        long,
    "Where is your God?"
⁴ These things I remember
    as I pour out my soul:
    how I used to go to the house of
        God
    under the protection of the
        Mighty Oneᵉ
    with shouts of joy and praise
    among the festive throng.

⁵ Why, my soul, are you downcast?
    Why so disturbed within me?
    Put your hope in God,
    for I will yet praise him,
    my Savior and my God.

⁶ My soul is downcast within me;
    therefore I will remember you
    from the land of the Jordan,
    the heights of Hermon — from
        Mount Mizar.
⁷ Deep calls to deep
    in the roar of your waterfalls;
    all your waves and breakers
    have swept over me.

*ᵃ 9* Hebrew *has lifted up his heel*    *ᵇ* In many Hebrew manuscripts Psalms 42 and 43 constitute
one psalm.    *ᶜ* In Hebrew texts 42:1-11 is numbered 42:2-12.    *ᵈ* Title: Probably a literary
or musical term    *ᵉ 4* See Septuagint and Syriac; the meaning of the Hebrew for this line is
uncertain.

8 By day the LORD directs his love,
   at night his song is with me —
    a prayer to the God of my life.

9 I say to God my Rock,
   "Why have you forgotten me?
Why must I go about mourning,
   oppressed by the enemy?"
10 My bones suffer mortal agony
   as my foes taunt me,
saying to me all day long,
   "Where is your God?"

11 Why, my soul, are you downcast?
   Why so disturbed within me?
Put your hope in God,
   for I will yet praise him,
    my Savior and my God.

## Psalm 43[a]

1 Vindicate me, my God,
   and plead my cause
    against an unfaithful nation.
Rescue me from those who are
   deceitful and wicked.
2 You are God my stronghold.
   Why have you rejected me?
Why must I go about mourning,
   oppressed by the enemy?
3 Send me your light and your
    faithful care,
   let them lead me;
let them bring me to your holy
    mountain,
   to the place where you dwell.
4 Then I will go to the altar of God,
   to God, my joy and my delight.
I will praise you with the lyre,
   O God, my God.

5 Why, my soul, are you downcast?
   Why so disturbed within me?
Put your hope in God,
   for I will yet praise him,
    my Savior and my God.

## Psalm 44[b]

*For the director of music. Of the Sons of*
*   Korah. A maskil.[c]*

1 We have heard it with our ears,
   O God;
our ancestors have told us
   what you did in their days,
    in days long ago.
2 With your hand you drove out
    the nations
   and planted our ancestors;
you crushed the peoples
   and made our ancestors
    flourish.
3 It was not by their sword that
    they won the land,
   nor did their arm bring them
    victory;
it was your right hand, your
    arm,
   and the light of your face, for
    you loved them.

4 You are my King and my God,
   who decrees[d] victories for
    Jacob.
5 Through you we push back our
    enemies;
   through your name we
    trample our foes.
6 I put no trust in my bow,
   my sword does not bring me
    victory;
7 but you give us victory over our
    enemies,
   you put our adversaries to
    shame.
8 In God we make our boast all
    day long,
   and we will praise your name
    forever.[e]

9 But now you have rejected and
    humbled us;

---

[a] In many Hebrew manuscripts Psalms 42 and 43 constitute one psalm.   [b] In Hebrew texts 44:1-26 is numbered 44:2-27.   [c] Title: Probably a literary or musical term   [d] 4 Septuagint, Aquila and Syriac; Hebrew *King, O God;* / command   [e] 8 The Hebrew has *Selah* (a word of uncertain meaning) here.

you no longer go out with our
armies.
10 You made us retreat before the
enemy,
and our adversaries have
plundered us.
11 You gave us up to be devoured
like sheep
and have scattered us among
the nations.
12 You sold your people for a
pittance,
gaining nothing from their
sale.
13 You have made us a reproach to
our neighbors,
the scorn and derision of those
around us.
14 You have made us a byword
among the nations;
the peoples shake their heads
at us.
15 I live in disgrace all day long,
and my face is covered with
shame
16 at the taunts of those who
reproach and revile me,
because of the enemy, who is
bent on revenge.
17 All this came upon us,
though we had not forgotten
you;
we had not been false to your
covenant.
18 Our hearts had not turned back;
our feet had not strayed from
your path.
19 But you crushed us and made us
a haunt for jackals;
you covered us over with deep
darkness.
20 If we had forgotten the name of
our God
or spread out our hands to a
foreign god,

21 would not God have discovered
it,
since he knows the secrets of
the heart?
22 Yet for your sake we face death
all day long;
we are considered as sheep to
be slaughtered.
23 Awake, Lord! Why do you sleep?
Rouse yourself! Do not reject
us forever.
24 Why do you hide your face
and forget our misery and
oppression?
25 We are brought down to the
dust;
our bodies cling to the ground.
26 Rise up and help us;
rescue us because of your
unfailing love.

Psalm 45[a]

*For the director of music. To the tune of
"Lilies." Of the Sons of Korah. A maskil.[b]
A wedding song.*

1 My heart is stirred by a noble
theme
as I recite my verses for the
king;
my tongue is the pen of a
skillful writer.

2 You are the most excellent of
men
and your lips have been
anointed with grace,
since God has blessed you
forever.

3 Gird your sword on your side,
you mighty one;
clothe yourself with splendor
and majesty.
4 In your majesty ride forth
victoriously

---

[a] In Hebrew texts 45:1-17 is numbered 45:2-18.    [b] Title: Probably a literary or musical term

in the cause of truth, humility
and justice;
let your right hand achieve
awesome deeds.
⁵ Let your sharp arrows pierce
the hearts of the king's
enemies;
let the nations fall beneath
your feet.
⁶ Your throne, O God,ᵃ will last for
ever and ever;
a scepter of justice will be
the scepter of your
kingdom.
⁷ You love righteousness and hate
wickedness;
therefore God, your God,
has set you above your
companions
by anointing you with the oil
of joy.
⁸ All your robes are fragrant with
myrrh and aloes and
cassia;
from palaces adorned with
ivory
the music of the strings makes
you glad.
⁹ Daughters of kings are among
your honored women;
at your right hand is the royal
bride in gold of Ophir.

¹⁰ Listen, daughter, and pay careful
attention:
Forget your people and your
father's house.
¹¹ Let the king be enthralled by
your beauty;
honor him, for he is your lord.
¹² The city of Tyre will come with a
gift,ᵇ
people of wealth will seek your
favor.
¹³ All glorious is the princess
within her chamber;

her gown is interwoven with
gold.
¹⁴ In embroidered garments she is
led to the king;
her virgin companions follow
her —
those brought to be with her.
¹⁵ Led in with joy and gladness,
they enter the palace of the
king.

¹⁶ Your sons will take the place of
your fathers;
you will make them princes
throughout the land.

¹⁷ I will perpetuate your memory
through all generations;
therefore the nations will
praise you for ever and
ever.

## Psalm 46ᶜ

*For the director of music. Of the Sons of
Korah. According to* alamoth.ᵈ *A song.*

¹ God is our refuge and strength,
an ever-present help in
trouble.
² Therefore we will not fear,
though the earth give way
and the mountains fall into
the heart of the sea,
³ though its waters roar and foam
and the mountains quake with
their surging.ᵉ

⁴ There is a river whose streams
make glad the city of God,
the holy place where the Most
High dwells.
⁵ God is within her, she will not
fall;
God will help her at break of
day.
⁶ Nations are in uproar, kingdoms
fall;

---

ᵃ 6 Here the king is addressed as God's representative.     ᵇ 12 Or A Tyrian robe is among the
*gifts*     ᶜ In Hebrew texts 46:1-11 is numbered 46:2-12.     ᵈ Title: Probably a musical term
ᵉ 3 The Hebrew has Selah (a word of uncertain meaning) here and at the end of verses 7 and 11.

he lifts his voice, the earth
melts.
<sup>7</sup> The LORD Almighty is with us;
the God of Jacob is our
fortress.

<sup>8</sup> Come and see what the LORD has
done,
the desolations he has brought
on the earth.
<sup>9</sup> He makes wars cease
to the ends of the earth.
He breaks the bow and shatters
the spear;
he burns the shields[a] with
fire.
<sup>10</sup> He says, "Be still, and know that
I am God;
I will be exalted among the
nations,
I will be exalted in the earth."

<sup>11</sup> The LORD Almighty is with us;
the God of Jacob is our
fortress.

## Psalm 47[b]

*For the director of music. Of the Sons of
Korah. A psalm.*

<sup>1</sup> Clap your hands, all you nations;
shout to God with cries of joy.

<sup>2</sup> For the LORD Most High is
awesome,
the great King over all the
earth.
<sup>3</sup> He subdued nations under us,
peoples under our feet.
<sup>4</sup> He chose our inheritance for us,
the pride of Jacob, whom he
loved.[c]

<sup>5</sup> God has ascended amid shouts
of joy,
the LORD amid the sounding
of trumpets.

<sup>6</sup> Sing praises to God, sing
praises;
sing praises to our King, sing
praises.
<sup>7</sup> For God is the King of all the
earth;
sing to him a psalm of praise.

<sup>8</sup> God reigns over the nations;
God is seated on his holy
throne.
<sup>9</sup> The nobles of the nations
assemble
as the people of the God of
Abraham,
for the kings[d] of the earth belong
to God;
he is greatly exalted.

## Psalm 48[e]

*A song. A psalm of the Sons of Korah.*

<sup>1</sup> Great is the LORD, and most
worthy of praise,
in the city of our God, his holy
mountain.

<sup>2</sup> Beautiful in its loftiness,
the joy of the whole earth,
like the heights of Zaphon[f] is
Mount Zion,
the city of the Great King.
<sup>3</sup> God is in her citadels;
he has shown himself to be her
fortress.

<sup>4</sup> When the kings joined forces,
when they advanced together,
<sup>5</sup> they saw her and were
astounded;
they fled in terror.
<sup>6</sup> Trembling seized them there,
pain like that of a woman in
labor.
<sup>7</sup> You destroyed them like ships of
Tarshish
shattered by an east wind.

---

<sup>a</sup> 9 Or *chariots*    <sup>b</sup> In Hebrew texts 47:1-9 is numbered 47:2-10.    <sup>c</sup> 4 The Hebrew has *Selah*
(a word of uncertain meaning) here.    <sup>d</sup> 9 Or *shields*    <sup>e</sup> In Hebrew texts 48:1-14 is numbered
48:2-15.    <sup>f</sup> 2 *Zaphon* was the most sacred mountain of the Canaanites.

⁸ As we have heard,
so we have seen
in the city of the LORD Almighty,
in the city of our God:
God makes her secure
forever.ᵃ

⁹ Within your temple, O God,
we meditate on your unfailing
love.
¹⁰ Like your name, O God,
your praise reaches to the ends
of the earth;
your right hand is filled with
righteousness.
¹¹ Mount Zion rejoices,
the villages of Judah are glad
because of your judgments.

¹² Walk about Zion, go around
her,
count her towers,
¹³ consider well her ramparts,
view her citadels,
that you may tell of them
to the next generation.

¹⁴ For this God is our God for ever
and ever;
he will be our guide even to
the end.

## Psalm 49ᵇ

*For the director of music. Of the Sons of
Korah. A psalm.*

¹ Hear this, all you peoples;
listen, all who live in this
world,
² both low and high,
rich and poor alike:
³ My mouth will speak words of
wisdom;
the meditation of my heart will
give you understanding.
⁴ I will turn my ear to a proverb;

with the harp I will expound
my riddle:

⁵ Why should I fear when evil days
come,
when wicked deceivers
surround me —
⁶ those who trust in their wealth
and boast of their great riches?
⁷ No one can redeem the life of
another
or give to God a ransom for
them —
⁸ the ransom for a life is costly,
no payment is ever enough —
⁹ so that they should live on
forever
and not see decay.
¹⁰ For all can see that the wise die,
that the foolish and the
senseless also perish,
leaving their wealth to others.
¹¹ Their tombs will remain their
housesᶜ forever,
their dwellings for endless
generations,
though they hadᵈ named
lands after themselves.

¹² People, despite their wealth, do
not endure;
they are like the beasts that
perish.

¹³ This is the fate of those who trust
in themselves,
and of their followers, who
approve their sayings.ᵉ
¹⁴ They are like sheep and are
destined to die;
death will be their shepherd
(but the upright will prevail
over them in the
morning).
Their forms will decay in the
grave,

---

ᵃ 8 The Hebrew has *Selah* (a word of uncertain meaning) here.    ᵇ In Hebrew texts 49:1-20
is numbered 49:2-21.    ᶜ 11 Septuagint and Syriac; Hebrew *In their thoughts their houses
will remain*    ᵈ 11 Or *generations, / for they have*    ᵉ 13 The Hebrew has *Selah* (a word of
uncertain meaning) here and at the end of verse 15.

far from their princely
   mansions.
<sup>15</sup> But God will redeem me from
   the realm of the dead;
  he will surely take me to
   himself.
<sup>16</sup> Do not be overawed when others
   grow rich,
  when the splendor of their
   houses increases;
<sup>17</sup> for they will take nothing with
   them when they die,
  their splendor will not
   descend with them.
<sup>18</sup> Though while they live they
   count themselves
   blessed—
  and people praise you when
   you prosper—
<sup>19</sup> they will join those who have
   gone before them,
  who will never again see the
   light of life.

<sup>20</sup> People who have wealth but lack
   understanding
  are like the beasts that perish.

## Psalm 50

*A psalm of Asaph.*

<sup>1</sup> The Mighty One, God, the LORD,
  speaks and summons the
   earth
  from the rising of the sun to
   where it sets.
<sup>2</sup> From Zion, perfect in beauty,
  God shines forth.
<sup>3</sup> Our God comes
  and will not be silent;
  a fire devours before him,
  and around him a tempest
   rages.
<sup>4</sup> He summons the heavens above,
  and the earth, that he may
   judge his people:

<sup>5</sup> "Gather to me this consecrated
   people,
  who made a covenant with me
   by sacrifice."
<sup>6</sup> And the heavens proclaim his
   righteousness,
  for he is a God of justice.<sup>a,b</sup>

<sup>7</sup> "Listen, my people, and I will
   speak;
  I will testify against you,
   Israel:
  I am God, your God.
<sup>8</sup> I bring no charges against you
   concerning your sacrifices
  or concerning your burnt
   offerings, which are ever
   before me.
<sup>9</sup> I have no need of a bull from
   your stall
  or of goats from your pens,
<sup>10</sup> for every animal of the forest is
   mine,
  and the cattle on a thousand
   hills.
<sup>11</sup> I know every bird in the
   mountains,
  and the insects in the fields
   are mine.
<sup>12</sup> If I were hungry I would not tell
   you,
  for the world is mine, and all
   that is in it.
<sup>13</sup> Do I eat the flesh of bulls
  or drink the blood of goats?

<sup>14</sup> "Sacrifice thank offerings to
   God,
  fulfill your vows to the Most
   High,
<sup>15</sup> and call on me in the day of
   trouble;
  I will deliver you, and you will
   honor me."

<sup>16</sup> But to the wicked person, God
   says:

---

<sup>a</sup> 6   With a different word division of the Hebrew; Masoretic Text *for God himself is judge*
<sup>b</sup> 6   The Hebrew has *Selah* (a word of uncertain meaning) here.

"What right have you to recite
        my laws
    or take my covenant on your
        lips?
17 You hate my instruction
    and cast my words behind you.
18 When you see a thief, you join
        with him;
    you throw in your lot with
        adulterers.
19 You use your mouth for evil
    and harness your tongue to
        deceit.
20 You sit and testify against your
        brother
    and slander your own
        mother's son.
21 When you did these things and I
        kept silent,
    you thought I was exactly[a] like
        you.
    But I now arraign you
    and set my accusations before
        you.

22 "Consider this, you who forget
        God,
    or I will tear you to pieces,
        with no one to rescue you:
23 Those who sacrifice thank
        offerings honor me,
    and to the blameless[b] I will
        show my salvation."

## Psalm 51[c]

*For the director of music. A psalm
of David. When the prophet Nathan
came to him after David had committed
adultery with Bathsheba.*

1 Have mercy on me, O God,
        according to your unfailing
        love;
    according to your great
        compassion
    blot out my transgressions.

2 Wash away all my iniquity
    and cleanse me from my sin.

3 For I know my transgressions,
    and my sin is always before
        me.
4 Against you, you only, have I
        sinned
    and done what is evil in your
        sight;
    so you are right in your verdict
    and justified when you judge.
5 Surely I was sinful at birth,
    sinful from the time my
        mother conceived me.
6 Yet you desired faithfulness
        even in the womb;
    you taught me wisdom in that
        secret place.

7 Cleanse me with hyssop, and I
        will be clean;
    wash me, and I will be whiter
        than snow.
8 Let me hear joy and gladness;
    let the bones you have crushed
        rejoice.
9 Hide your face from my sins
    and blot out all my iniquity.

10 Create in me a pure heart,
        O God,
    and renew a steadfast spirit
        within me.
11 Do not cast me from your
        presence
    or take your Holy Spirit from
        me.
12 Restore to me the joy of your
        salvation
    and grant me a willing spirit,
        to sustain me.
13 Then I will teach transgressors
        your ways,
    so that sinners will turn back
        to you.

a 21 Or *thought the 'I AM' was*     b 23 Probable reading of the original Hebrew text; the meaning
of the Masoretic Text for this phrase is uncertain.     c In Hebrew texts 51:1-19 is numbered
51:3-21.

14 Deliver me from the guilt of
  bloodshed, O God,
    you who are God my Savior,
  and my tongue will sing of
    your righteousness.
15 Open my lips, Lord,
    and my mouth will declare
      your praise.
16 You do not delight in sacrifice, or
    I would bring it;
  you do not take pleasure in
    burnt offerings.
17 My sacrifice, O God, is[a] a broken
    spirit;
  a broken and contrite heart
  you, God, will not despise.

18 May it please you to prosper
    Zion,
  to build up the walls of
    Jerusalem.
19 Then you will delight in the
    sacrifices of the righteous,
  in burnt offerings offered
    whole;
  then bulls will be offered on
    your altar.

## Psalm 52[b]

*For the director of music. A maskil[c]
of David. When Doeg the Edomite had
gone to Saul and told him: "David has
gone to the house of Ahimelek."*

1 Why do you boast of evil, you
    mighty hero?
  Why do you boast all day long,
    you who are a disgrace in the
      eyes of God?
2 You who practice deceit,
    your tongue plots destruction;
  it is like a sharpened razor.
3 You love evil rather than good,
    falsehood rather than
      speaking the truth.[d]

4 You love every harmful word,
    you deceitful tongue!

5 Surely God will bring you down
    to everlasting ruin:
  He will snatch you up and
    pluck you from your tent;
  he will uproot you from the
    land of the living.
6 The righteous will see and fear;
    they will laugh at you,
      saying,
7 "Here now is the man
    who did not make God his
      stronghold
  but trusted in his great wealth
    and grew strong by destroying
      others!"

8 But I am like an olive tree
    flourishing in the house of
      God;
  I trust in God's unfailing love
    for ever and ever.
9 For what you have done I will
    always praise you
  in the presence of your faithful
    people.
  And I will hope in your name,
    for your name is good.

## Psalm 53[e]

*For the director of music. According to
mahalath.[f] A maskil[c] of David.*

1 The fool says in his heart,
    "There is no God."
  They are corrupt, and their ways
    are vile;
  there is no one who does good.

2 God looks down from heaven
    on all mankind
  to see if there are any who
    understand,
  any who seek God.

---

[a] 17 Or *The sacrifices of God are*
Probably a literary or musical term
here and at the end of verse 5.   [b] In Hebrew texts 52:1-9 is numbered 52:3-11.   [c] Title:
[d] 3 The Hebrew has *Selah* (a word of uncertain meaning)
[e] In Hebrew texts 53:1-6 is numbered 53:2-7.   [f] Title:
Probably a musical term

³ Everyone has turned away, all
        have become corrupt;
    there is no one who does good,
        not even one.

⁴ Do all these evildoers know
        nothing?

    They devour my people as
        though eating bread;
    they never call on God.
⁵ But there they are, overwhelmed
        with dread,
    where there was nothing to
        dread.
    God scattered the bones of those
        who attacked you;
    you put them to shame, for
        God despised them.

⁶ Oh, that salvation for Israel
        would come out of Zion!
    When God restores his people,
        let Jacob rejoice and Israel be
        glad!

## Psalm 54[a]

*For the director of music. With stringed
instruments. A maskil[b] of David. When
the Ziphites had gone to Saul and said,
"Is not David hiding among us?"*

¹ Save me, O God, by your name;
    vindicate me by your might.
² Hear my prayer, O God;
    listen to the words of my
        mouth.

³ Arrogant foes are attacking me;
    ruthless people are trying to
        kill me —
    people without regard for
        God.[c]

⁴ Surely God is my help;
    the Lord is the one who
        sustains me.

⁵ Let evil recoil on those who
        slander me;
    in your faithfulness destroy
        them.

⁶ I will sacrifice a freewill offering
        to you;
    I will praise your name, LORD,
        for it is good.
⁷ You have delivered me from all
        my troubles,
    and my eyes have looked in
        triumph on my foes.

## Psalm 55[d]

*For the director of music. With stringed
instruments. A maskil of David.*

¹ Listen to my prayer, O God,
    do not ignore my plea;
²   hear me and answer me.
    My thoughts trouble me and I
        am distraught
³   because of what my enemy is
        saying,
    because of the threats of the
        wicked;
    for they bring down suffering on
        me
    and assail me in their anger.

⁴ My heart is in anguish within
        me;
    the terrors of death have fallen
        on me.
⁵ Fear and trembling have beset
        me;
    horror has overwhelmed me.
⁶ I said, "Oh, that I had the wings
        of a dove!
    I would fly away and be at rest.
⁷ I would flee far away
    and stay in the desert;[e]
⁸ I would hurry to my place of
        shelter,

---

[a] In Hebrew texts 54:1-7 is numbered 54:3-9.    [b] Title: Probably a literary or musical term
[c] 3 The Hebrew has *Selah* (a word of uncertain meaning) here.    [d] In Hebrew texts 55:1-23 is
numbered 55:2-24.    [e] 7 The Hebrew has *Selah* (a word of uncertain meaning) here and in the
middle of verse 19.

far from the tempest and
   storm."

9 Lord, confuse the wicked,
   confound their words,
   for I see violence and strife in
      the city.
10 Day and night they prowl about
      on its walls;
   malice and abuse are within it.
11 Destructive forces are at work in
      the city;
   threats and lies never leave its
      streets.

12 If an enemy were insulting me,
   I could endure it;
   if a foe were rising against me,
   I could hide.
13 But it is you, a man like myself,
   my companion, my close
      friend,
14 with whom I once enjoyed sweet
      fellowship
   at the house of God,
   as we walked about
      among the worshipers.

15 Let death take my enemies by
      surprise;
   let them go down alive to the
      realm of the dead,
   for evil finds lodging among
      them.

16 As for me, I call to God,
   and the LORD saves me.
17 Evening, morning and noon
   I cry out in distress,
   and he hears my voice.
18 He rescues me unharmed
   from the battle waged against
      me,
   even though many oppose
      me.
19 God, who is enthroned from of
      old,
   who does not change —

he will hear them and humble
   them,
because they have no fear of
   God.

20 My companion attacks his
      friends;
   he violates his covenant.
21 His talk is smooth as butter,
   yet war is in his heart;
   his words are more soothing
      than oil,
   yet they are drawn swords.

22 Cast your cares on the LORD
   and he will sustain you;
   he will never let
      the righteous be shaken.
23 But you, God, will bring down
      the wicked
   into the pit of decay;
   the bloodthirsty and deceitful
   will not live out half their days.

But as for me, I trust in you.

## Psalm 56[a]

*For the director of music. To the tune*
*of "A Dove on Distant Oaks." Of David.*
*A miktam.[b] When the Philistines had*
*seized him in Gath.*

1 Be merciful to me, my God,
   for my enemies are in hot
      pursuit;
   all day long they press their
      attack.
2 My adversaries pursue me all
      day long;
   in their pride many are
      attacking me.

3 When I am afraid, I put my trust
      in you.
4   In God, whose word I praise —
   in God I trust and am not afraid.
   What can mere mortals do
      to me?

a In Hebrew texts 56:1-13 is numbered 56:2-14.     b Title: Probably a literary or musical term

⁵ All day long they twist my words;
    all their schemes are for my
        ruin.
⁶ They conspire, they lurk,
    they watch my steps,
        hoping to take my life.
⁷ Because of their wickedness do
        not[a] let them escape;
    in your anger, God, bring the
        nations down.

⁸ Record my misery;
    list my tears on your scroll[b] —
        are they not in your record?
⁹ Then my enemies will turn back
        when I call for help.
    By this I will know that God is
        for me.

¹⁰ In God, whose word I praise,
    in the LORD, whose word I
        praise —
¹¹ in God I trust and am not afraid.
    What can man do to me?

¹² I am under vows to you, my God;
    I will present my thank
        offerings to you.
¹³ For you have delivered me from
        death
    and my feet from stumbling,
    that I may walk before God
        in the light of life.

## Psalm 57[c]

*For the director of music. To the tune of
"Do Not Destroy." Of David. A miktam.[d]
When he had fled from Saul into the
cave.*

¹ Have mercy on me, my God,
        have mercy on me,
    for in you I take refuge.
    I will take refuge in the shadow
        of your wings
    until the disaster has passed.

² I cry out to God Most High,
    to God, who vindicates me.
³ He sends from heaven and saves
        me,
    rebuking those who hotly
        pursue me — [e]
    God sends forth his love and
        his faithfulness.

⁴ I am in the midst of lions;
    I am forced to dwell among
        ravenous beasts —
    men whose teeth are spears and
        arrows,
    whose tongues are sharp
        swords.

⁵ Be exalted, O God, above the
        heavens;
    let your glory be over all the
        earth.

⁶ They spread a net for my feet —
    I was bowed down in
        distress.
    They dug a pit in my path —
    but they have fallen into it
        themselves.

⁷ My heart, O God, is steadfast,
    my heart is steadfast;
    I will sing and make music.
⁸ Awake, my soul!
    Awake, harp and lyre!
    I will awaken the dawn.

⁹ I will praise you, Lord, among
        the nations;
    I will sing of you among the
        peoples.
¹⁰ For great is your love, reaching
        to the heavens;
    your faithfulness reaches to
        the skies.

¹¹ Be exalted, O God, above the
        heavens;

---

[a] 7 Probable reading of the original Hebrew text; Masoretic Text does not have *do not.*  [b] 8 Or *misery; / put my tears in your wineskin*  [c] In Hebrew texts 57:1-11 is numbered 57:2-12.  [d] Title: Probably a literary or musical term (uncertain meaning) here and at the end of verse 6.  [e] 3 The Hebrew has *Selah* (a word of uncertain meaning)

let your glory be over all the
earth.

## Psalm 58[a]

*For the director of music. To the tune*
*of "Do Not Destroy." Of David.*
*A miktam.[b]*

[1] Do you rulers indeed speak
justly?
Do you judge people with
equity?
[2] No, in your heart you devise
injustice,
and your hands mete out
violence on the earth.

[3] Even from birth the wicked go
astray;
from the womb they are
wayward, spreading
lies.
[4] Their venom is like the venom of
a snake,
like that of a cobra that has
stopped its ears,
[5] that will not heed the tune of the
charmer,
however skillful the enchanter
may be.

[6] Break the teeth in their mouths,
O God;
LORD, tear out the fangs of
those lions!
[7] Let them vanish like water that
flows away;
when they draw the bow, let
their arrows fall short.
[8] May they be like a slug that melts
away as it moves along,
like a stillborn child that never
sees the sun.

[9] Before your pots can feel the
heat of the thorns—

whether they be green or
dry—the wicked will be
swept away.[c]
[10] The righteous will be glad when
they are avenged,
when they dip their feet in the
blood of the wicked.
[11] Then people will say,
"Surely the righteous still are
rewarded;
surely there is a God who
judges the earth."

## Psalm 59[d]

*For the director of music. To the tune of*
*"Do Not Destroy." Of David. A miktam.[b]*
*When Saul had sent men to watch*
*David's house in order to kill him.*

[1] Deliver me from my enemies,
O God;
be my fortress against those
who are attacking me.
[2] Deliver me from evildoers
and save me from those who
are after my blood.

[3] See how they lie in wait for me!
Fierce men conspire against me
for no offense or sin of mine,
LORD.
[4] I have done no wrong, yet they
are ready to attack me.
Arise to help me; look on my
plight!
[5] You, LORD God Almighty,
you who are the God of Israel,
rouse yourself to punish all the
nations;
show no mercy to wicked
traitors.[e]

[6] They return at evening,
snarling like dogs,
and prowl about the city.

---

[a] In Hebrew texts 58:1-11 is numbered 58:2-12.     [b] Title: Probably a literary or musical term
[c] 9 The meaning of the Hebrew for this verse is uncertain.     [d] In Hebrew texts 59:1-17 is
numbered 59:2-18.     [e] 5 The Hebrew has *Selah* (a word of uncertain meaning) here and at the
end of verse 13.

⁷ See what they spew from their
        mouths—
    the words from their lips are
        sharp as swords,
    and they think, "Who can hear
        us?"
⁸ But you laugh at them, LORD;
    you scoff at all those nations.

⁹ You are my strength, I watch for
        you;
    you, God, are my fortress,
¹⁰    my God on whom I can rely.

God will go before me
    and will let me gloat over those
        who slander me.
¹¹ But do not kill them, Lord our
        shield,ᵃ
    or my people will forget.
In your might uproot them
    and bring them down.
¹² For the sins of their mouths,
    for the words of their lips,
    let them be caught in their
        pride.
For the curses and lies they
        utter,
¹³    consume them in your
        wrath,
    consume them till they are no
        more.
Then it will be known to the
        ends of the earth
    that God rules over Jacob.

¹⁴ They return at evening,
    snarling like dogs,
    and prowl about the city.
¹⁵ They wander about for food
    and howl if not satisfied.
¹⁶ But I will sing of your strength,
    in the morning I will sing of
        your love;
    for you are my fortress,
    my refuge in times of trouble.

¹⁷ You are my strength, I sing
        praise to you;
    you, God, are my fortress,
    my God on whom I can rely.

### Psalm 60ᵇ

*For the director of music. To the tune of
"The Lily of the Covenant." A miktamᶜ
of David. For teaching. When he fought
Aram Naharaimᵈ and Aram Zobah,ᵉ
and when Joab returned and struck
down twelve thousand Edomites in the
Valley of Salt.*

¹ You have rejected us, God, and
        burst through our defenses;
    you have been angry— now
        restore us!
² You have shaken the land and
        torn it open;
    mend its fractures, for it is
        quaking.
³ You have shown your people
        desperate times;
    you have given us wine that
        makes us stagger.
⁴ But for those who fear you, you
        have raised a banner
    to be unfurled against the
        bow.ᶠ

⁵ Save us and help us with your
        right hand,
    that those you love may be
        delivered.
⁶ God has spoken from his
        sanctuary:
    "In triumph I will parcel out
        Shechem
    and measure off the Valley of
        Sukkoth.
⁷ Gilead is mine, and Manasseh is
        mine;
    Ephraim is my helmet,
    Judah is my scepter.

---

ᵃ 11 Or *sovereign*    ᵇ In Hebrew texts 60:1-12 is numbered 60:3-14.    ᶜ Title: Probably a
literary or musical term    ᵈ Title: That is, Arameans of Northwest Mesopotamia    ᵉ Title:
That is, Arameans of central Syria    ᶠ 4  The Hebrew has Selah (a word of uncertain meaning)
here.

8 Moab is my washbasin,
    on Edom I toss my sandal;
    over Philistia I shout in
        triumph."

9 Who will bring me to the
        fortified city?
    Who will lead me to Edom?
10 Is it not you, God, you who have
        now rejected us
    and no longer go out with our
        armies?
11 Give us aid against the enemy,
    for human help is worthless.
12 With God we will gain the
        victory,
    and he will trample down our
        enemies.

## Psalm 61[a]

*For the director of music. With stringed
    instruments. Of David.*

1 Hear my cry, O God;
    listen to my prayer.

2 From the ends of the earth I call
        to you,
    I call as my heart grows faint;
    lead me to the rock that is
        higher than I.
3 For you have been my refuge,
    a strong tower against the foe.

4 I long to dwell in your tent
        forever
    and take refuge in the shelter
        of your wings.[b]
5 For you, God, have heard my
        vows;
    you have given me the heritage
        of those who fear your
        name.

6 Increase the days of the king's
        life,

his years for many
    generations.
7 May he be enthroned in God's
        presence forever;
    appoint your love and
        faithfulness to protect
        him.

8 Then I will ever sing in praise of
        your name
    and fulfill my vows day after
        day.

## Psalm 62[c]

*For the director of music. For Jeduthun.
    A psalm of David.*

1 Truly my soul finds rest in God;
    my salvation comes from
        him.
2 Truly he is my rock and my
        salvation;
    he is my fortress, I will never
        be shaken.

3 How long will you assault me?
    Would all of you throw me
        down—
    this leaning wall, this tottering
        fence?
4 Surely they intend to topple me
    from my lofty place;
    they take delight in lies.
With their mouths they bless,
    but in their hearts they curse.[d]

5 Yes, my soul, find rest in God;
    my hope comes from him.
6 Truly he is my rock and my
        salvation;
    he is my fortress, I will not be
        shaken.
7 My salvation and my honor
        depend on God[e];
    he is my mighty rock, my
        refuge.

---

*a* In Hebrew texts 61:1-8 is numbered 61:2-9.    *b 4* The Hebrew has *Selah* (a word of uncertain
meaning) here.    *c* In Hebrew texts 62:1-12 is numbered 62:2-13.    *d 4* The Hebrew has *Selah*
(a word of uncertain meaning) here and at the end of verse 8.    *e 7* Or *I God Most High is my
salvation and my honor*

⁸Trust in him at all times, you
people;
pour out your hearts to him,
for God is our refuge.

⁹Surely the lowborn are but a
breath,
the highborn are but a lie.
If weighed on a balance, they are
nothing;
together they are only a
breath.

¹⁰Do not trust in extortion
or put vain hope in stolen
goods;
though your riches increase,
do not set your heart on them.

¹¹One thing God has spoken,
two things I have heard:
"Power belongs to you, God,

¹²     and with you, Lord, is
unfailing love";
and, "You reward everyone
according to what they have
done."

## Psalm 63ᵃ

*A psalm of David. When he was in the
Desert of Judah.*

¹You, God, are my God,
earnestly I seek you;
I thirst for you,
my whole being longs for you,
in a dry and parched land
where there is no water.

²I have seen you in the
sanctuary
and beheld your power and
your glory.

³Because your love is better than
life,
my lips will glorify you.

⁴I will praise you as long as I live,
and in your name I will lift up
my hands.

⁵I will be fully satisfied as with
the richest of foods;
with singing lips my mouth
will praise you.

⁶On my bed I remember you;
I think of you through the
watches of the night.

⁷Because you are my help,
I sing in the shadow of your
wings.

⁸I cling to you;
your right hand upholds me.

⁹Those who want to kill me will
be destroyed;
they will go down to the
depths of the earth.

¹⁰They will be given over to the
sword
and become food for jackals.

¹¹But the king will rejoice in God;
all who swear by God will
glory in him,
while the mouths of liars will
be silenced.

## Psalm 64ᵇ

*For the director of music. A psalm
of David.*

¹Hear me, my God, as I voice my
complaint;
protect my life from the threat
of the enemy.

²Hide me from the conspiracy of
the wicked,
from the plots of evildoers.

³They sharpen their tongues like
swords
and aim cruel words like
deadly arrows.

⁴They shoot from ambush at the
innocent;
they shoot suddenly, without
fear.

---

ᵃ In Hebrew texts 63:1-11 is numbered 63:2-12.     ᵇ In Hebrew texts 64:1-10 is numbered 64:2-11.

⁵They encourage each other in
  evil plans,
  they talk about hiding their
    snares;
  they say, "Who will see it*a*?"
⁶They plot injustice and say,
  "We have devised a perfect
    plan!"
  Surely the human mind and
    heart are cunning.

⁷But God will shoot them with his
  arrows;
  they will suddenly be struck
    down.
⁸He will turn their own tongues
  against them
  and bring them to ruin;
  all who see them will shake
    their heads in scorn.
⁹All people will fear;
  they will proclaim the works of
    God
  and ponder what he has done.

¹⁰The righteous will rejoice in the
    LORD
  and take refuge in him;
  all the upright in heart will
    glory in him!

## Psalm 65*b*

*For the director of music. A psalm
of David. A song.*

¹Praise awaits*c* you, our God, in
    Zion;
  to you our vows will be
    fulfilled.
²You who answer prayer,
  to you all people will come.
³When we were overwhelmed by
    sins,
  you forgave*d* our
    transgressions.
⁴Blessed are those you choose

and bring near to live in your
    courts!
We are filled with the good
    things of your house,
  of your holy temple.

⁵You answer us with awesome
    and righteous deeds,
  God our Savior,
  the hope of all the ends of the
    earth
  and of the farthest seas,
⁶who formed the mountains by
    your power,
  having armed yourself with
    strength,
⁷who stilled the roaring of the
    seas,
  the roaring of their waves,
  and the turmoil of the nations.
⁸The whole earth is filled with
  awe at your wonders;
  where morning dawns, where
    evening fades,
  you call forth songs of joy.

⁹You care for the land and water
    it;
  you enrich it abundantly.
The streams of God are filled
    with water
  to provide the people with
    grain,
  for so you have ordained it.*e*
¹⁰You drench its furrows and level
    its ridges;
  you soften it with showers and
    bless its crops.
¹¹You crown the year with your
    bounty,
  and your carts overflow with
    abundance.
¹²The grasslands of the wilderness
    overflow;
  the hills are clothed with
    gladness.

---

*a 5* Or *us*    *b* In Hebrew texts 65:1-13 is numbered 65:2-14.    *c 1* Or *befits*; the meaning of the
Hebrew for this word is uncertain.    *d 3* Or *made atonement for*    *e 9* Or *for that is how you
prepare the land*

¹³ The meadows are covered with
   flocks
   and the valleys are mantled
      with grain;
   they shout for joy and sing.

## Psalm 66

*For the director of music. A song.*
*A psalm.*

¹ Shout for joy to God, all the
   earth!
²    Sing the glory of his name;
      make his praise glorious.
³ Say to God, "How awesome are
   your deeds!
   So great is your power
      that your enemies cringe
         before you.
⁴ All the earth bows down to you;
   they sing praise to you,
   they sing the praises of your
      name." ᵃ

⁵ Come and see what God has
   done,
   his awesome deeds for
      mankind!
⁶ He turned the sea into dry land,
   they passed through the
      waters on foot—
   come, let us rejoice in him.
⁷ He rules forever by his power,
   his eyes watch the nations—
   let not the rebellious rise up
      against him.

⁸ Praise our God, all peoples,
   let the sound of his praise be
      heard;
⁹ he has preserved our lives
   and kept our feet from
      slipping.
¹⁰ For you, God, tested us;
   you refined us like silver.
¹¹ You brought us into prison

and laid burdens on our backs.
¹² You let people ride over our
   heads;
   we went through fire and
      water,
   but you brought us to a place
      of abundance.

¹³ I will come to your temple with
   burnt offerings
   and fulfill my vows to you—
¹⁴ vows my lips promised and my
   mouth spoke
   when I was in trouble.
¹⁵ I will sacrifice fat animals to you
   and an offering of rams;
   I will offer bulls and goats.

¹⁶ Come and hear, all you who fear
   God;
   let me tell you what he has
      done for me.
¹⁷ I cried out to him with my
   mouth;
   his praise was on my tongue.
¹⁸ If I had cherished sin in my
   heart,
   the Lord would not have
      listened;
¹⁹ but God has surely listened
   and has heard my prayer.
²⁰ Praise be to God,
   who has not rejected my
      prayer
   or withheld his love from me!

## Psalm 67 ᵇ

*For the director of music. With stringed*
*instruments. A psalm. A song.*

¹ May God be gracious to us and
   bless us
   and make his face shine on
      us— ᶜ
² so that your ways may be known
   on earth,

---

ᵃ 4  The Hebrew has *Selah* (a word of uncertain meaning) here and at the end of verses 7 and 15.
ᵇ In Hebrew texts 67:1-7 is numbered 67:2-8.    ᶜ 1  The Hebrew has *Selah* (a word of uncertain
meaning) here and at the end of verse 4.

your salvation among all
nations.

³ May the peoples praise you,
God;
may all the peoples praise you.

⁴ May the nations be glad and sing
for joy,
for you rule the peoples with
equity
and guide the nations of the
earth.

⁵ May the peoples praise you,
God;
may all the peoples praise you.

⁶ The land yields its harvest;
God, our God, blesses us.

⁷ May God bless us still,
so that all the ends of the earth
will fear him.

## Psalm 68ᵃ

*For the director of music. Of David.*
*A psalm. A song.*

¹ May God arise, may his enemies
be scattered;
may his foes flee before him.

² May you blow them away like
smoke—
as wax melts before the fire,
may the wicked perish before
God.

³ But may the righteous be glad
and rejoice before God;
may they be happy and joyful.

⁴ Sing to God, sing in praise of his
name,
extol him who rides on the
cloudsᵇ;
rejoice before him—his name
is the LORD.

⁵ A father to the fatherless, a
defender of widows,

is God in his holy dwelling.

⁶ God sets the lonely in families,ᶜ
he leads out the prisoners with
singing;
but the rebellious live in a sun-
scorched land.

⁷ When you, God, went out before
your people,
when you marched through
the wilderness,ᵈ

⁸ the earth shook, the heavens
poured down rain,
before God, the One of Sinai,
before God, the God of Israel.

⁹ You gave abundant showers,
O God;
you refreshed your weary
inheritance.

¹⁰ Your people settled in it,
and from your bounty, God,
you provided for the poor.

¹¹ The Lord announces the word,
and the women who proclaim
it are a mighty throng:

¹² "Kings and armies flee in haste;
the women at home divide the
plunder.

¹³ Even while you sleep among the
sheep pens,ᵉ
the wings of my dove are
sheathed with silver,
its feathers with shining
gold."

¹⁴ When the Almightyᶠ scattered
the kings in the land,
it was like snow fallen on
Mount Zalmon.

¹⁵ Mount Bashan, majestic
mountain,
Mount Bashan, rugged
mountain,

¹⁶ why gaze in envy, you rugged
mountain,

---

ᵃ In Hebrew texts 68:1-35 is numbered 68:2-36.
*rides through the deserts*   ᶜ 6 Or *the desolate in a homeland*
*word of uncertain meaning)* here and at the end of verses 19 and 32.
*the saddlebags*   ᶠ 14 Hebrew *Shaddai*

ᵇ 4 Or *name, / prepare the way for him who*   ᵈ 7 The Hebrew has *Selah* (a
ᵉ 13 Or *the campfires;* or

at the mountain where God
　chooses to reign,
　where the LORD himself will
　　dwell forever?
17 The chariots of God are tens of
　thousands
　and thousands of thousands;
　the Lord has come from Sinai
　　into his sanctuary.[a]
18 When you ascended on high,
　you took many captives;
　you received gifts from
　　people,
even from[b] the rebellious—
　that you,[c] LORD God, might
　　dwell there.

19 Praise be to the Lord, to God our
　Savior,
　who daily bears our burdens.
20 Our God is a God who saves;
　from the Sovereign LORD
　comes escape from death.
21 Surely God will crush the heads
　of his enemies,
　the hairy crowns of those who
　　go on in their sins.
22 The Lord says, "I will bring them
　from Bashan;
　I will bring them from the
　　depths of the sea,
23 that your feet may wade in the
　blood of your foes,
　while the tongues of your dogs
　　have their share."

24 Your procession, God, has come
　into view,
　the procession of my God and
　　King into the sanctuary.
25 In front are the singers, after
　them the musicians;
　with them are the young
　　women playing the
　　timbrels.

26 Praise God in the great
　congregation;
　praise the LORD in the
　　assembly of Israel.
27 There is the little tribe of
　Benjamin, leading them,
　there the great throng of
　　Judah's princes,
　and there the princes of
　　Zebulun and of Naphtali.

28 Summon your power, God[d];
　show us your strength, our God,
　　as you have done before.
29 Because of your temple at
　Jerusalem
　kings will bring you gifts.
30 Rebuke the beast among the
　reeds,
　the herd of bulls among the
　　calves of the nations.
Humbled, may the beast bring
　bars of silver.
Scatter the nations who
　delight in war.
31 Envoys will come from Egypt;
　Cush[e] will submit herself to
　　God.

32 Sing to God, you kingdoms of the
　earth,
　sing praise to the Lord,
33 to him who rides across the
　highest heavens, the
　　ancient heavens,
　who thunders with mighty
　　voice.
34 Proclaim the power of God,
　whose majesty is over Israel,
　whose power is in the heavens.
35 You, God, are awesome in your
　sanctuary;
　the God of Israel gives power
　　and strength to his people.

Praise be to God!

---

a 17 Probable reading of the original Hebrew text; Masoretic Text *Lord is among them at Sinai in
holiness*　　b 18 Or *gifts for people,* / *even*　　c 18 Or *they*　　d 28 Many Hebrew manuscripts,
Septuagint and Syriac; most Hebrew manuscripts *Your God has summoned power for you*
e 31 That is, the upper Nile region

## Psalm 69[a]

*For the director of music. To the tune of
"Lilies." Of David.*

1 Save me, O God,
   for the waters have come up to
      my neck.
2 I sink in the miry depths,
   where there is no foothold.
I have come into the deep
      waters;
   the floods engulf me.
3 I am worn out calling for help;
   my throat is parched.
My eyes fail,
   looking for my God.
4 Those who hate me without
      reason
   outnumber the hairs of my
      head;
many are my enemies without
      cause,
   those who seek to destroy me.
I am forced to restore
   what I did not steal.

5 You, God, know my folly;
   my guilt is not hidden from
      you.

6 Lord, the LORD Almighty,
   may those who hope in you
   not be disgraced because of
      me;
God of Israel,
   may those who seek you
   not be put to shame because of
      me.
7 For I endure scorn for your sake,
   and shame covers my face.
8 I am a foreigner to my own
      family,
   a stranger to my own mother's
      children;
9 for zeal for your house consumes
      me,
   and the insults of those who
      insult you fall on me.

10 When I weep and fast,
   I must endure scorn;
11 when I put on sackcloth,
   people make sport of me.
12 Those who sit at the gate mock
      me,
   and I am the song of the
      drunkards.

13 But I pray to you, LORD,
   in the time of your favor;
in your great love, O God,
   answer me with your sure
      salvation.
14 Rescue me from the mire,
   do not let me sink;
deliver me from those who hate
      me,
   from the deep waters.
15 Do not let the floodwaters engulf
      me
or the depths swallow me up
   or the pit close its mouth over
      me.

16 Answer me, LORD, out of the
      goodness of your love;
   in your great mercy turn to
      me.
17 Do not hide your face from your
      servant;
   answer me quickly, for I am in
      trouble.
18 Come near and rescue me;
   deliver me because of my foes.

19 You know how I am scorned,
   disgraced and shamed;
   all my enemies are before you.
20 Scorn has broken my heart
   and has left me helpless;
I looked for sympathy, but there
      was none,
   for comforters, but I found
      none.
21 They put gall in my food
   and gave me vinegar for my
      thirst.

---

a In Hebrew texts 69:1-36 is numbered 69:2-37.

²²May the table set before them
　　become a snare;
　　may it become retribution
　　　and[a] a trap.
²³May their eyes be darkened so
　　they cannot see,
　　and their backs be bent
　　　forever.
²⁴Pour out your wrath on them;
　　let your fierce anger overtake
　　　them.
²⁵May their place be deserted;
　　let there be no one to dwell in
　　　their tents.
²⁶For they persecute those you
　　wound
　　and talk about the pain of
　　　those you hurt.
²⁷Charge them with crime upon
　　crime;
　　do not let them share in your
　　　salvation.
²⁸May they be blotted out of the
　　book of life
　　and not be listed with the
　　　righteous.
²⁹But as for me, afflicted and in
　　pain —
　　may your salvation, God,
　　　protect me.

³⁰I will praise God's name in song
　　and glorify him with
　　　thanksgiving.
³¹This will please the LORD more
　　than an ox,
　　more than a bull with its horns
　　　and hooves.
³²The poor will see and be glad —
　　you who seek God, may your
　　　hearts live!
³³The LORD hears the needy
　　and does not despise his
　　　captive people.
³⁴Let heaven and earth praise
　　him,

the seas and all that move in
　　them,
³⁵for God will save Zion
　　and rebuild the cities of
　　　Judah.
Then people will settle there and
　　possess it;
³⁶　the children of his servants
　　will inherit it,
　　and those who love his name
　　　will dwell there.

## Psalm 70[b]

*For the director of music. Of David.
A petition.*

¹Hasten, O God, to save me;
　　come quickly, LORD, to help
　　　me.

²May those who want to take my
　　life
　　be put to shame and
　　　confusion;
　　may all who desire my ruin
　　　be turned back in disgrace.
³May those who say to me, "Aha!
　　Aha!"
　　turn back because of their
　　　shame.
⁴But may all who seek you
　　rejoice and be glad in you;
　　may those who long for your
　　　saving help always say,
　　"The LORD is great!"

⁵But as for me, I am poor and
　　needy;
　　come quickly to me, O God.
You are my help and my
　　deliverer;
　　LORD, do not delay.

## Psalm 71

¹In you, LORD, I have taken
　　refuge;
　　let me never be put to shame.

---

[a] 22 Or *snare / and their fellowship become*　　[b] In Hebrew texts 70:1-5 is numbered 70:2-6.

² In your righteousness, rescue
  me and deliver me;
    turn your ear to me and save
      me.
³ Be my rock of refuge,
    to which I can always go;
  give the command to save me,
    for you are my rock and my
      fortress.
⁴ Deliver me, my God, from the
    hand of the wicked,
    from the grasp of those who
      are evil and cruel.

⁵ For you have been my hope,
    Sovereign LORD,
  my confidence since my
    youth.
⁶ From birth I have relied on you;
    you brought me forth from my
      mother's womb.
  I will ever praise you.
⁷ I have become a sign to many;
    you are my strong refuge.
⁸ My mouth is filled with your
    praise,
    declaring your splendor all
      day long.

⁹ Do not cast me away when I am
    old;
  do not forsake me when my
    strength is gone.
¹⁰ For my enemies speak against
    me;
    those who wait to kill me
      conspire together.
¹¹ They say, "God has forsaken
    him;
  pursue him and seize him,
    for no one will rescue him."
¹² Do not be far from me, my God;
    come quickly, God, to help me.
¹³ May my accusers perish in
    shame;
  may those who want to harm
    me
    be covered with scorn and
      disgrace.

¹⁴ As for me, I will always have
    hope;
  I will praise you more and
    more.
¹⁵ My mouth will tell of your
    righteous deeds,
    of your saving acts all day
      long—
  though I know not how to
    relate them all.
¹⁶ I will come and proclaim your
    mighty acts, Sovereign
      LORD;
  I will proclaim your righteous
    deeds, yours alone.
¹⁷ Since my youth, God, you have
    taught me,
  and to this day I declare your
    marvelous deeds.
¹⁸ Even when I am old and gray,
    do not forsake me, my God,
  till I declare your power to the
    next generation,
    your mighty acts to all who are
      to come.

¹⁹ Your righteousness, God,
    reaches to the heavens,
  you who have done great
    things.
  Who is like you, God?
²⁰ Though you have made me see
    troubles,
    many and bitter,
  you will restore my life again;
  from the depths of the earth
    you will again bring me up.
²¹ You will increase my honor
    and comfort me once more.

²² I will praise you with the harp
    for your faithfulness, my
      God;
  I will sing praise to you with the
    lyre,
  Holy One of Israel.
²³ My lips will shout for joy
    when I sing praise to you—
  I whom you have delivered.

24 My tongue will tell of your
        righteous acts
    all day long,
for those who wanted to harm me
        have been put to shame and
        confusion.

## Psalm 72

*Of Solomon.*

1 Endow the king with your
        justice, O God,
    the royal son with your
        righteousness.
2 May he judge your people in
        righteousness,
    your afflicted ones with
        justice.

3 May the mountains bring
        prosperity to the people,
    the hills the fruit of
        righteousness.
4 May he defend the afflicted
        among the people
    and save the children of the
        needy;
    may he crush the oppressor.
5 May he endure[a] as long as the
        sun,
    as long as the moon, through
        all generations.
6 May he be like rain falling on a
        mown field,
    like showers watering the
        earth.
7 In his days may the righteous
        flourish
    and prosperity abound till the
        moon is no more.

8 May he rule from sea to sea
        and from the River[b] to the
        ends of the earth.
9 May the desert tribes bow before
        him

and his enemies lick the dust.
10 May the kings of Tarshish and of
        distant shores
    bring tribute to him.
    May the kings of Sheba and Seba
        present him gifts.
11 May all kings bow down to him
    and all nations serve him.

12 For he will deliver the needy who
        cry out,
    the afflicted who have no one
        to help.
13 He will take pity on the weak
        and the needy
    and save the needy from
        death.
14 He will rescue them from
        oppression and violence,
    for precious is their blood in
        his sight.

15 Long may he live!
    May gold from Sheba be given
        him.
    May people ever pray for him
    and bless him all day long.
16 May grain abound throughout
        the land;
    on the tops of the hills may it
        sway.
    May the crops flourish like
        Lebanon
    and thrive[c] like the grass of
        the field.
17 May his name endure forever;
    may it continue as long as the
        sun.

Then all nations will be blessed
        through him,[d]
    and they will call him blessed.

18 Praise be to the LORD God, the
        God of Israel,
    who alone does marvelous
        deeds.

---

a 5 Septuagint; Hebrew *You will be feared*    b 8 That is, the Euphrates    c 16 Probable
reading of the original Hebrew text; Masoretic Text *Lebanon, / from the city*    d 17 *Or will use
his name in blessings* (see Gen. 48:20)

<sup>19</sup>Praise be to his glorious name
forever;
may the whole earth be filled
with his glory.
Amen and Amen.

<sup>20</sup>This concludes the prayers
of David son of Jesse.

# BOOK III

*Psalms 73 – 89*

Psalm 73

*A psalm of Asaph.*

<sup>1</sup>Surely God is good to Israel,
to those who are pure in heart.

<sup>2</sup>But as for me, my feet had almost
slipped;
I had nearly lost my foothold.

<sup>3</sup>For I envied the arrogant
when I saw the prosperity of
the wicked.

<sup>4</sup>They have no struggles;
their bodies are healthy and
strong.<sup>a</sup>

<sup>5</sup>They are free from common
human burdens;
they are not plagued by
human ills.

<sup>6</sup>Therefore pride is their
necklace;
they clothe themselves with
violence.

<sup>7</sup>From their callous hearts comes
iniquity<sup>b</sup>;
their evil imaginations have
no limits.

<sup>8</sup>They scoff, and speak with
malice;
with arrogance they threaten
oppression.

<sup>9</sup>Their mouths lay claim to
heaven,
and their tongues take
possession of the earth.

<sup>10</sup>Therefore their people turn to
them
and drink up waters in
abundance.<sup>c</sup>

<sup>11</sup>They say, "How would God know?
Does the Most High know
anything?"

<sup>12</sup>This is what the wicked are like —
always free of care, they go on
amassing wealth.

<sup>13</sup>Surely in vain I have kept my
heart pure
and have washed my hands in
innocence.

<sup>14</sup>All day long I have been
afflicted,
and every morning brings new
punishments.

<sup>15</sup>If I had spoken out like that,
I would have betrayed your
children.

<sup>16</sup>When I tried to understand all
this,
it troubled me deeply

<sup>17</sup>till I entered the sanctuary of
God;
then I understood their final
destiny.

<sup>18</sup>Surely you place them on
slippery ground;
you cast them down to ruin.

<sup>19</sup>How suddenly are they destroyed,
completely swept away by
terrors!

<sup>20</sup>They are like a dream when one
awakes;
when you arise, Lord,
you will despise them as
fantasies.

<sup>21</sup>When my heart was grieved
and my spirit embittered,

---

<sup>a</sup> 4 With a different word division of the Hebrew; Masoretic Text *struggles at their death; /
their bodies are healthy*   <sup>b</sup> 7 Syriac (see also Septuagint); Hebrew *Their eyes bulge with fat*
<sup>c</sup> 10 The meaning of the Hebrew for this verse is uncertain.

²² I was senseless and ignorant;
    I was a brute beast before you.
²³ Yet I am always with you;
    you hold me by my right hand.
²⁴ You guide me with your counsel,
    and afterward you will take
    me into glory.
²⁵ Whom have I in heaven but you?
    And earth has nothing I desire
    besides you.
²⁶ My flesh and my heart may fail,
    but God is the strength of my
    heart
    and my portion forever.
²⁷ Those who are far from you will
    perish;
    you destroy all who are
    unfaithful to you.
²⁸ But as for me, it is good to be
    near God.
    I have made the Sovereign
    Lord my refuge;
    I will tell of all your deeds.

## Psalm 74

*A maskil[a] of Asaph.*

¹ O God, why have you rejected us
    forever?
    Why does your anger smolder
    against the sheep of your
    pasture?
² Remember the nation you
    purchased long ago,
    the people of your inheritance,
    whom you redeemed —
    Mount Zion, where you dwelt.
³ Turn your steps toward these
    everlasting ruins,
    all this destruction the enemy
    has brought on the
    sanctuary.
⁴ Your foes roared in the place
    where you met with us;

they set up their standards as
    signs.
⁵ They behaved like men wielding
    axes
    to cut through a thicket of
    trees.
⁶ They smashed all the carved
    paneling
    with their axes and hatchets.
⁷ They burned your sanctuary to
    the ground;
    they defiled the dwelling place
    of your Name.
⁸ They said in their hearts,
    "We will crush them
    completely!"
    They burned every place
    where God was worshiped
    in the land.

⁹ We are given no signs from God;
    no prophets are left,
    and none of us knows how
    long this will be.
¹⁰ How long will the enemy mock
    you, God?
    Will the foe revile your name
    forever?
¹¹ Why do you hold back your
    hand, your right hand?
    Take it from the folds of your
    garment and destroy
    them!

¹² But God is my King from long
    ago;
    he brings salvation on the
    earth.

¹³ It was you who split open the sea
    by your power;
    you broke the heads of the
    monster in the waters.
¹⁴ It was you who crushed the
    heads of Leviathan
    and gave it as food to the
    creatures of the desert.

---

a Title: Probably a literary or musical term

15 It was you who opened up
    springs and streams;
  you dried up the ever-flowing
    rivers.
16 The day is yours, and yours also
    the night;
  you established the sun and
    moon.
17 It was you who set all the
    boundaries of the earth;
  you made both summer and
    winter.

18 Remember how the enemy has
    mocked you, LORD,
  how foolish people have
    reviled your name.
19 Do not hand over the life of your
    dove to wild beasts;
  do not forget the lives of your
    afflicted people forever.
20 Have regard for your covenant,
  because haunts of violence
    fill the dark places of the
    land.
21 Do not let the oppressed retreat
    in disgrace;
  may the poor and needy praise
    your name.
22 Rise up, O God, and defend your
    cause;
  remember how fools mock you
    all day long.
23 Do not ignore the clamor of your
    adversaries,
  the uproar of your enemies,
    which rises continually.

## Psalm 75[a]

*For the director of music. To the tune
of "Do Not Destroy." A psalm of Asaph.
A song.*

1 We praise you, God,
  we praise you, for your Name
    is near;

people tell of your wonderful
    deeds.

2 You say, "I choose the appointed
    time;
  it is I who judge with equity.
3 When the earth and all its
    people quake,
  it is I who hold its pillars firm.[b]
4 To the arrogant I say, 'Boast no
    more,'
  and to the wicked, 'Do not lift
    up your horns.[c]
5 Do not lift your horns against
    heaven;
  do not speak so defiantly.'"

6 No one from the east or the west
  or from the desert can exalt
    themselves.
7 It is God who judges:
  He brings one down, he exalts
    another.
8 In the hand of the LORD is a cup
  full of foaming wine mixed
    with spices;
  he pours it out, and all the
    wicked of the earth
  drink it down to its very dregs.

9 As for me, I will declare this
    forever;
  I will sing praise to the God of
    Jacob,
10 who says, "I will cut off the horns
    of all the wicked,
  but the horns of the righteous
    will be lifted up."

## Psalm 76[d]

*For the director of music. With stringed
instruments. A psalm of Asaph. A song.*

1 God is renowned in Judah;
  in Israel his name is great.
2 His tent is in Salem,
  his dwelling place in Zion.

---

[a] In Hebrew texts 75:1-10 is numbered 75:2-11. meaning) here.   [c] 4 *Horns* here symbolize strength; also in verses 5 and 10.   [b] 3 The Hebrew has *Selah* (a word of uncertain   [d] In Hebrew texts 76:1-12 is numbered 76:2-13.

3 There he broke the flashing
      arrows,
   the shields and the swords, the
      weapons of war.[a]

4 You are radiant with light,
   more majestic than mountains
      rich with game.
5 The valiant lie plundered,
   they sleep their last sleep;
   not one of the warriors
      can lift his hands.
6 At your rebuke, God of Jacob,
   both horse and chariot lie still.

7 It is you alone who are to be
      feared.
   Who can stand before you
      when you are angry?
8 From heaven you pronounced
      judgment,
   and the land feared and was
      quiet—
9 when you, God, rose up to judge,
   to save all the afflicted of the
      land.
10 Surely your wrath against
      mankind brings you praise,
   and the survivors of your
      wrath are restrained.[b]

11 Make vows to the LORD your God
      and fulfill them;
   let all the neighboring lands
      bring gifts to the One to be
      feared.
12 He breaks the spirit of rulers;
   he is feared by the kings of the
      earth.

## Psalm 77[c]

*For the director of music. For Jeduthun.
   Of Asaph. A psalm.*

1 I cried out to God for help;
   I cried out to God to hear me.

2 When I was in distress, I sought
      the Lord;
   at night I stretched out
      untiring hands,
   and I would not be comforted.

3 I remembered you, God, and I
      groaned;
   I meditated, and my spirit
      grew faint.[d]
4 You kept my eyes from closing;
   I was too troubled to speak.
5 I thought about the former days,
   the years of long ago;
6 I remembered my songs in the
      night.
   My heart meditated and my
      spirit asked:

7 "Will the Lord reject forever?
   Will he never show his favor
      again?
8 Has his unfailing love vanished
      forever?
   Has his promise failed for all
      time?
9 Has God forgotten to be merciful?
   Has he in anger withheld his
      compassion?"

10 Then I thought, "To this I will
      appeal:
   the years when the Most High
      stretched out his right
      hand.
11 I will remember the deeds of the
      LORD;
   yes, I will remember your
      miracles of long ago.
12 I will consider all your works
      and meditate on all your
      mighty deeds."

13 Your ways, God, are holy.
   What god is as great as our
      God?

---

*a 3* The Hebrew has *Selah* (a word of uncertain meaning) here and at the end of verse 9.
*b 10* Or *Surely the wrath of mankind brings you praise, / and with the remainder of wrath you arm yourself    c* In Hebrew texts 77:1-20 is numbered 77:2-21.    *d 3* The Hebrew has *Selah* (a word of uncertain meaning) here and at the end of verses 9 and 15.

<sup>14</sup>You are the God who performs
  miracles;
    you display your power among
      the peoples.
<sup>15</sup>With your mighty arm you
  redeemed your people,
    the descendants of Jacob and
      Joseph.

<sup>16</sup>The waters saw you, God,
    the waters saw you and
      writhed;
    the very depths were
      convulsed.
<sup>17</sup>The clouds poured down water,
    the heavens resounded with
      thunder;
    your arrows flashed back and
      forth.
<sup>18</sup>Your thunder was heard in the
  whirlwind,
    your lightning lit up the world;
    the earth trembled and
      quaked.
<sup>19</sup>Your path led through the sea,
    your way through the mighty
      waters,
    though your footprints were
      not seen.

<sup>20</sup>You led your people like a flock
    by the hand of Moses and
      Aaron.

## Psalm 78

*A maskil<sup>a</sup> of Asaph.*

<sup>1</sup>My people, hear my teaching;
    listen to the words of my
      mouth.
<sup>2</sup>I will open my mouth with a
  parable;
    I will utter hidden things,
      things from of old —
<sup>3</sup>things we have heard and
  known,
    things our ancestors have told
      us.

<sup>4</sup>We will not hide them from their
  descendants;
    we will tell the next generation
      the praiseworthy deeds of the
        LORD,
    his power, and the wonders he
      has done.
<sup>5</sup>He decreed statutes for Jacob
    and established the law in
      Israel,
    which he commanded our
      ancestors
    to teach their children,
<sup>6</sup>so the next generation would
  know them,
    even the children yet to be
      born,
    and they in turn would tell
      their children.
<sup>7</sup>Then they would put their trust
  in God
    and would not forget his deeds
    but would keep his
      commands.
<sup>8</sup>They would not be like their
  ancestors —
    a stubborn and rebellious
      generation,
    whose hearts were not loyal to
      God,
    whose spirits were not faithful
      to him.

<sup>9</sup>The men of Ephraim, though
  armed with bows,
    turned back on the day of
      battle;
<sup>10</sup>they did not keep God's
  covenant
    and refused to live by his law.
<sup>11</sup>They forgot what he had done,
    the wonders he had shown
      them.
<sup>12</sup>He did miracles in the sight of
  their ancestors
    in the land of Egypt, in the
      region of Zoan.

<sup>a</sup> Title: Probably a literary or musical term

¹³ He divided the sea and led them
through;
he made the water stand up
like a wall.
¹⁴ He guided them with the cloud
by day
and with light from the fire all
night.
¹⁵ He split the rocks in the
wilderness
and gave them water as
abundant as the seas;
¹⁶ he brought streams out of a
rocky crag
and made water flow down
like rivers.
¹⁷ But they continued to sin against
him,
rebelling in the wilderness
against the Most High.
¹⁸ They willfully put God to the
test
by demanding the food they
craved.
¹⁹ They spoke against God;
they said, "Can God really
spread a table in the
wilderness?
²⁰ True, he struck the rock,
and water gushed out,
streams flowed abundantly,
but can he also give us bread?
Can he supply meat for his
people?"
²¹ When the LORD heard them, he
was furious;
his fire broke out against
Jacob,
and his wrath rose against
Israel,
²² for they did not believe in God
or trust in his deliverance.
²³ Yet he gave a command to the
skies above
and opened the doors of the
heavens;
²⁴ he rained down manna for the
people to eat,

he gave them the grain of
heaven.
²⁵ Human beings ate the bread of
angels;
he sent them all the food they
could eat.
²⁶ He let loose the east wind from
the heavens
and by his power made the
south wind blow.
²⁷ He rained meat down on them
like dust,
birds like sand on the
seashore.
²⁸ He made them come down
inside their camp,
all around their tents.
²⁹ They ate till they were gorged —
he had given them what they
craved.
³⁰ But before they turned from
what they craved,
even while the food was still in
their mouths,
³¹ God's anger rose against them;
he put to death the sturdiest
among them,
cutting down the young men
of Israel.
³² In spite of all this, they kept on
sinning;
in spite of his wonders, they
did not believe.
³³ So he ended their days in
futility
and their years in terror.
³⁴ Whenever God slew them, they
would seek him;
they eagerly turned to him
again.
³⁵ They remembered that God was
their Rock,
that God Most High was their
Redeemer.
³⁶ But then they would flatter him
with their mouths,
lying to him with their
tongues;

37 their hearts were not loyal to
    him,
      they were not faithful to his
        covenant.
38 Yet he was merciful;
      he forgave their iniquities
        and did not destroy them.
    Time after time he restrained his
        anger
      and did not stir up his full
        wrath.
39 He remembered that they were
        but flesh,
      a passing breeze that does not
        return.

40 How often they rebelled against
        him in the wilderness
      and grieved him in the
        wasteland!
41 Again and again they put God to
        the test;
      they vexed the Holy One of
        Israel.
42 They did not remember his
        power—
      the day he redeemed them
        from the oppressor,
43 the day he displayed his signs in
        Egypt,
      his wonders in the region of
        Zoan.
44 He turned their river into
        blood;
      they could not drink from
        their streams.
45 He sent swarms of flies that
        devoured them,
      and frogs that devastated
        them.
46 He gave their crops to the
        grasshopper,
      their produce to the locust.
47 He destroyed their vines with
        hail
      and their sycamore-figs with
        sleet.
48 He gave over their cattle to the
        hail,

their livestock to bolts of
        lightning.
49 He unleashed against them his
        hot anger,
      his wrath, indignation and
        hostility—
    a band of destroying angels.
50 He prepared a path for his anger;
      he did not spare them from
        death
    but gave them over to the
        plague.
51 He struck down all the firstborn
        of Egypt,
      the firstfruits of manhood in
        the tents of Ham.
52 But he brought his people out
        like a flock;
      he led them like sheep
        through the wilderness.
53 He guided them safely, so they
        were unafraid;
      but the sea engulfed their
        enemies.
54 And so he brought them to the
        border of his holy land,
      to the hill country his right
        hand had taken.
55 He drove out nations before
        them
      and allotted their lands to
        them as an inheritance;
    he settled the tribes of Israel in
        their homes.

56 But they put God to the test
      and rebelled against the Most
        High;
    they did not keep his statutes.
57 Like their ancestors they were
        disloyal and faithless,
      as unreliable as a faulty bow.
58 They angered him with their
        high places;
      they aroused his jealousy with
        their idols.
59 When God heard them, he was
        furious;
      he rejected Israel completely.

60 He abandoned the tabernacle of
  Shiloh,
    the tent he had set up among
      humans.
61 He sent the ark of his might into
  captivity,
    his splendor into the hands of
      the enemy.
62 He gave his people over to the
  sword;
    he was furious with his
      inheritance.
63 Fire consumed their young men,
  and their young women had
    no wedding songs;
64 their priests were put to the
  sword,
    and their widows could not
      weep.
65 Then the Lord awoke as from
  sleep,
    as a warrior wakes from the
      stupor of wine.
66 He beat back his enemies;
    he put them to everlasting
      shame.
67 Then he rejected the tents of
  Joseph,
    he did not choose the tribe of
      Ephraim;
68 but he chose the tribe of Judah,
    Mount Zion, which he loved.
69 He built his sanctuary like the
  heights,
    like the earth that he
      established forever.
70 He chose David his servant
    and took him from the sheep
      pens;
71 from tending the sheep he
  brought him
    to be the shepherd of his
      people Jacob,
      of Israel his inheritance.
72 And David shepherded them
    with integrity of heart;
    with skillful hands he led
      them.

## Psalm 79

*A psalm of Asaph.*

1 O God, the nations have invaded
  your inheritance;
    they have defiled your holy
      temple,
    they have reduced Jerusalem
      to rubble.
2 They have left the dead bodies of
  your servants
    as food for the birds of the sky,
    the flesh of your own people
      for the animals of the wild.
3 They have poured out blood like
  water
    all around Jerusalem,
    and there is no one to bury the
      dead.
4 We are objects of contempt to
  our neighbors,
    of scorn and derision to those
      around us.

5 How long, LORD? Will you be
  angry forever?
    How long will your jealousy
      burn like fire?
6 Pour out your wrath on the
  nations
    that do not acknowledge you,
  on the kingdoms
    that do not call on your name;
7 for they have devoured Jacob
    and devastated his homeland.

8 Do not hold against us the sins of
  past generations;
    may your mercy come quickly
      to meet us,
    for we are in desperate need.
9 Help us, God our Savior,
    for the glory of your name;
    deliver us and forgive our sins
      for your name's sake.
10 Why should the nations say,
    "Where is their God?"

Before our eyes, make known
    among the nations

that you avenge the outpoured
   blood of your servants.
[11] May the groans of the prisoners
      come before you;
   with your strong arm preserve
      those condemned to die.
[12] Pay back into the laps of our
      neighbors seven times
   the contempt they have hurled
      at you, Lord.
[13] Then we your people, the sheep
      of your pasture,
   will praise you forever;
   from generation to generation
      we will proclaim your praise.

Psalm 80[a]

*For the director of music. To the tune of*
*"The Lilies of the Covenant." Of Asaph.*
*A psalm.*

[1] Hear us, Shepherd of Israel,
   you who lead Joseph like a
      flock.
   You who sit enthroned between
      the cherubim,
   shine forth [2] before Ephraim,
      Benjamin and Manasseh.
   Awaken your might;
   come and save us.

[3] Restore us, O God;
   make your face shine on us,
   that we may be saved.

[4] How long, LORD God Almighty,
   will your anger smolder
   against the prayers of your
      people?
[5] You have fed them with the
      bread of tears;
   you have made them drink
      tears by the bowlful.
[6] You have made us an object of
      derision[b] to our neighbors,
   and our enemies mock us.

[7] Restore us, God Almighty;
   make your face shine on us,
   that we may be saved.

[8] You transplanted a vine from
      Egypt;
   you drove out the nations and
      planted it.
[9] You cleared the ground for it,
   and it took root and filled the
      land.
[10] The mountains were covered
      with its shade,
   the mighty cedars with its
      branches.
[11] Its branches reached as far as
      the Sea,[c]
   its shoots as far as the River.[d]

[12] Why have you broken down its
      walls
   so that all who pass by pick its
      grapes?
[13] Boars from the forest ravage it,
   and insects from the fields
      feed on it.
[14] Return to us, God Almighty!
   Look down from heaven and
      see!
   Watch over this vine,
[15]   the root your right hand has
         planted,
   the son[e] you have raised up for
      yourself.
[16] Your vine is cut down, it is
      burned with fire;
   at your rebuke your people
      perish.
[17] Let your hand rest on the man at
      your right hand,
   the son of man you have raised
      up for yourself.
[18] Then we will not turn away from
      you;
   revive us, and we will call on
      your name.

---

[a] In Hebrew texts 80:1-19 is numbered 80:2-20.
text; Masoretic Text *contention*   [c] 11 Probably the Mediterranean   [d] 11 That is, the
Euphrates   [e] 15 Or *branch*      [b] 6 Probable reading of the original Hebrew

¹⁹ Restore us, LORD God Almighty;
    make your face shine on us,
    that we may be saved.


## Psalm 81 [a]

*For the director of music. According to
gittith.[b] Of Asaph.*

¹ Sing for joy to God our strength;
    shout aloud to the God of
    Jacob!
² Begin the music, strike the
    timbrel,
    play the melodious harp and
    lyre.
³ Sound the ram's horn at the New
    Moon,
    and when the moon is full, on
    the day of our festival;
⁴ this is a decree for Israel,
    an ordinance of the God of
    Jacob.
⁵ When God went out against
    Egypt,
    he established it as a statute
    for Joseph.

I heard an unknown voice say:

⁶ "I removed the burden from
    their shoulders;
    their hands were set free from
    the basket.
⁷ In your distress you called and I
    rescued you,
    I answered you out of a
    thundercloud;
    I tested you at the waters of
    Meribah.[c]
⁸ Hear me, my people, and I will
    warn you —
    if you would only listen to me,
    Israel!
⁹ You shall have no foreign god
    among you;

    you shall not worship any god
    other than me.
¹⁰ I am the LORD your God,
    who brought you up out of
    Egypt.
    Open wide your mouth and I will
    fill it.
¹¹ "But my people would not listen
    to me;
    Israel would not submit to me.
¹² So I gave them over to their
    stubborn hearts
    to follow their own devices.
¹³ "If my people would only listen
    to me,
    if Israel would only follow my
    ways,
¹⁴ how quickly I would subdue
    their enemies
    and turn my hand against
    their foes!
¹⁵ Those who hate the LORD would
    cringe before him,
    and their punishment would
    last forever.
¹⁶ But you would be fed with the
    finest of wheat;
    with honey from the rock I
    would satisfy you."


## Psalm 82

*A psalm of Asaph.*

¹ God presides in the great
    assembly;
    he renders judgment among
    the "gods":

² "How long will you[d] defend the
    unjust
    and show partiality to the
    wicked?[c]
³ Defend the weak and the
    fatherless;

---

*a* In Hebrew texts 81:1-16 is numbered 81:2-17.    *b* Title: Probably a musical term
Hebrew has *Selah* (a word of uncertain meaning) here.    *c 7,2* The
*d 2* The Hebrew is plural.

uphold the cause of the poor
and the oppressed.
4 Rescue the weak and the
needy;
deliver them from the hand of
the wicked.

5 "The 'gods' know nothing, they
understand nothing.
They walk about in darkness;
all the foundations of the
earth are shaken.

6 "I said, 'You are "gods";
you are all sons of the Most
High.'
7 But you will die like mere
mortals;
you will fall like every other
ruler."

8 Rise up, O God, judge the
earth,
for all the nations are your
inheritance.

## Psalm 83[a]

*A song. A psalm of Asaph.*

1 O God, do not remain silent;
do not turn a deaf ear,
do not stand aloof, O God.
2 See how your enemies growl,
how your foes rear their
heads.
3 With cunning they conspire
against your people;
they plot against those you
cherish.
4 "Come," they say, "let us destroy
them as a nation,
so that Israel's name is
remembered no more."
5 With one mind they plot
together;
they form an alliance against
you—

6 the tents of Edom and the
Ishmaelites,
of Moab and the Hagrites,
7 Byblos, Ammon and Amalek,
Philistia, with the people of
Tyre.
8 Even Assyria has joined them
to reinforce Lot's
descendants.[b]

9 Do to them as you did to
Midian,
as you did to Sisera and Jabin
at the river Kishon,
10 who perished at Endor
and became like dung on the
ground.
11 Make their nobles like Oreb and
Zeeb,
all their princes like Zebah
and Zalmunna,
12 who said, "Let us take
possession
of the pasturelands of God."

13 Make them like tumbleweed, my
God,
like chaff before the wind.
14 As fire consumes the forest
or a flame sets the mountains
ablaze,
15 so pursue them with your
tempest
and terrify them with your
storm.
16 Cover their faces with shame,
LORD,
so that they will seek your
name.

17 May they ever be ashamed and
dismayed;
may they perish in disgrace.
18 Let them know that you, whose
name is the LORD—
that you alone are the Most
High over all the earth.

---

[a] In Hebrew texts 83:1-18 is numbered 83:2-19.
here.    [b] 8 The Hebrew has *Selah* (a word of
uncertain meaning) here.

## Psalm 84[a]

*For the director of music. According to gittith.[b] Of the Sons of Korah. A psalm.*

1 How lovely is your dwelling place,
      LORD Almighty!
2 My soul yearns, even faints,
      for the courts of the LORD;
   my heart and my flesh cry out
      for the living God.
3 Even the sparrow has found a
         home,
      and the swallow a nest for
         herself,
   where she may have her
         young—
   a place near your altar,
      LORD Almighty, my King and
         my God.
4 Blessed are those who dwell in
      your house;
   they are ever praising you.[c]

5 Blessed are those whose
         strength is in you,
      whose hearts are set on
         pilgrimage.
6 As they pass through the Valley
         of Baka,
      they make it a place of springs;
   the autumn rains also cover it
      with pools.[d]
7 They go from strength to
         strength,
   till each appears before God in
      Zion.

8 Hear my prayer, LORD God
         Almighty;
   listen to me, God of Jacob.
9 Look on our shield,[e] O God;
   look with favor on your
      anointed one.

10 Better is one day in your courts
      than a thousand elsewhere;

I would rather be a doorkeeper
      in the house of my God
   than dwell in the tents of the
      wicked.
11 For the LORD God is a sun and
         shield;
   the LORD bestows favor and
         honor;
   no good thing does he withhold
      from those whose walk is
         blameless.

12 LORD Almighty,
   blessed is the one who trusts
      in you.

## Psalm 85[f]

*For the director of music. Of the Sons of
Korah. A psalm.*

1 You, LORD, showed favor to your
         land;
   you restored the fortunes of
      Jacob.
2 You forgave the iniquity of your
         people
   and covered all their sins.[g]
3 You set aside all your wrath
   and turned from your fierce
      anger.

4 Restore us again, God our
         Savior,
   and put away your displeasure
      toward us.
5 Will you be angry with us
         forever?
   Will you prolong your anger
      through all generations?
6 Will you not revive us again,
   that your people may rejoice in
      you?
7 Show us your unfailing love,
         LORD,
   and grant us your salvation.

---

[a] In Hebrew texts 84:1-12 is numbered 84:2-13.    [b] Title: Probably a musical term
[c] 4 The Hebrew has Selah (a word of uncertain meaning) here and at the end of verse 8.
[d] 6 Or blessings    [e] 9 Or sovereign    [f] In Hebrew texts 85:1-13 is numbered 85:2-14.    [g] 2 The
Hebrew has Selah (a word of uncertain meaning) here.

8 I will listen to what God the
LORD says;
    he promises peace to his
        people, his faithful
        servants—
    but let them not turn to folly.
9 Surely his salvation is near those
      who fear him,
    that his glory may dwell in our
      land.

10 Love and faithfulness meet
      together;
    righteousness and peace kiss
      each other.
11 Faithfulness springs forth from
      the earth,
    and righteousness looks down
      from heaven.
12 The LORD will indeed give what
      is good,
    and our land will yield its
      harvest.
13 Righteousness goes before him
    and prepares the way for his
      steps.

## Psalm 86

*A prayer of David.*

1 Hear me, LORD, and answer
      me,
    for I am poor and needy.
2 Guard my life, for I am faithful to
      you;
    save your servant who trusts
      in you.
    You are my God; 3 have mercy on
      me, Lord,
    for I call to you all day long.
4 Bring joy to your servant, Lord,
    for I put my trust in you.

5 You, Lord, are forgiving and
      good,
    abounding in love to all who
      call to you.
6 Hear my prayer, LORD;
    listen to my cry for mercy.

7 When I am in distress, I call to
      you,
    because you answer me.
8 Among the gods there is none
      like you, Lord;
    no deeds can compare with
      yours.
9 All the nations you have made
      will come and worship before
      you, Lord;
    they will bring glory to your
      name.
10 For you are great and do
      marvelous deeds;
    you alone are God.

11 Teach me your way, LORD,
    that I may rely on your
      faithfulness;
    give me an undivided heart,
    that I may fear your name.
12 I will praise you, Lord my God,
      with all my heart;
    I will glorify your name
      forever.
13 For great is your love toward me;
    you have delivered me from
      the depths,
    from the realm of the dead.

14 Arrogant foes are attacking me,
      O God;
    ruthless people are trying to
      kill me—
    they have no regard for you.
15 But you, Lord, are a
      compassionate and
      gracious God,
    slow to anger, abounding in
      love and faithfulness.
16 Turn to me and have mercy on
      me;
    show your strength in behalf
      of your servant;
    save me, because I serve you
      just as my mother did.
17 Give me a sign of your goodness,
    that my enemies may see it
      and be put to shame,

for you, LORD, have helped me
and comforted me.

## Psalm 87

*Of the Sons of Korah. A psalm. A song.*

[1] He has founded his city on the
holy mountain.
[2] The LORD loves the gates of Zion
more than all the other
dwellings of Jacob.

[3] Glorious things are said of you,
city of God:[a]
[4] "I will record Rahab[b] and
Babylon
among those who
acknowledge me—
Philistia too, and Tyre, along
with Cush[c]—
and will say, 'This one was
born in Zion.' "[d]
[5] Indeed, of Zion it will be said,
"This one and that one were
born in her,
and the Most High himself will
establish her."
[6] The LORD will write in the
register of the peoples:
"This one was born in Zion."

[7] As they make music they will
sing,
"All my fountains are in you."

## Psalm 88[e]

*A song. A psalm of the Sons of Korah.
For the director of music. According
to* mahalath leannoth.[f] *A maskil[g] of
Heman the Ezrahite.*

[1] LORD, you are the God who saves
me;

day and night I cry out to you.
[2] May my prayer come before you;
turn your ear to my cry.

[3] I am overwhelmed with troubles
and my life draws near to
death.
[4] I am counted among those who
go down to the pit;
I am like one without
strength.
[5] I am set apart with the dead,
like the slain who lie in the
grave,
whom you remember no more,
who are cut off from your care.

[6] You have put me in the lowest
pit,
in the darkest depths.
[7] Your wrath lies heavily on me;
you have overwhelmed me
with all your waves.[h]
[8] You have taken from me my
closest friends
and have made me repulsive
to them.
I am confined and cannot
escape;
[9]   my eyes are dim with grief.

I call to you, LORD, every day;
I spread out my hands to you.
[10] Do you show your wonders to
the dead?
Do their spirits rise up and
praise you?
[11] Is your love declared in the
grave,
your faithfulness in
Destruction[i]?
[12] Are your wonders known in the
place of darkness,

---

*a 3* The Hebrew has *Selah* (a word of uncertain meaning) here and at the end of verse 6.    *b 4* A poetic name for Egypt    *c 4* That is, the upper Nile region    *d 4* Or *"I will record concerning those who acknowledge me: / 'This one was born in Zion.' / Hear this, Rahab and Babylon, / and you too, Philistia, Tyre and Cush."*    *e* In Hebrew texts 88:1-18 is numbered 88:2-19.    *f* Title: Possibly a tune, "The Suffering of Affliction"    *g* Title: Probably a literary or musical term    *h 7* The Hebrew has *Selah* (a word of uncertain meaning) here and at the end of verse 10.    *i 11* Hebrew *Abaddon*

or your righteous deeds in the
land of oblivion?

13 But I cry to you for help, LORD;
    in the morning my prayer
        comes before you.
14 Why, LORD, do you reject me
    and hide your face from me?

15 From my youth I have suffered
        and been close to death;
    I have borne your terrors and
        am in despair.
16 Your wrath has swept over me;
    your terrors have destroyed
        me.
17 All day long they surround me
        like a flood;
    they have completely engulfed
        me.
18 You have taken from me friend
        and neighbor —
    darkness is my closest friend.

## Psalm 89[a]

*A maskil[b] of Ethan the Ezrahite.*

1 I will sing of the LORD's great
        love forever;
    with my mouth I will make
        your faithfulness known
        through all generations.
2 I will declare that your love
        stands firm forever,
    that you have established your
        faithfulness in heaven
        itself.
3 You said, "I have made a
        covenant with my chosen
        one,
    I have sworn to David my
        servant,
4 'I will establish your line
        forever
    and make your throne firm
        through all generations.' "[c]

5 The heavens praise your
        wonders, LORD,
    your faithfulness too, in the
        assembly of the holy
        ones.
6 For who in the skies above can
        compare with the LORD?
    Who is like the LORD among
        the heavenly beings?
7 In the council of the holy ones
        God is greatly feared;
    he is more awesome than all
        who surround him.
8 Who is like you, LORD God
        Almighty?
    You, LORD, are mighty,
        and your faithfulness
        surrounds you.

9 You rule over the surging sea;
    when its waves mount up, you
        still them.
10 You crushed Rahab like one of
        the slain;
    with your strong arm you
        scattered your enemies.
11 The heavens are yours, and
        yours also the earth;
    you founded the world and all
        that is in it.
12 You created the north and the
        south;
    Tabor and Hermon sing for joy
        at your name.
13 Your arm is endowed with
        power;
    your hand is strong, your right
        hand exalted.
14 Righteousness and justice are
        the foundation of your
        throne;
    love and faithfulness go before
        you.
15 Blessed are those who have
        learned to acclaim you,

---

[a] In Hebrew texts 89:1-52 is numbered 89:2-53.     [b] Title: Probably a literary or musical term
[c] 4  The Hebrew has *Selah* (a word of uncertain meaning) here and at the end of verses 37, 45
and 48.

who walk in the light of your
     presence, LORD.
16 They rejoice in your name all
        day long;
     they celebrate your
        righteousness.
17 For you are their glory and
        strength,
     and by your favor you exalt our
        horn.[a]
18 Indeed, our shield[b] belongs to
        the LORD,
     our king to the Holy One of
        Israel.

19 Once you spoke in a vision,
     to your faithful people you said:
  "I have bestowed strength on a
        warrior;
     I have raised up a young man
        from among the people.
20 I have found David my servant;
     with my sacred oil I have
        anointed him.
21 My hand will sustain him;
     surely my arm will strengthen
        him.
22 The enemy will not get the better
        of him;
     the wicked will not oppress
        him.
23 I will crush his foes before him
     and strike down his
        adversaries.
24 My faithful love will be with him,
     and through my name his
        horn[c] will be exalted.
25 I will set his hand over the sea,
     his right hand over the rivers.
26 He will call out to me, 'You are
        my Father,
     my God, the Rock my Savior.'
27 And I will appoint him to be my
        firstborn,
     the most exalted of the kings of
        the earth.

28 I will maintain my love to him
        forever,
     and my covenant with him
        will never fail.
29 I will establish his line forever,
     his throne as long as the
        heavens endure.

30 "If his sons forsake my law
     and do not follow my statutes,
31 if they violate my decrees
     and fail to keep my
        commands,
32 I will punish their sin with the
        rod,
     their iniquity with flogging;
33 but I will not take my love from
        him,
     nor will I ever betray my
        faithfulness.
34 I will not violate my covenant
     or alter what my lips have
        uttered.
35 Once for all, I have sworn by my
        holiness—
     and I will not lie to David—
36 that his line will continue
        forever
     and his throne endure before
        me like the sun;
37 it will be established forever like
        the moon,
     the faithful witness in the sky."

38 But you have rejected, you have
        spurned,
     you have been very angry with
        your anointed one.
39 You have renounced the
        covenant with your
        servant
     and have defiled his crown in
        the dust.
40 You have broken through all his
        walls
     and reduced his strongholds
        to ruins.

---

*a* 17 *Horn* here symbolizes strong one.     *b* 18 Or *sovereign*     *c* 24 *Horn* here symbolizes
strength.

41 All who pass by have plundered
　　him;
　　he has become the scorn of his
　　　neighbors.
42 You have exalted the right hand
　　　of his foes;
　　you have made all his enemies
　　　rejoice.
43 Indeed, you have turned back
　　　the edge of his sword
　　and have not supported him in
　　　battle.
44 You have put an end to his
　　　splendor
　　and cast his throne to the
　　　ground.
45 You have cut short the days of
　　　his youth;
　　you have covered him with a
　　　mantle of shame.

46 How long, LORD? Will you hide
　　　yourself forever?
　　How long will your wrath burn
　　　like fire?
47 Remember how fleeting is my
　　　life.
　　For what futility you have
　　　created all humanity!
48 Who can live and not see death,
　　or who can escape the power
　　　of the grave?
49 Lord, where is your former great
　　　love,
　　which in your faithfulness you
　　　swore to David?
50 Remember, Lord, how your
　　　servant has[a] been
　　　mocked,
　　how I bear in my heart the
　　　taunts of all the nations,
51 the taunts with which your
　　　enemies, LORD, have
　　　mocked,
　　with which they have mocked
　　　every step of your
　　　anointed one.

52 Praise be to the LORD forever!
　　Amen and Amen.

## BOOK IV

*Psalms 90–106*

### Psalm 90

*A prayer of Moses the man of God.*

1 Lord, you have been our
　　　dwelling place
　　throughout all generations.
2 Before the mountains were born
　　or you brought forth the whole
　　　world,
　　from everlasting to everlasting
　　　you are God.

3 You turn people back to dust,
　　saying, "Return to dust, you
　　　mortals."
4 A thousand years in your sight
　　are like a day that has just
　　　gone by,
　　or like a watch in the night.
5 Yet you sweep people away in
　　　the sleep of death—
　　they are like the new grass of
　　　the morning:
6 In the morning it springs up
　　　new,
　　but by evening it is dry and
　　　withered.

7 We are consumed by your anger
　　and terrified by your
　　　indignation.
8 You have set our iniquities
　　　before you,
　　our secret sins in the light of
　　　your presence.
9 All our days pass away under
　　　your wrath;
　　we finish our years with a
　　　moan.
10 Our days may come to seventy
　　　years,

---

a 50 Or *your servants have*

or eighty, if our strength
    endures;
yet the best of them are but
    trouble and sorrow,
for they quickly pass, and we
    fly away.
¹¹ If only we knew the power of
    your anger!
Your wrath is as great as the
    fear that is your due.
¹² Teach us to number our days,
    that we may gain a heart of
    wisdom.

¹³ Relent, Lord! How long will it be?
    Have compassion on your
    servants.
¹⁴ Satisfy us in the morning with
    your unfailing love,
that we may sing for joy and be
    glad all our days.
¹⁵ Make us glad for as many days as
    you have afflicted us,
for as many years as we have
    seen trouble.
¹⁶ May your deeds be shown to
    your servants,
your splendor to their
    children.

¹⁷ May the favor[a] of the Lord our
    God rest on us;
establish the work of our
    hands for us —
yes, establish the work of our
    hands.

## Psalm 91

¹ Whoever dwells in the shelter of
    the Most High
will rest in the shadow of the
    Almighty.[b]
² I will say of the Lord, "He is my
    refuge and my fortress,
my God, in whom I trust."

³ Surely he will save you
    from the fowler's snare

and from the deadly
    pestilence.
⁴ He will cover you with his
    feathers,
and under his wings you will
    find refuge;
his faithfulness will be your
    shield and rampart.
⁵ You will not fear the terror of
    night,
nor the arrow that flies by
    day,
⁶ nor the pestilence that stalks in
    the darkness,
nor the plague that destroys at
    midday.
⁷ A thousand may fall at your side,
    ten thousand at your right
    hand,
but it will not come near you.
⁸ You will only observe with your
    eyes
and see the punishment of the
    wicked.

⁹ If you say, "The Lord is my
    refuge,"
and you make the Most High
    your dwelling,
¹⁰ no harm will overtake you,
    no disaster will come near
    your tent.
¹¹ For he will command his angels
    concerning you
to guard you in all your ways;
¹² they will lift you up in their
    hands,
so that you will not strike your
    foot against a stone.
¹³ You will tread on the lion and
    the cobra;
you will trample the great lion
    and the serpent.

¹⁴ "Because he[c] loves me," says the
    Lord, "I will rescue him;
I will protect him, for he
    acknowledges my name.

---

a 17 Or *beauty*    b 1 Hebrew *Shaddai*    c 14 That is, probably the king

15 He will call on me, and I will
   answer him;
  I will be with him in trouble,
   I will deliver him and honor
    him.
16 With long life I will satisfy him
   and show him my salvation."

## Psalm 92ᵃ

*A psalm. A song. For the Sabbath day.*

1 It is good to praise the LORD
   and make music to your name,
    O Most High,
2 proclaiming your love in the
    morning
   and your faithfulness at night,
3 to the music of the ten-stringed
    lyre
   and the melody of the harp.

4 For you make me glad by your
    deeds, LORD;
  I sing for joy at what your
    hands have done.
5 How great are your works,
    LORD,
  how profound your thoughts!
6 Senseless people do not know,
   fools do not understand,
7 that though the wicked spring
    up like grass
  and all evildoers flourish,
   they will be destroyed forever.

8 But you, LORD, are forever
    exalted.

9 For surely your enemies, LORD,
   surely your enemies will
    perish;
  all evildoers will be scattered.
10 You have exalted my hornᵇ like
    that of a wild ox;
  fine oils have been poured on
    me.
11 My eyes have seen the defeat of
   my adversaries;

  my ears have heard the rout of
    my wicked foes.

12 The righteous will flourish like a
    palm tree,
  they will grow like a cedar of
    Lebanon;
13 planted in the house of the
    LORD,
  they will flourish in the courts
    of our God.
14 They will still bear fruit in old
    age,
  they will stay fresh and
    green,
15 proclaiming, "The LORD is
    upright;
  he is my Rock, and there is no
    wickedness in him."

## Psalm 93

1 The LORD reigns, he is robed in
    majesty;
  the LORD is robed in majesty
    and armed with strength;
  indeed, the world is
    established, firm and
    secure.
2 Your throne was established
    long ago;
  you are from all eternity.

3 The seas have lifted up, LORD,
  the seas have lifted up their
    voice;
  the seas have lifted up their
    pounding waves.
4 Mightier than the thunder of the
    great waters,
  mightier than the breakers of
    the sea —
  the LORD on high is mighty.

5 Your statutes, LORD, stand
    firm;
  holiness adorns your house
    for endless days.

---

ᵃ In Hebrew texts 92:1-15 is numbered 92:2-16.    ᵇ 10 *Horn* here symbolizes strength.

## Psalm 94

1 The LORD is a God who avenges.
   O God who avenges, shine
      forth.
2 Rise up, Judge of the earth;
   pay back to the proud what
      they deserve.
3 How long, LORD, will the wicked,
   how long will the wicked be
      jubilant?

4 They pour out arrogant words;
   all the evildoers are full of
      boasting.
5 They crush your people, LORD;
   they oppress your inheritance.
6 They slay the widow and the
      foreigner;
   they murder the fatherless.
7 They say, "The LORD does not
      see;
   the God of Jacob takes no
      notice."

8 Take notice, you senseless ones
      among the people;
   you fools, when will you
      become wise?
9 Does he who fashioned the ear
      not hear?
   Does he who formed the eye
      not see?
10 Does he who disciplines nations
      not punish?
   Does he who teaches mankind
      lack knowledge?
11 The LORD knows all human
      plans;
   he knows that they are futile.

12 Blessed is the one you discipline,
      LORD,
   the one you teach from your
      law;
13 you grant them relief from days
      of trouble,
   till a pit is dug for the wicked.
14 For the LORD will not reject his
      people;

he will never forsake his
      inheritance.
15 Judgment will again be founded
      on righteousness,
   and all the upright in heart
      will follow it.

16 Who will rise up for me against
      the wicked?
   Who will take a stand for me
      against evildoers?
17 Unless the LORD had given me
      help,
   I would soon have dwelt in the
      silence of death.
18 When I said, "My foot is
      slipping,"
   your unfailing love, LORD,
      supported me.
19 When anxiety was great within
      me,
   your consolation brought me
      joy.

20 Can a corrupt throne be allied
      with you—
   a throne that brings on misery
      by its decrees?
21 The wicked band together
      against the righteous
   and condemn the innocent to
      death.
22 But the LORD has become my
      fortress,
   and my God the rock in whom
      I take refuge.
23 He will repay them for their sins
   and destroy them for their
      wickedness;
   the LORD our God will destroy
      them.

## Psalm 95

1 Come, let us sing for joy to the
      LORD;
   let us shout aloud to the Rock
      of our salvation.
2 Let us come before him with
      thanksgiving

and extol him with music and
song.

3 For the LORD is the great God,
 the great King above all gods.
4 In his hand are the depths of the
  earth,
 and the mountain peaks
  belong to him.
5 The sea is his, for he made it,
 and his hands formed the dry
  land.

6 Come, let us bow down in
  worship,
 let us kneel before the LORD
  our Maker;
7 for he is our God
 and we are the people of his
  pasture,
 the flock under his care.

Today, if only you would hear his
 voice,
8 "Do not harden your hearts as
  you did at Meribah,*a*
 as you did that day at Massah*b*
  in the wilderness,
9 where your ancestors tested me;
 they tried me, though they had
  seen what I did.
10 For forty years I was angry with
  that generation;
 I said, 'They are a people
  whose hearts go astray,
 and they have not known my
  ways.'
11 So I declared on oath in my anger,
 'They shall never enter my
  rest.'"

## Psalm 96

1 Sing to the LORD a new song;
 sing to the LORD, all the earth.
2 Sing to the LORD, praise his
  name;
 proclaim his salvation day
  after day.

3 Declare his glory among the
  nations,
 his marvelous deeds among
  all peoples.

4 For great is the LORD and most
  worthy of praise;
 he is to be feared above all
  gods.
5 For all the gods of the nations
  are idols,
 but the LORD made the
  heavens.
6 Splendor and majesty are before
  him;
 strength and glory are in his
  sanctuary.

7 Ascribe to the LORD, all you
  families of nations,
 ascribe to the LORD glory and
  strength.
8 Ascribe to the LORD the glory
  due his name;
 bring an offering and come
  into his courts.
9 Worship the LORD in the
  splendor of his*c* holiness;
 tremble before him, all the
  earth.
10 Say among the nations, "The
  LORD reigns."
 The world is firmly
  established, it cannot be
  moved;
 he will judge the peoples with
  equity.

11 Let the heavens rejoice, let the
  earth be glad;
 let the sea resound, and all
  that is in it.
12 Let the fields be jubilant, and
  everything in them;
 let all the trees of the forest
  sing for joy.
13 Let all creation rejoice before the
  LORD, for he comes,

*a 8 Meribah means quarreling.*   *b 8 Massah means testing.*   *c 9 Or LORD with the splendor of*

he comes to judge the earth.
He will judge the world in
righteousness
and the peoples in his
faithfulness.

## Psalm 97

[1] The LORD reigns, let the earth be
glad;
let the distant shores rejoice.
[2] Clouds and thick darkness
surround him;
righteousness and justice
are the foundation of his
throne.
[3] Fire goes before him
and consumes his foes on
every side.
[4] His lightning lights up the world;
the earth sees and trembles.
[5] The mountains melt like wax
before the LORD,
before the Lord of all the
earth.
[6] The heavens proclaim his
righteousness,
and all peoples see his glory.

[7] All who worship images are put
to shame,
those who boast in idols —
worship him, all you gods!

[8] Zion hears and rejoices
and the villages of Judah are
glad
because of your judgments,
LORD.
[9] For you, LORD, are the Most High
over all the earth;
you are exalted far above all
gods.
[10] Let those who love the LORD
hate evil,
for he guards the lives of his
faithful ones

and delivers them from the
hand of the wicked.
[11] Light shines[a] on the righteous
and joy on the upright in
heart.
[12] Rejoice in the LORD, you who are
righteous,
and praise his holy name.

## Psalm 98

*A psalm.*

[1] Sing to the LORD a new song,
for he has done marvelous
things;
his right hand and his holy arm
have worked salvation for him.
[2] The LORD has made his salvation
known
and revealed his righteousness
to the nations.
[3] He has remembered his love
and his faithfulness to Israel;
all the ends of the earth have
seen
the salvation of our God.

[4] Shout for joy to the LORD, all the
earth,
burst into jubilant song with
music;
[5] make music to the LORD with the
harp,
with the harp and the sound of
singing,
[6] with trumpets and the blast of
the ram's horn —
shout for joy before the LORD,
the King.

[7] Let the sea resound, and
everything in it,
the world, and all who live in
it.
[8] Let the rivers clap their hands,
let the mountains sing
together for joy;

a 11 One Hebrew manuscript and ancient versions (see also 112:4); most Hebrew manuscripts
*Light is sown*

⁹ let them sing before the LORD,
   for he comes to judge the
      earth.
He will judge the world in
   righteousness
   and the peoples with equity.

## Psalm 99

¹ The LORD reigns,
   let the nations tremble;
he sits enthroned between the
   cherubim,
   let the earth shake.
² Great is the LORD in Zion;
   he is exalted over all the
      nations.
³ Let them praise your great and
      awesome name —
   he is holy.

⁴ The King is mighty, he loves
      justice —
   you have established equity;
in Jacob you have done
   what is just and right.
⁵ Exalt the LORD our God
   and worship at his footstool;
   he is holy.

⁶ Moses and Aaron were among
      his priests,
   Samuel was among those who
      called on his name;
they called on the LORD
   and he answered them.
⁷ He spoke to them from the pillar
      of cloud;
   they kept his statutes and the
      decrees he gave them.

⁸ LORD our God,
   you answered them;
you were to Israel a forgiving
      God,
   though you punished their
      misdeeds.ᵃ
⁹ Exalt the LORD our God

and worship at his holy
      mountain,
   for the LORD our God is holy.

## Psalm 100

*A psalm. For giving grateful praise.*

¹ Shout for joy to the LORD, all the
      earth.
²    Worship the LORD with
         gladness;
   come before him with joyful
      songs.
³ Know that the LORD is God.
   It is he who made us, and we
      are hisᵇ;
   we are his people, the sheep of
      his pasture.

⁴ Enter his gates with
      thanksgiving
   and his courts with praise;
   give thanks to him and praise
      his name.
⁵ For the LORD is good and his love
      endures forever;
   his faithfulness continues
      through all generations.

## Psalm 101

*Of David. A psalm.*

¹ I will sing of your love and justice;
   to you, LORD, I will sing praise.
² I will be careful to lead a
      blameless life —
   when will you come to me?

I will conduct the affairs of my
      house
   with a blameless heart.
³ I will not look with approval
   on anything that is vile.

I hate what faithless people do;
   I will have no part in it.
⁴ The perverse of heart shall be far
   from me;

ᵃ 8 Or *God, / an avenger of the wrongs done to them*    ᵇ 3 Or *and not we ourselves*

I will have nothing to do with
what is evil.

5 Whoever slanders their neighbor
in secret,
I will put to silence;
whoever has haughty eyes and a
proud heart,
I will not tolerate.

6 My eyes will be on the faithful in
the land,
that they may dwell with me;
the one whose walk is blameless
will minister to me.

7 No one who practices deceit
will dwell in my house;
no one who speaks falsely
will stand in my presence.

8 Every morning I will put to
silence
all the wicked in the land;
I will cut off every evildoer
from the city of the LORD.

## Psalm 102[a]

*A prayer of an afflicted person who has
grown weak and pours out a lament
before the LORD.*

1 Hear my prayer, LORD;
let my cry for help come to you.
2 Do not hide your face from me
when I am in distress.
Turn your ear to me;
when I call, answer me
quickly.

3 For my days vanish like smoke;
my bones burn like glowing
embers.
4 My heart is blighted and
withered like grass;
I forget to eat my food.
5 In my distress I groan aloud
and am reduced to skin and
bones.

6 I am like a desert owl,
like an owl among the ruins.
7 I lie awake; I have become
like a bird alone on a roof.
8 All day long my enemies taunt
me;
those who rail against me use
my name as a curse.
9 For I eat ashes as my food
and mingle my drink with tears
10 because of your great wrath,
for you have taken me up and
thrown me aside.
11 My days are like the evening
shadow;
I wither away like grass.

12 But you, LORD, sit enthroned
forever;
your renown endures through
all generations.
13 You will arise and have
compassion on Zion,
for it is time to show favor to
her;
the appointed time has come.
14 For her stones are dear to your
servants;
her very dust moves them to
pity.
15 The nations will fear the name of
the LORD,
all the kings of the earth will
revere your glory.
16 For the LORD will rebuild Zion
and appear in his glory.
17 He will respond to the prayer of
the destitute;
he will not despise their plea.
18 Let this be written for a future
generation,
that a people not yet created
may praise the LORD:
19 "The LORD looked down from
his sanctuary on high,
from heaven he viewed the
earth,

---

[a] In Hebrew texts 102:1-28 is numbered 102:2-29.

20 to hear the groans of the
     prisoners
  and release those condemned
     to death."
21 So the name of the LORD will be
     declared in Zion
  and his praise in Jerusalem
22 when the peoples and the
     kingdoms
  assemble to worship the LORD.

23 In the course of my life[a] he broke
     my strength;
  he cut short my days.
24 So I said:
  "Do not take me away, my God,
     in the midst of my days;
  your years go on through all
     generations.
25 In the beginning you laid the
     foundations of the earth,
  and the heavens are the work
     of your hands.
26 They will perish, but you
     remain;
  they will all wear out like a
     garment.
  Like clothing you will change
     them
  and they will be discarded.
27 But you remain the same,
  and your years will never
     end.
28 The children of your servants
     will live in your presence;
  their descendants will be
     established before you."

Psalm 103

Of David.

1 Praise the LORD, my soul;
  all my inmost being, praise his
     holy name.
2 Praise the LORD, my soul,
  and forget not all his
     benefits—

3 who forgives all your sins
  and heals all your diseases,
4 who redeems your life from the
     pit
  and crowns you with love and
     compassion,
5 who satisfies your desires with
     good things
  so that your youth is renewed
     like the eagle's.

6 The LORD works righteousness
  and justice for all the
     oppressed.

7 He made known his ways to
     Moses,
  his deeds to the people of
     Israel:
8 The LORD is compassionate and
     gracious,
  slow to anger, abounding in
     love.
9 He will not always accuse,
  nor will he harbor his anger
     forever;
10 he does not treat us as our sins
     deserve
  or repay us according to our
     iniquities.
11 For as high as the heavens are
     above the earth,
  so great is his love for those
     who fear him;
12 as far as the east is from the west,
  so far has he removed our
     transgressions from us.

13 As a father has compassion on
     his children,
  so the LORD has compassion
     on those who fear him;
14 for he knows how we are formed,
  he remembers that we are
     dust.
15 The life of mortals is like grass,
  they flourish like a flower of
     the field;

a 23 Or By his power

<sup>16</sup> the wind blows over it and it is
  gone,
  and its place remembers it no
  more.
<sup>17</sup> But from everlasting to
  everlasting
  the LORD's love is with those
  who fear him,
  and his righteousness with
  their children's children—
<sup>18</sup> with those who keep his covenant
  and remember to obey his
  precepts.

<sup>19</sup> The LORD has established his
  throne in heaven,
  and his kingdom rules over all.

<sup>20</sup> Praise the LORD, you his angels,
  you mighty ones who do his
  bidding,
  who obey his word.
<sup>21</sup> Praise the LORD, all his heavenly
  hosts,
  you his servants who do his
  will.
<sup>22</sup> Praise the LORD, all his works
  everywhere in his dominion.

Praise the LORD, my soul.

## Psalm 104

<sup>1</sup> Praise the LORD, my soul.

LORD my God, you are very
  great;
  you are clothed with splendor
  and majesty.

<sup>2</sup> The LORD wraps himself in light
  as with a garment;
  he stretches out the heavens
  like a tent
<sup>3</sup>   and lays the beams of his
  upper chambers on their
  waters.
He makes the clouds his chariot
  and rides on the wings of the
  wind.

<sup>4</sup> He makes winds his
  messengers,<sup>a</sup>
  flames of fire his servants.

<sup>5</sup> He set the earth on its
  foundations;
  it can never be moved.
<sup>6</sup> You covered it with the watery
  depths as with a garment;
  the waters stood above the
  mountains.
<sup>7</sup> But at your rebuke the waters
  fled,
  at the sound of your thunder
  they took to flight;
<sup>8</sup> they flowed over the mountains,
  they went down into the
  valleys,
  to the place you assigned for
  them.
<sup>9</sup> You set a boundary they cannot
  cross;
  never again will they cover the
  earth.

<sup>10</sup> He makes springs pour water
  into the ravines;
  it flows between the
  mountains.
<sup>11</sup> They give water to all the beasts
  of the field;
  the wild donkeys quench their
  thirst.
<sup>12</sup> The birds of the sky nest by the
  waters;
  they sing among the branches.
<sup>13</sup> He waters the mountains from
  his upper chambers;
  the land is satisfied by the fruit
  of his work.
<sup>14</sup> He makes grass grow for the
  cattle,
  and plants for people to
  cultivate—
  bringing forth food from the
  earth:
<sup>15</sup> wine that gladdens human
  hearts,

<sup>a</sup> 4  Or angels

oil to make their faces shine,
and bread that sustains their
hearts.
<sup>16</sup>The trees of the LORD are well
watered,
the cedars of Lebanon that he
planted.
<sup>17</sup>There the birds make their
nests;
the stork has its home in the
junipers.
<sup>18</sup>The high mountains belong to
the wild goats;
the crags are a refuge for the
hyrax.
<sup>19</sup>He made the moon to mark the
seasons,
and the sun knows when to go
down.
<sup>20</sup>You bring darkness, it becomes
night,
and all the beasts of the forest
prowl.
<sup>21</sup>The lions roar for their prey
and seek their food from God.
<sup>22</sup>The sun rises, and they steal
away;
they return and lie down in
their dens.
<sup>23</sup>Then people go out to their
work,
to their labor until evening.
<sup>24</sup>How many are your works,
LORD!
In wisdom you made them all;
the earth is full of your
creatures.
<sup>25</sup>There is the sea, vast and
spacious,
teeming with creatures
beyond number—
living things both large and
small.
<sup>26</sup>There the ships go to and fro,
and Leviathan, which you
formed to frolic there.

<sup>27</sup>All creatures look to you
to give them their food at the
proper time.
<sup>28</sup>When you give it to them,
they gather it up;
when you open your hand,
they are satisfied with good
things.
<sup>29</sup>When you hide your face,
they are terrified;
when you take away their breath,
they die and return to the dust.
<sup>30</sup>When you send your Spirit,
they are created,
and you renew the face of the
ground.

<sup>31</sup>May the glory of the LORD
endure forever;
may the LORD rejoice in his
works—
<sup>32</sup>he who looks at the earth, and it
trembles,
who touches the mountains,
and they smoke.

<sup>33</sup>I will sing to the LORD all my life;
I will sing praise to my God as
long as I live.
<sup>34</sup>May my meditation be pleasing
to him,
as I rejoice in the LORD.
<sup>35</sup>But may sinners vanish from the
earth
and the wicked be no more.

Praise the LORD, my soul.

Praise the LORD.<sup>a</sup>


## Psalm 105

<sup>1</sup>Give praise to the LORD,
proclaim his name;
make known among the
nations what he has done.
<sup>2</sup>Sing to him, sing praise to him;
tell of all his wonderful acts;
<sup>3</sup>Glory in his holy name;

---

<sup>a</sup> 35 Hebrew *Hallelu Yah*; in the Septuagint this line stands at the beginning of Psalm 105.

let the hearts of those who
        seek the LORD rejoice.
4 Look to the LORD and his
        strength;
    seek his face always.

5 Remember the wonders he has
        done,
    his miracles, and the
        judgments he
        pronounced,
6 you his servants, the
        descendants of Abraham,
    his chosen ones, the children
        of Jacob.
7 He is the LORD our God;
    his judgments are in all the
        earth.

8 He remembers his covenant
        forever,
    the promise he made, for a
        thousand generations,
9 the covenant he made with
        Abraham,
    the oath he swore to Isaac.
10 He confirmed it to Jacob as a
        decree,
    to Israel as an everlasting
        covenant:
11 "To you I will give the land of
        Canaan
    as the portion you will
        inherit."

12 When they were but few in
        number,
    few indeed, and strangers in it,
13 they wandered from nation to
        nation,
    from one kingdom to another.
14 He allowed no one to oppress
        them;
    for their sake he rebuked
        kings:
15 "Do not touch my anointed ones;
    do my prophets no harm."

16 He called down famine on the
        land

and destroyed all their
        supplies of food;
17 and he sent a man before
        them —
    Joseph, sold as a slave.
18 They bruised his feet with
        shackles,
    his neck was put in irons,
19 till what he foretold came to
        pass,
    till the word of the LORD
        proved him true.
20 The king sent and released him,
    the ruler of peoples set him
        free.
21 He made him master of his
        household,
    ruler over all he possessed,
22 to instruct his princes as he
        pleased
    and teach his elders wisdom.

23 Then Israel entered Egypt;
    Jacob resided as a foreigner in
        the land of Ham.
24 The LORD made his people very
        fruitful;
    he made them too numerous
        for their foes,
25 whose hearts he turned to hate
        his people,
    to conspire against his
        servants.
26 He sent Moses his servant,
    and Aaron, whom he had
        chosen.
27 They performed his signs among
        them,
    his wonders in the land of Ham.
28 He sent darkness and made the
        land dark —
    for had they not rebelled
        against his words?
29 He turned their waters into
        blood,
    causing their fish to die.
30 Their land teemed with frogs,
    which went up into the
        bedrooms of their rulers.

³¹ He spoke, and there came
swarms of flies,
and gnats throughout their
country.
³² He turned their rain into hail,
with lightning throughout
their land;
³³ he struck down their vines and
fig trees
and shattered the trees of their
country.
³⁴ He spoke, and the locusts came,
grasshoppers without number;
³⁵ they ate up every green thing in
their land,
ate up the produce of their
soil.
³⁶ Then he struck down all the
firstborn in their land,
the firstfruits of all their
manhood.
³⁷ He brought out Israel, laden with
silver and gold,
and from among their tribes
no one faltered.
³⁸ Egypt was glad when they left,
because dread of Israel had
fallen on them.

³⁹ He spread out a cloud as a
covering,
and a fire to give light at
night.
⁴⁰ They asked, and he brought
them quail;
he fed them well with the
bread of heaven.
⁴¹ He opened the rock, and water
gushed out;
it flowed like a river in the
desert.

⁴² For he remembered his holy
promise
given to his servant Abraham.
⁴³ He brought out his people with
rejoicing,

his chosen ones with shouts of
joy;
⁴⁴ he gave them the lands of the
nations,
and they fell heir to what
others had toiled for —
⁴⁵ that they might keep his
precepts
and observe his laws.

Praise the LORD.ᵃ

## Psalm 106

¹ Praise the LORD.ᵇ

Give thanks to the LORD, for he is
good;
his love endures forever.

² Who can proclaim the mighty
acts of the LORD
or fully declare his praise?
³ Blessed are those who act justly,
who always do what is right.

⁴ Remember me, LORD, when you
show favor to your people,
come to my aid when you save
them,
⁵ that I may enjoy the prosperity of
your chosen ones,
that I may share in the joy of
your nation
and join your inheritance in
giving praise.

⁶ We have sinned, even as our
ancestors did;
we have done wrong and acted
wickedly.
⁷ When our ancestors were in
Egypt,
they gave no thought to your
miracles;
they did not remember your
many kindnesses,
and they rebelled by the sea,
the Red Sea.ᶜ

---

ᵃ 45 Hebrew *Hallelu Yah*    ᵇ 1 Hebrew *Hallelu Yah*; also in verse 48    ᶜ 7 Or *the Sea of Reeds*;
also in verses 9 and 22

⁸ Yet he saved them for his name's
      sake,
   to make his mighty power
      known.
⁹ He rebuked the Red Sea, and it
      dried up;
   he led them through the
      depths as through a
      desert.
¹⁰ He saved them from the hand of
      the foe;
   from the hand of the enemy he
      redeemed them.
¹¹ The waters covered their
      adversaries;
   not one of them survived.
¹² Then they believed his
      promises
   and sang his praise.

¹³ But they soon forgot what he had
      done
   and did not wait for his plan to
      unfold.
¹⁴ In the desert they gave in to their
      craving;
   in the wilderness they put God
      to the test.
¹⁵ So he gave them what they asked
      for,
   but sent a wasting disease
      among them.

¹⁶ In the camp they grew envious
      of Moses
   and of Aaron, who was
      consecrated to the LORD.
¹⁷ The earth opened up and
      swallowed Dathan;
   it buried the company of
      Abiram.
¹⁸ Fire blazed among their
      followers;
   a flame consumed the wicked.
¹⁹ At Horeb they made a calf
   and worshiped an idol cast
      from metal.
²⁰ They exchanged their glorious
      God

for an image of a bull, which
      eats grass.
²¹ They forgot the God who saved
      them,
   who had done great things in
      Egypt,
²² miracles in the land of Ham
   and awesome deeds by the
      Red Sea.
²³ So he said he would destroy
      them —
   had not Moses, his chosen
      one,
stood in the breach before him
   to keep his wrath from
      destroying them.

²⁴ Then they despised the pleasant
      land;
   they did not believe his
      promise.
²⁵ They grumbled in their tents
   and did not obey the LORD.
²⁶ So he swore to them with
      uplifted hand
   that he would make them fall
      in the wilderness,
²⁷ make their descendants fall
      among the nations
   and scatter them throughout
      the lands.

²⁸ They yoked themselves to the
      Baal of Peor
   and ate sacrifices offered to
      lifeless gods;
²⁹ they aroused the LORD's anger
   by their wicked deeds,
   and a plague broke out among
      them.
³⁰ But Phinehas stood up and
      intervened,
   and the plague was checked.
³¹ This was credited to him as
      righteousness
   for endless generations to
      come.
³² By the waters of Meribah they
      angered the LORD,

and trouble came to Moses
because of them;
<sup>33</sup> for they rebelled against the
Spirit of God,
and rash words came from
Moses' lips.*a*

<sup>34</sup> They did not destroy the
peoples
as the LORD had commanded
them,
<sup>35</sup> but they mingled with the
nations
and adopted their customs.
<sup>36</sup> They worshiped their idols,
which became a snare to
them.
<sup>37</sup> They sacrificed their sons
and their daughters to false
gods.
<sup>38</sup> They shed innocent blood,
the blood of their sons and
daughters,
whom they sacrificed to the idols
of Canaan,
and the land was desecrated
by their blood.
<sup>39</sup> They defiled themselves by what
they did;
by their deeds they prostituted
themselves.

<sup>40</sup> Therefore the LORD was angry
with his people
and abhorred his inheritance.
<sup>41</sup> He gave them into the hands of
the nations,
and their foes ruled over them.
<sup>42</sup> Their enemies oppressed them
and subjected them to their
power.
<sup>43</sup> Many times he delivered them,
but they were bent on
rebellion
and they wasted away in their
sin.
<sup>44</sup> Yet he took note of their distress
when he heard their cry;

<sup>45</sup> for their sake he remembered his
covenant
and out of his great love he
relented.
<sup>46</sup> He caused all who held them
captive
to show them mercy.

<sup>47</sup> Save us, LORD our God,
and gather us from the
nations,
that we may give thanks to your
holy name
and glory in your praise.

<sup>48</sup> Praise be to the LORD, the God of
Israel,
from everlasting to
everlasting.

Let all the people say, "Amen!"

Praise the LORD.

## BOOK V

### *Psalms 107 – 150*

### Psalm 107

<sup>1</sup> Give thanks to the LORD, for he is
good;
his love endures forever.

<sup>2</sup> Let the redeemed of the LORD
tell their story—
those he redeemed from the
hand of the foe,
<sup>3</sup> those he gathered from the
lands,
from east and west, from north
and south.*b*

<sup>4</sup> Some wandered in desert
wastelands,
finding no way to a city where
they could settle.
<sup>5</sup> They were hungry and thirsty,
and their lives ebbed away.
<sup>6</sup> Then they cried out to the LORD
in their trouble,

---

*a 33 Or against his spirit, / and rash words came from his lips*     *b 3 Hebrew north and the sea*

and he delivered them from
their distress.

⁷ He led them by a straight way
to a city where they could
settle.

⁸ Let them give thanks to the
LORD for his unfailing love
and his wonderful deeds for
mankind,

⁹ for he satisfies the thirsty
and fills the hungry with good
things.

¹⁰ Some sat in darkness, in utter
darkness,
prisoners suffering in iron
chains,

¹¹ because they rebelled against
God's commands
and despised the plans of the
Most High.

¹² So he subjected them to bitter
labor;
they stumbled, and there was
no one to help.

¹³ Then they cried to the LORD in
their trouble,
and he saved them from their
distress.

¹⁴ He brought them out of
darkness, the utter
darkness,
and broke away their chains.

¹⁵ Let them give thanks to the
LORD for his unfailing love
and his wonderful deeds for
mankind,

¹⁶ for he breaks down gates of
bronze
and cuts through bars of iron.

¹⁷ Some became fools through
their rebellious ways
and suffered affliction
because of their iniquities.

¹⁸ They loathed all food
and drew near the gates of
death.

¹⁹ Then they cried to the LORD in
their trouble,
and he saved them from their
distress.

²⁰ He sent out his word and healed
them;
he rescued them from the
grave.

²¹ Let them give thanks to the
LORD for his unfailing
love
and his wonderful deeds for
mankind.

²² Let them sacrifice thank
offerings
and tell of his works with
songs of joy.

²³ Some went out on the sea in
ships;
they were merchants on the
mighty waters.

²⁴ They saw the works of the LORD,
his wonderful deeds in the
deep.

²⁵ For he spoke and stirred up a
tempest
that lifted high the waves.

²⁶ They mounted up to the heavens
and went down to the
depths;
in their peril their courage
melted away.

²⁷ They reeled and staggered like
drunkards;
they were at their wits' end.

²⁸ Then they cried out to the LORD
in their trouble,
and he brought them out of
their distress.

²⁹ He stilled the storm to a whisper;
the waves of the sea*a* were
hushed.

³⁰ They were glad when it grew
calm,
and he guided them to their
desired haven.

*a 29* Dead Sea Scrolls; Masoretic Text / *their waves*

31 Let them give thanks to the
LORD for his unfailing love
and his wonderful deeds for
mankind.
32 Let them exalt him in the
assembly of the people
and praise him in the council
of the elders.

33 He turned rivers into a desert,
flowing springs into thirsty
ground,
34 and fruitful land into a salt
waste,
because of the wickedness of
those who lived there.
35 He turned the desert into pools
of water
and the parched ground into
flowing springs;
36 there he brought the hungry to
live,
and they founded a city where
they could settle.
37 They sowed fields and planted
vineyards
that yielded a fruitful harvest;
38 he blessed them, and their
numbers greatly
increased,
and he did not let their herds
diminish.

39 Then their numbers decreased,
and they were humbled
by oppression, calamity and
sorrow;
40 he who pours contempt on
nobles
made them wander in a
trackless waste.
41 But he lifted the needy out of
their affliction
and increased their families
like flocks.
42 The upright see and rejoice,
but all the wicked shut their
mouths.

43 Let the one who is wise heed
these things
and ponder the loving deeds of
the LORD.

## Psalm 108[a]

*A song. A psalm of David.*

1 My heart, O God, is steadfast;
I will sing and make music
with all my soul.
2 Awake, harp and lyre!
I will awaken the dawn.
3 I will praise you, LORD, among
the nations;
I will sing of you among the
peoples.
4 For great is your love, higher
than the heavens;
your faithfulness reaches to
the skies.
5 Be exalted, O God, above the
heavens;
let your glory be over all the
earth.

6 Save us and help us with your
right hand,
that those you love may be
delivered.
7 God has spoken from his
sanctuary:
"In triumph I will parcel out
Shechem
and measure off the Valley of
Sukkoth.
8 Gilead is mine, Manasseh is
mine;
Ephraim is my helmet,
Judah is my scepter.
9 Moab is my washbasin,
on Edom I toss my sandal;
over Philistia I shout in
triumph."
10 Who will bring me to the
fortified city?
Who will lead me to Edom?

a In Hebrew texts 108:1-13 is numbered 108:2-14.

11 Is it not you, God, you who have
        rejected us
    and no longer go out with our
        armies?
12 Give us aid against the enemy,
    for human help is worthless.
13 With God we will gain the
        victory,
    and he will trample down our
        enemies.

## Psalm 109

*For the director of music. Of David.*
*A psalm.*

1 My God, whom I praise,
    do not remain silent,
2 for people who are wicked and
        deceitful
    have opened their mouths
        against me;
    they have spoken against me
        with lying tongues.
3 With words of hatred they
        surround me;
    they attack me without cause.
4 In return for my friendship they
        accuse me,
    but I am a man of prayer.
5 They repay me evil for good,
    and hatred for my friendship.

6 Appoint someone evil to oppose
        my enemy;
    let an accuser stand at his
        right hand.
7 When he is tried, let him be
        found guilty,
    and may his prayers condemn
        him.
8 May his days be few;
    may another take his place of
        leadership.
9 May his children be fatherless
    and his wife a widow.
10 May his children be wandering
        beggars;

may they be driven[a] from their
    ruined homes.
11 May a creditor seize all he has;
    may strangers plunder the
        fruits of his labor.
12 May no one extend kindness to
        him
    or take pity on his fatherless
        children.
13 May his descendants be cut off,
    their names blotted out from
        the next generation.
14 May the iniquity of his fathers
    be remembered before the
        LORD;
    may the sin of his mother
        never be blotted out.
15 May their sins always remain
        before the LORD,
    that he may blot out their
        name from the earth.

16 For he never thought of doing a
        kindness,
    but hounded to death the poor
        and the needy and the
        brokenhearted.
17 He loved to pronounce a curse —
    may it come back on him.
    He found no pleasure in
        blessing —
    may it be far from him.
18 He wore cursing as his garment;
    it entered into his body like
        water,
    into his bones like oil.
19 May it be like a cloak wrapped
        about him,
    like a belt tied forever around
        him.
20 May this be the LORD's payment
        to my accusers,
    to those who speak evil of me.

21 But you, Sovereign LORD,
    help me for your name's sake;
    out of the goodness of your
        love, deliver me.

a 10 Septuagint; Hebrew *sought*

²²For I am poor and needy,
  and my heart is wounded
    within me.
²³I fade away like an evening
    shadow;
  I am shaken off like a locust.
²⁴My knees give way from fasting;
  my body is thin and gaunt.
²⁵I am an object of scorn to my
    accusers;
  when they see me, they shake
    their heads.

²⁶Help me, LORD my God;
  save me according to your
    unfailing love.
²⁷Let them know that it is your
    hand,
  that you, LORD, have done it.
²⁸While they curse, may you
    bless;
  may those who attack me be
    put to shame,
  but may your servant rejoice.
²⁹May my accusers be clothed
    with disgrace
  and wrapped in shame as in a
    cloak.

³⁰With my mouth I will greatly
    extol the LORD;
  in the great throng of
    worshipers I will praise
      him.
³¹For he stands at the right hand of
    the needy,
  to save their lives from those
    who would condemn
      them.

## Psalm 110

*Of David. A psalm.*

¹The LORD says to my lord:ᵃ

  "Sit at my right hand

until I make your enemies
    a footstool for your feet."

²The LORD will extend your
    mighty scepter from Zion,
      saying,
  "Rule in the midst of your
    enemies!"
³Your troops will be willing
    on your day of battle.
  Arrayed in holy splendor,
    your young men will come to
      you
  like dew from the morning's
    womb.ᵇ
⁴The LORD has sworn
    and will not change his mind:
  "You are a priest forever,
    in the order of Melchizedek."
⁵The Lord is at your right hand;ᶜ
  he will crush kings on the day
    of his wrath.
⁶He will judge the nations,
    heaping up the dead
  and crushing the rulers of the
    whole earth.
⁷He will drink from a brook along
    the way,ᵈ
  and so he will lift his head
    high.

## Psalm 111ᵉ

¹Praise the LORD.ᶠ

  I will extol the LORD with all my
    heart
  in the council of the upright
    and in the assembly.

²Great are the works of the LORD;
  they are pondered by all who
    delight in them.
³Glorious and majestic are his
    deeds,

---

ᵃ *1* Or *Lord*    ᵇ *3* The meaning of the Hebrew for this sentence is uncertain.    ᶜ *5* Or *My lord is at your right hand, LORD*    ᵈ *7* The meaning of the Hebrew for this clause is uncertain.
ᵉ This psalm is an acrostic poem, the lines of which begin with the successive letters of the Hebrew alphabet.    ᶠ *1* Hebrew *Hallelu Yah*

and his righteousness endures
forever.
[4] He has caused his wonders to be
remembered;
the LORD is gracious and
compassionate.
[5] He provides food for those who
fear him;
he remembers his covenant
forever.
[6] He has shown his people the
power of his works,
giving them the lands of other
nations.
[7] The works of his hands are
faithful and just;
all his precepts are
trustworthy.
[8] They are established for ever
and ever,
enacted in faithfulness and
uprightness.
[9] He provided redemption for his
people;
he ordained his covenant
forever—
holy and awesome is his name.
[10] The fear of the LORD is the
beginning of wisdom;
all who follow his precepts
have good understanding.
To him belongs eternal praise.

## Psalm 112[a]

[1] Praise the LORD.[b]

Blessed are those who fear the
LORD,
who find great delight in his
commands.

[2] Their children will be mighty in
the land;
the generation of the upright
will be blessed.

[3] Wealth and riches are in their
houses,
and their righteousness
endures forever.
[4] Even in darkness light dawns for
the upright,
for those who are gracious
and compassionate and
righteous.
[5] Good will come to those who are
generous and lend freely,
who conduct their affairs with
justice.

[6] Surely the righteous will never
be shaken;
they will be remembered
forever.
[7] They will have no fear of bad
news;
their hearts are steadfast,
trusting in the LORD.
[8] Their hearts are secure, they will
have no fear;
in the end they will look in
triumph on their foes.
[9] They have freely scattered their
gifts to the poor,
their righteousness endures
forever;
their horn[c] will be lifted high
in honor.
[10] The wicked will see and be
vexed,
they will gnash their teeth and
waste away;
the longings of the wicked will
come to nothing.

## Psalm 113

[1] Praise the LORD.[d]

Praise the LORD, you his
servants;
praise the name of the LORD.

---

*a* This psalm is an acrostic poem, the lines of which begin with the successive letters of
the Hebrew alphabet.    *b 1* Hebrew *Hallelu Yah*    *c 9* *Horn* here symbolizes dignity.
*d 1* Hebrew *Hallelu Yah*; also in verse 9

2 Let the name of the LORD be
praised,
both now and forevermore.
3 From the rising of the sun to the
place where it sets,
the name of the LORD is to be
praised.

4 The LORD is exalted over all the
nations,
his glory above the heavens.
5 Who is like the LORD our God,
the One who sits enthroned on
high,
6 who stoops down to look
on the heavens and the earth?

7 He raises the poor from the dust
and lifts the needy from the
ash heap;
8 he seats them with princes,
with the princes of his people.
9 He settles the childless woman
in her home
as a happy mother of children.

Praise the LORD.

## Psalm 114

1 When Israel came out of Egypt,
Jacob from a people of foreign
tongue,
2 Judah became God's sanctuary,
Israel his dominion.

3 The sea looked and fled,
the Jordan turned back;
4 the mountains leaped like rams,
the hills like lambs.

5 Why was it, sea, that you fled?
Why, Jordan, did you turn
back?
6 Why, mountains, did you leap
like rams,
you hills, like lambs?

7 Tremble, earth, at the presence
of the Lord,
at the presence of the God of
Jacob,

8 who turned the rock into a pool,
the hard rock into springs of
water.

## Psalm 115

1 Not to us, LORD, not to us
but to your name be the glory,
because of your love and
faithfulness.

2 Why do the nations say,
"Where is their God?"
3 Our God is in heaven;
he does whatever pleases
him.
4 But their idols are silver and
gold,
made by human hands.
5 They have mouths, but cannot
speak,
eyes, but cannot see.
6 They have ears, but cannot
hear,
noses, but cannot smell.
7 They have hands, but cannot
feel,
feet, but cannot walk,
nor can they utter a sound
with their throats.
8 Those who make them will be
like them,
and so will all who trust in
them.

9 All you Israelites, trust in the
LORD —
he is their help and shield.
10 House of Aaron, trust in the
LORD —
he is their help and shield.
11 You who fear him, trust in the
LORD —
he is their help and shield.

12 The LORD remembers us and
will bless us:
He will bless his people Israel,
he will bless the house of
Aaron,

[13] he will bless those who fear the
Lord —
small and great alike.

[14] May the Lord cause you to
flourish,
both you and your children.

[15] May you be blessed by the Lord,
the Maker of heaven and
earth.

[16] The highest heavens belong to
the Lord,
but the earth he has given to
mankind.

[17] It is not the dead who praise the
Lord,
those who go down to the
place of silence;

[18] it is we who extol the Lord,
both now and forevermore.

Praise the Lord.[a]

## Psalm 116

[1] I love the Lord, for he heard my
voice;
he heard my cry for mercy.

[2] Because he turned his ear to me,
I will call on him as long as I
live.

[3] The cords of death entangled
me,
the anguish of the grave came
over me;
I was overcome by distress and
sorrow.

[4] Then I called on the name of the
Lord:
"Lord, save me!"

[5] The Lord is gracious and
righteous;
our God is full of compassion.

[6] The Lord protects the unwary;
when I was brought low, he
saved me.

[7] Return to your rest, my soul,
for the Lord has been good to
you.

[8] For you, Lord, have delivered
me from death,
my eyes from tears,
my feet from stumbling,

[9] that I may walk before the Lord
in the land of the living.

[10] I trusted in the Lord when I
said,
"I am greatly afflicted";

[11] in my alarm I said,
"Everyone is a liar."

[12] What shall I return to the Lord
for all his goodness to me?

[13] I will lift up the cup of salvation
and call on the name of the
Lord.

[14] I will fulfill my vows to the Lord
in the presence of all his
people.

[15] Precious in the sight of the
Lord
is the death of his faithful
servants.

[16] Truly I am your servant, Lord;
I serve you just as my mother
did;
you have freed me from my
chains.

[17] I will sacrifice a thank offering
to you
and call on the name of the
Lord.

[18] I will fulfill my vows to the
Lord
in the presence of all his
people,

[19] in the courts of the house of the
Lord —
in your midst, Jerusalem.

Praise the Lord.[a]

[a] 18,19 Hebrew *Hallelu Yah*

## Psalm 117

¹ Praise the LORD, all you nations;
    extol him, all you peoples.
² For great is his love toward us,
    and the faithfulness of the
        LORD endures forever.

Praise the LORD.[a]

## Psalm 118

¹ Give thanks to the LORD, for he is
    good;
    his love endures forever.

² Let Israel say:
    "His love endures forever."
³ Let the house of Aaron say:
    "His love endures forever."
⁴ Let those who fear the LORD
    say:
    "His love endures forever."

⁵ When hard pressed, I cried to
    the LORD;
    he brought me into a spacious
    place.
⁶ The LORD is with me; I will not
    be afraid.
    What can mere mortals do to
    me?
⁷ The LORD is with me; he is my
    helper.
    I look in triumph on my
    enemies.

⁸ It is better to take refuge in the
    LORD
    than to trust in humans.
⁹ It is better to take refuge in the
    LORD
    than to trust in princes.
¹⁰ All the nations surrounded me,
    but in the name of the LORD I
    cut them down.
¹¹ They surrounded me on every
    side,
    but in the name of the LORD I
    cut them down.

¹² They swarmed around me like
    bees,
    but they were consumed as
    quickly as burning thorns;
    in the name of the LORD I cut
    them down.
¹³ I was pushed back and about to
    fall,
    but the LORD helped me.
¹⁴ The LORD is my strength and my
    defense[b];
    he has become my salvation.

¹⁵ Shouts of joy and victory
    resound in the tents of the
    righteous:
    "The LORD's right hand has done
    mighty things!
¹⁶   The LORD's right hand is lifted
    high;
    the LORD's right hand has
    done mighty things!"
¹⁷ I will not die but live,
    and will proclaim what the
    LORD has done.
¹⁸ The LORD has chastened me
    severely,
    but he has not given me over to
    death.
¹⁹ Open for me the gates of the
    righteous;
    I will enter and give thanks to
    the LORD.
²⁰ This is the gate of the LORD
    through which the righteous
    may enter.
²¹ I will give you thanks, for you
    answered me;
    you have become my
    salvation.

²² The stone the builders rejected
    has become the cornerstone;
²³ the LORD has done this,
    and it is marvelous in our
    eyes.
²⁴ The LORD has done it this very
    day;

---

a 2 Hebrew *Hallelu Yah*    b 14 Or *song*

let us rejoice today and be
glad.
²⁵ LORD, save us!
LORD, grant us success!

²⁶ Blessed is he who comes in the
name of the LORD.
From the house of the LORD we
bless you.ᵃ
²⁷ The LORD is God,
and he has made his light
shine on us.
With boughs in hand, join in the
festal procession
upᵇ to the horns of the altar.
²⁸ You are my God, and I will praise
you;
you are my God, and I will
exalt you.
²⁹ Give thanks to the LORD, for he is
good;
his love endures forever.

## Psalm 119ᶜ

### א Aleph

¹ Blessed are those whose ways
are blameless,
who walk according to the law
of the LORD.
² Blessed are those who keep his
statutes
and seek him with all their
heart—
³ they do no wrong
but follow his ways.
⁴ You have laid down precepts
that are to be fully obeyed.
⁵ Oh, that my ways were
steadfast
in obeying your decrees!
⁶ Then I would not be put to
shame

when I consider all your
commands.
⁷ I will praise you with an upright
heart
as I learn your righteous laws.
⁸ I will obey your decrees;
do not utterly forsake me.

### ב Beth

⁹ How can a young person stay on
the path of purity?
By living according to your
word.
¹⁰ I seek you with all my heart;
do not let me stray from your
commands.
¹¹ I have hidden your word in my
heart
that I might not sin against
you.
¹² Praise be to you, LORD;
teach me your decrees.
¹³ With my lips I recount
all the laws that come from
your mouth.
¹⁴ I rejoice in following your
statutes
as one rejoices in great
riches.
¹⁵ I meditate on your precepts
and consider your ways.
¹⁶ I delight in your decrees;
I will not neglect your word.

### ג Gimel

¹⁷ Be good to your servant while I
live,
that I may obey your word.
¹⁸ Open my eyes that I may see
wonderful things in your law.
¹⁹ I am a stranger on earth;
do not hide your commands
from me.

---

ᵃ 26 The Hebrew is plural.    ᵇ 27 Or *Bind the festal sacrifice with ropes / and take it*    ᶜ This
psalm is an acrostic poem, the stanzas of which begin with successive letters of the Hebrew
alphabet; moreover, the verses of each stanza begin with the same letter of the Hebrew
alphabet.

²⁰My soul is consumed with
longing
for your laws at all times.
²¹You rebuke the arrogant, who
are accursed,
those who stray from your
commands.
²²Remove from me their scorn and
contempt,
for I keep your statutes.
²³Though rulers sit together and
slander me,
your servant will meditate on
your decrees.
²⁴Your statutes are my delight;
they are my counselors.

## ד Daleth

²⁵I am laid low in the dust;
preserve my life according to
your word.
²⁶I gave an account of my ways
and you answered me;
teach me your decrees.
²⁷Cause me to understand the way
of your precepts,
that I may meditate on your
wonderful deeds.
²⁸My soul is weary with sorrow;
strengthen me according to
your word.
²⁹Keep me from deceitful ways;
be gracious to me and teach
me your law.
³⁰I have chosen the way of
faithfulness;
I have set my heart on your
laws.
³¹I hold fast to your statutes,
LORD;
do not let me be put to shame.
³²I run in the path of your
commands,
for you have broadened my
understanding.

## ה He

³³Teach me, LORD, the way of your
decrees,
that I may follow it to the end.ᵃ
³⁴Give me understanding, so that I
may keep your law
and obey it with all my heart.
³⁵Direct me in the path of your
commands,
for there I find delight.
³⁶Turn my heart toward your
statutes
and not toward selfish gain.
³⁷Turn my eyes away from
worthless things;
preserve my life according to
your word.ᵇ
³⁸Fulfill your promise to your
servant,
so that you may be feared.
³⁹Take away the disgrace I dread,
for your laws are good.
⁴⁰How I long for your precepts!
In your righteousness preserve
my life.

## ו Waw

⁴¹May your unfailing love come to
me, LORD,
your salvation, according to
your promise;
⁴²then I can answer anyone who
taunts me,
for I trust in your word.
⁴³Never take your word of truth
from my mouth,
for I have put my hope in your
laws.
⁴⁴I will always obey your law,
for ever and ever.
⁴⁵I will walk about in freedom,
for I have sought out your
precepts.
⁴⁶I will speak of your statutes
before kings

---

ᵃ 33 Or *follow it for its reward*   ᵇ 37 Two manuscripts of the Masoretic Text and Dead Sea
Scrolls; most manuscripts of the Masoretic Text *life in your way*

and will not be put to shame,
⁴⁷ for I delight in your commands
because I love them.
⁴⁸ I reach out for your commands,
which I love,
that I may meditate on your
decrees.

### ז Zayin

⁴⁹ Remember your word to your
servant,
for you have given me hope.
⁵⁰ My comfort in my suffering is
this:
Your promise preserves my
life.
⁵¹ The arrogant mock me
unmercifully,
but I do not turn from your
law.
⁵² I remember, LORD, your ancient
laws,
and I find comfort in them.
⁵³ Indignation grips me because of
the wicked,
who have forsaken your law.
⁵⁴ Your decrees are the theme of
my song
wherever I lodge.
⁵⁵ In the night, LORD, I remember
your name,
that I may keep your law.
⁵⁶ This has been my practice:
I obey your precepts.

### ח Heth

⁵⁷ You are my portion, LORD;
I have promised to obey your
words.
⁵⁸ I have sought your face with all
my heart;
be gracious to me according to
your promise.
⁵⁹ I have considered my ways
and have turned my steps to
your statutes.
⁶⁰ I will hasten and not delay
to obey your commands.
⁶¹ Though the wicked bind me with
ropes,
I will not forget your law.
⁶² At midnight I rise to give you
thanks
for your righteous laws.
⁶³ I am a friend to all who fear you,
to all who follow your
precepts.
⁶⁴ The earth is filled with your love,
LORD;
teach me your decrees.

### ט Teth

⁶⁵ Do good to your servant
according to your word, LORD.
⁶⁶ Teach me knowledge and good
judgment,
for I trust your commands.
⁶⁷ Before I was afflicted I went
astray,
but now I obey your word.
⁶⁸ You are good, and what you do is
good;
teach me your decrees.
⁶⁹ Though the arrogant have
smeared me with lies,
I keep your precepts with all
my heart.
⁷⁰ Their hearts are callous and
unfeeling,
but I delight in your law.
⁷¹ It was good for me to be
afflicted
so that I might learn your
decrees.
⁷² The law from your mouth is
more precious to me
than thousands of pieces of
silver and gold.

### י Yodh

⁷³ Your hands made me and
formed me;
give me understanding to
learn your commands.

74 May those who fear you rejoice
    when they see me,
  for I have put my hope in your
    word.
75 I know, LORD, that your laws are
    righteous,
  and that in faithfulness you
    have afflicted me.
76 May your unfailing love be my
    comfort,
  according to your promise to
    your servant.
77 Let your compassion come to me
    that I may live,
  for your law is my delight.
78 May the arrogant be put to
    shame for wronging me
    without cause;
  but I will meditate on your
    precepts.
79 May those who fear you turn to
    me,
  those who understand your
    statutes.
80 May I wholeheartedly follow
    your decrees,
  that I may not be put to shame.

 כ Kaph

81 My soul faints with longing for
    your salvation,
  but I have put my hope in your
    word.
82 My eyes fail, looking for your
    promise;
  I say, "When will you comfort
    me?"
83 Though I am like a wineskin in
    the smoke,
  I do not forget your decrees.
84 How long must your servant
    wait?
  When will you punish my
    persecutors?
85 The arrogant dig pits to trap me,
    contrary to your law.
86 All your commands are
    trustworthy;

help me, for I am being
    persecuted without cause.
87 They almost wiped me from the
    earth,
  but I have not forsaken your
    precepts.
88 In your unfailing love preserve
    my life,
  that I may obey the statutes of
    your mouth.

ל Lamedh

89 Your word, LORD, is eternal;
  it stands firm in the heavens.
90 Your faithfulness continues
    through all generations;
  you established the earth, and
    it endures.
91 Your laws endure to this day,
  for all things serve you.
92 If your law had not been my
    delight,
  I would have perished in my
    affliction.
93 I will never forget your precepts,
  for by them you have
    preserved my life.
94 Save me, for I am yours;
  I have sought out your
    precepts.
95 The wicked are waiting to
    destroy me,
  but I will ponder your statutes.
96 To all perfection I see a limit,
  but your commands are
    boundless.

מ Mem

97 Oh, how I love your law!
  I meditate on it all day long.
98 Your commands are always
    with me
  and make me wiser than my
    enemies.
99 I have more insight than all my
    teachers,
  for I meditate on your statutes.

100 I have more understanding
       than the elders,
    for I obey your precepts.
101 I have kept my feet from every
       evil path
    so that I might obey your
       word.
102 I have not departed from your
       laws,
    for you yourself have taught
       me.
103 How sweet are your words to my
       taste,
    sweeter than honey to my
       mouth!
104 I gain understanding from your
       precepts;
    therefore I hate every wrong
       path.

 נ Nun

105 Your word is a lamp for my feet,
    a light on my path.
106 I have taken an oath and
       confirmed it,
    that I will follow your
       righteous laws.
107 I have suffered much;
    preserve my life, LORD,
       according to your word.
108 Accept, LORD, the willing praise
       of my mouth,
    and teach me your laws.
109 Though I constantly take my life
       in my hands,
    I will not forget your law.
110 The wicked have set a snare
       for me,
    but I have not strayed from
       your precepts.
111 Your statutes are my heritage
       forever;
    they are the joy of my heart.
112 My heart is set on keeping your
       decrees
    to the very end.[a]

ס Samekh

113 I hate double-minded people,
    but I love your law.
114 You are my refuge and my
       shield;
    I have put my hope in your
       word.
115 Away from me, you evildoers,
    that I may keep the commands
       of my God!
116 Sustain me, my God, according
       to your promise, and I will
       live;
    do not let my hopes be dashed.
117 Uphold me, and I will be
       delivered;
    I will always have regard for
       your decrees.
118 You reject all who stray from
       your decrees,
    for their delusions come to
       nothing.
119 All the wicked of the earth you
       discard like dross;
    therefore I love your statutes.
120 My flesh trembles in fear of
       you;
    I stand in awe of your laws.

ע Ayin

121 I have done what is righteous
       and just;
    do not leave me to my
       oppressors.
122 Ensure your servant's well-
       being;
    do not let the arrogant oppress
       me.
123 My eyes fail, looking for your
       salvation,
    looking for your righteous
       promise.
124 Deal with your servant
       according to your love
    and teach me your decrees.

a 112 Or *decrees / for their enduring reward*

125I am your servant; give me
　　discernment
　　that I may understand your
　　statutes.
126It is time for you to act, LORD;
　　your law is being broken.
127Because I love your commands
　　more than gold, more than
　　pure gold,
128and because I consider all your
　　precepts right,
　　I hate every wrong path.

 פ Pe

129Your statutes are wonderful;
　　therefore I obey them.
130The unfolding of your words
　　gives light;
　　it gives understanding to the
　　simple.
131I open my mouth and pant,
　　longing for your commands.
132Turn to me and have mercy
　　on me,
　　as you always do to those who
　　love your name.
133Direct my footsteps according
　　to your word;
　　let no sin rule over me.
134Redeem me from human
　　oppression,
　　that I may obey your
　　precepts.
135Make your face shine on your
　　servant
　　and teach me your decrees.
136Streams of tears flow from my
　　eyes,
　　for your law is not obeyed.

צ Tsadhe

137You are righteous, LORD,
　　and your laws are right.
138The statutes you have laid down
　　are righteous;
　　they are fully trustworthy.
139My zeal wears me out,
　　for my enemies ignore your
　　words.
140Your promises have been
　　thoroughly tested,
　　and your servant loves them.
141Though I am lowly and
　　despised,
　　I do not forget your precepts.
142Your righteousness is
　　everlasting
　　and your law is true.
143Trouble and distress have come
　　upon me,
　　but your commands give me
　　delight.
144Your statutes are always
　　righteous;
　　give me understanding that I
　　may live.

ק Qoph

145I call with all my heart; answer
　　me, LORD,
　　and I will obey your decrees.
146I call out to you; save me
　　and I will keep your statutes.
147I rise before dawn and cry for
　　help;
　　I have put my hope in your
　　word.
148My eyes stay open through the
　　watches of the night,
　　that I may meditate on your
　　promises.
149Hear my voice in accordance
　　with your love;
　　preserve my life, LORD,
　　according to your laws.
150Those who devise wicked
　　schemes are near,
　　but they are far from your law.
151Yet you are near, LORD,
　　and all your commands are
　　true.
152Long ago I learned from your
　　statutes
　　that you established them to
　　last forever.

## ר Resh

<sup>153</sup>Look on my suffering and
  deliver me,
  for I have not forgotten your
    law.
<sup>154</sup>Defend my cause and
    redeem me;
  preserve my life according to
    your promise.
<sup>155</sup>Salvation is far from the wicked,
  for they do not seek out your
    decrees.
<sup>156</sup>Your compassion, LORD, is
    great;
  preserve my life according to
    your laws.
<sup>157</sup>Many are the foes who
    persecute me,
  but I have not turned from
    your statutes.
<sup>158</sup>I look on the faithless with
    loathing,
  for they do not obey your
    word.
<sup>159</sup>See how I love your precepts;
  preserve my life, LORD, in
    accordance with your
    love.
<sup>160</sup>All your words are true;
  all your righteous laws are
    eternal.

## ש Sin and Shin

<sup>161</sup>Rulers persecute me without
    cause,
  but my heart trembles at your
    word.
<sup>162</sup>I rejoice in your promise
  like one who finds great spoil.
<sup>163</sup>I hate and detest falsehood
  but I love your law.
<sup>164</sup>Seven times a day I praise you
  for your righteous laws.
<sup>165</sup>Great peace have those who
    love your law,
  and nothing can make them
    stumble.

<sup>166</sup>I wait for your salvation, LORD,
  and I follow your commands.
<sup>167</sup>I obey your statutes,
  for I love them greatly.
<sup>168</sup>I obey your precepts and your
    statutes,
  for all my ways are known to
    you.

## ת Taw

<sup>169</sup>May my cry come before you,
    LORD;
  give me understanding
    according to your word.
<sup>170</sup>May my supplication come
    before you;
  deliver me according to your
    promise.
<sup>171</sup>May my lips overflow with
    praise,
  for you teach me your
    decrees.
<sup>172</sup>May my tongue sing of your
    word,
  for all your commands are
    righteous.
<sup>173</sup>May your hand be ready to
    help me,
  for I have chosen your
    precepts.
<sup>174</sup>I long for your salvation, LORD,
  and your law gives me delight.
<sup>175</sup>Let me live that I may praise
    you,
  and may your laws sustain me.
<sup>176</sup>I have strayed like a lost sheep.
  Seek your servant,
  for I have not forgotten your
    commands.

## Psalm 120

*A song of ascents.*

<sup>1</sup>I call on the LORD in my distress,
  and he answers me.
<sup>2</sup>Save me, LORD,
  from lying lips
  and from deceitful tongues.

3 What will he do to you,
and what more besides,
you deceitful tongue?
4 He will punish you with a
warrior's sharp arrows,
with burning coals of the
broom bush.

5 Woe to me that I dwell in
Meshek,
that I live among the tents of
Kedar!
6 Too long have I lived
among those who hate peace.
7 I am for peace;
but when I speak, they are for
war.

## Psalm 121

*A song of ascents.*

1 I lift up my eyes to the
mountains—
where does my help come
from?
2 My help comes from the LORD,
the Maker of heaven and
earth.

3 He will not let your foot slip—
he who watches over you will
not slumber;
4 indeed, he who watches over
Israel
will neither slumber nor
sleep.

5 The LORD watches over you—
the LORD is your shade at your
right hand;
6 the sun will not harm you by
day,
nor the moon by night.

7 The LORD will keep you from all
harm—
he will watch over your life;
8 the LORD will watch over your
coming and going
both now and forevermore.

## Psalm 122

*A song of ascents. Of David.*

1 I rejoiced with those who said to
me,
"Let us go to the house of the
LORD."
2 Our feet are standing
in your gates, Jerusalem.

3 Jerusalem is built like a city
that is closely compacted
together.
4 That is where the tribes go
up—
the tribes of the LORD—
to praise the name of the
LORD
according to the statute given
to Israel.
5 There stand the thrones for
judgment,
the thrones of the house
of David.

6 Pray for the peace of
Jerusalem:
"May those who love you be
secure.
7 May there be peace within your
walls
and security within your
citadels."
8 For the sake of my family and
friends,
I will say, "Peace be within
you."
9 For the sake of the house of the
LORD our God,
I will seek your prosperity.

## Psalm 123

*A song of ascents.*

1 I lift up my eyes to you,
to you who sit enthroned in
heaven.
2 As the eyes of slaves look to the
hand of their master,

as the eyes of a female slave
    look to the hand of her
    mistress,
so our eyes look to the LORD our
    God,
    till he shows us his mercy.

3 Have mercy on us, LORD, have
    mercy on us,
for we have endured no end of
    contempt.
4 We have endured no end
    of ridicule from the
    arrogant,
    of contempt from the proud.

## Psalm 124

*A song of ascents. Of David.*

1 If the LORD had not been on our
    side—
    let Israel say—
2 if the LORD had not been on our
    side
    when people attacked us,
3 they would have swallowed us
    alive
    when their anger flared
    against us;
4 the flood would have engulfed
    us,
    the torrent would have swept
    over us,
5 the raging waters
    would have swept us away.

6 Praise be to the LORD,
    who has not let us be torn by
    their teeth.
7 We have escaped like a bird
    from the fowler's snare;
    the snare has been broken,
    and we have escaped.
8 Our help is in the name of the
    LORD,
    the Maker of heaven and
    earth.

## Psalm 125

*A song of ascents.*

1 Those who trust in the LORD are
    like Mount Zion,
    which cannot be shaken but
    endures forever.
2 As the mountains surround
    Jerusalem,
so the LORD surrounds his
    people
    both now and forevermore.

3 The scepter of the wicked will
    not remain
    over the land allotted to the
    righteous,
for then the righteous might use
    their hands to do evil.

4 LORD, do good to those who are
    good,
    to those who are upright in
    heart.
5 But those who turn to crooked
    ways
    the LORD will banish with the
    evildoers.

Peace be on Israel.

## Psalm 126

*A song of ascents.*

1 When the LORD restored the
    fortunes of a Zion,
    we were like those who
    dreamed.b
2 Our mouths were filled with
    laughter,
    our tongues with songs of joy.
Then it was said among the
    nations,
    "The LORD has done great
    things for them."
3 The LORD has done great things
    for us,
    and we are filled with joy.

---

a 1 Or LORD brought back the captives to    b 1 Or those restored to health

4 Restore our fortunes,[a] LORD,
  like streams in the Negev.
5 Those who sow with tears
  will reap with songs of joy.
6 Those who go out weeping,
  carrying seed to sow,
  will return with songs of joy,
  carrying sheaves with them.

## Psalm 127

*A song of ascents. Of Solomon.*

1 Unless the LORD builds the
    house,
  the builders labor in vain.
  Unless the LORD watches over
    the city,
  the guards stand watch in
    vain.
2 In vain you rise early
  and stay up late,
  toiling for food to eat —
  for he grants sleep to[b] those he
    loves.

3 Children are a heritage from the
    LORD,
  offspring a reward from him.
4 Like arrows in the hands of a
    warrior
  are children born in one's
    youth.
5 Blessed is the man
  whose quiver is full of them.
  They will not be put to shame
  when they contend with their
    opponents in court.

## Psalm 128

*A song of ascents.*

1 Blessed are all who fear the
    LORD,
  who walk in obedience to
    him.
2 You will eat the fruit of your
    labor;

blessings and prosperity will
  be yours.
3 Your wife will be like a fruitful
    vine
  within your house;
  your children will be like olive
    shoots
  around your table.
4 Yes, this will be the blessing
  for the man who fears the
    LORD.

5 May the LORD bless you from
    Zion;
  may you see the prosperity of
    Jerusalem
  all the days of your life.
6 May you live to see your
    children's children —
  peace be on Israel.

## Psalm 129

*A song of ascents.*

1 "They have greatly oppressed
    me from my youth,"
  let Israel say;
2 "they have greatly oppressed me
    from my youth,
  but they have not gained the
    victory over me.
3 Plowmen have plowed my
    back
  and made their furrows long.
4 But the LORD is righteous;
  he has cut me free from the
    cords of the wicked."

5 May all who hate Zion
  be turned back in shame.
6 May they be like grass on the
    roof,
  which withers before it can
    grow;
7 a reaper cannot fill his hands
    with it,
  nor one who gathers fill his
    arms.

---

a 4 Or *Bring back our captives*     b 2 Or *eat — / for while they sleep he provides for*

8 May those who pass by not say to
   them,
      "The blessing of the LORD be
         on you;
      we bless you in the name of the
         LORD."

## Psalm 130

*A song of ascents.*

1 Out of the depths I cry to you,
      LORD;
2   Lord, hear my voice.
   Let your ears be attentive
      to my cry for mercy.

3 If you, LORD, kept a record of
      sins,
   Lord, who could stand?
4 But with you there is
      forgiveness,
   so that we can, with reverence,
      serve you.

5 I wait for the LORD, my whole
      being waits,
   and in his word I put my hope.
6 I wait for the Lord
      more than watchmen wait for
         the morning,
      more than watchmen wait for
         the morning.

7 Israel, put your hope in the
      LORD,
   for with the LORD is unfailing
      love
   and with him is full
      redemption.
8 He himself will redeem Israel
   from all their sins.

## Psalm 131

*A song of ascents. Of David.*

1 My heart is not proud, LORD,
   my eyes are not haughty;

I do not concern myself with
      great matters
   or things too wonderful for
      me.
2 But I have calmed and quieted
      myself,
   I am like a weaned child with
      its mother;
   like a weaned child I am
      content.

3 Israel, put your hope in the
      LORD
   both now and forevermore.

## Psalm 132

*A song of ascents.*

1 LORD, remember David
   and all his self-denial.

2 He swore an oath to the LORD,
   he made a vow to the Mighty
      One of Jacob:
3 "I will not enter my house
   or go to my bed,
4 I will allow no sleep to my eyes
   or slumber to my eyelids,
5 till I find a place for the LORD,
   a dwelling for the Mighty One
      of Jacob."

6 We heard it in Ephrathah,
   we came upon it in the fields of
      Jaar:[a]
7 "Let us go to his dwelling place,
   let us worship at his footstool,
      saying,
8 'Arise, LORD, and come to your
      resting place,
   you and the ark of your might.
9 May your priests be clothed with
      your righteousness;
   may your faithful people sing
      for joy.' "

10 For the sake of your servant
      David,

---

[a] 6 Or *heard of it in Ephrathah, / we found it in the fields of Jearim.* (See 1 Chron. 13:5,6) (And no
quotation marks around verses 7-9)

do not reject your anointed
one.

¹¹ The LORD swore an oath to
David,
a sure oath he will not revoke:
"One of your own descendants
I will place on your throne.
¹² If your sons keep my covenant
and the statutes I teach them,
then their sons will sit
on your throne for ever and
ever."

¹³ For the LORD has chosen Zion,
he has desired it for his
dwelling, saying,
¹⁴ "This is my resting place for ever
and ever;
here I will sit enthroned, for I
have desired it.
¹⁵ I will bless her with abundant
provisions;
her poor I will satisfy with food.
¹⁶ I will clothe her priests with
salvation,
and her faithful people will
ever sing for joy.

¹⁷ "Here I will make a horn*a* grow
for David
and set up a lamp for my
anointed one.
¹⁸ I will clothe his enemies with
shame,
but his head will be adorned
with a radiant crown."

## Psalm 133

*A song of ascents. Of David.*

¹ How good and pleasant it is
when God's people live
together in unity!

² It is like precious oil poured on
the head,
running down on the beard,

running down on Aaron's beard,
down on the collar of his robe.
³ It is as if the dew of Hermon
were falling on Mount Zion.
For there the LORD bestows his
blessing,
even life forevermore.

## Psalm 134

*A song of ascents.*

¹ Praise the LORD, all you servants
of the LORD
who minister by night in the
house of the LORD.
² Lift up your hands in the
sanctuary
and praise the LORD.

³ May the LORD bless you from
Zion,
he who is the Maker of heaven
and earth.

## Psalm 135

¹ Praise the LORD.*b*

Praise the name of the LORD;
praise him, you servants of the
LORD,
² you who minister in the house of
the LORD,
in the courts of the house of
our God.

³ Praise the LORD, for the LORD is
good;
sing praise to his name, for
that is pleasant.
⁴ For the LORD has chosen Jacob
to be his own,
Israel to be his treasured
possession.

⁵ I know that the LORD is great,
that our Lord is greater than
all gods.

---

*a* 17 *Horn* here symbolizes strong one, that is, king.
3 and 21                *b* 1 Hebrew *Hallelu Yah*; also in verses

⁶ The LORD does whatever pleases
him,
in the heavens and on the
earth,
in the seas and all their
depths.
⁷ He makes clouds rise from the
ends of the earth;
he sends lightning with the
rain
and brings out the wind from
his storehouses.

⁸ He struck down the firstborn of
Egypt,
the firstborn of people and
animals.
⁹ He sent his signs and wonders
into your midst, O Egypt,
against Pharaoh and all his
servants.
¹⁰ He struck down many nations
and killed mighty kings—
¹¹ Sihon king of the Amorites,
Og king of Bashan,
and all the kings of
Canaan—
¹² and he gave their land as an
inheritance,
an inheritance to his people
Israel.

¹³ Your name, LORD, endures
forever,
your renown, LORD, through
all generations.
¹⁴ For the LORD will vindicate his
people
and have compassion on his
servants.

¹⁵ The idols of the nations are silver
and gold,
made by human hands.
¹⁶ They have mouths, but cannot
speak,
eyes, but cannot see.
¹⁷ They have ears, but cannot hear,
nor is there breath in their
mouths.

¹⁸ Those who make them will be
like them,
and so will all who trust in
them.

¹⁹ All you Israelites, praise the
LORD;
house of Aaron, praise the
LORD;
²⁰ house of Levi, praise the LORD;
you who fear him, praise the
LORD.
²¹ Praise be to the LORD from Zion,
to him who dwells in
Jerusalem.

Praise the LORD.

Psalm 136

¹ Give thanks to the LORD, for he is
good.
*His love endures forever.*
² Give thanks to the God of gods.
*His love endures forever.*
³ Give thanks to the Lord of lords:
*His love endures forever.*

⁴ to him who alone does great
wonders,
*His love endures forever.*
⁵ who by his understanding made
the heavens,
*His love endures forever.*
⁶ who spread out the earth upon
the waters,
*His love endures forever.*
⁷ who made the great lights—
*His love endures forever.*
⁸ the sun to govern the day,
*His love endures forever.*
⁹ the moon and stars to govern the
night;
*His love endures forever.*

¹⁰ to him who struck down the
firstborn of Egypt
*His love endures forever.*
¹¹ and brought Israel out from
among them
*His love endures forever.*

<sup>12</sup> with a mighty hand and
outstretched arm;
*His love endures forever.*

<sup>13</sup> to him who divided the Red Sea<sup>a</sup>
asunder
*His love endures forever.*

<sup>14</sup> and brought Israel through the
midst of it,
*His love endures forever.*

<sup>15</sup> but swept Pharaoh and his army
into the Red Sea;
*His love endures forever.*

<sup>16</sup> to him who led his people
through the wilderness;
*His love endures forever.*

<sup>17</sup> to him who struck down great
kings,
*His love endures forever.*

<sup>18</sup> and killed mighty kings —
*His love endures forever.*

<sup>19</sup> Sihon king of the Amorites
*His love endures forever.*

<sup>20</sup> and Og king of Bashan —
*His love endures forever.*

<sup>21</sup> and gave their land as an
inheritance,
*His love endures forever.*

<sup>22</sup> an inheritance to his servant
Israel.
*His love endures forever.*

<sup>23</sup> He remembered us in our low
estate
*His love endures forever.*

<sup>24</sup> and freed us from our enemies.
*His love endures forever.*

<sup>25</sup> He gives food to every creature.
*His love endures forever.*

<sup>26</sup> Give thanks to the God of
heaven.
*His love endures forever.*

## Psalm 137

<sup>1</sup> By the rivers of Babylon we sat
and wept

when we remembered Zion.
<sup>2</sup> There on the poplars
we hung our harps,
<sup>3</sup> for there our captors asked us for
songs,
our tormentors demanded
songs of joy;
they said, "Sing us one of the
songs of Zion!"

<sup>4</sup> How can we sing the songs of the
Lord
while in a foreign land?
<sup>5</sup> If I forget you, Jerusalem,
may my right hand forget its
skill.
<sup>6</sup> May my tongue cling to the roof
of my mouth
if I do not remember you,
if I do not consider Jerusalem
my highest joy.

<sup>7</sup> Remember, Lord, what the
Edomites did
on the day Jerusalem fell.
"Tear it down," they cried,
"tear it down to its
foundations!"
<sup>8</sup> Daughter Babylon, doomed to
destruction,
happy is the one who repays
you
according to what you have
done to us.
<sup>9</sup> Happy is the one who seizes your
infants
and dashes them against the
rocks.

## Psalm 138

*Of David.*

<sup>1</sup> I will praise you, Lord, with all
my heart;
before the "gods" I will sing
your praise.
<sup>2</sup> I will bow down toward your
holy temple

---

<sup>a</sup> 13 Or *the Sea of Reeds*; also in verse 15

and will praise your name
    for your unfailing love and
        your faithfulness,
for you have so exalted your
        solemn decree
    that it surpasses your fame.
3 When I called, you answered
        me;
    you greatly emboldened me.

4 May all the kings of the earth
        praise you, LORD,
    when they hear what you have
        decreed.
5 May they sing of the ways of the
        LORD,
    for the glory of the LORD is
        great.
6 Though the LORD is exalted, he
        looks kindly on the lowly;
    though lofty, he sees them
        from afar.
7 Though I walk in the midst of
        trouble,
    you preserve my life.
You stretch out your hand
        against the anger of my
        foes;
    with your right hand you save
        me.
8 The LORD will vindicate me;
    your love, LORD, endures
        forever—
    do not abandon the works of
        your hands.

## Psalm 139

*For the director of music. Of David.*
*A psalm.*

1 You have searched me, LORD,
    and you know me.
2 You know when I sit and when I
        rise;
    you perceive my thoughts
        from afar.
3 You discern my going out and
    my lying down;

    you are familiar with all my
        ways.
4 Before a word is on my tongue
    you, LORD, know it
        completely.
5 You hem me in behind and
        before,
    and you lay your hand upon
        me.
6 Such knowledge is too
        wonderful for me,
    too lofty for me to attain.

7 Where can I go from your
        Spirit?
    Where can I flee from your
        presence?
8 If I go up to the heavens, you are
        there;
    if I make my bed in the depths,
        you are there.
9 If I rise on the wings of the
        dawn,
    if I settle on the far side of the
        sea,
10 even there your hand will guide
        me,
    your right hand will hold me
        fast.
11 If I say, "Surely the darkness will
        hide me
    and the light become night
        around me,"
12 even the darkness will not be
        dark to you;
    the night will shine like the
        day,
    for darkness is as light to
        you.

13 For you created my inmost
        being;
    you knit me together in my
        mother's womb.
14 I praise you because I am
        fearfully and wonderfully
        made;
    your works are wonderful,
    I know that full well.

15 My frame was not hidden from
      you
    when I was made in the secret
          place,
    when I was woven together in
          the depths of the earth.
16 Your eyes saw my unformed
      body;
    all the days ordained for me
          were written in your
          book
    before one of them came to
          be.
17 How precious to me are your
      thoughts,[a] God!
    How vast is the sum of them!
18 Were I to count them,
    they would outnumber the
          grains of sand—
    when I awake, I am still with
          you.

19 If only you, God, would slay the
      wicked!
    Away from me, you who are
          bloodthirsty!
20 They speak of you with evil
      intent;
    your adversaries misuse your
          name.
21 Do I not hate those who hate
      you, LORD,
    and abhor those who are in
          rebellion against you?
22 I have nothing but hatred for
      them;
    I count them my enemies.
23 Search me, God, and know my
      heart;
    test me and know my anxious
          thoughts.
24 See if there is any offensive way
      in me,
    and lead me in the way
          everlasting.

## Psalm 140[b]

*For the director of music. A psalm
of David.*

1 Rescue me, LORD, from
      evildoers;
    protect me from the violent,
2 who devise evil plans in their
      hearts
    and stir up war every day.
3 They make their tongues as
      sharp as a serpent's;
    the poison of vipers is on their
          lips.[c]

4 Keep me safe, LORD, from the
      hands of the wicked;
    protect me from the violent,
    who devise ways to trip my
          feet.
5 The arrogant have hidden a
      snare for me;
    they have spread out the cords
          of their net
    and have set traps for me along
          my path.

6 I say to the LORD, "You are my
      God."
    Hear, LORD, my cry for mercy.
7 Sovereign LORD, my strong
      deliverer,
    you shield my head in the day
          of battle.
8 Do not grant the wicked their
      desires, LORD;
    do not let their plans succeed.

9 Those who surround me proudly
      rear their heads;
    may the mischief of their lips
          engulf them.
10 May burning coals fall on them;
    may they be thrown into the
          fire,
    into miry pits, never to rise.

---

[a] 17 Or *How amazing are your thoughts concerning me*     [b] In Hebrew texts 140:1-13 is
numbered 140:2-14.     [c] 3 The Hebrew has *Selah* (a word of uncertain meaning) here and at the
end of verses 5 and 8.

11 May slanderers not be
established in the land;
may disaster hunt down the
violent.
12 I know that the LORD secures
justice for the poor
and upholds the cause of the
needy.
13 Surely the righteous will praise
your name,
and the upright will live in
your presence.

## Psalm 141

*A psalm of David.*

1 I call to you, LORD, come quickly
to me;
hear me when I call to you.
2 May my prayer be set before you
like incense;
may the lifting up of my
hands be like the evening
sacrifice.

3 Set a guard over my mouth,
LORD;
keep watch over the door of my
lips.
4 Do not let my heart be drawn to
what is evil
so that I take part in wicked
deeds
along with those who are
evildoers;
do not let me eat their
delicacies.

5 Let a righteous man strike me —
that is a kindness;
let him rebuke me — that is oil
on my head.
My head will not refuse it,
for my prayer will still be
against the deeds of
evildoers.

6 Their rulers will be thrown
down from the cliffs,
and the wicked will learn
that my words were well
spoken.
7 They will say, "As one plows and
breaks up the earth,
so our bones have been
scattered at the mouth of
the grave."

8 But my eyes are fixed on you,
Sovereign LORD;
in you I take refuge — do not
give me over to death.
9 Keep me safe from the traps set
by evildoers,
from the snares they have laid
for me.
10 Let the wicked fall into their own
nets,
while I pass by in safety.

## Psalm 142[a]

*A maskil[b] of David. When he was in the
cave. A prayer.*

1 I cry aloud to the LORD;
I lift up my voice to the LORD
for mercy.
2 I pour out before him my
complaint;
before him I tell my trouble.

3 When my spirit grows faint
within me,
it is you who watch over my
way.
In the path where I walk
people have hidden a snare for
me.
4 Look and see, there is no one at
my right hand;
no one is concerned for me.
I have no refuge;
no one cares for my life.

---

a In Hebrew texts 142:1-7 is numbered 142:2-8.　　b Title: Probably a literary or musical term

5 I cry to you, LORD;
    I say, "You are my refuge,
    my portion in the land of the
        living."

6 Listen to my cry,
    for I am in desperate need;
rescue me from those who
        pursue me,
    for they are too strong for me.
7 Set me free from my prison,
    that I may praise your name.
Then the righteous will gather
        about me
    because of your goodness to
        me.


## Psalm 143

*A psalm of David.*

1 LORD, hear my prayer,
    listen to my cry for mercy;
in your faithfulness and
        righteousness
    come to my relief.

2 Do not bring your servant into
        judgment,
    for no one living is righteous
        before you.
3 The enemy pursues me,
    he crushes me to the ground;
he makes me dwell in the
        darkness
    like those long dead.
4 So my spirit grows faint within
        me;
    my heart within me is
        dismayed.
5 I remember the days of long
        ago;
    I meditate on all your works
    and consider what your hands
        have done.
6 I spread out my hands to you;
    I thirst for you like a parched
        land.*a*

7 Answer me quickly, LORD;
    my spirit fails.
Do not hide your face from me
    or I will be like those who go
        down to the pit.
8 Let the morning bring me word
        of your unfailing love,
    for I have put my trust in you.
Show me the way I should go,
    for to you I entrust my life.
9 Rescue me from my enemies,
        LORD,
    for I hide myself in you.
10 Teach me to do your will,
    for you are my God;
may your good Spirit
    lead me on level ground.

11 For your name's sake, LORD,
        preserve my life;
    in your righteousness, bring
        me out of trouble.
12 In your unfailing love, silence
        my enemies;
    destroy all my foes,
    for I am your servant.


## Psalm 144

*Of David.*

1 Praise be to the LORD my Rock,
    who trains my hands for war,
    my fingers for battle.
2 He is my loving God and my
        fortress,
    my stronghold and my
        deliverer,
my shield, in whom I take
        refuge,
    who subdues peoples*b* under
        me.

3 LORD, what are human beings
        that you care for them,
    mere mortals that you think of
        them?

---

*a 6* The Hebrew has *Selah* (a word of uncertain meaning) here.    *b 2* Many manuscripts of the
Masoretic Text, Dead Sea Scrolls, Aquila, Jerome and Syriac; most manuscripts of the Masoretic
Text *subdues my people*

4 They are like a breath;
  their days are like a fleeting
    shadow.
5 Part your heavens, LORD, and
    come down;
  touch the mountains, so that
    they smoke.
6 Send forth lightning and scatter
    the enemy;
  shoot your arrows and rout
    them.
7 Reach down your hand from on
    high;
  deliver me and rescue me
from the mighty waters,
  from the hands of foreigners
8 whose mouths are full of lies,
  whose right hands are
    deceitful.

9 I will sing a new song to you, my
    God;
  on the ten-stringed lyre I will
    make music to you,
10 to the One who gives victory to
    kings,
  who delivers his servant
    David.

From the deadly sword 11 deliver
    me;
  rescue me from the hands of
    foreigners
whose mouths are full of lies,
  whose right hands are
    deceitful.

12 Then our sons in their youth
  will be like well-nurtured
    plants,
and our daughters will be like
    pillars
  carved to adorn a palace.
13 Our barns will be filled
  with every kind of provision.

Our sheep will increase by
    thousands,
  by tens of thousands in our
    fields;
14 our oxen will draw heavy
    loads.[a]
There will be no breaching of
    walls,
  no going into captivity,
  no cry of distress in our
    streets.
15 Blessed is the people of whom
    this is true;
  blessed is the people whose
    God is the LORD.

Psalm 145[b]

*A psalm of praise. Of David.*

1 I will exalt you, my God the
    King;
  I will praise your name for
    ever and ever.
2 Every day I will praise you
  and extol your name for ever
    and ever.

3 Great is the LORD and most
    worthy of praise;
  his greatness no one can
    fathom.
4 One generation commends your
    works to another;
  they tell of your mighty acts.
5 They speak of the glorious
    splendor of your
    majesty—
  and I will meditate on your
    wonderful works.[c]
6 They tell of the power of your
    awesome works—
  and I will proclaim your great
    deeds.
7 They celebrate your abundant
    goodness

---

[a] 14 Or *our chieftains will be firmly established*
of which (including verse 13b) begin with the successive letters of the Hebrew alphabet.
[b] This psalm is an acrostic poem, the verses
[c] 5 Dead Sea Scrolls and Syriac (see also Septuagint); Masoretic Text *On the glorious splendor of
your majesty / and on your wonderful works I will meditate*

and joyfully sing of your
righteousness.

8 The LORD is gracious and
compassionate,
slow to anger and rich in love.

9 The LORD is good to all;
he has compassion on all he
has made.

10 All your works praise you, LORD;
your faithful people extol you.

11 They tell of the glory of your
kingdom
and speak of your might,

12 so that all people may know of
your mighty acts
and the glorious splendor of
your kingdom.

13 Your kingdom is an everlasting
kingdom,
and your dominion endures
through all generations.

The LORD is trustworthy in all he
promises
and faithful in all he does.[a]

14 The LORD upholds all who fall
and lifts up all who are bowed
down.

15 The eyes of all look to you,
and you give them their food
at the proper time.

16 You open your hand
and satisfy the desires of every
living thing.

17 The LORD is righteous in all his
ways
and faithful in all he does.

18 The LORD is near to all who call
on him,
to all who call on him in truth.

19 He fulfills the desires of those
who fear him;
he hears their cry and saves
them.

20 The LORD watches over all who
love him,
but all the wicked he will
destroy.

21 My mouth will speak in praise of
the LORD.
Let every creature praise his
holy name
for ever and ever.

## Psalm 146

1 Praise the LORD.[b]

Praise the LORD, my soul.

2 I will praise the LORD all my life;
I will sing praise to my God as
long as I live.

3 Do not put your trust in princes,
in human beings, who cannot
save.

4 When their spirit departs, they
return to the ground;
on that very day their plans
come to nothing.

5 Blessed are those whose help is
the God of Jacob,
whose hope is in the LORD
their God.

6 He is the Maker of heaven and
earth,
the sea, and everything in
them —
he remains faithful forever.

7 He upholds the cause of the
oppressed
and gives food to the hungry.
The LORD sets prisoners free,

8 the LORD gives sight to the
blind,
the LORD lifts up those who are
bowed down,
the LORD loves the righteous.

9 The LORD watches over the
foreigner

---

a 13 One manuscript of the Masoretic Text, Dead Sea Scrolls and Syriac (see also Septuagint);
most manuscripts of the Masoretic Text do not have the last two lines of verse 13.    b 1 Hebrew
*Hallelu Yah*; also in verse 10

and sustains the fatherless
and the widow,
but he frustrates the ways of
the wicked.

¹⁰ The LORD reigns forever,
your God, O Zion, for all
generations.

Praise the LORD.

Psalm 147

¹ Praise the LORD.ᵃ

How good it is to sing praises to
our God,
how pleasant and fitting to
praise him!

² The LORD builds up Jerusalem;
he gathers the exiles of Israel.
³ He heals the brokenhearted
and binds up their wounds.
⁴ He determines the number of
the stars
and calls them each by name.
⁵ Great is our Lord and mighty in
power;
his understanding has no
limit.
⁶ The LORD sustains the humble
but casts the wicked to the
ground.

⁷ Sing to the LORD with grateful
praise;
make music to our God on the
harp.

⁸ He covers the sky with clouds;
he supplies the earth with rain
and makes grass grow on the
hills.
⁹ He provides food for the cattle
and for the young ravens when
they call.

¹⁰ His pleasure is not in the
strength of the horse,
nor his delight in the legs of
the warrior;
¹¹ the LORD delights in those who
fear him,
who put their hope in his
unfailing love.

¹² Extol the LORD, Jerusalem;
praise your God, Zion.
¹³ He strengthens the bars of your
gates
and blesses your people
within you.
¹⁴ He grants peace to your
borders
and satisfies you with the
finest of wheat.

¹⁵ He sends his command to the
earth;
his word runs swiftly.
¹⁶ He spreads the snow like wool
and scatters the frost like
ashes.
¹⁷ He hurls down his hail like
pebbles.
Who can withstand his icy
blast?
¹⁸ He sends his word and melts
them;
he stirs up his breezes, and the
waters flow.

¹⁹ He has revealed his word to
Jacob,
his laws and decrees to Israel.
²⁰ He has done this for no other
nation;
they do not know his laws.ᵇ

Praise the LORD.

Psalm 148

¹ Praise the LORD.ᶜ

Praise the LORD from the
heavens;

---

ᵃ 1 Hebrew *Hallelu Yah*; also in verse 20    ᵇ 20 Masoretic Text; Dead Sea Scrolls and Septuagint
nation; / he has not made his laws known to them    ᶜ 1 Hebrew *Hallelu Yah*; also in verse 14

praise him in the heights
above.
2 Praise him, all his angels;
praise him, all his heavenly
hosts.
3 Praise him, sun and moon;
praise him, all you shining
stars.
4 Praise him, you highest
heavens
and you waters above the
skies.

5 Let them praise the name of the
LORD,
for at his command they were
created,
6 and he established them for ever
and ever—
he issued a decree that will
never pass away.

7 Praise the LORD from the earth,
you great sea creatures and all
ocean depths,
8 lightning and hail, snow and
clouds,
stormy winds that do his
bidding,
9 you mountains and all hills,
fruit trees and all cedars,
10 wild animals and all cattle,
small creatures and flying
birds,
11 kings of the earth and all
nations,
you princes and all rulers on
earth,
12 young men and women,
old men and children.

13 Let them praise the name of the
LORD,
for his name alone is exalted;
his splendor is above the earth
and the heavens.
14 And he has raised up for his
people a horn,[a]

the praise of all his faithful
servants,
of Israel, the people close to
his heart.

Praise the LORD.

## Psalm 149

1 Praise the LORD.[b]

Sing to the LORD a new song,
his praise in the assembly of
his faithful people.

2 Let Israel rejoice in their
Maker;
let the people of Zion be glad
in their King.
3 Let them praise his name with
dancing
and make music to him with
timbrel and harp.
4 For the LORD takes delight in his
people;
he crowns the humble with
victory.
5 Let his faithful people rejoice in
this honor
and sing for joy on their beds.

6 May the praise of God be in their
mouths
and a double-edged sword in
their hands,
7 to inflict vengeance on the
nations
and punishment on the
peoples,
8 to bind their kings with
fetters,
their nobles with shackles of
iron,
9 to carry out the sentence written
against them—
this is the glory of all his
faithful people.

Praise the LORD.

---

a 14 *Horn* here symbolizes strength.　　b 1 Hebrew *Hallelu Yah*; also in verse 9

## Psalm 150

[1] Praise the LORD.[a]

Praise God in his sanctuary;
 praise him in his mighty
 heavens.
[2] Praise him for his acts of power;
 praise him for his surpassing
 greatness.
[3] Praise him with the sounding of
 the trumpet,
 praise him with the harp and
 lyre,
[4] praise him with timbrel and
 dancing,
 praise him with the strings
 and pipe,
[5] praise him with the clash of
 cymbals,
 praise him with resounding
 cymbals.

[6] Let everything that has breath
 praise the LORD.

Praise the LORD.

---

[a] 1 Hebrew *Hallelu Yah*; also in verse 6

# PROVERBS

Israel understood that the Creator had placed an order in his world that could be discovered. The book of Proverbs captures these lessons in compact, memorable sayings passed down from the wisest among their elders. Many of them are from Solomon, a king renowned for his wisdom. These proverbs are especially designed to help younger people avoid common pitfalls and find the path to prosperity, health and security.

After a short section of teaching, wisdom itself, personified as a woman, calls out to the simple and invites them to grow in knowledge. This section ends by presenting two banquets, one hosted by Wisdom and one by Folly, illustrating the essential choice to be made in life. A collection of 375 proverbs of Solomon follows, reflecting the numerical value of his name in Hebrew. (Hebrew letters were also used as numbers, so words had a value equal to the sum of their letters.) After some "sayings of the wise," next is a collection of Solomon's wisdom compiled by the men of Hezekiah, king of Judah. Here the count is 130, equaling the value of Hezekiah's name. The book closes with sayings from Agur and Lemuel, ending with a poem whose 22 parts begin with consecutive letters of the Hebrew alphabet. The character qualities praised throughout the book are seen in a description of the ideal wife.

This rich book of short, pithy wisdom presents a consistent theme: *the fear of the LORD is the beginning of knowledge.*

---

1 The proverbs of Solomon son of David, king of Israel:

2 for gaining wisdom and instruction;
   for understanding words of insight;
3 for receiving instruction in prudent behavior,
   doing what is right and just and fair;
4 for giving prudence to those who are simple,[a]
   knowledge and discretion to the young—
5 let the wise listen and add to their learning,
   and let the discerning get guidance—
6 for understanding proverbs and parables,
   the sayings and riddles of the wise.[b]

7 The fear of the LORD is the beginning of knowledge,
   but fools[c] despise wisdom and instruction.

8 Listen, my son, to your father's instruction
   and do not forsake your mother's teaching.
9 They are a garland to grace your head
   and a chain to adorn your neck.

10 My son, if sinful men entice you,
   do not give in to them.

---

[a] 4 The Hebrew word rendered *simple* in Proverbs denotes a person who is gullible, without moral direction and inclined to evil.   [b] 6 Or *understanding a proverb, namely, a parable, / and the sayings of the wise, their riddles*   [c] 7 The Hebrew words rendered *fool* in Proverbs, and often elsewhere in the Old Testament, denote a person who is morally deficient.

[11] If they say, "Come along with us;
  let's lie in wait for innocent
    blood,
  let's ambush some harmless
    soul;
[12] let's swallow them alive, like the
    grave,
  and whole, like those who go
    down to the pit;
[13] we will get all sorts of valuable
    things
  and fill our houses with
    plunder;
[14] cast lots with us;
  we will all share the loot"—
[15] my son, do not go along with
    them,
  do not set foot on their paths;
[16] for their feet rush into evil,
  they are swift to shed blood.
[17] How useless to spread a net
  where every bird can see it!
[18] These men lie in wait for their
    own blood;
  they ambush only
    themselves!
[19] Such are the paths of all who go
    after ill-gotten gain;
  it takes away the life of those
    who get it.

[20] Out in the open wisdom calls
    aloud,
  she raises her voice in the
    public square;
[21] on top of the wall[a] she cries out,
  at the city gate she makes her
    speech:

[22] "How long will you who are
    simple love your simple
    ways?
  How long will mockers delight
    in mockery
  and fools hate knowledge?
[23] Repent at my rebuke!
  Then I will pour out my
    thoughts to you,
  I will make known to you my
    teachings.
[24] But since you refuse to listen
    when I call
  and no one pays attention
    when I stretch out my
    hand,
[25] since you disregard all my
    advice
  and do not accept my rebuke,
[26] I in turn will laugh when
    disaster strikes you;
  I will mock when calamity
    overtakes you—
[27] when calamity overtakes you
    like a storm,
  when disaster sweeps over you
    like a whirlwind,
  when distress and trouble
    overwhelm you.

[28] "Then they will call to me but I
    will not answer;
  they will look for me but will
    not find me,
[29] since they hated knowledge
  and did not choose to fear the
    LORD.
[30] Since they would not accept my
    advice
  and spurned my rebuke,
[31] they will eat the fruit of their
    ways
  and be filled with the fruit of
    their schemes.
[32] For the waywardness of the
    simple will kill them,
  and the complacency of fools
    will destroy them;
[33] but whoever listens to me will
    live in safety
  and be at ease, without fear of
    harm."

2 My son, if you accept my words
  and store up my commands
    within you,
[2] turning your ear to wisdom

---

[a] 21 Septuagint; Hebrew / at noisy street corners

and applying your heart to
    understanding—
³ indeed, if you call out for insight
    and cry aloud for
    understanding,
⁴ and if you look for it as for silver
    and search for it as for hidden
    treasure,
⁵ then you will understand the
    fear of the LORD
    and find the knowledge of
    God.
⁶ For the LORD gives wisdom;
    from his mouth come
    knowledge and
    understanding.
⁷ He holds success in store for the
    upright,
    he is a shield to those whose
    walk is blameless,
⁸ for he guards the course of the
    just
    and protects the way of his
    faithful ones.

⁹ Then you will understand what
    is right and just
    and fair—every good path.
¹⁰ For wisdom will enter your
    heart,
    and knowledge will be
    pleasant to your soul.
¹¹ Discretion will protect you,
    and understanding will guard
    you.
¹² Wisdom will save you from the
    ways of wicked men,
    from men whose words are
    perverse,
¹³ who have left the straight paths
    to walk in dark ways,
¹⁴ who delight in doing wrong
    and rejoice in the perverseness
    of evil,
¹⁵ whose paths are crooked
    and who are devious in their
    ways.

¹⁶ Wisdom will save you also from
    the adulterous woman,
    from the wayward woman
    with her seductive words,
¹⁷ who has left the partner of her
    youth
    and ignored the covenant she
    made before God.ᵃ
¹⁸ Surely her house leads down to
    death
    and her paths to the spirits of
    the dead.
¹⁹ None who go to her return
    or attain the paths of life.

²⁰ Thus you will walk in the ways of
    the good
    and keep to the paths of the
    righteous.
²¹ For the upright will live in the
    land,
    and the blameless will remain
    in it;
²² but the wicked will be cut off
    from the land,
    and the unfaithful will be torn
    from it.

3 My son, do not forget my
    teaching,
    but keep my commands in
    your heart,
² for they will prolong your life
    many years
    and bring you peace and
    prosperity.

³ Let love and faithfulness never
    leave you;
    bind them around your neck,
    write them on the tablet of
    your heart.
⁴ Then you will win favor and a
    good name
    in the sight of God and man.

⁵ Trust in the LORD with all your
    heart

ᵃ 17 Or covenant of her God

and lean not on your own
understanding;
⁶in all your ways submit to him,
and he will make your paths
straight.ᵃ

⁷Do not be wise in your own
eyes;
fear the LORD and shun evil.
⁸This will bring health to your
body
and nourishment to your
bones.

⁹Honor the LORD with your
wealth,
with the firstfruits of all your
crops;
¹⁰then your barns will be filled to
overflowing,
and your vats will brim over
with new wine.

¹¹My son, do not despise the
LORD's discipline,
and do not resent his rebuke,
¹²because the LORD disciplines
those he loves,
as a father the son he delights
in.ᵇ

¹³Blessed are those who find
wisdom,
those who gain
understanding,
¹⁴for she is more profitable than
silver
and yields better returns than
gold.
¹⁵She is more precious than
rubies;
nothing you desire can
compare with her.
¹⁶Long life is in her right hand;
in her left hand are riches and
honor.
¹⁷Her ways are pleasant ways,
and all her paths are peace.

¹⁸She is a tree of life to those who
take hold of her;
those who hold her fast will be
blessed.

¹⁹By wisdom the LORD laid the
earth's foundations,
by understanding he set the
heavens in place;
²⁰by his knowledge the watery
depths were divided,
and the clouds let drop the
dew.

²¹My son, do not let wisdom and
understanding out of your
sight,
preserve sound judgment and
discretion;
²²they will be life for you,
an ornament to grace your
neck.
²³Then you will go on your way in
safety,
and your foot will not stumble.
²⁴When you lie down, you will not
be afraid;
when you lie down, your sleep
will be sweet.
²⁵Have no fear of sudden disaster
or of the ruin that overtakes
the wicked,
²⁶for the LORD will be at your side
and will keep your foot from
being snared.

²⁷Do not withhold good from
those to whom it is due,
when it is in your power to act.
²⁸Do not say to your neighbor,
"Come back tomorrow and I'll
give it to you" —
when you already have it with
you.
²⁹Do not plot harm against your
neighbor,
who lives trustfully near you.

---

ᵃ 6 Or will direct your paths   ᵇ 12 Hebrew; Septuagint loves, / and he chastens everyone he
accepts as his child

³⁰Do not accuse anyone for no reason—
  when they have done you no harm.

³¹Do not envy the violent
  or choose any of their ways.

³²For the LORD detests the perverse
  but takes the upright into his confidence.

³³The LORD's curse is on the house of the wicked,
  but he blesses the home of the righteous.

³⁴He mocks proud mockers
  but shows favor to the humble and oppressed.

³⁵The wise inherit honor,
  but fools get only shame.

4 Listen, my sons, to a father's instruction;
  pay attention and gain understanding.

²I give you sound learning,
  so do not forsake my teaching.

³For I too was a son to my father,
  still tender, and cherished by my mother.

⁴Then he taught me, and he said to me,
  "Take hold of my words with all your heart;
  keep my commands, and you will live.

⁵Get wisdom, get understanding;
  do not forget my words or turn away from them.

⁶Do not forsake wisdom, and she will protect you;
  love her, and she will watch over you.

⁷The beginning of wisdom is this: Get\a wisdom.
  Though it cost all you have,\b get understanding.

⁸Cherish her, and she will exalt you;
  embrace her, and she will honor you.

⁹She will give you a garland to grace your head
  and present you with a glorious crown."

¹⁰Listen, my son, accept what I say,
  and the years of your life will be many.

¹¹I instruct you in the way of wisdom
  and lead you along straight paths.

¹²When you walk, your steps will not be hampered;
  when you run, you will not stumble.

¹³Hold on to instruction, do not let it go;
  guard it well, for it is your life.

¹⁴Do not set foot on the path of the wicked
  or walk in the way of evildoers.

¹⁵Avoid it, do not travel on it;
  turn from it and go on your way.

¹⁶For they cannot rest until they do evil;
  they are robbed of sleep till they make someone stumble.

¹⁷They eat the bread of wickedness
  and drink the wine of violence.

¹⁸The path of the righteous is like the morning sun,
  shining ever brighter till the full light of day.

¹⁹But the way of the wicked is like deep darkness;
  they do not know what makes them stumble.

²⁰My son, pay attention to what I say;

---

ᵃ 7 Or *Wisdom is supreme; therefore get*    ᵇ 7 Or *wisdom. / Whatever else you get*

turn your ear to my words.
21 Do not let them out of your sight,
    keep them within your heart;
22 for they are life to those who find
    them
    and health to one's whole
    body.
23 Above all else, guard your heart,
    for everything you do flows
    from it.
24 Keep your mouth free of
    perversity;
    keep corrupt talk far from your
    lips.
25 Let your eyes look straight
    ahead;
    fix your gaze directly before
    you.
26 Give careful thought to the[a]
    paths for your feet
    and be steadfast in all your
    ways.
27 Do not turn to the right or the
    left;
    keep your foot from evil.

5 My son, pay attention to my
    wisdom,
    turn your ear to my words of
    insight,
2 that you may maintain
    discretion
    and your lips may preserve
    knowledge.
3 For the lips of the adulterous
    woman drip honey,
    and her speech is smoother
    than oil;
4 but in the end she is bitter as
    gall,
    sharp as a double-edged
    sword.
5 Her feet go down to death;
    her steps lead straight to the
    grave.
6 She gives no thought to the way
    of life;

her paths wander aimlessly,
    but she does not know it.

7 Now then, my sons, listen to me;
    do not turn aside from what I
    say.
8 Keep to a path far from her,
    do not go near the door of her
    house,
9 lest you lose your honor to others
    and your dignity[b] to one who
    is cruel,
10 lest strangers feast on your
    wealth
    and your toil enrich the house
    of another.
11 At the end of your life you will
    groan,
    when your flesh and body are
    spent.
12 You will say, "How I hated
    discipline!
    How my heart spurned
    correction!
13 I would not obey my teachers
    or turn my ear to my
    instructors.
14 And I was soon in serious
    trouble
    in the assembly of God's
    people."

15 Drink water from your own
    cistern,
    running water from your own
    well.
16 Should your springs overflow in
    the streets,
    your streams of water in the
    public squares?
17 Let them be yours alone,
    never to be shared with
    strangers.
18 May your fountain be blessed,
    and may you rejoice in the
    wife of your youth.
19 A loving doe, a graceful deer—

a 26 Or *Make level*   b 9 Or *years*

may her breasts satisfy you
always,
may you ever be intoxicated
with her love.

20 Why, my son, be intoxicated
with another man's wife?
Why embrace the bosom of a
wayward woman?

21 For your ways are in full view of
the LORD,
and he examines all your
paths.

22 The evil deeds of the wicked
ensnare them;
the cords of their sins hold
them fast.

23 For lack of discipline they will
die,
led astray by their own great
folly.

6 My son, if you have put up
security for your neighbor,
if you have shaken hands in
pledge for a stranger,

2 you have been trapped by what
you said,
ensnared by the words of your
mouth.

3 So do this, my son, to free
yourself,
since you have fallen into your
neighbor's hands:
Go — to the point of
exhaustion — a
and give your neighbor no rest!

4 Allow no sleep to your eyes,
no slumber to your eyelids.

5 Free yourself, like a gazelle from
the hand of the hunter,
like a bird from the snare of
the fowler.

6 Go to the ant, you sluggard;
consider its ways and be wise!

7 It has no commander,
no overseer or ruler,

8 yet it stores its provisions in
summer
and gathers its food at harvest.

9 How long will you lie there, you
sluggard?
When will you get up from
your sleep?

10 A little sleep, a little slumber,
a little folding of the hands to
rest —

11 and poverty will come on you
like a thief
and scarcity like an armed
man.

12 A troublemaker and a villain,
who goes about with a corrupt
mouth,

13 who winks maliciously with
his eye,
signals with his feet
and motions with his fingers,

14 who plots evil with deceit in
his heart —
he always stirs up conflict.

15 Therefore disaster will overtake
him in an instant;
he will suddenly be
destroyed — without
remedy.

16 There are six things the LORD
hates,
seven that are detestable to
him:

17 haughty eyes,
a lying tongue,
hands that shed innocent
blood,

18 a heart that devises wicked
schemes,
feet that are quick to rush
into evil,

19 a false witness who pours
out lies
and a person who stirs up
conflict in the community.

---

a 3 Or *Go and humble yourself,*

20 My son, keep your father's
    command
    and do not forsake your
      mother's teaching.
21 Bind them always on your heart;
    fasten them around your neck.
22 When you walk, they will guide
      you;
    when you sleep, they will
      watch over you;
    when you awake, they will
      speak to you.
23 For this command is a lamp,
    this teaching is a light,
    and correction and instruction
    are the way to life,
24 keeping you from your
      neighbor's wife,
    from the smooth talk of a
      wayward woman.

25 Do not lust in your heart after
      her beauty
    or let her captivate you with
      her eyes.
26 For a prostitute can be had for a
      loaf of bread,
    but another man's wife preys
      on your very life.
27 Can a man scoop fire into his
      lap
    without his clothes being
      burned?
28 Can a man walk on hot coals
    without his feet being
      scorched?
29 So is he who sleeps with another
      man's wife;
    no one who touches her will go
      unpunished.

30 People do not despise a thief if
      he steals
    to satisfy his hunger when he
      is starving.
31 Yet if he is caught, he must pay
      sevenfold,
    though it costs him all the
      wealth of his house.

32 But a man who commits
      adultery has no sense;
    whoever does so destroys
      himself.
33 Blows and disgrace are his lot,
    and his shame will never be
      wiped away.
34 For jealousy arouses a husband's
      fury,
    and he will show no mercy
      when he takes revenge.
35 He will not accept any
      compensation;
    he will refuse a bribe, however
      great it is.

7 My son, keep my words
    and store up my commands
      within you.
2 Keep my commands and you
      will live;
    guard my teachings as the
      apple of your eye.
3 Bind them on your fingers;
    write them on the tablet of
      your heart.
4 Say to wisdom, "You are my
      sister,"
    and to insight, "You are my
      relative."
5 They will keep you from the
      adulterous woman,
    from the wayward woman
      with her seductive words.

6 At the window of my house
    I looked down through the
      lattice.
7 I saw among the simple,
    I noticed among the young
      men,
    a youth who had no sense.
8 He was going down the street
      near her corner,
    walking along in the direction
      of her house
9 at twilight, as the day was
      fading,
    as the dark of night set in.

10 Then out came a woman to meet
   him,
     dressed like a prostitute and
       with crafty intent.
11 (She is unruly and defiant,
     her feet never stay at home;
12 now in the street, now in the
     squares,
     at every corner she lurks.)
13 She took hold of him and kissed
   him
     and with a brazen face she
       said:

14 "Today I fulfilled my vows,
     and I have food from my
       fellowship offering at
       home.
15 So I came out to meet you;
     I looked for you and have
       found you!
16 I have covered my bed
     with colored linens from
       Egypt.
17 I have perfumed my bed
     with myrrh, aloes and
       cinnamon.
18 Come, let's drink deeply of love
     till morning;
     let's enjoy ourselves with
       love!
19 My husband is not at home;
     he has gone on a long journey.
20 He took his purse filled with
     money
     and will not be home till full
       moon."

21 With persuasive words she led
     him astray;
     she seduced him with her
       smooth talk.
22 All at once he followed her
     like an ox going to the
       slaughter,
     like a deer[a] stepping into a
       noose[b]

23 till an arrow pierces his liver,
   like a bird darting into a snare,
     little knowing it will cost him
       his life.

24 Now then, my sons, listen to
     me;
     pay attention to what I say.
25 Do not let your heart turn to her
     ways
     or stray into her paths.
26 Many are the victims she has
     brought down;
     her slain are a mighty throng.
27 Her house is a highway to the
     grave,
     leading down to the chambers
       of death.

8 Does not wisdom call out?
   Does not understanding raise
     her voice?
2 At the highest point along the
     way,
     where the paths meet, she
       takes her stand;
3 beside the gate leading into the
     city,
     at the entrance, she cries
       aloud:
4 "To you, O people, I call out;
   I raise my voice to all
       mankind.
5 You who are simple, gain
     prudence;
     you who are foolish, set your
       hearts on it.[c]
6 Listen, for I have trustworthy
     things to say;
     I open my lips to speak what is
       right.
7 My mouth speaks what is true,
     for my lips detest wickedness.
8 All the words of my mouth are
     just;
     none of them is crooked or
       perverse.

a 22 Syriac (see also Septuagint); Hebrew fool    b 22 The meaning of the Hebrew for this line is
uncertain.    c 5 Septuagint; Hebrew foolish, instruct your minds

⁹To the discerning all of them are
   right;
     they are upright to those who
       have found knowledge.
¹⁰Choose my instruction instead
   of silver,
     knowledge rather than choice
       gold,
¹¹for wisdom is more precious
   than rubies,
     and nothing you desire can
       compare with her.

¹²"I, wisdom, dwell together with
   prudence;
     I possess knowledge and
       discretion.
¹³To fear the LORD is to hate evil;
   I hate pride and arrogance,
     evil behavior and perverse
       speech.
¹⁴Counsel and sound judgment
   are mine;
     I have insight, I have power.
¹⁵By me kings reign
   and rulers issue decrees that
     are just;
¹⁶by me princes govern,
   and nobles — all who rule on
     earth.ᵃ
¹⁷I love those who love me,
   and those who seek me find
     me.
¹⁸With me are riches and honor,
   enduring wealth and
     prosperity.
¹⁹My fruit is better than fine gold;
   what I yield surpasses choice
     silver.
²⁰I walk in the way of
   righteousness,
     along the paths of justice,
²¹bestowing a rich inheritance on
   those who love me
     and making their treasuries
       full.

²²"The LORD brought me forth as
   the first of his works,ᵇ,ᶜ
     before his deeds of old;
²³I was formed long ages ago,
   at the very beginning, when
     the world came to be.
²⁴When there were no watery
   depths, I was given birth,
     when there were no springs
       overflowing with water;
²⁵before the mountains were
   settled in place,
     before the hills, I was given
       birth,
²⁶before he made the world or its
   fields
     or any of the dust of the
       earth.
²⁷I was there when he set the
   heavens in place,
     when he marked out the
       horizon on the face of the
         deep,
²⁸when he established the clouds
   above
     and fixed securely the
       fountains of the deep,
²⁹when he gave the sea its
   boundary
     so the waters would not
       overstep his command,
   and when he marked out the
     foundations of the earth.
³⁰   Then I was constantlyᵈ at his
     side.
   I was filled with delight day after
     day,
     rejoicing always in his
       presence,
³¹rejoicing in his whole world
   and delighting in mankind.

³²"Now then, my children, listen
   to me;
     blessed are those who keep my
       ways.

---

ᵃ 16 Some Hebrew manuscripts and Septuagint; other Hebrew manuscripts *all righteous rulers*
ᵇ 22 Or *way*; or *dominion*   ᶜ 22 Or *The LORD possessed me at the beginning of his work*; or *The LORD brought me forth at the beginning of his work*   ᵈ 30 Or *was the artisan*; or *was a little child*

³³ Listen to my instruction and be
wise;
  do not disregard it.
³⁴ Blessed are those who listen to
me,
  watching daily at my doors,
    waiting at my doorway.
³⁵ For those who find me find life
  and receive favor from the
    LORD.
³⁶ But those who fail to find me
harm themselves;
  all who hate me love death."

9 Wisdom has built her house;
  she has set up[a] its seven
    pillars.
² She has prepared her meat and
mixed her wine;
  she has also set her table.
³ She has sent out her servants,
  and she calls
from the highest point of the
city,
⁴   "Let all who are simple come
to my house!"
  To those who have no sense she
says,
⁵   "Come, eat my food
  and drink the wine I have
    mixed.
⁶ Leave your simple ways and you
will live;
  walk in the way of insight."

⁷ Whoever corrects a mocker
invites insults;
  whoever rebukes the wicked
    incurs abuse.
⁸ Do not rebuke mockers or they
will hate you;
  rebuke the wise and they will
    love you.
⁹ Instruct the wise and they will
be wiser still;
  teach the righteous and they
    will add to their learning.

¹⁰ The fear of the LORD is the
beginning of wisdom,
  and knowledge of the Holy
    One is understanding.
¹¹ For through wisdom[b] your days
will be many,
  and years will be added to
    your life.
¹² If you are wise, your wisdom will
reward you;
  if you are a mocker, you alone
    will suffer.

¹³ Folly is an unruly woman;
  she is simple and knows
    nothing.
¹⁴ She sits at the door of her house,
  on a seat at the highest point of
    the city,
¹⁵ calling out to those who pass
by,
  who go straight on their way,
¹⁶   "Let all who are simple come
to my house!"
  To those who have no sense she
says,
¹⁷   "Stolen water is sweet;
  food eaten in secret is
    delicious!"
¹⁸ But little do they know that the
dead are there,
  that her guests are deep in the
    realm of the dead.

10 The proverbs of Solomon:

A wise son brings joy to his
father,
  but a foolish son brings grief to
    his mother.
² Ill-gotten treasures have no
lasting value,
  but righteousness delivers
    from death.
³ The LORD does not let the
righteous go hungry,

---

*a 1* Septuagint, Syriac and Targum; Hebrew *has hewn out*    *b 11* Septuagint, Syriac and Targum; Hebrew *me* but he thwarts the craving of the wicked.

4 Lazy hands make for poverty,
but diligent hands bring wealth.

5 He who gathers crops in summer is a prudent son,
but he who sleeps during harvest is a disgraceful son.

6 Blessings crown the head of the righteous,
but violence overwhelms the mouth of the wicked.[a]

7 The name of the righteous is used in blessings,[b]
but the name of the wicked will rot.

8 The wise in heart accept commands,
but a chattering fool comes to ruin.

9 Whoever walks in integrity walks securely,
but whoever takes crooked paths will be found out.

10 Whoever winks maliciously causes grief,
and a chattering fool comes to ruin.

11 The mouth of the righteous is a fountain of life,
but the mouth of the wicked conceals violence.

12 Hatred stirs up conflict,
but love covers over all wrongs.

13 Wisdom is found on the lips of the discerning,
but a rod is for the back of one who has no sense.

14 The wise store up knowledge,
but the mouth of a fool invites ruin.

15 The wealth of the rich is their fortified city,
but poverty is the ruin of the poor.

16 The wages of the righteous is life,
but the earnings of the wicked are sin and death.

17 Whoever heeds discipline shows the way to life,
but whoever ignores correction leads others astray.

18 Whoever conceals hatred with lying lips
and spreads slander is a fool.

19 Sin is not ended by multiplying words,
but the prudent hold their tongues.

20 The tongue of the righteous is choice silver,
but the heart of the wicked is of little value.

21 The lips of the righteous nourish many,
but fools die for lack of sense.

22 The blessing of the LORD brings wealth,
without painful toil for it.

23 A fool finds pleasure in wicked schemes,
but a person of understanding delights in wisdom.

24 What the wicked dread will overtake them;
what the righteous desire will be granted.

---

a 6 Or righteous, / but the mouth of the wicked conceals violence    b 7 See Gen. 48:20.

25 When the storm has swept by,
　　the wicked are gone,
　but the righteous stand firm
　　forever.

26 As vinegar to the teeth and
　　smoke to the eyes,
　so are sluggards to those who
　　send them.

27 The fear of the LORD adds length
　　to life,
　but the years of the wicked are
　　cut short.

28 The prospect of the righteous is
　　joy,
　but the hopes of the wicked
　　come to nothing.

29 The way of the LORD is a refuge
　　for the blameless,
　but it is the ruin of those who
　　do evil.

30 The righteous will never be
　　uprooted,
　but the wicked will not remain
　　in the land.

31 From the mouth of the righteous
　　comes the fruit of
　　wisdom,
　but a perverse tongue will be
　　silenced.

32 The lips of the righteous know
　　what finds favor,
　but the mouth of the wicked
　　only what is perverse.

11 The LORD detests dishonest
　　scales,
　but accurate weights find favor
　　with him.

2 When pride comes, then comes
　　disgrace,
　but with humility comes
　　wisdom.

3 The integrity of the upright
　　guides them,
　but the unfaithful are
　　destroyed by their
　　duplicity.

4 Wealth is worthless in the day of
　　wrath,
　but righteousness delivers
　　from death.

5 The righteousness of the
　　blameless makes their
　　paths straight,
　but the wicked are brought
　　down by their own
　　wickedness.

6 The righteousness of the upright
　　delivers them,
　but the unfaithful are trapped
　　by evil desires.

7 Hopes placed in mortals die
　　with them;
　all the promise ofª their power
　　comes to nothing.

8 The righteous person is rescued
　　from trouble,
　and it falls on the wicked
　　instead.

9 With their mouths the godless
　　destroy their neighbors,
　but through knowledge the
　　righteous escape.

10 When the righteous prosper, the
　　city rejoices;
　when the wicked perish, there
　　are shouts of joy.

11 Through the blessing of the
　　upright a city is exalted,
　but by the mouth of the wicked
　　it is destroyed.

12 Whoever derides their neighbor
　　has no sense,

ª 7 Two Hebrew manuscripts; most Hebrew manuscripts, Vulgate, Syriac and Targum *When the
wicked die, their hope perishes; / all they expected from*

but the one who has understanding holds their tongue.

13 A gossip betrays a confidence, but a trustworthy person keeps a secret.

14 For lack of guidance a nation falls, but victory is won through many advisers.

15 Whoever puts up security for a stranger will surely suffer, but whoever refuses to shake hands in pledge is safe.

16 A kindhearted woman gains honor, but ruthless men gain only wealth.

17 Those who are kind benefit themselves, but the cruel bring ruin on themselves.

18 A wicked person earns deceptive wages, but the one who sows righteousness reaps a sure reward.

19 Truly the righteous attain life, but whoever pursues evil finds death.

20 The LORD detests those whose hearts are perverse, but he delights in those whose ways are blameless.

21 Be sure of this: The wicked will not go unpunished, but those who are righteous will go free.

22 Like a gold ring in a pig's snout is a beautiful woman who shows no discretion.

23 The desire of the righteous ends only in good,

but the hope of the wicked only in wrath.

24 One person gives freely, yet gains even more; another withholds unduly, but comes to poverty.

25 A generous person will prosper; whoever refreshes others will be refreshed.

26 People curse the one who hoards grain, but they pray God's blessing on the one who is willing to sell.

27 Whoever seeks good finds favor, but evil comes to one who searches for it.

28 Those who trust in their riches will fall, but the righteous will thrive like a green leaf.

29 Whoever brings ruin on their family will inherit only wind, and the fool will be servant to the wise.

30 The fruit of the righteous is a tree of life, and the one who is wise saves lives.

31 If the righteous receive their due on earth, how much more the ungodly and the sinner!

12 Whoever loves discipline loves knowledge, but whoever hates correction is stupid.

2 Good people obtain favor from the LORD, but he condemns those who devise wicked schemes.

3 No one can be established
    through wickedness,
  but the righteous cannot be
    uprooted.

4 A wife of noble character is her
    husband's crown,
  but a disgraceful wife is like
    decay in his bones.

5 The plans of the righteous are just,
  but the advice of the wicked is
    deceitful.

6 The words of the wicked lie in
    wait for blood,
  but the speech of the upright
    rescues them.

7 The wicked are overthrown and
    are no more,
  but the house of the righteous
    stands firm.

8 A person is praised according to
    their prudence,
  and one with a warped mind is
    despised.

9 Better to be a nobody and yet
    have a servant
  than pretend to be somebody
    and have no food.

10 The righteous care for the needs
    of their animals,
  but the kindest acts of the
    wicked are cruel.

11 Those who work their land will
    have abundant food,
  but those who chase fantasies
    have no sense.

12 The wicked desire the
    stronghold of evildoers,
  but the root of the righteous
    endures.

13 Evildoers are trapped by their
    sinful talk,
  and so the innocent escape
    trouble.

14 From the fruit of their lips
    people are filled with good
    things,
  and the work of their hands
    brings them reward.

15 The way of fools seems right to
    them,
  but the wise listen to advice.

16 Fools show their annoyance at
    once,
  but the prudent overlook an
    insult.

17 An honest witness tells the
    truth,
  but a false witness tells lies.

18 The words of the reckless pierce
    like swords,
  but the tongue of the wise
    brings healing.

19 Truthful lips endure forever,
  but a lying tongue lasts only a
    moment.

20 Deceit is in the hearts of those
    who plot evil,
  but those who promote peace
    have joy.

21 No harm overtakes the
    righteous,
  but the wicked have their fill of
    trouble.

22 The LORD detests lying lips,
  but he delights in people who
    are trustworthy.

23 The prudent keep their
    knowledge to themselves,
  but a fool's heart blurts out
    folly.

24 Diligent hands will rule,
  but laziness ends in forced
    labor.

25 Anxiety weighs down the
    heart,
  but a kind word cheers it up.

26 The righteous choose their
     friends carefully,
   but the way of the wicked leads
     them astray.

27 The lazy do not roast[a] any game,
   but the diligent feed on the
     riches of the hunt.

28 In the way of righteousness
     there is life;
   along that path is
     immortality.

13 A wise son heeds his father's
     instruction,
   but a mocker does not respond
     to rebukes.

2 From the fruit of their lips
   people enjoy good things,
   but the unfaithful have an
     appetite for violence.

3 Those who guard their lips
   preserve their lives,
   but those who speak rashly
     will come to ruin.

4 A sluggard's appetite is never
     filled,
   but the desires of the diligent
     are fully satisfied.

5 The righteous hate what is
     false,
   but the wicked make
     themselves a stench
   and bring shame on
     themselves.

6 Righteousness guards the
     person of integrity,
   but wickedness overthrows
     the sinner.

7 One person pretends to be rich,
     yet has nothing;
   another pretends to be poor,
     yet has great wealth.

8 A person's riches may ransom
     their life,
   but the poor cannot respond to
     threatening rebukes.

9 The light of the righteous shines
     brightly,
   but the lamp of the wicked is
     snuffed out.

10 Where there is strife, there is
     pride,
   but wisdom is found in those
     who take advice.

11 Dishonest money dwindles away,
   but whoever gathers money
     little by little makes it grow.

12 Hope deferred makes the heart
     sick,
   but a longing fulfilled is a tree
     of life.

13 Whoever scorns instruction will
     pay for it,
   but whoever respects a
     command is rewarded.

14 The teaching of the wise is a
     fountain of life,
   turning a person from the
     snares of death.

15 Good judgment wins favor,
   but the way of the unfaithful
     leads to their destruction.[b]

16 All who are prudent act with[c]
     knowledge,
   but fools expose their folly.

17 A wicked messenger falls into
     trouble,
   but a trustworthy envoy brings
     healing.

18 Whoever disregards discipline
     comes to poverty and
     shame,

---

[a] 27 The meaning of the Hebrew for this word is uncertain;
the meaning of the Hebrew for this phrase is uncertain.    [b] 15 Septuagint and Syriac;
    [c] 16 Or prudent protect themselves
through

but whoever heeds correction
is honored.

19 A longing fulfilled is sweet to the
soul,
but fools detest turning from
evil.

20 Walk with the wise and become
wise,
for a companion of fools
suffers harm.

21 Trouble pursues the sinner,
but the righteous are rewarded
with good things.

22 A good person leaves an
inheritance for their
children's children,
but a sinner's wealth is stored
up for the righteous.

23 An unplowed field produces
food for the poor,
but injustice sweeps it away.

24 Whoever spares the rod hates
their children,
but the one who loves their
children is careful to
discipline them.

25 The righteous eat to their hearts'
content,
but the stomach of the wicked
goes hungry.

14 The wise woman builds her
house,
but with her own hands the
foolish one tears hers
down.

2 Whoever fears the LORD walks
uprightly,
but those who despise him are
devious in their ways.

3 A fool's mouth lashes out with
pride,
but the lips of the wise protect
them.

4 Where there are no oxen, the
manger is empty,
but from the strength of an ox
come abundant harvests.

5 An honest witness does not
deceive,
but a false witness pours out
lies.

6 The mocker seeks wisdom and
finds none,
but knowledge comes easily to
the discerning.

7 Stay away from a fool,
for you will not find knowledge
on their lips.

8 The wisdom of the prudent is to
give thought to their ways,
but the folly of fools is
deception.

9 Fools mock at making amends
for sin,
but goodwill is found among
the upright.

10 Each heart knows its own
bitterness,
and no one else can share its
joy.

11 The house of the wicked will be
destroyed,
but the tent of the upright will
flourish.

12 There is a way that appears to be
right,
but in the end it leads to
death.

13 Even in laughter the heart may
ache,
and rejoicing may end in
grief.

14 The faithless will be fully repaid
for their ways,
and the good rewarded for
theirs.

15 The simple believe anything,
　　but the prudent give thought
　　　to their steps.

16 The wise fear the LORD and shun
　　evil,
　　but a fool is hotheaded and yet
　　　feels secure.

17 A quick-tempered person does
　　foolish things,
　　and the one who devises evil
　　　schemes is hated.

18 The simple inherit folly,
　　but the prudent are crowned
　　　with knowledge.

19 Evildoers will bow down in the
　　presence of the good,
　　and the wicked at the gates of
　　　the righteous.

20 The poor are shunned even by
　　their neighbors,
　　but the rich have many
　　　friends.

21 It is a sin to despise one's
　　neighbor,
　　but blessed is the one who is
　　　kind to the needy.

22 Do not those who plot evil go
　　astray?
　　But those who plan what
　　　is good find$^a$ love and
　　　faithfulness.

23 All hard work brings a profit,
　　but mere talk leads only to
　　　poverty.

24 The wealth of the wise is their
　　crown,
　　but the folly of fools yields
　　　folly.

25 A truthful witness saves lives,
　　but a false witness is
　　　deceitful.

26 Whoever fears the LORD has a
　　secure fortress,
　　and for their children it will be
　　　a refuge.

27 The fear of the LORD is a
　　fountain of life,
　　turning a person from the
　　　snares of death.

28 A large population is a king's
　　glory,
　　but without subjects a prince
　　　is ruined.

29 Whoever is patient has great
　　understanding,
　　but one who is quick-tempered
　　　displays folly.

30 A heart at peace gives life to the
　　body,
　　but envy rots the bones.

31 Whoever oppresses the poor
　　shows contempt for their
　　　Maker,
　　but whoever is kind to the
　　　needy honors God.

32 When calamity comes, the
　　wicked are brought
　　　down,
　　but even in death the
　　　righteous seek refuge in
　　　God.

33 Wisdom reposes in the heart of
　　the discerning
　　and even among fools she lets
　　　herself be known.$^b$

34 Righteousness exalts a nation,
　　but sin condemns any people.

35 A king delights in a wise servant,
　　but a shameful servant
　　　arouses his fury.

15 A gentle answer turns away
　　wrath,

$^a$ 22 Or show　$^b$ 33 Hebrew; Septuagint and Syriac *discerning / but in the heart of fools she is not known*

but a harsh word stirs up
    anger.

2 The tongue of the wise adorns
        knowledge,
    but the mouth of the fool
        gushes folly.

3 The eyes of the LORD are
        everywhere,
    keeping watch on the wicked
        and the good.

4 The soothing tongue is a tree of
        life,
    but a perverse tongue crushes
        the spirit.

5 A fool spurns a parent's
        discipline,
    but whoever heeds correction
        shows prudence.

6 The house of the righteous
        contains great treasure,
    but the income of the wicked
        brings ruin.

7 The lips of the wise spread
        knowledge,
    but the hearts of fools are not
        upright.

8 The LORD detests the sacrifice of
        the wicked,
    but the prayer of the upright
        pleases him.

9 The LORD detests the way of the
        wicked,
    but he loves those who pursue
        righteousness.

10 Stern discipline awaits anyone
        who leaves the path;
    the one who hates correction
        will die.

11 Death and Destruction[a] lie open
        before the LORD —
    how much more do human
        hearts!

12 Mockers resent correction,
    so they avoid the wise.

13 A happy heart makes the face
        cheerful,
    but heartache crushes the
        spirit.

14 The discerning heart seeks
        knowledge,
    but the mouth of a fool feeds
        on folly.

15 All the days of the oppressed are
        wretched,
    but the cheerful heart has a
        continual feast.

16 Better a little with the fear of the
        LORD
    than great wealth with
        turmoil.

17 Better a small serving of
        vegetables with love
    than a fattened calf with
        hatred.

18 A hot-tempered person stirs up
        conflict,
    but the one who is patient
        calms a quarrel.

19 The way of the sluggard is
        blocked with thorns,
    but the path of the upright is a
        highway.

20 A wise son brings joy to his
        father,
    but a foolish man despises his
        mother.

21 Folly brings joy to one who has
        no sense,
    but whoever has
        understanding keeps a
        straight course.

22 Plans fail for lack of counsel,
    but with many advisers they
        succeed.

a 11 Hebrew *Abaddon*

<sup>23</sup>A person finds joy in giving an
apt reply—
and how good is a timely word!

<sup>24</sup>The path of life leads upward for
the prudent
to keep them from going down
to the realm of the dead.

<sup>25</sup>The Lord tears down the house
of the proud,
but he sets the widow's
boundary stones in place.

<sup>26</sup>The Lord detests the thoughts of
the wicked,
but gracious words are pure in
his sight.

<sup>27</sup>The greedy bring ruin to their
households,
but the one who hates bribes
will live.

<sup>28</sup>The heart of the righteous
weighs its answers,
but the mouth of the wicked
gushes evil.

<sup>29</sup>The Lord is far from the wicked,
but he hears the prayer of the
righteous.

<sup>30</sup>Light in a messenger's eyes
brings joy to the heart,
and good news gives health to
the bones.

<sup>31</sup>Whoever heeds life-giving
correction
will be at home among the
wise.

<sup>32</sup>Those who disregard discipline
despise themselves,
but the one who heeds
correction gains
understanding.

<sup>33</sup>Wisdom's instruction is to fear
the Lord,
and humility comes before
honor.

**16** To humans belong the plans
of the heart,
but from the Lord comes
the proper answer of the
tongue.

<sup>2</sup>All a person's ways seem pure to
them,
but motives are weighed by
the Lord.

<sup>3</sup>Commit to the Lord whatever
you do,
and he will establish your
plans.

<sup>4</sup>The Lord works out everything
to its proper end—
even the wicked for a day of
disaster.

<sup>5</sup>The Lord detests all the proud
of heart.
Be sure of this: They will not
go unpunished.

<sup>6</sup>Through love and faithfulness
sin is atoned for;
through the fear of the Lord
evil is avoided.

<sup>7</sup>When the Lord takes pleasure
in anyone's way,
he causes their enemies to
make peace with them.

<sup>8</sup>Better a little with righteousness
than much gain with injustice.

<sup>9</sup>In their hearts humans plan
their course,
but the Lord establishes their
steps.

<sup>10</sup>The lips of a king speak as an
oracle,
and his mouth does not betray
justice.

<sup>11</sup>Honest scales and balances
belong to the Lord;
all the weights in the bag are of
his making.

12 Kings detest wrongdoing,
  for a throne is established
    through righteousness.

13 Kings take pleasure in honest
      lips;
  they value the one who speaks
    what is right.

14 A king's wrath is a messenger of
      death,
  but the wise will appease it.

15 When a king's face brightens, it
    means life;
  his favor is like a rain cloud in
    spring.

16 How much better to get wisdom
    than gold,
  to get insight rather than
    silver!

17 The highway of the upright
    avoids evil;
  those who guard their ways
    preserve their lives.

18 Pride goes before destruction,
  a haughty spirit before a fall.

19 Better to be lowly in spirit along
    with the oppressed
  than to share plunder with the
    proud.

20 Whoever gives heed to
    instruction prospers,ᵃ
  and blessed is the one who
    trusts in the LORD.

21 The wise in heart are called
    discerning,
  and gracious words promote
    instruction.ᵇ

22 Prudence is a fountain of life to
    the prudent,
  but folly brings punishment to
    fools.

23 The hearts of the wise make
    their mouths prudent,
  and their lips promote
    instruction.ᶜ

24 Gracious words are a
    honeycomb,
  sweet to the soul and healing
    to the bones.

25 There is a way that appears to be
    right,
  but in the end it leads to death.

26 The appetite of laborers works
    for them;
  their hunger drives them on.

27 A scoundrel plots evil,
  and on their lips it is like a
    scorching fire.

28 A perverse person stirs up
    conflict,
  and a gossip separates close
    friends.

29 A violent person entices their
    neighbor
  and leads them down a path
    that is not good.

30 Whoever winks with their eye is
    plotting perversity;
  whoever purses their lips is
    bent on evil.

31 Gray hair is a crown of
    splendor;
  it is attained in the way of
    righteousness.

32 Better a patient person than a
    warrior,
  one with self-control than one
    who takes a city.

33 The lot is cast into the lap,
  but its every decision is from
    the LORD.

ᵃ 20 Or *whoever speaks prudently finds what is good*   ᵇ 21 Or *words make a person persuasive*
ᶜ 23 Or *prudent / and make their lips persuasive*

**17** Better a dry crust with peace and quiet
than a house full of feasting, with strife.

2 A prudent servant will rule over a disgraceful son
and will share the inheritance as one of the family.

3 The crucible for silver and the furnace for gold,
but the LORD tests the heart.

4 A wicked person listens to deceitful lips;
a liar pays attention to a destructive tongue.

5 Whoever mocks the poor shows contempt for their Maker;
whoever gloats over disaster will not go unpunished.

6 Children's children are a crown to the aged,
and parents are the pride of their children.

7 Eloquent lips are unsuited to a godless fool —
how much worse lying lips to a ruler!

8 A bribe is seen as a charm by the one who gives it;
they think success will come at every turn.

9 Whoever would foster love covers over an offense,
but whoever repeats the matter separates close friends.

10 A rebuke impresses a discerning person
more than a hundred lashes a fool.

11 Evildoers foster rebellion against God;
the messenger of death will be sent against them.

12 Better to meet a bear robbed of her cubs
than a fool bent on folly.

13 Evil will never leave the house of one who pays back evil for good.

14 Starting a quarrel is like breaching a dam;
so drop the matter before a dispute breaks out.

15 Acquitting the guilty and condemning the innocent —
the LORD detests them both.

16 Why should fools have money in hand to buy wisdom,
when they are not able to understand it?

17 A friend loves at all times,
and a brother is born for a time of adversity.

18 One who has no sense shakes hands in pledge
and puts up security for a neighbor.

19 Whoever loves a quarrel loves sin;
whoever builds a high gate invites destruction.

20 One whose heart is corrupt does not prosper;
one whose tongue is perverse falls into trouble.

21 To have a fool for a child brings grief;
there is no joy for the parent of a godless fool.

22 A cheerful heart is good medicine,
but a crushed spirit dries up the bones.

23 The wicked accept bribes in secret
to pervert the course of justice.

24 A discerning person keeps
wisdom in view,
but a fool's eyes wander to the
ends of the earth.

25 A foolish son brings grief to his
father
and bitterness to the mother
who bore him.

26 If imposing a fine on the
innocent is not good,
surely to flog honest officials is
not right.

27 The one who has knowledge
uses words with restraint,
and whoever has
understanding is even-
tempered.

28 Even fools are thought wise if
they keep silent,
and discerning if they hold
their tongues.

18 An unfriendly person pursues
selfish ends
and against all sound
judgment starts quarrels.

2 Fools find no pleasure in
understanding
but delight in airing their own
opinions.

3 When wickedness comes, so
does contempt,
and with shame comes
reproach.

4 The words of the mouth are deep
waters,
but the fountain of wisdom is a
rushing stream.

5 It is not good to be partial to the
wicked
and so deprive the innocent of
justice.

6 The lips of fools bring them
strife,
and their mouths invite a
beating.

7 The mouths of fools are their
undoing,
and their lips are a snare to
their very lives.

8 The words of a gossip are like
choice morsels;
they go down to the inmost
parts.

9 One who is slack in his work
is brother to one who destroys.

10 The name of the LORD is a
fortified tower;
the righteous run to it and are
safe.

11 The wealth of the rich is their
fortified city;
they imagine it a wall too high
to scale.

12 Before a downfall the heart is
haughty,
but humility comes before
honor.

13 To answer before listening—
that is folly and shame.

14 The human spirit can endure in
sickness,
but a crushed spirit who can
bear?

15 The heart of the discerning
acquires knowledge,
for the ears of the wise seek it
out.

16 A gift opens the way
and ushers the giver into the
presence of the great.

17 In a lawsuit the first to speak
seems right,
until someone comes forward
and cross-examines.

18 Casting the lot settles disputes
and keeps strong opponents
apart.

19 A brother wronged is more
unyielding than a fortified
city;
disputes are like the barred
gates of a citadel.

20 From the fruit of their mouth a
person's stomach is filled;
with the harvest of their lips
they are satisfied.

21 The tongue has the power of life
and death,
and those who love it will eat
its fruit.

22 He who finds a wife finds what is
good
and receives favor from the
LORD.

23 The poor plead for mercy,
but the rich answer harshly.

24 One who has unreliable friends
soon comes to ruin,
but there is a friend who sticks
closer than a brother.

19 Better the poor whose walk is
blameless
than a fool whose lips are
perverse.

2 Desire without knowledge is not
good—
how much more will hasty feet
miss the way!

3 A person's own folly leads to
their ruin,
yet their heart rages against
the LORD.

4 Wealth attracts many friends,
but even the closest friend of
the poor person deserts
them.

5 A false witness will not go
unpunished,
and whoever pours out lies
will not go free.

6 Many curry favor with a ruler,
and everyone is the friend of
one who gives gifts.

7 The poor are shunned by all
their relatives—
how much more do their
friends avoid them!
Though the poor pursue them
with pleading,
they are nowhere to be
found.ᵃ

8 The one who gets wisdom loves
life;
the one who cherishes
understanding will soon
prosper.

9 A false witness will not go
unpunished,
and whoever pours out lies
will perish.

10 It is not fitting for a fool to live in
luxury—
how much worse for a slave to
rule over princes!

11 A person's wisdom yields
patience;
it is to one's glory to overlook
an offense.

12 A king's rage is like the roar of a
lion,
but his favor is like dew on the
grass.

13 A foolish child is a father's ruin,
and a quarrelsome wife is like
the constant dripping of a
leaky roof.

14 Houses and wealth are inherited
from parents,

ᵃ 7 The meaning of the Hebrew for this sentence is uncertain.

but a prudent wife is from the
LORD.

¹⁵ Laziness brings on deep sleep,
and the shiftless go hungry.

¹⁶ Whoever keeps commandments
keeps their life,
but whoever shows contempt
for their ways will die.

¹⁷ Whoever is kind to the poor
lends to the LORD,
and he will reward them for
what they have done.

¹⁸ Discipline your children, for in
that there is hope;
do not be a willing party to
their death.

¹⁹ A hot-tempered person must pay
the penalty;
rescue them, and you will have
to do it again.

²⁰ Listen to advice and accept
discipline,
and at the end you will be
counted among the wise.

²¹ Many are the plans in a person's
heart,
but it is the LORD's purpose
that prevails.

²² What a person desires is
unfailing love*ᵃ*;
better to be poor than a liar.

²³ The fear of the LORD leads to
life;
then one rests content,
untouched by trouble.

²⁴ A sluggard buries his hand in the
dish;
he will not even bring it back
to his mouth!

²⁵ Flog a mocker, and the simple
will learn prudence;

rebuke the discerning, and
they will gain knowledge.

²⁶ Whoever robs their father and
drives out their mother
is a child who brings shame
and disgrace.

²⁷ Stop listening to instruction, my
son,
and you will stray from the
words of knowledge.

²⁸ A corrupt witness mocks at
justice,
and the mouth of the wicked
gulps down evil.

²⁹ Penalties are prepared for
mockers,
and beatings for the backs of
fools.

20 Wine is a mocker and beer a
brawler;
whoever is led astray by them
is not wise.

² A king's wrath strikes terror like
the roar of a lion;
those who anger him forfeit
their lives.

³ It is to one's honor to avoid
strife,
but every fool is quick to
quarrel.

⁴ Sluggards do not plow in
season;
so at harvest time they look
but find nothing.

⁵ The purposes of a person's heart
are deep waters,
but one who has insight draws
them out.

⁶ Many claim to have unfailing
love,
but a faithful person who can
find?

---

*ᵃ 22 Or Greed is a person's shame*

7 The righteous lead blameless
      lives;
   blessed are their children after
      them.

8 When a king sits on his throne to
      judge,
   he winnows out all evil with
      his eyes.

9 Who can say, "I have kept my
      heart pure;
   I am clean and without sin"?

10 Differing weights and differing
      measures—
   the LORD detests them both.

11 Even small children are known
      by their actions,
   so is their conduct really pure
      and upright?

12 Ears that hear and eyes that
      see—
   the LORD has made them both.

13 Do not love sleep or you will
      grow poor;
   stay awake and you will have
      food to spare.

14 "It's no good, it's no good!" says
      the buyer—
   then goes off and boasts about
      the purchase.

15 Gold there is, and rubies in
      abundance,
   but lips that speak knowledge
      are a rare jewel.

16 Take the garment of one who
      puts up security for a
      stranger;
   hold it in pledge if it is done for
      an outsider.

17 Food gained by fraud tastes
      sweet,
   but one ends up with a mouth
      full of gravel.

18 Plans are established by seeking
      advice;
   so if you wage war, obtain
      guidance.

19 A gossip betrays a confidence;
   so avoid anyone who talks too
      much.

20 If someone curses their father or
      mother,
   their lamp will be snuffed out
      in pitch darkness.

21 An inheritance claimed too soon
   will not be blessed at the end.

22 Do not say, "I'll pay you back for
      this wrong!"
   Wait for the LORD, and he will
      avenge you.

23 The LORD detests differing
      weights,
   and dishonest scales do not
      please him.

24 A person's steps are directed by
      the LORD.
   How then can anyone
      understand their own
      way?

25 It is a trap to dedicate something
      rashly
   and only later to consider
      one's vows.

26 A wise king winnows out the
      wicked;
   he drives the threshing wheel
      over them.

27 The human spirit is[a] the lamp of
      the LORD
   that sheds light on one's
      inmost being.

28 Love and faithfulness keep a
      king safe;
   through love his throne is
      made secure.

a 27 Or A person's words are

29 The glory of young men is their
     strength,
  gray hair the splendor of the
     old.

30 Blows and wounds scrub away
     evil,
  and beatings purge the inmost
     being.

21 In the LORD's hand the king's
     heart is a stream of water
  that he channels toward all
     who please him.

2 A person may think their own
     ways are right,
  but the LORD weighs the heart.

3 To do what is right and just
  is more acceptable to the LORD
     than sacrifice.

4 Haughty eyes and a proud
     heart—
  the unplowed field of the
     wicked—produce sin.

5 The plans of the diligent lead to
     profit
  as surely as haste leads to
     poverty.

6 A fortune made by a lying
     tongue
  is a fleeting vapor and a deadly
     snare.[a]

7 The violence of the wicked will
     drag them away,
  for they refuse to do what is
     right.

8 The way of the guilty is devious,
  but the conduct of the
     innocent is upright.

9 Better to live on a corner of the
     roof
  than share a house with a
     quarrelsome wife.

10 The wicked crave evil;
  their neighbors get no mercy
     from them.

11 When a mocker is punished, the
     simple gain wisdom;
  by paying attention to the wise
     they get knowledge.

12 The Righteous One[b] takes note
     of the house of the
     wicked
  and brings the wicked to ruin.

13 Whoever shuts their ears to the
     cry of the poor
  will also cry out and not be
     answered.

14 A gift given in secret soothes
     anger,
  and a bribe concealed in the
     cloak pacifies great
     wrath.

15 When justice is done, it brings
     joy to the righteous
  but terror to evildoers.

16 Whoever strays from the path of
     prudence
  comes to rest in the company
     of the dead.

17 Whoever loves pleasure will
     become poor;
  whoever loves wine and olive
     oil will never be rich.

18 The wicked become a ransom for
     the righteous,
  and the unfaithful for the
     upright.

19 Better to live in a desert
  than with a quarrelsome and
     nagging wife.

20 The wise store up choice food
     and olive oil,
  but fools gulp theirs down.

---

[a] 6 Some Hebrew manuscripts, Septuagint and Vulgate; most Hebrew manuscripts *vapor for those who seek death*    [b] 12 Or *The righteous person*

21 Whoever pursues righteousness
and love
 finds life, prosperity[a] and
honor.

22 One who is wise can go up
against the city of the
mighty
 and pull down the stronghold
in which they trust.

23 Those who guard their mouths
and their tongues
 keep themselves from
calamity.

24 The proud and arrogant
person— "Mocker" is his
name—
 behaves with insolent fury.

25 The craving of a sluggard will be
the death of him,
 because his hands refuse to
work.

26 All day long he craves for more,
 but the righteous give without
sparing.

27 The sacrifice of the wicked is
detestable—
 how much more so when
brought with evil intent!

28 A false witness will perish,
 but a careful listener will
testify successfully.

29 The wicked put up a bold front,
 but the upright give thought to
their ways.

30 There is no wisdom, no insight,
no plan
 that can succeed against the
LORD.

31 The horse is made ready for the
day of battle,
 but victory rests with the
LORD.

22 A good name is more
desirable than great
riches;
 to be esteemed is better than
silver or gold.

2 Rich and poor have this in
common:
 The LORD is the Maker of them
all.

3 The prudent see danger and take
refuge,
 but the simple keep going and
pay the penalty.

4 Humility is the fear of the LORD;
 its wages are riches and honor
and life.

5 In the paths of the wicked are
snares and pitfalls,
 but those who would preserve
their life stay far from
them.

6 Start children off on the way
they should go,
 and even when they are old
they will not turn from it.

7 The rich rule over the poor,
 and the borrower is slave to
the lender.

8 Whoever sows injustice reaps
calamity,
 and the rod they wield in fury
will be broken.

9 The generous will themselves be
blessed,
 for they share their food with
the poor.

10 Drive out the mocker, and out
goes strife;
 quarrels and insults are ended.

11 One who loves a pure heart and
who speaks with grace
 will have the king for a friend.

a 21 Or *righteousness*

12 The eyes of the LORD keep watch
　　over knowledge,
　　but he frustrates the words of
　　　　the unfaithful.

13 The sluggard says, "There's a
　　lion outside!
　　I'll be killed in the public
　　　　square!"

14 The mouth of an adulterous
　　woman is a deep pit;
　　a man who is under the LORD's
　　　　wrath falls into it.

15 Folly is bound up in the heart of
　　a child,
　　but the rod of discipline will
　　　　drive it far away.

16 One who oppresses the poor to
　　increase his wealth
　　and one who gives gifts to
　　　　the rich — both come to
　　　　poverty.

17 Pay attention and turn your ear
　　to the sayings of the wise;
　　apply your heart to what I
　　　　teach,

18 for it is pleasing when you keep
　　them in your heart
　　and have all of them ready on
　　　　your lips.

19 So that your trust may be in the
　　LORD,
　　I teach you today, even you.

20 Have I not written thirty sayings
　　for you,
　　sayings of counsel and
　　　　knowledge,

21 teaching you to be honest and to
　　speak the truth,
　　so that you bring back truthful
　　　　reports
　　to those you serve?

22 Do not exploit the poor because
　　they are poor

and do not crush the needy in
　　court,

23 for the LORD will take up their
　　case
　　and will exact life for life.

24 Do not make friends with a hot-
　　tempered person,
　　do not associate with one
　　　　easily angered,

25 or you may learn their ways
　　and get yourself ensnared.

26 Do not be one who shakes hands
　　in pledge
　　or puts up security for debts;

27 if you lack the means to pay,
　　your very bed will be snatched
　　　　from under you.

28 Do not move an ancient
　　boundary stone
　　set up by your ancestors.

29 Do you see someone skilled in
　　their work?
　　They will serve before kings;
　　they will not serve before
　　　　officials of low rank.

23 When you sit to dine with a
　　ruler,
　　note well what[a] is before you,

2 and put a knife to your throat
　　if you are given to gluttony.

3 Do not crave his delicacies,
　　for that food is deceptive.

4 Do not wear yourself out to get
　　rich;
　　do not trust your own
　　　　cleverness.

5 Cast but a glance at riches, and
　　they are gone,
　　for they will surely sprout wings
　　and fly off to the sky like an
　　　　eagle.

6 Do not eat the food of a
　　begrudging host,

---

a 1 Or who

do not crave his delicacies;
7 for he is the kind of person
    who is always thinking about
    the cost.a
"Eat and drink," he says to you,
    but his heart is not with you.
8 You will vomit up the little you
    have eaten
    and will have wasted your
    compliments.

9 Do not speak to fools,
    for they will scorn your
    prudent words.

10 Do not move an ancient
    boundary stone
    or encroach on the fields of the
    fatherless,
11 for their Defender is strong;
    he will take up their case
    against you.

12 Apply your heart to instruction
    and your ears to words of
    knowledge.

13 Do not withhold discipline from
    a child;
    if you punish them with the
    rod, they will not die.
14 Punish them with the rod
    and save them from death.

15 My son, if your heart is wise,
    then my heart will be glad
    indeed;
16 my inmost being will rejoice
    when your lips speak what is
    right.

17 Do not let your heart envy
    sinners,
    but always be zealous for the
    fear of the LORD.
18 There is surely a future hope for
    you,
    and your hope will not be cut
    off.

19 Listen, my son, and be wise,
    and set your heart on the right
    path:
20 Do not join those who drink too
    much wine
    or gorge themselves on meat,
21 for drunkards and gluttons
    become poor,
    and drowsiness clothes them
    in rags.

22 Listen to your father, who gave
    you life,
    and do not despise your
    mother when she is old.
23 Buy the truth and do not sell it —
    wisdom, instruction and
    insight as well.
24 The father of a righteous child
    has great joy;
    a man who fathers a wise son
    rejoices in him.
25 May your father and mother
    rejoice;
    may she who gave you birth be
    joyful!

26 My son, give me your heart
    and let your eyes delight in my
    ways,
27 for an adulterous woman is a
    deep pit,
    and a wayward wife is a
    narrow well.
28 Like a bandit she lies in wait
    and multiplies the unfaithful
    among men.

29 Who has woe? Who has sorrow?
    Who has strife? Who has
    complaints?
    Who has needless bruises?
    Who has bloodshot eyes?
30 Those who linger over wine,
    who go to sample bowls of
    mixed wine.
31 Do not gaze at wine when it is
    red,

a 7 Or *for as he thinks within himself, / so he is*; or *for as he puts on a feast, / so he is*

when it sparkles in the cup,
when it goes down smoothly!
<sup>32</sup>In the end it bites like a snake
and poisons like a viper.
<sup>33</sup>Your eyes will see strange sights,
and your mind will imagine
confusing things.
<sup>34</sup>You will be like one sleeping on
the high seas,
lying on top of the rigging.
<sup>35</sup>"They hit me," you will say, "but
I'm not hurt!
They beat me, but I don't feel
it!
When will I wake up
so I can find another drink?"

24 Do not envy the wicked,
do not desire their company;
<sup>2</sup>for their hearts plot violence,
and their lips talk about
making trouble.

<sup>3</sup>By wisdom a house is built,
and through understanding it
is established;
<sup>4</sup>through knowledge its rooms
are filled
with rare and beautiful
treasures.

<sup>5</sup>The wise prevail through great
power,
and those who have
knowledge muster their
strength.
<sup>6</sup>Surely you need guidance to
wage war,
and victory is won through
many advisers.

<sup>7</sup>Wisdom is too high for fools;
in the assembly at the gate
they must not open their
mouths.

<sup>8</sup>Whoever plots evil
will be known as a schemer.
<sup>9</sup>The schemes of folly are sin,
and people detest a mocker.

<sup>10</sup>If you falter in a time of
trouble,
how small is your strength!
<sup>11</sup>Rescue those being led away to
death;
hold back those staggering
toward slaughter.
<sup>12</sup>If you say, "But we knew nothing
about this,"
does not he who weighs the
heart perceive it?
Does not he who guards your life
know it?
Will he not repay everyone
according to what they
have done?

<sup>13</sup>Eat honey, my son, for it is good;
honey from the comb is sweet
to your taste.
<sup>14</sup>Know also that wisdom is like
honey for you:
If you find it, there is a future
hope for you,
and your hope will not be cut
off.

<sup>15</sup>Do not lurk like a thief near the
house of the righteous,
do not plunder their dwelling
place;
<sup>16</sup>for though the righteous fall
seven times, they rise
again,
but the wicked stumble when
calamity strikes.

<sup>17</sup>Do not gloat when your enemy
falls;
when they stumble, do not let
your heart rejoice,
<sup>18</sup>or the LORD will see and
disapprove
and turn his wrath away from
them.

<sup>19</sup>Do not fret because of evildoers
or be envious of the wicked,
<sup>20</sup>for the evildoer has no future
hope,

and the lamp of the wicked
    will be snuffed out.

²¹ Fear the LORD and the king, my
    son,
and do not join with rebellious
    officials,
²² for those two will send sudden
    destruction on them,
and who knows what
    calamities they can bring?

²³ These also are sayings of the
    wise:

To show partiality in judging is
    not good:
²⁴ Whoever says to the guilty, "You
    are innocent,"
will be cursed by peoples and
    denounced by nations.
²⁵ But it will go well with those who
    convict the guilty,
and rich blessing will come on
    them.

²⁶ An honest answer
    is like a kiss on the lips.

²⁷ Put your outdoor work in order
    and get your fields ready;
after that, build your house.

²⁸ Do not testify against your
    neighbor without cause—
would you use your lips to
    mislead?
²⁹ Do not say, "I'll do to them as
    they have done to me;
I'll pay them back for what
    they did."

³⁰ I went past the field of a
    sluggard,
past the vineyard of someone
    who has no sense;
³¹ thorns had come up
    everywhere,
the ground was covered with
    weeds,

and the stone wall was in
    ruins.
³² I applied my heart to what I
    observed
and learned a lesson from
    what I saw:
³³ A little sleep, a little slumber,
a little folding of the hands to
    rest—
³⁴ and poverty will come on you
    like a thief
and scarcity like an armed
    man.

25 These are more proverbs of
    Solomon, compiled by the
men of Hezekiah king of Judah:

² It is the glory of God to conceal a
    matter;
to search out a matter is the
    glory of kings.
³ As the heavens are high and the
    earth is deep,
so the hearts of kings are
    unsearchable.

⁴ Remove the dross from the
    silver,
and a silversmith can produce
    a vessel;
⁵ remove wicked officials from the
    king's presence,
and his throne will be
    established through
    righteousness.

⁶ Do not exalt yourself in the
    king's presence,
and do not claim a place
    among his great men;
⁷ it is better for him to say to you,
    "Come up here,"
than for him to humiliate you
    before his nobles.

What you have seen with your
    eyes
⁸   do not bring*a* hastily to court,

---

*a* 7,8 Or *nobles / on whom you had set your eyes.* / *⁸Do not go*

for what will you do in the end
if your neighbor puts you to
shame?

9 If you take your neighbor to
court,
do not betray another's
confidence,

10 or the one who hears it may
shame you
and the charge against you
will stand.

11 Like apples[a] of gold in settings of
silver
is a ruling rightly given.

12 Like an earring of gold or an
ornament of fine gold
is the rebuke of a wise judge to
a listening ear.

13 Like a snow-cooled drink at
harvest time
is a trustworthy messenger to
the one who sends him;
he refreshes the spirit of his
master.

14 Like clouds and wind without
rain
is one who boasts of gifts never
given.

15 Through patience a ruler can be
persuaded,
and a gentle tongue can break
a bone.

16 If you find honey, eat just
enough—
too much of it, and you will
vomit.

17 Seldom set foot in your
neighbor's house—
too much of you, and they will
hate you.

18 Like a club or a sword or a sharp
arrow

is one who gives false
testimony against a
neighbor.

19 Like a broken tooth or a lame
foot
is reliance on the unfaithful in
a time of trouble.

20 Like one who takes away a
garment on a cold day,
or like vinegar poured on a
wound,
is one who sings songs to a
heavy heart.

21 If your enemy is hungry, give
him food to eat;
if he is thirsty, give him water
to drink.

22 In doing this, you will heap
burning coals on his head,
and the LORD will reward you.

23 Like a north wind that brings
unexpected rain
is a sly tongue—which
provokes a horrified look.

24 Better to live on a corner of the
roof
than share a house with a
quarrelsome wife.

25 Like cold water to a weary soul
is good news from a distant
land.

26 Like a muddied spring or a
polluted well
are the righteous who give way
to the wicked.

27 It is not good to eat too much
honey,
nor is it honorable to search
out matters that are too
deep.

28 Like a city whose walls are
broken through
is a person who lacks
self-control.

a 11 Or possibly apricots

26 Like snow in summer or rain in harvest,
    honor is not fitting for a fool.
² Like a fluttering sparrow or a darting swallow,
    an undeserved curse does not come to rest.
³ A whip for the horse, a bridle for the donkey,
    and a rod for the backs of fools!
⁴ Do not answer a fool according to his folly,
    or you yourself will be just like him.
⁵ Answer a fool according to his folly,
    or he will be wise in his own eyes.
⁶ Sending a message by the hands of a fool
    is like cutting off one's feet or drinking poison.
⁷ Like the useless legs of one who is lame
    is a proverb in the mouth of a fool.
⁸ Like tying a stone in a sling
    is the giving of honor to a fool.
⁹ Like a thornbush in a drunkard's hand
    is a proverb in the mouth of a fool.
¹⁰ Like an archer who wounds at random
    is one who hires a fool or any passer-by.
¹¹ As a dog returns to its vomit,
    so fools repeat their folly.
¹² Do you see a person wise in their own eyes?
    There is more hope for a fool than for them.
¹³ A sluggard says, "There's a lion in the road,
    a fierce lion roaming the streets!"

¹⁴ As a door turns on its hinges,
    so a sluggard turns on his bed.
¹⁵ A sluggard buries his hand in the dish;
    he is too lazy to bring it back to his mouth.
¹⁶ A sluggard is wiser in his own eyes
    than seven people who answer discreetly.
¹⁷ Like one who grabs a stray dog by the ears
    is someone who rushes into a quarrel not their own.
¹⁸ Like a maniac shooting flaming arrows of death
¹⁹ is one who deceives their neighbor
    and says, "I was only joking!"
²⁰ Without wood a fire goes out;
    without a gossip a quarrel dies down.
²¹ As charcoal to embers and as wood to fire,
    so is a quarrelsome person for kindling strife.
²² The words of a gossip are like choice morsels;
    they go down to the inmost parts.
²³ Like a coating of silver dross on earthenware
    are fervent[a] lips with an evil heart.
²⁴ Enemies disguise themselves with their lips,
    but in their hearts they harbor deceit.
²⁵ Though their speech is charming, do not believe them,
    for seven abominations fill their hearts.
²⁶ Their malice may be concealed by deception,

---

*a 23* Hebrew; Septuagint *smooth*

but their wickedness will be
exposed in the assembly.

27 Whoever digs a pit will fall into
it;
if someone rolls a stone, it will
roll back on them.

28 A lying tongue hates those it
hurts,
and a flattering mouth works
ruin.

27 Do not boast about tomorrow,
for you do not know what a
day may bring.

2 Let someone else praise you, and
not your own mouth;
an outsider, and not your own
lips.

3 Stone is heavy and sand a
burden,
but a fool's provocation is
heavier than both.

4 Anger is cruel and fury
overwhelming,
but who can stand before
jealousy?

5 Better is open rebuke
than hidden love.

6 Wounds from a friend can be
trusted,
but an enemy multiplies
kisses.

7 One who is full loathes honey
from the comb,
but to the hungry even what is
bitter tastes sweet.

8 Like a bird that flees its nest
is anyone who flees from
home.

9 Perfume and incense bring joy
to the heart,
and the pleasantness of a
friend

springs from their heartfelt
advice.

10 Do not forsake your friend or a
friend of your family,
and do not go to your relative's
house when disaster
strikes you —
better a neighbor nearby than
a relative far away.

11 Be wise, my son, and bring joy to
my heart;
then I can answer anyone who
treats me with contempt.

12 The prudent see danger and take
refuge,
but the simple keep going and
pay the penalty.

13 Take the garment of one who
puts up security for a
stranger;
hold it in pledge if it is done for
an outsider.

14 If anyone loudly blesses their
neighbor early in the
morning,
it will be taken as a curse.

15 A quarrelsome wife is like the
dripping
of a leaky roof in a rainstorm;

16 restraining her is like
restraining the wind
or grasping oil with the hand.

17 As iron sharpens iron,
so one person sharpens
another.

18 The one who guards a fig tree
will eat its fruit,
and whoever protects their
master will be honored.

19 As water reflects the face,
so one's life reflects the
heart.[a]

a 19 Or so others reflect your heart back to you

²⁰ Death and Destruction[a] are
    never satisfied,
    and neither are human eyes.

²¹ The crucible for silver and the
    furnace for gold,
    but people are tested by their
    praise.

²² Though you grind a fool in a
    mortar,
    grinding them like grain with
    a pestle,
    you will not remove their folly
    from them.

²³ Be sure you know the condition
    of your flocks,
    give careful attention to your
    herds;

²⁴ for riches do not endure forever,
    and a crown is not secure for
    all generations.

²⁵ When the hay is removed and
    new growth appears
    and the grass from the hills is
    gathered in,

²⁶ the lambs will provide you with
    clothing,
    and the goats with the price of
    a field.

²⁷ You will have plenty of goats'
    milk to feed your family
    and to nourish your female
    servants.

**28** The wicked flee though no
    one pursues,
    but the righteous are as bold
    as a lion.

² When a country is rebellious, it
    has many rulers,
    but a ruler with discernment
    and knowledge maintains
    order.

³ A ruler[b] who oppresses the poor
    is like a driving rain that
    leaves no crops.

⁴ Those who forsake instruction
    praise the wicked,
    but those who heed it resist
    them.

⁵ Evildoers do not understand
    what is right,
    but those who seek the Lᴏʀᴅ
    understand it fully.

⁶ Better the poor whose walk is
    blameless
    than the rich whose ways are
    perverse.

⁷ A discerning son heeds
    instruction,
    but a companion of gluttons
    disgraces his father.

⁸ Whoever increases wealth by
    taking interest or profit
    from the poor
    amasses it for another, who
    will be kind to the poor.

⁹ If anyone turns a deaf ear to my
    instruction,
    even their prayers are
    detestable.

¹⁰ Whoever leads the upright along
    an evil path
    will fall into their own trap,
    but the blameless will receive
    a good inheritance.

¹¹ The rich are wise in their own
    eyes;
    one who is poor and
    discerning sees how
    deluded they are.

¹² When the righteous triumph,
    there is great elation;
    but when the wicked rise to
    power, people go into
    hiding.

¹³ Whoever conceals their sins
    does not prosper,

---

a 20 Hebrew *Abaddon*   b 3 Or *A poor person*

but the one who confesses
and renounces them finds
mercy.

¹⁴ Blessed is the one who always
trembles before God,
but whoever hardens their
heart falls into trouble.

¹⁵ Like a roaring lion or a charging
bear
is a wicked ruler over a
helpless people.

¹⁶ A tyrannical ruler practices
extortion,
but one who hates ill-gotten
gain will enjoy a long
reign.

¹⁷ Anyone tormented by the guilt of
murder
will seek refuge in the grave;
let no one hold them back.

¹⁸ The one whose walk is blameless
is kept safe,
but the one whose ways are
perverse will fall into the
pit.ᵃ

¹⁹ Those who work their land will
have abundant food,
but those who chase fantasies
will have their fill of
poverty.

²⁰ A faithful person will be richly
blessed,
but one eager to get rich will
not go unpunished.

²¹ To show partiality is not good —
yet a person will do wrong for
a piece of bread.

²² The stingy are eager to get rich
and are unaware that poverty
awaits them.

²³ Whoever rebukes a person will
in the end gain favor

rather than one who has a
flattering tongue.

²⁴ Whoever robs their father or
mother
and says, "It's not wrong,"
is partner to one who destroys.

²⁵ The greedy stir up conflict,
but those who trust in the
LORD will prosper.

²⁶ Those who trust in themselves
are fools,
but those who walk in wisdom
are kept safe.

²⁷ Those who give to the poor will
lack nothing,
but those who close their eyes
to them receive many
curses.

²⁸ When the wicked rise to power,
people go into hiding;
but when the wicked perish,
the righteous thrive.

29 Whoever remains stiff-
necked after many
rebukes
will suddenly be destroyed —
without remedy.

² When the righteous thrive, the
people rejoice;
when the wicked rule, the
people groan.

³ A man who loves wisdom brings
joy to his father,
but a companion of prostitutes
squanders his wealth.

⁴ By justice a king gives a country
stability,
but those who are greedy forᵇ
bribes tear it down.

⁵ Those who flatter their
neighbors
are spreading nets for their feet.

---

ᵃ 18 Syriac (see Septuagint); Hebrew *into one*    ᵇ 4 Or *who give*

6 Evildoers are snared by their
    own sin,
  but the righteous shout for joy
    and are glad.

7 The righteous care about justice
    for the poor,
  but the wicked have no such
    concern.

8 Mockers stir up a city,
  but the wise turn away
    anger.

9 If a wise person goes to court
    with a fool,
  the fool rages and scoffs, and
    there is no peace.

10 The bloodthirsty hate a person
    of integrity
  and seek to kill the upright.

11 Fools give full vent to their
    rage,
  but the wise bring calm in the
    end.

12 If a ruler listens to lies,
  all his officials become
    wicked.

13 The poor and the oppressor have
    this in common:
  The LORD gives sight to the
    eyes of both.

14 If a king judges the poor with
    fairness,
  his throne will be established
    forever.

15 A rod and a reprimand impart
    wisdom,
  but a child left undisciplined
    disgraces its mother.

16 When the wicked thrive, so does
    sin,
  but the righteous will see their
    downfall.

17 Discipline your children, and
    they will give you peace;

  they will bring you the
    delights you desire.

18 Where there is no revelation,
    people cast off restraint;
  but blessed is the one
    who heeds wisdom's
    instruction.

19 Servants cannot be corrected by
    mere words;
  though they understand, they
    will not respond.

20 Do you see someone who speaks
    in haste?
  There is more hope for a fool
    than for them.

21 A servant pampered from
    youth
  will turn out to be insolent.

22 An angry person stirs up
    conflict,
  and a hot-tempered person
    commits many sins.

23 Pride brings a person low,
  but the lowly in spirit gain
    honor.

24 The accomplices of thieves are
    their own enemies;
  they are put under oath and
    dare not testify.

25 Fear of man will prove to be a
    snare,
  but whoever trusts in the LORD
    is kept safe.

26 Many seek an audience with a
    ruler,
  but it is from the LORD that one
    gets justice.

27 The righteous detest the
    dishonest;
  the wicked detest the
    upright.

30 The sayings of Agur son of Ja-
    keh — an inspired utterance.

This man's utterance to Ithiel:

"I am weary, God,
     but I can prevail.[a]
2 Surely I am only a brute, not a
     man;
  I do not have human
     understanding.
3 I have not learned wisdom,
  nor have I attained to the
     knowledge of the Holy
     One.
4 Who has gone up to heaven and
     come down?
  Whose hands have gathered
     up the wind?
  Who has wrapped up the waters
     in a cloak?
  Who has established all the
     ends of the earth?
  What is his name, and what is
     the name of his son?
  Surely you know!

5 "Every word of God is flawless;
  he is a shield to those who take
     refuge in him.
6 Do not add to his words,
  or he will rebuke you and
     prove you a liar.

7 "Two things I ask of you, LORD;
  do not refuse me before I die:
8 Keep falsehood and lies far from
     me;
  give me neither poverty nor
     riches,
  but give me only my daily
     bread.
9 Otherwise, I may have too much
     and disown you
  and say, 'Who is the LORD?'
  Or I may become poor and
     steal,
  and so dishonor the name of
     my God.

10 "Do not slander a servant to
     their master,
  or they will curse you, and you
     will pay for it.

11 "There are those who curse their
     fathers
  and do not bless their
     mothers;
12 those who are pure in their own
     eyes
  and yet are not cleansed of
     their filth;
13 those whose eyes are ever so
     haughty,
  whose glances are so
     disdainful;
14 those whose teeth are swords
  and whose jaws are set with
     knives
  to devour the poor from the
     earth
  and the needy from among
     mankind.

15 "The leech has two daughters.
  'Give! Give!' they cry.

  "There are three things that are
     never satisfied,
  four that never say, 'Enough!':
16 the grave, the barren womb,
  land, which is never satisfied
     with water,
  and fire, which never says,
     'Enough!'

17 "The eye that mocks a father,
  that scorns an aged mother,
  will be pecked out by the ravens
     of the valley,
  will be eaten by the vultures.

18 "There are three things that are
     too amazing for me,
  four that I do not understand:
19 the way of an eagle in the sky,
  the way of a snake on a rock,

---

a 1  With a different word division of the Hebrew; Masoretic Text *utterance to Ithiel, / to Ithiel and Ukal:*

the way of a ship on the high
    seas,
and the way of a man with a
    young woman.

20 "This is the way of an adulterous
    woman:
    She eats and wipes her mouth
    and says, 'I've done nothing
        wrong.'

21 "Under three things the earth
    trembles,
    under four it cannot bear up:
22 a servant who becomes king,
    a godless fool who gets plenty
        to eat,
23 a contemptible woman who gets
    married,
    and a servant who displaces
        her mistress.

24 "Four things on earth are small,
    yet they are extremely wise:
25 Ants are creatures of little
    strength,
    yet they store up their food in
        the summer;
26 hyraxes are creatures of little
    power,
    yet they make their home in
        the crags;
27 locusts have no king,
    yet they advance together in
        ranks;
28 a lizard can be caught with the
    hand,
    yet it is found in kings'
        palaces.

29 "There are three things that are
    stately in their stride,
    four that move with stately
        bearing:
30 a lion, mighty among beasts,
    who retreats before nothing;
31 a strutting rooster, a he-goat,
    and a king secure against
        revolt.[a]

32 "If you play the fool and exalt
    yourself,
    or if you plan evil,
    clap your hand over your
        mouth!
33 For as churning cream produces
    butter,
    and as twisting the nose
        produces blood,
    so stirring up anger produces
        strife."

31 The sayings of King Lemu-
    el—an inspired utterance his
mother taught him.

2 Listen, my son! Listen, son of my
    womb!
    Listen, my son, the answer to
        my prayers!
3 Do not spend your strength[b] on
    women,
    your vigor on those who ruin
        kings.

4 It is not for kings, Lemuel—
    it is not for kings to drink
        wine,
    not for rulers to crave beer,
5 lest they drink and forget what
    has been decreed,
    and deprive all the oppressed
        of their rights.
6 Let beer be for those who are
    perishing,
    wine for those who are in
        anguish!
7 Let them drink and forget their
    poverty
    and remember their misery no
        more.

8 Speak up for those who cannot
    speak for themselves,
    for the rights of all who are
        destitute.
9 Speak up and judge fairly;
    defend the rights of the poor
        and needy.

a 31 The meaning of the Hebrew for this phrase is uncertain.    b 3 Or *wealth*

10 [a]A wife of noble character who
    can find?
  She is worth far more than
    rubies.
11 Her husband has full confidence
    in her
  and lacks nothing of value.
12 She brings him good, not harm,
  all the days of her life.
13 She selects wool and flax
  and works with eager hands.
14 She is like the merchant ships,
  bringing her food from afar.
15 She gets up while it is still
    night;
  she provides food for her
    family
  and portions for her female
    servants.
16 She considers a field and buys it;
  out of her earnings she plants
    a vineyard.
17 She sets about her work
    vigorously;
  her arms are strong for her
    tasks.
18 She sees that her trading is
    profitable,
  and her lamp does not go out
    at night.
19 In her hand she holds the distaff
  and grasps the spindle with
    her fingers.
20 She opens her arms to the poor
  and extends her hands to the
    needy.
21 When it snows, she has no fear
    for her household;

for all of them are clothed in
    scarlet.
22 She makes coverings for her bed;
  she is clothed in fine linen and
    purple.
23 Her husband is respected at the
    city gate,
  where he takes his seat among
    the elders of the land.
24 She makes linen garments and
    sells them,
  and supplies the merchants
    with sashes.
25 She is clothed with strength and
    dignity;
  she can laugh at the days to
    come.
26 She speaks with wisdom,
  and faithful instruction is on
    her tongue.
27 She watches over the affairs of
    her household
  and does not eat the bread of
    idleness.
28 Her children arise and call her
    blessed;
  her husband also, and he
    praises her:
29 "Many women do noble things,
  but you surpass them all."
30 Charm is deceptive, and beauty
    is fleeting;
  but a woman who fears the
    Lord is to be praised.
31 Honor her for all that her hands
    have done,
  and let her works bring her
    praise at the city gate.

---

[a] 10 Verses 10-31 are an acrostic poem, the verses of which begin with the successive letters of
the Hebrew alphabet.

# TABLE OF WEIGHTS AND MEASURES

| | Biblical Unit | Approximate American Equivalent | Approximate Metric Equivalent |
|---|---|---|---|
| **Weights** | talent (60 minas) | 75 pounds | 34 kilograms |
| | mina (50 shekels) | 1 1/4 pounds | 560 grams |
| | shekel (2 bekas) | 2/5 ounce | 11.5 grams |
| | pim (2/3 shekel) | 1/4 ounce | 7.8 grams |
| | beka (10 gerahs) | 1/5 ounce | 5.7 grams |
| | gerah | 1/50 ounce | 0.6 gram |
| | daric | 1/3 ounce | 8.4 grams |
| **Length** | cubit | 18 inches | 45 centimeters |
| | span | 9 inches | 23 centimeters |
| | handbreadth | 3 inches | 7.5 centimeters |
| | stadion (pl. stadia) | 600 feet | 183 meters |
| **Capacity** | | | |
| *Dry Measure* | cor [homer] (10 ephahs) | 6 bushels | 220 liters |
| | lethek (5 ephahs) | 3 bushels | 110 liters |
| | ephah (10 omers) | 3/5 bushel | 22 liters |
| | seah (1/3 ephah) | 7 quarts | 7.5 liters |
| | omer (1/10 ephah) | 2 quarts | 2 liters |
| | cab (1/18 ephah) | 1 quart | 1 liter |
| *Liquid Measure* | bath (1 ephah) | 6 gallons | 22 liters |
| | hin (1/6 bath) | 1 gallon | 3.8 liters |
| | log (1/72 bath) | 1/3 quart | 0.3 liter |

The figures of the table are calculated on the basis of a shekel equaling 11.5 grams, a cubit equaling 18 inches and an ephah equaling 22 liters. The quart referred to is either a dry quart (slightly larger than a liter) or a liquid quart (slightly smaller than a liter), whichever is applicable. The ton referred to in the footnotes is the American ton of 2,000 pounds. These weights are calculated relative to the particular commodity involved. Accordingly, the same measure of capacity in the text may be converted into different weights in the footnotes.

This table is based upon the best available information, but it is not intended to be mathematically precise; like the measurement equivalents in the footnotes, it merely gives approximate amounts and distances. Weights and measures differed somewhat at various times and places in the ancient world. There is uncertainty particularly about the ephah and the bath; further discoveries may shed more light on these units of capacity.

# ABOUT THE NIV

The goal of the New International Version (NIV) is to enable English-speaking people from around the world to read and hear God's eternal Word in their own language. Our work as translators is motivated by our conviction that the Bible is God's Word in written form. We believe that the Bible contains the divine answer to the deepest needs of humanity, sheds unique light on our path in a dark world and sets forth the way to our eternal well-being. Out of these deep convictions, we have sought to recreate as far as possible the experience of the original audience — blending transparency to the original text with accessibility for the millions of English speakers around the world. We have prioritized accuracy, clarity and literary quality with the goal of creating a translation suitable for public and private reading, evangelism, teaching, preaching, memorizing and liturgical use. We have also sought to preserve a measure of continuity with the long tradition of translating the Scriptures into English.

The complete NIV Bible was first published in 1978. It was a completely new translation made by over a hundred scholars working directly from the best available Hebrew, Aramaic and Greek texts. The translators came from the United States, Great Britain, Canada, Australia and New Zealand, giving the translation an international scope. They were from many denominations and churches — including Anglican, Assemblies of God, Baptist, Brethren, Christian Reformed, Church of Christ, Evangelical Covenant, Evangelical Free, Lutheran, Mennonite, Methodist, Nazarene, Presbyterian, Wesleyan and others. This breadth of denominational and theological perspective helped to safeguard the translation from sectarian bias. For these reasons, and by the grace of God, the NIV has gained a wide readership in all parts of the English-speaking world.

The work of translating the Bible is never finished. As good as they are, English translations must be regularly updated so that they will continue to communicate accurately the meaning of God's Word. Updates are needed in order to reflect the latest developments in our understanding of the biblical world and its languages and to keep pace with changes in English usage. Recognizing, then, that the NIV would retain its ability to communicate God's Word accurately only if it were regularly updated, the original translators established the Committee on Bible Translation (CBT). The Committee is a self-perpetuating group of biblical scholars charged with keeping abreast of advances in biblical scholarship and changes in English and issuing periodic updates to the NIV. The CBT is an independent, self-governing body and has sole responsibility for the NIV text. The Committee mirrors the original group of translators in its diverse international and denominational makeup and in its unifying commitment to the Bible as God's inspired Word.

In obedience to its mandate, the Committee has issued periodic updates to the NIV. An initial revision was released in 1984. A more thorough revision process was completed in 2005, resulting in the separately published TNIV. The updated NIV you now have in your hands builds on both the original NIV and the TNIV and represents the latest effort of the Committee to articulate God's unchanging Word in the way the original authors might have said it had they been speaking in English to the global English-speaking audience today.

## Translation Philosophy

The Committee's translating work has been governed by three widely accepted principles about the way people use words and about the way we understand them.

First, the meaning of words is determined by the way that users of the language actually use them at any given time. For the biblical languages, therefore, the Committee utilizes the best and most recent scholarship on the way Hebrew, Aramaic and Greek words were being used in biblical times. At the same time, the Committee carefully studies the state of modern English. Good translation is like good communication: one must know the target audience so that the appropriate choices can be made about which English words to use to represent the original words of Scripture. From its inception, the NIV has had as its target the general English-speaking population all over the world, the "International" in its title reflecting this concern. The aim of the Committee is to put the Scriptures into natural English that will communicate effectively with the broadest possible audience of English speakers.

Modern technology has enhanced the Committee's ability to choose the right English words to convey the meaning of the original text. The field of computational linguistics harnesses the power of computers to provide broadly applicable and current data about the state of the language. Translators can now access huge databases of modern English to better understand the current meaning and usage of key words. The Committee utilized this resource in preparing the 2011 edition of the NIV. An area of especially rapid and significant change in English is the way certain nouns and pronouns are used to refer to human beings. The Committee therefore requested experts in computational linguistics at Collins Dictionaries to pose some key questions about this usage to its database of English — the largest in the world, with over 4.4 billion words, gathered from several English-speaking countries and including both spoken and written English. (The Collins Study, called "The Development and Use of Gender Language in Contemporary English," can be accessed at *http://www.thenivbible.com/about-the-niv/about-the-2011-edition/*.) The study revealed that the most popular words to describe the human race in modern U.S. English were "humanity," "man" and "mankind." The Committee then used this data in the updated NIV, choosing from among these three words (and occasionally others also) depending on the context.

A related issue creates a larger problem for modern translations: the move away from using the third-person masculine singular pronouns — "he/him/his" — to refer to men and women equally. This usage does persist in some forms of English, and this revision therefore occasionally uses these pronouns in a generic sense. But the tendency, recognized in day-to-day usage and confirmed by the Collins study, is away from the generic use of "he," "him" and "his." In recognition of this shift in language and in an effort to translate into the natural English that people are actually using, this revision of the NIV generally uses other constructions when the biblical text is plainly addressed to men and women equally. The reader will encounter especially frequently a "they," "their" or "them" to express a generic singular idea. Thus, for instance, Mark 8:36 reads: "What good is it for someone to gain the whole world, yet forfeit their soul?" This generic use of the "distributive" or "singular" "they/them/their" has been used for many centuries by respected writers of English and has now become established as standard English, spoken and written, all over the world.

A second linguistic principle that feeds into the Committee's translation work is that meaning is found not in individual words, as vital as they are, but in larger clusters: phrases, clauses, sentences, discourses. Translation is not, as many people think, a matter of word substitution: English word x in place of Hebrew word y. Translators must first determine the meaning of the words of the biblical languages in the context of the passage and then select English words that accurately communicate that meaning to modern listeners and readers. This means that accurate translation will not always reflect the exact structure of the original language. To be sure, there is debate over the degree to which translators should try to preserve the "form" of the original text in English. From the beginning, the NIV has taken a mediating position on this issue. The manual produced when the translation that became the NIV was first being planned states: "If the Greek or Hebrew syntax has a good parallel in modern English, it should be used. But if there is no good parallel, the English syntax appropriate to the meaning of the original is to be chosen." It is fine, in other words, to carry over the form of the biblical languages into English—but not at the expense of natural expression. The principle that meaning resides in larger clusters of words means that the Committee has not insisted on a "word-for-word" approach to translation. We certainly believe that every word of Scripture is inspired by God and therefore to be carefully studied to determine what God is saying to us. It is for this reason that the Committee labors over every single word of the original texts, working hard to determine how each of those words contributes to what the text is saying. Ultimately, however, it is how these individual words function in combination with other words that determines meaning.

A third linguistic principle guiding the Committee in its translation work is the recognition that words have a spectrum of meaning. It is popular to define a word by using another word, or "gloss," to substitute for it. This substitute word is then sometimes called the "literal" meaning of a word. In fact, however, words have a range of possible meanings. Those meanings will vary depending on the context, and words in one language will usually not occupy the same semantic range as words in another language. The Committee therefore studies each original word of Scripture in its context to identify its meaning in a particular verse and then chooses an appropriate English word (or phrase) to represent it. It is impossible, then, to translate any given Hebrew, Aramaic or Greek word with the same English word all the time. The Committee does try to translate related occurrences of a word in the original languages with the same English word in order to preserve the connection for the English reader. But the Committee generally privileges clear natural meaning over a concern with consistency in rendering particular words.

## Textual Basis

For the Old Testament the standard Hebrew text, the Masoretic Text as published in the latest edition of *Biblia Hebraica*, has been used throughout. The Masoretic Text tradition contains marginal notations that offer variant readings. These have sometimes been followed instead of the text itself. Because such instances involve variants within the Masoretic tradition, they have not been indicated in the textual notes. In a few cases, words in the basic consonantal text have been divided differently than in the Masoretic Text. Such cases are usually indicated in the textual footnotes. The Dead Sea Scrolls contain biblical texts that represent an earlier stage of the transmission of the Hebrew text. They have been consulted, as have been the Samaritan Pentateuch and the ancient scribal traditions concerning deliberate textual changes. The translators also consulted the more important early versions. Readings from these versions, the Dead Sea Scrolls and the scribal traditions were occasionally followed where the Masoretic Text seemed doubtful and where accepted principles of textual criticism showed that one or more of these textual witnesses appeared to provide the correct reading. In rare cases, the translators have emended the Hebrew text where it appears to have become corrupted at an even earlier stage of its transmission. These departures from the Masoretic Text are also indicated in the textual footnotes. Sometimes the vowel indicators (which are later additions to the basic consonantal text) found in the Masoretic Text did not, in the judgment of the translators, represent the correct vowels for the original text. Accordingly, some words have been read with a different set of vowels. These instances are usually not indicated in the footnotes.

The Greek text used in translating the New Testament has been an eclectic one, based on the latest editions of the Nestle-Aland/ United Bible Societies' Greek New Testament. The translators have made their choices among the variant readings in accordance with widely accepted principles of New Testament textual criticism. Footnotes call attention to places where uncertainty remains.

The New Testament authors, writing in Greek, often quote the Old Testament from its ancient Greek version, the Septuagint. This is one reason why some of the Old Testament quotations in the NIV New Testament are not identical to the corresponding passages in the NIV Old Testament. Such quotations in the New Testament are indicated with the footnote "(see Septuagint)."

**Footnotes and Formatting**

Footnotes in this version are of several kinds, most of which need no explanation. Those giving alternative translations begin with "Or" and generally introduce the alternative with the last word preceding it in the text, except when it is a single-word alternative. When poetry is quoted in a footnote a slash mark indicates a line division.

It should be noted that references to diseases, minerals, flora and fauna, architectural details, clothing, jewelry, musical instruments and other articles cannot always be identified with precision. Also, linear measurements and measures of capacity can only be approximated (see the Table of Weights and Measures). Although *Selah*, used mainly in the Psalms, is probably a musical term, its meaning is uncertain. Since it may interrupt reading and distract the reader, this word has not been kept in the English text, but every occurrence has been signaled by a footnote.

As an aid to the reader, sectional headings have been inserted. They are not to be regarded as part of the biblical text and are not intended for oral reading. It is the Committee's hope that these headings may prove more helpful to the reader than the traditional chapter divisions, which were introduced long after the Bible was written.

Sometimes the chapter and/or verse numbering in English translations of the Old Testament differs from that found in published Hebrew texts. This is particularly the case in the Psalms, where the traditional titles are included in the Hebrew verse numbering. Such differences are indicated in the footnotes at the bottom of the page. In the New Testament, verse numbers that marked off portions of the traditional English text not supported by the best Greek manuscripts now appear in brackets, with a footnote indicating the text that has been omitted (see, for example, Matthew 17:[21]).

Mark 16:9–20 and John 7:53—8:11, although long accorded virtually equal status with the rest of the Gospels in which they stand, have a questionable standing in the textual history of the New Testament, as noted in the bracketed annotations with which they are set off. A different typeface has been chosen for these passages to indicate their uncertain status.

Basic formatting of the text, such as lining the poetry, paragraphing (both prose and poetry), setting up of (administrative-like) lists, indenting letters and lengthy prayers within narratives and the insertion of sectional headings, has been the work of the Committee. However, the choice between single-column and double-column formats has been left to the publishers. Also the issuing of "red-letter" editions is a publisher's choice—one that the Committee does not endorse.

The Committee has again been reminded that every human effort is flawed—including this revision of the NIV. We trust, however, that many will find in it an improved representation of the Word of God, through which they hear his call to faith in our Lord Jesus Christ and to service in his kingdom. We offer this version of the Bible to him in whose name and for whose glory it has been made.

The Committee on Bible Translation